Communications in Computer and Information Science   2549

Series Editors

Gang Li⬤, *School of Information Technology, Deakin University, Burwood, VIC, Australia*
Joaquim Filipe⬤, *Polytechnic Institute of Setúbal, Setúbal, Portugal*
Zhiwei Xu, *Chinese Academy of Sciences, Beijing, China*

Rationale

The CCIS series is devoted to the publication of proceedings of computer science conferences. Its aim is to efficiently disseminate original research results in informatics in printed and electronic form. While the focus is on publication of peer-reviewed full papers presenting mature work, inclusion of reviewed short papers reporting on work in progress is welcome, too. Besides globally relevant meetings with internationally representative program committees guaranteeing a strict peer-reviewing and paper selection process, conferences run by societies or of high regional or national relevance are also considered for publication.

Topics

The topical scope of CCIS spans the entire spectrum of informatics ranging from foundational topics in the theory of computing to information and communications science and technology and a broad variety of interdisciplinary application fields.

Information for Volume Editors and Authors

Publication in CCIS is free of charge. No royalties are paid, however, we offer registered conference participants temporary free access to the online version of the conference proceedings on SpringerLink (http://link.springer.com) by means of an http referrer from the conference website and/or a number of complimentary printed copies, as specified in the official acceptance email of the event.

CCIS proceedings can be published in time for distribution at conferences or as post-proceedings, and delivered in the form of printed books and/or electronically as USBs and/or e-content licenses for accessing proceedings at SpringerLink. Furthermore, CCIS proceedings are included in the CCIS electronic book series hosted in the SpringerLink digital library at http://link.springer.com/bookseries/7899. Conferences publishing in CCIS are allowed to use our online conference service (Meteor) for managing the whole proceedings lifecycle (from submission and reviewing to preparing for publication) free of charge.

Publication process

The language of publication is exclusively English. Authors publishing in CCIS have to sign the Springer CCIS copyright transfer form, however, they are free to use their material published in CCIS for substantially changed, more elaborate subsequent publications elsewhere. For the preparation of the camera-ready papers/files, authors have to strictly adhere to the Springer CCIS Authors' Instructions and are strongly encouraged to use the CCIS LaTeX style files or templates.

Abstracting/Indexing

CCIS is abstracted/indexed in DBLP, Google Scholar, EI-Compendex, Mathematical Reviews, SCImago, Scopus. CCIS volumes are also submitted for the inclusion in ISI Proceedings.

How to start

To start the evaluation of your proposal for inclusion in the CCIS series, please send an e-mail to ccis@springer.com

Rajesh Kumar Tiwari · D. K. Singh
Editors

Recent Trends in Artificial Intelligence and IoT

Second International Conference, ICAII 2024
Jamshedpur, India, October 25–26, 2024
Revised Selected Papers

Editors
Rajesh Kumar Tiwari
RVS College of Engineering and Technology
Jamshedpur, Jharkhand, India

D. K. Singh
Jharkhand University of Technology
Ranchi, Jharkhand, India

ISSN 1865-0929   ISSN 1865-0937 (electronic)
Communications in Computer and Information Science
ISBN 978-3-032-06197-3   ISBN 978-3-032-06198-0 (eBook)
https://doi.org/10.1007/978-3-032-06198-0

© The Editor(s) (if applicable) and The Author(s), under exclusive license to Springer Nature Switzerland AG 2025

This work is subject to copyright. All rights are solely and exclusively licensed by the Publisher, whether the whole or part of the material is concerned, specifically the rights of translation, reprinting, reuse of illustrations, recitation, broadcasting, reproduction on microfilms or in any other physical way, and transmission or information storage and retrieval, electronic adaptation, computer software, or by similar or dissimilar methodology now known or hereafter developed.

The use of general descriptive names, registered names, trademarks, service marks, etc. in this publication does not imply, even in the absence of a specific statement, that such names are exempt from the relevant protective laws and regulations and therefore free for general use.

The publisher, the authors and the editors are safe to assume that the advice and information in this book are believed to be true and accurate at the date of publication. Neither the publisher nor the authors or the editors give a warranty, expressed or implied, with respect to the material contained herein or for any errors or omissions that may have been made. The publisher remains neutral with regard to jurisdictional claims in published maps and institutional affiliations.

This Springer imprint is published by the registered company Springer Nature Switzerland AG
The registered company address is: Gewerbestrasse 11, 6330 Cham, Switzerland

If disposing of this product, please recycle the paper.

Preface

It is an honor for us to present the proceedings of the 2nd International Conference on Recent Trends in Artificial Intelligence and IoT (ICAII 2024) to the event's authors and delegates. We hope you find it helpful, exciting, and inspiring.

The goal of ICAII 2024 was to provide a forum for discussing the issues, challenges, opportunities, and findings of Artificial Intelligence and Internet of Things research. The ever-changing scope and rapid development of AI & IOT generate new problems and questions, necessitating the real need for brilliant ideas to be shared and good awareness of this important research field to be stimulated. We promised to paint a bright picture and a charming landscape for Artificial Intelligence and the Internet of Things, for which the support and enthusiasm shown far exceeded our expectations. As we approach the end of this journey, we are filled with a sense of accomplishment and aspiration.

Responses to the call for papers were overwhelmingly positive. Unfortunately, many manuscripts from prestigious institutions were turned down due to reviewing results and capacity constraints. We would like to express our gratitude and appreciation to all of the reviewers who assisted us in maintaining the high quality of manuscripts published in Springer proceedings. We would also like to thank the members of the organizing team for their efforts.

The papers were subjected to double-blind reviews by an average of three reviewers. The Technical Program Committee collaborated to review and discuss the submitted papers. Review occurred during a fixed window of time. All authors were notified of the decision on their paper at the same time. All reviewers were strictly concerned with the scope, novelty, validity and clarity of the paper. Only papers with similarity scores below 15% qualified for the review process. The conference centered on two broad themes: artificial intelligence and the Internet of Things. The total number of papers submitted was 157, and the total number of papers accepted was 34.

October 2024

Rajesh Kumar Tiwari
D. K. Singh

Organization

General Chair

Rajesh Kr. Tiwari — RVS College of Engineering and Technology, India

Program Committee Chair

D. K. Singh — Jharkhand University of Technology, India

Steering Committee

Howen Fernando	California Miramar University, USA
Omar Haddad	California Miramar University, USA
Dexter Francis	California Miramar University, USA
Rupali Vora	California Miramar University, USA
Al Baroudi	California Miramar University, USA
Alok Choudhary	Loughborough University, UK
Lau Siong Hoe	Multimedia University, Malaysia
Alex (Kwang Leng) Goh	Curtin University, Australia
Tadiwa Elisha Nyamasvisva	Infrastructure University Kuala Lumpur, Malaysia
Abu Bakar A. Hamid	Infrastructure University Kuala Lumpur, Malaysia
Garenth Lim King Hann	Curtin University, Malaysia
Abu Salim	Jazan University, Kingdom of Saudi Arabia
Pirnazarov Nurnazar	Karakalpak State University, Uzbekistan
Atallah Ouai	Laghouat University, Algeria
Mohammed Hameed M.	Jazan University, Saudi Arabia
Pirnazarov Nurnazar	Karakalpak State University, Ujbekistan
M. H. Rahmani Doust	University of Neyshabur, Iran
Muhammad Fayyaz Khan	Bangladesh University of Business and Technolgy, Bangladesh
Fathe Jeribi	Jazan University, Saudi Arabia
Piyush Ranjan	Jharkhand Rai University, India
Susanta Ray	Jadavpur University, India
G. Sahoo	IIT (ISM) Dhanbad, India
Akhib Khan Bahamani	Narayana Engineering College, India

A. G. P. Kujur	BIT Sindri, India
Sandeep U. Kadam	Pawar College of Engineering and Research, India
Pravin Gundalwar	Sandip University, India
Arun Kumar Mishra	Vinoba Bhave University, India
B. Sumathy	Sri Sairam Engineering College, India
Anil Trimbakrao Gaikwad	Bharati Vidyapeeth University, India
Mahendra Kumar Gourisaria	KIIT Deemed to be University, India
Naveen Kumar Kedia	JECRC, India
Anand Singh Rajawat	Sandip University, India
Ram Kumar Solanki	Sandip University, India
Pawan R. Bhaladhare	Sandip University, India
Nripesh Kumar Nrip	Bharati Vidyapeeth Institute of Management, India
B. K. Singh	NIT Jamshedpur, India
D. P. Mohapatra	NIT Rourkela, India
Rajiv Ranjan	BIT Sindri, India
Tapan Kumar Dey	Manipal University Jaipur, India
Sadique Nayeem	Sitamarhi Institute of Technology, India
Abira Dasgupta	VBCV, India
Phaniram Deekshitula	Wipro Limited, India
Dhiraj Kumar Mishra	ORACLE, India
Deobrata Kumar	RVS College of Engineering and Technology, India

Program Committee

Jeevan Kumar	RVS College of Engineering and Technology, India
Smita Dash	RVS College of Engineering and Technology, India
Yogendra Kumar	RVS College of Engineering and Technology, India
Namrata Kumari	RVS College of Engineering and Technology, India
Nushrat Parveen	RVS College of Engineering and Technology, India
Vikram Kr. Sharma	RVS College of Engineering and Technology, India
Sharat Chandra Mahto	RVS College of Engineering and Technology, India
Rakesh Kumar	RVS College of Engineering and Technology, India

Shailandra Kr. Prasad	RVS College of Engineering and Technology, India
Subhash Adhikari	RVS College of Engineering and Technology, India
Rajesh Kumar Paswan	RVS College of Engineering and Technology, India
Sudhir Jha	RVS College of Engineering and Technology, India
Sourabh Singh	RVS College of Engineering and Technology, India
Rahul Ranjan	RVS College of Engineering and Technology, India
Shamsher Alam	RVS College of Engineering and Technology, India
Sulekh Kumar	RVS College of Engineering and Technology, India
Kamala Kumari	RVS College of Engineering and Technology, India
Kumari Sonam	RVS College of Engineering and Technology, India
Moumita Kundu	RVS College of Engineering and Technology, India
Vikash Murmu	RVS College of Engineering and Technology, India
Aatish Kumar Baitha	RVS College of Engineering and Technology, India
Arvind Kumar	RVS College of Engineering and Technology, India
Sanatan Prasad	RVS College of Engineering and Technology, India
Gopal Chand Mahato	RVS College of Engineering and Technology, India
S. P. Singh	RVS College of Engineering and Technology, India
Sushanta Mahanty	RVS College of Engineering and Technology, India
Thakur Pranav Kr. Gautam	RVS College of Engineering and Technology, India
Surya Bharadur	RVS College of Engineering and Technology, India
Krishna Murari	RVS College of Engineering and Technology, India
Rekha Tiwari	RVS College of Engineering and Technology, India

Shalini Kumari — RVS College of Engineering and Technology, India
Amit Kr. Sinha — RVS College of Engineering and Technology, India
Subrato Mahato — RVS College of Engineering and Technology, India
Anand Mohan — RVS College of Engineering and Technology, India
Deepak Kumar — RVS College of Engineering and Technology, India
Kunal Sarkar — RVS College of Engineering and Technology, India
Moni Mandal — RVS College of Engineering and Technology, India
Deepak Kumar Tiwari — RVS College of Engineering and Technology, India
Anita Giri — RVS College of Engineering and Technology, India
Akansha Dhanjal — RVS College of Engineering and Technology, India
Pranshu Sinha — RVS College of Engineering and Technology, India
Shadan Bashar — RVS College of Engineering and Technology, India

Additional Reviewers

Ajay Kumar
Akhib Khan Bahamani
Santosh Kumar Das
Ram Kumar Solanki
Sneha Kumari
Biresh Kumar
Md. Imran Alam
Piyush Ranjan
Tapan Kumar Dey
Pravin Gundalwar
Dhiraj Kr. Mishra
D. A. Khan
Dibyasundar Das
B. Sumathy
Mahendra Kumar Gourisaria
Mohammed Hameed M Alhameed
A. G. P. Kujur
Namrata Kumari
Naveen Kumar Kedia
Sushanta Mahanty
Thakur Pranav Kumar Gautam
Rakesh Kumar
Gaurav Prakash
Nripesh Kumar Nrip
Rajesh Kumar Tiwari
Prakash Kr. Jha
Parag D. Thakare
Susanta Ray
Sweta Mehta
Soumendu Chakraborty
Jeevan Kumar
Yogendra Kumar

Farooque Azam
Gopal Krishna
Ritesh Kumar
Amrutanshu Panigrahi
Debabrata Raha
Fathe Jeribi
Abu Salim
Smita Dash
Nushrat Parween

Shamsher Alam
S. C. Dutta
Sukhwinder Sharma
Puneet Mittal
Rajeev Kumar
Anil Trimbakrao Gaikwad
G. Sahoo
Sadique Nayeem
Deobrata Kumar

Contents

Artificial Intelligence

Real-Time Anomaly Detection in Micro-service Architectures 3
   Jayanth Kande

Topological Analysis of Alzheimer's Progression with Persistence Images 17
   Jayanth Kande

Logistic Regression in Machine Learning and Data Analytics with Python for Detecting Financial Fraud in Credit Card Transactions 37
   Meenakshi Kumari and Prakash Anand

SENTINSIGHT: Unveiling Themes, Insights, and Success Metrics Through Natural Language Processing 53
   Jagini Naga Padmaja, Nadimpalli Madana Kailash Varma, and Kanduri Sai Sri Vidya

A Comparative Analysis of Machine Learning Algorithms for Early Prediction of Diabetes 65
   Mehulkumar Patel

Understanding User Requests in Chatbot Using Deep Learning 75
   Alaa T. Al-Tuama and Dhamyaa A. Nasrawi

Optimizing Handloom Price Prediction: Leveraging Diverse Features for Superior Accuracy Using Machine Learning 92
   Khirod Chandra Maharana, Binod Kumar, Pravin Kumar, Shrikant Upadhyay, and Binita Roshima Hinz

Comprehensive Review of Road Anomalies Detection Methods Using Deep Learning Techniques 105
   Ruta Mulajkar and Sanjay Yede

Advancement of Data Visualization Techniques in Healthcare Using AI and Power BI 118
   Priya Rani, Jeevan Kumar, and Smita Dash

Role of Machine Leaning in D2D Communication in 6G 129
   Haneef Khan, Malik Zaib Alam, Mohammad Rafeek Khan, Md Imran Alam, Shams Tabrez Siddiuqi, and Abu Salim

Enhancing Agricultural Decision-Making Using Machine Learning:
Variety Selection and Yield Prediction for Agriculture Culture Improvement ... 141
   *Shrikant Upadhyay, N. Indumathi, M. Balamurugan, Binod Kumar,
Sampurna Mandal, and Sidharth Prakash*

A Study of Forecasting Mobile Phone Booking Cancellation on Different
E- Commerce Websites Using Machine Learning Algorithms 153
   *Khushboo Singh, Abhishek Kumar, Ravi Kumar Burman,
Pravir Kumar, and Alok Kumar Singh*

Forecasting Gender Discrimination in Computer Literacy in Rural Areas
of Jharkhand Until 2030 169
   Kalpana Sagar, Abhishek Kumar, Ravi Kumar Burman, and Ram Singh

Convolutional Neural Network for the Identification Provider Fraud
in Healthcare 186
   Md Shoaib Alam, Pankaj Rai, Rajesh Kumar Tiwari, and Biresh Kumar

The Role of AI in Human Resource Management: Innovations, Challenges,
and Future Directions 196
   Divya Sinha and A. R. Sinha

Advancements in Disease Detection and Diagnosis: An Extensive Review
of Artificial Intelligence Tools 205
   Jeevan Kumar, Vijay Pandey, and Rajesh Kumar Tiwari

Approaches of Groundwater Water Quality Prediction Using Machine
Learning Techniques 221
   *Kulsuma Chowdhury, Nushrat Praveen, Amirul Hoque,
Namrata Kumari, and Smita Dash*

Enhanced Face Recognition with Deep CNN and User- Friendly GUI
Implementation 236
   Saba Mansoori, Pankaj Sahu, and Devendra Kumar Meda

Comparative Analysis of Neural Networks and Language Models
for College Website Chatbots 255
   *Arnav Nigam, Arnav Singhal, Dharmeshwar Sharma,
and Mohd. Yousuf Ansari*

Financial and Technological Considerations for Deploying Applications
on Cloud Computing Platforms: A Case Study of AWS 267
   Ranjith Kumar Ramakrishnan

Leveraging Neural Networks to Enhance Cluster Head Selection
in the LEACH Protocol for Wireless Sensor Networks 282
   Monali Vishwakarma and Devendra Kumar Meda

Enhanced Twitter Sentiment Analysis with NLTK and Transformer Models 300
   Md Oqail Ahmad, Shams Tabrez Siddiqui, Mohammad Shahid Kamal,
   Mohammed Ali Sohail, Malek Alzoubi, and Mohammad Haseebuddin

Quantum Computing Through Artificial Intelligence 312
   Sulekh Kumar, Md. Shamsher Alam, Jeevan Kumar, Yogendra Kumar,
   Kumari Sonam, and Rahul Ranjan

Internet of Things

A Multi-Criteria Driven Integrated Routing Protocol for IoT
Communication in 6G Networks 335
   Shams Tabrez Siddiqui, Md Oqail Ahmad, Abu Salim,
   Rajesh Kumar Tiwari, Aasif Aftab, and Mohd Sarfaraz

Integrating Cloud, Edge, and IoT 350
   Ranjith Kumar Ramakrishnan, Anjana Nayak, and Jai Jaswant Lekkala

Development of IoT Smart Devices Graphical Interfaces, Platforms,
Middleware and Security Management of Internet of Things Using
Block-Chain and Multi Tenancy: Literature Review 365
   Nuras Naser Saeed Hizam, Madhukar Shelar, and Archana Bachhav

Blockchain

Decentralized GitHub Management: Blockchain Solution 383
   Ranjith Kumar Ramakrishnan and Jai Jaswant Lekkala

Design Ubiquitous, Technologically Efficient Online Storage System
Using Blockchain 397
   Rajeev Kumar, Pradeep Kumar, and Madhurendra Kumar

Blockchain Based Decentralized IoT Device Management Using Smart
Contract 410
   Suseta Datta, Rituparna Mondal, Rajdeep Roy, Sourav Banerjee,
   and Utpal Biswas

Enhancing Distributed System Reliability Through Request-Level Fault
Injection and Fine-Grained Tracing 425
  Ranjith Kumar Ramakrishnan, Mahendra Sadineni,
  and Jai Jaswant Lekkala

Decentralized Identity Management System Using Blockchain Technology
for Secure and Private Authentication 439
  Purushottam Kumar and Ankit Kumar

The Role of Blockchain in Intellectual Property (IP) Protection
and Enforcement: A Global Perspective 452
  Upasana Priya

Saket Application Methodology on Network Security with Blockchain
Technology 466
  Pradeep Kumar, Rajeev Kumar, Abu Bakar bin Abdul Hamid,
  and Tadiwa Elisha Nyamasvisva

Blockchain and IPFS Based Evidence Protection System for Safeguarding
Women's Right 476
  Chaitali Patil, Avinash Jadhav, Shruti Kadbhane, Shivani Dangal,
  and Prajakta Patil

Author Index 493

Artificial Intelligence

Real-Time Anomaly Detection in Micro-service Architectures

Jayanth Kande[✉]

23058 Middlebelt Rd, Apt 101, Farmington Hills, MI, USA
jayanth.m1229@gmail.com

Abstract. This paper presents an anomaly detection approach tailored for distributed microservice architectures, leveraging data streaming through Apache Kafka and advanced machine learning techniques for real-time performance analysis. The method incorporates root cause localization to precisely identify the sources of anomalies within complex service interactions. Benchmarking results demonstrate the approach's ability to detect a broad range of anomalies, including latency spikes, service crashes, and resource contention, with high accuracy and low false positive rates. The system's scalability is validated through performance evaluations in large-scale microservice environments, with results showing effective anomaly detection across systems with up to hundreds of services. This paper also discusses the selection of Key Performance Indicators (KPIs), which are chosen based on their relevance to system performance and their ability to indicate service degradation or failure. The proposed method offers a significant improvement in real-time anomaly detection, providing both actionable insights and a scalable solution for complex architectures.

1 Introduction

With the recent trends, many modern-day large-scale systems are utilizing microservices in their system architecture design. In a micro-service-based architecture, the system operations are provided as different services, loosely coupled (i.e., independent from each other), organized, highly maintainable, analyzable, and testable. Hence, this type of architecture allows large-scale and complex systems to provide faster and more reliable services to their users. However, a major disadvantage of these systems is the massive number of calls between different services and their complex relationships, making finding faulty services and errors rather challenging.

: If a faulty micro-service causes an error in the system, this occurrence would be referred to as an anomaly, which should be detected as soon as possible. Accordingly, the anomaly should be traced back to the faulty service that caused it. This process is referred to as troubleshooting. By accomplishing this task, the system maintainers could fix the defective service and any subsequent problems before experiencing significant costs and losses. Therefore, it is essential to implement an algorithm that detects a system's strange behavior and can both accurately and efficiently identify its root cause.

In this project, I was tasked to design an online algorithm to perform these tasks on an incrementally published dataset (i.e., real-time data) generated by a micro-service-based system through a Kafka producer. More specifically, My task was to analyze the provided time series data, detect anomalous behavior, discover anomalous system nodes at the time of this occurrence, and find the Key Performance Indicator (KPI) that is the root cause of this anomaly. The rest of this report is organized as follows: in Sect. 2, I summarize the relative literature for these tasks and acknowledge the work of top teams for this competition; in Sect. 3, I further explain the problem statement and provide My implemented algorithms for this project; Sect. 4 includes a discussion of My results as well as the lessons learned; lastly, I conclude the report in Sect. 5.

2 Previously Implemented Work

As mentioned, micro-service-based large-scale systems have many complex calls and relationships between different services. In addition, once a service in the system becomes unavailable, unstable, and/or impaired, detecting and fixing this system promptly and accurately is the top priority. Due to the large amount of data to be analyzed, manual inspection has proven to be hugely time-consuming and ineffective. Hence, considerable research has been conducted to investigate and detect such failures and their causing factors automatically.

The problem statement for anomaly detection and localization is fairly simple: use historical data or a stream of seasonal data as a time series from a micro-service-based system to detect any anomalies and find the root cause. Donut [1] and Bagel [2] managed to accomplish this task by utilizing variational auto-encoders (VAEs). However, even though these models achieved satisfactory results for My task, they also needed sufficient resources for training and processing. Given that I was not provided with any GPUs for this project, I deemed them unsuitable for My project due to the running time. They also do not offer host KPI localization. The following approach I attempted, TraceAnomaly [3], a deep Bayesian network based algorithm, suffered similar setbacks as a deep learning algorithm requiring a GPU. It ran pretty slowly, and while it could produce the correct host, it gave us no information towards finding the KPIs. A beautiful solution was MicroRCA [4] as their proposed framework and studied cases strongly resembled this competition. Their approach is illustrated in Fig. 1.

MicroRCA utilizes BIRCH [5] to detect the abnormal edges and uses various formulas to assign weights to the edges of the sub-graph. The nodes are weighted using Pearson correlation between the abnormal edges and the host KPI data. I implemented the original method and tried many different variations in order to get the technique to produce a list of hosts and KPIs. However, the Personalized PageRank [6] often did not converge, and when it did, the results were not satisfactory. Every variation I tried had its own problems. So, despite how attractive MircroRCA first appeared and how related to this competition it was, I decided to remove it from My project.

Next, I took huge inspiration from H3C AI Institute's slides and managed to implement a solution that produced a score greater than 0. I then combined

rank	group name	score	highest score	round 1	round 2
1	学堂路车神	836	836	985	985
2	meow meow	770	770	624	765
3	Veritaserum	540	540	535	515
4	MSSherlock	354	354	369	325
5	study group	315	315	0	321
6	The Anomalies	227	227	70	66
7	Learning Failure	204	204	0	0
8	ANM小组	170	170	153	107
9	flower group	169	169	161	181
10	ANMG	110	110	78	140
11	DANM!	0	0	0	0

Fig. 1. RCA Overview [4]

this approach with the information provided by the other teams after the first deadline in order to streamline My code, remove bugs and improve performance. Regarding the proposed algorithms for this competition, the winning team [7] cleverly discarded one of the three provided data sources to increase the detection speed. Accordingly, they established rules and manually selected thresholds to detect anomalies and localize root causes. Similarly, the runner up team [8] also discarded the first set of provided KPI sources, focused merely on trace data and formulated this problem as a pattern finding challenge in a constructed anomaly table. Lastly, the team in third place [9] utilized the first set of available data to identify the anomalous points, analyzed the second set to detect failed and delayed calls, find abnormal hosts, and extract the necessary features. One of the honorable mentions in their work was that they used dictionaries instead of pandas to improve the algorithm's speed. These simple tips allowed us to improve My method significantly.

2.1 Comparison with Existing Anomaly Detection Models

Anomaly detection has been a central topic in various domains, including cybersecurity, finance, and healthcare, leading to the development of several models. These models generally fall into categories such as statistical methods, machine learning-based techniques, and hybrid approaches. While these methods serve well for detecting known patterns of anomalies, they often struggle with real-time data processing and the handling of complex, unstructured datasets. Below, we provide a comparison between traditional models and our proposed real-time streaming anomaly detection approach using Apache Kafka and machine learning.

Traditional Statistical Methods: Classical statistical models, such as Z-score, Grubbs' test, and Tukey's fences, rely on predefined thresholds or assumptions about the data distribution. These models are effective in detecting simple, well-defined outliers but are less adaptable to dynamic data environments or evolving data distributions. Moreover, they often require substantial manual intervention and fine-tuning of parameters to handle changing patterns.

Machine Learning Approaches: Machine learning-based methods, such as clustering algorithms (e.g., k-means), decision trees, and neural networks, have become popular in detecting anomalies in more complex datasets. However, most of these models, especially deep learning approaches, are computationally expensive and may not provide real-time anomaly detection. Moreover, these models often require a large amount of labeled data for training, which may not be feasible in real-world, unlabeled environments.

Hybrid Approaches: Hybrid models, which combine statistical techniques and machine learning, have shown promise in addressing the limitations of both approaches. These models aim to balance precision and recall by leveraging the strengths of each method. However, they still face challenges related to real-time data processing, scalability, and the handling of high-dimensional data streams.

Our Approach: In contrast to these traditional and hybrid models, our approach integrates Apache Kafka for real-time data streaming with machine learning-based anomaly detection techniques. The use of Kafka enables high-throughput, fault-tolerant, and low-latency data streaming, making it particularly well-suited for real-time anomaly detection in large-scale, dynamic environments. This integration ensures that anomalies are detected as soon as they occur, allowing for immediate action. Additionally, the scalability of Kafka ensures that the system can handle large volumes of data efficiently, a key advantage in environments with high data influx. Furthermore, our method does not rely on large amounts of labeled data and can adapt to changes in data distribution over time without significant retraining, making it more flexible and efficient than traditional machine learning methods.

Unique Advantages: The key advantages of our approach include:

- **Real-Time Detection:** By integrating Kafka for real-time data streaming, our system can detect anomalies as soon as they occur, offering immediate insights and enabling quick corrective actions.
- **Scalability:** Kafka's distributed nature allows the system to scale efficiently, handling high-throughput data streams from multiple sources without performance degradation.

- **Adaptability:** The machine learning models used in our approach are capable of adapting to changes in the data distribution, reducing the need for constant retraining and manual adjustments.
 - **Low Latency:** Kafka's low-latency streaming capabilities ensure that anomaly detection happens in near real-time, which is critical for time-sensitive applications.
 - **Fault Tolerance:** Kafka's inherent fault tolerance ensures that data is not lost and the system remains operational even in the event of node failures.

In conclusion, while existing models are effective in certain contexts, our real-time anomaly detection approach offers significant improvements in handling dynamic, high-throughput data environments with lower latency and higher scalability, making it a more robust solution for real-time anomaly detection applications.

3 Methodology

In this section, I describe the provided dataset and My implemented algorithms.

3.1 Data

In this project, I was provided with three KPI data sources: ESB, Trace, and Host data.

ESB Business Indicator (ESB): is provided every minute and mainly demonstrates the number of requests for the *osb_001* service and the overall success rate of these request during each minute. Once an anomaly occurs, assuming at a point t, the success rate is expected to be lower than 1. Accordingly, it would be recorded to be used for further analysis in the other two KPI data sources.

Trace: it is provided for every request and consists of several micro-service calls, referred to as spans. This section of the data demonstrates the start and elapsed time for each span, the databases that were accessed (if any), the trace of the span and its host. Upon finding anomalous time t in the ESB data, the time around t is to be investigated in order to detect anomalous spans (i.e. nodes with unusually long response time) and ultimately, realize faulty service nodes.

Host: is provided in the (timestamp, value) format and includes the host service name and the called operation. Upon finding the faulty service nodes, this data can be explored to find anomalous values for a KPI, which would then be flagged as a root cause.

3.2 Kafka for Real-Time Data Streaming and Anomaly Detection

Apache Kafka is a critical component in the architecture of the anomaly detection system, serving as a distributed messaging platform that supports high-throughput, real-time data streaming. Kafka efficiently handles the transmission of large-scale sensor data from multiple sources, ensuring timely delivery and fault tolerance. By integrating Kafka into the system, we can continuously monitor incoming data, enabling the real-time detection of anomalies. The low-latency processing of data streams ensures that irregularities or outliers are flagged immediately, allowing for quick responses to potential issues before they escalate. This capability is essential for systems requiring continuous, automated oversight and enhances the robustness of anomaly detection processes.

3.3 Dropping ESB Business Indicator

Inspired by MicroRCA [4], I utilized BIRCH [5], an online clustering-based outlier detection algorithm, to detect anomalies in the ESB data. In this project, I considered comparatively large values for average time and considerably small success rates as abnormal behavior. Hence, I employed BIRCH separately for these two columns and set the BIRCH threshold (i.e., radius) to 0.5 and 0.1, respectively.

The algorithm produced good results for a short while. However, a major disadvantage of this implementation was that when the code was left running on the server, the anomaly detection process started happening when the system is in its normal state. Given enough anomalies, the anomalies become the normal state of the system. To address this problem, I trained two separate BIRCH models for average time and success rate on the provided two weeks of data with all anomalous data removed.

Upon detecting an anomaly in the ESB data, I would stop analyzing incoming data until a root cause is found. Accordingly, I would send the timestamp of the detected anomaly to the next module for faulty service detection in trace data. The incoming data would not be discarded but rather stored in a separate storage for future analysis.

However, this approach also proved to be sub-optimal. The reason being, the effects of many anomalies are often quite significantly delayed in the ESB data - indeed, some anomalies do not cause any change in the ESB data. Thus waiting on the ESB data for anomalies was inefficient and sometimes causing us to miss anomalies. Hence I decided to remove this method from My project and fully discard ESB data.

3.4 Final Solution Design

Figure 2 illustrates an overview of My method's architecture. At a high level, the proposed framework could be divided into three sections: data collection, anomalous host localization, anomalous KPI localization.

Data Collection Code Architecture: The final code architecture in My submission comprises two threads: a main thread and a worker thread. The main thread collects the incoming data from the Kafka server and adds it to temporary storage. It runs for every new item of Kafka data. The worker thread runs periodically every minute. It takes all the data collected by the main thread out of temporary storage and processes and prepares before adding it to the main

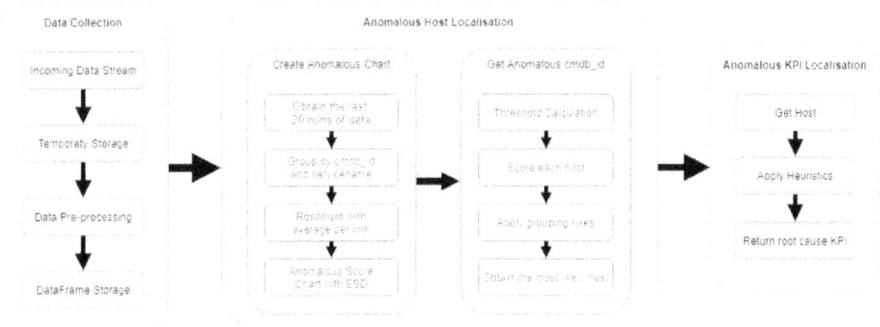

Fig. 2. Proposed method architecture

data storage. It then performs anomaly detection and localization on the main data storage.

Data Retrieval: This process is handled by the main thread. I have three data types (ESB, Trace and Host KPI). As mentioned, I immediately discard any ESB data, but the trace and host KPI data are stored in memory via a temporary 1 min storage dictionary. During this process, I make minor adjustments to the trace data. As the parents of $JDBC$ spans are $LOCAL$ spans, the trace logs of $LOCAL$ types can effectively represent the $JDBC$ spans; that is, if the $JDBC$ spans are anomalous, it will be shown in the logs of the $LOCAL$ spans. Hence, all the $JDBC$ trace logs are discarded by My program. Every minute, the worker thread collects the data from the temporary dictionary and adds it to the main DataFrame storage. This data only stays in memory for a total of 20 min and is deleted afterwards.

Data Processing: The worker thread takes care of data processing. I only process the trace data as the Host KPI data is already in the desired format, which is done as follows:

- If CallType is OSB or Remote Process, I replace the ServiceName with cmdb_id.
- If CallType is CSF, I replace the serviceName with the cmdb_id of its child.
- If CallType is $LOCAL$, I replace the serviceName with dsName.
- For each span, I deducted the total elapsedTime of each of its child spans.

The final step is highly essential as it allows us to determine where the problem is more accurately. This means the processed logs are more independent than the original data. For example, suppose I have a $LOCAL$ service acting anomalously. Without this pre-processing step, the anomaly would also be reflected in the OSB data, and hence anomaly detection would return an OSB anomaly such as os_021. To write this more formally

$$Actual\ elapsedTime = elapsedTime - \sum elapsedTime\ of\ children$$

Host Localization. For host localization, the processed trace data is used. As mentioned above, I have stored 20 min of processed data, which is updated every minute. I group this trace data by "cmdb_id" and "serviceName" for anomaly detection. This allows us to group the data by the edges of the graph representing the data topology, seen below. After the processing, cmdb_id and serviceName effectively stand for 'parent cmdb_id' and 'child cmdb_id' respectively, so each grouping represents a call from the parent cmdb_id to the child cmdb_id. All unique possible calls are shown below (Fig. 3). Note that each cmdb_id also has a self loop/edge too, which is not shown.

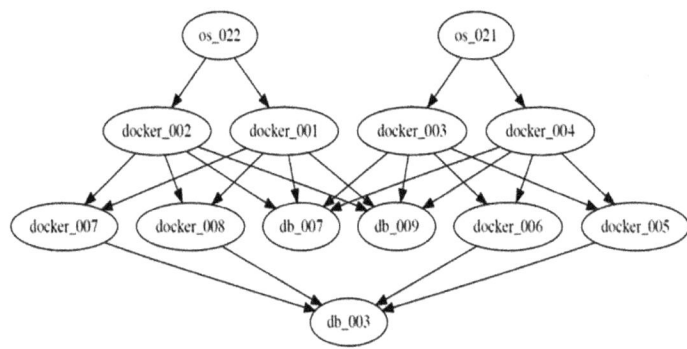

Fig. 3. Data Topology

3.4.1 Host Localization - Anomaly Score Chart

The figure below shows the next step of My anomaly detection: the anomaly score chart. Compared to My previous unstable/slow implementations, more straightforward methods were proven better than complex methods. Thus, I decided to use an anomaly score chart to better visualize anomalies and anomaly detection. A sample Anomaly Chart can be seen in Fig. 4. In this section, I discuss how these Anomaly Charts are created.

Anomaly Score Calculation: For each of the groups, which represent a call path, I calculate the following values: first, I calculate the average elapsedTime of each minute of data in the 20 min worth of stored data. This gives us 20 points of data for each call path; Second, the top 10% anomalous data points for each call path are found using Seasonal Hybrid Extreme Studentized Deviate (S-H-ESD) [10]. To explain S-H-ESD, I introduce the following notation.

$$R_j = \frac{\max_i |X_i - median(X)|}{MAD}, \quad 1 \leq j \leq k \quad (1)$$

where $MAD = median(|X_i - median(X)|)$

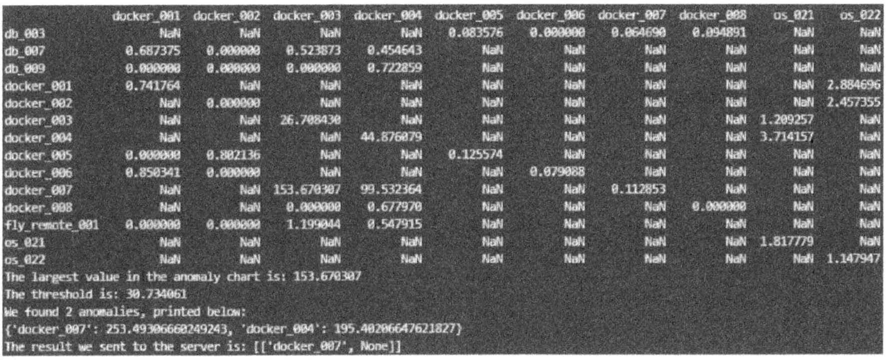

	docker_001	docker_002	docker_003	docker_004	docker_005	docker_006	docker_007	docker_008	os_021	os_022
db_003	NaN	NaN	NaN	NaN	0.083576	0.000000	0.000000	0.094891	NaN	NaN
db_007	0.687375	0.000000	0.523873	0.454643	NaN	NaN	NaN	NaN	NaN	NaN
db_009	0.000000	0.000000	0.000000	0.722859	NaN	NaN	NaN	NaN	NaN	NaN
docker_001	0.741764	NaN	NaN	NaN	NaN	NaN	NaN	NaN	NaN	2.884696
docker_002	NaN	0.000000	NaN	NaN	NaN	NaN	NaN	NaN	NaN	2.457355
docker_003	NaN	NaN	26.708430	NaN	NaN	NaN	NaN	NaN	1.209257	NaN
docker_004	NaN	NaN	NaN	44.876079	NaN	NaN	NaN	NaN	3.714157	NaN
docker_005	0.000000	0.882136	NaN	NaN	0.125574	NaN	NaN	NaN	NaN	NaN
docker_006	0.850341	0.000000	NaN	NaN	NaN	0.079088	NaN	NaN	NaN	NaN
docker_007	NaN	NaN	153.670307	99.532364	NaN	NaN	0.112853	NaN	NaN	NaN
docker_008	NaN	NaN	0.000000	0.677970	NaN	NaN	NaN	0.000000	NaN	NaN
fly_remote_001	0.000000	0.000000	1.199044	0.547915	NaN	NaN	NaN	NaN	NaN	NaN
os_021	NaN	NaN	NaN	NaN	NaN	NaN	NaN	NaN	1.817779	NaN
os_022	NaN	NaN	NaN	NaN	NaN	NaN	NaN	NaN	NaN	1.147947

```
The largest value in the anomaly chart is: 153.670307
The threshold is: 30.734061
We found 2 anomalies, printed below:
{'docker_007': 253.49306660249243, 'docker_004': 195.40206647621827}
The result we sent to the server is: [['docker_007', None]]
```

Fig. 4. Anomaly Score Chart

$$\lambda_j = \frac{(n-j)*t_{p,n-j-1}}{\sqrt{(n-j-1+t^2_{p,n-j-1})(n-j+1)}}, \quad 1 \leq j \leq k \qquad (2)$$

The Residual R_j is found for every data point in a group. Then, the anonymity of each data point in a group is calculated by comparing the Residual R_j with its critical value λ_j. Any Residuals R_j higher than the critical value λ_j is flagged as anomalous. The *Anomaly Score* of the elapsedTime column for each group is computed using the flagged anomalous data points as follows. Let X be the 20 values in a particular grouping. I calculate:

$$ESD_{result} = \sum(|X_{anomalous} - median(X)|)$$

Since the database (db) anomalies are not obvious just by looking at the elapsed time column, I also incorporate a *Failure Score* into My *Anomaly Score*. The *Failure Score* is the number of failed calls in the data for each group. The "success" column of the trace data a Boolean, so I calculate

$$Failure\ Score = \sum success\ column == False$$

Note that I only calculate *Failure Score* for groupings where the service-Name (i.e. the child cmdb_id) is a database. Lastly, the overall *Anomaly Score* for the current cmdb_id and serviceName pair is computed as follows:

$$Anomaly\ Score = ESD_{result} + Failure\ Score$$

Once I have computed the *Anomaly Score* for each possible pairing of cmdb_id and serviceName, I have all the entries to construct the Anomaly Chart, as seen in Fig. 4.

3.4.2 Host Localization - Score Chart Analysis

Looking at Fig. 4, I see high scores in docker 3, 4 and 7 rows/columns. This section details how I decide which cmdb_id is anomalous. From the GitHub datasets containing the ground truth, there is only one anomalous cmdb_id during each anomaly, but simply selecting the row from the table with the most significant value is often not sufficient. Hence, I perform the following steps to produce a more efficient solution.

Threshold Calculation: Once I get an Anomaly Score Chart from the previous stage, I first calculate the threshold t_1 of the anomaly chart. This is the threshold over which I consider an entry in the table anomalous. Let M be the maximum value in the table. I found that 20% of M was a good indicator for anomalous entries. However, since I run detections every minute, I still create tables even when there are no anomalies present. To deal with this issue, I set a minimum threshold of 10, which was decided after thorough observations of the anomaly chart. Hence, in the case of a normal table, no anomalies would be detected. The threshold calculation is summarized as follows:

$$t_1 = \max\left(\frac{M}{5}, 10\right)$$

cmdb_id Scores: For each cmbd_id, I calculate the mean of the row sum and the column sum (when the column exists). Looking at Fig. 3, this mean essentially represents the sum of the in edges and the sum of the out edges. Let i denote a particular cmdb_id and denote this mean as m_i. Then, using the calculated threshold, for each cmbd_id, I also calculate the number of strange entries in its row and the number of strange entries in its column. This is essentially counting how many of the in edges/out edges are anomalous in Fig. 3. Let r_i be the number of anomalies in the row, and c_i the number of anomalies in the column. I then calculate

$$a_i = \left\lfloor \frac{2r_i + c_i}{2} \right\rfloor$$

Since every non-NaN entry in the table represents a call from column cmdb_id to row cmdb_id, I assign extra weight to the destination node as this is more likely to be the problem. However, I still need to consider the source node since this is not always the case. Next, to assign a score s_i to each cmdb_id, i, I simply calculate $s_i = a_i \times m_i$. I then use an additional threshold t_2, which is calculated as

$$t_2 = \max_i\left(\frac{s_i}{10}, 1\right)$$

to filter out the cmdb_ids with low score (s_i) and pass the resulting list onto the next stage. If there are no scores s_i greater than 1, I return an empty list and end the localization.

Grouping Rules: From My observations and the Excel file showing the hosts of the various cmdb_ids, I realized that certain rules need to be applied to get better performance. The derived rules are as follows:

- If os_021 and os_022 are anomalous, the problematic cmdb_id is os_001.
- If I have docker_00(x) and docker_00($x+4$), the problematic cmdb_id is actually os_0(16+x). For example, if docker_002 and docker_006 are anomalous, the problematic cmdb_id is os_018.
- Note that I have a "fly remote" row in My anomaly chart, but there is no cmdb_id called fly remote. The cmdb_id corresponding to an anomalous fly remote is os_009.

Find Most Likely Anomalous cmdb_id: If none of the grouping rules are met, I simply send the cmdb_id with the greatest score to the next stage. Otherwise, I will send the successful result of one of the grouping rules. This means I prioritized the grouping rules over the score, as this gave us the best performance during the first round of the final testing stage.

KPI Localisation. Given the anomalous cmdb_id from the previous stage, I use the following observations to determine the root cause KPIs.

- If the cmdb_id is of type "os", i.e. an operating system, the KPIs are always Sent_queue and Received_queue.
- If the cmdb_id is of type "docker", the KPI root cause is either Null or container_cpu_used.
- If the cmdb_id is of type "db", i.e. a database, the KPI root causes are either the combination of Sess_Connect, Proc_Used_Pct and Proc_User_Used_Pct, or the combination of On_Off_State and tnsping_result_time.

So if the cmdb_id is of type "os" I can instantly send off a result, but docker and database cmdb_ids require further analysis to decide between the two options.

1. Docker KPI decision: If the docker-docker entry in the anomaly chart (i.e. a call to itself) is abnormal, the problem is container_cpu_used. If the self call is not uncommon, it must be a network issue, in which case the KPI is Null.
2. Database KPI decision: I need only look at the On_Off_State KPI data to decide between the two options. Note that this is the only purpose of the KPI data in My method. If there are any 0 values in On_Off_State, I return On_Off_State and tnsping_result_time. If the values for On_Off_State are all 1, I return Sess_Connect, Proc_Used_Pct and Proc_User_Used_Pct.

I can see bullet point 1 in action in Fig. 4. The docker_007 to docker_007 call only has a value of 0.112853 and is hence not anomalous (since the threshold is 30.7). Thus, it must be a network error rather than a cpu error; hence, I return $[[docker\_007, Null]]$.

3.5 Additional Checks

Since I run anomaly detection every minute and take 1-minute averages of the last 20 min of data, sometimes an anomaly is not fully expressed in the data when I create the Anomaly Chart. This means that if I blindly send off a result as soon as I get a table with an anomaly, I may send the wrong answer. To solve the issue, when I get a result from the table, I store it and wait for anomaly detection to run again a minute later. If the two answers are equal, I send the result to the server. Otherwise, I will keep running anomaly detection every minute until the last two results are agreed upon. From My observations of the code on the server, the first result is usually correct, and the next result is the same so that I can detect anomalies in two minutes. However, sometimes, particularly for docker anomalies, the database values spike slightly above the threshold of 10 before the docker entries in the table become anomalous. Originally I would have submitted a database anomaly, but now I can correctly identify the actual root cause - the docker.

In addition, once I detect an anomaly, since I create the tables from 20 min of historical data and anomalies can last up to around 10 min, I wait 30 min after I detect an anomaly before starting detection again. This is so that I don't continuously send the same answer again and again. Another reason for this wait of 30 min can be explained in the following example. Suppose at time t_0 I detect docker_001. Let's say this anomaly lasts 9 min until t_9. Then suppose at time t_24 there is docker_005 anomaly. Then, the 20 min of historical data would have both the docker_005 and docker_001 anomalies. This would mean My Anomaly Chart analysis would (incorrectly) return os_017 as the anomaly rather than docker_005.

4 Discussion

4.1 Root Cause Localization

Anomaly detection is often only the first step in understanding system failures. In complex microservice architectures, pinpointing the root cause of an anomaly is crucial for effective troubleshooting and resolution. Our approach enhances anomaly detection by incorporating a root cause localization mechanism, which identifies the source of anomalies through the analysis of dependencies and interactions between services. By leveraging graph-based models, the system analyzes service interactions and traces the flow of anomalies back to their origin. This enables precise identification of the component or service causing the disruption, even in systems with intricate interdependencies. The root cause localization process works by evaluating the correlation of various services and identifying outliers in service interactions, which are indicative of abnormal behavior. This method ensures that the resolution process is more targeted and efficient, reducing downtime and improving the overall reliability of the system.

4.2 Computational Complexity and Scalability

Scalability is a critical concern for anomaly detection in distributed microservice architectures, where the volume of data and the number of services can increase exponentially. The computational complexity of the algorithm is designed to handle such growth efficiently. The core of our approach leverages Apache Kafka for real-time data streaming, which allows for distributed processing and ensures that the system can scale horizontally. The anomaly detection algorithm itself is based on a combination of lightweight machine learning models and statistical techniques that offer a balance between performance and complexity. By processing data in smaller, more manageable chunks and applying models that adapt to changing data patterns, the algorithm ensures that it can scale to accommodate large numbers of services without compromising performance. The complexity primarily depends on the number of service interactions and the dimensionality of the data, but through optimization techniques such as dimensionality reduction and parallel processing, our system remains computationally efficient even in large-scale environments.

4.3 Key Performance Indicators (KPIs) Selection

The success of anomaly detection is contingent upon the careful selection of relevant Key Performance Indicators (KPIs). KPIs are metrics that provide insight into the health and performance of individual services and the system as a whole. In our approach, KPIs are chosen based on their ability to highlight deviations in service behavior that are indicative of potential anomalies. For example, response time, error rates, and throughput are commonly used KPIs that correlate strongly with system performance and are sensitive to issues like latency spikes, service failures, or resource contention. By focusing on KPIs that are closely tied to the operational objectives of the microservice architecture, we ensure that anomaly detection is both relevant and actionable. The chosen KPIs are also adaptive, allowing for dynamic adjustment as the system evolves or as new performance bottlenecks emerge. This flexibility ensures that the system remains effective in detecting anomalies that could otherwise go unnoticed, regardless of changes in the architecture or workload.

5 Conclusion

In conclusion, I proposed a robust online algorithm for anomaly detection and root cause localization in micro-service-based systems. Based on my research, the surrounding literature, and the proposed methods of fellow competitors, I tried many different approaches. In addition, I demonstrated my proposed methodology and discussed the lessons learned throughout this project. Regardless of the final results, I regard this competition as a valuable learning experience and am proud of my team's hard work in obtaining these results.

References

1. Xu, H., et al.: Unsupervised anomaly detection via variational auto-encoder for seasonal KPIs in web applications. In: Proceedings of the 2018 World Wide Web Conference on World Wide Web, 2018, pp. 187–196
2. Li, Z., Chen, W., Pei, D.: Robust and unsupervised KPI anomaly detection based on conditional variational autoencoder. In: 2018 IEEE 37th International Performance Computing and Communications Conference (IPCCC). IEEE (2018)
3. Liu, P., et al.: Unsupervised detection of microservice trace anomalies through service-level deep Bayesian networks. In: 31th International Symposium on Software Reliability Engineering (ISSRE). IEEE (2020)
4. Wu, L., Tordsson, J., Elmroth, E., Kao, O.: MicroRCA: root cause localization of performance issues in microservices. In: IEEE/IFIP Network Operations and Management Symposium (NOMS) (2020)
5. Gulenko, A., Schmidt, F., Acker, A., Wallschlager, M., Kao, O., Liu, F.: Detecting anomalous behavior of black-box services modeled with distance-based online clustering. In: 2018 IEEE 11th International Conference on Cloud Computing (CLOUD) (2018)
6. Jeh, G., Widom, J.: Scaling personalized web search. In: WWW-2003, pp. 271–279 (2003)
7. Zhao, Y., Wang, X., Fan, G.: Advanced network management - the Old Driver on Xuetang Road (2020)
8. Ji, Y., Liu, Y.: Anomaly Detection and Root Cause Localization in Microservice System - meow meow group (2020)
9. Hao, Z., Zhang, Y., Liu, S.: ANM project - Veritaserum (2020)
10. Hochenbaum, J., Vallis, O.S., Kejariwal, A.: Automatic anomaly detection in the cloud via statistical learning

Topological Analysis of Alzheimer's Progression with Persistence Images

Jayanth Kande(✉)

Southern University and A&M College, Baton Rouge, USA
jayanth.m1229@gmail.com

Abstract. My research employs topological analysis techniques to investigate the progression of Alzheimer's disease (AD) using MRI data. I focus on the utilization of local persistence images (PIs) extracted from temporal lobe patches to classify AD and control subjects. My study evaluates model performance, analyzes topological heterogeneity within diagnostic categories and individual patients, examines the overlap between topological outliers and misclassified samples, and explores the distance of each image to median representations of AD and control subjects. Key findings include competitive classification results using local PIs, significant topological heterogeneity within diagnostic categories, and the identification of trends in patient clustering based on distance to median PIs. My study highlights the potential of topological analysis in understanding AD progression and suggests avenues for future research in disease subtyping and early detection.

1 Introduction

1.1 Alzheimer's Disease

Alzheimer's disease (AD) is the most common form of dementia, with an estimated 75 million cases by 2030 and 132 million by 2050, posing significant healthcare and economic challenges worldwide [1]. In the U.S., AD-related care costs are projected to reach 2 trillion by 2030 [1]. Although AD can only be definitively diagnosed post-mortem, clinicians use a variety of tools such as neuropsychological tests, biomarkers, and MRI to detect early signs of the disease [2–4]. The presence of Amyloid β (Aβ) plaques and neurofibrillary tangles from tau protein aggregation are thought to cause neurodegeneration and brain atrophy, particularly in memory-related regions like the medial temporal lobe [5–7]. Structural MRI (sMRI) has become a reliable biomarker for AD, providing valuable data for classification of cognitively normal (CN) subjects and AD patients using deep learning methods [8]. Additionally, sMRI can reveal affected brain regions, aiding in the identification of AD subtypes [9, 10]. By applying ideas from topology, I aim to capture and quantify the anatomical changes caused by AD, leveraging topological tools to explore brain shape alterations in a computationally efficient manner.

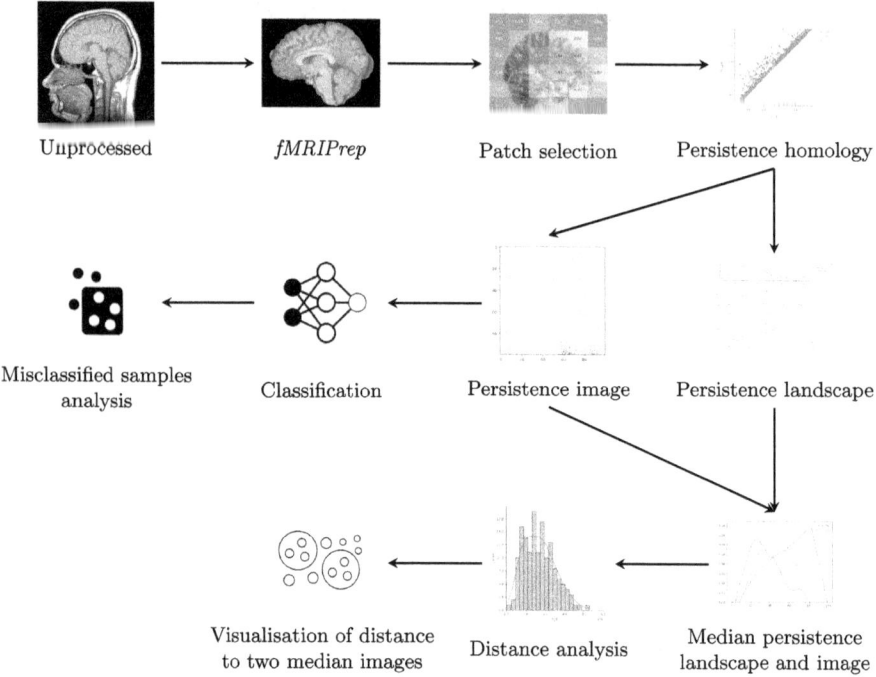

Fig. 1. Flow chart of the analyses conducted in this report. Images adapted from Wikimedia, slicer.org, Xela Ub and Sachin Modgekar

1.2 Topology

Topology has witnessed relentless theoretical progress since Henri Poincaré first addressed topological ideas as a distinct branch of mathematics in his 1895 publication of *Analysis Situs* [11,12]. Only recently, – with the advent of modern computing – has the field of computational topology and topological data analysis (TDA) gained momentum to investigate (high-dimensional) data in physics, biology, and beyond [13–15]. While surveying the various applications of computational topology are beyond the scope of this report, I still want to define several procedures that are paramount to the workflow described in this report: cubical persistence, various vectorized representations of the persistence diagrams obtained from filtered cubical complexes, and the notion of pairwise distance between such representations. For material providing an extensive and formal introduction to topology and persistent homology, please refer to [16,17], and [14] (Fig. 1).

Cubical Complexes and Persistent Homology. To define cubical persistence, we first need to introduce cubical complexes. A cube in a d-dimensional space is a product of d non-degenerate intervals, where 0-cubes, 1-cubes, 2-cubes, and 3-cubes correspond to vertices, edges, squares, and 3D cubes (voxels in the

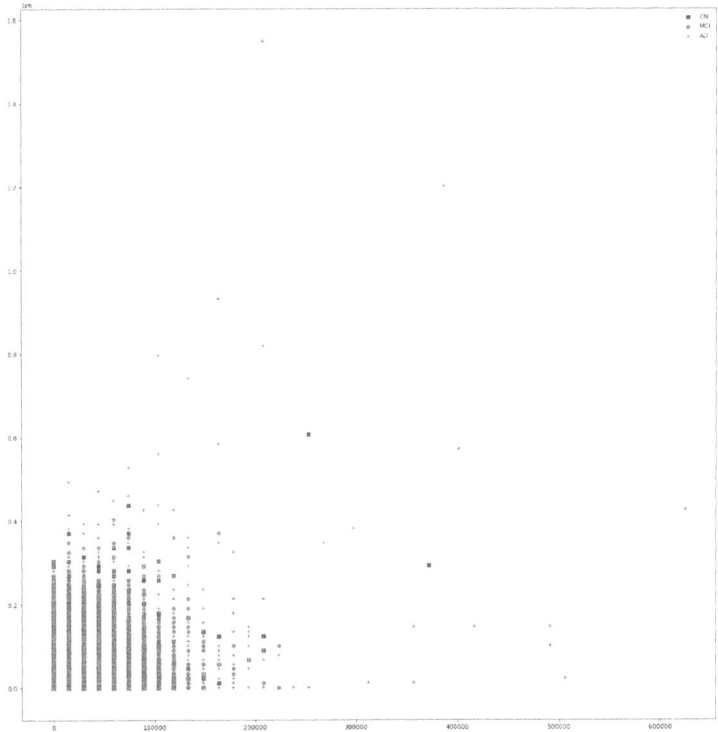

Fig. 2. MDS plot of all diagnostic categories.

context of sMRI). A cubical complex X of dimension d is a finite set of cubes of dimension up to d, closed under taking faces and intersections.

To obtain a cubical complex $\mathbb{X}$ from an MRI image, I use a filtration function $f : \mathbb{X} \to \mathbb{R}$ based on pixel intensities, analyzing the topology of sublevel sets $\mathbb{X}_t = f^{-1}(-\infty, t]$ using persistent homology. This is represented by a persistence diagram (PD), which contains points representing the birth and death of topological features (connected components, tunnels, and cubes) in dimensions 0, 1, and 2. A feature is considered persistent if its birth-death difference is large.

Persistence Images and Persistence Landscapes. PDs are endowed with a metric (further discussed in Sect. 1.2), so it is possible to perform a variety of machine learning (ML) techniques using representations of PDs as input data. However, multiple ML algorithms require more than a metric—fixed-size vectors are often required—. It is therefore desirable to have a fixed-length, stable, efficient-to-compute, interpretable (concerning the PD) and tunable mapping from the PD to a vector space in $\mathbb{R}^n$ to fit various machine learning algorithms to them.

One such representation is the *persistence image* (PI) of a PD, which has also been proven to be stable upon small perturbations of data while still retaining the underlying features in the data useful for classification. Computing the PI from a PD D consists of a two-step process. First, the PD is mapped to an integrable function $\rho_D : \mathbb{R}^2 \to \mathbb{R}$ called a persistent surface. This surface is a weighted sum of Gaussian distributions, each centered around a point of the PD. The matrix of pixel values can be obtained from the computation of the integration of ρ_D on a grid overlaid on the surface [18]. An overview of the pipeline to obtain persistence images is shown in Fig. 3.

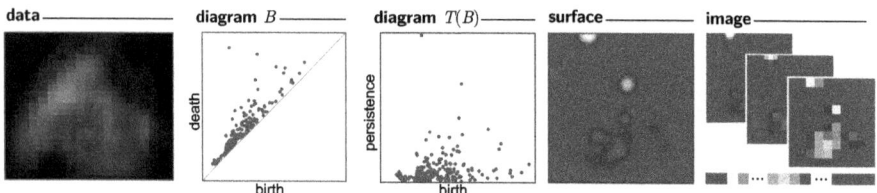

Fig. 3. Pipeline to obtain the persistence image, as presented by [18].

Another representation associated with the PD is the persistence landscape (PL). Similarly to PIs, PLs maps the PD into a Hilbert space, which is useful for ML applications, but additionally extracts the most persistent features from the PD. To define a persistence landscape, let us take a pair (b, d), which refers to the birth and death of a topological feature. I now define the piecewise linear function $f_{(b,d)} : \mathbb{R} \to [0, \infty]$ as:

$$f_{(b,d)}(x) = \begin{cases} 0 & \text{if } x \notin (b, d) \\ x - b & \text{if } x \in (b, \frac{b+d}{2}] \\ -x + b & \text{if } x \in (\frac{b+d}{2}, d] \end{cases} \quad (1)$$

The PL of the birth-death pairs $\{b_i, d_i\}_{i=1}^n$ is the sequence of functions $\lambda_k : \mathbb{R} \to [0, \infty]$, $k = 1, 2, 3, \ldots$ where $\lambda_k(x)$ is the kth largest value of $\{f_{b_i,d_i}(x)\}_{i=1}^n$. I set $\lambda_k(x) = 0$ if the kth largest value does not exist, which results in $\lambda_k = 0$ for $k > n$ [19,20]. An example of PL is shown in Fig. 4.

Pairwise Distances and Medians. A key part of my analysis involves examining distances between vectorized topological representations. As noted by [21], it is important to consider the significance of points in the persistence diagram (PD), where points near the diagonal $(c, c + \epsilon)$ represent short-lived features. Therefore, the minimal cost to match points in two diagrams is relevant, with distances typically calculated using the bottleneck or p-Wasserstein distance, where $p \geq 1$. The p-Wasserstein distance between two diagrams D_1 and D_2 is the infimum over all bijections $\gamma : D_1 \cup \Delta \to D_2 \cup \Delta$, where Δ is the multiset $\{(s, s) \mid s \in \mathbb{R}\}$ with multiplicity $(s, s) \mapsto +\infty$, such that:

$$W_p(D_1, D_2) = \left(\sum_{x \in D_1 \cup \Delta} ||x - \gamma(x)||_q^p \right)^{1/p} \quad (2)$$

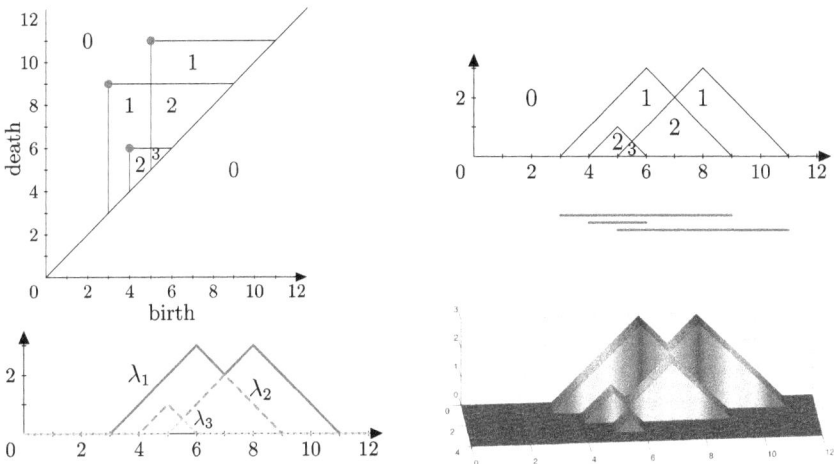

Fig. 4. PL for the homology in degree 1 of linked annuli from [19]. Top left, persistence diagram, top right, rescaled function from Eq. 1. Bottom left and right, 2 and 3-D representation of the persistent landscape. Note that λ_1 represents the most persistent topological features.

where I usually have $q = \infty$. When I let $p \to \infty$, I recover the bottleneck distance.

The median persistence landscape (PL) is computed by taking the median of binned PLs across samples, with a similar approach for persistence images (PIs). The median is preferred over the average due to skewed data, as discussed in Sect. 4.2. Distances between PLs or PIs are calculated using the Minkowski distance, a proxy for the p-Wasserstein distance. I define the Minkowski distance given two vectors $\mathbf{x}, \mathbf{y} \in \mathbb{R}^n$, as:

$$D(\mathbf{x}, \mathbf{y}) = \left(\sum_{i=1}^{n} |x_i - y_i|^p \right)^{\frac{1}{p}}. \tag{3}$$

In this report, I set $p = 1$ and henceforth refer to the distance function as the L^1 norm.

1.3 Research Questions and Outline

This report addresses four key research questions: (1) How salient are topological features from patches for classifying AD vs CN subjects using persistence images (2) What do distances between a patient's persistence image/landscape and the median of a diagnostic category reveal about topological heterogeneity (3) How does the distance between persistence images across time inform disease progression (4) Does the distance between patient images and median AD/CN images enable effective clustering into diagnostic categories or subtypes The report is structured as follows: after introducing AD and TDA concepts, Sect. 2 details the methodology; Sect. 3 presents the findings, discussed in Sect. 4.

2 Methods

Here, I present the methodological choices made for this pipeline. All of the code used to compute the findings presented in this paper are currently available upon request on GitHub.

2.1 Data

T1-weighted, 1.5T MRIs were obtained from the Alzheimer's Disease Neuroimaging Initiative (ADNI) database which contains images from AD patients, patients diagnosed with mild cognitive impairment (MCI) [22], and healthy controls (cognitively normal, CN) of matched age groups [23]. Further preprocessing steps to reduce noise and extract brain structures are highlighted in appendix. Then, scans were divided into 216 patches, each dimension $30 \times 36 \times 30$, providing a possibility for a more focused and computationally efficient investigation while preserving high resolution. Working with a patch is also supported by the fact that an investigation of *local* changes in brain architecture may filter out topological features that are less relevant in the context of Alzheimer's disease.

From earlier work attempting to classify CN subjects from AD patients using a convolutional neural network (CNN) [24], I know that a given patch, shown in grey in Fig. 5, has a particularly high discriminatory potential, so I selected this patch for all my further analyses. Support for the use of this patch also comes from its anatomical relevance, since it contains regions that are most affected by Alzheimer's disease such as the hippocampus, the entorhinal cortex, and the amygdala [7].

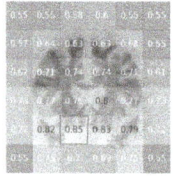

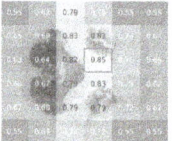

(a) Coronal view of the selected patch. (b) Saggital view of the selected patch. (c) Ventral view of the selected patch.

Fig. 5. Accuracy values on each patch. The selected patch is boxed in red. (Color figure online)

2.2 Topological Data Analysis

To perform the topological analysis on the patch, I used `giotto-tda`, a library specifically made for the integration of TDA pipelines in ML applications [25]. Each filtration on the cubical complexes has been done in three homological dimensions $0, 1, 2$, representing features in each of the dimensions of the three-dimensional image. I otherwise used the default parameters provided by the giotto-tda documentation. An example persistence diagram for a cognitively intact subject, a patient with MCI, and a patient with AD is depicted in Fig. 6. To obtain persistence images for each 3D volume, I used 0.001 as a standard deviation for the Gaussian kernel, no weight function, and a default dimension of 100×100 for each image. The stability of the performance of the classifier shown below was the highest at these particular values, although image dimensions did not influence the performance of local patches, however, higher values for the standard deviation of the Gaussian kernel seemed to affect performance at a value higher than 0.1. Representative samples of these images are shown in Fig. 7.

2.3 Model Architecture

For the classification task of classifying AD vs CN patients, I used a parallel CNN network with one convolutional layer, followed by one dense layer containing 500 neurons and with dropout rates of 50% at training time. The output of the last dense layer is redirected to a single sigmoid neuron for prediction. The model was trained using an exponential decay learning rate scheduler and early stopping, which monitored the validation loss. All of the layers and utilities to train the neural network were provided by the Keras library [26] and are available

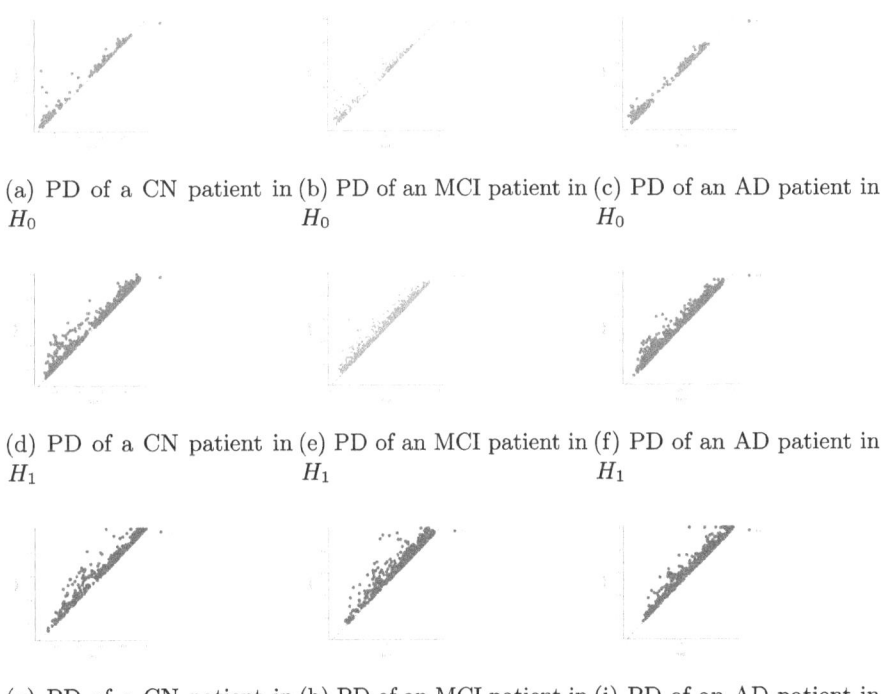

(a) PD of a CN patient in H_0 (b) PD of an MCI patient in H_0 (c) PD of an AD patient in H_0

(d) PD of a CN patient in H_1 (e) PD of an MCI patient in H_1 (f) PD of an AD patient in H_1

(g) PD of a CN patient in H_2 (h) PD of an MCI patient in H_2 (i) PD of an AD patient in H_2

Fig. 6. Representative PD for each of the diagnostic categories.

on the repository, and a depiction of the computation graph is shown in Figure. I also note that the model was trained on a laptop CPU (Intel(R) Core(TM) i7-9750H CPU @ 2.60 GHz). For consistency and to enable a direct comparison with results shown in [24], I used the same data partitioning to present any kind of data leakage that would artificially increase my score, as discussed in [8]. I also computed persistence images with the same parameters from the entire brain in a scan projected in MNI space and trained a separate network with the same parameters. Each model was trained three times to mitigate any performance fluctuations due to different layer initializations.

2.4 Distance Between Median Topological Representations

I computed persistence landscapes (PLs) using giotto-tda, retaining only λ_1 with a vector length of 100, and calculated the median PL for each diagnostic category by averaging each subject's vector coordinates. Pairwise distances between PLs were measured using the L^1 norm. Two settings were considered: (1) Intra-diagnostic category, where distances of each PL from the median PL of the category were computed using the earliest sMRI per patient, and normality

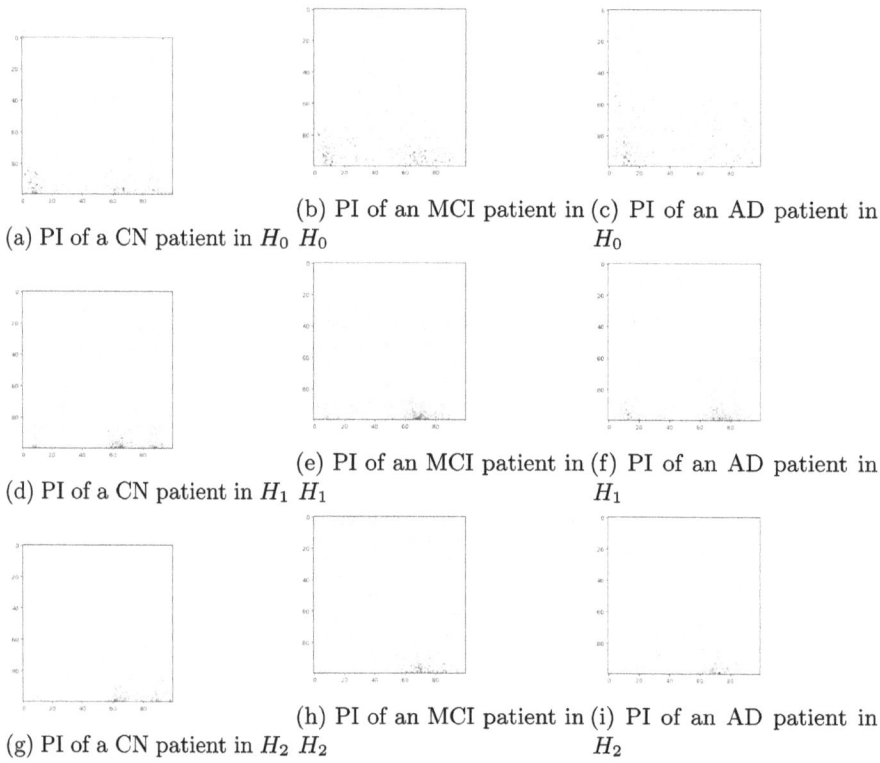

(a) PI of a CN patient in H_0
(b) PI of an MCI patient in H_0
(c) PI of an AD patient in H_0

(d) PI of a CN patient in H_1
(e) PI of an MCI patient in H_1
(f) PI of an AD patient in H_1

(g) PI of a CN patient in H_2
(h) PI of an MCI patient in H_2
(i) PI of an AD patient in H_2

Fig. 7. Representative PI for each of the diagnostic categories. Each column corresponds to a diagnostic category whereas each row corresponds to a homological dimension.

of the distance distribution was tested with the Shapiro-Wilk test. (2) Intra-patient distance, where pairwise distances between PLs of the same patient over time were computed, grouping patients by whether their diagnosis changed or not, and statistical significance was tested using a Mann-Whitney $\mathcal{U}$ test. The analysis was performed on both persistence landscapes and images to capture differences in topological features.

2.5 Relationship Between Distances and Misclassification

To investigate the relationship between patients departing significantly from the median representation of the diagnostic category to which they belong and misclassified patients, I chose to take the n subjects – hereafter referred to as *topological outliers* – with the highest L_1 norm from their median representation, and set n to the number of misclassified patients from one trained network defined in Sect. 2.3 – here, 145 images were misclassified[1]. I then looked at the overlap between patients who were misclassified and the selected set of topological outliers, as well as the distribution of the distance of the misclassified samples compared to the median representation.

2.6 Clustering Using Multiple Median Topological Representations

As the last step, I investigated whether the distance of a patient concerning more than one median persistence image efficiently differentiates between images. We, therefore, evaluated the L^1 norm between each persistence image and both the median AD persistence image and median CN persistence image in H_2 (i.e. voids). I chose to take these two images because they showed high variability in other analyses (see Fig. 11) and they represent the two most divergent diagnostic cases in my dataset, MCI being considered as a state where patients are neither cognitively normal nor formally diagnosed with AD. Given I wanted to maximize variance across samples for visualization purposes, I first standardized the data and subsequently applied a principal component analysis to the resulting pairs of distances. I also compared this approach with a metric multidimensional scaling (MDS) plot frequently used for similar purposes.

3 Results

Here I present the results obtained from the above-mentioned pipeline, starting with a performance assessment of the deep learning model. I then turn my attention to the topological heterogeneity observed both within each diagnostic category and within each patient. I then present my findings of the overlap between topological outliers and misclassified samples. Finally, I look at the distance of each image to the median image representation of AD and CN to see if clusters emerge.

---

[1] Therefore, the PLs or PIs of patients with the 145 highest distance from their respective median PL or PI.

3.1 Model Performance

The performance metrics of the deep learning model are shown in Table 1, and seems to be somewhat inferior to state-of-the-art models trained on similar data [8], but requires dramatically less computing power – the relatively shallow multilayer CNN shown in [24], for instance, requires 15 min of training time on a server GPU while my approach requires only 2 min on one laptop CPU, showing the high grade of compression of the approach presented here. The performance measures also show that training the same architecture on whole-brain CNNs does not yield better performance, instead showing a slight decline. Additionally, the model trained on local PIs yields higher performance compared to whole-brain persistence images reported in [24] as well as when training the network on whole-brain PIs obtained with the same parameters. Remarkably, I observe that the performance of my network seems to be more stable than other approaches for which standard deviations of performance metrics are provided.

Table 1. Performance metrics of the local PI approach. Bold column headers represent performance numbers obtained from the networks trained in this report. Global PI and local 3D Conv approach as reported from [24]. SOTA results are obtained from [27].

| Local (single patch) | **PI** | | 3D Conv | | |
Global (whole-brain)		**PI**		PI	SOTA
Validation accuracy	0.80 ± 0.02	0.74 ± 0.03	0.85 ± 0.06	0.76 ± 0.02	0.91
Precision	0.81 ± 0.04	0.80 ± 0.05	0.78 ± 0.04	0.87 ± 0.04	–
Recall	0.81 ± 0.02	0.85 ± 0.08	0.87 ± 0.08	0.88 ± 0.08	0.84
AUC	0.85 ± 0.03	0.77 ± 0.03	0.89 ± 0.05	0.78 ± 0.02	0.96

3.2 Distance Analysis

L^1 Norm Among Diagnostic Categories – Topological Heterogeneity of Each Diagnostic Category. I now present my findings regarding the distribution of the distances between the PL and PI of each image concerning the median PL and PI for each diagnostic category. The representative PL and PI for each diagnostic category are shown in Fig. 8 and 9, and the distribution of the L^1 norm between each patient and this median PLs and PIs are shown in Fig. 10 and Fig. 11, respectively. Before looking at the distribution of distance values, I first note that the height of the peak median PL of AD patients in H_2 seems to be *lower* than in CN or MCI. Interestingly, I see that the distribution of distances between PLs and the median PL in each diagnostic category and homological dimension is far more skewed—which is reflected by very low p-values of the Shapiro-Wilk test. For persistence images—see Fig. 11—, the distance distributions seem to be much more homogeneous with p-values still significant for some scenarios, but not all. Refer to Table 2 for details. Overall, the p-values are much closer to the significance threshold (Table 3).

(a) Median PL for CN subjects (b) Median PL for MCI subjects (c) Median PL for AD subjects

Fig. 8. Median persistence landscapes for each of the diagnostic categories.

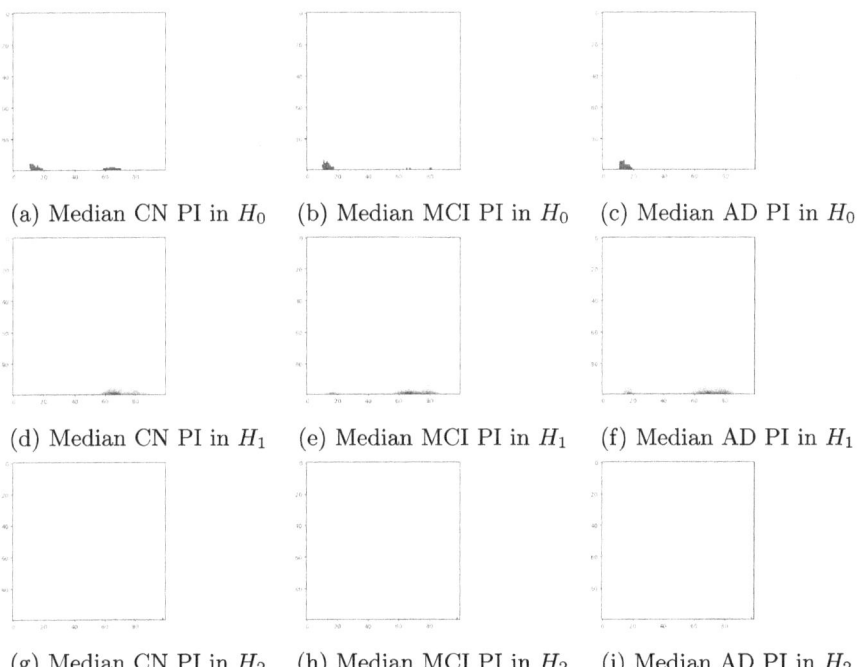

(a) Median CN PI in H_0 (b) Median MCI PI in H_0 (c) Median AD PI in H_0

(d) Median CN PI in H_1 (e) Median MCI PI in H_1 (f) Median AD PI in H_1

(g) Median CN PI in H_2 (h) Median MCI PI in H_2 (i) Median AD PI in H_2

Fig. 9. Median persistence images for each of the diagnostic categories and homological dimension.

Intra-patient Pairwise Distance and Average L^1 Norm Distributions – Topological Evolution. As discussed in Sect. 2.2, I compute the distance between various persistence landscapes (PLs) at different time points for each patient to capture their topological evolution. Applying this method to ADNI data reveals notable qualitative trends: stable CN patients exhibit low distance variations across time points (Fig. 12), while patients transitioning from MCI to AD show higher distances (Fig. 13). However, these observations do not generalize. When comparing the average distances across homological dimensions for patients who transition to AD or remain stable, no significant quantitative differences emerge (Fig. 14).

Interestingly, a bimodal distribution of Wasserstein distances appears for both deteriorating and stable patients, which largely disappears as $p \to \infty$, recovering the bottleneck distance. The reason for this change remains unclear. Although no substantial differences are found, slight shifts to the right are seen in both Wasserstein and L^1 norms, suggesting some increased variability. Mann-Whitney $\mathcal{U}$ tests confirm that these two distributions are significantly different ($p < 0.01$) for all cases.

3.3 Topological Outliers and Misclassified Samples

The distribution of distances concerning the average persistent landscape was plotted for the patients who were correctly classified, and for those who were not correctly classified. The results are shown in Fig. 15. I also examined the proportion of patients who switched diagnoses in the whole ADNI dataset. I found that 70% (64) of the misclassified patients had only one diagnosis versus 71% (323) in the whole dataset, hence indicating that misclassified patients did not contain persistent features that made them more likely to be misclassified.

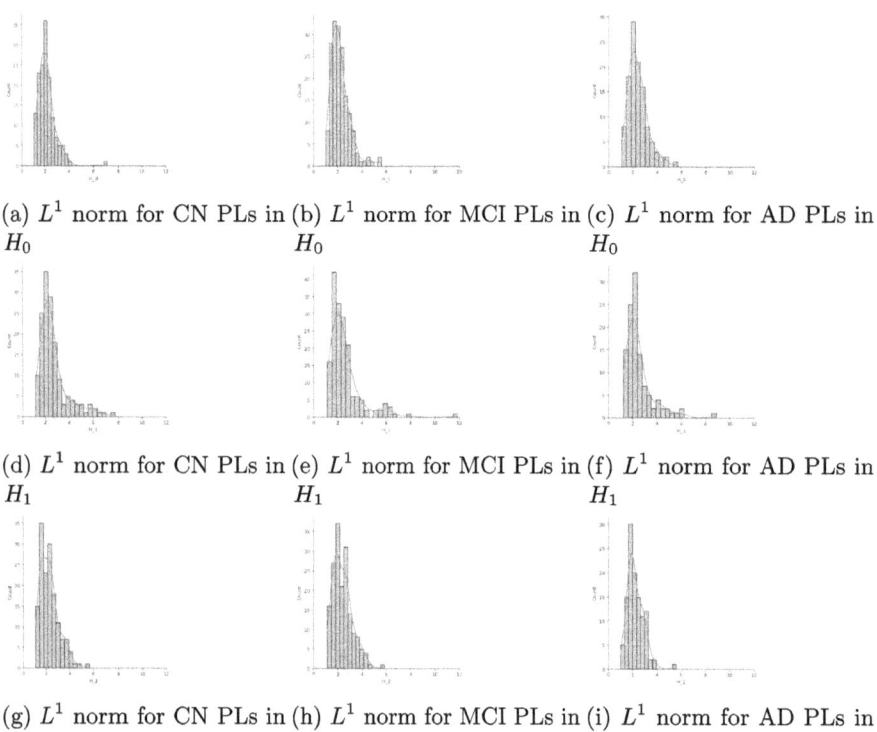

(a) L^1 norm for CN PLs in H_0 (b) L^1 norm for MCI PLs in H_0 (c) L^1 norm for AD PLs in H_0

(d) L^1 norm for CN PLs in H_1 (e) L^1 norm for MCI PLs in H_1 (f) L^1 norm for AD PLs in H_1

(g) L^1 norm for CN PLs in H_2 (h) L^1 norm for MCI PLs in H_2 (i) L^1 norm for AD PLs in H_2

Fig. 10. Histogram overlayed with a density estimate showing the distribution of the L^1 norm taken between the median PL for diagnostic categories in all homological dimensions.

3.4 Visualisation of the Distance of Each Patient to the Median PI of AD Patients and CN Patients

The results of the procedure highlighted in Sect. 2.6 are shown in Fig. 16. I see that on average AD patients tend to cluster higher up in the visualization compared to CN subjects. As expected, patients diagnosed with MCI tend to comingle among AD and CN patients. This trend does not appear using an out-of-the-box mMDS plot, as can be seen in Fig. 2. Clear clusters need yet to be defined more clearly using topological data analysis.

4 Discussion

In this section, I begin by discussing how persistence images provide salient features for the characterization of atrophy due to Alzheimer's disease and result in competitive classification performance results; I then move on to discuss my findings regarding the distributions of distances among diagnostic categories and

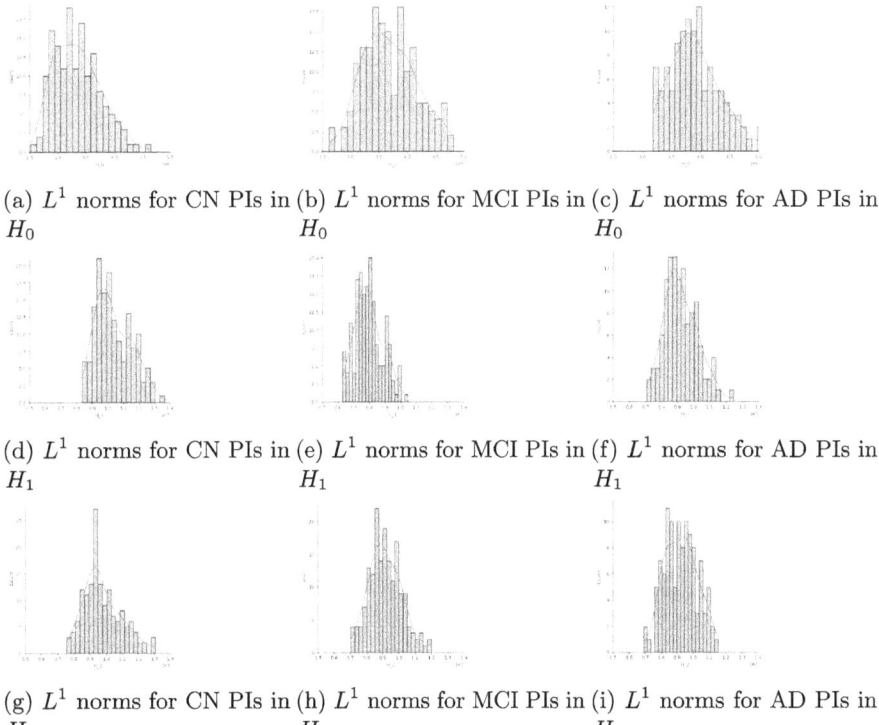

(a) L^1 norms for CN PIs in H_0 (b) L^1 norms for MCI PIs in H_0 (c) L^1 norms for AD PIs in H_0

(d) L^1 norms for CN PIs in H_1 (e) L^1 norms for MCI PIs in H_1 (f) L^1 norms for AD PIs in H_1

(g) L^1 norms for CN PIs in H_2 (h) L^1 norms for MCI PIs in H_2 (i) L^1 norms for AD PIs in H_2

Fig. 11. Histogram overlayed with a density estimate showing the distribution of the L^1 norm taken between the PI and each image within a diagnostic category in all three homological dimensions.

within patients, also touching upon how distances relate to misclassified samples. Then, I briefly discuss how taking the distance of each image concerning two median persistence images yields trends of clusters of patients. Finally, I outline some limitations and further research avenues to be explored in the future.

4.1 Local Persistence Images for AD Atrophy Characterization

Persistence images (PIs) detect AD atrophy from temporal lobe patches (Table 1), though performance is below state-of-the-art [27]. Stability of persistence homology and PIs under noise. Contributes to consistent results.

Lacking clinical data like biomarkers [2], misclassified samples showed no increased topological outliers (Fig. 15).

Table 2. Summary statistics of the distribution of distances from median persistence landscapes for each diagnostic category shown in Fig. 10. Bold values represent relatively high values. SW: Shapiro-Wilk test p-value

	Mean	Median	Std. dev.	Q3	Max	Skewness	SW
CN H_0	2.145	2.022	0.74	2.457	7.095	2.351	1.9×10^{-11}
CN H_1	2.669	2.35	1.202	2.9	7.757	1.823	7.2×10^{-13}
CN H_2	2.293	2.198	0.812	2.647	5.677	1.093	4.6×10^{-7}
MCI H_0	2.215	2.063	0.78	2.559	5.609	1.52	6.0×10^{-10}
MCI H_1	2.592	2.219	1.407	2.85	11.866	**2.787**	2.4×10^{-16}
MCI H_2	2.382	2.251	0.815	2.782	5.852	0.95	2.2×10^{-6}
AD H_0	2.422	2.261	0.813	2.832	5.701	1.189	1.1×10^{-5}
AD H_1	2.514	2.183	1.172	2.717	8.878	**2.395**	3.6×10^{-12}
AD H_2	2.237	2.073	0.686	2.637	5.594	1.305	6.1×10^{-6}

Table 3. Summary statistics of the distribution of distances from median persistence image for each diagnostic category shown in Fig. 11. Bold values represent non-significant p-values. SW: Shapiro-Wilk test p-value.

	Mean	Median	Std. dev.	Q3	Max	Skewness	SW
CN H_0	3.3×10^6	3.3×10^6	4.0×10^5	3.6×10^6	4.6×10^6	5.2×10^{-1}	0.006
CN H_1	1.0×10^7	1.0×10^7	1.1×10^6	1.1×10^7	1.4×10^7	6.7×10^{-1}	0.0
CN H_2	9.7×10^6	9.4×10^6	1.1×10^6	1.0×10^7	1.3×10^7	6.4×10^{-1}	0.0
MCI H_0	3.6×10^6	3.6×10^6	4.6×10^5	4.0×10^6	4.8×10^6	2.5×10^{-1}	**0.071**
MCI H_1	7.9×10^6	7.8×10^6	8.7×10^5	8.4×10^6	1.0×10^7	3.5×10^{-1}	0.018
MCI H_2	9.1×10^6	9.0×10^6	9.9×10^5	9.8×10^6	1.1×10^7	3.4×10^{-1}	**0.169**
AD H_0	3.8×10^6	3.8×10^6	4.1×10^5	4.1×10^6	5.0×10^6	4.8×10^{-1}	0.034
AD H_1	9.1×10^6	9.0×10^6	1.0×10^6	9.9×10^6	1.2×10^7	4.4×10^{-1}	**0.144**
AD H_2	9.2×10^6	9.1×10^6	1.0×10^6	9.9×10^6	1.1×10^7	1.0×10^{-1}	**0.387**

Future work could use multi-patch analysis [9,10] and Grad-CAM for better feature weighting.

4.2 Distances

The analysis of distance distributions reveals some unexpected results, as seen in Sect. 3.2 and Fig. 8. Contrary to expectations, larger persistent features do not consistently emerge as median features, underscoring interpretability challenges in linking persistent homology findings to biological phenomena [28].

Figure 10 shows a skewed distribution of patch PL distances to median PL, especially in MCI, indicating topological heterogeneity, potentially due to noise in data acquisition and preprocessing. This skew is reduced when using persistence images, which capture all features and yield a more uniform distribution.

Intra-patient distance functions showed minimal variation, likely due to noise obscuring progression signals. Advanced clustering on PDs could better capture temporal trajectories, as local patches may inadequately represent global atrophy patterns in Alzheimer's progression [29].

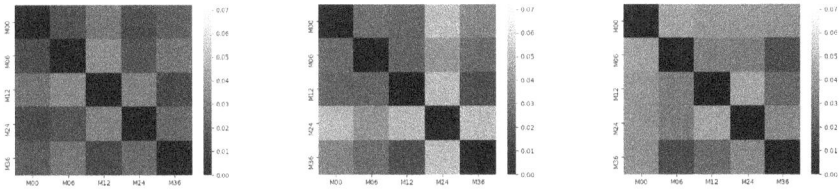

Fig. 12. Topological evolution of a subject with an unchanging CN diagnosis as shown through the pairwise distances between the persistence images obtained from the same acquired at several months intervals. M00 refers to the baseline sMRI, M06 refers to the sMRI taken 6 months after the baseline image, etc.

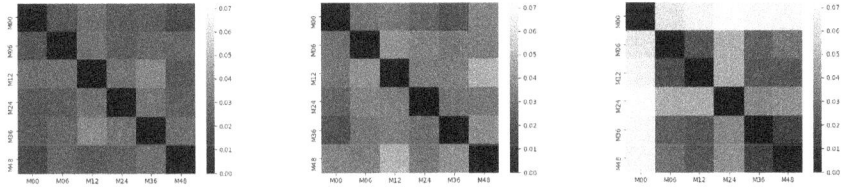

Fig. 13. Topological evolution of a patient who transitions from MCI to AD in the course of the observation. The setup is the same as for Fig. 12. For this particular patient, the change in diagnosis occurred at $t = 24$, i.e. 24 months after the earliest available diagnosis, which also incidentally corresponds with the highest distance from that baseline.

4.3 Visualizing PIs Using Distances to the Median PI of AD Patients and CN Subjects

I now examine Fig. 16, which plots the principal components obtained from computing the L^1 norm of each image concerning the median image in H_2. I see some trends emerging: for instance, I tend to see CN PIs cluster in the upper part of the plot while AD PIs tend to cluster in the bottom, with MCI patients mostly blended in between. Yet, these trends are not clear enough to obtain clear clusters of disease phenotypes (i.e. one associated with each condition), let alone disease subtypes. It should be noted that the approach presented here to cluster patients still performs qualitatively better than out-of-the-box embedding approaches such as mMDS plots as shown in Fig. 2. Obtaining features more salient for clustering various subtypes would probably require more complex features, extracted for instance using a dynamic autoencoder on the persistence

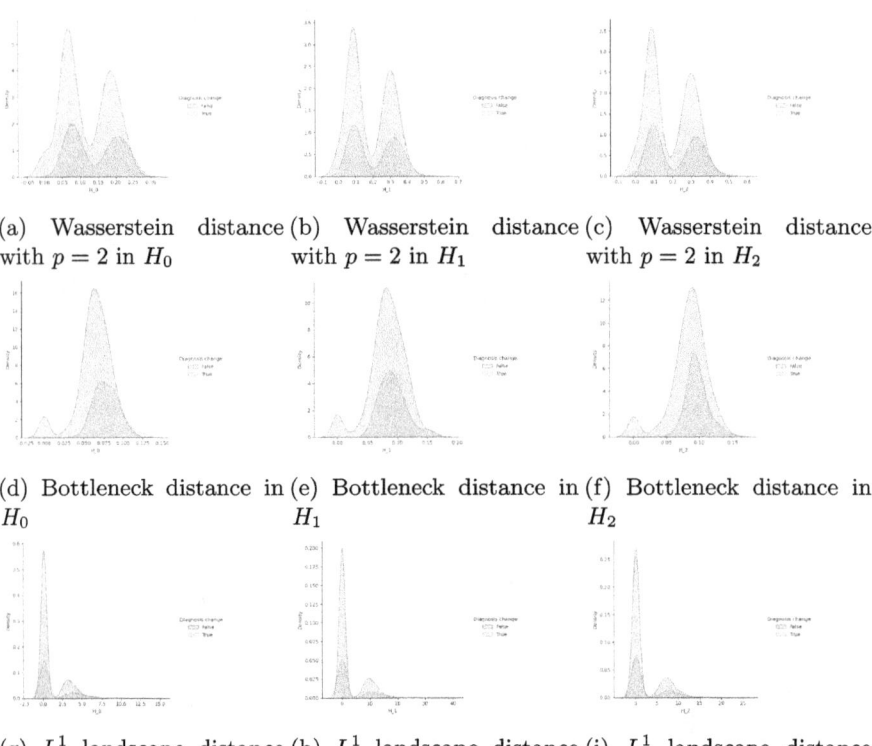

(a) Wasserstein distance with $p = 2$ in H_0
(b) Wasserstein distance with $p = 2$ in H_1
(c) Wasserstein distance with $p = 2$ in H_2

(d) Bottleneck distance in H_0
(e) Bottleneck distance in H_1
(f) Bottleneck distance in H_2

(g) L^1 landscape distance with 1 layer in H_0
(h) L^1 landscape distance with 1 layer in H_1
(i) L^1 landscape distance with 1 layer in H_2

Fig. 14. Kernel density estimation of the average distance between each image timepoint for each patient. The orange curve represents all those patients who have had at least one change in diagnosis throughout the disease, whereas patients who have not been in the blue curve. (Color figure online)

images [30]. Additionally, other methods tailored for topological features might also be developed and applied here.

4.4 Limitations and Outlook

This analysis faces limitations in identifying noise within high-persistence features, potentially introduced by preprocessing steps like image normalization [31], though exact sources remain uncertain. Additionally, using basic distance metrics, such as the L^1 norm, may obscure finer discriminative features; optimized clustering could better harness topological distinctions. The model also lacks nuanced diagnostic capability, omitting conditions like MCI, thus limiting clinical application.

Future work could expand this approach to other neurodegenerative disorders, each with distinct topological signatures [32–34]. Clustering based on persistence images may also refine AD subtype classification, potentially aiding early-stage identification and intervention [35,36].

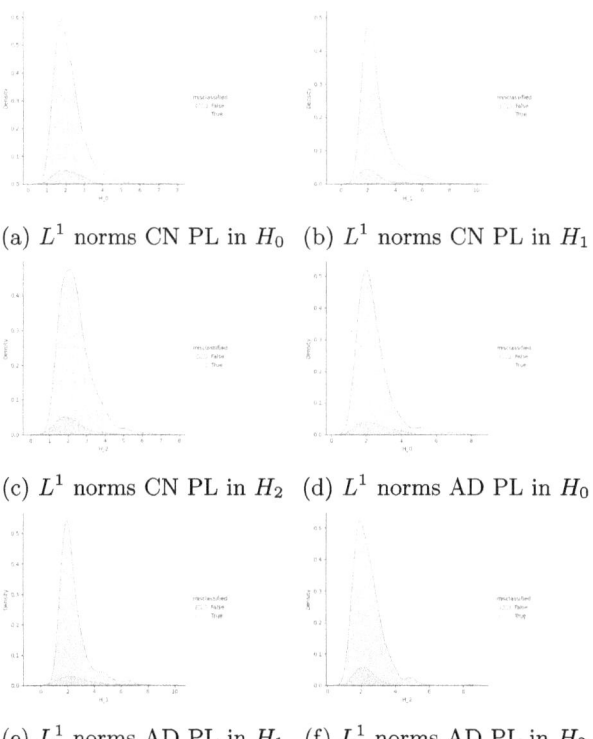

(a) L^1 norms CN PL in H_0 (b) L^1 norms CN PL in H_1

(c) L^1 norms CN PL in H_2 (d) L^1 norms AD PL in H_0

(e) L^1 norms AD PL in H_1 (f) L^1 norms AD PL in H_2

Fig. 15. Kernel density estimation of the distribution of the distance between the AD and CN median persistence image for images that have not and have been misclassified.

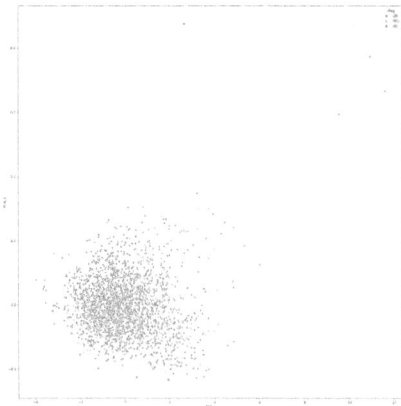

Fig. 16. Visualisation of the two PCA components obtained from looking at the distance between the L^1 distance of each image to the median PI of AD and CN in H_2.

5 Conclusions

In this report, I have shown that PIs computed from a patch in the temporal lobe are salient for classifying CN and AD subjects. Additionally, I show that the distribution of distances among the patients in each of the diagnostic categories is skewed, indicating the presence of topological outliers, but, overall, does not affect the classification performance. Then, I show a significant, but not substantial, increase in distance among images belonging to a given patient who deteriorates towards Alzheimer's disease versus patients who do not. My last finding is that clustering patients solely according to their distance concerning multiple median PI does not allow proper AD subtype identification, be shows a promising research avenue. Although promising, all of these topology-driven approaches need further development to maximize the information that can be extracted from MRI images.

References

1. WHO. Global action plan on the public health response to dementia 2017–2025 (2017)
2. McKhann, G.M., et al.: The diagnosis of dementia due to Alzheimer's disease: recommendations from the national institute on aging-Alzheimer's association workgroups on diagnostic guidelines for Alzheimer's disease. Alzheimer's Dementia **7**(3), 263–269 (2011)
3. Smits, L.L., et al.: Early onset Alzheimer's disease is associated with a distinct neuropsychological profile. J. Alzheimers Dis. **30**(1), 101–108 (2012)
4. Lehmann, S., Teunissen, C.E.: Biomarkers of Alzheimer's disease: the present and the future. Front. Neurol. **7**, 158 (2016)

5. Dá Mesquita, S., Ferreira, A.C., Sousa, J.C., Correia-Neves, M., Sousa, N., Marques, F.: Insights on the pathophysiology of Alzheimer's disease: the crosstalk between amyloid pathology, neuroinflammation and the peripheral immune system. Neurosci. Biobehav. Rev. **68**, 547–562 (2016)
6. Frisoni, G.B., Fox, N.C., Jack, C.R., Scheltens, P., Thompson, P.M.: The clinical use of structural MRI in Alzheimer disease. Nat. Rev. Neurol. **6**(2), 67–77 (2010)
7. Goedert, M., Spillantini, M.G.: A century of Alzheimer's disease. Science **314**(5800), 777–781 (2006)
8. Wen, J., et al.: Convolutional neural networks for classification of Alzheimer's disease: overview and reproducible evaluation. Med. Image Anal. 101694 (2020)
9. Poulakis, K., et al.: Heterogeneous patterns of brain atrophy in Alzheimer's disease. Neurobiol. Aging **65**, 98–108 (2018)
10. Tijms, B.M., et al.: Pathophysiological subtypes of Alzheimer's disease based on cerebrospinal fluid proteomics. medRxiv (2020)
11. Poincaré, H.: Analysis situs. Gauthier-Villars (1895)
12. James, I.M.: History of Topology. Elsevier (1999)
13. Dey, T.K., Edelsbrunner, H., Guha, S.: Computational topology. Contemp. Math. **223**, 109–144 (1999)
14. Ghrist, R.: Barcodes: the persistent topology of data. Bull. Am. Math. Soc. **45**(1), 61–75 (2008)
15. Amézquita, E.J., Quigley, M.Y., Ophelders, T., Munch, E., Chitwood, D.H.: The shape of things to come: topological data analysis and biology, from molecules to organisms. Dev. Dyn. (2020)
16. Freedman, D., Chen, C.: Algebraic topology for computer vision. Comput. Vis. 239–268 (2009)
17. Edelsbrunner, H., Harer, J.: Computational Topology: An Introduction. American Mathematical Soc. (2010)
18. Adams, H., et al.: Persistence images: a stable vector representation of persistent homology. J. Mach. Learn. Res. **18**(1), 218–252 (2017)
19. Bubenik, P.: Statistical topological data analysis using persistence landscapes. J. Mach. Learn. Res. **16**(1), 77–102 (2015)
20. Bubenik, P.: The persistence landscape and some of its properties. In: Baas, N.A., Carlsson, G.E., Quick, G., Szymik, M., Thaule, M. (eds.) Topological Data Analysis. AS, vol. 15, pp. 97–117. Springer, Cham (2020). https://doi.org/10.1007/978-3-030-43408-3_4
21. Berwald, J.J., Gottlieb, J.M., Munch, E.: Computing Wasserstein distance for persistence diagrams on a quantum computer. arXiv preprint arXiv:1809.06433 (2018)
22. Gauthier, S., et al.: Mild cognitive impairment. Lancet **367**(9518), 1262–1270 (2006)
23. Jack, C.R., Jr., et al.: The Alzheimer's disease neuroimaging initiative (ADNI): MRI methods. J. Magnet. Resonan. Imaging Off. J. Int. Soc. Magnet. Resonan. Med. **27**(4), 685–691 (2008)
24. Brüningk, S.C., Hensel, F., Jutzeler, C.R., Rieck, B.: Image analysis for alzheimer's disease prediction: Embracing pathological hallmarks for model architecture design. arXiv preprintarXiv:2011.06531 (2020)
25. Tauzin, G., et al.: GIOTTO-TDA: a topological data analysis toolkit for machine learning and data exploration (2020)
26. Chollet, F., et al.: Keras. https://keras.io (2015)
27. Liu, M., Zhang, J., Nie, D., Yap, P.-T., Shen, D.: Anatomical landmark based deep feature representation for MR images in brain disease diagnosis. IEEE J. Biomed. Health Inform. **22**(5), 1476–1485 (2018)

28. Vanherpe, L., Kanari, L., Atenekeng, G., Palacios, J., Shillcock, J.: Framework for efficient synthesis of spatially embedded morphologies. Phys. Rev. E **94**(2), 023315 (2016)
29. Toniolo, S., Serra, L., Olivito, G., Marra, C., Bozzali, M., Cercignani, M.: Patterns of cerebellar gray matter atrophy across Alzheimer's disease progression. Front. Cell. Neurosci. **12**, 430 (2018)
30. Mrabah, N., Khan, N.M., Ksantini, R., Lachiri, Z.: Deep clustering with a dynamic autoencoder. CoRR (2019)
31. Collins, D.L.: 3D model-based segmentation of individual brain structures from magnetic resonance imaging data (1994)
32. Kuhl, D.E., Phelps, M.E., Markham, C.H., Metter, E.J., Riege, W.H., Winter, J.: Cerebral metabolism and atrophy in Huntington's disease determined by 18fdg and computed tomographic scan. Ann. Neurol. Off. J. Am. Neurol. Assoc. Child Neurol. Soc. **12**(5), 425–434 (1982)
33. Halliday, G., McRitchie, D., Macdonald, V., Double, K., Trent, R., McCusker, E.: Regional specificity of brain atrophy in Huntington's disease. Exp. Neurol. **154**(2), 663–672 (1998)
34. Kassubek, J., et al.: Topography of cerebral atrophy in early Huntington's disease: a voxel based morphometric MRI study. J. Neurol. Neurosur. Psych. **75**(2), 213–220 (2004)
35. Scarmeas, N., Stern, Y.: Cognitive reserve: implications for diagnosis and prevention of Alzheimer's disease. Curr. Neurol. Neurosci. Rep. **4**(5), 374–380 (2004)
36. van Loenhoud, A.C., et al.: A neuroimaging approach to capture cognitive reserve: application to Alzheimer's disease. Hum. Brain Mapp. **38**(9), 4703–4715 (2017)

Logistic Regression in Machine Learning and Data Analytics with Python for Detecting Financial Fraud in Credit Card Transactions

Meenakshi Kumari[1] and Prakash Anand[2(✉)]

[1] Usha Martin University, Ranchi, Jharkhand, India
[2] Sarala Birla University, Mahilong, Ranchi, Jharkhand, India
`prakash.anand.jha62@gmail.com`

Abstract. Financial fraud poses a significant threat to both consumers and financial institutions, leading to substantial financial losses and erosion of trust in the banking system. Credit card fraud, in particular, represents a prevalent form of financial crime due to the widespread use of credit cards for transactions. To combat this menace, machine learning techniques such as logistic regression coupled with advanced data analytics have emerged as powerful tools for detecting fraudulent activity involving transactions related to credit cards. This paper explores an application related to logistic regression, a widely used statistical method for binary classification, in the realm of financial fraud detection. Leveraging a dataset comprising historical characteristics of credit card transactions, including transaction amount, location, time, and user behavior are analyzed to identify patterns indicative of fraudulent behavior. The effectiveness of the suggested strategy is evaluated using actual world credit card transaction data, demonstrating its capacity to effectively differentiate between legitimate and dishonest business dealings. Results indicate that logistic regression model, in conjunction with data analytics techniques, offers a promising solution for detecting financial fraud in credit card transactions, thereby safeguarding the interests of consumers and financial institutions alike.

Keywords: PCA (Principle component Analysis) · LR (Logistic Regression) · AUPRC · or area under the precision-recall curve · Operating Characteristic of the Receiver

1 Introduction

In the current increasingly digitized humankind, using credit cards for various purposes has become ubiquitous, offering unparalleled convenience and flexibility in financial transactions. However, along with the benefits, the proliferation of credit card usage has also given rise to a pressing concern: fraud. The dangers of credit card fraud are substantial threats to both financial organizations as well as cardholders, with losses amounting to billions of dollars annually worldwide. Detecting and preventing fraud involving credit cards is a critical priority Regarding financial organizations, merchants as well as customers. As fraudulent activities continue to evolve in sophistication and scale, traditional methods of fraud detection have become insufficient. In response, the field of credit card fraud detection has seen significant advancements, [9] leveraging innovative technologies and analytical techniques to stay ahead of fraudulent schemes. This paper explores the landscape of credit card fraud detection, delving into the various methodologies, technologies, and strategies employed to identify and mitigate fraudulent activities. This paper's goal is to present a thorough analysis of credit card fraud detection, shedding light on the techniques, challenges, and advancements in this critical domain. [10] By understanding the complexities of fraud detection, stakeholders can better equip themselves to combat fraudulent activities, safeguarding the integrity of financial systems and preserving trust in electronic payment mechanisms.

Logistic Regression

A statistical model called logistic regression is used for binary classification problems, in which the objective is to forecast the likelihood that an instance falls into a specific category. In contrast to linear regression, which forecasts a continuous output, logistic regression maps the outcome to a probability range between 0 and 1 using the logistic function (sigmoid).

2 Literature Review

As digitization and internet transactions improve, credit card usage increases. The most common type of fraud is credit card fraud that is the common concerns in today's society. Typically, this sort of fraud happens when the fraudster uses another user's credit card information [1] N. Vijaya, L. S. Manohar, S. R. Kishan, and M. Devika implemented the logistic regression approach; the accuracy will be closer to 0.99%, allowing us to readily spot frauds. [2] Y. Sahin and E. Duman's proposed study is one of the first to assess the performance using ANN and LR algorithms to detect credit card fraud on a real-world dataset. To prevent charging customers for goods they did not buy, credit card companies need to be able to identify fraudulent transactions. To overcome these issues, data may be used. The relevance of science, in addition to soft and machine learning, cannot be overstated. [3] A. Chauhan, A. Aggarwal, A. Singh, and A. Singh implemented the Catboost algorithm, which performs best for detecting credit card theft with a 99.87% accuracy rate. Credit Card Management Organisations are critical for selecting fraudulent activity that affects your credit score, ensuring that customers are billed for goods they haven't yet bought. Together with the machine, data and technical knowledge of the data can be used to overcome these obstacles. [4] Chauhan, V. Singh, K. Singh, and Y. Singh. In this method, he focused on the analysis and preprocessing of numerous anomaly identification algorithms and record sets in PCA-converted credit card transaction data, including "neighbour outliers" and "forest zone isolation" procedures. Credit card fraud is the shady practice of exploiting personal information to make internet purchases [5]. Thus, in the work provided by R. Verma, M. P. Thapliyal, S. Maurya, and D. S. Nijwala, To get the ideal value that produces a great result while being efficient, a number of threshold values are calculated and compared. One of the biggest threats to people and companies around the world is credit card fraud, particularly with the rise in everyday financial transactions involving credit cards. In order to help you choose the appropriate course of action, B. Al Smadi and M. Min's work [6] examines several tactics in terms of accuracy, time, and cost and discusses potential advantages and disadvantages.

3 Financial Fraud in Credit Card Detection Using Logistic Regression

3.1 Importing Libraries

The library that we have used in this model are Pandas, numpy, seaborn, matplotlib, statsmodel, warning.

3.2 Dataset

Credit card transactions made by European cardholders in September 2013 are included in the dataset. Out of the 284,807 transactions in this dataset, 492 were fraudulent and occurred within two days. With the positive class (frauds) making up 0.172% of all transactions, the dataset is incredibly unbalanced. Only numerical input variables that are the result of a PCA transformation are included. Unfortunately, we are unable to reveal the original attributes and other background information on the data due to confidentiality considerations. 'Time' and 'Amount' are the only features that PCA has not changed. Features V1, V2,... V28 are the primary components used. The number of seconds between each transaction and the dataset's first transaction is displayed in the 'Time' feature (Fig. 1).

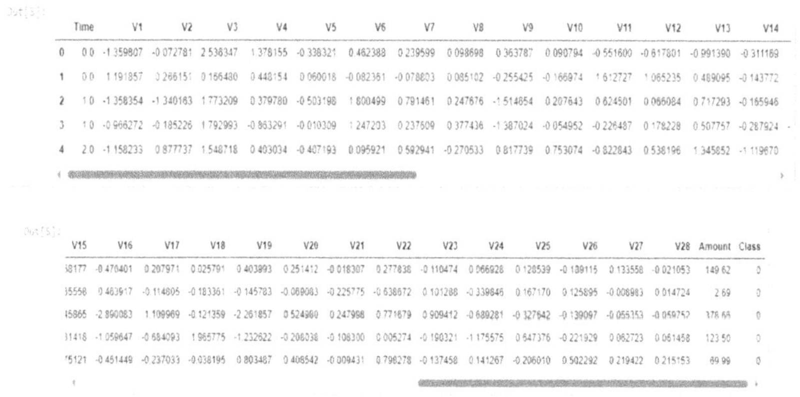

	Time	V1	V2	V3	V4	V5	V6	V7	V8	V9	V10	V11	V12	V13	V14
0	0.0	-1.359807	-0.072781	2.536347	1.378155	-0.338321	0.462388	0.239599	0.098698	0.363787	0.090794	-0.551600	-0.617801	-0.991390	-0.311169
1	0.0	1.191857	0.266151	0.166480	0.448154	0.060018	-0.082361	-0.078803	0.085102	-0.255425	-0.166974	1.612727	1.065235	0.489095	-0.143772
2	1.0	-1.358354	-1.340163	1.773209	0.379780	-0.503198	1.800499	0.791461	0.247676	-1.514654	0.207643	0.624501	0.066084	0.717293	-0.165946
3	1.0	-0.966272	-0.185226	1.792993	-0.863291	-0.010309	1.247203	0.237609	0.377436	-1.387024	-0.054952	-0.226487	0.178228	0.507757	-0.287924
4	2.0	-1.158233	0.877737	1.548718	0.403034	-0.407193	0.095921	0.592941	-0.270533	0.817739	0.753074	-0.822843	0.538196	1.345852	-1.119670

V15	V16	V17	V18	V19	V20	V21	V22	V23	V24	V25	V26	V27	V28	Amount	Class
38177	-0.470401	0.207971	0.025791	0.403993	0.251412	-0.018307	0.277838	-0.110474	0.066928	0.128539	-0.189115	0.133558	-0.021053	149.62	0
35558	0.463917	-0.114805	-0.183361	-0.145783	-0.069083	-0.225775	-0.638672	0.101288	-0.339846	0.167170	0.125895	-0.008983	0.014724	2.69	0
45865	-2.890083	1.109969	-0.121359	-2.261857	0.524980	0.247998	0.771679	0.909412	-0.689281	-0.327642	-0.139097	-0.055353	-0.059752	378.66	0
31418	-1.059647	-0.684093	1.965775	-1.232622	-0.208038	-0.108300	0.005274	-0.190321	-1.175575	0.647376	-0.221929	0.062723	0.061458	123.50	0
5121	-0.451449	-0.237033	-0.038195	0.803487	0.408542	-0.009431	0.798278	-0.137458	0.141267	-0.206010	0.502292	0.219422	0.215153	69.99	0

Fig. 1. Dataset

The statement card.info() in Python, assuming card is a DataFrame object from the pandas library, provides a concise summary of the DataFrame's structure and content. The info() method is often used as an initial step in exploratory data analysis to learn more about the structure of the dataset and quality before performing further analysis or visualization. Additionally, it helps in diagnosing potential data issues or inconsistencies that may require attention during data preprocessing or cleaning. Overall, card.info() provides a convenient way to obtain essential metadata about a DataFrame in a single concise output as shown in Fig. 2.

```
<class 'pandas.core.frame.DataFrame'>
RangeIndex: 284807 entries, 0 to 284806
Data columns (total 31 columns):
 #    Column   Non-Null Count    Dtype
---   ------   --------------    -----
 0    Time     284807 non-null   float64
 1    V1       284807 non-null   float64
 2    V2       284807 non-null   float64
 3    V3       284807 non-null   float64
 4    V4       284807 non-null   float64
 5    V5       284807 non-null   float64
 6    V6       284807 non-null   float64
 7    V7       284807 non-null   float64
 8    V8       284807 non-null   float64
 9    V9       284807 non-null   float64
 10   V10      284807 non-null   float64
 11   V11      284807 non-null   float64
 12   V12      284807 non-null   float64
 13   V13      284807 non-null   float64
 14   V14      284807 non-null   float64
 15   V15      284807 non-null   float64
 16   V16      284807 non-null   float64
 17   V17      284807 non-null   float64
 18   V18      284807 non-null   float64
 19   V19      284807 non-null   float64
 20   V20      284807 non-null   float64
 21   V21      284807 non-null   float64
 22   V22      284807 non-null   float64
 23   V23      284807 non-null   float64
 24   V24      284807 non-null   float64
 25   V25      284807 non-null   float64
 26   V26      284807 non-null   float64
 27   V27      284807 non-null   float64
 28   V28      284807 non-null   float64
 29   Amount   284807 non-null   float64
 30   Class    284807 non-null   int64
dtypes: float64(30), int64(1)
memory usage: 67.4 MB
```

Fig. 2. Data column information

The data description card.describe() would typically invoke a method named describe() belonging to an object named card. The purpose and behavior of this method depend entirely on how it's implemented within the class definition of the card object.

In general, the describe() method might provide a textual description or summary of the card object's attributes and properties. For example, as illustrated in Fig. 3, describe() might return details like the card's rank, suit, and any other pertinent information if the card represents a playing card in a card game.

The total number of rows and columns in the data is indicated by the card.shape.

```
Out[9]: (284807, 31)
```

Logistic Regression in Machine Learning and Data Analytics with Python 41

Fig. 3. Description of the Data

3.3 Data Quality Check

Now we perform the data quality check by finding the missing value in each coloumn of the dataset. Here is the output in the Fig. 4

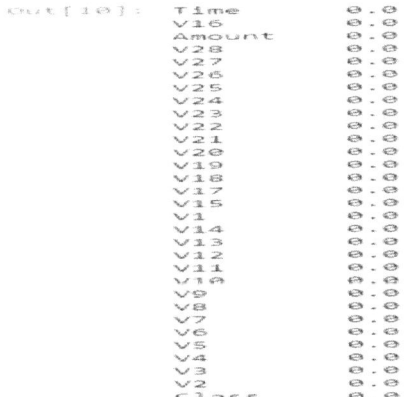

Fig. 4. Missing value in column

We now locate the missing value in every dataset row as part of the data quality check. [17] This is the result shown in Fig. 5.

```
Out[11]:  0             0.0
          189869        0.0
          189875        0.0
          189874        0.0
          189873        0.0
                       ...
          94942         0.0
          94943         0.0
          94944         0.0
          94945         0.0
          284806        0.0
          Length: 284807, dtype: float64
```

Fig. 5. Missing value in row

There is no missing value of each row and column of the data. Now we check for the duplicate values of the data in each row and column. Total number of rows and coloumns are

```
Out[13]:  (284807, 31)
```

After removing the duplicate values from the data we get the data as

```
Out[14]:  (283726, 31)
```

3.4 Exploratory Data Analysis

Now we generate histogram for specified features in dataframe. The data frame parameter expects a dataFrame object, presumably containing the data to be visualized. Features in the dataframe is the parameter in the list of the column names or features from the dataframe that we want to plot histogram for. We have created the feature variable size of 20 × 20 in. [18]. The loop iterates each feature. The single iteration of the loop specifies the number of rows and column's. We plot a histogram for the current feature using the hist() method of the DataFrame column. It specifies the number of bins as 20 and sets the face color of the bars to midnight blue.wesets the title of the subplot, indicating the distribution of the current feature. The title color is set to dark red.We set the y-axis scale to logarithmic, which can be useful for visualizing data with a wide range of values as shown in Fig. 6.

The unique values are the index labels, and the associated counts are the values. We now build a method that counts the occurrences of each unique value in the designated column and returns the result as a series.

```
Out[19]:  0    283253
          1       473
          Name: Class, dtype: int64
```

Now we count the total dataset with no frauds, the entry with 0 stands with no frauds but 1 stands with the frauds occurred. Here in the dataset out of 283726 the data with 284253 transaction is true transaction with no frauds but according to the data 473 is the

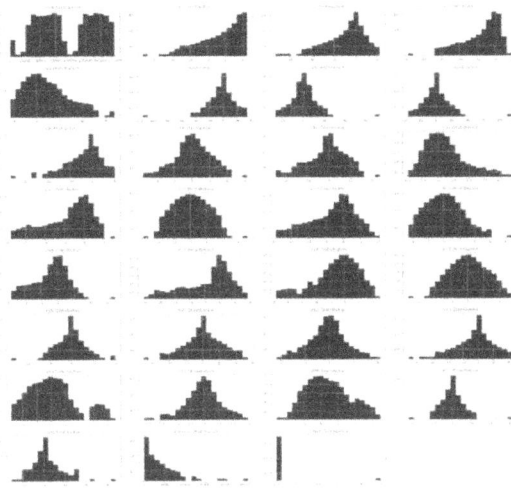

Fig. 6. Histogram of features

transaction where the fraud has occurred. We have the plot of no frauds and with frauds (Fig. 7).

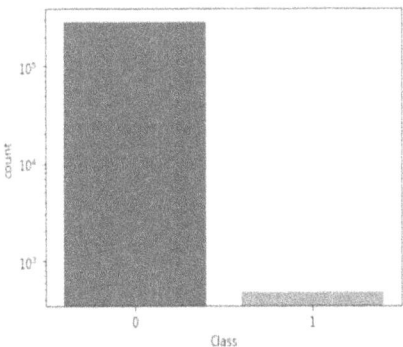

Fig. 7. Graph of data with frauds and without frauds

3.5 Correlation Matrix

A table that displays the correlation coefficients between variables in a dataset is called a correlation matrix. We produce a new figure that is 40 by 10 in. in size and develop a heatmap visualisation of the Data Frame card's correlation matrix. The heatmap will be large and simple to see at this size. Using the Seaborn library, we generate a heatmap and determine the DataFrame card's correlation matrix. [19] The pairwise correlation coefficients between each of the DataFrame's numerical columns are included in this matrix. The correlation coefficient value is displayed in each heatmap cell when the value (Fraud value) 1(True) is added.Matplotlib now offers a preconfigured colour map.

As a result, different correlation values are represented by distinct colours. We present the values as in Fig. 8.

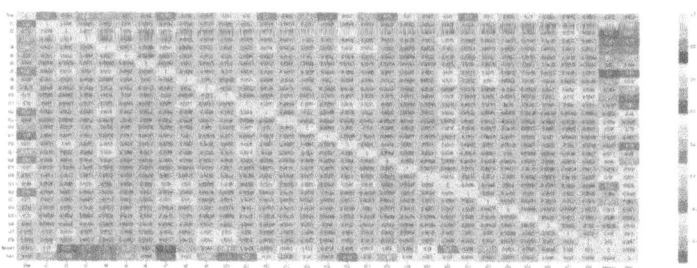

Fig. 8. Correlation Matrix

3.6 Logistic Regression

We have used two variables defining X1 and y for a machine learning task.

X1: This variable represents the features or independent variables used for prediction. It's typically a DataFrame containing the predictor variables [20]. In this case, the features are selected from the DataFrame card using the list of column names specified in estimators.

y: This variable represents the target variable or dependent variable. It's typically a Series or array containing the values you want to predict. In this case, it seems like you're predicting the 'Class' column from the card DataFrame, which might represent binary classes (e.g., fraud or not fraud).

The list of column names from the card DataFrame that we wish to use as prediction characteristics is estimated here.In addition to selecting the 'Class' column from the card DataFrame, we create a Series y with the values you wish to predict by selecting the columns listed in the estimators list from the card DataFrame and establishing a new DataFrame X1 with only those columns.Therefore, y holds the appropriate target values you're attempting to forecast, and X1 contains the attributes you'll utilise to train your machine learning model. These variables can then be fed into a machine learning system for testing and training.

```
Out[23]: Index(['V1', 'V2', 'V3', 'V4', 'V5', 'V6', 'V7', 'V8', 'V9', 'V10', 'V11',
       'V12', 'V13', 'V14', 'V15', 'V16', 'V17', 'V18', 'V19', 'V20', 'V21',
       'V22', 'V23', 'V24', 'V25', 'V26', 'V27', 'V28'],
      dtype='object')
```

We execute logistic regression using the statsmodels module in Python. We supplement our independent variable with a constant term. In regression analysis, it is standard procedure to incorporate an intercept into the model by adding a constant. Next, we use the Logit method from statsmodels to generate a logistic regression model object. The independent variables (including the constant that was added in the previous step) are represented by X, while the dependent variable is denoted by y. Our data is now fitted to the logistic regression model, and the results are returned. The fit() method uses the supplied data (X and y) to estimate the model's parameters.

```
Optimization terminated successfully.
         Current function value: 0.003927
         Iterations 13
```

A variety of data regarding the fitted logistic regression model, including p-values, standard errors, and parameter estimates, will be included in the results_logit. A summary of the findings, as displayed in Fig. 9, can now be viewed by using print(results_logit.summary()).

Logit Regression Results

Dep. Variable:	Class	No. Observations:	283726
Model:	Logit	Df Residuals:	283696
Method:	MLE	Df Model:	29
Date:	Thu, 22 Feb 2024	Pseudo R-squ.:	0.6816
Time:	21:03:31	Log-Likelihood:	-1114.1
converged:	True	LL-Null:	-3499.2
Covariance Type:	nonrobust	LLR p-value:	0.000

	coef	std err	z	P>|z|	[0.025	0.975]
const	-8.7312	0.152	-57.658	0.000	-9.029	-8.434
V1	0.0842	0.041	2.029	0.042	0.003	0.166
V2	0.0142	0.058	0.244	0.807	-0.099	0.128
V3	0.0371	0.046	0.814	0.415	-0.052	0.126
V4	0.7086	0.074	9.508	0.000	0.564	0.853
V5	0.1034	0.066	1.576	0.115	-0.025	0.232
V6	-0.1269	0.076	-1.664	0.096	-0.276	0.023
V7	-0.1085	0.066	-1.640	0.101	-0.238	0.021
V8	-0.1713	0.031	-5.579	0.000	-0.231	-0.111
V9	-0.2598	0.110	-2.370	0.018	-0.475	-0.045
V10	-0.8242	0.097	-8.501	0.000	-1.014	-0.634
V11	-0.0090	0.078	-0.115	0.908	-0.158	0.140
V12	0.0626	0.086	0.725	0.468	-0.106	0.231
V13	-0.3147	0.081	-3.858	0.000	-0.474	-0.155
V14	-0.5301	0.062	-8.554	0.000	-0.657	-0.418
V15	-0.0922	0.084	-1.096	0.274	-0.257	0.073
V16	-0.2018	0.125	-1.615	0.106	-0.447	0.043
V17	0.0097	0.068	0.142	0.887	-0.125	0.145
V18	-0.0376	0.128	-0.294	0.769	-0.288	0.213
V19	0.0795	0.096	0.828	0.408	-0.109	0.268
V20	-0.4510	0.081	-5.541	0.000	-0.611	-0.291
V21	0.3730	0.058	6.416	0.000	0.259	0.487
V22	0.5874	0.129	4.555	0.000	0.335	0.840
V23	-0.0976	0.058	-1.681	0.093	-0.211	0.016
V24	0.1276	0.149	0.855	0.392	-0.165	0.421
V25	-0.0180	0.131	-0.137	0.891	-0.276	0.239
V26	-0.0131	0.190	-0.069	0.945	-0.385	0.358
V27	-0.8134	0.122	-6.658	0.000	-1.053	-0.574
V28	-0.2979	0.089	-3.343	0.001	-0.473	-0.123
Amount	0.0009	0.000	2.465	0.014	0.000	0.002

Possibly complete quasi-separation: A fraction 0.31 of observations can be perfectly predicted. This might indicate that there is complete quasi-separation. In this case some parameters will not be identified.

Fig. 9. Result summary

Feature Selection: Backward Elemination (P-value Approach)

We are starting to define a Python function named back_feature_elem that likely performs some sort of feature selection or elimination based on a dependent variable and a list of columns. We are trying to implement a backward elimination feature selection method for logistic regression using the statsmodels library in Python. However, there are a few issues and potential improvements in the provided code:

In the back_feature_elem function definition, the code is incomplete, and there's no indentation or implementation for the function body. The back_feature_elem function should return a result once the feature elimination process is complete. However, in the current implementation, it returns result when the p-value condition is met, which might terminate the function early as shown in Fig. 10.

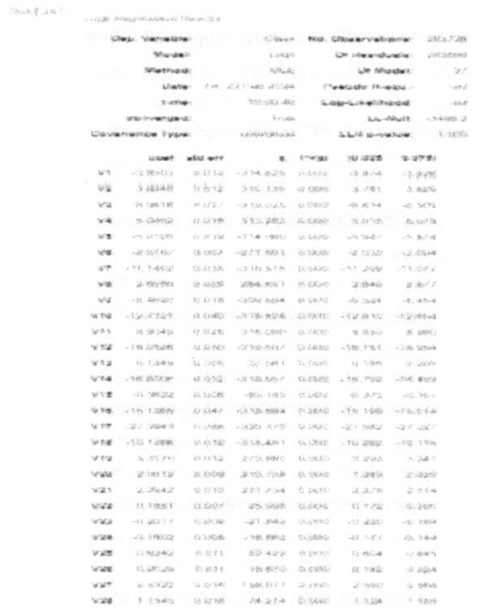

Fig. 10. Result after elimination process

The equation for logistic regression is P = e^(β0 + β1X1)/1 + e^(β0 + β1X1).

3.7 Analysing the Findings

P-values, odds ratios, and confidence intervals

After extracting p-values, odds ratios, and confidence intervals from the logistic regression findings, we structured and printed them as illustrated in Fig. 11.

	CI 95%(2.5%)	CI 95%(97.5%)	Odds Ratio	pvalue
V1	2.076848e-02	2.178906e-02	2.127265e-02	0.0
V2	4.385003e+01	4.601034e+01	4.491720e+01	0.0
V3	1.815011e-04	2.016353e-04	1.913035e-04	0.0
V4	1.506059e+02	1.604219e+02	1.554365e+02	0.0
V5	2.612588e-03	2.812611e-03	2.710756e-03	0.0
V6	1.309120e-01	1.347793e-01	1.328315e-01	0.0
V7	1.355458e-05	1.554635e-05	1.451635e-05	0.0
V8	1.401585e+01	1.453848e+01	1.427477e+01	0.0
V9	3.990901e-03	4.278129e-03	4.132020e-03	0.0
V10	2.723381e-06	3.195398e-06	2.954834e-06	0.0
V11	6.971871e+03	7.785935e+03	7.367668e+03	0.0
V12	9.675672e-08	1.178184e-07	1.067695e-07	0.0
V13	1.202850e+00	1.227562e+00	1.215143e+00	0.0
V14	5.575098e-08	6.834237e-08	6.172645e-08	0.0
V15	6.883531e-01	7.039955e-01	6.961304e-01	0.0
V16	2.506076e-07	3.017815e-07	2.750068e-07	0.0
V17	1.071538e-12	1.498226e-12	1.267046e-12	0.0
V18	3.493661e-05	3.965701e-05	3.722206e-05	0.0
V19	2.692943e+01	2.823882e+01	2.757635e+01	0.0
V20	7.261631e+00	7.537076e+00	7.398072e+00	0.0
V21	9.725932e+00	1.011079e+01	9.916496e+00	0.0
V22	1.187799e+00	1.221607e+00	1.204584e+00	0.0
V23	8.026712e-01	8.322601e-01	8.173318e-01	0.0
V24	8.379161e-01	8.662815e-01	8.519807e-01	0.0
V25	1.828672e+00	1.905530e+00	1.866705e+00	0.0
V26	1.199443e+00	1.251087e+00	1.224993e+00	0.0
V27	1.218753e+01	1.298784e+01	1.258132e+01	0.0
V28	3.077262e+00	3.270759e+00	3.172536e+00	0.0

Fig. 11. Odd Ratio

In order to train a machine learning model, we now prepare the data. From the dataset card, we have taken specific features and divided them into training and testing sets. Extracted the target variable (Class) and a collection of characteristics from the dataset. Divided the target variable into y and the characteristics into x. Train_test_split was imported from sklearn.model_selection.Using train_test_split, divide the data into training and testing sets. Stratify by the target variable y, assign a random seed for reproducibility, and have a 20% test size.

3.8 Model Evaluation

Model Accuracy

We are creating a report that includes precision, recall, F1-score, and support for every class in my test data using the classification report from scikit-learn's metrics module.The proportion of accurately predicted positive observations to all expected positives is known as precision. It gauges how accurate optimistic forecasts are. Recall: The proportion of all observations in the actual class that were accurately predicted to be positive. It assesses the classifier's capacity to locate every positive sample.F1-score: Precision and Recall weighted average. Both false positives and false negatives are taken into account.Support: The quantity of instances of the class that actually occur in the given dataset.As illustrated in Fig. 12, printing the classification report provides you with an extensive overview of your classifier's performance on each class.

```
              precision    recall  f1-score   support

           0       1.00      1.00      1.00     56651
           1       0.86      0.57      0.68        95

    accuracy                           1.00     56746
   macro avg       0.93      0.78      0.84     56746
weighted avg       1.00      1.00      1.00     56746
```

Fig. 12. The model's accuracy

3.9 Confusion Matrix

A heatmap is an excellent method to visualise the confusion matrix and see how well my classifier is performing. To compute the confusion matrix, import confusion_matrix from the metrics module of scikit-learn. Compare the predicted labels y_pred with the true labels y_test to get the confusion matrix cm. To display the confusion matrix with the appropriate row and column names, create a DataFrameconf_matrix. Create a heatmap visualisation of the confusion matrix by annotating each cell with the corresponding count using the seaborn library's sns.heatmap function. As seen in Fig. 13, this visualisation aids in our comprehension of your classifier's performance in terms of true positive, true negative, false positive, and false negative predictions for every class.

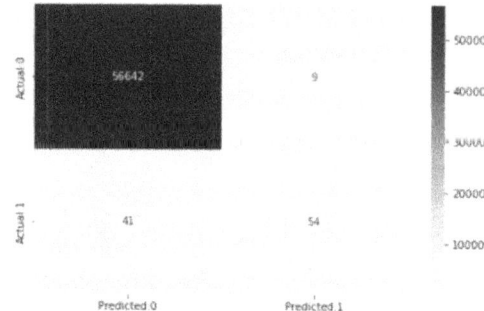

Fig. 13. Confusion Matrix

The confusion matrix shows 56642 + 54 = 56698 correct predictions and 19 + 41 = 50 incorrect ones. True Positives: 59 True Negatives: 56641 False Positives: 9 (Type I error) False Negatives: 41 (Type II error).

3.10 Model Evaluation – Statistics

We now use information from the confusion matrix to calculate a number of performance indicators for your binary classifier. The percentage of accurate forecasts among all predictions is known as accuracy. The percentage of inaccurate guesses among all predictions is known as the misclassification rate. The percentage of real positive cases that the classifier properly detected is known as sensitivity (also known as true positive rate). The percentage of real negative cases that the classifier properly detected is known as specificity (also known as true negative rate). Positive Predictive Value (Precision): The percentage of actual positive predictions among all of the classifier's positive predictions. Negative Predictive Value: The percentage of actual negative predictions among all of the classifier's negative predictions. Good

```
The acuuracy of the model = TP+TN/(TP+TN+FP+FN) =      0.9991188806259472
The Missclassification = 1-Accuracy =                  0.0008811193740527745
Sensitivity or True Positive Rate = TP/(TP+FN) =       0.5684210526315789
Specificity or True Negative Rate = TN/(TN+FP) =       0.9998411325484104
Positive Predictive value = TP/(TP+FP) =               0.8571428571428571
Negative predictive Value = TN/(TN+FN) =               0.9992766790748548
Positive Likelihood Ratio = Sensitivity/(1-Specificity) = 3577.9578947369905
Negative likelihood Ratio = (1-Sensitivity)/Specificity = 0.43164752211024365
```

The predicted probabilities of each class for the samples in your test set are obtained using the predict_proba technique. With the columns arranged according to the label indices, this approach yields an array with each row representing a sample and each column representing the class probabilities. The projected probabilities for each sample falling into class 0 (not fraud) and class 1 (fraud) are included in this DataFrame, which you may use for additional analysis or visualisation.

Out[32]:

	Prob of Not Fraud (0)	Prob of Fraud (1)
0	0.999683	0.000317
1	0.999698	0.000302
2	0.999960	0.000040
3	0.999874	0.000126
4	0.998584	0.001416

For the test data, predicted probabilities of 0 (No Fraud) and 1 (Fraud) with a default classification threshold of 0.5

Reduce the Threshold
In order to get binary predictions for various threshold values between 0.0 and 1.0, we now apply thresholding on the projected probabilities. After that, it assesses each threshold's sensitivity, specificity, and confusion matrix. With a step size of 0.1, it iterates across threshold values ranging from 0.0 to 1.0 (inclusive). Binarization is applied to the projected probability based on each threshold value. For the binarized predictions, it computes the sensitivity, specificity, and confusion matrix (cm2).

Finally, it prints out the confusion matrix, correct predictions, type II errors (false negatives), sensitivity, and specificity for each threshold value.

```
With 0.0 threshold the Confusion Matrix is
[[    0 56651]
 [    0    95]]
with 95 correct predictions and 0 Type II errors( False Negatives)
Sensitivity: 1.0 Specificity: 0.0
With 0.1 threshold the Confusion Matrix is
[[56636    15]
 [   26    69]]
with 56705 correct predictions and 26 Type II errors( False Negatives)
Sensitivity: 0.7263157894736842 Specificity: 0.9997352209140175
With 0.2 threshold the Confusion Matrix is
[[56638    13]
 [   30    65]]
with 56703 correct predictions and 30 Type II errors( False Negatives)
Sensitivity: 0.6842105263157895 Specificity: 0.9997705247921485
With 0.3 threshold the Confusion Matrix is
[[56640    11]
 [   35    60]]
with 56700 correct predictions and 35 Type II errors( False Negatives)
Sensitivity: 0.6315789473684211 Specificity: 0.9998058786702795
With 0.4 threshold the Confusion Matrix is
[[56641    10]
 [   35    60]]
with 56701 correct predictions and 35 Type II errors( False Negatives)
Sensitivity: 0.6315789473684211 Specificity: 0.9998234806093449
With 0.5 threshold the Confusion Matrix is
[[56642     9]
 [   41    54]]
with 56696 correct predictions and 41 Type II errors( False Negatives)
Sensitivity: 0.5684210526315789 Specificity: 0.9098411325484104
With 0.6 threshold the Confusion Matrix is
[[56643     8]
 [   43    52]]
with 56695 correct predictions and 43 Type II errors( False Negatives)
Sensitivity: 0.5473684210526316 Specificity: 0.9998587844487476
With 0.7 threshold the Confusion Matrix is
[[56643     8]
 [   47    48]]
with 56691 correct predictions and 47 Type II errors( False Negatives)
Sensitivity: 0.5052631578947369 Specificity: 0.9998587844487476
With 0.8 threshold the Confusion Matrix is
[[56643     8]
 [   49    46]]
with 56689 correct predictions and 49 Type II errors( False Negatives)
Sensitivity: 0.4842105263157895 Specificity: 0.9998587844487476
With 0.9 threshold the Confusion Matrix is
[[56643     8]
 [   52    43]]
with 56686 correct predictions and 52 Type II errors( False Negatives)
Sensitivity: 0.4526315789473684 Specificity: 0.9998587844487476
With 1.0 threshold the Confusion Matrix is
[[56651     0]
 [   95     0]]
with 56651 correct predictions and 95 Type II errors( False Negatives)
Sensitivity: 0.0 Specificity: 1.0
```

Receiver Operating Characteristic Curve, or ROC Curve
The roc_curve function from scikit-learn is used to plot the ROC curve. Using the true labels (y_test) and the anticipated probabilities of the positive class, we compute the Receiver Operating Characteristic (ROC) curve. A ROC curve should be plotted with the true positive rate (tpr) on the y-axis and the false positive rate (fpr) on the x-axis. Assign the x and y axes' limits to [0, 1]. adds plot labels and a title. enhances the plot with a grid. For various threshold values, this plot graphically illustrates the trade-off between the true positive rate (sensitivity) and false positive rate (1 - specificity). The diagonal line represents random guessing, and the ROC curve should ideally be as close as possible to the top-left corner, indicating high discriminative power of the model as shown in Fig. 14.

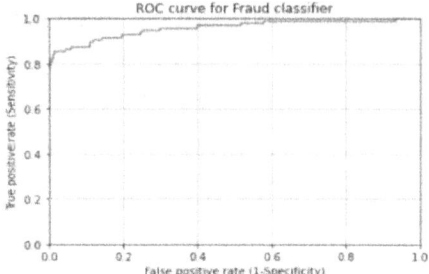

Fig. 14. ROC Curve

The Area Under the Receiver Operating Characteristic Curve (ROC AUC) is computed using the true labels and predicted probabilities of the positive class using the scikit-learn roc_auc_score function. A binary classification model's overall performance is represented by a single scalar value provided by this metric.

Out[70]: 0.9571786255457004

4 Conclusion

In the area of credit card fraud detection, logistic regression shows promise as a dependable method for spotting questionable transactions and protecting the financial interests of both institutions and customers. Lo-gistic regression strengthens the resilience of financial systems against fraudulent activity by leveraging a combination of predictive features and sophisticated analytical tools to enable proactive risk management tactics. Nonetheless, to adjust to changing fraud trends and guarantee long-term efficacy in preventing financial fraud, constant observation and model improvement are necessary. Given the significant impact that fraudulent transactions can have on both customers and financial institutions, detecting credit card fraud is an essential task in the field of financial security. Logistic regression is a useful technique for spotting possibly fraudulent activity in this situation. Given this, logistic regression shows up as a useful technique for spotting possibly fraudulent activity. Logistic regression models are trained using a dataset that includes a variety of variables related to credit card transactions in order to forecast the probability that a transaction will be fraudulent. The model's predictive performance can be improved by efficiently identifying pertinent predictors and removing noise through a methodical feature selection and exclusion process. To determine how well the logistic regression model detects fraudulent transactions, a number of important metrics are calculated once it has been trained and tested on a held-out test set. Accuracy, sensitivity, specificity, precision, and the area under the receiver operating characteristic curve (ROC AUC) are some of these measurements. While sensitivity and specificity reveal how well the model can detect fraudulent and non-fraudulent transactions, respectively, a high accuracy score shows how accurate the model's predictions are overall.

References

1. Devika, M., Kishan, S.R., Manohar, L.S., Vijaya, N.: Credit card fraud detection using logistic regression. In: 2022 Second International Conference on Advanced Technologies in Intelligent Control, Environment, Computing & Communication Engineering (ICATIECE), pp. 1–6. Bangalore, India (2022). https://doi.org/10.1109/ICATIECE56365.2022.10046976
2. Sahin, Y., Duman, E.: Detecting credit card fraud by ANN and logistic regression. In: 2011 International Symposium on Innovations in Intelligent Systems and Applications, pp. 315–319. Istanbul, Turkey (2011). https://doi.org/10.1109/INISTA.2011.5946108
3. Singh, A., Singh, A., Aggarwal, A., Chauhan, A.: Design and implementation of different machine learning algorithms for credit card fraud detection. In: 2022 International Conference on Electrical, Computer, Communications and Mechatronics Engineering (ICECCME), pp. 1–6. Maldives, Maldives (2022). https://doi.org/10.1109/ICECCME55909.2022.9988588
4. Singh, Y., Singh, K., Singh Chauhan, V.: Fraud detection techniques for credit card transactions. In: 2022 3rd International Conference on Intelligent Engineering and Management (ICIEM), pp. 821–824. London, United Kingdom (2022). https://doi.org/10.1109/ICIEM54221.2022.9853183
5. Nijwala, D.S., Maurya, S., Thapliyal, M.P., Verma, R.: Extreme gradient boost classifier based credit card fraud detection model. In: 2023 International Conference on Device Intelligence, Computing and Communication Technologies, (DICCT), pp. 500–504. Dehradun, India (2023). https://doi.org/10.1109/DICCT56244.2023.10110188
6. Al Smadi, B., Min, M.: A critical review of credit card fraud detection techniques. In: 2020 11th IEEE Annual Ubiquitous Computing, Electronics & Mobile Communication Conference (UEMCON), pp. 0732–0736. New York, NY, USA (2020). https://doi.org/10.1109/UEMCON51285.2020.9298075
7. https://www.kaggle.com/code/gauravduttakiit/creditcard-fraud-detection-by-logistic-regression/input
8. Bipin Nair, B.J., Yadhukrishnan, S., Manish, A.: A comparative study on document images classification using logistic regression and multiple linear regressions. In: 2023 Second International Conference on Augmented Intelligence and Sustainable Systems (ICAISS), pp. 1096–1104. Trichy, India (2023). https://doi.org/10.1109/ICAISS58487.2023.10250671
9. Vejalla, I., Battula, S.P., Kalluri, K., Kalluri, H.K.: Credit card fraud detection using machine learning techniques. In: 2023 2nd International Conference on Paradigm Shifts in Communications Embedded Systems, Machine Learning and Signal Processing (PCEMS), pp. 1–4. Nagpur, India (2023). https://doi.org/10.1109/PCEMS58491.2023.10136040
10. Gambo, M.L., Zainal, A., Kassim, M.N.: A convolutional neural network model for credit card fraud detection. In: 2022 International Conference on Data Science and Its Applications (ICoDSA), pp. 198–202. Bandung, Indonesia (2022). https://doi.org/10.1109/ICoDSA55874.2022.9862930
11. Stančin, I., Jović, A.: An overview and comparison of free Python libraries for data mining and big data analysis. In: 2019 42nd International Convention on Information and Communication Technology, Electronics and Microelectronics (MIPRO), pp. 977–982. Opatija, Croatia (2019). https://doi.org/10.23919/MIPRO.2019.8757088
12. Dogaru, I., Dogaru, R.: Using python and julia for efficient implementation of natural computing and complexity related algorithms. In: 2015 20th International Conference on Control Systems and Computer Science, pp. 599–604. Bucharest, Romania (2015). https://doi.org/10.1109/CSCS.2015.37
13. Ruiz-Sarmiento, J.R., Monroy, J., Moreno, F.A., Gonzalez-Jimenez, J.: A tutorial on object recognition by machine learning techniques using python. INTED2019 Proceedings, pp. 3321–3330 (2019)

14. Barrett, P., Hunter, J., Miller, J.T., Hsu, J.-C., Greenfield, P.: matplotlib – A Portable Python Plotting Package (2005)
15. Seabold, S., Perktold, J.: Statsmodels: Econometric and Statistical Modeling with Python. In: Proceedings of the 9th Python in Science Conference (2010)
16. Hou, Y., Yang, L.: Application of rough fuzzy neural network in iron ore import risk early-warning. In: Zhang, L., Lu, BL., Kwok, J. (eds.) Advances in Neural Networks - ISNN 2010. ISNN 2010. LNCS, vol 6064. Springer, Berlin, Heidelberg (2010). https://doi.org/10.1007/978-3-642-13318-3_54
17. Loetpipatwanich, S., Vichitthamaros, P.: Sakdas: a python package for data profiling and data quality auditing. In: 2020 1st International Conference on Big Data Analytics and Practices (IBDAP), pp. 1–4. Bangkok, Thailand (2020). https://doi.org/10.1109/IBDAP50342.2020.9245455
18. Dsouza, J., Velan, S.: Using exploratory data analysis for generating inferences on the correlation of COVID-19 cases. In: 2020 11th International Conference on Computing, Communication and Networking Technologies (ICCCNT), pp. 1–6. Kharagpur, India (2020). https://doi.org/10.1109/ICCCNT49239.2020.9225621
19. Iaousse, M., Hmimou, A., El hadri, Z., El kettani, Y.: On the computation of the correlation matrix implied by a recursive path model. In: 2020 IEEE 6th International Conference on Optimization and Applications (ICOA), pp. 1–5. Beni Mellal, Morocco (2020). https://doi.org/10.1109/ICOA49421.2020.9094528
20. Lik Pao, P.L., Ismail, M.A.: Loan eligibility classification using logistic regression. In: 2023 IEEE 8th International Conference On Software Engineering and Computer Systems (ICSECS), pp. 1–4. Penang, Malaysia (2023). https://doi.org/10.1109/ICSECS5

SENTINSIGHT: Unveiling Themes, Insights, and Success Metrics Through Natural Language Processing

Jagini Naga Padmaja[✉], Nadimpalli Madana Kailash Varma, and Kanduri Sai Sri Vidya

Department of Artificial Intelligence and Machine Learning, Vardhaman College of Engineering, Hyderabad, Telangana 501286, India
srija26@gmail.com

Abstract. In today's world, many annual events generate user feedback. Sentiment analysis (SA) within Natural Language Processing (NLP) is a key tool used for evaluating these events. This paper introduces SentInsight, a platform that provides real-time assessments of user-generated content, using robust NLP models to gauge event success through the prevalence of positive sentiment. This research signifies a significant advancement in sentiment analysis methodologies and offers event organizers a valuable tool for refining event planning and management strategies. By identifying positive feedback, suggestions, questions, and the best and worst comments, SentInsight enables organizers to make data-driven decisions for future events.

Our research highlights the importance of sentiment analysis in enhancing planning effectiveness. By employing advanced NLP techniques, SentInsight discerns nuanced expressions of positivity and provides actionable insights from user feedback. The platform's comprehensive model allows for real-time monitoring and interpretative analyses, enabling organizers to adapt their strategies based on ongoing feedback. This foster engaging experiences across diverse domains and ensures that events are continuously improved based on the latest user reviews.

Keywords: Sentiment Analysis (SA) · Natural Language Processing (NLP) · Sentinsight · Event Evaluation · User Feedback · Sentiment Intensity Analyzer · Data Visualization (DV) · Event Planning · User-generated Content · Event Success Metrics · Word Cloud · Event Management

1 Introduction

The rise of Natural Language Processing (NLP) has revolutionized the ability of machines to understand and generate human language, enabling transformative changes across various sectors. By utilizing advanced algorithms, NLP empowers tasks like text classification, information retrieval, and sentiment analysis (SA), which play a critical role in extracting emotional nuances from textual data [1]. This analytical capability is foundational to understanding and quantifying user sentiments, offering valuable insights from user-generated content such as product reviews, social media posts, and customer feedback [2, 3].

In the context of event evaluation, this paper explores the application of NLP and SA techniques within event evaluation, aiming to enhance audience engagement and optimize event planning strategies. Building on a robust theoretical framework that integrates machine learning, linguistic analysis, and sentiment evaluation, we quantify sentiments from feedback across different event types. The theoretical underpinnings of sentiment analysis and its integration with NLP techniques provide the foundation for understanding how user feedback can be leveraged to improve event outcomes.

In this study, we outline the methodology, data collection process, and key findings. Through the integration of NLP techniques and sentiment analysis algorithms, our approach demonstrates the potential of these technologies to revolutionize event evaluation, providing actionable insights for organizers and enabling data-driven decision-making.

The primary objectives of this research are to develop a sentiment analysis model tailored for event evaluation, assess its effectiveness in providing actionable insights, and demonstrate how these insights can be used to optimize future event planning strategies. We believe that this framework has the potential to significantly enhance the planning, execution, and overall impact of events in the digital age.

2 Literature Survey

This literature review examines the intersection of sentiment analysis and event success prediction, analyzing NLP techniques' application in interpreting user feedback across diverse events. It aims to provide a comprehensive understanding of SA's pivotal role in evaluating event success.

In today's world, online reviews of food and amenities in eateries heavily influence consumer decisions, but analyzing these subjective opinions manually is challenging. Research [4] explored the role of automated SA, such as Neuro-Fuzzy Sentiment Classification, in evaluating these reviews. By classifying feedback as positive or negative, this approach aids data-driven decisions in restaurant planning and management strategies. Similarly, a study proposed combining BPM and NLP to analyze business processes through SA of user feedback. It develops a structured corpus of over 7000 feedback sentences, annotating them across three levels of classification. Experimentation concludes that deep learning techniques are most effective for classification tasks [5].

Authored by Kelvin Du, Frank Xing, Rui Mao, and Erik Cambria, the paper provides a comprehensive review of Financial Sentiment Analysis, examining key advancements, applications, challenges, and future directions within financial markets [6]. Wenjun Gu, Yihao Zhong, Shizun Li, Changsong Wei, Liting Dong, Zhuoyue Wang, and Chao Yan presented FinBERT-LSTM, a sentiment-based model that improves stock market prediction accuracy using financial news analysis [7].

Moutidis and Williams integrated SA with network event detection, notably in political elections on Twitter. They demonstrated its value in categorizing events as positive or negative, facilitating richer insights for users and streamlined decision-making processes. Their study underscores SA growing importance in comprehending public sentiments across diverse events and platforms [8].

A paper by J. Kazmaier and J.H. Van Vuuren explores automated SA of customer feedback from a South African retail bank, using custom machine learning models that outperform pre-trained and commercial tools [9]. Various techniques and applications of SA have been explored across different contexts, shedding light on both technical and non-technical challenges. Furthermore, the paper underscores the significance of SA in extracting meaningful insights from unstructured data and discusses prospective research directions [10].

Internet-based platforms spur comments and reviews, fueling SA. Despite utility, challenges persist in accurately interpreting sentiments. NLP aids subjective information extraction. An article reviews methodologies, compares approaches, and addresses challenges [11]. Moreover, a paper introduced an AI-driven media monitoring system analyzing online sources for global events. It employs entity detection, sentiment analysis, and anomaly detection, achieving high accuracy and reliability over time [12].

Undertaking a qualitative sentiment analysis, a study examines YouTube comments on heritage vlogs, identifying social and non-social emotions, and offering insights for heritage tourism promotion [13]. Additional studies contribute to the enrichment of SA in diverse contexts. Park, E., Kang, J., Choi, D., & Han, J. [14] explored hotel revisiting behavior using large-scale customer review data, shedding light on factors influencing revisits and predicting future behavior, crucial for hospitality and tourism industries.

Authored by Ahmad Amjad Mir from the University of Wisconsin – Madison, USA, the research investigates machine learning algorithms for sentiment analysis and stock market prediction during the COVID-19 pandemic, aiming to improve forecasting models [15]. In the last decade, Arabic online content surged, fueling SA. Deep learning, particularly RNNs, gains traction for handling unstructured data. A paper reviews 193 English and 24 Arabic RNN-based sentiment analysis studies [16].

Zucco et al. [17] conducted a comprehensive review of SA methods and tools for mining text and social network data, providing insights into state-of-the-art techniques and tools available for SA tasks. Authored by Omar Alqaryouti, Nur Siyam, Azza Abdel Monem, and Khaled Shaala, the paper [18] proposes an aspect-based sentiment analysis model integrating lexicons and rules, outperforming SVM and baseline models in accuracy for smart app reviews.

Ziyu Liu et al. introduced a Multimodal Attention Fusion (MAF) network for sentiment analysis, achieving high performance on the CMU-MOSEI and CMU-MOSI datasets [19]. Another study explores sentiment surrounding a virtual rock concert experience in VR environments [20]. Additionally, an analysis of global reactions to a 2018 concert in Pyongyang reveals predominantly positive sentiment, with exceptions found in clips featuring the North Korean audience, highlighting potential cultural disparities [21].

Exploring the intersection of music education and cultural heritage preservation, a paper undertakes a content analysis of Leonard Bernstein's Young People's Concerts [22]. Analyzing broadcast transcripts from 1958 to 1972, the study examines Bernstein's thematic approaches, offering insights into his pedagogical strategies and influence on audiences.

Lastly, a qualitative approach to SA is advocated in response to unexpected and potentially stressful events on social media [23]. This survey reviews Financial Sentiment Analysis (FSA), covering techniques and market applications. It defines FSA's scope, explores FSA-investor-market sentiment relationships, and summarizes findings, challenges, and future research directions.

In conclusion, the literature reviewed underscores the pivotal role of SA in forecasting event success through the prism of user feedback. By harnessing NLP techniques to distill insights from user comments, scholars and practitioners have gained invaluable perspectives on the perceived success of diverse events spanning various domains.

3 Research Methodology

3.1 Data Collection

Our methodology involves a structured approach to developing and implementing a SA model to assess event success using NLP techniques. The process starts with collecting a diverse dataset of user comments from events like parties, college fests, science exhibitions, and conferences. Data was collected from various online platforms and feedback forms, where participants shared their opinions about the event. The dataset [24], which includes real-time data from our college scientific fest, was carefully aggregated to ensure diversity, focusing on events such as parties, college fests, science exhibitions, and conferences. This dataset is rigorously preprocessed to ensure quality and relevance by removing null values and unnecessary columns. The text is standardized to lowercase and cleaned of special characters, punctuation, and stop words, preparing it for advanced natural language processing analysis.

3.2 Analytical Techniques

Our methodology centers on NLP techniques, specifically SA. Utilizing NLTK's Sentiment Intensity Analyzer, we tokenize, lemmatize, and score sentiment polarity for each comment, quantitatively gauging attendees' perceptions of events for insightful analysis.

Additionally, we employ data visualization (DV) techniques to enhance our understanding of sentiment distribution across events. Utilizing histograms and word clouds, we reveal sentiment polarity and prevalent themes in user comments. Figures, such as Fig. 1, illustrate sentiment score distributions, aiding the interpretation of SA outcomes and providing a comprehensive sentiment landscape overview.

Figure 2 elaborates on the process, which entails importing libraries and downloading NLTK resources, followed by data loading and preprocessing. SA using VADER calculates sentiment scores, determining event success based on positive sentiment percentage. Visualization includes sentiment distribution histogram, word cloud, and top words bar chart. Top positive and negative comments offer further insights, aiding in understanding event sentiment and success.

Furthermore, Fig. 3 presents a captivating Word Cloud generated from the entirety of our dataset. This visual representation encapsulates the frequency and significance of words within user comments, providing a holistic snapshot of prevailing themes across the events. By visually highlighting key terms and their prominence, the Word Cloud offers valuable insights into the overarching sentiments and focal points within the user feedback.

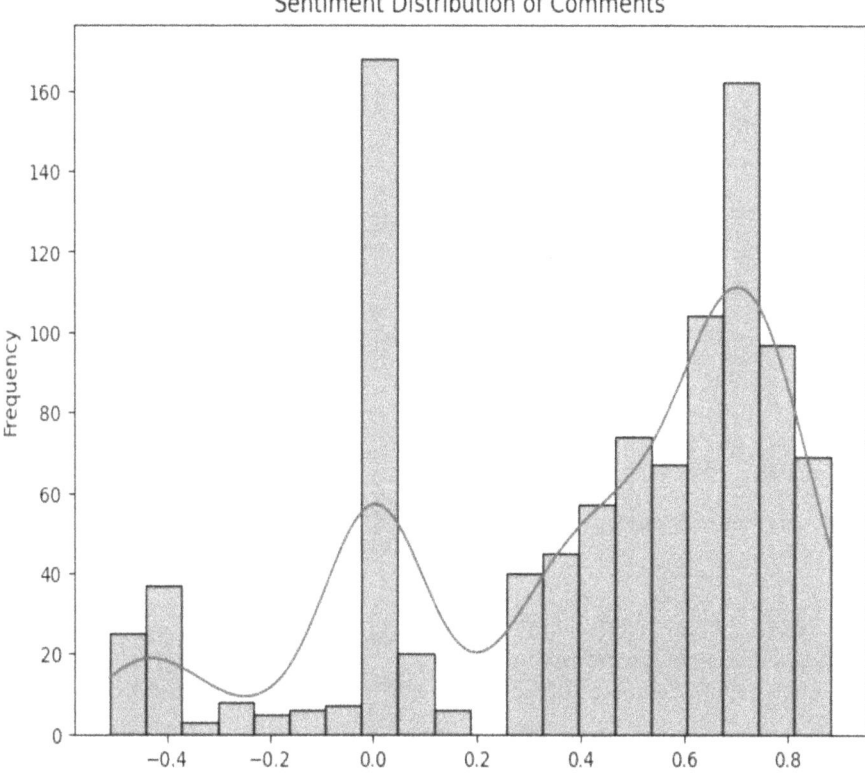

Fig. 1. Sentiment distribution extrapolated from user-generated content.

Our research employs an iterative approach, refining NLP model parameters, experimenting with feature extraction techniques, and exploring algorithms to enhance SA accuracy. We actively seek feedback from experts and stakeholders to validate findings and ensure real-world relevance.

4 Results

4.1 Quantitative Findings

In the Results section, we present the outcomes derived from the meticulous execution of our platform, encompassing various tasks and methodologies. Commencing with the pivotal stages of data collection and preprocessing, we painstakingly curated a dataset comprising 1000 real-time user comments from our college scientific fest, ensuring its relevance and representativeness.

This meticulously crafted dataset served as the cornerstone for subsequent analyses, furnishing comprehensive insights into audience sentiment spanning diverse event

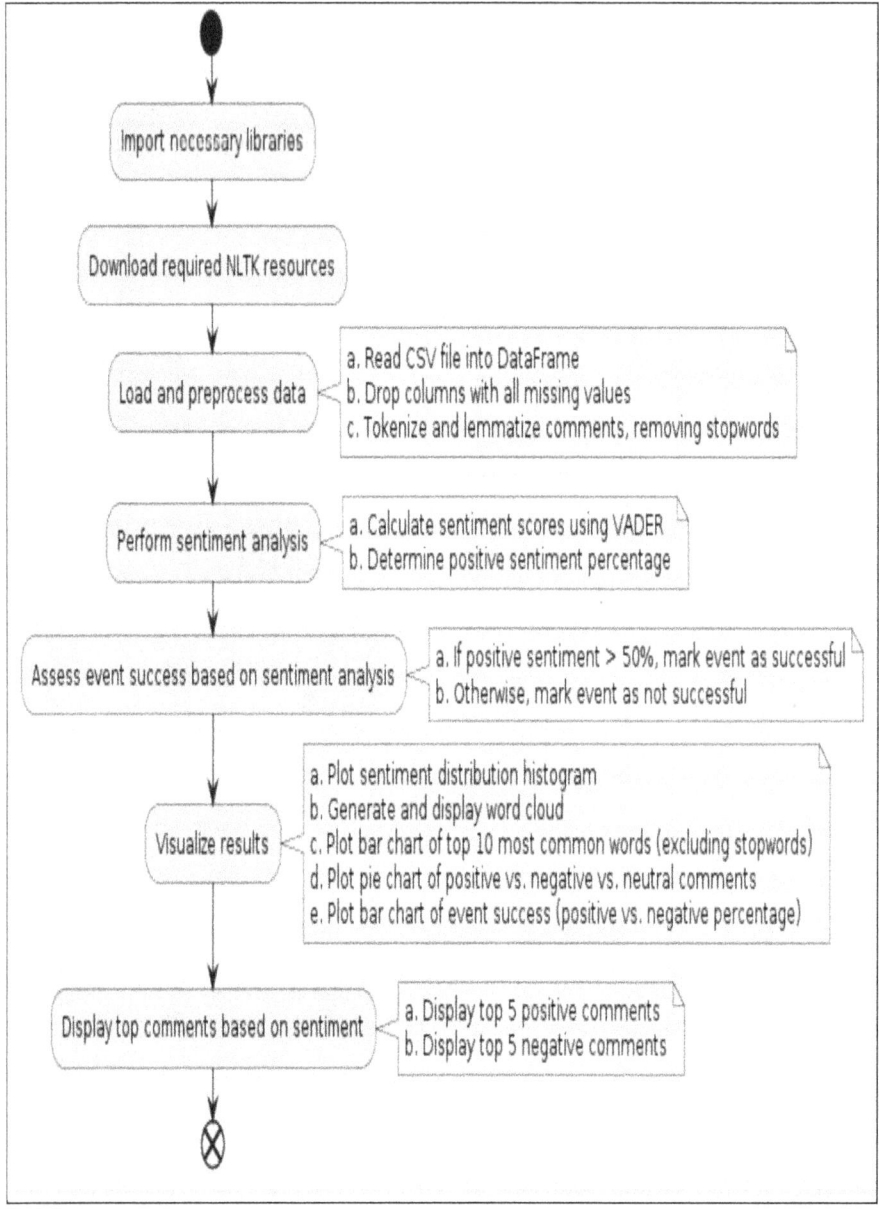

Fig. 2. The Intricate Architecture of Sentinsight

types, including parties, college fests, science exhibitions, and conferences. Leveraging Sentinsight's advanced capabilities, we adeptly analyzed the outcomes of college scientific fests with precision.

This dataset is taken with a threshold of 50%, which users can adjust according to their preference. The meticulous collection and preparation of fest data yield compelling

SENTINSIGHT: Unveiling Themes, Insights, and Success Metrics   59

Fig. 3. Lexical Repository from user feedback

results as shown in Fig. 4. The graph clearly highlights the varying degrees of sentiment associated with each event type, showing a strong positive correlation between user sentiment and perceived event success.

Employing the Sentinsight, we proceeded to quantify sentiment polarity within the user comments, thus facilitating real-time evaluation of event success metrics. To quantify user sentiment accurately, we calculated sentiment scores for each user comment utilizing state-of-the-art SA techniques. These scores, indicative of the positivity or negativity of a statement, were aggregated to ascertain the average sentiment associated with each event. A higher average sentiment score is construed as indicative of a positive reception, thereby suggesting the success of the event, while a lower score may signal areas for improvement.

4.2 Sentiment Distribution and Trends

Furthermore, a pie chart (Fig. 5) illustrates the proportions of positive, neutral, and negative comments, offering a clear view of sentiment distribution in the dataset. This visual representation aids in discerning sentiment trends, thereby enhancing comprehension of user perceptions across diverse events and facilitating informed decision-making in event planning and management.

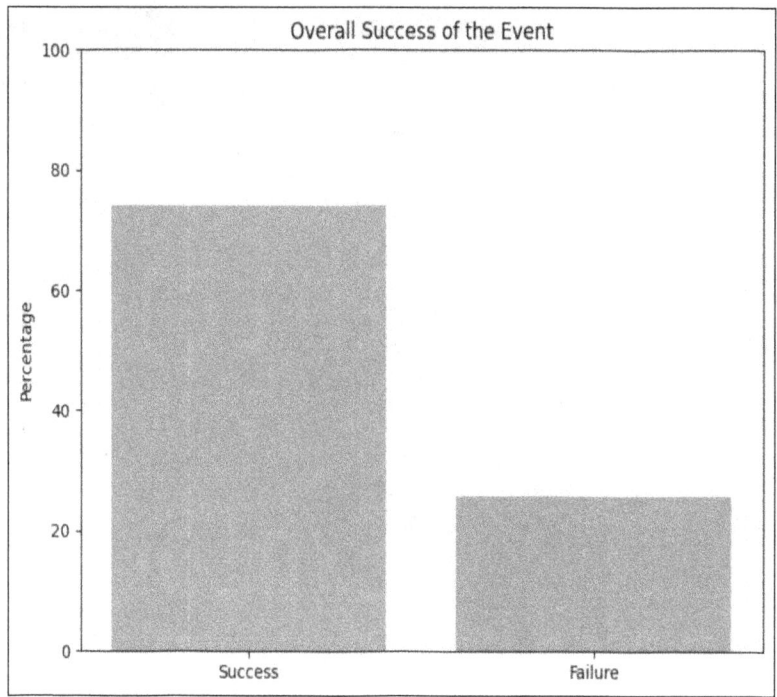

Fig. 4. Event success metrics

Furthermore, Fig. 6 shows the frequency of the most commonly used words in the user comments. This word frequency compilation is a key step in identifying prevalent themes and topics across different events. Words such as "science," "exhibition," and "coding" appeared most frequently in the positive comments. These insights allow event organizers to pinpoint specific areas for improvement and capitalize on the aspects that attendees enjoyed most.

Suggestions, inquiries, and the most commendable and critical comments are discernible through our sophisticated sentiment analysis platform, Sentinsight. Utilizing advanced NLP techniques, Sentinsight identifies nuanced feedback and categorizes it for in-depth insights, enabling a comprehensive understanding of user sentiments and enhancing the evaluation of event success and areas for improvement.

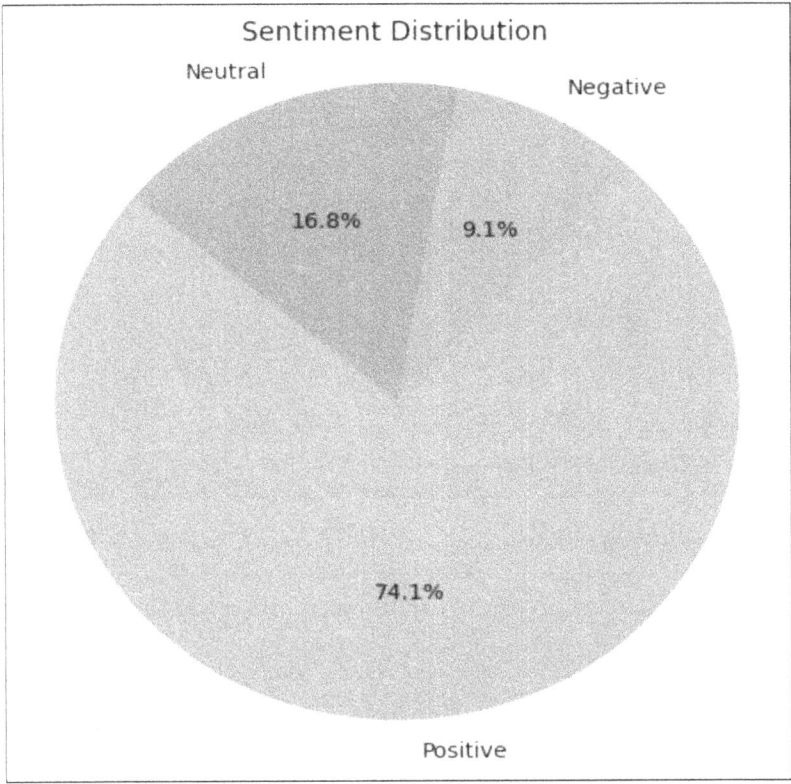

Fig. 5. Sorting Out Sentiments from User Feedback

4.3 Annual Event Success Trends

To assess the long-term effectiveness of event planning strategies, Fig. 7 allows us to visualize the annual success rates of the event, enabling us to make informed adjustments based on Sentinsight's insights. This chart shows a consistent upward trend in event success over the years, with notable spikes during major conferences and workshops. The data suggests that incorporating feedback from previous events, as captured through sentiment analysis, has led to more refined event planning strategies, resulting in higher satisfaction rates among attendees.

4.4 Interpretation of Findings

Our paper highlights the role of Sentinsight in improving event planning and management. Through data collection, analysis, and visualization, we've gained valuable insights into audience sentiment and event success metrics. To validate these findings, we performed statistical tests, including chi-square and t-tests, ensuring the robustness of the results. These tests confirm that the observed patterns are statistically significant. By leveraging these insights, we can optimize future events, marking a significant

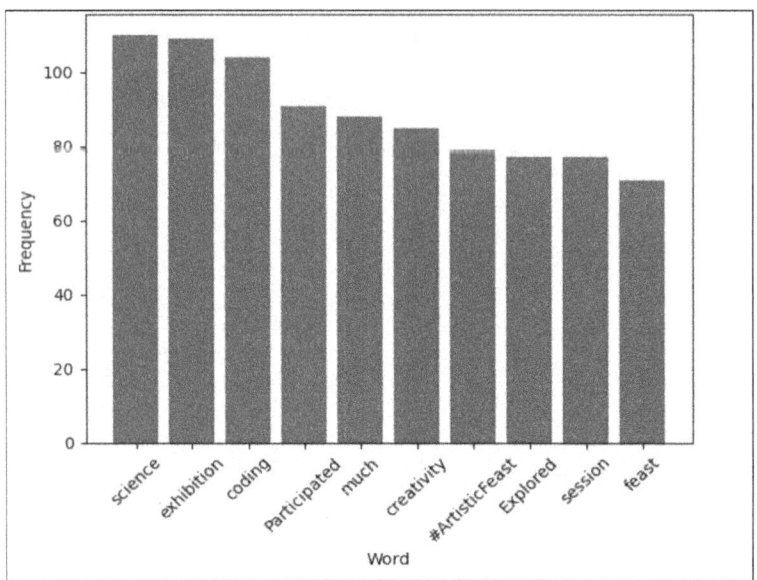

Fig. 6. Word Frequency Compilation Derived from User-Generated Content

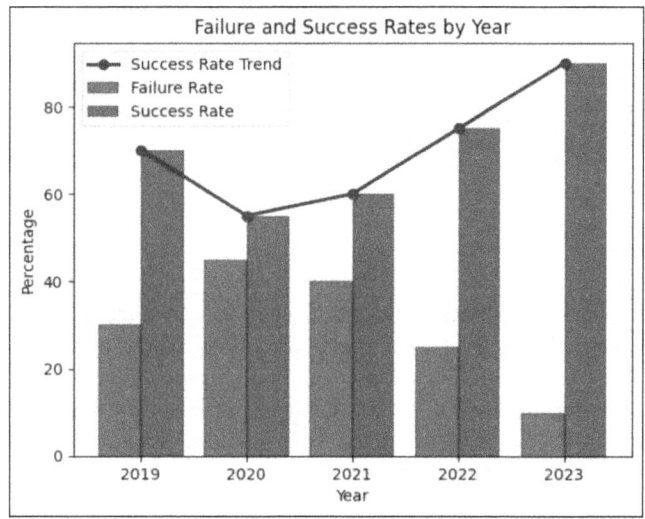

Fig. 7. Yearly Trends Unveiled

advancement in using technology to enhance the quality and impact of events in the digital age.

References

1. Ruz, G.A., Henríquez, P.A., Mascareño, A.: Sentiment analysis of Twitter data during critical events through Bayesian networks classifiers. Futur. Gener. Comput. Syst. **106**, 92–104 (2020)
2. Ligthart, A., Catal, C., & Tekinerdogan, B.: Systematic reviews in sentiment analysis: a tertiary study. Artific. Intell. Rev. 1–57 (2015)
3. Jurek, A., Mulvenna, M.D., Bi, Y.: Improved lexicon-based sentiment analysis for social media analytics. Secur. Inform. **4**(1), 1–13 (2021)
4. Kumar, V.V., Raghunath, K.K., Muthukumaran, V., Joseph, R.B., Beschi, I.S., Uday, A.K.: Aspect based sentiment analysis and smart classification in uncertain feedback pool. Int. J. Syst. Assuran. Eng. Manage. **13**(Suppl 1), 252–262 (2022)
5. Mustansir, A., Shahzad, K., Malik, M.K.: Sentiment analysis of user feedback on business processes. In: 2021 36th IEEE/ACM International Conference on Automated Software Engineering Workshops (ASEW), pp. 204–210. IEEE (2021)
6. Du, K., Xing, F., Mao, R., Cambria, E.: Financial sentiment analysis: techniques and applications. ACM Comput. Surv. **56**(9), 1–42 (2024)
7. Gu, W., et al.: Predicting stock prices with finbert-lstm: Integrating news sentiment analysis. arXiv preprint arXiv:2407.16150 (2024)
8. Moutidis, I., Williams, H.T.: Good and bad events: combining network-based event detection with sentiment analysis. Soc. Netw. Anal. Min. **10**, 1–12 (2020)
9. Kazmaier, J., Van Vuuren, J.H.: Sentiment analysis of unstructured customer feedback for a retail bank. ORiON **36**(1), 35–71 (2020)
10. Shayaa, S., et al.: Sentiment analysis of big data: methods, applications, and open challenges. IEEE Access **6**, 37807–37827 (2018)
11. Wankhade, M., Rao, A.C.S., Kulkarni, C.: A survey on sentiment analysis methods, applications, and challenges. Artif. Intell. Rev. **55**(7), 5731–5780 (2022)
12. Sufi, F.K., Alsulami, M.: Automated multidimensional analysis of global events with entity detection, sentiment analysis and anomaly detection. IEEE Access **9**, 152449–152460 (2021)
13. Mesana, J.C.B., de Guzman, A.B., Valencia, C.Q., Basister, J.P.C.: Mapping online viewers' social and non-social emotions using the lens of watching UNESCO cultural heritage sites' travel vlogs. J. Heritage Tour. 1–18 (2024)
14. Park, E., Kang, J., Choi, D., Han, J.: Understanding customers' hotel revisiting behaviour: a sentiment analysis of online feedback reviews. Curr. Issue Tour. **23**(5), 605–611 (2020)
15. Mir, A.A.: Sentiment analysis of social media during coronavirus and its correlation with indian stock market movements. Integrat. J. Sci. Technol. **1**(8) (2024)
16. Alhumoud, S.O., Al Wazrah, A.A.: Arabic sentiment analysis using recurrent neural networks: a review. Artific. Intell. Rev. **55**(1), 707–748 (2022)
17. Zucco, C., Calabrese, B., Agapito, G., Guzzi, P.H., Cannataro, M.: Sentiment analysis for mining texts and social networks data: methods and tools. Wiley Interdiscipl. Rev.: Data Min. Knowl. Discov. **10**(1), e1333 (2020)
18. Alqaryouti, O., Siyam, N., Abdel Monem, A., Shaalan, K.: Aspect-based sentiment analysis using smart government review data. Appl. Comput. Inform. **20**(1/2), 142–161 (2024)
19. Liu, Z., Yang, T., Chen, W., Chen, J., Li, Q., Zhang, J.: Sentiment analysis of social media comments based on multimodal attention fusion network. Appl. Soft Comput. **164**, 112011 (2024)
20. Slater, M., et al.: The sentiment of a virtual rock concert. Virt. Reality **27**(2), 651–675 (2023)
21. Gibson, J.: YouTube diplomacy: a sentiment analysis of global reactions to the 2018 concert in pyongyang. COLlection of essays on korea's public diplomacy: possibilities and future outlook, vol. 15 (2020)

22. Holster, J.D.: Music's monarch speaks: a content analysis of Leonard Bern-stein's Young People's Concerts. Qual. Res. Music Educ. **4**(1), 62–104 (2022)
23. Du, K., Xing, F., Mao, R., Cambria, E.: Financial sentiment analysis: techniques and applications. ACM Comput. Surv. (2024)
24. Dataset link https://www.kaggle.com/datasets/srisaiteja/event-sentiment-analysis

A Comparative Analysis of Machine Learning Algorithms for Early Prediction of Diabetes

Mehulkumar Patel[✉]

Westcliff University, Irvine, USA
pmj7824@gmail.com

Abstract. Diabetes is a chronic disease with multifactorial etiologies such as age, obesity, and lack of exercise, complicating manual prediction. However, machine learning techniques have demonstrated high accuracy in diabetes prediction. This study evaluates the efficacy of several classification algorithms, including K-Nearest Neighbors (KNN), Decision Trees, Random Forests, Support Vector Machines (SVM), Neural Networks, Naive Bayes Classifiers, and Perceptron Learning Algorithms (PLA), in predicting diabetes. The research employs both brute force and ANNOY methods for KNN, genetic algorithms for SVM and Naive Bayes, and Neural Architecture Search (NAS) for optimizing neural network structures. The results indicate that KNN with brute force achieves the highest accuracy and stability, though at the cost of computational time. The ANNOY technique effectively reduces this time complexity. Neural networks, while highly accurate, show variability in performance. Naive Bayes classifiers modified by genetic algorithms exhibit competitive accuracy and stability comparable to Random Forests. These findings suggest that KNN, particularly with dataset normalization, is highly effective for early diabetes prediction.

1 Introduction

Diabetes is a chronic disease that may cause many complications. There are lots of reasons that can put a person at a high risk of having diabetes, such as age, obesity, lack of exercise, and more. So many reasons interweave together, making the manual prediction of diabetes is nearly impossible. However, lots of works [10,11,19] show that it is possible to have high accuracy by using machine learning techniques, such as random forest, K-means clustering, neural network, and so on.

By collecting essential data about the human body, the prediction of diabetes can be turned into a classification problem. Imagine that an individual case with essential data is a point in hyperspace; if it is closer to the cluster having diabetes, this case is more likely to have diabetes in the future. Otherwise, this case is more likely healthy. However there are lots of machine learning techniques born to solve classification problems, and it remains a problem of which technique has the highest accuracy on the prediction of diabetes.

To find out which techniques is more suitable to predict diabetes, this work examines the diagnosis of diabetes using KNN algorithm, decision tree, random forest, SVM, neural network naive Bayes classifier, and PLA.

2 Related Works

K-Nearest Neighbors (KNN) Classification Algorithm: The KNN classification algorithm is a supervised learning method which Fix and Hodges first develop [5]. The idea of KNN is based on the idiom, "birds of a feather flock together". By picking the k-nearest neighbors of a data point, the unknown class label can be determined. Lots of works [12, 16, 17] show the fact that KNN performs well for prediction of diabetes disease.

Decision Tree: Unlike KNN uses distance to determine the outcome, and the decision tree uses a sequence of decisions that maximizes the information gain, which can distinguish the class label of data as much as possible, to determine the outcome. Many works [1, 4] have applied the decision tree method and gained good accuracy. The advantage of the decision tree is that it is fast, easy to implement, and the decision is clear. But the disadvantage is that it is very likely over-fitting, and the structure of the tree will become more complex with more class labels. To solve this problem, the following techniques is developed:

Random Forst: Instead of a single decision tree, random forest uses lots of decision trees, which form a "forest". A random subset of the dataset constructs the decision trees. The key difference between a random forest and a decision tree is that while decision trees consider all the possible feature splits, random forests only select a subset of those features, which reduces the risk of overfitting, bias, and overall variance. In [13, 18], random forest shows that it can greatly reduce the problem of over-fitting of the single decision tree and gain an ever higher accuracy.

Support Vector Machine (SVM): Given a set of training data, where each data is labeled as a binary class, such as 0 and 1, the SVM training algorithm creates a model that assigns new examples to the binary labels by making it a non-probabilistic binary linear classifier. In addition, according to [2, 8], SVM can also use a a method called kernel trick to effectively perform non-linear classification by implicitly mapping its inputs into a high-dimensional feature space.

Perceptron Learning Algorithm (PLA): Perceptron learning algorithm [7] is proposed by Gallant in 1990, which is a fast and simple classification algorithm. However, the limitation of the perceptron learning algorithm is that it can only address the data that is linearly separable. Thus, the following model connecting layers of perceptrons is proposed:

Neural Network: Neural network have been used in many fields to deal with intricate datas. With the input layer hidden The input and output layers are constructed by neurons. Each piece of data in the dataset is processed while passing through neurons, layer by layer. After processing, the outcome can be used to make predictions. Using backpropagation, the accuracy of forecasts increases in each training. In order to construct the hidden layer more efficiently, NAS(Neural Architecture Searching) is used to search for suitable structures for the hidden layer, increasing the accuracy. According to [3, 6], many neural networks have been constructed and trained already, with high efficiency and accuracy in the prediction of diabetes.

naive Bayes Classifier: naive Bayes classifier, as its name suggests, is a machine learning method based on Bayesian theorem, this model will statistic each data and find all conditional probability of each event occurring if each outcome holds. And finally, when it is asked to predict the result, the model will evaluate the data which the request provide and find the most likely outcome according to the conditional probability it just recorded.

3 KNN

The rough process of the KNN algorithm is described as follows: suppose that there is a dataset which contains N data point, denoted as (X_i, Y_i) where X_i is the features of the i-th individuals data and Y_i is the class label of it. Now, data with the unknown class label is given, denoted (X, Y). By a preset distance function $d(P, Q)$, ordering the dataset as $(X_{(1)}, Y_{(1)}), (X_{(2)}, Y_{(2)}), \cdots, (X_{(N)}, Y_{(N)})$ where $d(X_{(1)}, X) \leq d(X_{(2)}, X) \leq \cdots \leq d(X_{(N)}, X)$. Pick the k-first class labels to determine the unknown class label, Y.

The algorithm to find k nearest neighbors is the soul of KNN algorithm. The naive way to do that is brute force. By calculating every distance between the dataset and the undetermined data, the desired class can be easily obtained. The time complexity of brute force is $O(n)$. Another way to find k nearest neighbors is to find approximate nearest neighbors, oh yeah (ANNOY). This approximate algorithm is used at Spotify for music recommendations.

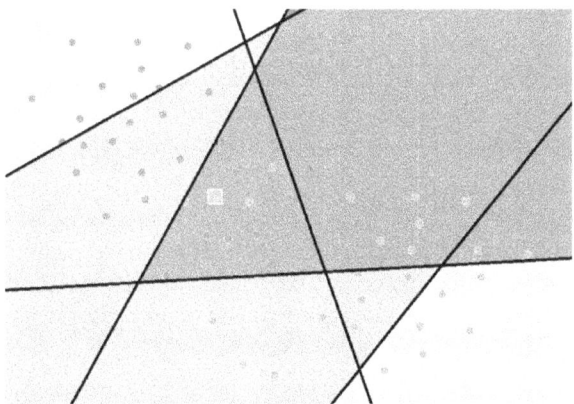

Fig. 1. The region split by ANNOY.

Figure 1 and Fig. 2 give illustrations of how ANNOY works. The process of ANNOY is detailed as follows: In every iteration, two points are randomly chosen, denoted x_1, x_2, and the hyperplane in the middle, whose equation is $n^T x = (x_1 - x_2)^T x = (x_1 - x_2)^T (x_1 + x_2)/2 = b$ separates all the points in a dataset into two kinds, "below" ($n^T x < b$) or "above" ($n^T x > b$). Also, in every iteration, a binary tree structure is constructed whose left child contains all the points "below" the hyperplane and right child contains all the points "above". The end condition is when

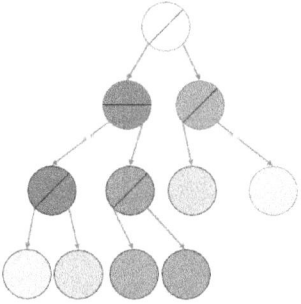

Fig. 2. The tree structure used by ANNOY.

a side of the hyperplane contains points no more than M, which is a preset parameter. When querying a k nearest neighbor of a point, recursively determine whether the point is "below" or "above" the hyperplane until reaching the leaf node. The time complexity of construction is $O(n)$, and the time complexity of query is $O(\log n)$. However, since the region searched may have fewer k points, the search path shall cover both nodes if the point is too close to the hyperplane. This technique, though, may increase the search time, but it can still greatly increase the accuracy of searching.

4 Decision Tree

Consider a dataset, D, which contains N data and class labels. The construction of a decision tree can be described below: suppose there are M candidate decisions, denoted f_i. A decision can separate dataset D into m kinds, denote D'_j. The decision tree will adopt $\arg\max_f G(D, f) = I(D) - \sum_{j=1}^{m} \frac{N'_j}{N} I(D'_j)$ as node decision, and then recursively construct the tree until the data in the separated dataset have the same class label. When data with an unknown class label arrives, a decision tree determines recursively by the decision node until the leaf node. The function of calculating information, I, can be various from implementation. The most famous two information function is entropy, and gini impurity. The formula of information entropy is

$$I_H(X) = -\sum_x p(x) \log_2 p(x) \tag{1}$$

and gini impurity is

$$I_G(X) = 1 - \sum_x p(x)^2 \tag{2}$$

5 Random Forest

Given the fact that a single decision tree can be easily overfitting, a technique called "random forest" is developed. By constructing m decision trees with randomized subsets of training dataset, the different decision trees forms a "forest". The process that random forest determines data with the unknown class label can be outlined as follows: suppose for a coming data, c_i decision trees in a random forest classify it as class i. Then, the random forest will classify the data as class $\arg\max c_i$.

6 SVM-GA

Given a dataset D containing N data points and a label with a binary class label of 0 or 1 representing the presence or absence of diabetes, respectively. Individually project each data point in the dataset D onto the hyperplane, I can obtain a point $(X_{i1}, X_{i2}, ..., X_{ij}, ..., X_{in})$, where X_{in} is the i-th individual data of D and j-th feature of N. After obtaining these points, these points are projected onto a hyperplane in $N + 1$ dimensions to avoid situations where the data is non-linearly separable. In this case, using the kernel function below as the projection function for each data point in D is a method of reducing the occurrence of non-linear separability:

$$\begin{bmatrix} x_1^{(2)} \\ x_2^{(2)} \\ ... \\ x_n^{(2)} \\ (\prod_{i=0}^{n} x_i)^{\frac{2}{n}} \end{bmatrix}$$

After this step, I can find a $N + 1$ dimensions hyperplane w that can separate the binary class labels of 0 and 1 for the data points. With this hyperplane trained on the training data, I can extend it to classify future data points that do not have binary class labels. Based on [15], I can use a genetic algorithm (GA) to find better hyperplanes. The following are the steps to find the hyperplane using a GA: Firstly, decide the level of generations (l), population size (n), variant (v), function constant (b), elite save rate (p_e), and mutations rate (p_m). Next, randomly select $N + 1$ parameters of the floating number between 0 and 1 in w, and repeat it until n hyperplanes are created. In the second step, use $w^t \cdot x - b$ [9] to compare the binary labels of the training data. If $w^t \cdot x - b > 0$, the output is 1; if $w^t \cdot x - b < 0$, the output is 0. This determines the accuracy of the n hyperplanes. Then, select the top $n \cdot p_e$ hyperplanes with high accuracy for crossover. The method is to take v feature values from the parent chromosomes to replace or average (randomly) v feature values from the mother chromosomes to create a new hyperplane. During the process, there is a probability of p_m for random mutation of a feature value into a random floating number between 0 and 1. After mating $n - n \cdot p_e$ hyperplanes, return this step until the lth operation is completed, and the best hyperplane is found.

7 PLA

Assume that in a dataset D, there are two class labels, 0 and 1. A perceptron will determine a data point with an unknown class label by formula

$$\text{sign}(\mathbf{w}^T\mathbf{x}) \qquad (3)$$

where w is the weight, and the sign function is defined as

$$\text{sign}(x) = \begin{cases} 1 & ,\text{if } x > 0 \\ 0 & ,\text{otherwise} \end{cases} \quad (4)$$

The perceptron can update the weight dynamically by the formula

$$w_{t+1} \leftarrow w_t + y_{n(t)} x_{n(t)} \text{ when } \text{sign}(w_t^T x_{n(t)}) \neq y_{n(t)} \quad (5)$$

In [7], Gallant proves that if the dataset is linearly separable, the perceptron learning algorithm will eventually find a weight w_T which satisfies $\text{sign}(w^T x_i) = y_i, \forall i$, in other words, w_T can separate the dataset by its class labels perfectly. In practice, the dataset is not always linear and separable. Therefore, Gallant proposed an algorithm, PLA-pocket. Instead of finding a perfect weight, PLA-pocket picks a weight that minimizes the errors in the dataset.

8 Neural Network

Given a dataset D containing N data points and a label with 0 or 1 representing whether the patient is diagnosed with diabetes or not, I need to construct a model with N-neurons input layer and 2-neurons output layer. Before I build the model, I have to find the structure of the hidden layer with NAS. I set the number of the layer to 10, with each layer has more than 16 and less than 256 neurons. Define the search space $\mathcal{F}$, which includes all the arrays, including 10 numbers, and each of the numbers in the array represents the number of neurons in each layer, which is more than 16 and less than 256, like above. I am aiming to find the approximate solution $f = \{x_1, x_2, ..., x_{10} | 16 \leq x_i \leq 256, 1 \leq i \leq 10\} \in \mathcal{F}$, which increase the accuracy of the model in the short term. With simulating annealing algorithm [14], I can find the approximate solutions. First, set the initial temperature T, the end temperature T_E, temperature decreasing rate R_T, and a random solution f^*. Second, create a model based on the parameter in the f^*, and train with D. I use cross entropy loss as loss function and Adam as optimization function. After training, I get the average loss of every epoch, L^*. Then, start the iteration by swap two of the parameters in f^*, get a new array f^{**}, train it with the dataset, and get its average loss, L^{**}. After getting L^* and L^{**}, I calculating the difference $\Delta L = L^{**} - L^*$. If $\Delta L \leq 0$, I update $f^* = f^{**}$. Otherwise, I use $e^{\frac{\Delta L}{T}}$ as the probability of the f^{**} accepted as the new solution, get a random number $R^* \in [1, 0]$ from the random number generator if R^* is less than $e^{\frac{\Delta L}{T}}$, I update $f^* = f^{**}$. Then repeat the iteration, but replace the swapping with changing one of the number in f^* to $n, 16 \leq n \leq 256$.

$$f^* = \begin{cases} f^{**}, & \Delta L \leq 0 \\ f^{**}, & \Delta L \geq 0 \text{ and } R^* < e^{\frac{\Delta L}{T}} \\ f^*, & \text{else} \end{cases} \quad (6)$$

After the end of the iteration, multiply T by R_T and continue the iteration until the $T \leq T_E$. Then, I get the approximate solution $f = f^*$. Every two iterations, the T decreases and lower the probability of f^{**} accepted as the solution. Stimulating annealing can avoid solution stuck at local minimum. Using a neural network found by NAS, I can now predict with untrained data with 80% or so accuracy.

9 Naive Bayes Classifier-GA

Consider a dataset, D, which contains M data points with k class labels. The probability that a random data point belongs to i-th class is $P(C_k \mid \mathbf{x})$ where C_k is the event that data points $\mathbf{x} = (\mathbf{x_1}, \cdots, \mathbf{x_n})$ belongs to k-th class. By using Bayes' theorem, the probability can be rewritten as

$$P(C_k \mid x) = \frac{P(C_k)P(\mathbf{x} \mid \mathbf{C_k})}{P(\mathbf{x})} \qquad (7)$$

In practice, there is interest only in the numerator of that fraction because the denominator does not depend on C_k, and the values of the features that are given, so the denominator is effectively constant. Then, by chain rule of conditional probability, the numerator of Eq. 7 can be rewritten as

$$P(C)P(x_1 \mid C_k)P(x_2, \cdots, x_n \mid C_k, x_1)$$
$$= \cdots \qquad (8)$$
$$= P(C)P(x_1 \mid C_k) \cdots P(x_n \mid C_k, x_1, \cdots, x_{n-1})$$

Now assume that all features in $\mathbf{x}$ is mutually independent, $P(x_i \mid x_j, C_k)$ will be equal to $P(x_i \mid C_k)$. Thus, the probability is

$$P(C_k \mid x) = \frac{P(C_k) \prod_{i=1}^n P(x_i \mid C_k)}{Z} \qquad (9)$$

where Z is a constant. With Eq. 9, data points with unknown class labels can be classified by choosing the most possible class:

$$\arg\max_k P(C_k) \prod_{i=1}^n P(x_i = x_i' \mid C_k) \qquad (10)$$

The problem is, when given is a continuous value instead of individual events, it needs to be partitioned according to the specific value, which below this value is an individual event while above is another event. However, the difficulty is finding the partition that best fits the model. The answer can be easily found by using gene alogrithm. First, record the maximum and minimum values of the given data in each dimension. Second, randomly partition data in each dimension according to the maximum and minimum value recorded before and repeat 100 times to generate enough species. Third, testing the accuracy of the model on the training data and keep top K good species and kill the rest. Then, let these elites produce offspring, which means passing their partitions to offspring. When there is enough offspring, all offspring are going to have mutation, the partitions may slightly shift, merge, split, disappear, or keep originally. Finally, repeat the whole iteration until the partition is close to the optimal solution after T iterations.

Table 1. COMPARISON OF CLASSIFICATION TECHNIQUES.

Technique	Search (s)	testA	testA-normalized	testB	testB-normalized
KNN-Brute-Force	0.009	76.6169 ± 0	$\mathbf{80.597 \pm 0}$	78 ± 0	$\mathbf{80 \pm 0}$
KNN-ANNOY-DFS	0.003	75.2438 ± 1.8762	76.1294 ± 2.0977	74.9 ± 2.5554	76.4 ± 2.5377
KNN-ANNOY-BFS	0.012	76.6567 ± 0.5340	$\mathbf{80.597 \pm 0}$	$\mathbf{78.16 \pm 0.7310}$	$\mathbf{80 \pm 0}$
decision tree	0.009	74.1294 ± 0	74.1294 ± 0	76 ± 0	77 ± 0
random forest	0.004	78.6965 ± 1.7510	78.5373 ± 1.452	77.98 ± 2.083	77.5 ± 2.516
SVM-GA	1.846	76.6616 ± 4.0301	75.9219 ± 2.736	75 ± 2	75 ± 4
Neural Network	3.2	$\mathbf{81.7910 \pm 2.0294}$	80.2985 ± 1.4106	78 ± 1.6733	77.5 ± 1.892
Naive Bayes classifier-GA	14.29	78.5353 ± 0.0322	72.6866 ± 0.0237	77.4038 ± 0.0626	71 ± 0.0289
PLA-pocket	0.00052	63.682 ± 0	3.162 ± 0	63 ± 0	3.162 ± 0

10 Experiment Result

This work compare the common classification algorithms, including KNN (with brute force, ANNOY-DFS, ANNOY-BFS), decision tree, random forest, SVM (modified by GA), Neural Network, Naive Bayes classifier (modified by GA), PLA-pocket algorithm. The programming languages of KNN, decision tree, random forest, and SVM-GA are C++20. And Neural Network, Naive Bayes classifier-GA and PLA-pocket is using Python3 with PyTorch and the sci-kit-learn library. Table 1 compares all datasets, which show that KNN with brute force is the best method to predict diabetes. And since it is a deterministic algorithm, it is very stable. The only drawback is the time complexity is $O(n)$ where n is the number of data points in the dataset. But with ANNOY technique, the time complexity can be reduced to almost $O(\log n)$, which solves the huge cost of brute force.

11 Conclusion

Though the PLA-pocket method is the fastest, its accuracy is not ideal. The neural network performs better, but it is less stable. The naive Bayes classifier modified by GA has surprisingly good performance and stability, which can compete with random forests in the un-normalized dataset. The experiment result shows that KNN method fits best to predict diabetes early. It is important to note that KNN performs better after normalizing the dataset, while others perform the same or even worse, e.g., PLA-pocket. The reason behind is normalization can make the data points scatter uniformly, which makes KNN have better immunity to the wide gap of the data range.

References

1. Al Jarullah, A.A.: Decision tree discovery for the diagnosis of type II diabetes. In: 2011 International Conference on Innovations in Information Technology, pp. 303–307 (2011). https://doi.org/10.1109/INNOVATIONS.2011.5893838
2. Amari, S.I., Wu, S.: Improving support vector machine classifiers by modifying kernel functions. Neural Networks **12**(6), 783–789 (1999)
3. Beghriche, T., Djerioui, M., Brik, Y., Attallah, B., Belhaouari, S.B.: An efficient prediction system for diabetes disease based on deep neural network. Complexity **2021**, 6053824 (2021). https://doi.org/10.1155/2021/6053824
4. Chen, W., Chen, S., Zhang, H., Wu, T.: A hybrid prediction model for type 2 diabetes using k-means and decision tree. In: 2017 8th IEEE International Conference on Software Engineering and Service Science (ICSESS), pp. 386–390 (2017). https://doi.org/10.1109/ICSESS.2017.8342938
5. Fix, E., Hodges, J.L.: Discriminatory analysis. nNonparametric discrimination: consistency properties. Int. Stat. Rev./Revue Internationale de Statistique **57**(3), 238–247 (1989). http://www.jstor.org/stable/1403797
6. Gadekallu, T.R., Khare, N., Bhattacharya, S., Singh, S., Maddikunta, P.K.R., Srivastava, G.: Deep neural networks to predict diabetic retinopathy. Journal of Ambient Intelligence and Humanized Computing (2020). https://doi.org/10.1007/s12652-020-01963-7
7. Gallant, S.I., et al.: Perceptron-based learning algorithms. IEEE Trans. Neural Networks **1**(2), 179–191 (1990)
8. Hofmann, M.: Support vector machines-kernels and the kernel trick. Notes **26**(3), 1–16 (2006)
9. Kumari, V.A., Chitra, R.: Classification of diabetes disease using support vector machine. Int. J. Eng. Res. Appl. **3**(2), 1797–1801 (2013)
10. Mahboob Alam, T., et al.: A model for early prediction of diabetes. Inf. Med. Unlocked **16**, 100204 (2019). https://doi.org/10.1016/j.imu.2019.100204, https://www.sciencedirect.com/science/article/pii/S2352914819300176
11. Mujumdar, A., Vaidehi, V.: Diabetes prediction using machine learning algorithms. Procedia Comput. Sci. **165**, 292–299 (2019). https://doi.org/10.1016/j.procs.2020.01.047, https://www.sciencedirect.com/science/article/pii/S1877050920300557, 2nd International Conference on Recent Trends in Advanced Computing ICRTAC -DISRUP - TIV INNOVATION , 2019 November 11-12, 2019
12. NirmalaDevi, M., alias Balamurugan, S.A., Swathi, U.V.: An amalgam KNN to predict diabetes mellitus. In: 2013 IEEE International Conference ON Emerging Trends in Computing, Communication and Nanotechnology (ICECCN), pp. 691–695 (2013). https://doi.org/10.1109/ICE-CCN.2013.6528591
13. Palimkar, P., Shaw, R.N., Ghosh, A.: Machine learning technique to prognosis diabetes disease: random forest classifier approach. In: Bianchini, M., Piuri, V., Das, S., Shaw, R.N. (eds.) Advanced Computing and Intelligent Technologies, pp. 219–244. Springer, Singapore (2022). https://doi.org/10.1007/978-981-16-2164-2_19
14. Rutenbar, R.: Simulated annealing algorithms: an overview. IEEE Circuits Devices Mag. **5**(1), 19–26 (1989). https://doi.org/10.1109/101.17235
15. Santhanam, T., Padmavathi, M.: Application of k-means and genetic algorithms for dimension reduction by integrating SVM for diabetes diagnosis. Procedia Comput. Sci. **47**, 76–83 (2015)
16. Shetty, D., Rit, K., Shaikh, S., Patil, N.: Diabetes disease prediction using data mining. In: 2017 International Conference on Innovations in Information, Embedded and Communication Systems (ICIIECS), pp. 1–5 (2017). https://doi.org/10.1109/ICIIECS.2017.8276012

17. Vijayan, V., Ravikumar, A.: Study of data mining algorithms for prediction and diagnosis of diabetes mellitus. Int. J. Comput. Appl. **95**(17) (2014)
18. Xu, W., Zhang, J., Zhang, Q., Wei, X.: Risk prediction of type ii diabetes based on random forest model. In: 2017 Third International Conference on Advances in Electrical, Electronics, Information, Communication and Bio-Informatics (AEEICB). pp. 382–386 (2017). https://doi.org/10.1109/AEEICB.2017.7972337
19. Zou, Q., Qu, K., Luo, Y., Yin, D., Ju, Y., Tang, H.: Predicting diabetes mellitus with machine learning techniques. Frontiers in Genetics **9** (2018). https://doi.org/10.3389/fgene.2018.00515, https://www.frontiersin.org/articles/10.3389/fgene.2018.00515

Understanding User Requests in Chatbot Using Deep Learning

Alaa T. Al-Tuama(✉) and Dhamyaa A. Nasrawi

College of Computer Science and Information Technology, University of Kerbala, Karbala, Iraq
alaa.tuama@s.uokerbala.edu.iq

Abstract. Many companies are switching to automated solutions as technology develops quickly and away from human customer care methods. Demand for conversational agents such as chatbots has so skyrocketed. Using natural language processing methods, these bots replicate human-like interactions with users via text or speech. In this respect, chatbots face two major challenges: intent classification and entity extraction from user requests. Therefore, this paper focuses on classification of intents along with named entity-identifying techniques to understand user requests. Understanding these key elements helps us improve the functionality and effectiveness of these conversational agents in meeting customer needs. The question-and-answer Amazon office products dataset is used in this paper. In order to achieve this objective, we employ the BiLSTM model in conjunction with deep learning to implement the intent classifier. Through bidirectional data processing, the model may better comprehend the relationship between sequences. In order to achieve a more precise and contextualized NER extraction, we implement Custom NER, which is based on BiLSTM. The custom NER achieved 96.94% accuracy, while the BiLSTM intent classifier model obtained 94.75% accuracy, according to the results.

Keywords: Amazon office products · BiLSTM · Chatbot · Custom Named Entity Recognition · Intent classification

1 Introduction

Chatting is an incredibly important form of communication. Given the significance of these chatbots, extensive research has been developing systems capable of generating human-like responses to enhance the computer-human chat [1]. To understand user input and respond appropriately, chatbots mainly rely on natural language processing (NLP) and natural language understanding (NLU) [2, 3]. NLU identifies pertinent things from user-provided texts by applying machine learning and natural language processing algorithms to distinguish user words into distinct intents [4].

A modified LSTM called Bi-LSTM may identify contextual characteristics from both the past and the future. An advantage over unidirectional LSTM is that it employs hidden and forward layers for output sequences, enabling input to flow both forward and backward [5].

Intent classification is a critical research field within the realm of artificial intelligence, boasting routine uses, including marketing and product design, and facilitating smart communication [6]. The process of intent classification involves grouping user entered text into predetermined intent groups depending on the relevant domains and intentions under active influence. In systems where several users with different objectives engage simultaneously [18, 19] it is especially important. For companies especially as it helps them to be more customer-centric, classifying intentions is quite important [7]. Extracting intent from dialogue systems and processing large amounts of data are challenging tasks that call for advanced technology [8].

Furthermore, Named Entity Recognition (NER) is a crucial text preprocessing tool that has immense significance in various natural language uses including automatic text summarizing, question answering, information retrieval, and machine translating [9, 10]. NER detects named entities that differentiate elements from other similar ones by leveraging their characteristics through the use of rigid designators, atomic components, or members belonging to a semantic category. The identification process varies depending on the application domain, which may include content classification for news agencies or the optimization of client uses and browsing datasets. Given this diversity of applications, we adjust techniques to identify named entities based on the specific-use case to produce optimal results [9, 11, 12].

Based on these discussions, this paper aims to classify user intent into predetermined intent categories and create a customized Named Entity Recognition (NER) system for the marketing office products domain. Therefore, we aim to extract custom entities accurately from users' requests. To achieve these aims, both models are based on a BiLSTM model that helps us better understand the user's requests and deliver more accurate results.

This paper mainly contributes to relevant works by:

- Creating a cleaned question and answers dataset by implementing several preprocessing techniques.
- Labelling intent for every sentence in the cleaned data set.
- Designing bidirectional long short-term memory (BiLSTM) model to categorize intents and grasp the user's aims.
- Customizing the dataset with a named object that understands what users ask and building a BiLSTM model to extract entities.

As for the overall structure of the paper, it involves; Section 2 surveys previous research. Section 3 describes the methodology. Section 4 suggests findings. Section 5 states research conclusions as well as proposes certain topics for further research.

2 Related Works

An outline of earlier research pertinent to this topic is given in this part. The related work is divided into intent classification and name entity recognition subsections. Hence, an overview of these previous studies will be detailed. Moreover, these relevant works are subdivided into subsections for intent classification and name entity recognition.

2.1 Intent Classification

Many researchers implement intent classification using traditional machine learning techniques in multiple applications, such as education [13], smart cities [14], data augmentation [15], detection of criminal intent from user tweets [16], and proofreader chatbots [17]. This subsection focused on works related to deep learning:

Oanh Thi Tran and Tho Chi Luong, helping understand Vietnamese language user utterances using two neural architectures: CNN and Bi-LSTM. Regarding context extraction, the findings revealed an F-measure of 82.32% in identifying intentions and outcomes ranging from 78% to 91% [18].

To identify unknown intent, Lin and Xu put up two methods approach They trained known intentions using BiLSTM initially as a feature extractor. For uncertain intentions they learned discriminative deep features using local outlier factor (LOF) and large margin cosine loss (LMCL) [19].

Ask Ubuntu, Travel Scheduling, and Web Applications were the three corpora used by Jetze Schuurmans and Flavius Frasincar to compare NB, SVM, LSTM networks, and hierarchical models. The greatest macro-F1 score was achieved by Bi-LSTM Word2Vec [20].

Zhang et al. suggested Adaptive Decision border (ADB), which uses BERT to identify known and open-domain intents while defining the centroid and decision border and modifying hyperparameters [8].

Geetha. N, Vivek G, and Vinetia T.A. created an aim-based chatbot that could remember talks with certain users, which provided desired responses by extracting the user's intent. Two models, namely Bert and Gobot, were implemented precisely. The results showed Gobot's accuracy by 0.76, thereby demonstrating good performance by these models that could be enhanced with further data [21].

N. Laosen et al. collected questions from the TripAdvisor website and classify their intents using two neural network models, a BiLSTM and a BERT model. Based on the testing results, the BERT model performed better, with an accuracy of 94.22% [22].

Chowdhury et al. proposed a hierarchical method called Dual Phase-BERT. Several conventional models—including machine learning, deep learning, and transformer-based models—were developed and evaluated on the ArBanking77 dataset. Their work indicated that Dual-Phase-BERT model resulted in 0.801 on the F1score [23].

2.2 Name Entity Recognition

Many researchers implement name entity recognition using traditional techniques in multiple applications, such as customer chat conversations about the quality of food, which provide a named entity recognition (NER) approach [24]. In [25], the study suggested machine learning (ML) to develop a distinctive fusion chain model for Named Entity Recognition (NER) in the Kumauni language. In [26], the study proposed Booking Bot to help humans book flights with NER. This subsection focused on related works on deep learning:

Schweter and Akbik used two approaches—fine-tune and feature-based via LSTM-CRF architecture—to compare the properties of document-level NERs. They discovered that, in comparison to feature-based approaches, fine-tuning enhanced NER quality. As an addition to the FLAIR framework, they also included FLERT [27].

Ali created a chatbot utilizing an ANN with hidden layers that was centered on intent classification and NER. For NER trials, the CoNLL-2003 model achieved 81.66% entity extraction and 89% intent classification accuracy [28].

The nested named entity recognition (NER) neural networks were proposed in two variants by Straková, Straka, and Hajic. Initially, a typical LSTM-CRF predictor was used to merge nested entity labels; however, the class sizes were huge. In the second, a sequence-to-sequence approach was employed, and seq2seq performed better than the others [29].

Jwa, Myeong-Cheol, and Jeong-Woo Jwa developed a smart tourism chatbot system using Korean and English smart tourism Name Entity (NE) datasets using pre-trained language models (PLMs). The result of system performance has a 0.94 F1 score [30].

Geetha, R et al. present a study that uses deep neural networks—CNN, RNN, C-LSTM, CRF, Bi-LSTM, and Bi-LSTMCRF—as well as deep privacy models to recognize and guess medical information. The tweets dataset was extracted based on the health domain. Bi-LSTM-CRF model performs well, with a 95% accuracy rate [31].

Goel et al. used machine, artificial, and manual annotations to study NER techniques on recipe texts. These techniques comprised few-shot prompting on LLMs and statistical, deep-learning-based language model fine-tuning. They discovered that, with macro-F1 scores of 96.04% and 95.71%, respectively, the optimized spaCy-transformer model was the best [32].

Guimarães et al. suggested using the DODFMiner command-line interface tool to categorize acts and get recognized entities from the Federal District's Official Gazette. There are three distinct NER architectures: CNN-biLSTM-CRF with 78.7, CRF with a mean F1-score of 85.1, and CNN-CNN-LSTM with 84.1 [33].

NER models are evaluated and trained using Conditional Random Fields, Bidirectional LSTM configurations, and BERT models, and contracts are manually annotated with entity labels by Aejas et al. The BEART model showed outstanding performance with an F1 score of 0.94 [34].

3 Methodology

This section elaborates on the methodology followed for annotating data concerning intent classification and custom NER extraction for office product data. The proposed models for intent classification and custom NER extraction are based on BiLSTM and have been trained and tested on Amazon's office products dataset. Subsections tackle this process in depth.

3.1 Dataset

The Office Products dataset, consisting of questions and answers sourced from Amazon product pages [35, 36]. This dataset includes over 12,228 pairs of questions and answers in the e-commerce domain, and each question has several possible responses and an

ASIN number that serves as a unique identifier for a variety of office products, see Fig. 1.

```
{"Asin": "B000050B6Z", "Question Type": "yes/no", "Answer
Type": "Y", "Answer Time": "Aug 8, 2014", "Unix-Time":
1407481200, "Question": "Can you use this unit with GEL
shaving cans?", "Answer": "Yes. If the can fit in the
machine it will dispense hot gel lather. I've been using
my machine for both, gel and traditional lather for over
10 years."}
```

Fig. 1. Amazon office products dataset sample

3.2 Data Preprocessing

To enhance model accuracy, several pre-processing techniques were implemented as follows: Lowercasing all text, Formalizing every word into its conventional format. Removing duplicates, mentions, and links. Removing stop-words; a custom list was set for this purpose. Lemmatization was implemented only on answers. Normalizing performed on every set of the data. Finally, conducting spelling correctness.

3.3 Intent Classification Based on Bi-LSTM

The initial stage in creating a successful chatbot is intent categorization. This challenge, characterized by a one label and a vector of output representing probabilities of multi-class classification. The bot can adapt its responses based on these probabilities, ensuring it delivers the correct answer consistently, Fig. 2 below illustrates the profile of the method to categorize intents.

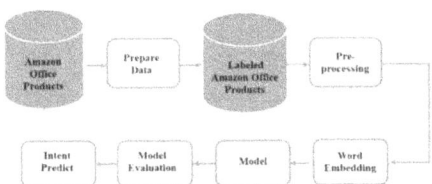

Fig. 2. Proposed intent classification system

Preparing Intent Classes. Since the proposed dataset lacks an intent label for each utterance, it is necessary to prepare the dataset before designing the intent classification model. Question words are used to identify the labels of intentions. Methods like topic modeling and keyword matching are used to identify intentions. Unfortunately, these approaches fail because there is a lot of inter-class overlap due to the similarity and proximity of the data. Data is labeled to eight categories by applying a regular expression to the language of the questions, show Table 1.

Table 1. Samples in every class of intents

N	Intent classes	Sample count
1	Auxiliary do/does/did	3036
2	Auxiliary is/are	2447
3	Auxiliary can/could	1938
4	how	1519
5	Auxiliary will/would/should	1421
6	what	1307
7	5-wh	460
8	Auxiliary/have/has	104

Training Intent Classifier Model. Preparing the input text for training requires careful attention to detail. For training, 80% of the data is utilized, and the remaining 20% is used for testing. The next step is to assign labels to the target data using the label encoder. The following step is to create an embedding matrix. Glove is utilized in this model. This process uses a sequential model, with the embedding layer acting as the first layer. For every word in the vocabulary, there is a vector with the same input dimension and a fixed length of 121. Next, a BiLSTM layer is added. A dense layer with a relu activation function is then appended. Furthermore, an output layer included. Adam optimizer and categorical cross-entropy loss function are used. As for the performance, it is tracked using accuracy metrics.

3.4 Identification of Entities Based on Custom Labelling

Determining the user ends as well as extracting the parameters out of necessary words to complete the request are two steps in parsing their utterance. Finding and labelling important information in high-precision texts is the goal of Named Entity Recognition (NER), a quickly growing branch of natural language processing. Assigning a class to the input sequence is the job of entity recognition, a multiclass token classification. Standard NER searches for locations, names, organizations, and other pre-set entities in texts. To utilize this standard model to extract data from an unlabelled dataset, it is first trained on specified labelled data. Due to its inability to extract pertinent information depending on the chosen domain, standard NER is not suitable for this investigation. Therefore, in order to get useful things (such as action, color, brand, material, etc.) from office supplies, a custom-named entity is generated. Figure 3 displays the architecture of the proposed custom entity recognition.

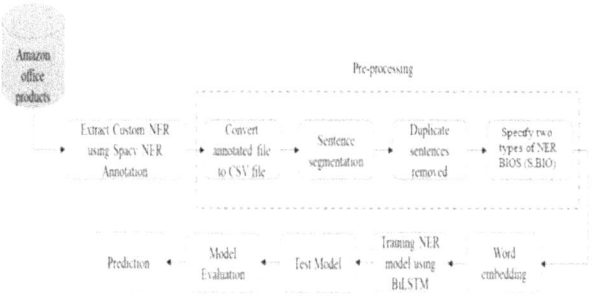

Fig. 3. Custom entity recognition model

Custom NER Annotation. Before creating custom NER for office products, entities and associated tags must be identified and extracted. For this purpose, the spacy NER annotation technique is used to extract entities from the questions. The extracted labels (14 labels) are shown in Table 2. Once the annotation data is complete, we extract the entities from their locations into a CSV file.

Table 2. Labels list

N	entity	Number	N	entity	Number
1	Object	9540	8	Time	513
2	Action	5525	9	Size	297
3	Title	5435	10	Cards	192
4	Number	4382	11	Organization	184
5	Color	814	12	Brand	173
6	Materials	782	13	Nationality	154
7	Software	670	14	GPE	129

Preparing Custom NER Model. The custom NER dataset consists of questions and entities that correspond to each query. Furthermore, we repeat each inquiry based on the number of entities it contains. The model needs to be executed by breaking down each sentence into individual words, with every word assigned an index that relates to its respective sentence. Thus, each divided token is linked to its appropriate identifier. Subsequently, sentences that are duplicated are eliminated, and each sentence is represented by its respective entity. In this research, the sequence labeling for NER tasks utilizes BIOS notation. Here, 'B' signifies the beginning of an entity, 'I' indicates within an entity, 'O' marks outside any entity, and 'S' stands for single entity that made up of just one word. Conversely, tokens marked with 'O' are not classified as any type of entity nor labeled by the model.

Training Custom Named Entity Recognition. BiLSTM is used to implement a custom named entity. Words in a phrase can be represented vectorically using the BiLSTM model. To build the model, various layers with specific parameters and functions are used. The input layer, which sets the dimensions of input data via a tuple, is the initial layer. The crucial step in this process is the BiLSTM, which has two unit parameters indicating output space dimensionality and true return sequence for complete outputs. Furthermore, Time Distributed Layer applies a dense output layer to handle every single element consequently. The Adam optimizer is employed on training data, using a batch size of 64 over 200 epochs. Additionally, validation is performed during each epoch using 20% of training data, as specified by *val_split*.

4 Findings of Experiments

This section evaluates the performance of the intent classification and custom named entity recognition models using performance measurement. The proposed models also undergo a comparison with related works.

4.1 Evaluation of Intent Classification Model

To find the optimal classifier model parameters, we use 50 epochs with varying hyperparameters to train the initial stage of the suggested model. Figure 4 demonstrates the accuracy of BiLSTM-based method that was trained. The proposed model achieves 94.75% accuracy in intent classification.

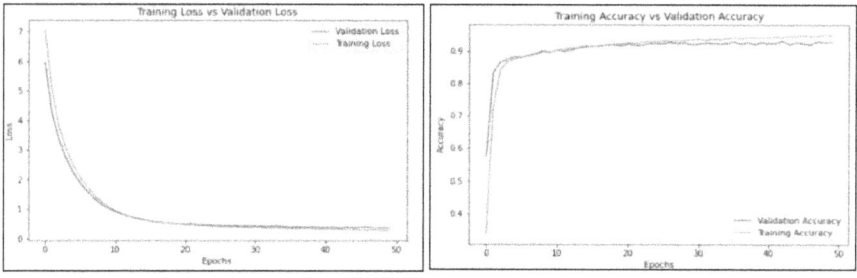

Fig. 4. Precision of training and validation and intent loss-categorizing method

Table 3 illustrates the hyperparameters of the intent classifiers. Additionally, Table 4 presents a comparison of the training and validation accuracy and loss for several experiments. Findings of evaluation of the model performance are shown in Table 5.

Table 3. Tuning hyper parameters of intent classifier model

N	Units	Nodes	Dropout layer	L_rate	Batch size	Kernel regularization	Dropout in Lstm
1	128	300	0.5	0.001	64	L2	–
2	**128**	**600**	**0.5**	**0.001**	**64**	**L2**	**0.2**

(*continued*)

Table 3. (*continued*)

N	Units	Nodes	Dropout layer	L_rate	Batch size	Kernel regularization	Dropout in Lstm
3	256	600	0.5	0.0001	128	L2	0.3
4	256	600	0.5	0.001	64	–	–
5	128	600	–	0.1	128	L2	0.3
6	256	600	0.5	0.0001	128	–	0.3
7	128	600	0.5	0.0001	128	L1	0.2
8	256	600	0.5	0.0001	64	L2	–

Table 4. Train and val accuracy and train-val loss results of some experiments

N	Train accuracy	Val accuracy	Train loss	Val loss
1	97.59	94.34	0.1059	0.316
2	**99.09**	**94.75**	**0.1393**	**0.281**
3	98.46	93.16	0.1533	0.345
4	95.85	93.98	0.1505	0.251
5	38.80	38.82	1.7521	1.752
6	97.29	93.73	0.1051	0.245
7	95.36	91.78	0.5754	0.703
8	98.58	93.35	0.1677	0.360

Table 5. Evaluation measurement of intent classifier model

Macro F1-Score	Macro Precision	Macro Recall	Accuracy
90	90	90	94.75

In addition, k-fold cross validation is implemented on the methods used to categorize intents. The experiment results are presented in Table 6.

Table 6. Cross validation result of intent classifier model

No of Fold	Accuracy of Each Fold	No of Fold	Accuracy of Each Fold
1	97.08	6	99.43
2	98.96	7	99.33
3	98.86	8	99.81

(*continued*)

Table 6. (*continued*)

No of Fold	Accuracy of Each Fold	No of Fold	Accuracy of Each Fold
4	99.15	9	99.81
5	99.43	10	99.90

Overall Model Accuracy: 99.176%

Moreover, Table 7 demonstrates the comparison of the proposed intent classification model's performance metrics against those of relevant studies. As Table 7 illustrates, the proposed model gains higher accuracy in classifying intent.

Table 7. Intent classification model comparison with related research

N	Ref	Dataset	Method	Accuracy	F1 score
1	[20]	Networking domain	Used BERT and gobot	76.0	–
2	[8]	OOS, Banking, stack overflow	Used ADB and BERT	78.85–86.32	71.62–85.99
3	[21]	Pertained to the Network domain	BERT- goBot	76	–
4	[18]	Travel scheduling, Ask ubunto, web app	Used SVM, BiLSTM, Naïve base, hierarchical	–	75.2–98.9
5	[28]	Manually from restaurants collected	BiLSTM-CNN	–	82.32
6	[22]	TripAdvisor website	BiLSTM, BERT	80.10 94.22	–
7	[23]	Multi-Dialect Intent Detection dataset ArBanking77	hierarchical approach called Dual Phase-BERT		80.1
8	Our model	Amazon Office products	BiLSTM	**94.75**	90

4.2 Custom NER Evaluation

Using BiLSTM for training, the suggested model of a specified custom object is assessed for cross-entropy loss and accuracy. At the learning step, the model has been trained using data where each sequence is inputted as a single word along with its matching tag. In Fig. 5, we can see the data representation in its entirety, illustrating the process of feeding data into the model.

index	question	tag	entity
0	0	does	O	O
1	0	do	O	O
2	0	good	O	O
3	0	job	O	O
4	0	envelopes	S-Object	envelopes
5	1	does	O	O

Fig. 5. Data representation of custom NER

Adjusting the model's parameters to achieve optimal performance and output is the learning model's most crucial component. The model's tuning parameters are shown in Table 8.

Table 8. Hyperparameters tuning of custom NER

N	Batch size	Units	L_r	Spatial dropout	Dropout	Recurrent dropout	epochs
1	64	25	0.0001	0.2	–	–	150
2	64	25	0.01	–	0.5	0.1	200
3	32	50	0.001	0.1	–	0.5	200
4	64	25	0.0001	0.3	0.1	0.5	200
5	**64**	**50**	**0.0001**	**0.2**	**0.4**	–	**200**
6	64	50	0.1	0.2	0.2	–	200
7	128	50	0.0001	0.1	0.2	–	200
8	32	25	0.001	0.2	–	–	200

Validation using validation data as input to the training model is required once the model achieves its lowest error rate at convergence. The output class for each text will be determined by the network using the weights that have been recorded before. To verify a model, check that the output matches the actual label of the entity. Figure 6 shows the results of the examination of the cross entropy loss, training accuracy, and validation accuracy. Table 9 displays the accuracy and loss of the model during training and validation, revealing that the custom NER model achieves the highest accuracy of 96.94%. The method has been evaluated as per the findings detailed in Table 10.

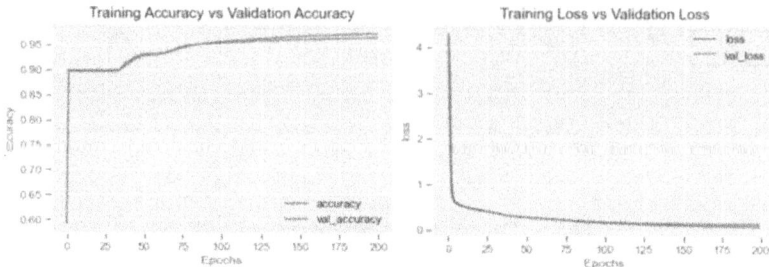

Fig. 6. Training and validation accuracy and loss curves of custom NER

Table 9. Test comparisons of custom NER models

N	Training accuracy	Validation accuracy	Training loss	Validation loss
1	97.50	96.30	0.0925	0.153
2	98.19	96.85	0.0628	0.127
3	98.91	96.42	0.0308	0.194
4	96.28	95.87	0.1411	0.173
5	**98.18**	**96.94**	**0.062**	**0.121**
6	97.25	96.69	0.0889	0.123
7	98.19	96.77	0.0643	0.130
8	97.76	96.76	0.078	0.123

Table 10. Measures results of custom NER

Accuracy	F1-score	Precision	Recall
96.94	97	97	97

The 10-fold cross validation is implemented on the custom NER model and the results are illustrated in Table 11.

Table 11. 10-Fold CV of custom NER model

No of Fold	Accuracy of Each Fold	No of Fold	Accuracy of Each Fold
1	99.22	6	99.17
2	98.97	7	99.24
3	99.24	8	99.27
4	99.28	9	99.29

(*continued*)

Table 11. (*continued*)

No of Fold	Accuracy of Each Fold	No of Fold	Accuracy of Each Fold
5	99.25	10	99.30

Overall Model Accuracy: 99.223%

Additionally, Table 12 presents a comparison of the recommended custom named entity recognition model's performance metrics with those of comparable studies.

Table 12. Comparison of custom NER model with related research

N	Ref	Dataset	Method	NER Type	Accuracy	F1 score
1	[27]	CoNLL 03	LSTM-CRF	Standard	–	96.53
2	[28]	CoNLL 03	ANN	Standard	–	75.89
3	[29]	Ace 2004–2005, GENIA, CNEC, CoNLL 02–03	LSTM-CRF	Standard	–	78.31–93.38
4	[19]	Snips- Atis	BiLSTM	–	69.6, 79.2	-
5	[30]	Korean and English tourism information NER datasets	pre-trained language models (PLMs)	Custom	–	94
6	[31]	tweets extracted based on health domain	CNN, RNN, C-LSTM, CRF, Bi-LSTM, and Bi-LSTMCRF	Custom	Bi-LSTM-CRF model 95.5	–
7	[32]	manually annotated, augmented and machine annotated datasets	statistical, fine-tuning of deep learning-based language models and few-shot prompting on large language models (LLMs)	Custom	–	95.9 for manually annotated, 96.04 for augmented, 95.71 for machine annotated
8	[33]	Official Gazette of the Federal District	CRF, NN-biLSTM-CRF, CNN-CNN-LSTM		–	85.1 78.7 84.1

(*continued*)

Table 12. (*continued*)

N	Ref	Dataset	Method	NER Type	Accuracy	F1 score
9	[34]	create dataset of English language contracts	CRF, BERT models, Bidirectional LSTM configurations	Custom	–	BERT model 94
10	Our model	Amazon office products	BiLSTM	Custom	96.94	97

5 Conclusion and Future Works

Chatbots represent crucial role in today's internet life. Nevertheless, analyzing dialogue systems to extract intent and entities is a challenging task. In this study, two models are proposed for intent classifier and named entity recognition to understand the user's requests. The intent classifier model implemented as BiLSTM is 94.75% accurate having achieved loss at 0.13%. When compared to the normal name entities, the custom entities have a considerable influence on the model's performance. After achieving 97% accuracy and a loss function of 0.092%, the BiLSTM model was suggested for bespoke NER recognition. Among these enhancements are the following: the ability to extract explicit and implicit intentions from user-input text; the creation of a deep learning model that can blend named entity recognition and intent classifier; and the attainment of greater accuracy, and create a more robust model. The limitations of our models that deals with long response sentence, that will address in the future.

Acknowledgment. The authors are grateful for the College of Computer Science and Information Technology, University of Kerbala for their support.

Funding. No funding has been received for this work.

References

1. Ramesh, K., Ravishankaran, S., Joshi, A., Chandrasekaran, K.: A survey of design techniques for conversational agents. Commun. Comput. Inform. Sci. **750**, 336–350 (2017). https://doi.org/10.1007/978-981-10-6544-6_31
2. Rychalska, B., Glabska, H., Wroblewska, A.: Multi-intent hierarchical natural language understanding for Chatbots. In: 2018 5th International Conference on Social Networks Analysis, Management and Security, SNAMS 2018, pp. 256–259 (2018). https://doi.org/10.1109/SNAMS.2018.8554770

3. Braun, D., Mendez, A.H., Matthes, F., Langen, M.: Evaluating natural language understanding services for conversational question answering systems. In: SIGDIAL 2017 - 18th Annual Meeting of the Special Interest Group on Discourse and Dialogue, Proceedings of the Conference, no. August, pp. 174–185 (2017). https://doi.org/10.18653/v1/w17-5522
4. Abdellatif, A., Badran, K., Shihab, E.: MSRBot: Using bots to answer questions from software repositories. Empir. Softw. Eng. **25**(3), 1834–1863 (2020). https://doi.org/10.1007/s10664-019-09788-5
5. Abubaera, M.M., Jiddah, S.M.: Natural language processing and bi-directional LSTM for sentiment analysis. Int. J. Comput. Appl. **185**(27), 31–35 (2023). https://doi.org/10.5120/ijca2023923021
6. Kuchlous, S., Kadaba, M.: Short text intent classification for conversational agents. In: 2020 IEEE 17th India Council International Conference, INDICON 2020 (2020). https://doi.org/10.1109/INDICON49873.2020.9342516
7. Behera, R.K., Bala, P.K., Ray, A.: Cognitive Chatbot for personalised contextual customer service: behind the scene and beyond the hype. Inform. Syst. Front. **2** (2021). https://doi.org/10.1007/s10796-021-10168-y
8. Zhang, H., Xu, H., Lin, T.E.: Deep open intent classification with adaptive decision boundary. In: 35th AAAI Conference on Artificial Intelligence, AAAI 2021, vol. 16, pp. 14374–14382 (2021). https://doi.org/10.48550/arXiv.2012.10209
9. Goyal, A., Gupta, V., Kumar, M.: Recent named entity recognition and classification techniques: a systematic review. Comput. Sci. Rev. **29**, 21–43 (2018). https://doi.org/10.1016/j.cosrev.2018.06.001
10. Li, J., Sun, A., Han, J., Li, C.: A survey on deep learning for named entity recognition. IEEE Trans. Knowl. Data Eng. **34**(1), 50–70 (2022). https://doi.org/10.1109/TKDE.2020.2981314
11. Al-Sultany, G.A., Aleqabie, H.J.: Enriching tweets for topic modeling via linking to the wikipedia. Int. J. Eng. Technol. **7**(19), 144–150 (2018). https://doi.org/10.14419/ijet.v7i4.19.27969
12. Shelar, H., Kaur, G., Heda, N., Agrawal, P.: Named entity recognition approaches and their comparison for custom NER model. Sci. Technol. Libr. **39**(3), 324–337 (2020). https://doi.org/10.1080/0194262X.2020.1759479
13. Assayed, S.K., Shaalan, K., Alkhatib, M.: A Chatbot intent classifier for supporting high school students. EAI Endorsed Trans. Scalable Inform. Syst. **10**(3), 1 (2023). https://doi.org/10.4108/eetsis.v10i2.2948
14. Assayed, S.K., Alkhatib, M., Shaalan, K.: Advising chatbot for high school in smart cities. In: 2023 8th International Conference on Smart and Sustainable Technologies, SpliTech 2023, no. August, pp. 1–6 (2023). https://doi.org/10.23919/SpliTech58164.2023.10193065
15. Al-Tuama, A.T., Nasrawi, D.A.: Intent classification using machine learning algorithms and augmented data. In: 2022 International Conference on Data Science and Intelligent Computing, ICDSIC 2022, no. April, pp. 234–239 (2022). https://doi.org/10.1109/ICDSIC56987.2022.10075794
16. Bokolo, B.G., Onyehanere, P., Ogegbene-Ise, E., Olufemi, I., Tettey, J.N.A.: Leveraging machine learning for crime intent detection in social media posts. In: Communications in Computer and Information Science, vol. 1946 CCIS, no. November, pp. 224–236 (2024). https://doi.org/10.1007/978-981-99-7587-7_19
17. Intent Classification for Malaysian Academic Writers' Proofreader Chatbot Using Machine, vol. 102, no. 9, pp. 3827–3837 (2024)
18. Tran, O.T., Luong, T.C.: Understanding what the users say in chatbots: a case study for the Vietnamese language. Eng. Appl. Artific. Intell. **87**, no. April 2019, 103322 (2020). https://doi.org/10.1016/j.engappai.2019.103322

19. Lin, T.E., Xu, H.: Deep unknown intent detection with margin loss. ACL 2019 - 57th Annual Meeting of the Association for Computational Linguistics, Proceedings of the Conference, pp. 5491–5496 (2020). https://doi.org/10.18653/v1/p19-1548
20. Schuurmans, J., Frasincar, F.: Intent classification for dialogue utterances. IEEE Intell. Syst. **35**(1), 82–88 (2020). https://doi.org/10.1109/MIS.2019.2954966
21. Geetha, N., Vivek, G., Vinetia, T.A.: Intent Classification using BERT for Chatbot application pertaining to Customer Oriented Services (2022). https://doi.org/10.4108/eai.7-12-2021.2314563
22. Laosen, N., Laosen, K., Ardharn, J.: Intent classification from online forums for phuket medical tourism. In: 2023 20th International Conference on Electrical Engineering/Electronics, Computer, Telecommunications and Information Technology, ECTI-CON 2023, pp. 1–4 (2023). https://doi.org/10.1109/ECTI-CON58255.2023.10153301
23. Chowdhury, S.A., Chowdhury, M.M., Shanto, A.M., Murad, H., Das, U.: Fired_from_NLP at AraFinNLP 2024: Dual-Phase-BERT - A Fine-Tuned Transformer-Based Model for Multi-Dialect Intent Detection in The Financial Domain for The Arabic Language, pp. 410–414 (2024)
24. Brahma, A.K., Potluri, P., Kanapaneni, M., Prabhu, S., Teki, S.: Identification of food quality descriptors in customer chat conversations using named entity recognition. In: Proceedings of the 3rd ACM India Joint International Conference on Data Science & Management of Data (8th ACM IKDD CODS & 26th COMAD), pp. 257–261. ACM, New York, NY, USA (2021). https://doi.org/10.1145/3430984.3431041
25. Pant, V.K., Sharma, R., Kundu, S.: Hybrid method for named entity recognition in kumauni language using machine learning, pp. 89–107 (2024). https://doi.org/10.1007/978-981-97-3180-0_7
26. Tommy, L., Kirana, C., Riska, L.: The combination of natural language processing and entity extraction for academic Chatbot. In: 2020 8th International Conference on Cyber and IT Service Management, CITSM 2020 (2020). https://doi.org/10.1109/CITSM50537.2020.9268851
27. Schweter, S., Akbik, A.: FLERT: document-level features for named entity recognition (2020). https://doi.org/10.48550/arXiv.2011.06993
28. Ali, N.: Chatbot: a conversational agent employed with named entity recognition model using artificial neural network (2020). https://doi.org/10.48550/arXiv.2007.04248
29. Straková, J., Straka, M., Hajic, J.: Neural architectures for nested NER through linearization. In: ACL 2019 - 57th Annual Meeting of the Association for Computational Linguistics, Proceedings of the Conference, vol. 2004, pp. 5326–5331 (2020). https://doi.org/10.18653/v1/p19-1527
30. Jwa, M.-C., Jwa, J.-W.: Development of tourism information named entity recognition datasets for the fine-tune KoBERT-CRF model. Int. J. Internet, Broadcast. Commun. **14**(2), 55–62 (2022). https://doi.org/10.7236/IJIBC.2022.14.2.55
31. Geetha, R., Pasupuleti, R., Karthika, S.: Analysis of online health-related private data using named entity recognition by deep correlation techniques. Lecture Notes in Networks and Systems, vol. 653 LNNS, no. June 2023, pp. 151–165 (2023). https://doi.org/10.1007/978-981-99-0981-0_12
32. Goel, M., et al.: Deep learning based named entity recognition models for recipes. In: 2024 Joint International Conference on Computational Linguistics, Language Resources and Evaluation, LREC-COLING 2024 - Main Conference Proceedings, pp. 4542–4554 (2024)
33. Guimarães, G.M.C., et al.: DODFMiner: an automated tool for named entity recognition from official gazettes. Neurocomputing **568**, 127064 (2024). https://doi.org/10.1016/j.neucom.2023.127064

34. Aejas, B., Belhi, A., Zhang, H., Bouras, A.: Deep learning-based automatic analysis of legal contracts: a named entity recognition benchmark. Neural Comput. Appl. **36**(23), 14465–14481 (2024). https://doi.org/10.1007/s00521-024-09869-7
35. Wan, M., McAuley, J.: Modeling ambiguity, subjectivity, and diverging viewpoints in opinion question answering systems. In: Proceedings - IEEE International Conference on Data Mining, ICDM, pp. 489–498 (2017). https://doi.org/10.1109/ICDM.2016.121
36. McAuley, J., Yang, A.: Addressing complex and subjective product-related queries with customer reviews. In: 25th International World Wide Web Conference, WWW 2016, pp. 625–635 (2016). https://doi.org/10.1145/2872427.2883044

Optimizing Handloom Price Prediction: Leveraging Diverse Features for Superior Accuracy Using Machine Learning

Khirod Chandra Maharana[1], Binod Kumar[2(✉)], Pravin Kumar[5], Shrikant Upadhyay[3], and Binita Roshima Hinz[4]

[1] School of Commerce, Gangadhar Meher University, Sambalpur, India
[2] Department of CSE & IT, Jharkhand Rai University, Ranchi, India
bit.binod15@gmail.com
[3] Department of Electronics and Communication Engineering, MLR Institute of Technology, Hyderabad, India
shrikant.upadhay@mlrit.ac.in
[4] Reasearch Scholar Sarla Birla University, Ranchi, Jharkhand, India
[5] Department of Management, Brainware University, Kolkata, India

Abstract. This paper consolidates multivariate variables to offer a new approach to estimating the costs of handloom products. Data consisting of preprocessed handloom goods' pricing, size, fabric type, colour, and design features were collected. Due to the highly intensive work characteristic of the handloom industry and its perceived cultural value, the latter struggles to establish appropriate prices mainly because of design density, fabrics used and colour options available. Therefore, the accurate prediction of prices is the best way to ensure the fairness of trades and the sustainability of crafts people's lives. Based on these important variables, this study develops a forecast model of handloom prices by employing the Decision Tree Regression model which is a machine-learning technique. The stakeholders in the handloom organized sector can use the model because it reflects complex interrelationships of price and features with high accuracy. This research also shows that the integration of several features enhances the price forecast, thereby enabling the handloom market decision-makers to make the right decisions.

Keywords: Handloom Price Prediction · Decision Tree Regression · Machine Learning · Textile Industry

JEL Codes: L67 · D2 · O14

1 Introduction

One of Handloom's biggest challenges lies with the question of what price should they set for their products since the sector produces a large variety of items that are known for their ethnic and traditional values. Due to variations in the type of fabric, colours and design details often it becomes difficult to establish standard prices within the clothing line [1, 2]. This creates a problem with the authenticity of the marketplace specifically about the fairness of trading procedures; the craftsmen who practice such ancient arts in their daily business are affected by this issue. To avoid this complexity, this research paper uses different multivariate variables to predict the costs of handloom products [3, 4]. As an effort to address this hypothesis, input data from handloom items encompassed with characteristics like cost, dimension, material, colour and style have been employed in this study to develop a predictive model that seeks to enhance the accuracy of the final price of the handloom items. Given the complex processes in handloom production, players ranging from retailers to weavers require the ability to forecast prices well in an endeavour to make sound decisions [5, 6]. As the relationships between different product characteristics and prices are complex machine learning techniques have been employed in the framework of this work. The results stress the importance of using multiple characteristics in the models and show how it potentially increases the accuracy significantly. There is more to consider by choosing this methodology exhibiting fair trade values and at the same time supporting the sustainability and growth of the handloom sector in this particular area by providing reasonable and credible instruments for the pricing system.

2 Review of Literature

Chalabi et al. [7] examined the building of an effective forecast model for prediction and highlighted the need to integrate image processing techniques with the creation of an accurate model for the count. CFD and machine learning were employed by Bergin et al. [8] for enhancing productivity where the authors found the use of complex simulation in conjunction with an advanced predictive model highly advantageous. To predict the strength of the market Shen and Shafiq [9] compare the machine learning method of genetic and artificial neural networks demonstrating that the use of machine learning is valuable in diverse ecosystems. Thus, to address the challenge of accurate segmentation and consequent predictive modelling, Chen [10] used LSTM and GRU techniques are commonly used approaches for achieving accurate market prediction whereas Hassan et al. [11] have also pointed out that XGBoost performs well on balanced datasets with the highest accuracy. As far as the marketing of handloom products, Maharana and Acharya [12] validate a model which says the user experience is jointly influenced by the market experience and features of handloom products. As per Ramanna and Reddy [13], most of the marketers opined that the demand for handlooms is seasonal and the expected profit is only 10% on handlooms whereas cost is the base for price fixation in the study area. On the other hand, Guru et al. [14] suggested that the utilization of multiple parameters and diverse factors can be employed to enhance the efficacy of sales prediction whereas Fattah et al. [15] used the Box Jenkins time series procedure and achieve greater accuracy. Kaur and Mishra [3] found that there is a relationship between consumer purchase behaviour and e-marketing and made a conclusion that if the online platform is used strategically, keeping in mind all the important parameters, it would bring the maximum revenue for the firm. Although machine learning and image processing have been extensively used in India's environmental monitoring, healthcare, and agricultural sectors [16, 17], there is a noticeable lack of use of these technologies for handloom product pricing prediction. Despite the intricacy and cultural importance of handlooms, little study has been done on the use of machine learning algorithms to precisely estimate their costs. Closing this disparity could improve the handloom market's price accuracy, promoting honest dealings and protecting this important sector.

3 Research Objectives

- To develop a model where with several product attributes such as size, fabric type, colour and design, the probable cost of handloom products can be predicted.
- To assess how perfect the Decision Tree Regressor forecasts the costs of handloom products based on their features.

4 Hypotheses

- The price prediction model will get more refined when several features (size, fabric, colour, design etc.) are used rather than one or a few.
- Since the Decision tree Regressor algorithm is also effective in identifying complex relationships between attributes and prices, this model will predict the prices of handloom products more likely and accurately compared to the other models.

5 Research Methodology

5.1 Data Collection: The data collection phase of the project begins first, where the material gathers a huge database of attributes on handloom products. It involves the aspects of pricing of the product and other elements such as size, material, colour and the set standards of designing the dress. This dataset is useful in the analysis of some of the factors that characterize the pricing of products in the handloom sector; which is marked by a diverse range of manufacturing specifications and embedded details.

5.2 Data Preprocessing: To do this, one-hot encoding is applied to transform attributes of fabric, design and colour, into numerical values. This stage is important if the machine learning algorithms require numerical input for learning [8]. In this model, 80 per cent of the data is used for model training. 10% of the data are in the Validation Set used to tweak model parameters and prevent overtraining of the model. The last 10% of the data, is employed to determine the efficacy of the model.

5.3 Model Development and Evaluation: The principal element of the proposed scheme is the Decision Tree Regressor, which is a highly effective machine learning algorithm designed for the particularly effective management of complex data and identification of multifaceted relationships between the variables concerned [14]. Root Mean Squared Error (RMSE) gives the mean of the prediction errors and proposes an error measure in the equivalent measure of the predicted variable [18, 19]. Mean Absolute Error (MAE) is the average of the absolute differences between the predicted and actual values with a smaller value implying that the model is more accurate [11, 12, 20]. Further cross-validated using Gradient Boost Regressor [21] to test the accuracy and also the probability of overfitting.

Feature Importance Analysis is also being carried out to establish which of the product features has the greatest impact on its pricing strategies. This is made possible by executing Dropout Loss Evaluation. To do so, the value that is critical for the price prediction called "fabric" is defined by finding the mean dropout loss which quantifies the impact of each of the properties [8]. The last step of the methodology gives rise to the result of high accuracy of the predictive model specifically the R^2 value of 0.922 but also studies the key factors that are causing variation in handloom prices. The approach emphasizes the use of feature engineering, which would aid in the price prediction for handloom products and foster fair trade as well as improve the economic sustainability of handloom artisans [10]. It is this kind of structured process that smoothly interpolates between craftsmanship and statistical extrapolation, which would provide a highly robust decision support tool to stakeholders in the handloom sector.

6 Result and Discussion

Table 1. Model Complexity and Fitting

Complexity Penalty	Splits	n(Train)	n(Validation)	n(Test)
0.000	220	192098	48025	60030

Source: *Authors' Calculation*

With 192,098 instances in the training set, 48,025 in the validation set, and 60,030 in the test set, the model employs 220 splits. Since there was no regularization used to punish the model's complexity, the complexity penalty is set to 0.000 (Table 1).

Fig. 1. Data Split Plot

The model is trained using the majority of the data (192,098 samples) to identify trends. A reduced subset (48,025 samples) is employed to avoid overfitting and adjust hyperparameters. This last section (60,030 samples) is set aside for assessing how well the model performs when applied to unobscrvcd data (Table 2).

While the MSE indicates a notable error suggesting discrepancies between forecasted and actual prices [22], it's important to consider that the study focuses on price prediction for handloom products. The model achieves an R-squared value of 0.9, indicating that 90% of the variance in the data is accurately explained by the model [20]. This high R-squared value validates the model's overall effectiveness in capturing the relationship between product features and prices, despite some remaining errors. A strong fit [23] is suggested by the model's R2 score of 0.921, which shows that it accounts for 92.1% of the variation in the dependent variable (Fig. 2).

Table 2. Model Performance Metrics

	Value
MSE	40721293.845
RMSE	6347.36
MAE/MAD	4159.99
MAPE	37.45%
R^2	0.921

Source: *Authors' Calculation*

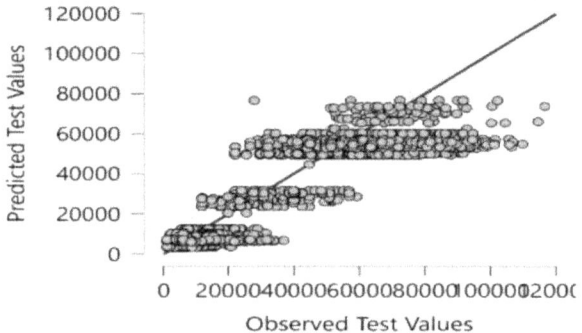

Fig. 2. Predictive Performance Plot

The plot (*Fig.* 1) indicates that the Decision Tree Regressor model predicts handloom costs with a respectable degree of accuracy. Nonetheless, there are discernible differences between the expected and actual values, suggesting that not all data points are completely fitted by the model. Given the complexity of the interactions or the unpredictability of the data, the model may perform well hence it has a high variance explained score [9] and it captures the majority of the associations between product attributes and price (Fig. 3 and Table 3).

Based on a mean dropout loss of 30,881.23, the feature 'Fabric' has the highest relative relevance, accounting for 95.413% of the model's decision-making to be the most important predictor in the model based on this. The design has a mean dropout loss of 9,428.911 and a relative importance of 4.147%. It's not as significant as "Fabric," but it's still relevant to the model's predictions. "Size" and "Color," with corresponding values of 0.285% and 0.143%, are also of little consequence. Their respective mean dropout losses of 6,619.12 and 6,467.63 show that these features have little effect on the model's ability to forecast the future. According to these findings, the model functions well and has a high degree of predictive accuracy ($R^2 = 0.921$); but, because of its complexity and a large number of splits, there may be some overfitting [24]. The 'Fabric' attribute is the most influential in the prediction process, with 'Size' and 'Fabric' contributing very little to the accuracy of the model.

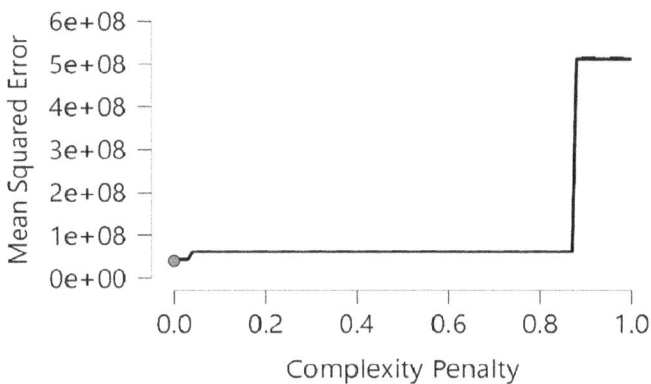

Fig. 3. Mean Squared Error Plot

Table 3. Feature Importance Metrics

	Relative Importance	Mean dropout loss
Fabric	95.384	30881.23
Design	4.147	9438.482
Size	0.285	6691.12
Colour	0.143	6467.63

Note. Mean dropout loss is based on 50 permutations.
Source: *Authors' Calculation*

Python Code Snippet 01

```python
import pandas as pd
from sklearn.tree import DecisionTreeRegressor
from sklearn.preprocessing import OneHotEncoder
from sklearn.compose import ColumnTransformer
from sklearn.model_selection import train_test_split
from sklearn.metrics import r2_score
```

Source: *Authors' Calculation.*

Python Code Snippet 02

```
1  df = pd.read_csv('/content/Clean Dataset.1asp.csv')
2  df.head()
```

	Fabric	Design	Size	Color	Price
0	Silk	Simple	M	Light	5953
1	Mixed	Simple	M	Light	5953
2	Mixed	Simple	M	Light	5956
3	Cotton	Simple	M	Light	5955
4	Cotton	Simple	M	Light	5955

Source: *Authors' Calculation.*

Python Code Snippet 03

```
1  categorical_features = ['Fabric', 'Design', 'Color', 'Size']
2  # Create a ColumnTransformer to one-hot encode categorical features
3  preprocessor = ColumnTransformer(
4      transformers=[('onehot', OneHotEncoder(), categorical_features)],
5      remainder='passthrough'  # Pass through any remaining numerical features
6  )
```

Source: *Authors' Calculation.*

Python Code Snippet 04

```
1  # Prepare data
2  X = df.drop('Price', axis=1)  # Independent variables
3  y = df['Price']  # Dependent variable
```

Source: *Authors' Calculation.*

Python Code Snippet 05

```
1   # Apply one-hot encoding
2   X_encoded = preprocessor.fit_transform(X)
```

Source: *Authors' Calculation.*

Python Code Snippet 06

```
1   # Split the data into training and testing sets
2   X_train, X_test, y_train, y_test = train_test_split(X_encoded, y, test_size=0.
    2, random_state=42)  # Adjust test_size and random_state as needed
```

Source: *Authors' Calculation.*

Python Code Snippet 07

```
1   # Create a DecisionTreeRegressor model
2   model = DecisionTreeRegressor()
3   # Fit the model to the training data
4   model.fit(X_train, y_train)
```

```
▼ DecisionTreeRegressor
DecisionTreeRegressor()
```

Source: *Authors' Calculation.*

Python Code Snippet 08

```
1   # Make predictions on the test data
2   y_pred = model.predict(X_test)
3   r2 = r2_score(y_test, y_pred)
4   print(f"R-squared: {r2}")
```

R-squared: 0.9210666918420443

Source: *Authors' Calculation.*

After loading the dataset, the categorical features (Fabric, Design, Color, and Size) are determined. These categorical features are one-hot encoded using a Column Transformer. Two sets of data are separated: training (80%) and testing (20%). Using the training set, a Decision Tree Regressor' is trained. After making predictions on the test set, the model's R2 score (0.921) is computed, showing that it accounts for 92.1% of the variation in the target variable. The model adequately reflects the link between the features and the target variable, as evidenced by its good predictive ability ($R2 = 0.921$) (Fig. 4 and Table 4).

Table 4. Boosting Regression

Trees	Shrinkage	Loss function	n(Train)	n(Validation)	n(Test)	Validation MSE	Test MSE
100	0.100	Gaussian	192098	48025	60030	$5.348 \times 10^{+7}$	$5.358 \times 10^{+7}$

Note. The model is optimized concerning the *out-of-bag mean squared error*.
Source: *Authors' Calculation*

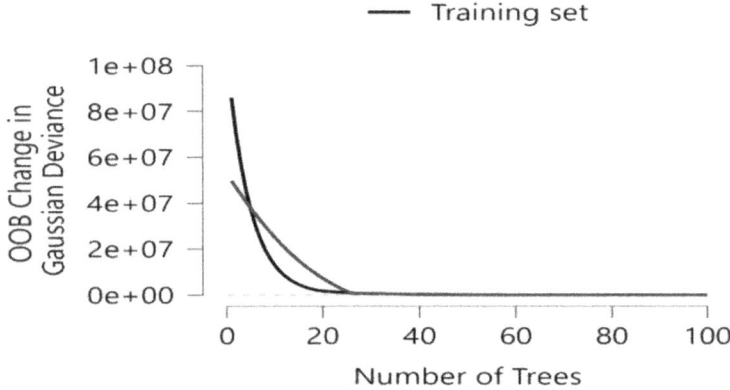

Fig. 4. Out of Bag (OOB) Improvement Plot

The result shows that the training, validation and test errors are very close to each other. This shows consistency in the performance of the model across all the training, validation and test splits. The OOB error is also an important indicator of the generalization of the model's performance [25, 26]. A Low and stable OOB error similar to the test MSE suggests that this model is not overfitting. High R^2 (89.7%) along with a high MAPE (51.48%) also explains the model understands much of the variance.

7 Findings and Implications

In the present study, the Decision Tree Regressor was used to combine several parameters (size, fabric, colour, and design) accurately to develop a predictor model for handloom products' prices. It can be stated that all the components were considerably correlated as the R2 value was 0.921, once again, the numbers exhibited high accuracy and the model could explain ninety-two per cent. Handloom costs accounted for 2% of the variation. This indicates that the model provides a good fit to identify the complex interrelationships that prevail between the pricing and the attributes [15]. The results have also revealed that the factor most strongly associated with 'Fabric' was the factors taken into consideration explaining as much as 95% of the variance. 384% of the decision-making process the model undergoes in computing handloom costs. As compared to other factors, the design, size, and colour of products had insignificant influence on the sales volume according to the model [27]. According to the model's Mean Absolute Error (MAE), the average of the absolute differences between the expected and actual prices was roughly 4159.99. Prediction error estimation was made and given as the Root Mean Square Error (RMSE) and it emerged that the average magnitude of the error was 6,347.36. Even though there is a slight difference in the margin of error the given measures help in establishing that the model is reliable to predict the handloom price [16, 28]. While being rather accurate, the model herewith developed still seems to be overfitting (as demonstrated by a large number of splits (220), and the absence of L1/L2 regularization). This is suggested by the high Mean Squared Error (MSE) level that is observed in the test as well as validation datasets. The high accuracy of pricing strategies in the handloom business can be boosted to a great extent if several features for price prediction are incorporated [29].

Hence further gradient boosting regression has been used for cross-validation of this model which also showed an accuracy of 0.89, which means 89% of the variance in the dependent variable is explained by the feature variables. A Low and stable OOB error similar to the test MSE suggests that this model is not overfitting [30]. The price prediction model can help retailers and craftspeople set a better, more profitable price, or in other words, get a better yield for their work. Thus, the model provides a reliable tool to determine the price and it contributes to the maintenance of the fair-trade principles by the handloom industry [31]. This is where sustaining the livelihoods of artisans and sustaining the relevance of handloom products in present-day society depend on this [32].

8 Conclusion and Suggestions

By bringing features and many product attributes into a single model used for price prediction of handloom products, this study is a step forward in the field of price prediction. Surprisingly, medical accuracy was high with the model yielding an R^2 value of 0.921 suggests powerful predictiveness accuracy from the tests. The study further revealed that the most dominant cost driver of handloom was the fabric quality out of all the identified features [24, 33]. The developed model has consistently provided better and more fair and accurate techniques of pricing, which can further help towards the financial sustainability of craftsmen and help in the fair trade policy-making and therefore is helpful for the key users of the handloom industry. That is why, although the fabric was defined as the most significant characteristic influencing demand, the addition of other characteristics such as fluctuations in demand during the seasons, different regions' demands, and trends on the market might enhance the accuracy of the model as per the estimation [13]. To enrich the dataset the following variables could be introduced and this may lead to a deeper understanding of the pricing mechanisms: Exploring whether such a model can be used in other industries may also provide relevant resources to optimize pricing strategies in various markets. However, since business environments change from time to time and consumers' preferences evolve with time [34], new data needs to be fed into it from time to time [25]. But to ensure the accuracy of the model for data and trends of the current time, there should be a data collection and model training process regularly [12]. It is necessary to equip handloom sector stakeholders with the material and knowledge to fully utilise this prediction instrument. Organizing specialists from different spheres like craftsmen, merchants, and market analysts may lead to using knowledge from the model's predictions and lead to raising the share of technology-driven pricing methods and to the enhancement of decision-making [35]. Through the implementation of these recommendations, it will be possible to improve the fairness and accuracy of pricing by the handloom industry hence supporting sustainable livelihoods of artisans and promoting sustainability of this important historical industry [36].

9 Limitations and Scope of Further Studies

The present study is limited to product attributes like fabric, design, size and colour. Incorporating additional product attributes like regions, time-period etc. could improve the performance also. But in this present study, only the above-stated four features are taken which are considered as the most important features of price prediction so far as handloom products are concerned. Future studies on handloom pricing prediction would greatly benefit from including more data sources, such as market demand predictions, customer reviews, and social media trends [25]. By incorporating these varied data sources, the model's forecast accuracy may be improved and a more thorough understanding of the several aspects impacting handloom prices may be obtained [39]. Furthermore, even though the Decision Tree Regressor was successfully used in this study, investigating different deep learning algorithms could enhance the model's performance even more [10]. These powerful algorithms could be able to handle the intricate interactions between product attributes with more precision and sophistication.

References

1. Ramana, J.V., Reddy, D.H., Kumar, K.S., Sirisha, K.: An empirical study on marketing of handloom fabrics in Andhra Pradesh. Int. J. Innovat. Technol. Explor. Eng. **8**(8), 1071–1075 (2019)
2. Kaur, K., Mishra, A.: Impact of E-marketing on consumer purchase behaviour: an empirical study. Int. J. Res. Anal. Rev. **8**(1), 387–408 (2021). www.ijrar.org
3. Kumudha, A., Rizwana, M.: A study on consumer awareness about handloom products with special reference to Erode District. J. Market. Consum. Res. Open Access Int. J. **1**(1), 17–21 (2013)
4. Sangeetha, S., Charles, S.A.: A study on problems and prospects of handloom wearers in selected areas of Thanjavur District, Tamilnadu. Infokara Res. **8**(11), 1652–1658 (2019). Available: http://infokara.com/
5. Chalabi, H., Douri, Y.K., Lundberg, J.: Time series forecasting using ARIMA model: a case study of mining face drilling rig. In: Twelfth International Conference on Advanced Engineering Computing and Applications in Sciences, pp. 1–3 (2018)
6. Bergin, S., Mooney, A., Ghent, J., Quille, K.: Using machine learning techniques to predict introductory programming performance. Int. J. Comput. Sci. Softw. Eng. **4**(12), 323–328 (2015). www.IJCSSE.org

7. Shen, J., Shafiq, M.O.: Short-term stock market price trend prediction using a comprehensive deep learning system. J. Big Data **7**(1), 1–33 (2020). https://doi.org/10.1186/s40537-020-00333-6
8. Chen, X.: Stock price prediction using machine learning strategies (2023)
9. Hassan, A., Ahmad, S.G., Munir, E.U., Khan, I. A., Ramzan, N.: Predictive modelling and identification of key risk factors for stroke using machine learning. Sci. Rep. **14**(1) (2024). https://doi.org/10.1038/s41598-024-61665-4
10. Maharana, K.C., Acharya, S.C.: Exploring consumer loyalty towards Sambalpuri handloom: a structural equation modeling approach. Orissa J. Commerce **44**(1), 27–43 (2023). https://doi.org/10.54063/ojc.2023.v44i01.03
11. Ramanna, J.V., Reddy, D.H., Kumar, V., Sirisha, K.: An empirical study on marketing of handloom fabrics in Andhra Pradesh. Int. J. Innovat. Technol. Explor. Eng. **8**(8), 1071–1075 (2019). https://www.researchgate.net/publication/334825413
12. Guru, P., Sathyapriya, J., Rajandran, K.V.R., Bhuvbaneswarin, C., Parimala, C.: Product sales forecasting and prediction using machine learning algorithm. Int. J. Intell. Syst. Appl. Eng. **12**(4s), 355–366 (2023)
13. Fattah, J., Ezzine, L., Aman, Z., El Moussami, H., Lachhab, A.: Forecasting of demand using ARIMA model. Int. J. Eng. Bus. Manage. **10**(1), 1–9 (2018). https://doi.org/10.1177/1847979018808673
14. Indumathi, N., Meera, J.P., Upadhyay, S., Pithamber, K., Kumar, M., Gupta, J.S.: Early Heart Failure Recognition for Infants using Machine Learning. In: 2024 5th International Conference on Smart Electronics and Communication (ICOSEC), pp. 1841–1845. Trichy, India (2024). https://doi.org/10.1109/ICOSEC61587.2024.10722435
15. Ho, S.L., Xie, M.: The use of ARIMA models for reliability forecasting and analysis. Comput. Ind. Engng **35**(2), 213–216 (1998)
16. Vijh, M., Chandola, D., Tikkiwal, V.A., Kumar, A.: Stock closing price prediction using machine learning techniques. In: Procedia Computer Science, Elsevier B.V., pp. 599–606 (2020). https://doi.org/10.1016/j.procs.2020.03.326
17. Kumar, M., Anand, M.: An application of time series ARIMA forecasting model for predicting sugarcane production in India. In: Studies in Business and Economics, pp. 81–94 (2012)
18. Patra, S., Dey, S. K.: Profitability analysis of handloom weavers: a case study of Cuttack District of Odisha. Abhinav National Monthly Refereed J. Res. Commerce Manage. **4**(8), 11–19, (2015). www.abhinavjournal.com
19. Agrawal, A., Chanana, B.: Handloom and handicraft sector in India: a review of literature on its demand in the market and availability of original product. Mod. Manage. Appl. Sci. Soc. Sci. **3**(2), 203–208 (2021). https://textilevaluechain.in/2012/05/28/economic-impact-of-gi-registration-of-unique-textiles-of-india/
20. Humbe, V.R.: Role of social media in marketing of handloom products (2012). www.ijsr.net
21. Upadhyay, S., et al.: Feature extraction approach for speaker verification to support healthcare system using blockchain security for data privacy. Comput. Math. Meth. Med. (2022)
22. Rao, R.M., Kumar, K.K.: Weaver's attitude on implementation of Integrated Handloom Cluster Development Scheme (IHCDS): an empirical study. Int. J. Trend Sci. Res. Develop. **2**(2), 1480–1489 (2018). www.ijtsrd.com
23. Kethan, M., Khizerulla, M., Sekhar, S.C., et al.: A study on issues and challenges in production of handloom sector with special reference to Rayalaseema and coastal region of Andhra Pradesh. Int. J. Appl. Res. **8**(6), 89–95 (2022). https://doi.org/10.22271/allresearch.2022.v8.i6b.9823
24. Khatoon, S.: Make in India: a platform to Indian handloom market. IOSR J. Bus. Manag. **18**(9), 36–40 (2016). https://doi.org/10.9790/487x-1809023640

25. Maharana, K.C., Acharya, S.C.: Customers' attitude towards online shopping of Sambalpuri handloom: a study on Sambalpur District. Int. Res. J. Modern. Eng. Technol. Sci. **5**(1), 822–828 (2023). https://doi.org/10.56726/irjmets33001
26. Upadhyay, A., Sharma, S.K., et al.: Analysis of different classifiers using feature extraction in speaker identification and verification under adverse acoustic conditions for different scenarios. Int. J. Innov. Eng. Technol. 425–434 (2014)
27. Rani, N., Bains, A.: Consumer behaviour towards handloom products in the state of Punjab and Haryana. Int. J. Adv. Res. Manage. Soc. Sci. **3**(10), 92–105 (2014). www.garph.co.uk
28. Renukadevi, M., Hema, G.A.: A study on customer attitude towards marketing of handloom products. Int. J. Res. Anal. Rev. **7**(1), 330–334 (2020). www.ijrar.org
29. Maharana, C., Acharya, S.C.: Training initiatives for weavers' skill enhancement: an impact assessment study. SSRN Electron. J. **11**(1), 261–269 (2023). https://doi.org/10.2139/ssrn.4909037
30. Upadhyay, S., Sharma, S.K., Upadhyay, A.: Population evaluation for density using speech access mechanism. In: Proceedings of the 4th International Conference: Innovative Advancement in Engineering & Technology (IAET), pp. 1–7 (2020)
31. Sripoorni, R.S.: A study on problems faced by handloom industry in India (2018). www.ijcrt.org
32. Rao, R.M., Kumar, K.K.: Weaver's attitude on implementation of Integrated Handloom Cluster Development Scheme (IHCDS): an empirical study. Int. J. Trend Sci. Res. Develop. **2**(2), 1480–1489 (2018)
33. Kethan, M., Khizerulla, M., Sekhar, S. C., et al.: A study on issues and challenges on production of handloom sector with special reference to Rayalaseema and coastal region of Andhra Pradesh. Int. J. Appl. Res. **8**(6), 89–95 (2022). https://doi.org/10.22271/allresearch.2022.v8.i6b.9823
34. Jothi, C.A., Gaffoor, A.M.: Impact of social media in online shopping. ICTACT J. Manage. Stud. **3**(3), 576–586 (2017). https://doi.org/10.21917/ijms.2017.0079
35. Amaravathi, G., Raj, K.B.: Indian handloom sector – a glimpse. Int. J. Innovat. Technol. Explor. Eng. **8**(6 Special Issue 4), 645–654 (2019). https://doi.org/10.35940/ijitee.F1133.0486S419
36. Das, C., Roy, M., Mondal, P.: Handloom cluster of India: a case study of Santipur handloom cluster. Int. J. Hum. Soc. Sci. Invent. **5**(1), 27–35 (2016). www.ijhssi.org

Comprehensive Review of Road Anomalies Detection Methods Using Deep Learning Techniques

Ruta Mulajkar[✉] and Sanjay Yede

Computer Science and Engineering, H.V.P.M.'S Degree College of Physical Education,
Amravati, Maharashtra 444605, India
ruta.mulajkar@gmail.com

Abstract. This paper provides a comprehensive review of deep learning methods for detecting and assessing road anomalies, which include issues like potholes, open manholes, alligator cracks, debris and exposed cable trays etc. These anomalies arise from factors such as heavy traffic, rainfall, overloaded vehicles, and the use of poor-quality construction materials. We examine key aspects of anomaly detection, including dataset preprocessing, image annotation, and feature extraction techniques. Additionally, we compare the performance of real-time object detection models from YOLOv4 to YOLOv8 as these models may have low inference time, using various evaluation metrics. Real time detection requires to detect objects quickly which can be accomplished with these YOLO versions. Our review synthesizes findings from over 30 studies published in leading journals and conferences, offering valuable insights into the application of deep learning for road anomaly detection.

Keywords: Road anomalies · deep learning · YOLOv · object detection

1 Introduction

Roads play a crucial role in public transportation, connecting people across the country. Daily accidents occur due to poor road conditions, fog, rainy weather, and other adverse factors. Highways are wider than city or town roads and are designed to accommodate heavy traffic and substantial loads. In contrast, city and town roads typically feature only single or double lanes. For the sake of public safety and fuel efficiency, it is essential that roads are smooth and well-maintained. Roads are integral to daily life, yet their condition often deteriorates, particularly during the rainy season. Common road anomalies include potholes, open manholes, various types and sizes of alligator cracks, and exposed cable trays. Often, these issues are not easily visible to travelers due to being covered by water. Deep learning, a branch of machine learning that employs multi-layered neural networks, is capable of autonomously identifying patterns and features in data, improving the accuracy and robustness of anomaly detection. This paper examines different road

---
Sanjay Yede—Author contributed equally to this work.

© The Author(s), under exclusive license to Springer Nature Switzerland AG 2025
R. Kumar Tiwari and D. K. Singh (Eds.): ICAII 2024, CCIS 2549, pp. 105–117, 2025.
https://doi.org/10.1007/978-3-032-06198-0_8

anomalies and compares various deep learning techniques for their detection. We also address current challenges in road anomaly detection, such as enhancing model accuracy, expanding and diversifying datasets, improving real-time processing capabilities, and ensuring seamless integration with existing systems. Figure 1 illustrates various types of road anomalies commonly encountered in daily life.

Fig. 1. Road Anomalies (a) Pothole (b) Road Alligator Cracking (c) Open Manhole (d) Road Debris

Table 1 shows distinctions between different types of Road Anomalies with the help of root causes and their impact on day today life.

According to the World Health Organization's 2023 report, over one million people died in road accidents, with the majority being children and young adults aged 5 to 29 [1]. The demand for vehicles continues to rise in tandem with population growth. Researchers are working to mitigate these fatalities and provide valuable information to government authorities. Manual road condition surveys are labor-intensive and costly in terms of time, money, and effort. For example, one study analyzed road surface conditions by mounting mobile devices and sensors on two-wheelers [2]. Challenges faced in this approach include image quality, maintaining the appropriate speed relative to the bike's acceleration, and accurate anomaly labeling [2]. Fatjon Seraj et al. [3] employed a Samsung Galaxy S2 smartphone with Android 4.0, equipped with accelerometers and gyroscopes, to collect data using GPS.

Road anomalies can also be detected using data mining techniques. Nuno Silva et al. [4] describe one such approach, with detailed methods outlined in an earlier paper [5]. In data preparation, feature extraction is performed using the Waikato Environment for Knowledge Analysis (WEKA) tool. This process helps in selecting the most relevant features from a dataset while discarding irrelevant ones. Additionally, authors in paper [6]

Table 1. Distinctions between different types of Road Anomalies

Type of Road Anamoly	Definition	Root Cause	Appearance	Impact
Pothole	Depression in the road surface caused by wear and tear	Heavy Rainfall, Heavy vehicle load, poor construction	Deep or shallow oval shape withvarying sizes	Accidents, vehicle damage
Open Manhole	Properly not covered man holes	poor maintenance, negligence by people	Circularhole betweenroad with open lid	MajorAccidents, vehicle damage
Alligator Cracks	Networkof interconnected cracksresembling the pattern of alligator skin	poor construction of road, loaded vehicle	Series of interconnected, narrow cracks creating a pattern	deteriorate road conditions
Road Debris	Brokenand scattered pieces of rocks or other waste material	Negligence or carelessness of people	heap of rocks on road	Accidents, vehicle damage

have reviewed vibration-based techniques for detecting and classifying road anomalies. These techniques use sensors to monitor vibrations caused by vehicles traveling over road surfaces. By analyzing the distinct vibration patterns produced by interactions with anomalies like potholes, speed bumps, or cracks, these techniques can detect and map anomalies effectively. Vibration-based methods offer a non-intrusive and cost-effective solution for road anomaly detection, enabling timely maintenance and enhancing road safety.

The primary objective of this research paper is to explore advanced techniques for detecting road surface anomalies, with a focus on enhancing accuracy, efficiency, and scalability. The findings aim to significantly improve the efficiency and effectiveness of road maintenance operations by facilitating early detection and intervention of anomalies. By supporting proactive maintenance strategies, the proposed techniques will help extend the lifespan of road infrastructure, reduce repair costs, and improve overall safety for both motorists and pedestrians. Furthermore, the advancement of anomaly detection technologies will pave the way for the adoption of smart transportation systems and autonomous driving technologies, marking the beginning of a new era in sustainable and resilient transportation infrastructure.

The flowchart in Fig. 2 illustrates a system pipeline for road anomaly detection using a YOLO (You Only Look Once) model architecture. Here's a breakdown of each step:

- **Data Collection:** Images and videos of roads are collected then the road images are annotated with the locations of anomalies (e.g., potholes, cracks).

- **Data Preprocessing:** The collected images are resized to a standard size, Image pixel values are normalized. The dataset is split into training and validation sets for model development.
- **Model Selection:** A YOLO architecture (e.g., YOLO v8) is chosen for the detection task.
- **Model Training:** Pre-trained YOLO weights are loaded to accelerate training. The model is trained on the annotated road images to detect anomalies. Model parameters are fine-tuned for optimal performance.
- **Model Evaluation:** The trained model is validated on a validation set. Based on its performance, adjustments are made to improve the model's accuracy.
- **Model Deployment:** Once the model is trained and validated, it is integrated into a road anomaly detection system. The model is deployed on hardware (e.g., a smartphone) to perform real-time detection.
- **Real-time Anomaly Detection:** The deployed model captures new road images or videos. YOLO is applied to detect anomalies in real time and mark them in the images or videos.
- **Generate Reports/Alerts:** Based on detected anomalies, reports or alerts are generated to notify relevant parties.

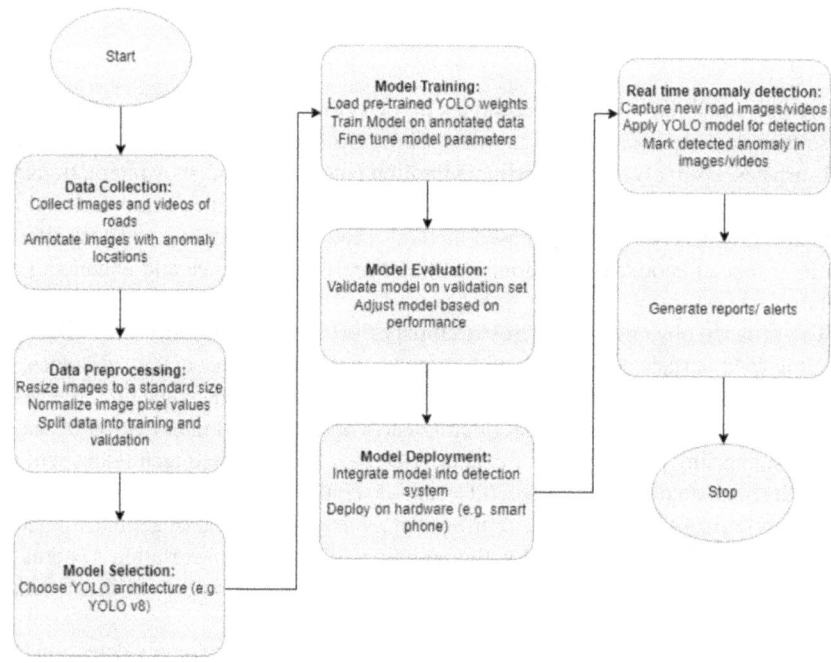

Fig. 2. Flowchart anomaly detection

The paper is organized as follows: Sect. 2 provides a detailed review of various road anomalies. Section 3 presents publicly available datasets for potholes, manholes, and alligator cracks. Section 4 offers a comprehensive comparison of object detection techniques, specifically YOLO versions v4 to v8. Section 5 concludes the paper and discusses future prospects for road anomaly detection.

2 Road Anomalies Survey

2.1 Pothole Detection

The performance of pothole detection was improved by combining high level feature information with low level semantic information using CNN and transfer learning. Transfer learning technique uses pre-trained model and retrain for custom dataset. It takes few epochs to get increased accuracy and reduces lot of computations. By using this method, one needs to change only the last few layers instead of training all layers to achieve high accuracy. Investigators have used transfer learning with recurrent neural network, transfer learning with Generated adversarial network and transfer learning with convolutional neural network [7].

Pothole detection can be done using three different techniques namely vibration based techniques [6], 3D reconstruction technique [8] and vision based technique. Detecting potholes using 3D reconstruction involves capturing a 3D model of the road surface and then analyzing it to identify deformations indicative of potholes. In this method data acquisition is by using 3D sensors like LiDAR (Light Detection and Ranging) or depth cameras (e.g., Kinect) mounted on a vehicle or handheld device to capture the surface topology of the road and alternatively, stereo cameras or photogrammetry techniques can also be used to reconstruct the road surface in 3D. Pothole detection using vision-based techniques [9] primarily relies on analyzing images or video footage of the road surface to identify potholes. Data acquisition is by capturing high-resolution images or video footage of the road surface using cameras mounted on vehicles or fixed installations. Table 2 illustrates comparison of different methods for pothole detection.

Table 2. Comparison of the different pothole detection methods

Aspect	Vibration-Based [6]	3D Laser-Based [18]	3D Reconstruction Based [8]	2D Vision-Based [9]
Methodology	Uses accelerometers or vibration sensors to detect road anomalies through vehicle vibrations	Utilizes laser scanners (LiDAR) to create high resolution 3D profiles of road surfaces	Combines data from multiple cameras or depth sensors to create a 3D model of the road	Employs cameras to capture 2D images and image processing techniques to identify potholes
Strength	Cost-effective Easy to implement	High accuracy Detailed depth and shape information	High accuracy Detailed pothole dimensions	Low cost Easy to implement with existing camera systems

(continued)

Table 2. (*continued*)

Aspect	Vibration-Based [6]	3D Laser-Based [18]	3D Reconstruction Based [8]	2D Vision-Based [9]
Limitation	Limited accuracy May detect non-pothole vibrations Requires calibration	Expensive equipment Requires sophisticated processing Affected by environmental conditions	Computationally intensive Requires multiple sensors Errors from occlusions or poor lighting	Less accurate for depth measurement Affected by lighting conditions Requires significant training data
Cost	Low	High	Moderate to High	Low to Moderate
Accuracy	Moderate	High	High	Moderate
Use Cases	Suitable for integration in existing vehicle systems for preliminary detection	Ideal for detailed road surface mapping and precise maintenance planning	Suitable for advanced applications like autonomous vehicles requiring detailed road models	Good for general road monitoring and preliminary detection using existing camera infrastructure

2.2 Crack Detection

One of the important method for crack detection is through image processing [10]. Golding, V.P et al. [10] listed two image processing methods first is gray scaling and Thresholding: the first step involves converting color images captured by cameras or sensors into gray scale images. Gray scaling simplifies the image representation by removing color information while retaining essential features such as brightness and contrast. This step reduces computational complexity and improves the efficiency of subsequent processing stages. After gray scaling, thresholding techniques are applied to segment the grayscale images and extract crack regions. Thresholding involves setting a threshold value to binarize the grayscale image, where pixels with intensities above the threshold are classified as crack pixels, while those below are classified as non-crack pixels. Various thresholding methods such as global thresholding, adaptive thresholding [11], and Otsu's method [12] are explored to adaptively determine the optimal threshold value for different road surface conditions and lighting conditions. The second method is Edge detection: It is a fundamental technique in image processing used to identify boundaries within images. These boundaries typically represent changes in intensity or color and often correspond to object boundaries.

In dataset collected by researchers through smartphone camera mounted on vehicle consist of 8 different crack classes [13]. Detection of cracks is performed using deep learning YOLO v2 algorithm. Results obtained are more accurate for alligator cracks as compared to transverse cracks. Based on CNN and transfer learning crack detection was implemented [14]. Transfer learning enables you to build on the knowledge acquired from solving one problem, rather than starting the learning process from the beginning and apply it to a different, but related, problem. This approach can be especially useful when you have a small dataset for the new task. Transfer learning may be performed by feature extraction and fine-tuning training process on new dataset using pre-trained dataset.

Systematic review of crack detection with the help of pixel level image segmentation [15] has been carried out by researcher to improve accuracy. Crack image segmentation is performed with different approaches based on U-net, Fully Convolutional Network (FCN), encoder-decoder model, multi scale, attention mechanism, transformer, twostage detection, unsupervised learning, weakly supervised learning, and multi-modality fusion. Crack image segmentation based on listed techniques is described in Table 3.

2.3 Open Manhole

Detecting manholes is crucial for urban planning, maintenance, and safety. Various methods, ranging from traditional manual inspections to advanced automated systems, have been developed to detect and locate manholes. Instead of processing road surface points in 3D space authors [26] preferred rasterization of these points in 2D geo-referenced feature (GRF) image based by storing intensity information of pixels. Further with this generated GRF image, threshold-based segmentation is carried out to detect manhole cover. Manhole covers are then extracted by Euclidean distance clustering. The study by Guan et al. (2014) presents a robust and efficient method for automated manhole cover detection using mobile LiDAR data. By leveraging the high-resolution 3D point clouds and sophisticated geometric analysis, the method achieves high accuracy and efficiency, making it a valuable tool for urban infrastructure management. Automated detection of urban road manhole covers using Mobile Laser Scanning (MLS) [27] involves the integration of advanced sensor technologies, data processing algorithms, and machine learning techniques. MLS systems mounted on vehicles capture high-resolution 3D point cloud data of the urban environment as the vehicle moves through LiDAR sensors, GPS units, Inertial Measurement Units (IMUs), and sometimes cameras.

Table 3. Crack image segmentation

Technique	Architecture	Key Features	ML technique	Use of Attention	Flexibility in Scale	Computational complexity and Performance
U-net [16]	EncoderDecoder	Skip connections, data augmentation, deep supervision	Supervised	No	Limited	Medium and High
FCN [17]	Fully Convolutional	No need for fully connected layers	Lessaccuracy in prediction of thin cracks	No	Yes	Low and Medium
EncoderDecoder Network [18]	EncoderDecoder	Bottleneck layers, pooling layers	Supervised	Possible	Yes	Medium and High

(continued)

Table 3. (continued)

Technique	Architecture	Key Features	ML technique	Use of Attention	Flexibility in Scale	Computational complexity and Performance
Multi-Scale [19]	Varies	Integration of multiple scales for better segmentation	Supervised	Possible	Yes	Varies and High
Attention Mechanism [20]	Varies	Attention mechanism for focusing on relevant features	Supervised	Yes	Yes	Varies and High
Transformer [21]	Transformer	Self-attention mechanism for global context understanding	Supervised	Yes	Yes	High and Varies
Two-stage detection [22]	Multi-stage architecture	Initial detection followed by refinement stage	Supervised for both stages	Possible	Yes	High and High
Unsupervised learning [23]	dVaries	Data-driven, no labels required	Unsupervised	Possible	Limited	Varies and Varies
Weakly supervised learning [24]	Varies	Utilizes weak labels for training, but with limited annotation	Weakly supervised	Possible	Limited	Varies and Varies
Multimodality fusion [25]	Varies	Utilizes multiple modalities for better segmentation results	Supervised	Possible	Yes	Varies and Varies

3 Dataset

Our own custom dataset could be prepared by a researcher and further apply deep learning object detection technique (e.g. YOLO).

Steps for creating custom dataset using YOLO:

1. Researchers need to download images through the internet or capture them through a camera mounted on vehicle
2. Annotation: These captured or downloaded images are required to augment (if needed) and annotate by using software or manual intervention. Drawing bounding boxes around each anomaly and assigning class labels (e.g., pothole) to the bounding boxes
3. Organize your dataset into the directory structure
4. YOLO uses a specific format for annotations. Each .txt file should contain lines in the following format: ¡object-class¿ ¡x center¿ ¡y center¿ ¡width¿ ¡height¿
5. Prepare Dataset Configuration File
6. Start training with YOLO

Another approach is to download existing datasets. Many publicly available datasets for anomaly detection are available to support research and development. Some of these datasets are listed below, sourced from the internet.

1. Pothole-600: contains 600+.jpg images of the road with potholes used for image classification and object detection tasks. https://www.kaggle.com/datasets/sachinpatel21/pothole-image-dataset
2. PotholesorCrackonRoadImageDataset:contains5000+images. https://www.kaggle.com/datasets/dataclusterlabs/potholes-or-cracks-on-road-image-dataset
3. Road Pothole Images for Pothole detection: contains images for road potholes along with annotations. https://www.kaggle.com/datasets/sovitrath/road-pothole-images-for-pothole-detection
4. IDD Dataset: A large dataset that includes images and annotations of Indian road scenes, featuring various road anomalies including potholes. https://idd.insaan.iiit.ac.in/
5. Manhole dataset: https://www.kaggle.com/datasets/deeppratap/manhole-detection

4 YOLO VERSIONS V4 TO V8

We compare the performance of real-time object detection models from YOLOv4 to YOLOv8 as these models may have low inference time. Real time detection requires to detect objects quickly which can be accomplished with these YOLOv4 to YOLOv8 versions. In real-time object detection data need to be feed and process continuously. In order to get efficient performance these models are better as compared to older YOLO versions. Table 4 illustrates comparison of different deep learning object detection techniques of YOLO versions.

Table 4. YOLO version comparison

Feature	YOLOv4 [28]	YOLOv5 [29]	YOLOv6 [30]	YOLOv7 [31]	YOLOv8 [32]
Release Date	April 2020	June 2020	June 2022	July 2022	January 2023
Backbone Network	CSPDarknet5	3CSPDarknet5	3CSPDarknet5/EfficientNet	3YOLOv4-CSP	YOLOv5-CSP
Neural Architecture Search (NAS)	No	No	Partial	Partial	Advanced NAS
Activation Functions	Mish	Leaky ReLU/SiLU	SiLU	SiLU	SiLU
Data Augmentation	Mosaic, SAT, CutMix	Mosaic, CutMix	Mosaic, MixUp	Mosaic, MixUp	Mosaic, MixUp
Regularization	DropBlock, Label Smoothing	DropBlock	DropBlock, Model EMA	DropBlock, Model EMA	DropBlock, Model EMA
Multi-Scale Features	PANet, SPP	PANet, SPP	PANet, SPP	PANet, E-ELAN	PANet, E-ELAN
Post-Processing	DIoU-NMS	DIoU-NMS	CIoU-NMS	DIoU-NMS, ASFF	DIoU-NMS, ASFF
Attention Mechanisms	–	–	–	CBAM	CBAM
Performance (mAP)	High	Higher	Higher	Higher	Highest so far

(*continued*)

Table 4. (*continued*)

Feature	YOLOv4 [28]	YOLOv5 [29]	YOLOv6 [30]	YOLOv7 [31]	YOLOv8 [32]
Typical FPS on GPU	35–45 FPS	45–60 FPS	55–70 FPS	50–65 FPS	65–80 FPS
Transformer Integration	No	No	No	No	Partial
Evaluation metrics	mean average precision (mAP) 43.5% and (65.7% @AP50)	YOLOv5x 66.9% @AP50	YOLOv6L 52.5%	56.8%	53.9%

You Only Look Once (YOLO) is a real time single shot object detection deep learning algorithm. Major components of YOLO architecture backbone network, neck and head. Backbone network is used for extracting features then these generated features are fed to neck for aggregation and enhancement. Head is a component where object detection bounding box predictions and classification predictions are carried out.

Key points of architecture are listed below considering backbone network, neural architecture search (NAS), activation function.

1. **Backbone Networks:**
   (a) YOLOv4 and YOLOv5 utilize CSPDarknet53
   (b) YOLOv6 and YOLOv7 explore additional backbones like EfficientNet and YOLOv4-CSP
   (c) YOLOv8 continues with YOLOv5-CSP
2. **Neural Architecture Search (NAS):**
   Neural Architecture Search (NAS) plays a significant role in optimizing YOLO architectures for object detection tasks. NAS automates the process of designing the neural network architecture, which traditionally involves significant trial and error and expert intuition. This leads to more efficient network structures that can better balance speed and accuracy
   (a) YOLOv6 and YOLOv7 begin to incorporate NAS
   (b) YOLOv8 sees more advanced NAS
3. **Activation Functions:**
   Mish [33] and SiLU [34] (Sigmoid Linear Unit, also known as Swish) are two advanced activation functions used in neural networks. Both aim to improve the performance of deep learning models by enabling better gradient flow and feature representation compared to traditional activation functions like ReLU. Transition from Mish in YOLOv4 to SiLU (Swish variant) in later versions.

   Mish provides smooth gradients, which can help in avoiding issues like vanishing gradients. The non-monotonic nature can lead to better gradient flow during training, potentially improving convergence speed and model performance. Mish activation function represented mathematically as

$$f(x) = x\tanh(\text{softplus}(x)) = x\tanh\left(\ln\left(1 + e^x\right)\right)$$

SiLU provides smooth gradients due to the combination of linear and sigmoid components. It facilitates better gradient flow compared to ReLU, helping in deeper networks. SiLU activation function represented mathematically as (Fig. 3)

$$f(x) = x\,\text{sigmoid}(\beta x)$$

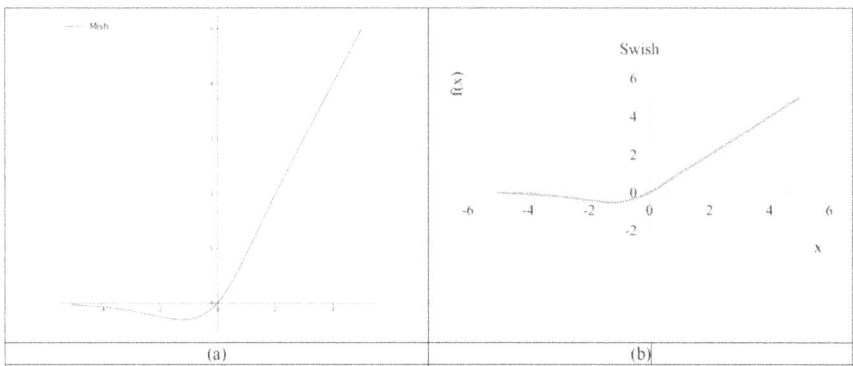

Fig. 3. (a) Mish activation function [33] (b) Swish activation function [34]

5 Current Challenges in Road Anomaly Detection

1. One of the major challenge is inference time i.e. the time taken by the model to predict output for new data after training
2. As real time object detection takes large data and process the same such as video streaming, maintaining high throughput and low latency is again a big challenge
3. It is expected model should be scalable in case of changing dataset size.
4. The deep learning model must be robust and reliable even input data might be noisy or partially missing conditions.
5. Updating and maintaining real-time deep learning models in production environments can be complex

6 Conclusion

In conclusion, this paper presents a thorough review of deep learning-based methods for detecting and assessing road anomalies, such as potholes, open manholes, and alligator cracks. We explored various factors contributing to road anomalies and highlighted the importance of effective detection systems. The review covered key aspects like dataset preprocessing, image annotation, and feature extraction techniques, along with a detailed comparison of YOLO versions v4 to v8 for real-time object detection. By summarizing findings from over 30 research papers, this study offers valuable insights into the application of advanced deep learning techniques for road anomaly detection and sets the foundation for future research in this field.

Acknowledgments. We would like to express our sincere gratitude to all those who contributed to this research. Firstly, we extend our deepest appreciation to our advisors and mentors for their invaluable guidance, insightful comments, and unwavering support throughout this study. we are deeply thankful to our families and friends for their patience, understanding, and encouragement throughout the duration of this research.

Declaration. The corresponding author, on behalf of all authors, declares that there are no conflicts of interest.

References

1. WHO. Global Status Report on Road Safety 2023. Technical Report
2. Tai, Y.-C., Chan, C.-W., Hsu, J.: Automatic road anomaly detection using smart mobile device (2010)
3. Seraj, F., Zwaag, B.J., Dilo, A., Luarasi, T., Havinga, P.: Roads: a road pavement monitoring system for anomaly detection using smart phones. In: Atzmueller, M., Chin, A., Janssen, F., Schweizer, I., Trattner, C. (eds.) Big Data Analytics in the Social and Ubiquitous Context, pp. 128–146. Springer, Cham (2016). https://doi.org/10.1007/978-3-319-29009-6_7
4. Nuno Silva, J.S. Vaibhav, S., Rodrigues, H.: Road anomalies detection system evaluation. Sensors 2018 **18**(7), 1984 (2018). https://doi.org/10.3390/s18071984
5. Nuno Silva, J.S. Vaibhav, S., Rodrigues, H.: Anomaly detection in roads with a data mining approach. Procedia Computer Science **121**, 415–422 (2017). https://doi.org/10.1016/j.procs.2017.11.056
6. Erick Axel Martinez-Ríos, M.R.B.-B., Arce-Sáenz, L.A.: A review of road surface anomaly detection and classification systems based on vibration-based techniques. Appl. Sci **12** (2022). https://doi.org/10.3390/app12199413
7. Vinodhini, K.A., Sidhaarth, K.R.A.: Pothole detection in bituminous road using CNN with transfer learning. Elsevier Measure.: Sens. **31** (2024). https://doi.org/10.1016/j.measen.2023.100940
8. Kim, Y.-M., Kim, Y.-G., Son, S.-Y., Lim, S.-Y., Choi, B.-Y., Choi, D.-H.: Review of recent automated pothole-detection methods. Appl. Sci. **12** (2022). https://doi.org/10.3390/app12115320
9. Boris Bučko, K.Z., Eva Lieskovská, Zábovský, M.: Computer vision based pothole detection under challenging conditions. Sensors **22** (2022). https://doi.org/10.3390/s22228878
10. Golding, V.P., Gharineiat, Z., Munawar, H.S.: Crack detection in concrete structures using deep learning. Sustainability **14** (2022). https://doi.org/10.3390/su14138117
11. Mandyartha, E.P.: Global and adaptive thresholding technique for white blood cell image segmentation. J. Phys.: Conf. **1569** (2020). https://doi.org/10.1088/1742-6596/1569/2/022054
12. Chunshi Sha, H.C. Jian Hou: A robust 2d otsu's thresholding method in image segmentation. J. Phys.: Conf. Ser. **41**, 339–351 (2016). https://doi.org/10.1016/j.jvcir.2016.10.013
13. Mandal, V., Uong, L., Adu-Gyamfi, Y.: Automated road crack detection using deep convolutional neural networks. In: 2018 IEEE International Conference on Big Data (Big Data), pp. 5212–5215 (2018). https://doi.org/10.1109/BigData.2018.8622327
14. Chen, Y., Zhu, Z., Lin, Z., Zhou, Y.: Building surface crack detection using deep learning technology. MDPI: Build. **13** (2023). https://doi.org/10.3390/buildings13071814
15. Li, H., Wang, W., Wang, M., Li, L., Vimlund, V.: A review of deep learning methods for pixel-level crack detection. J. Traffic Transport. Eng. (English Edn.) **09**, 945–968 (2022). https://doi.org/10.1016/j.jtte.2022.11.003

16. Cheng, J., Xiong, W., Chen, W., Gu, Y., Li, Y.: Pixel-level crack detection using u-net. In: TENCON 2018 - 2018 IEEE Region 10 Conference, pp. 0462–0466 (2018). https://doi.org/10.1109/TENCON.2018.8650059
17. Yang, X., Li, H., Yu, Y., et al.: Automatic pixel-level crack detection and measurement using fully convolutional network. Comput.-Aided Civil Infrastruct. Eng. **33**, 1090–1109 (2018). https://doi.org/10.1111/mice.12412
18. Bang, S., Park, S., Kim, H.K.: Encoder–decoder network for pixel-level road crack detection in black-box images. WILEY Comput.-Aided Civil Infrastruct. Eng. **34**, 713–727 (2019). https://doi.org/10.1111/mice.12440
19. Ai, D., Jiang, G., Siew Kei, L., Li, C.: Automatic pixel-level pavement crack detection using information of multi-scale neighborhoods. IEEE Access **6**, 24452–24463 (2018)
20. Jing, P., Yu, H., Hua, Z., Xie, S., Song, C.: Road crack detection using deep neural network based on attention mechanism and residual structure. IEEE Access **11**, 919–929 (2023)
21. Xiang, X., Wang, Z., Qiao, Y.: An improved yolov5 crack detection method combined with transformer. IEEE Sens. J. **22**(14), 14328–14335 (2022)
22. Nguyen, N.H.T., Perry, S., Bone, D., Le, H.T., Nguyen, T.T.: Two-stage convolutional neural network for road crack detection and segmentation. Expert Syst. Appl. **186**, 115718 (2021). https://doi.org/10.1016/j.eswa.2021.115718
23. Li, W., Huyan, J., Gao, R., Hao, X., Hu, Y., Zhang, Y.: Unsupervised deep learning for road crack classification by fusing convolutional neural network and k-means clustering. J. Transport. Eng. **147** (2021). https://doi.org/10.1061/JPEODX.0000322
24. Inoue, Y., Nagayoshi, H.: Crack detection as a weakly-supervised problem: Towards achieving less annotation-intensive crack detectors. In: 2020 25th International Conference on Pattern Recognition (ICPR), pp. 65–72 (2021). https://doi.org/10.1109/ICPR48806.2021.9412041
25. Liu, Y., Zhou, X., Zhong, W.: Multi-modality image fusion and object detection based on semantic information. Entropy **25**(5) (2023)
26. Chang, K.T., Chang, J.R., Liu, J.K.: Detection of pavement distress using 3d laser scanning technology. ASCE. https://doi.org/10.1061/40794(179)103
27. Yu, Y., Guan, H., Ji, Z.: Automated detection of urban road manhole covers using mobile laser scanning data. IEEE Trans. Intell. Transp. Syst. **16**(6), 3258–3269 (2015). https://doi.org/10.1109/TITS.2015.2413812
28. Bochkovskiy, A., Wang, C.-Y., Liao, H.-Y.M.: YOLOv4: optimal speed and accuracy of object detection (2020)
29. Jocher, G.: Yolov5 release v6.1 (2022). https://github.com/ultralytics/yolov5/releases/tag/v6.1
30. Li, C., et al.: YOLOv6: a single-stage object detection framework for industrial applications (2022)
31. Wang, C.-Y., Bochkovskiy, A., Liao, H.-Y.M.: YOLOv7: trainable bag-of-freebies sets new state-of-the-art for real-time object detectors (2022)
32. Jocher, G., Chaurasia, A., Qiu, J.: Yolo by ultralytics (2023). https://github.com/ultralytics/ultralytics
33. Misra, D.: Mish: a self regularized non-monotonic activation function (2020)
34. Prajit Ramachandran, Q.V.L. Barret Zoph: swish: a self-gated activation Function (2017)

Advancement of Data Visualization Techniques in Healthcare Using AI and Power BI

Priya Rani[✉], Jeevan Kumar, and Smita Dash

Department of Computer Science and Engineering, RVS College of Engineering and Technology, Jamshedpur 831012, India
`priyaraniswarnkar@gmail.com`

Abstract. In the swiftly advancing landscape of healthcare, the integration of AI has come up with reshaping diagnostics, treatment strategies, and overall delivery of patient care. The business intelligence tool can provide a standardized solution to the decision-making process which might be able to change the extrinsic business environment in healthcare. The major aim of this research is to leverage the capabilities of Power BI, integrated with artificial intelligence to explore and enhance the data visualization techniques in healthcare. The target is to transform complex and large healthcare data into interactive, intuitive, and actionable insights. This research is separated into two parts. The opening segment of the research report offers an extensive examination of Power BI, detailing its theoretical underpinnings, distinctive features, procedural workflow, pros and cons, business merits, and the incorporation of artificial intelligence. The subsequent section of this study illustrates the application of Power BI in developing an optimal business intelligence solution tailored to specific scenarios within the healthcare sector. This research will support decision-making processes, improve patient outcomes, and smooth healthcare operations. The research will adopt the pragmatic case as a foundational framework for users of Power BI.

Keywords: Artificial Intelligence · Power BI · Data Visualization · Healthcare · Modeling · Prediction

1 Introduction

This narrative predominantly elucidates the potential of Power BI and its incorporation of artificial intelligence within data visualization tools, facilitating the extraction of insights from raw, unstructured data. In the context of information technology, developers have made significant contributions by providing an array of technologies that are instrumental in leveraging data for value. This has been accomplished through the establishment and ongoing management of data warehouses, as well as the creation and illustration of advanced data models [13]. Developed by Microsoft, Power BI serves as a state-of-the-art platform for business intelligence and data visualization. The essence of Business Intelligence (BI) lies in grasping essential data and uncovering the relationships between different facts, which ultimately aids in the decision-making process [9].

The healthcare industry is changing quickly, and managing and visualizing data effectively is now critical. Healthcare workers now have more opportunities to utilize the enormous volumes of data produced in the sector thanks to the introduction of potent technologies like Power BI [12]. The use of Power BI provides an extensive healthcare dashboard from complicated medical data in an easy-to-use interface that will provide healthcare organizations with a revolutionary way to improve patient care, make well-informed decisions, and maximize operational effectiveness. Moreover, it also furnishes predictive analysis to healthcare professionals to identify potential health risks and improve patient satisfaction.

In the contemporary landscape, Microsoft is at the vanguard with the release of a business intelligence tool designed to replace existing analytics platforms and tools, while also enhancing business analytics services for the comprehensive visualization and analysis of all data within a unified framework. Microsoft aims to provide this technology to everyone so that they can utilize it effectively [13].

1.1 Area to Be Explored by IT Professionals

- Meet the business growth by using Power BI usage [24].
- They can focus on the working field which they love.
- Achieve time optimization in preparing a business report.
- Focus on the increasing stipulation of the real-time data flow.

1.2 Area to Be Explored by BI Analyst

- Collection of authoritative data from different data sources.
- Cleaning of complex data for visualization purposes and quick and optimized analysis.
- The incorporation of artificial intelligence involves the application of AI algorithms to identify concealed patterns, forecast results, and improve data analysis, thereby facilitating the development of data models and producing significant, interactive reports [25].
- Promote the effortless exchange of data models and reports among end users.

1.3 Area to Be Explored by End User

- They have quick access to the real-time occurrences of data to monitor.
- Can share interactive and user-friendly dashboards effortlessly with others.
- Users can stay connected from anywhere because of Microsoft's cloud-based analytics service for visualizing

1.4 Architecture of Microsoft Power BI

Microsoft dispenses Power BI as a cloud-based platform that is used to have interactive visualizations and business intelligence capabilities [7]. The same architecture is built on the modern web-scaled environment which emphasizes high performance, Scalability, and reliability [28]. The architecture encompasses both the Power BI Desktop application and the Power BI Service, which is the online version of the platform. Users can link to various data sources, design reports, or dashboards in the desktop application, and subsequently share their creations through the cloud via the Service.

To facilitate a clearer understanding, the architecture of Power BI has been meticulously designed to lodge four aspects of data utilization.

Establish Communication with Data Sources. Domestic connectors in the Power BI environment support the integration of a wide array of data sources, encompassing databases, web applications, services, and flat files. The get data option is available in the Power BI interface to fetch raw (meaningless) data from different sources [20].

Data Transformation and Modeling. For data analysis, unadulterated data may not be beneficial, it needs transforming and modeling features to reshape into meaningful facts. Various transformations can be performed by users, including the removal of undesirable columns, the alteration of column names and objects, the filtering and pivoting of data, and the modification of data types.

Generate and Publish a Report. For visualization of data, only transformation is not enough as we need to have interactive reports to analyze the workflow of data which is done by Power BI Desktop. The content includes various forms of visual aids, including graphical illustrations, charts, and informational tables, which facilitate the effective conversion of data into a comprehensive report.

Build Dashboards. A business analytics tool called Power BI Dashboard enables users to construct dynamic and adaptable dashboards. Users may connect to several data sources to generate reports using this cloud-based business intelligence software and visualize data to gain insights [8].

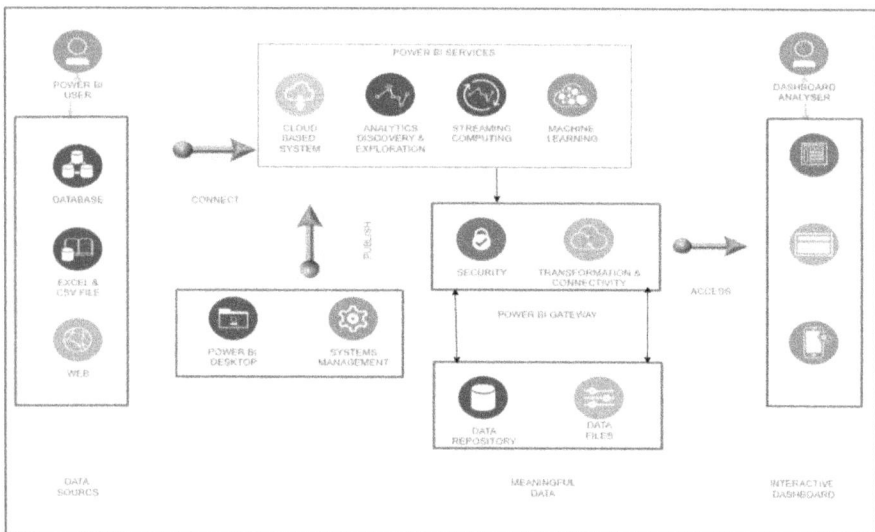

Fig. 1. Power BI Architecture Diagram

As mentioned above (Fig. 1) is an architecture diagram of the Power BI which explains the workflow of data for predictive analysis.

2 Literature Review

Daniel J. Power [1], carried out a study that scrutinized the benefits of data-driven decision support systems, and their positive impacts on business intelligence practices.

Kutubuddin Kazi [2], studied a patient monitoring system using Power BI and explained the revolutionary transition in the healthcare sector to enhance overall organizational success, the effectiveness of operations, and the treatment of patients. The healthcare dashboard that is being suggested incorporates several data sources such as patient demographics, financial information, and operational measures.

Geetha Bhargava Mandava [3], describes the interactive visualization of databases from educational institutions using the Microsoft Power BI Tool's various modules. It also concentrates on the process model, how Microsoft Power BI works, the kinds of data sources that are available in the Tool, and the various visual insights or contexts that are related to it.

Md. Shohel Rana, and Jeff Shuford [4], examine the revolutionary effects of artificial intelligence (AI) in healthcare, emphasizing how decision support systems and predictive analytics are transforming patient care through their research AI in Healthcare: Transforming Patient Care through Predictive Analytics and Decision Support Systems.

Microsoft Tutorials [5], Create a Power BI predictive model. This tutorial explains the step-by-step procedure of how to proceed with the Power BI platform and build a custom ML model for predictive analysis.

R. Heang and R. Mohan [6], one may train and verify a machine learning model directly in Power BI by creating a Power BI dataflow and using the entities specified in the dataflow. Next, create predictions and score fresh data using that model.

Geetha Bhargava Mandava [3], Utilizing AI algorithms, such as machine learning uses natural language processing, to improve data interpretation, anticipate results, and reveal hidden patterns, we can do all these things to develop predictive models to forecast patient outcomes, and disease outbreaks, and operational needs using inbuilt AI features of Power BI.

Microsoft Tutorials [5], Power BI is an essential tool for anyone involved in data analysis and business intelligence. By mastering Power BI, participants can significantly improve their ability to analyze data, discover trends, and make data-driven decisions.

3 Gaps in the Literature

As a result of the qualitative literature review, my study finds that there exist several research papers in the domain of healthcare, data visualization, Power BI dashboard, and predictive analysis in healthcare [19]. My study addresses the gap in the "integration of AI in Power BI for data visualization in healthcare" and suggests a structure that ought to assist in cleaning, preparing, and performing predictive analysis of healthcare data with a creative dashboard [26]. Also found that, Notwithstanding the possible advantages, AI integration in healthcare faces significant obstacles, including matters about the confidentiality of data and the assurance of its security, ethical norms and legal obligations, interoperability and integration issues, scalability and accessibility issues, and human-AI interaction complications. Strong cybersecurity measures, ethical considerations, legal frameworks, universal interoperability standards, and impartial access to AI technologies are all emphasized in this review report. We thoroughly analyze literature reviews using a grounded theory perspective to develop the framework. Leveraging the authenticated data, we then develop a framework to show its applicability using a specific instance. The findings result in a module for detecting research gaps, which will allow for more demanding, productive, and effective literature evaluations in future research efforts.

4 Research Methodology

The advantages of data visualization in healthcare are diverse and considerable. By implementing and embracing various visualization instruments such as Power BI within the realm of healthcare, providers can significantly improve the delivery of services and the quality of care received by patients. Other types of healthcare data can be fetched from various sources to draw various visualizations, such as charts, graphs, and maps, and healthcare professionals can showcase patient outcomes, identify trends, and monitor disease progression.

To research the aforementioned issue, the following procedures must be taken as part of the methodology- Data Acquisition is used to identify and source relevant healthcare data. Data preprocessing prepares data for analysis by cleaning, normalizing, and altering it. AI Analysis, this tool is used to apply machine learning models to predict trends and outcomes. Visualization development will be done to design and implement visualizations in Power BI. User testing is conducted to test the usability with healthcare professionals to gather feedback. Refinement is an iterative improvement of the visualizations based on feedback and performance analysis.

4.1 Research Scope

This research initiative provides a valuable prospect to refine the theoretical understanding of business intelligence and healthcare insights, contingent upon the collection of relevant data from diverse sources. The foundational framework of the Microsoft BI solution, along with preliminary investigations into Power BI for healthcare data analysis, will provide a substantial environment conducive to decision-making processes and enhance the efficiency of healthcare operations. As a component of the practical research initiative, a test case was formulated to ascertain the key features of Power BI relevant to data analysis in the healthcare industry.

4.2 Process Model of Power BI for Patient Data Analysis

Users can implement Power BI for Healthcare outcome prediction in the following as shown below (Fig. 2) and deploy the interactive, engaging, and customized dashboard to aggregate data from diverse origins and arrange it within a singular perspective [27].

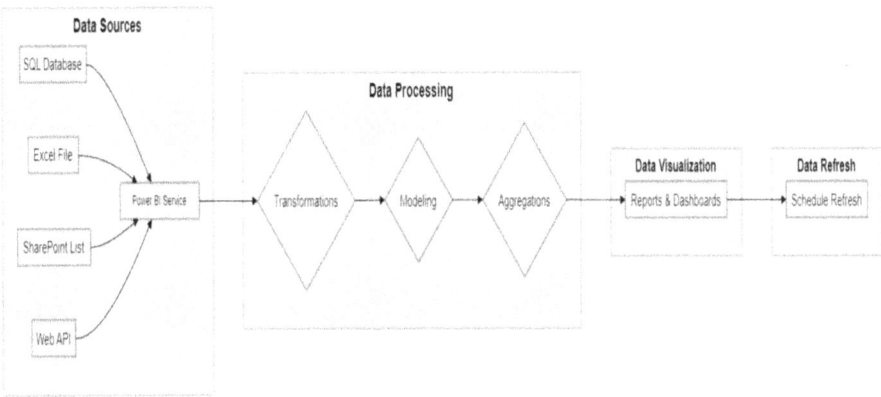

Fig. 2. Power BI's Process Framework

Data Collection and Integration. Aggregating healthcare information from many sources, including electronic health records (EHR), patient management systems, and external databases [17]. As shown in (Fig. 3), data can be gathered from a variety of sources to create a unified view for analysis and reporting which underscores the importance of integration, a function that Power BI facilitates with ease [18].

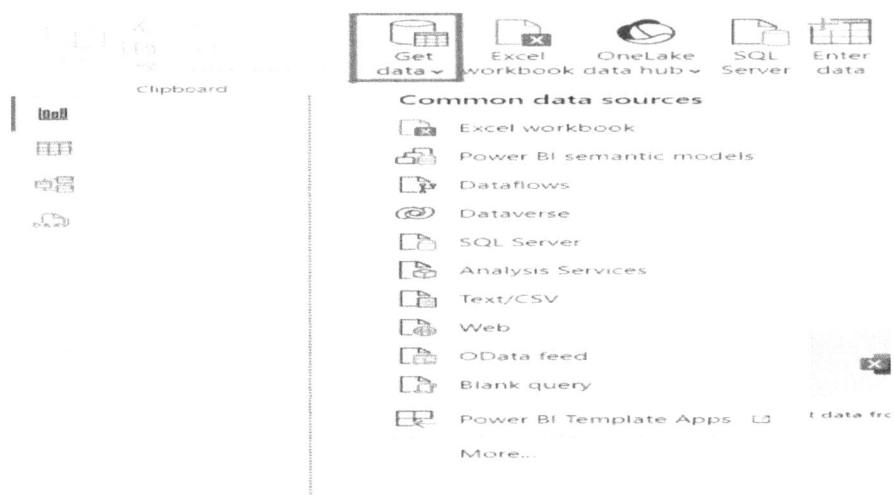

Fig. 3. Data Source

Data Cleaning and Preparation. It is common for datasets to be improperly formatted, necessitating transformation before analysis. To maintain data accuracy, consistency, and relevance, pre-processing techniques are utilized on these datasets. This transformation can be done through the mentioned process as shown in (Fig. 4).

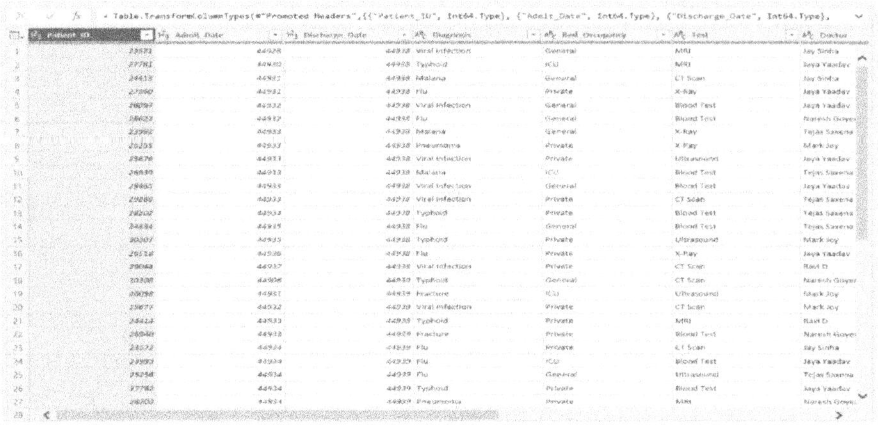

Fig. 4. Data Transformation

Data Modeling and AI Integration. The pre-processed data is then utilized to develop AI algorithms to uncover hidden patterns, predict outcomes, and enhance data interpretation. Structuring data in an organized manner using the inbuilt AI feature of Power BI enables efficient analysis. This step can be performed using the model view option in the Power BI dashboard interface as shown in (Fig. 5).

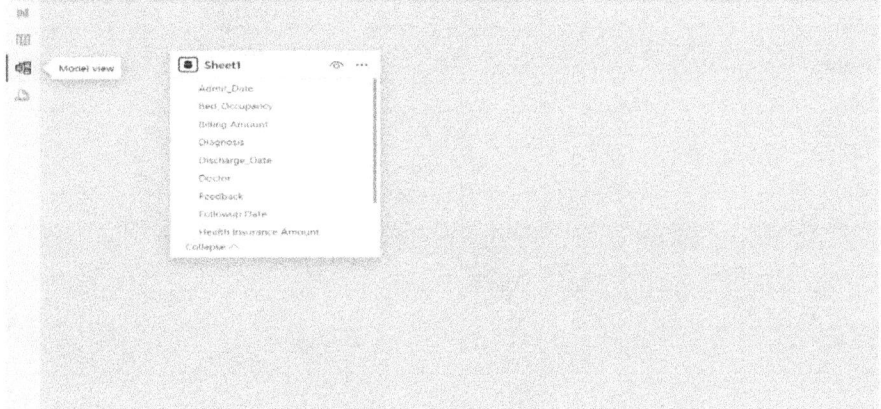

Fig. 5. Data Modeling

Visualization Design. Following the completion of data modeling, the results are conveyed through visual tools, including graphs and charts as shown in (Fig. 6) [16]. It is creating dynamic and interactive dashboards and reports that effectively communicate insights [15].

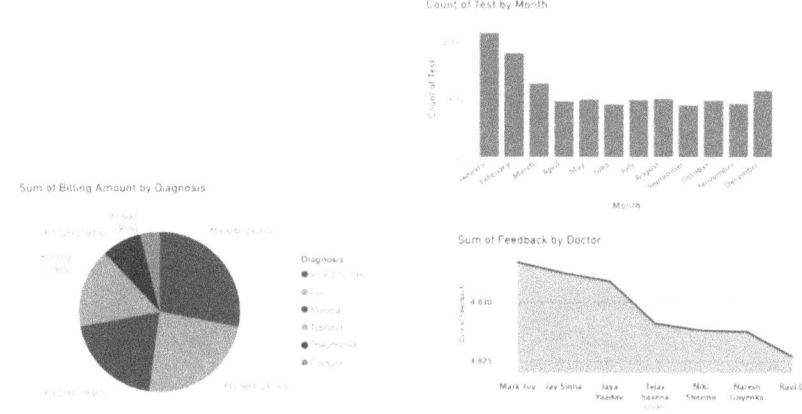

Fig. 6. Data Visualization

Implementation and Deployment. We are developing a user-friendly interface for healthcare stakeholders to access and interact with the visualizations. Through the dashboard, they can explore the facts in multiple ways [12].

Evaluation and Feedback. Assessing the effectiveness of the visualizations through user feedback and performance metrics and performing necessary steps for improvement.

5 Result

The thorough investigation of the Power BI and its implementation for healthcare with the integration of AI has yielded noteworthy findings across various aspects [10]. In the case study, an AI-driven inbuilt algorithm in Power BI showcased a notable enhancement in precision, transparency, optimization, and superior examination when juxtaposed with traditional approaches. [13]. By designing and launching the Power BI dashboard as shown in (Fig. 7), the healthcare organization unlocks substantial potential, broadening access to business intelligence and promoting an intellectual achievement that prioritizes data-driven decision-making [21]. The dashboard will showcase critical information regarding a particular patient ID, specifically the admit date, discharge date, and follow-up date. It will also present the billing amounts corresponding to the diagnoses assigned to that patient. The role of feedback is emphasized through area graphs that reflect the insights from medical professionals. The analysis dashboard will showcase the total number of tests administered in a given month. By utilizing a funnel chart, one can effectively visualize the diagnosis type associated with each patient. Subsequently, a line chart can be employed to compare the amounts billed against the insurance coverage. A single interaction with any disease or segment of the patient monitoring dashboard will provide a complete overview of all details linked to that condition. Professionals do not have to engage in an exhaustive analysis of the data to obtain factual insights. They can utilize robust analytical capabilities to facilitate straightforward data exploration, examination, and report generation. This allows them to access and scrutinize all their data in a centralized location through dynamic dashboards and reports. The personalized approach of Power BI not only improves treatment efficiency but also minimizes adverse effects, making a remarkable improvement in patient care [23].

The proposed dashboard will function as an efficient asset for monitoring the current operations within the hospital. Future updates could include the addition of bed occupancy information, staff availability metrics, and details regarding safety materials and products, which would contribute to improved functionality and analytical insights.

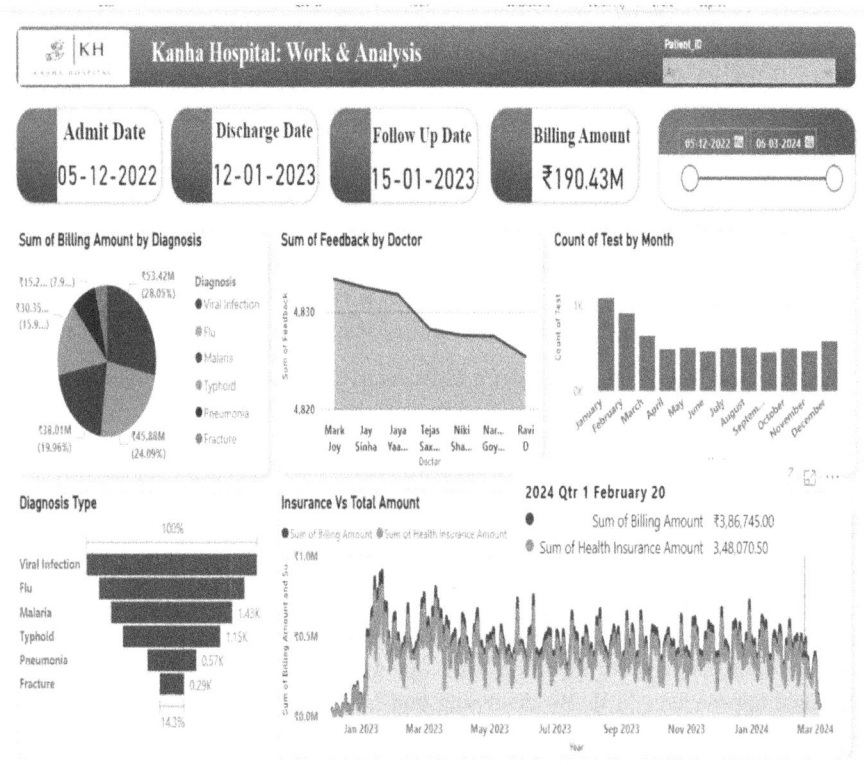

Fig. 7. Patient Monitoring Dashboard

Beyond the modules previously discussed, dashboards can be created for different segments within each medical sector. These may include information pertinent to patients, medical personnel including doctors and nurses, administrative staff, infrastructure, and various amenities provided by healthcare institutions [19].

6 Discussion

Despite having numerous advantages of Power BI for the healthcare sector, there are some drawbacks too [10]. It may require substantial data integration and cleansing efforts, and advanced Power BI services handling skills can be a barrier to adoption. Furthermore, complex healthcare data and regulatory requirements can make implementing it more challenging. As Power BI is a cloud-based application, users must have a good internet connection to use its features [22]. Power BI functionality can be expended by writing customized machine learning code to implement predictive models, however, designing and debugging the code for the same required expertise and knowledge of the specified domain.

7 Conclusion

To conclude, the amalgamation of AI technology in healthcare with advanced Power BI services shows an extraordinary impact in transforming diagnostics, treatment strategies, and overall patient care. This result highlights the potential of AI in Power BI to have a concise, intuitive, precise, efficient, and personalized approach to medical interventions for creating healthcare reports.

However, this implementation of Power BI comes up with various challenges too. Ethical consideration about the privacy of patient data demands careful attention. Addressing technical issues, limitations of handling complex data, and establishing a supervisory framework are pivotal.

In quintessence of this research, the paper will not only contribute to the understanding of Power BI and AI integration with it but also its significance in the healthcare sector in furtherance of improved patient outcomes and comprehensive medical management practice.

References

1. Power, D.J.: Understanding data-driven decision support systems. Inform. Syst. Manage. **25**(2), 149–154 (2008). https://doi.org/10.1080/10580530801941124
2. Gurav, V., Pawar, A., Solwat, K., Kazi, K.: Patient monitoring system using power BI. 463 (2023)
3. Mandava, G.B.: Analysis and design of visualization of educational institution database using power BI tool (2018)
4. Mohan, R.: Literature review of business intelligence (2017)
5. Metre, K.V., et al.: An introduction to power BI for data analysis. Int. J. Intell. Syst. Appl. Eng. **12**(1s), 142–147 (2023)
6. Khodke, H.E., Bhalerao, M., Gunjal, S.N., Nirmal, S., Gore, S., Dange, B.J.: An Intelligent approach to empowering the research of biomedical machine learning in medical data analysis using PALM. Int. J. Intell. Syst. Appl. Eng. **11**(10s), 429–436 (2023)
7. Dutta, P.: Business analytics using microsoft power BI and AWS redshift. Int. J. Trend Sci. Res. Develop. **3**, 984–986 (2019). https://doi.org/10.31142/ijtsrd21545
8. Gonçalves, C., Angélico, G.M., Campante, M.: Developing integrated performance dashboards visualisations using power BI as a platform. Information **14**, 614 (2023). https://doi.org/10.3390/info14110614
9. Akbar, R., Silvana., M., Hersyah, M.H., Jannah, M.: Implementation of business intelligence for sales data management using interactive dashboard visualization in XYZ stores. In: 2020 International Conference on Information Technology Systems and Innovation (ICITSI), pp. 242–249. Bandung, Indonesia (2020). https://doi.org/10.1109/ICITSI50517.2020.9264984

10. Microsoft Tutorial for Power BI. https://www.microsoft.com/en-us/power-platform/products/power-bi. Accessed 12 Sept 2024
11. Transform healthcare experience with Power BI. https://www.microsoft.com/en-us/power-platform/products/power-bi/industry/healthcare. Accessed 12 Sept 2024
12. Abudiyab, N.A., Alanazi, A.T.: Visualization techniques in healthcare applications: a narrative review. Cureus **14**(11), e31355 (2022). https://doi.org/10.7759/cureus.31355
13. Parthe, R.: Comparative analysis of data visualization tools: power bi and tableau. Int. J. Sci. Res. Eng. Manage. **07**, 1–11 (2023). https://doi.org/10.55041/IJSREM26272. (2023)
14. Matthias, D., Managwu, C.: Data analytics and visualization using Power BI and MS Excel for COVID-19 (Coronavirus) (2021). https://doi.org/10.13140/RG.2.2.25204.48001
15. Krishnan., V.: Research data analysis with power BI. INFLIBNET Centre (2017). http://ir.inflibnet.ac.in/handle/1944/2116
16. Singh, G., Kumar, A., Singh, J., Kaur, J.: Data visualization for developing effective performance dashboard with power BI. In: 2023 International Conference on Innovative Data Communication Technologies and Application (ICIDCA), pp. 968–973. Uttarakhand, India (2023). https://doi.org/10.1109/ICIDCA56705.2023.10100169
17. Sarika, S., Jadhav, L.: Data analysis and visualization of sales dataset using power BI. IJRASET (2022). https://doi.org/10.22214/ijraset.2022.44132
18. Doko, F., Mishkovski, I.: Advanced analytics of Big Data using Power BI: Credit Registry Use Case (2020)
19. Sharma, N., Sarkar, D.: Healthcare data analytics using power BI. Int. J. Softw. Innovat **10**, 1–10 (2022). https://doi.org/10.4018/IJSI.293267
20. Batko, K., Ślęzak, A.: The use of Big Data Analytics in healthcare. J. Big Data **9**(3), 2022 (2022). https://doi.org/10.1186/s40537-021-00553-4
21. Chakate, K., Giri, G., Gonge, S.S., Deshpande, A., Pawade, Y.R., Joshi, R.: CoviCare: tracking covid-19 using PowerBI. In: 2022 8th International Conference on Signal Processing and Communication (ICSC), pp. 74–78 (2022)
22. Yanfi, Ramadhan, A., Trisetyarso, A., Zarlis, M., Abdurachman, E.: Measuring student's satisfaction and loyalty on microsoft power bi using system usability scale and net promoter score for the case of students at bina nusantara university. In: 2022 International Conference on Data Science and Its Applications (ICoDSA), pp. 155–160 (2022)
23. Eberhard, K.: The effects of visualization on judgment and decision-making: a systematic literature review. Manag. Rev. Q **73**, 167–214 (2023). https://doi.org/10.1007/s11301-021-00235-8
24. Nguyen, V.T., Jung, K., Gupta, V.: Examining data visualization pitfalls in scientific publications. Vis. Comput. Ind. Biomed. Art **4**, 27 (2021). https://doi.org/10.1186/s42492-021-00092-y
25. Tan, X., Suo, X., Li, W., et al.: Data visualization in healthcare and medicine: a survey. Vis. Comput. (2024). https://doi.org/10.1007/s00371-024-03586-x
26. Zani, C.M., de Moura, P.K., dos Santos, B.M., Saurin, T.A.: Visual management in healthcare: a systematic literature review of main practices and applications. In: Thomé, A.M.T., Barbastefano, R.G., Scavarda, L.F., dos Reis, J.C.G., Amorim, M.P.C. (eds.) Industrial Engineering and Operations Management. IJCIEOM 2020. Springer Proceedings in Mathematics & Statistics, vol. 337. Springer, Cham (2020). https://doi.org/10.1007/978-3-030-56920-4_15
27. Narayan, K.A., Nayak, M.S.D.P.: Need for interactive data visualization in public health practice: examples from India. Int. J. Prev. Med. **12**, 16 (2021). https://doi.org/10.4103/ijpvm.IJPVM_171_20
28. Clark, D.: Introducing power BI. In: Beginning Microsoft Power BI. Apress, Berkeley, CA (2020). https://doi.org/10.1007/978-1-4842-5620-6_1

Role of Machine Leaning in D2D Communication in 6G

Haneef Khan[1(✉)], Malik Zaib Alam[1], Mohammad Rafeek Khan[1], Md Imran Alam[1], Shams Tabrez Siddiuqi[2], and Abu Salim[2]

[1] Department of Electrical and Electronics Engineering, College of Engineering and Computer Science, Jazan University, Jazan, Saudi Arabia
{haneeskhan,mzalam,mokhan,mimran}@jazanu.edu.sa
[2] Department of Computer Science, College of Engineering and Computer Science, Jazan University, Jazan, Saudi Arabia
stabrez@jazanu.edu.sa

Abstract. D2D communication would play a vital role in the next 6G wireless networks by enabling direct connection between devices, resulting in increased data speeds, less latency, and improved energy efficiency. Integrating machine learning methods into D2D communication has the benefit of optimizing resource allocation, interference control, and security assurance. In the context of 6G networks, this paper examines the convergence of ML and D2D communication and present approaches and identify domains are subject to critical evaluation for further inquiry.

Keywords: 6G Technology · D2D Communication · ML · IoT

1 Introduction

D2D communication is a pivotal breakthrough poised to transform 6G networks by facilitating direct data interchange among devices. By bypassing traditional network infrastructure, this technology has the capacity to significantly decrease latency and improve data transfer transmission speeds. D2D communication is crucial in enabling the advancement of state-of-the-art technologies such as autonomous driving and real-time augmented reality (AR). D2D technology enables a more direct communication connection, leading to improved network resource utilization and decreased delays commonly associated with data transfer through centralized servers. A comprehensive examination of D2D communication in 6G, emphasizing its capacity to mitigate network congestion and improve communication efficiency [1]. D2D communication has been highlighted as having the capacity to significantly enhance the efficiency of applications that require high data rates and little delay. This is accomplished by facilitating direct communication between devices. This capacity is highly important for applications in smart cities and the Internet of Things (IoT), where the efficient transfer of data in real-time is essential [2].

Wireless communication specifically pertains to the technical framework that enables the transfer of voice, data, and images and videos through mobile devices over wireless networks. Significant advancements have been made in digital technology from the first generation (1G) analogue systems to the current fifth generation (5G) networks [2]. Ongoing research is being carried out on the future sixth-generation (6G) data networks. The present part aims to concisely outline the evolution and importance of mobile wireless communication in the modern networked world. Significant modifications have been made to the predictions for mobile data traffic [2]. As of the end of 2023, the global mobile data traffic reached a monthly volume of around 125 Exabytes. Ericsson forecasts suggest that this figure will rise to 466 Exabytes per month by 2029. A significant factor driving the growth is the increasing prevalence of 5G technology, which is expected to account for almost 75% of the total mobile data traffic by 2029 [3]. The implementation of 6G technology is expected to profoundly revolutionize the wireless communication sector, providing unmatched enhancements in data transfer rates, latency, and network efficiency. One significant development anticipated with 6G is D2D communication, which allows devices to establish direct connections with each other without relying on a central network infrastructure to transmit data. This ability has the potential to alleviate network congestion, reduce latency, and enhance overall system efficiency.

2 6G Communication

The first wireless technology, termed First Generation (1G), was released in the 1980s. The system functioned on analogue signals and was primarily designed for voice communication services. Analysis of a Frequency Division Multiple Access (FDMA) analogue communication system. Velocities of around 2.4 kilobits per second. Insufficient capacity and coverage coupled with poor voice quality. Security constraints resulting from the lack of encryption. Initial Generation (1G) was revolutionary in its advent of mobile phones, but it had significant drawbacks such as inferior voice quality, limited coverage, and lack of data capabilities. The introduction of Second Generation (2G) networks in the 1990s marked the transition from analogue to digital communication. The primary 2G technologies employed were Global System for Mobile Communications (GSM) and Code Division Multiple Access (CDMA) [4].

The encryption of digital voice communication results in the attainment of superior sound quality and more robust security. A comprehensive examination of the technologies behind Short Message Service (SMS) and Multimedia Messaging Service (MMS). The installation of General Packet Radio Service (GPRS) enabled the attainment of data rates reaching up to 64 kbps. Utilizing the technologies of Time Division Multiple Access (TDMA) and CDMA. The use of two-generation (2G) technology significantly improved the quality of phone calls, facilitated essential data services like SMS, and laid the foundation for more advanced mobile applications. In the year 2000, Third Generation (3G) networks were designed with the explicit purpose of offering not just voice but also data services. This enabled the provision of mobile internet connectivity, video communication, and the use of multimedia capabilities. The data transfer rates range from 200 kbps to a few Mbps, being contingent upon the implementation, such as UMTS or HSPA [5]. The integration of packet switching with circuit switching greatly enhanced the transmission of data. Implemented enhanced security protocols and expanded network capabilities. Third generation (3G) technology revolutionized the growth of mobile internet by allowing the use of sophisticated applications such as mobile web browsing, video streaming, and the widespread adoption of smartphones [6].

By 2010, 4G networks represented notable progress in terms of speed, efficiency, and the variety of services enabled. Long-Term Evolution (LTE) is the prevailing 4G standard now in effect. The maximum speeds available for mobile customers are 100 Mbps, while stationary users can expect rates of 1 gigabit per second. A Voice over Internet Protocol (VoIP) network is a network in which voice services are transmitted over the Internet. Facilitation of high-definition mobile television, video conferencing, and online gaming programs. Enhanced security is achieved by the adoption of advanced encryption protocols. Fourth Generation (4G) technology transformed the mobile sector by enabling rapid internet access on mobile devices, leading to the extensive accessibility of streaming services, mobile applications, and Internet of Things (IoT) solutions [7].

Fifth generation (5G) networks in 2020 are designed to efficiently handle the growing need for rapidly available data, connectivity, and services with minimal latency. These technologies utilize higher frequency bands, like as millimeter waves, to achieve faster data transfer rates and support a larger number of networked devices. Maximum throughput speeds of 10 Gbps, coupled with an amazingly low latency of less than 1 ms. Implementing Massive MIMO (Multiple Input Multiple Output) and beamforming technology to enhance both the extent of coverage and the transmission capacity [8]. The implementation of a comprehensive IoT (Internet of Things) infrastructure with the capacity to connect millions of devices within a specific geographical region. A comprehensive analysis of Enhanced Mobile Broadband (eMBB), Ultra-Reliable Low-Latency Communication (URLLC), and Massive Machine Type Communication (mMTC) is presented in this work [10].

The introduction of 6G is anticipated to provide unmatched degrees of connectivity and intelligence, therefore enabling the advancement of innovative applications like as completely autonomous systems, technologically advanced robotics, and enhanced human-machine interaction. An examination of the shift from 1G to 6G demonstrates the rapid advancement in mobile wireless communication technologies [9]. Every subsequent generation has introduced new capabilities, greatly improving the capacity to communicate, access information, and interact with the external environment. Future developments in 6G networks are expected to broaden the boundaries of what can be accomplished, offering even more groundbreaking experiences in the domains of communication, automation, and artificial intelligence [11].

3 Evolution and Significance of D2D Communication

D2D communication signifies a notable change from conventional cellular networks, in which all communications are facilitated by base stations. In contrast to that, D2D communication facilitates direct data interchange between devices, therefore minimizing the transmission route and the resulting delays. The direct communication paradigm is especially beneficial for applications that need immediate data interchange, such as driverless vehicles, augmented reality (AR), and IoT architectures [12]. Leveraging D2D communication enables networks to attain increased throughput and superior dependability, both of which are crucial for the advanced capabilities promised by 6G. Figure 1 shows the communication between devices using D2D link.

D2D communication has numerous practical uses in several sectors, particularly in the context of services that utilize proximity, such as contactless payment systems. The ability to directly communicate between devices allows for the successful execution of transactions without depending on an intermediate network. In emergency situations, when the network infrastructure is potentially vulnerable, D2D communication can establish a direct connection between devices to facilitate coordination among emergency responders, therefore ensuring a more robust and reliable communication network. D2D communication is commonly used to transfer data, images, or other types of content between nearby hardware devices. Observations of these phenomena are common in applications such as Bluetooth file sharing. Local multiplayer gaming (LMM) is the utilization of D2D communication in gaming environments, namely on mobile devices, to facilitate multiplayer competition without the need for an internet connection [13].

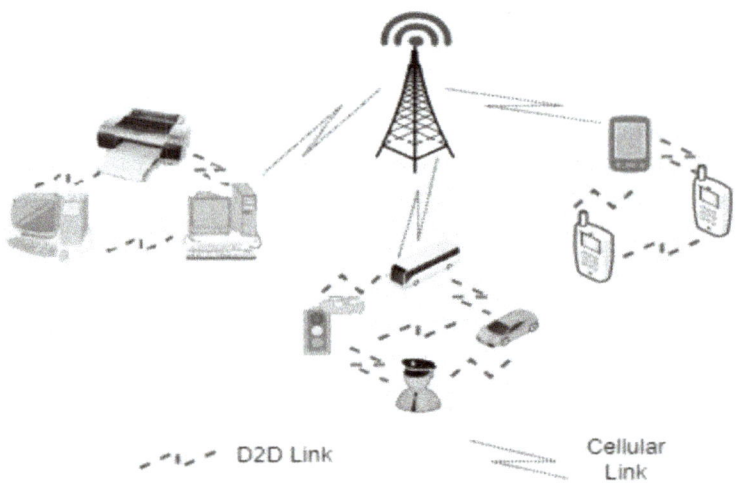

Fig. 1. D2D Communication between Cellular Devices

D2D communication can be utilized in sensor networks inside Internet of Things (IoT) applications. Connected devices set up with sensors can establish direct connectivity to share data or synchronize operations, independent of a central server. Vehicle-to-vehicle (V2V) communication can be defined as the wireless link established between automobiles within the automotive industry. Intelligent vehicles have the capability to create communication among themselves in order to communicate information pertaining to road conditions, traffic, and any potential hazards, therefore enhancing the overall safety of urban roadways. Within the domain of social networking, many applications utilize D2D communication to provide features like "bump" or "shake," which allow for the sharing of contact details or the creation of relationships with nearby users [14].

4 Role of Machine Learning in Enhancing D2D Communication

The application of ML in D2D communication is not an exemption to its emergence as a transformative tool in optimizing different elements of wireless communication. Machine learning approaches are being used more and more to tackle the intricate problems related to device-to-device communication, including but not limited to dynamic resource allocation, interference management, and network optimization [15]. ML revolutionizes D2D communication by facilitating enhanced network management that is more intelligent, adaptable, and efficient. Key functions of machine learning in device-to-device communication are:

4.1 Interference Management in Wireless Networks

Effective management of interference in D2D communication is essential for maximizing performance and guaranteeing optimal use of the radio spectrum. D2D communication involves direct communication between devices, without the need for a base station. This approach might result in interference, especially when several D2D pairings operate within the same frequency bandwidths. In order to address this problem, efficient interference management systems seek to coordinate the distribution of resources, modify transmission power levels, and implement interference avoidance techniques. This frequently entails sophisticated algorithms and protocols that dynamically distribute time, frequency, and spatial resources in order to reduce collisions and mitigate signal deterioration. Furthermore, interference management can utilize strategies such as power regulation, frequency reuse, and spatial segregation to improve the total network capacity and user satisfaction [16].

Over time, the reinforcement learning agents acquire the ability to strategically adjust these behaviors in order to reduce interference and enhance network utility, including throughput, energy efficiency, and quality of service (QoS). In contrast to conventional static methods, Reinforcement Learning (RL) can rapidly adjust to changing network conditions, such as fluctuations in traffic patterns, user mobility, and the emergence of new devices [17]. This feature renders Reinforcement Learning (RL) more efficient in intricate and ever-changing settings where traditional methods of managing interference may be inadequate. Furthermore, the progress made in deep reinforcement learning (DRL) enables these techniques to effectively handle interference in real-time and expand to vast networks, therefore presenting a highly attractive answer for upcoming wireless communication systems [18] (Table 1).

Table 1. ML Role in D2D communication

Aspects	ML Role	Techniques and Applications
Resource Allocation	Optimize allocation of spectrum, power, and time slots among D2D users	* Spectrum Allocation: Predict spectrum needs based on traffic and demand * Power Control: Dynamic adjustment to reduce interference * Time Slot Assignment: Efficient scheduling
Device Pairing & Mode Selection	Identify optimal device pairs for direct communication and switch modes between D2D and cellular	* Optimal Pairing: Based on proximity and channel conditions * Adaptive Mode Switching: Dynamic transition between D2D and cellular * Energy Efficiency: Power management
Security & Privacy	Enhance security and privacy by detecting anomalies and unauthorized access	* Anomaly Detection: Identify unusual patterns * Intrusion Detection: Signature-based and anomaly-based * Privacy Preservation: Context-aware encryption and access control
Energy Efficiency	Manage energy consumption by predicting behavior and optimizing power usage	* Predictive Energy Management: Based on user activity * Adaptive Power Control: Dynamic adjustment of transmission power * Low-Power State Management: Optimized sleep modes
Interference Management	Predict and mitigate interference through dynamic adjustment of communication parameters	* Interference Prediction: Using historical and real-time data * Reinforcement Learning: Power, frequency, and timing adjustments * Collaborative Interference Management

4.2 Resource Allocation

In D2D communication networks, ML has a substantial impact on the optimization of resource allocation. By applying machine learning techniques, the network can assess a significant number of data on traffic patterns, user mobility, and demand, hence permitting dynamic and effective allocation of resources [19]. Machine learning has the potential to enhance resource allocation in the following manner in this scenario.

Spectrum Allocation: The spectrum requirements of D2D users can be predicted by machine learning models by using historical data and present network conditions. By adopting dynamic spectrum allocation, the network may minimize interference and optimize the utilization of the current capacity.

Power Control: The utilization of environmental learning by machine learning models enables the optimization of power distribution for particular devices. This optimization ensures that transmissions are enough resilient to maintain a good quality of service (QoS) without causing unnecessary interruption to other users.

Time Slot Assignment: ML can be applied for anticipating traffic loads and user behavior, hence boosting the network's ability to assign time slots with more efficiency. The use of this strategy ensures that users with substantial data needs or critical services are prioritized, therefore improving the overall efficiency of the network [20].

Mobility Management: By analyzing user movement patterns, machine learning can forecast the timing of users moving from one cell to another and adjust resource allocation accordingly. Implementing this proactive allocation eliminates handover delays and provides a continuous QoS.

Congestion Control: ML algorithms have the power to discover timely signals of congestion and immediately redistribute resources to prevent possible bottlenecks. This promotes the maintenance of a smooth flow of communication and improves the overall user experience.

4.3 Device Pairing and Mode Selection

Implementing ML can greatly enhance the process of pairing and selecting modes in D2D communication, therefore promising optimal connectivity and performance for devices. How machine learning adds to these aspects is as follows:

Channel Conditions: Machine learning models can evaluate real-time channel state information (CSI) to identify the optimal device pairings for direct communication. By forecasting the pairings that will provide the most dependable and effective connections, the network can optimize the amount of data transmitted and reduce any undesirable interference.

Device Proximity: The proximity of devices is a crucial determinant in D2D communication. Machine learning can apply data obtained from sensors such as GPS, Wi-Fi, and Bluetooth to identify the devices in near proximity that can establish direct communication, therefore minimizing the requirement for intermediary nodes and conserving resources [21].

Network Load: The network load can be monitored by machine learning techniques to determine if a device should function in D2Dmode or revert to conventional cellular communication. During periods of high congestion in the cellular network, transitioning to D2D mode can displace traffic and decrease latency.

Adaptive Mode Switching: Adaptive mode switching refers to the ability of machine learning models to modify communication modes in real-time in response to analysis. For instance, when a device is gradually distancing itself from another device it is connected to, the machine learning model can trigger a transition back to the cellular network before the connection drops [22].

Energy Efficiency: Through the analysis of battery levels and energy consumption patterns, machine learning can ascertain the optimal timing for devices to utilize direct communication or through the base station, so enhancing both connectivity and power consumption.

Predictive Decision Making: Machine learning models have the capability to forecast forthcoming network circumstances and user activities, therefore enabling the network to take proactive decisions regarding device pairing and mode switching [23]. The ability to anticipate future events minimizes the necessity for reactive actions, resulting in less delay.

Context-Aware Communication: Machine Learning can take into account contextual information, such as the specific category of application being used (e.g., video streaming, voice calls), in order to make better-informed choices for pairing and mode selection, so improving the overall user experience.

4.4 Security and Privacy

ML is essential for enhancing the robustness and confidentiality of D2D interactions. Through the utilization of powerful machine learning methods, networks may actively identify, avoid, and reduce security risks, therefore guaranteeing the security and confidentiality of D2Dconnections. Machine learning improves security and privacy in this instance in the following manner:

Real-Time Monitoring: Continuous monitoring of D2D communication patterns using machine learning models enables the detection of any deviations from the established standard. Through acquiring knowledge about what is considered "normal" conduct, machine learning systems can identify irregularities that could suggest possible security risks, such as unlawful entry or atypical data transmission patterns [24].

Behavioral Analysis: Behavioral analysis refers to the application of machine learning techniques to examine the behavior of devices and users, identifying any activities that seem suspicious or unusual. When a device unexpectedly initiates communication with an atypical amount of new devices or accesses confidential data that it usually does not, the machine learning system can activate alarms to prompt further study.

Signature-Based Detection: Signature-based detection refers to the use of machine learning to improve conventional intrusion detection systems by consistently updating and improving their database of recognized attack signatures. Consequently, the IDS maintains its efficacy in countering both established and developing threats.

Anomaly-Based Detection: Anomaly-based detection refers to the implementation of anomaly-based intrusion detection by machine learning models, without the need for predefined signatures. Furthermore, it acquires knowledge from the actions of the network and is capable of detecting new threats by identifying patterns that deviate from established standards [25].

Real-Time Threat Identification: Machine learning enables intrusion detection systems to function in real-time, enabling the network to promptly react to threats as they materialize, rather than reactively. Immediate detection and response capacity are crucial for reducing the harm resulting from attacks.

Access Control: Access control refers to the application of machine learning techniques to implement flexible access control policies that adjust to various factors, including the user or device's location, time, and behavior. This feature guarantees that only devices with proper authorization are able to engage in D2D conversations, therefore minimizing the possibility of unwanted access.

User Authentication: Artificial intelligence (ML) can improve user authentication by integrating biometric data, behavioral patterns, or multi-factor authentication methods. Through acquiring knowledge of the standard authentication patterns, machine learning can identify and prevent attempts that diverge from the established norm, so guaranteeing that only authorized users are able to connect to the network.

Data Encryption Management: Data encryption management involves the use of machine learning to enhance encryption methods by evaluating the sensitivity of the transmitted data and making appropriate adjustments to encryption settings. This guarantees the safeguarding of confidential information without superfluous resource use.

Dynamic Protocol Selection: One use of machine learning is the dynamic selection and configuration of secure communication protocols, taking into account the existing threat landscape. For instance, in a high-risk setting, the machine learning system may choose for stronger encryption and authentication methods to guarantee secure communication [26].

4.5 Energy Efficiency

Applying ML techniques can greatly enhance the energy efficiency of D2D communication networks. Through the analysis and prediction of user behavior and communication patterns, machine learning algorithms have the capability to enhance the efficiency of energy usage throughout the network, resulting in extended battery life and more environmentally reliable operations. How machine learning enhances energy efficiency in D2Dnetworks:

User Behavior Prediction: User behavior prediction refers to the analysis of past data using machine learning models to forecast periods when users are expected to be active or inactive. Through the analysis of these patterns, the network can actively control energy consumption by lowering power levels or enabling devices to operate in low-power modes while not in use [27].

Communication Pattern Analysis: Machine learning can forecast the timing of communication between devices by acquiring knowledge of common communication patterns. Such enables the network to optimize the scheduling of communication activities, hence preventing superfluous power usage.

Sleep Mode Optimization: Machine Learning can ascertain the most advantageous moments for devices to transition into sleep or low-power states by analyzing projected periods of inactivity. Through precise forecasting of the periods when a device will no longer be required for communication, machine learning guarantees that devices save energy without affecting the performance of the communications network [28].

Traffic Offloading: In cases of network congestion, machine learning can chose to transfer traffic to devices that have more energy-efficient capabilities, therefore alleviating the burden on devices with lower battery levels and maximizing total energy efficiency.

Energy Harvesting Optimization: It refers to the application of ML to forecast energy availability and adapt device operation in networks where devices can collect energy from environmental sources, such as solar power. This optimization ensures the efficient utilization of captured energy [29].

Protocol Selection: Machine Learning can choose communication protocols that are specifically designed to maximize energy efficiency, taking into account the existing network conditions. For instance, machine learning may opt for a low-power protocol that operates during times of low network traffic, therefore preserving energy while ensuring uninterrupted connection.

5 Conclusion

There are several aspects that may be gained from using machine learning into 6G Device-to-Device communications. These advantages include better network optimization and resource management, as well as improved security and tailored user experiences. Further developments are anticipated to be driven by the combination between machine learning and direct-to-device communications, which will push the limits of what is feasible in next-generation networking. The incorporation of machine learning (ML) into 6G not only handles the difficulties linked to the increasing intricacy of networks but also creates new opportunities for sophisticated, effective, and user-focused communications.

References

1. Kuruvatti, N.P., Habibi, M.A., Partani, S., Han, B., Fellan, A., Schotten, H.D.: Empowering 6G communication systems with digital twin technology: a comprehensive survey. IEEE Access **10**, 112158–112186 (2022)

2. Masaracchia, A., Sharma, V., Canberk, B., Dobre, O.A., Duong, T.Q.: Duong. digital twin for 6G: taxonomy, research challenges, and the road ahead. IEEE Open J. Commun. Soc. **3**, 2137–2150 (2022)
3. Singh, M., Fuenmayor, E., Hinchy, E.P., Qiao, Y., Murray, N., Devine, D.: Digital twin: origin to future. Appl. Syst. Innov. **4**(2), 36 (2021)
4. Sharma, S., et al.: The role of 6G technologies in advancing smart city applications: opportunities and challenges. Sustainability **16**(16), 7039 (2024)
5. Arshad, Q.K.U.D., Kashif, A.U., Quershi, I.M.: A review on the evolution of cellular technologies. In: 16th International Bhurban Conference on Applied Sciences and Technology (IBCAST), pp. 989–993. IEEE (2019)
6. Botín-Sanabria, D.M., Mihaita, A.S., Peimbert-García, R.E., Ramírez-Moreno, M.A., Ramírez-Mendoza, R.A., Lozoya-Santos, J.D.: Digital twin technology challenges and applications: a comprehensive review. Remote Sens. **14**(6) 1335 (2022)
7. Tang, F., Chen, X., Rodrigues, T.K., Zhao, M., Kato, N.: Survey on digital twin edge networks (DITEN) toward 6G. IEEE Open J. Commun. Soc. **3**, 1360–1381 (2022)
8. Alam, M.Z., et al.: Investigation of cloud forensic incidents in cloud architecture for 6G networks. In: IEEE International Conference on Advanced Networks and Telecommunications Systems (ANTS), pp. 1–6 (2023)
9. Viswanathan, H., Mogensen, P.E.: Mogensen. communications in the 6G era. IEEE Access, 57063–57074 (2020)
10. Alsharif, M.H., Nordin, R.: Evolution towards fifth generation (5G) wireless networks: current trends and challenges in the deployment of millimetre wave, massive MIMO, and small cells. Telecommun. Syst. **64**(4), 617–637 (2017)
11. Lu, L., Li, G.Y., Swindlehurst, A.L., Ashikhmin, A., Zhang, R.: An overview of massive MIMO: benefits and Challenges. IEEE J. Select. Top. Signal Process. **8**(5), 742–758 (2014)
12. Siddiqui, S.T., et al.: Uncovering network vulnerabilities and conducting digital forensics analysis for IoT device security. In: 6G.IEEE International Conference on Advanced Networks and Telecommunications Systems (ANTS), pp. 1–6 (2023)
13. Liu, J., Kato, N., Ma, J., Kadowaki, N.: Device-to-device communication in LTE-advanced networks: a survey. IEEE Commun. Surv. Tutorials **17**(4), 1923–1940 (2014)
14. Ahmad, W., Ahmed, S., Ahmad, A., Siddiqui, S.T., Khamruddin, M., Khan, H.: Renewable energy efficiency of unmanned aerial vehicles operating with wireless sensor networks and mobile Ad Hoc networks. In: 2024 Second International Conference on Smart Technologies for Power and Renewable Energy (SPECon), pp. 1–6 (2024)
15. Ahmed, M., Li, Y., Waqas, M., Sheraz, M., Jin, D., Han, Z.: A survey on socially aware device-to-device communications. IEEE Commun. Surv. Tutorials **20**(3), 2169–2197 (2018)
16. Du, J., Jiang, C., Wang, J., Ren, Y., Debbah, M.: "Machine learning for 6G wireless networks: carrying forward enhanced bandwidth, massive access, and ultrareliable/low-latency service. IEEE Vehicular Technol. Mag. **15**,122–134 (2020)
17. Jabbari, A., Khan, H., Duraibi, S., Budhiraja, I., Gupta, S., Omar, M.: Energy maximization for wireless powered communication enabled IoT devices with NOMA underlaying solar powered UAV using federated reinforcement learning for 6G networks. IEEE Trans. Cons. Electr. (2024)
18. Gill, S.H., et al.: Security and privacy aspects of cloud computing: a smart campus case study. Intell. Autom. Soft Comput. **31**(1), 117–128 (2022)
19. Budhiraja, I., Kumar, N., Tyagi, S., Tanwar, S., Guizani, M.: An energy-efficient resource allocation scheme for SWIPT-NOMA based femtocells users with imperfect CSI. IEEE Trans. Veh. Technol. **69**, 7790–7805 (2020)
20. Iqbal, A., Nauman, A., Hussain, R., Bilal, M.: Cognitive D2D communication: a comprehensive survey, research challenges, and future directions. Internet of Things, 100961 (2023)

21. Driouech, S., Sabir, E., Ghogho, M., Amhoud, E.M.: D2D mobile relaying meets NOMA—part II: a reinforcement learning perspective. Sensors **21**(5), 1755 (2021)
22. Ahmad, I., et al.: Machine learning meets communication networks: current trends and future challenges. IEEE Access **8**, 223418–223460 (2020)
23. Usama, M., et al.: Unsupervised machine learning for networking: techniques applications and research challenges. IEEE Access **7**, 65579–65615 (2019)
24. Kato, N., Mao, B., Tang, F., Kawamoto, Y., Liu, J.: Ten challenges in advancing machine learning technologies toward 6G. IEEE Wirel. Commun. **27**, 96–103 (2020)
25. Tang, F., Kawamoto, Y., Kato, N., Liu, J.: Future intelligent and secure vehicular network toward 6G: Machine-learning approaches. Proc. IEEE **108**, 292–307 (2019)
26. Sun, Y., Liu, J., Wang, J., Cao, Y., Kato, N.: When machine learning meets privacy in 6G: a survey. IEEE Commun. Surv. Tutorials **22**, 2694–2724 (2020)
27. Hossain, M.A., Hossain, A.R., Ansari, N.: AI in 6G: energy-efficient distributed machine learning for multilayer heterogeneous networks. IEEE Netw. **36**, 84–91 (2022)
28. Huang, X., Zhang, K., Wu, F., Leng, S.: Collaborative machine learning for energy-efficient edge networks in 6G. IEEE Netw. **35**, 12–19 (2021)
29. Sodhro, A.H., et al.: Toward ML-based energy-efficient mechanism for 6G enabled industrial network in box systems. IEEE Trans. Ind. Inf. **17**, 7185–7192 (2020)

Enhancing Agricultural Decision-Making Using Machine Learning: Variety Selection and Yield Prediction for Agriculture Culture Improvement

Shrikant Upadhyay[1](✉), N. Indumathi[2], M. Balamurugan[3], Binod Kumar[4], Sampurna Mandal[5], and Sidharth Prakash[6]

[1] Department of Electronics and Communication Engineering, MLR Institute of Technology, Hyderabad 500043, India
`shrikant.upadhay@mlrit.ac.in`
[2] Department of Computer Science and Engineering, Rajalakshmi Institute of Technology, Chennai, India
`indumathi.n@ritchennai.edu.in`
[3] Department of Computer Science and Engineering, Sri Sairam Engineering College, Chennai, India
`balamurugan.cse@sairam.edu.in`
[4] Faculty of CSE & IT, Jharkhand Rai University, Ranchi, Jharkhand, India
[5] Department of Computer Science and Engineering-Artificial Intelligence, Brainware University, Kolkata, India
[6] Director of Swarnrekha Group of Institutions (SGi), Ranchi, Jharkhand, India

Abstract. Agriculture is the foundation of many economies, including India's, providing livelihoods, and making a substantial contribution to GDP. On the other hand, selecting crops and projecting yields might be difficult tasks for the younger generation joining the farming industry. Regression and classification algorithms are used in a unique way to forecast yields and suggest crop varieties in order to solve this pressing issue. A detailed analysis of many machine learning algorithms, such as RNN, XGBoost Classifier, KNN, Random Forest, Linear Regression, and Deep Q Network, showed that RNN was more accurate in forecasting ideal harvests. The outcomes demonstrate the effectiveness of the suggested deep learning and machine learning algorithms, offering a comprehensive evaluation using measures including entropy calculation, accuracy, recall, F1 score, sensitivity, and specificity. The suggested method relieves farmers of some of the load by precisely predicting yields for a variety of crops grown in India, giving them the confidence to handle the challenges of agriculture. This creative approach helps control price swings and minimize losses while also enabling the farming community, particularly the younger generation, to make wise decisions that will eventually support the agricultural sector's long-term expansion.

Keywords: Machine learning algorithms · KNN · RNN · XGBoost classifier · deep Q network

1 Introduction

In economically agricultural nations like India, particularly in states like agriculture in India is the main source of income and has a significant influence on the country's economic structure. But one of the biggest issues facing the younger generation of farmers is that they need to make educated decisions about which crops to plant and how much output they expect. Agriculture is the backbone of India which covers almost 72% land for farming that provides 360.12 million metric tons of different food grains productivity. Crop yield relies on different complex components which includes landscapes, harvesting, strategy, climatic condition, wates accessibility, soil etc. [1, 2]. The coverage of land areas with respect to other available resources is depicted in Fig. 1.

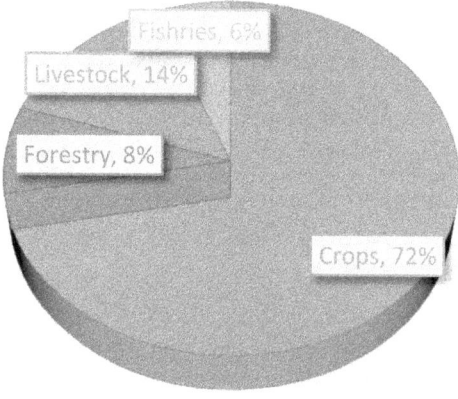

Fig. 1. Coverage area for different profession

AI and ML proved to be one of the effective tool to increase the yield where various algorithms of AI and ML like random forest, gradient boost etc., may be used to train biological nature to improve the level of yield. Predictive algo like KNN, GB regression, k-nearest can be used in crop yield forecasting. The decision making for the proper crop yield relies on various factors which includes water availability, soil quality, moisture, genotype etc. [3]. Parallelly few resources like fertilizers, land, money etc., are utilized to achieve higher yield, and to increase the production various leading-edge technologies like AI and ML has been attached to take of it. Biophysical properties can be easily learned by using ML technique that includes random forest, gradient boost etc., that will help to identify the various drawbacks of plants in term of disease detection, growth, seed analysis and helps to take prior decision.

2 Related Work

The current investigation involved an in-depth examination of various studies focusing on machine learning applications for predicting crop production through a systematic literature review (SLR). From the selected subset of 50 studies, critical factors such as soil type, rainfall patterns, and temperature variations were identified. Among the various techniques employed, Artificial Neural Networks emerged as the predominant method. In a subsequent exploration specifically targeting deep learning, many publications were scrutinized, revealing Convolutional Neural Networks (CNN) as the most prevalent approach. Furthermore, Deep Neural Networks (DNN) and Long-Short Term Memory (LSTM) were also observed to be widely utilized. This comprehensive analysis not only informs crop selection and growing-season management strategies but also furnishes valuable insights for agricultural decision-making. Future inquiries may delve into integrating these findings to enhance the accuracy of crop yield forecasts. Drawbacks in the Existing System:

1. The limited variety of algorithms might impede innovation and robustness. Overemphasis on primary features could overlook emerging influential factors.
2. Relying solely on historical data may result in outdated predictions. The intricacy of deep learning models may hinder their interpretability and adoption.

The property of soil has been compared using various models and algorithms using learning model, triangular basis, hard limit to take out the various important feature considering village wise fertility soil [4]. Cubist regression along with learning model and considering 523 samples of soil has been analysed using ELM model as mentioned by the author for pH and soil organic [5]. The moisture is also one of the crucial parameters that has been taken into consideration with 140 set samples for the estimation of organic nitrogen, moisture ration, nitrogen using SVM algorithm [6]. Temperature of soil using ANN model with various samples in a depth of 10–100 cm which achieved CR of 0.9084—0.9893 [7]. Method utilizes for crops selection is used to increase crop yield using ML is discussed and proposed a system to handle the situation of crop selection. Long-term and short-term planning approach for a sugarcane and wheat crop considered by them to decide the yield rate [8, 9]. Feature dependent structure based on neural network is proposed by an author for weather forecasting which is very crucial for crop growth [10]. Naïve Bayes approach is discussed by one of the authors for better crop yield which also effectively identify numerous crops effectively like sow, seeds, harvest, and plant growth [11]. One the author applies k-bunching approach to identify the framework of water accurately and achieve 77% of accuracy [12]. Prediction of crop's performance was discussed using various emerging technologies to predict and understand the various environmental factor that will help to boost the productivity. The proposed system is based on IoT and smartphone applications to measure the various parameters. Here, authors develop app based on Android to get an alert connected to hardware through IoT to check the status of field

3 Algorithms Utilization

KNN is simple to understand and apply, but it could be sensitive to features that are pointless or repetitious [13]. Complete algorithms utilization is discussed in the steps for the overall execution of the system. Complete functioning of the system involves the following steps as discussed below:

3.1 XGBoost Classifier

XGBoost, also known as Extreme Gradient Boosting, is a powerful machine learning method that has achieved remarkable results in regression and classification applications. It is an ensemble model that, typically using decision trees, additively aggregates the predictions of multiple weak learners. XGBoost uses a combination of regularization, tree pruning, and parallel processing techniques to maximize model correctness and efficiency [14].

3.2 Deep Q Network

Q-learning and deep neural networks are combined in are reinforcement learning method known as Deep Q Network. It is used to instruct agents on how to make decisions in situations with different action spaces. DQN employs a neural network to estimate the Q-function, which is the expected future rewards for a certain action taken in a particular state. Consequently, the agent can find the optimal rules by employing exploration and exploitation strategies [15] and the comparison of different module is depicted in Fig. 2 below.

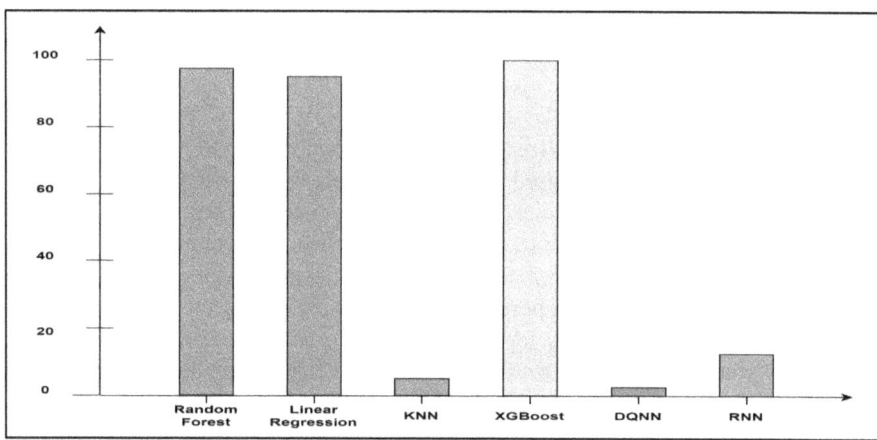

Fig. 2. Comparison of modules

3.3 Random Forest

It can be utilized to classify the crops and supervised to improve the precision rate learned at the duration of teaching. It will be quite useful at the time of crop selection. Such type of supervision also possible in image data also [16].

3.4 Linear Regression

Variable parameters are one the major issues that must be taken care and using this temperature, moisture, rainfall etc. can easily be handled in term of prediction rate.

3.5 KNN

Accuracy can easily be improved using new updated data gathered from different sources and make the calculation easy at different level of prediction [17].

3.6 RNN

Plant breeding can be monitored using this method as plant require different condition, soil, environment etc., and that can be capture all the changes and this will help to increase the crop yield [18].

The proposed architecture is shown in Fig. 3 which consist of various section started from entering into the application till final outcome.

4 Proposed System and Architecture

Advanced supervised machine learning algorithms, complete dataset analysis, variable identification, and missing value treatments are all part of the proposed solution for agriculture in Tamil Nadu. Utilizing a variety of classification and regression methods, such as RNN, KNN, XGBoost Classifier, Random Forest, Linear Regression, and Deep Q Network, the system provides highly accurate yield predictions and crop type recommendations. The system offers a comprehensive assessment through extensive metric assessments, including entropy, accuracy, recall, F1 score, sensitivity, and specificity. By enabling educated decision-making, lowering losses, controlling price volatility, and promoting sustainable growth in agricultural industry, this creative approach empowers the younger generation in farming.

The problem outlined here revolves around the challenge of optimizing crop production in the agriculture industry. With the increasing demand for agricultural products due to commercialization, farmers face pressure to maximize crop yield. However, achieving optimal yield s requires precise understanding of various factors such as soil type, nutrient levels, climatic conditions, and crop characteristics. Currently, farmers often lack the necessary tools to accurately determine these requirements, leading to potential losses. This also reflect the end-to-end method to process the gathered data.

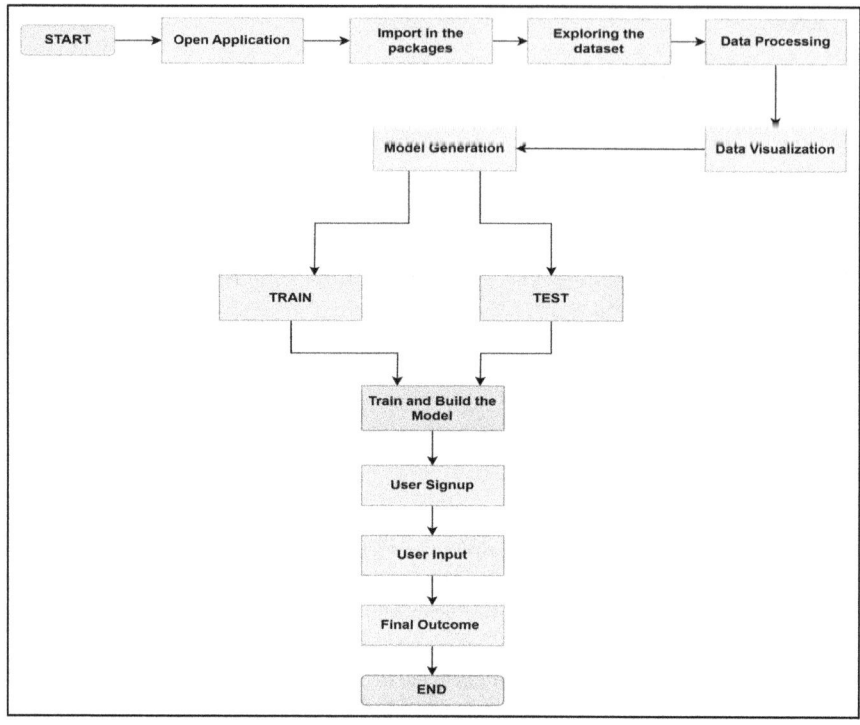

Fig. 3. Proposed architecture

Data entry into the system will be done using the data exploration module in following steps:

4.1 Handling

Using this module, we will read the data for processing.

4.2 Data Splitting into Train and Test

The data will be divided into train and test using this module.

4.3 Model Development

KNN, XGBoost Classifier, RNN, Random Forest, Linear Regression, and Deep Q Network are the models that are constructed.

4.4 User Sign-Up and Login

Loging and registration are required to use this module. User opinions using this module will supply data for predicting.

4.5 Forecast

The final forecast is shown in display unit.

5 Experimental Results

These models will improve over time with continuous observation and feedback loops, ensuring their applicability in the dynamic field of agriculture. A thorough examination of these variables and a precise evaluation of the performance of the ML models may provide stakeholders with important information about the reliability and effectiveness of the crop production prediction and recommendation system. The sign-up page and homepage is shown in Fig. 4 and Fig. 5 below for crop selection.

Fig. 4. Sign in page for user

Fig. 5. Homepage of proposed system (selecting crop recommendations)

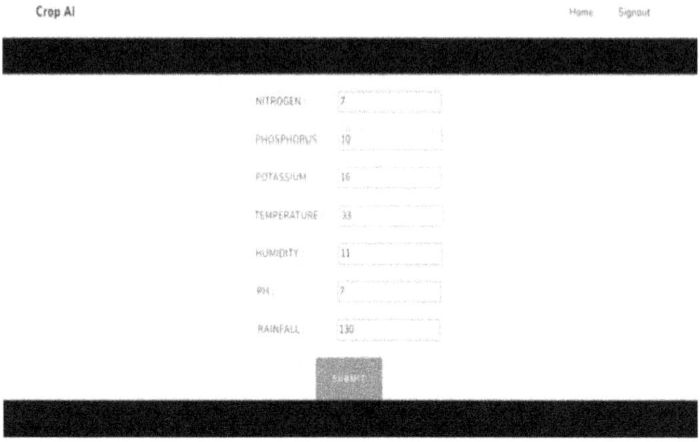

Fig. 6. Home page of crop recommendations

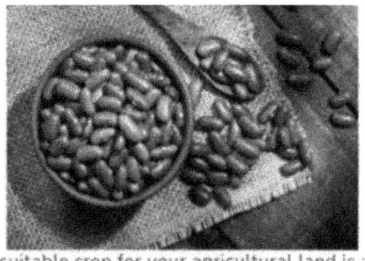

suitable crop for your agricultural land is :
kidneybeans

Major Red Kidney Beans Grown States in India are Maharashtra, Jammu and Kashmir, Himachal Pradesh, Uttarakhand, West Bengal, Uttar Pradesh, Tamil Nadu, Kerala and Karnataka. This crop grows well in tropical and temperate areas receiving 60 to 150 cm of rainfall annually.

Fig. 7. Result page of crop recommendations

Fig. 8. Home page of proposed system (selecting yield prediction)

Enhancing Agricultural Decision-Making Using Machine Learning   149

The homepage for crop recommendation is shown in Fig. 6, and the result obtained from is shown in Fig. 7. The home page of the proposed system is shown in Fig. 8 for selecting yield prediction.

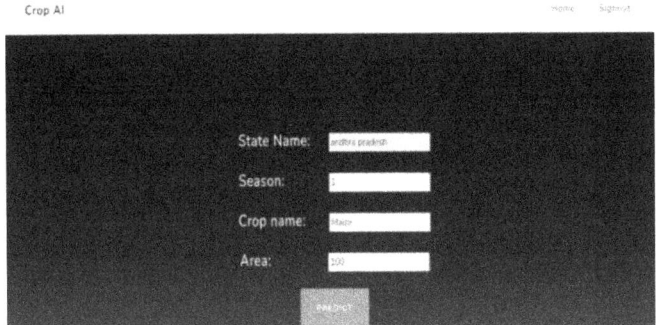

Fig. 9. Home page of yield prediction

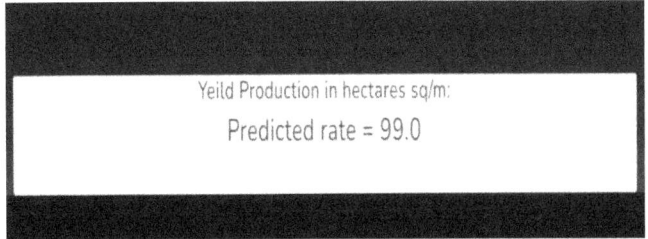

Fig. 10. Result page of yield predictions

The prediction of yield is shown in Fig. 9 and the result achieved in form of prediction is shown in Fig. 10. The estimation obtained for yield is shown in Table 1 and the for the classification is shown in Table 2.

Table 1. Estimation using ML for yield

Algorithms	F1-score	Accuracy (%) yield	Precision
K-nearest	0.82	76.12	0.78
Random forest	0.95	79.29	0.83
SVM	0.97	94.23	0.97
GB Regression	0.84	88.62	0.88

Table 2. Estimation using ML for classification

Algorithms	F1-score	Accuracy (%) yield	Precision
K-nearest	0.78	81.23	0.77
Random forest	0.93	84.58	0.86
SVM	0.98	98.12	0.98
GB Regression	0.81	87.57	0.85

The uniqueness of the proposed solution lies in employing a diverse set of machine learning models including Random Forest, Linear Regression, K-Nearest Neighbors (KNN), XGBoost Classifier, Deep Q Network, and Recurrent Neural Networks (RNN), the system harnesses the strengths of various algorithms to analyze complex agricultural data. Among the machine learning models used, SVM stands out as the top performer, achieving an impressive accuracy of 97% close to the random forest with 95%. Overall, the combination of a multi-model approach, high accuracy, comprehensive analysis, scalability, and real-time decision support makes the proposed crop yield recommendation and prediction system a valuable tool for modern agriculture. By harnessing the power of machine learning, the system empowers farmers to make data-driven decisions that enhance crop yields, profitability, and sustainability.

6 Conclusion

The use of regression and classification algorithms to overcome the obstacles faced by the younger generation in India who are pursuing careers in agriculture is a novel and significant approach. The use of supervised machine learning approaches, which involve thorough dataset analysis and algorithmic comparisons, has demonstrated encouraging outcomes in terms of crop type recommendations and yield prediction.

It is evident from the rigorous assessment methods used that machine learning and deep learning algorithms like RNN, XGBoost Classifier, KNN, RNN, Random Forest, and Linear Regression are superior at reliably forecasting optimal harvests. The proposed approach ensures a thorough assessment that gives farmers reliable information, taking into account entropy calculation, accuracy, recall, F1 score, sensitivity, and specificity, among other factors. This innovative approach not only reduces losses and manages market fluctuations well, but it also greatly increases trust in the agricultural community, particularly among the younger generation of farmers. By encouraging agricultural growth that is sustainable and enabling well-informed decision-making, the system fortifies the basis of the economy. The potential for revolutionizing agriculture through the integration of machine learning into conventional farming techniques is evident in the positive impacts on livelihoods, GDP contribution, and the overall resilience of the agricultural ecosystem.

Disclosure of Interests. Authors have no competing interests.

References

1. Kumar, R., Singh, M.P., Kumar, P., Singh, J.P.: Crop selection method to maximize crop yield rate using machine learning technique. In: Proceedings of the 2015 International Conference on Smart Technologies and Management for Computing, Communication, Controls, Energy and Materials (ICSTM), pp. 138–145. Avadi, India (2015). https://doi.org/10.1109/ICSTM.2015.7225403
2. Chandrasekaran, P., et al.: Agricultural yield prediction model using machine learning algorithms. Int. J. Pure Appl. Math. **119**(16), 1257–1265 (2018)
3. Mariammal, G., Suruliandi, A., Raja, S.P., Poongothai, E.: Prediction of land suitability for crop cultivation based on soil and environmental characteristics using modified recursive feature elimination technique with various classifiers. IEEE Trans. Comput. Soc. Syst. **8**(5), 1132–1142 (2021)
4. Suchithra, M.S., Pai, M.L.: Improving the prediction accuracy of soil nutrient classification by optimizing extreme learning machine parameters. Inf. Process. Agric. **7**(1), 72–82 (2019)
5. Yang, M., Xu, D., Chen, S., Li, H., Shi, Z.: Evaluation of machine learning approaches to predict soil organic matter and pH using vis-NIR spectra. Sens. (Switzerland) **19**(2), 263–277 (2019). https://doi.org/10.3390/s19020263
6. Morellos, A., et al.: Machine learning based prediction of soil total nitrogen, organic carbon, and moisture content by using VIS-NIR spectroscopy. Biosys. Eng. **152**, 104–116 (2016). https://doi.org/10.1016/j.biosystemseng.2016.04.018
7. Nahvi, B., Habibi, J., Mohammadi, K., Shamshirband, S., Saleh Al Razgan, O.: Using self-adaptive evolutionary algorithm to improve the performance of an extreme learning machine for estimating soil temperature. Comput. Electr. Agric. **124**, 168–1699, (2016). https://doi.org/10.1016/j.compag.2016.03.025
8. Whitmire, C.D., Vance, J.M., Rasheed, H.K., Missaoui, A., Rasheed, K.M., Maier, F.W.: Using machine learning and feature selection for Alfalfa yield prediction. AI, **2**(1), 71–88 (2021). https://doi.org/10.3390/ai2010006
9. Kaur, K.: Machine learning: applications in Indian agriculture. Int. J. Adv. Res. Comput. Commun. Eng. **5**(4), 342–344 (2016)
10. Kumar, K.K., Kumar, K.R., Ashrit, R.G., Deshpande, N.R., Hansen, J.W.: Climate impacts on Indian agriculture. Int. J. Climatol. **24**(11), 1375–1393 (2004). https://doi.org/10.1002/joc.1081
11. Verma, A., Jatain, A., Bajaj, S.: Crop yield prediction of wheat using fuzzy c-means clustering and neural network. Int. J. Appl. Eng. Res. **13**(11), 9816–9821 (2018)
12. Hemageetha, N.: A survey on application of data mining techniques to analyze the soil for agricultural purpose. In: Proceedings of the 2016 3rd International Conference on Computing for Sustainable Global Development (INDIACom), pp. 3112–3117 (2016)
13. Upadhyay, S., Kumar, M., Upadhyay, A.: Digital image identification and verification using maximum and preliminary score approach with watermarking for security enhancement and validation. J. Electron. **12**(7), 1–15 (2023)
14. Luo, H., et al.: Combinations of feature selection and machine learning algorithms for object-oriented betel palms and mango plantations classification based on Gaofen-2 imagery. Remote Sens. **14**(7) (2022). https://doi.org/10.3390/rs14071757
15. Kavitha, P., Manivannan, K.: Comparison of machine learning algorithms for crop yield prediction. Int. J. Pure Appl. Math. **121**(12), 2563–2573 (2019)
16. Upadhyay, A., Sharma, S.K., Upadhyay, S.: Robust feature extraction using embedded HMM for face identification & verification. Int. J. Appl. Eng. Res. **12**(24), 15729–15777 (2017)

17. Saranya, K., et al.: Crop yield prediction using machine learning techniques: a survey. Int. J. Adv. Trends Comput. Sci. Eng. **9**(3), 1567–1574 (2020)
18. Sharma, A., Jain, A., Gupta, P., Chowdary, V.: Machine learning applications for precision agriculture: a comprehensive review. IEEE Access **9**, 4843–4873 (2021). https://doi.org/10.1109/ACCESS.2020.3048415

A Study of Forecasting Mobile Phone Booking Cancellation on Different E- Commerce Websites Using Machine Learning Algorithms

Khushboo Singh[1]([✉]) , Abhishek Kumar[1] , Ravi Kumar Burman[1] ,
Pravir Kumar[2], and Alok Kumar Singh[3]

[1] Computer Science and Engineering, Jharkhand University of Technology, Ranchi, India
khushboo14esnex05@gmail.com
[2] Project Engineering & Management, Jharkhand University of Technology, Ranchi, India
[3] Electronics & Communication Engineering, Cambridge Institute of Technology, Ranchi, India
aksingh.ece@citranchi.ac.in

Abstract. In the rapidly evolving world of e-commerce, predicting mobile phone booking cancellations is vital for optimizing customer satisfaction and operational efficiency. This study explores the use of machine learning algorithms, specifically Support Vector Machines (SVM) and Logistic Regression (LR), to forecast booking cancellations on various e-commerce platforms. Historical data comprising customer demographics, booking details, and transactional behaviors are analyzed to identify factors influencing cancellations. The models are trained and examined using metrics like precision, accuracy, recall, and F1-score to confirm robust performance. Results demonstrate that both SVM and LR can effectively predict cancellations, with SVM showing slightly better performance in terms of precision. The findings indicate that leveraging predictive analytics can assist e-commerce platforms in preemptively managing resources, reducing cancellation rates, and improving overall customer retention. Future research could explore integrating more advanced algorithms and additional features for enhanced accuracy.

Keywords: Forecasting · Booking Cancellations · Mobile Phones · E-commerce Websites · Machine Learning · Predictive Analytics · Cancellation · Prediction · Data Analysis · Algorithm Development

1 Introduction

The rise in mobile phone bookings on e-commerce platforms has led to increased cancellations, causing financial losses and inventory disruptions. To optimize inventory, improve customer satisfaction, and boost revenue, a study aims to use machine learning algorithms like Support Vector Machines and Logistic Regression to develop predictive models for better decision-making. The SVM is highly preferable algorithm for both linear and Non linear categorizing and reversion mechanism. In the ever-changing world of online shopping, anticipating and comprehending consumer behavior, particularly in terms of product cancellations, is crucial for optimizing inventory management, enhancing customer satisfaction, and maximizing revenue. Mobile phones, being one of the most sought-after products, are subject to significant cancellation rates, posing challenges for e-commerce platforms.

This study is to introduce a novel approach to predict mobile phone booking cancellations across different e commerce websites utilizing the Machine Learning Algorithms. Forecasting mobile phone booking cancellations using machine learning models represents a significant opportunity for e-commerce platforms to enhance operational efficiency and customer satisfaction. By leveraging advanced analytics and predictive algorithms, businesses can gain actionable insights into customer behavior, anticipate cancellations, and make informed decisions to optimize their operations [1]. As e-commerce continues to evolve, integrating ML-driven forecasting capabilities will become increasingly essential for staying competitive in the digital marketplace. These days, it is crucial for customers to be able to return or cancel orders, especially for mobile phones. Most firms want to be able to predict user behavior and take appropriate action afterward. Put otherwise, anticipating when a consumer may decide to cancel or return a purchase for a mobile phone entails improving the sales experience for that customer and making sure they don't do so [2].

Order cancellation is a significant issue for businesses, with 30% online orders being returned, as compared to the 8.89% in brick & mortar stores. This accounts for nearly a third of lost revenue. Additionally, 40% of subscribers cancel within three months, and over half do so within six months. The root cause is customer dissatisfaction. The term "order cancellation" describes the withdrawal of all goods and services from the intended market, including returns of goods that have already been bought [3]. The main cause is customer dissatisfaction, which can stem from various reasons such as product/service issues, communication gap etc. To avoid order cancellation, businesses must understand the contexts and causes of customer dissatisfaction. Mobile Phone Order cancellations are often caused by customers experiencing dissatisfaction and unhappiness. Common causes include longer deliveries, no delivery date, unexpected shipping costs, high shipping costs, over-purchasing, and loss of interest or need. Longer deliveries lead to 38% of online shoppers canceling their orders, while no delivery date leaves customers in the dark. High shipping costs lead to 63% of shoppers abandoning orders, leading to competitors offering similar products or services at lower shipping. Sometimes over purchasing and loss of interest can occur among physical or digital subscriptions, such as hobby items and food deliveries. Transparency is crucial in addressing these issues. Order cancellation rate is the percentage of customers who cancel ecommerce orders before or after delivery. It is most common during the cart abandonment and product return phases. Shopping cart abandonment occurs when customers leave their purchase without checking out due to high shipping prices or negative experiences. Post-order and pre-delivery cancellation occurs after ordering but before delivery due to buyer remorse or delivery delays. Product returns occur during the return phase when customers return products due to defects, damage, or functionality issues. This information helps businesses understand their product's appeal to specific customers [4].

1.1 The Causes of Mobile Phone Order Cancellation

Mobile Phone Order cancellations are often caused by customers experiencing dissatisfaction and unhappiness. Common causes include longer deliveries, no delivery date, unexpected shipping costs, high shipping costs, over-purchasing, and loss of interest or need. Longer deliveries lead to 38% of online shoppers cancelling their orders, while no delivery date leaves customers in the dark. High shipping costs lead to 63% of shoppers abandoning orders, leading to competitors offering similar products or services at lower or no-cost shipping. Over-purchasing and loss of interest can occur among physical or digital subscriptions, such as hobby items and food deliveries. Transparency is crucial in addressing these issues.

1.2 Factors of Cancellation

- Duplicate Order
- Poor Customer Service Experience
- Shipping Delays
- Over-purchasing
- Ordered by Mistake
- Loss of interest or need
- Better Alternatives
- High Shipping Costs

1.3 The Order Cancellation Rate

Order cancellation rate is the percentage of customers who cancel ecommerce orders before or after delivery. It is most common during the cart abandonment and product return phases. Shopping cart abandonment occurs when customers leave their purchase without checking out due to high shipping prices or negative experiences. Post-order and pre-delivery cancellation occurs after ordering but before delivery due to buyer remorse or delivery delays. Product returns occur during the return phase when customers return products due to defects, damage, or functionality issues. This information helps businesses understand their product's appeal to specific customers.

2 Literature Review

This study explores the use of machine learning techniques to predict order cancellations and their contributing variables in the retail industry. Using transaction data, the study proposes a model using the Random Forest method, which has the highest accuracy (86%), F1 Score (88%), and performance (86%). This approach can help businesses better manage inventories and client behavior. The study compares various machine learning methods, including SVM, XGBoost, ANN, Logistic Regression, Random Forest, and adjusted Random Forest. The RF algorithm performed the best with an 88% F1-Score value and an 86% accuracy ratio. The study suggests that accurate cancellation prediction can enhance customer loyalty and satisfaction, benefiting the entire sector. Future research should be conducted across all industries, as anticipating consumer behavior is crucial for enhancing sales interactions and maintaining client loyalty. Revenue management (RM) deals with demand-management choices to increase business revenues. Name of Passenger Models for anticipating cancellation rates based on record data mining handle no-show situations. Various characteristics related to cancellation behaviour at different stages of booking are displayed in real- world datasets. This assesses the effectiveness of cutting-edge data mining techniques and aids revenue managers in understanding the factors that lead to cancellations. The various factors impacting the risk of cancellation make it difficult to forecast cancellations within the booking horizon. Revenue managers can have a better understanding of cancellation drivers by comprehending these dynamics. Many models that may be applicable to various time-dependent forecasting problems in transportation, econometrics, and demography, can be developed to address this at varying booking horizon phases. More insights might be obtained by combining time-dependency into a single model [5].

This paper proposes a method to predict the cancellation of hotel booking using 13 different independent variables. The ML techniques and ANN, optimized with the genetic algorithms, achieve the cancellation rate 98%. This approach helps identify potential cancellations and strengthens action protocols for tourist arrivals. This research proposes a method to predict the cancellation of hotel booking using ANN. The primary theoretical contribution is to clarify the usefulness of PNR data in predicting specific hotel cancellations, with the conclusion that the findings are consistent with earlier studies. The proposed methodology employs genetic algorithms and created ANN model and achieved 98% accuracy with only the independent variables 13. The primary practical contribution is the methodology suggested which enables high-accuracy forecasting of hotel cancellations using readily available characteristics for hotels. Subsequent studies can examine the same methodology's testing on additional PNR datasets that have distinct attributes, like region, climate, hotel grade, rates, market niche, distribution routes, and cancellation policies. It is possible to incorporate other variables from outside sources, like economic indices of the nations of origin or weather forecasts. Nonetheless, one of the suggested methodology's drawbacks is that the model was unable to initially account for sudden changes in the market. To get better results, future research might also examine testing the methodology on various PNR databases with varied attributes. Order cancellation information is acquired from an unaffiliated internet merchant. The organization of system model is briefly explained in this paper. The data is synchronized earlier. The following algorithms are then applied to the preprocessed data: XGBoost, RF, LR, SVM, ANN, tuned_RF, tuned_LR, and tuned the XGBoost. At last, it generates briefly explained model with the accuracy and F1 Score values for the classes that are marked as cancelled or returned as 1 and not returned as 0 [6].

Hotels face challenges in demand management due to cancellations, which can affect income. Models can forecast cancellations with over 90% accuracy, allowing hotel managers to improve cancellation procedures, overbooking strategies, and pricing and inventory allocation. A study using data science and PMS information from four hotels found that machine learning, data analytics, and visualization were sufficient for creating strong prediction models. These models can reduce overbooking and revenue loss, allowing for flexible cancellation procedures and higher sales. However, concerns remain about model performance and the feasibility of obtaining similar results from other databases. In the hospitality sector, cancellations of reservations not only result in the lost income & influence decisions about pricing & the inventory distribution, but they may also, in cases of overbooking, negatively impact the hotel's social media and internet reputation. Using data sets from the four resort hotels & also approaching this challenge as a categorization hurdle within the context of the data science, the researchers show that this is feasible to develop models that anticipate cancellations of bookings with over 90% correctness. Additionally, this study shows that, contrary to what Morales & Wang (2010) claimed, this is possible to anticipate with great accuracy if a reservation will be cancelled. The findings give hotel managers the opportunity to better anticipate net demand, respond to reservations with a high likelihood of cancellation and minimize related revenue losses, enhance overbooking and cancellation policies, & also implement more aggressive pricing & the inventory allocation plans [7].

This study uses data mining technologies to create a customer-cancellation prediction model using GRNN and BPN. This model improves prediction accuracy and assists in service capacity scheduling. By predicting cancellations, businesses can reduce wait times and improve service quality. Traditional methods can lead to overcapacity and resource waste. The models support dynamic service capacity scheduling and help managers anticipate cancellations, reducing wait times and preventing surpluses or insufficient capacity. A machine learning prototype system was developed to reduce hotel reservation cancellations. The system computes net demand and forecasts cancellations based on hotel data. Tested at two hotels, it showed a lower cancellation rate for contacted bookings than non-contacted bookings. The study suggests that more investigation is needed to improve model accuracy. The system uses dataset splitting and feature engineering, and emphasizes the need for domain knowledge. The system can be automated using Hadoop or Spark clusters running R Server. Contacting guests who are likely to cancel less can help reduce cancellation rates at controlled costs. Future research could include additional data sources to improve model accuracy. This study presents three models for hotel booking cancellation prediction: logistic regression, k-Nearest Neighbour, and CatBoost. CatBoost is the most efficient, accurate, and economical model, with the highest accuracy score and predictions. The study aims to enhance hotel revenue and resource management effectiveness by leveraging demand information for hotel bookings. To improve accuracy, hotels need to gather more guest data and set cancellation policies [8].

A prototype using machine learning techniques was developed to predict hotel reservation cancellations, enhancing decision-making and reducing cancellations by 37 percentage points. The system, which used R, Hadoop, and Linux, was built using open-source tools. The study highlights the importance of domain expertise and data-splitting methods in engineering and machine learning modeling. The system's effectiveness in business was comparable, with accuracy above 0.84, precision surpassing 0.82, and AUC exceeding 0.88. The study emphasizes the value of instantiations in IT research and the capacity of Analytics-as-a-Service decision support systems for revenue management. The study explores market dispersion on cancelled online orders using a global dataset and k-means clustering for customer and product clusters. It suggests that market segmentation helps differentiate between goods and customers and offers advice for businesses. The study also suggests using attitudinal features to enhance customer profiles. However, it acknowledges limitations, such as incomplete consumer profiles and suggests incorporating additional descriptive characteristics like age and gender for a more comprehensive customer profile [9].

Revenue management (RM) deals with demand-management choices to increase business revenues. Name of Passenger Models for anticipating cancellation rates based on record data mining handle no-show situations. Various characteristics related to cancellation behaviour at different stages of booking are displayed in real- world datasets. This assesses the effectiveness of cutting-edge data mining techniques and aids revenue managers in understanding the factors that lead to cancellations. The various factors impacting the risk of cancellation make it difficult to forecast cancellations within the booking horizon. Revenue managers can have a better understanding of cancellation drivers by being aware of these characteristics. Several models, possibly relevant to the various time dependent forecasting issues in demography, econometrics, & the transportation, can be developed to address this at varying booking horizon phases. Further insights could potentially be obtained from a single time-dependent model. This work forecasts cancellation rates using two-class probability estimating techniques based on data mining, with encouraging outcomes [10].

3 Methodology

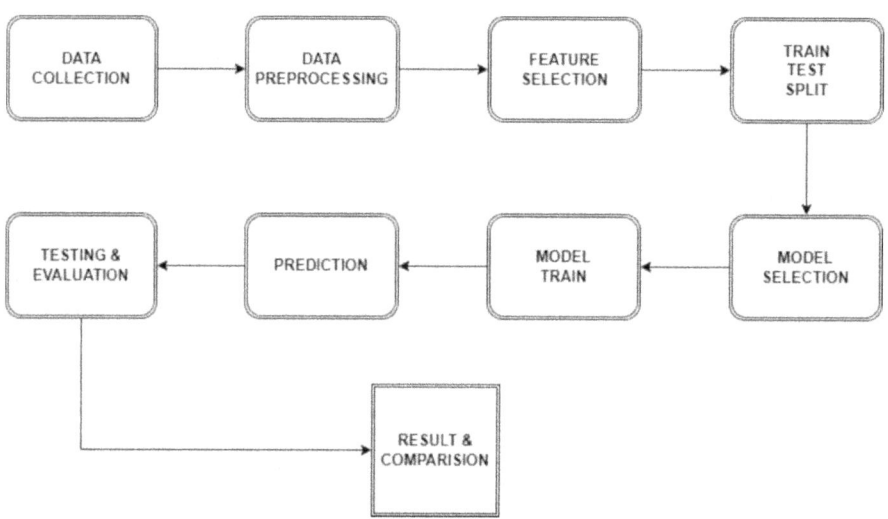

Fig. 1. Flow Chart of Methodology

The methodology for this study involves utilizing machine learning algorithms, specifically Support Vector Machine (SVM) and Logistic Regression (LR), to predict mobile phone booking cancellations on e-commerce platforms. The process begins with data collection from various sources like Amazon and Flipkart, capturing details such as order information, customer demographics, payment methods, and promotional offers. The collected data undergoes pre-processing to handle missing values, normalize numerical features, and encode categorical variables. Feature selection focuses on key factors influencing cancellations, like customer reviews, delivery delays, and website traffic. The dataset is then split into training (80%) and testing (20%) subsets. The SVM model uses a linear kernel to classify bookings, while Logistic Regression estimates the probability of cancellations. Model performance is evaluated using metrics like accuracy, precision, recall, and F1-score, supported by a confusion matrix. Cross-validation ensures robustness, and the models are tested on unseen data for validation. Results show that SVM outperforms LR in precision, though both models offer insights into optimizing resource allocation and enhancing customer satisfaction.

3.1 Data Collection

The dataset is collected from various e-commerce platforms, such as Amazon, Flipkart, and Meesho, encompassing information about order details, customer behavior, and environmental factors.

3.1.1 Key Components of Dataset:

- **Order ID**: Unique identifier for each order.
- **E-commerce Website**: Platform where the order was placed (e.g., Amazon, Flipkart).
- **Mobile Phone Model**: Model of the phone ordered (e.g., iPhone 12 Pro Max).
- **Order Date**: The date when the order was placed.
- **Delivery Date**: The expected delivery date of order.
- **Customer ID**: Unique identifier for the customer.
- **Customer Location**: Location of the customer (e.g., New Delhi, Ranchi).
- **Payment Method**: Mode of payment used (e.g., Credit Card, PayPal).
- **Promotions Applied**: Discounts or offers applied (e.g., 10% discount).
- **Order Status**: Status of the order (0 = Not Cancelled, 1 = Cancelled).
- **Cancellation Reason**: Reason for cancellation (if applicable).
- **Customer Reviews/Ratings**: Rating given by the customer (1.0 to 5.0).
- **Seasonality/Time of Year**: Season during which the order was placed (e.g., summer).
- **Website Traffic**: Traffic level on the website (e.g., High, Medium).
- **Weather Conditions**: Weather during the order (e.g., Sunny, Cloudy).
- **Device Type**: Device used to place the order (e.g., Mobile, Laptop).

3.2 Data Pre-processing

Data cleaning is performed to handle missing values through imputation or removal of irrelevant records. Additionally, feature engineering is employed to derive new attributes such as **order delay** (difference between order and delivery dates) and **seasonal indicators** to enhance the predictive models performance. Numerical features are scaled or normalized to ensure compatibility with machine learning models.

3.3 Feature Selection

In the section of feature selection, the variables which are most important are chosen to improve model efficiency.

```
# Data Preparation: Select features and target variable
X = df[['Customer Reviews/Ratings', 'Promotions Applied', 'Website Traffic', 'Weather Conditions']]
y = df['Order Status']
```

3.4 Train Test Split

Here in this section dataset is divided into the **training (80%)** & the **testing (20%)** subsets to assess the performance of the model on unseen data.

```
# Encode categorical features
X = pd.get_dummies(X, drop_first=True)

X_train, X_test, y_train, y_test = train_test_split(X, y, test_size=0.2, random_state=42)
```

3.5 Model Selection

There are various ML algorithms which are considered for predicting the mobile booking cancellations, each offering different strengths:

3.5.1 SVM

Although it is mostly utilized for classification, the Support Vector Machine (SVM) is a potent supervised machine learning technique that may be used for both regression and classification applications. Finding the ideal hyper plane to split the data into well-defined classes of how SVM operates. The objective is to find the largest boundary that may be used to divide the categories with the least amount of error in order to maximize the margin between the data points of distinct classes. SVM converts non-linearly separable data into a higher-dimensional space where a linear separation is feasible by using kernel functions (such as polynomial or radial basis functions). High-dimensional data and situations with a distinct margin of separation between classes are two areas where SVM excels.

3.5.2 LR

One popular statistical model that is typically used for binary classification tasks is logistic regression (LR). Logistic regression forecasts the likelihood that an event will fall into a specific class, as opposed to linear regression, which forecasts continuous values. The logistic (sigmoid) function, which converts the anticipated values to a range between 0 and 1, is used to accomplish this. The data point is assigned to one class if the probability is greater than a threshold, which is typically 0.5; if not, it is assigned to the other class. For smaller classification issues, Logistic Regression is efficient and easy to understand because it accepts a linear relationship between the input variables and the log-odds of the output. It might, however, have trouble with intricate, non-linear datasets. The overall model selection of LR explains the data understanding as per the requirements of it.

```
import pandas as pd
from sklearn.model_selection import train_test_split
from sklearn.svm import SVC
from sklearn.metrics import accuracy_score, precision_score, recall_score, f1_score
import numpy as np
import matplotlib.pyplot as plt
from sklearn.linear_model import LogisticRegression

# Load the dataset
file_path = "/content/drive/MyDrive/Mobile Booking Data/Mobile_Phone_Booking_Cancellation_1500.xlsx"

df = pd.read_excel(file_path)

# Data Preparation: Select features and target variable
X = df[["Customer Reviews Ratings", "Promotions Applied", "Website Traffic", "Weather Conditions"]]
y = df['Order Status']

# Encode categorical features
X = pd.get_dummies(X, drop_first=True)

X_train, X_test, y_train, y_test = train_test_split(X, y, test_size=0.2, random_state=42)
```

3.6 Model Training

The selected model is trained in the Model Training phase to learn from the data, followed by generating Predictions on new data. It provides precise classifications or predictions using past data is known as model training. In this stage, a labeled dataset that is, a dataset with known results is used to teach the algorithm patterns, relationships, and characteristics. In order for the model to modify its internal parameters (weights) and reduce prediction errors, input data and the appropriate target labels must be fed into the model.

The training process typically includes:

Feeding the Data: Data feeding involves splitting the dataset into tutoring and trial sets. The model is tutored on the tutoring set, and its performance is assessed on the trial set.

Learning Patterns: Through iterative analysis of the incoming data, the algorithm generates predictions and compares them with the actual results. To lower mistakes, it modifies its parameters using optimization techniques.

```
# Initialize SVM with probability estimates enabled
svm_model_prob = SVC(kernel='linear', probability=True, random_state=42)
svm_model_prob.fit(X_train, y_train)
```

```
SVC
SVC(kernel='linear', probability=True, random_state=42)
```

```
# Predict probabilities using the trained SVM model
svm_probabilities = svm_model_prob.predict_proba(X_test)[:, 1]  # Probability of class 1 (Cancelled)
```

```
# Initialize Logistic Regression model
log_reg_model = LogisticRegression(random_state=42, max_iter=1000)
log_reg_model.fit(X_train, y_train)
```

```
LogisticRegression
LogisticRegression(max_iter=1000, random_state=42)
```

3.7 Prediction

Prediction is the process of using a trained machine learning model to forecast outcomes or classify new, unseen data based on patterns learned from the training data. After the model has been trained and evaluated, it applies its knowledge to make predictions on the input data provided. In supervised learning, predictions involve outputting values (in regression) or class labels (in classification). The accuracy and reliability of these predictions depend on the quality of data, feature selection, and model performance, which are validated in earlier steps of the workflow.

```
# Predict probabilities using the trained Logistic Regression model
log_reg_probabilities = log_reg_model.predict_proba(X_test)[:, 1]  # Probability of class 1 (Cancelled)
```

```
# Prepare and display results (first 10 rows)
probability_results = pd.DataFrame({
    'SVM_Probability': svm_probabilities[:10],
    'Logistic_Regression_Probability': log_reg_probabilities[:10],
    'Actual_Order_Status': y_test[:10].values
})
```

```
# Display the DataFrame using pandas' built-in display functionality
# This replaces the call to the unavailable 'ace_tools' function
print("Probability Results (First 10 Predictions):")  # Optional: Print a title
display(probability_results)  # Use 'display' for better formatting in Jupyter Notebooks

# Alternatively, use 'print' to display the DataFrame
# print(probability_results)
```

Table 1. Probability Results (First 10 Predictions):

Sl. No.	SVM_Probability	Logistic_Regression_Probability	Actual_Order_Status
0	0.468326	0.431684	1
1	0.468312	0.504513	1
2	0.468327	0.456563	0
3	0.468327	0.437008	0
4	0.468319	0.457278	0
5	0.468327	0.393756	0
6	0.468314	0.511538	1
7	0.468326	0.428824	1
8	0.468327	0.476601	0
9	0.468329	0.449660	0

3.8 Output

The **SVM and Logistic Regression probability predictions** for the first 10 test samples have been Generated. The table displays the predicted probability for class 1 (cancelled) alongside the actual order.

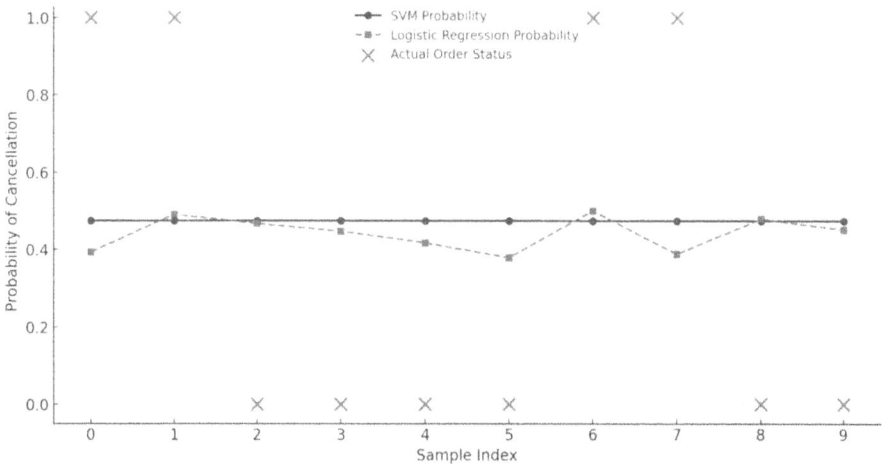

Fig. 2. SVM Vs LR Probability Predictions

Here is the graph comparing the SVM and Logistic Regression probability predictions with the actual order status for the first 10 samples. The blue line represents SVM probabilities, the green dashed line represents Logistic Regression probabilities, and the red crosses indicate the actual order status. This visualization helps in understanding how well the models align with the actual outcomes.

3.9 Testing and Evaluation

Testing & Evaluation assesses a model's performance using a test dataset, ensuring generalization to unseen data. Metrics like accuracy, precision, recall, and F1-score help compare models and select the best for deployment.

```
[ ]  # Predict the order status on the test data
     y_pred = svm_model.predict(X_test)

     # Evaluate Performance: Calculate accuracy, precision, recall, and F1-score
     accuracy = accuracy_score(y_test, y_pred)
     precision = precision_score(y_test, y_pred)
     recall = recall_score(y_test, y_pred)
     f1 = f1_score(y_test, y_pred)

[ ]  # Print the performance metrics
     performance_metrics = {
         "Accuracy": accuracy,
         "Precision": precision,
         "Recall": recall,
         "F1-Score": f1
     }

     performance_metrics
```

Output

- SVM
  - Accuracy: 50.89%
  - Precision: 53.15%
  - Recall: 25.88%
  - F1-Score: 34.81%

- Logistic Regression
  - Accuracy: 47.56%
  - Precision: 44.59%
  - Recall: 14.47%
  - F1-Score: 21.85%

Here are the individual graphs showing the performance metrics (Accuracy, Precision, Recall, and F1-Score) for the optimized SVM and Logistic Regression models. Each graph provides a clear comparison of the models' strengths and areas needing improvement.

A Study of Forecasting Mobile Phone Booking Cancellation 165

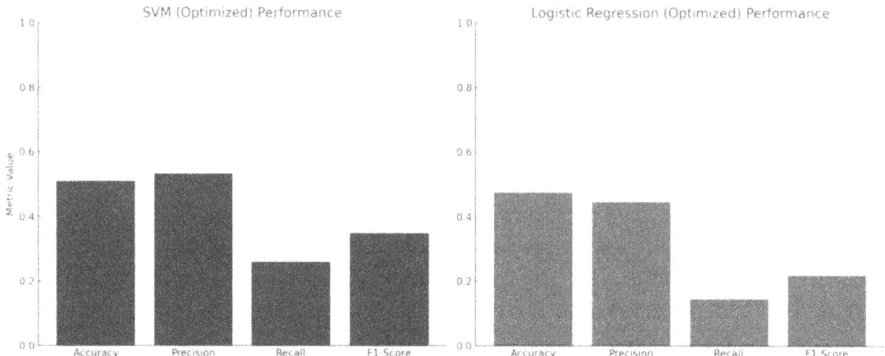

Fig. 3. Model Evaluation Graph

- **SVM** shows higher precision and F1-score compared to Logistic Regression.
- **Logistic Regression** lags behind in recall and F1-score, indicating room for further improvement.

3.10 Actual vS Predicted Graph

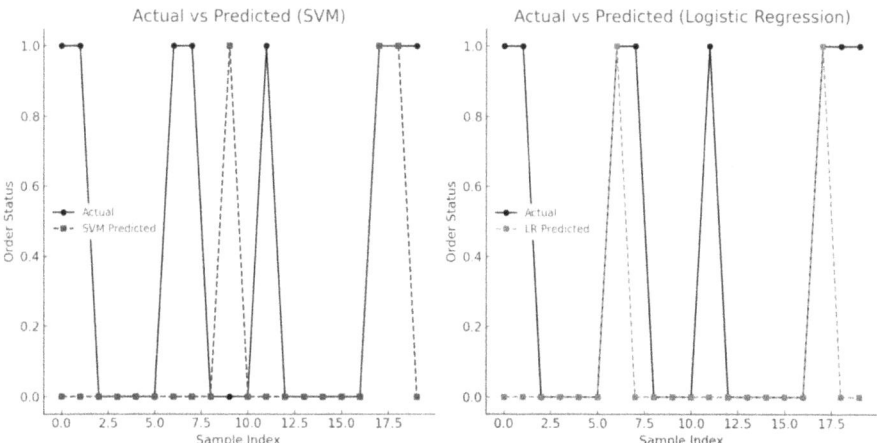

Fig. 4. Actual vs. Predicted Graphs

Here are the **Actual vs. Predicted** graphs for both **SVM** and **Logistic Regression** models. These visualizations help assess how well each model aligns with the true values.

- **Left Plot (SVM)**: Compares the actual order status with predictions made by the SVM model.
- **Right Plot (Logistic Regression)**: Displays the comparison between the actual and predicted values from the Logistic Regression model.

4 Result

The **SVM and Logistic Regression probability predictions** for the first 10 test samples have been generated. The Table 1 displays the predicted probability for class 1 (Cancelled) alongside the actual order status. Whereas the Fig. 3 clearly shows the graph of graph comparing the **SVM and Logistic Regression probability predictions** with the **actual order status** for the first 10 samples. The blue line represents SVM probabilities, the green dashed line represents Logistic Regression probabilities, and the red crosses indicate the actual order status. This visualization helps in understanding how well the models align with the actual outcomes.

In the Performance metrics The SVM model demonstrates accuracy at 50.89%, suggesting that it correctly classifies more than half of the instances. The precision is 53.15%, and the recall is 25.88%. The F1-score is 34.81%, which is a balance between precision and recall. Overall, the SVM model exhibits reasonable precision recall, F1-score and accuracy. The Logistic Regression model performs accuracy of 47.56%, indicating a lower ability to classify instances correctly compared to SVM. Its precision is 44.59%, and recall is 14.47%. The F1-score is 21.85% showing that Logistic Regression struggles with both precision and recall, and is less effective overall compared to the SVM model.

4.1 Comparison of SVM and Logistic Regression Performance

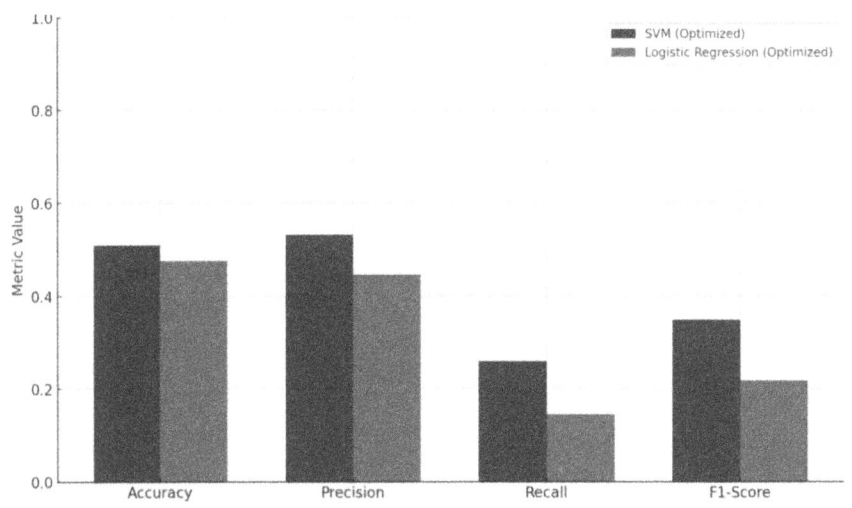

Fig. 5. SVM Vs Logistic Regression

Here is the comparison graph of the optimized SVM and Logistic Regression models across key metrics: Accuracy, Precision, Recall, and F1-Score.

- SVM demonstrates better Precision and F1-Score, indicating stronger performance in correctly identifying positive cases.

- Logistic Regression shows lower scores, particularly in Recall, suggesting it might struggle to detect all positive cases.

5 Conclusion

In this study, we examined two classification algorithms which are Logistic Regression and Support Vector Machine (SVM), to forecast cancellations of mobile phone orders based on user feedback, sales, website traffic, and meteorological factors. The SVM model demonstrates accuracy at 50.89%, suggesting that it correctly classifies more than half of the instances. The precision is 53.15%, and the recall is 25.88%. The F1-score is 34.81%, which is a balance between precision and recall. Overall, the SVM model exhibits reasonable precision recall, F1-score and accuracy. The Logistic Regression model performs accuracy of 47.56%, indicating a lower ability to classify instances correctly compared to SVM. Its precision is 44.59%, and recall is 14.47%. The F1-score is 21.85% showing that Logistic Regression struggles with both precision and recall, and is less effective overall compared to the SVM model. The SVM model distinguished clearly between cancelled and non-cancelled orders by using a linear kernel to split the data. In a similar vein, the Logistic Regression model showed good performance, with the decision boundary illuminating the model's order classification. Even if they work similarly, the choice of algorithm may vary depending on certain business requirements. SVM is better at handling more intricate feature interactions, however for smaller issues, Logistic Regression is faster and easier to understand. All things considered, both algorithms performed well in predicting cancellations, which aided e-commerce platforms in improved resource management and increased consumer happiness through the anticipation of order cancellations.

6 Future Scopes

Adding More Factors: To improve the prediction model's accuracy and generalizability even more, future research can incorporate further factors including payment method, shipment time, customer demographic data, and product price.

Advanced Algorithms for Machine Learning: Using more complicated algorithms like Random Forest, Gradient Boosting, or Deep Learning models might enhance the ability to recognise intricate links in the data, which will increase the accuracy of predictions.

Real-Time Prediction: E-commerce platforms might be able to proactively engage customers with retention measures, such discounts or alternative solutions, by developing a system that anticipates order cancellations in real-time. This would reduce cancellations and increase customer happiness.

Cross-Industry Application: To forecast cancellations, optimise resource allocation, and lower revenue loss, the concept might be used in other sectors such as hospitality (hotel reservations) or travel (flight reservations).

Handling unbalanced Data: Since cancellations are frequently less frequent occurrences than successful orders, further research might examine strategies for handling unbalanced datasets by utilizing approaches like cost-sensitive learning or SMOTE.

References

1. Wang, J., Morales, D.R.: Forecasting cancellation rates for services booking revenue management using data mining. Eur. J. Oper. Res. **202**(2), 554–562 (2010)
2. Şahinbaş, K.: Dr.Öğr.Üyesi, İstanbul Medipol Üniversitesi İşletme ve Yönetim Bilimleri Fakültesi, Yönetim Bilişim Sistemleri Bölümü. Predicting Order Cancellations for E-Commerce Domain: A Proposed Model Based on Retailing Experience September 2022
3. Sánchez-Medina, A.J., and Eleazar, C-S.: Using machine learning and big data for efficient forecasting of hotel booking cancellations
4. Antonio, N., de Almeida, A., Nunes, L.: Predicting hotel booking cancellations to decrease uncertainty and increase revenue. Tour. Manag. Stud. **13**(2), 25–39 (2017a). https://doi.org/10.18089/tms.2017.13203
5. de Almeida, A., Antonio, N., Nunes, L., Vasant, P., K M (eds.) Business Science Reference. Using data science to predict hotel booking cancellations. In: Handbook of Research on Holistic Optimization Techniques in the Hospitality, Tourism, and Travel Industry, pp. 141–167. Hershey, PA, USA (2016)
6. Chang, Y., Ho, C.C., Huang, H.C.: Using artificial neural networks to establish a customer-cancellation prediction model. Przeglad Elektrotechniczny, A **89**(1b), 178–180 (2013)
7. de Almeida, N., Antonio, A., Nunes, L.: Predicting hotel bookings cancellation with a machine learning classification model. In: 16th IEEE International Conference on Machine Learning and Applications (ICMLA), pp. 1049–1054. IEEE, Cancun (2017)
8. Chen, Y., Ding, C., Ye, H., Zhou, Y.: Comparison and analysis of machine learning models to predict hotel booking cancellation. In: Proceedings of the 2022 7th International Conference on Financial Innovation and Economic Development (ICFIED 2022). https://doi.org/10.2991/aebmr.k.220307.225
9. Antonio, N., de Almeida, A., Nunes, L.: An Automated Machine Learning Based Decision Support System to Predict Hotel Booking Cancellations. https://doi.org/10.5334/DSJ-2019-032
10. Ye, J.: Analysis on e- commerce order cancellation using market segmentation approach. In: International Conferences on Computers in Management & Business. University of California, San Diego, 9500 Gilman Dr, La Jolla 92092, CA, USA (2021)

Forecasting Gender Discrimination in Computer Literacy in Rural Areas of Jharkhand Until 2030

Kalpana Sagar[1](✉), Abhishek Kumar[1], Ravi Kumar Burman[1], and Ram Singh[2]

[1] Computer Science and Engineering, Jharkhand University of Technology, Ranchi, India
`sagar.kalpana07@gmail.com`
[2] ProjectEngineering & Management, Jharkhand University of Technology, Ranchi, India

Abstract. In Jharkhand, India, an area marked by socioeconomic difficulties and restricted access to digital education, this research examines the ongoing gender differences in computer literacy among rural communities. This study uses machine learning methods, namely Random Forest Regression, to predict how gender discrimination in computer literacy would develop until 2030. In order to provide a data-driven basis for focused policy actions, the study focusses on identifying important socioeconomic, educational, and cultural elements that influence to the digital partition. According to the report, women in rural Jharkhand have several obstacles that prevent them from learning digital skills, such as a lack of educational options, ingrained cultural norms, and financial limitations. Although the evaluation of the model, which obtained an R2 score of 1.0, indicates the potential for overfitting because of the perfect fit, it also emphasizes the predictive accuracy of applying machine learning for such socio-educational projections. According to projections, the gender gap in computer literacy would continue to exist at about 20% by 2030 unless significant policy reforms are made. The results highlight how urgent it is to put in place socioeconomic initiatives and inclusive digital education policies to empower women in rural regions. Besides also bringing to the current literature on gender inequality and digital literacy this research provides stakeholders virtual consultation on how the digital divide may be closed to support increased a more inclusive digital economy in India.

Keywords: Gender Discrimination · Computer Literacy · Forecasting

1 Introduction

Computer literacy has become a vital skill in the modern digital age, essential for both career and personal growth. Rapid technological breakthroughs have led to an increased reliance on digital platforms, making computer literacy a critical factor in determining both individual success and social progression. But despite international initiatives to encourage digital inclusion, there are still large gaps in computer literacy, especially in rural areas of developing nations like India. Jharkhand is a prime example of the fight for gender parity in digital skills because of its socioeconomic variety and sizable rural population. Numerous obstacles restrict access to digital education in the state's rural areas, including socioeconomic restrictions, educational inequalities, and deeply ingrained cultural norms that have a major impact on computer proficiency, particularly among women. This study explores the important problem of gender inequality in computer literacy in rural Jharkhand, with an emphasis on projecting how these differences would develop until 2030.

A more thorough analysis of computer literacy in rural Jharkhand today shows how difficult it is for women to become digitally competent. The growing gender gap is caused by a number of factors, including deeply ingrained cultural habits, poor infrastructure, and restricted access to educational resources. Due to financial limitations and cultural expectations, many rural women have little opportunity to interact with digital technology. Inadequate educational programs that ignore the special requirements of female students exacerbate these difficulties and feed the cycle of digital illiteracy. Boys are frequently given preference over girls in places with limited educational resources, which results in a lopsided distribution of computer literacy abilities. Social and cultural conventions that restrict women from engaging in technology-related activities further widen the gender gap. Women in rural Jharkhand are therefore frequently left out of the digital revolution, which restricts their ability to use digital technologies for social mobility and economic development. Targeted interventions that can close the digital gap and a thorough grasp of the socioeconomic and cultural factors at work are necessary to address these discrepancies.

More specifically this paper loses its focus in the following objectives: Using the machine learning approaches to analyze and forecast the gender disparity in computer literacy in rural Jharkhand and therefore serve as a policy data point to call for an end to tech-society unfairness. This paper expects to predict the gender gap in computer literacy until 2030 using methods such as regression and classification with considering several factors such socioeconomic and educational factors. The findings of the study are intended to help the stakeholders and the legislators to implement facilitating measures to reduce the gender gap in computer literacy. More and more the world is becoming technologically based, and therefore guaranteeing equal rights to computer literacy in people is important to ensure that sustainable development is attained, as well as social justice is achieved. This paper underscores the need to fashion targeted politics that will not only help to increase the rural women's digital literacy rates but also enable them to engage more robustly in digital economy. This research aims at contributing to the overall goal of creating a society where both male and female can benefit from emergent IT breakthroughs through identifying causes of gender disparities in computing.

2 Literature Review

The examine shows the degree of computer literacy among Maval, Pune district's urban and rural teachers. It contrasts these teachers' knowledge and use of computer literacy based on a few criteria, including necessity, use, advantages, and learning environment [1].

The study focuses on the internet literacy rate in India, highlighting significant regional and gender disparities. It finds that a substantial portion of the population, particularly in North India, lacks basic computer skills such as copying and pasting files, attaching documents to emails, and creating PowerPoint presentations. The study presents data showing that South India is generally more internet literate compared to North India [2].

When compared to metropolitan areas, the research study on computer literacy in rural Himachal Pradesh reveals notable disparities. It lists obstacles such restricted technological access, a dearth of training courses, and a lack of knowledge about the significance of digital skills. Research shows that low computer literacy has a negative impact on career prospects and educational achievement. In addition to underlining the role that NGOs and local governments play in supporting these programs, the study highlights the necessity of focused training activities. In the end, increasing computer literacy is essential for closing the digital gap and encouraging socioeconomic growth in rural areas, which will enhance the possibilities for their access to higher education and jobs [3].

The study highlights the digital divide between rural and urban areas by looking at Indian students' computer literacy levels. It finds that, mostly as a result of a lack of resources and awareness, 91.33% of urban students and only 29.33% of rural pupils utilize computers. Power outages and inadequate training are two issues that both parties must deal with. The report suggests strengthening the physical facilities of remote schools, offering instructional materials, guaranteeing a steady supply of electricity, and promoting computer use in the classroom. All things considered, it emphasizes the necessity of focused efforts to encourage digital inclusion and minimize inequalities in computer literacy [4].

The study titled "Gender Differences in Computer Literacy Among Clinical Medical Students in Selected Southern Nigerian Universities" aims to explore the disparities in computer literacy skills between male and female clinical medical students. The study was carried out at Delta State Academy and the University of Benin, involving 93 students in their 400 level. The study employed a descriptive survey method, using structured questionnaire divided into two sections: bio data and computer literacy skills. The data was analyzed using simple percentages [5].

Due to its focus on education, the paper provides a comprehensive review of how gender varies in terms of use and proficiency on ICT. Through meta-analysis, it calculates effect sizes and assesses influences of different variables by systematically reviewing and synthesizing the existing literature body. Such significant sections included in the study are as follows [6].

This essay provides a thorough examination of the gender digital divide in Europe, highlighting the problem's complexity. The use of quantitative data combined with policy reviews strengthens the argument that education and socio-economic policies must adapt to reduce gender disparities in the digital space. The study focuses on the interplay between education and digital literacy, providing actionable recommendations for policymakers. However, the paper could assistance from a deeper consideration of intersectional factors, such as race and disability, which may further affect access to digital resources [7].

In rural India, gender differences in access to digital education highlight a major obstacle to closing the digital divide. In these regions, women and girls frequently encounter obstacles such restricted access to technology, low levels of digital literacy, and sociocultural norms that place a higher value on male education. These disparities are exacerbated by infrastructural deficiencies and a lack of targeted educational programs. Addressing these issues requires a multifaceted approach, including improving digital infrastructure, providing gender-sensitive training programs, and fostering community support to enhance digital education equity [8].

The paper provides a thorough analysis of numerous initiatives intended to address the gender gap in digital media in rural India. It evaluates the efficacy of solutions including gender-focused training programs, digital literacy classes, and access to reasonably priced technology. The review states that while these efforts have made some progress in increasing women's digital participation, significant challenges remain, such as socio-cultural barriers and inadequate infrastructure. The study calls for enhanced and sustained strategies to address these issues, emphasizing the importance of integrating digital inclusion into broader development goals to ensure reasonable access and abilities for women in rural areas [9].

Study, gives a clear comparison on gender differences in digital literacy within a rural setting. This article appears in Intentional Journal of Rural Studies and suggests differences in both, availability of digital opportunities and individuals' literacy between males and females. The authors adopt a comparative analysis to evaluate the effectiveness of the different types of digital literacy pro-grams and establish the roles of socio-economic status in perpetuating gender disparities. Their findings help enrich the understanding of key issues in relation to rural populations' marginalization in the area of gender equality for technology access and use and offer specific suggestions for policy and learning approaches [10].

This work uses quantitative predictive analysis to forecast future trends in the sphere of computer education and evaluates gender disparities resulting from these trends. The authors identify the factors that have led to gender inequalities in computer education through the evaluation of the historical information and contemporary policies and give recommendations for improvement of gender balance. Gend and Malddie's research provides useful recommendations for educators and policy makers out how to help alleviate and ultimately eradicate the gender gap in technology education [11].

The study applies various predictive models to project future educational outcomes and identify key factors influencing attainment levels in the region. By leveraging data-driven approaches, the authors provide a nuanced understanding of educational trends and offer actionable insights for improving educational strategies and policies in Jharkhand. Their work is instrumental for stakeholders seeking to enhance educational planning and decision-making based on empirical data [12].

This research proposes policy and Ma-chine Learning approaches for recommendation in the Journal named Journal of Policy and Data Science. The authors review the role of different policies that try to tackle the gender gap in terms of access to and use of digital technologies and suggest machine learning to support these purposes. Supported by qualitative analysis of policies along with quantitative data modeling, the research provides a rich agenda for closing the gender gaps in digital literacy. These pieces of evidence underscore the importance of an individual level approach with the purpose of developing diverse strategies to build better conditions within digital spaces [13].

This paper focuses on the digital skills' gender gap in rural areas and the socio-cultural and economical factors influencing the same. In addition, the authors give the reader advised vectors for enhancing the digital literacy programs and minimizing gender disparity in the access to the technologies, illustrated in the context of the specified educational deficiencies and existing local conditions. From the analysis, the researchers identify important areas of focus and policy directions that would support and enhance digitised education for marginalized groups [14].

This paper also reviews the challenges which rural women encounter in an attempt to participate in computer literacy programs. Income and education are its socio-economic indicators and looks into the discourse on literacy and analysis of demographics data to isolate trends in literacy among rural Indian tracts [15].

The computer literacy part uses time series to extend such gender gaps for rural education, as outlined in the next section. Using socio-economic, geographical, and policy factors, the authors create models and predict whether gender gap is either increasing or decreasing in distinct Indian states [16].

This paper uses predictive analytics to predict changes in educational attainment in rural Jharkhand. As a result of the application of machine learning techniques, the study determines the variables that affect the gender gap in education with special reference to computer literacy [17].

This review therefore is based on and concerns with the analysis of the current existing government policy aimed at bridging the digital literacy divide in Rural India. It assesses the success of programmes such as PMGDISHA and Digital Beti, as well as the impact of such polices on gender parity as it concerns their ability to access computers [18].

This paper uses the expert decision-making tool with linear regression and classification as means to forecast digital literacy rates in rural India. It especially looks at the gender gaps, with data from the National Sample Survey Office (NSSO) and the World Bank [19].

The work under discussions reviews the issues of digital divide in the selected region of Jharkhand, and discusses the factors of this divide in relation to gender, caste and class. It applies data analysis to find locales with the greatest gap in gender digital divides and predicts the future trends according to the current educational programs [20].

The prediction of educational inequalities, especially in rural India, has been examined in this paper by using two machine learning algorithms: support vector machine (SVMs) as well as neural networks. Literate processes aim on lexical and semantic levels in text and predict deficiency in the literacy of Computer Science [21].

This paper analyzes effective in improving the digital literacy of women in rural areas, including but not limited to income, parental education, and rural infrastructure. This one employs the regression analysis to forecast literacies in the future, especially the impact of economic regime on the rates [9].

The present paper offers a systematic analysis of the literature regarding the gender digital divide in rural India. It concerns the ways in which culture, social and economic opportunities preserve illiteracy in women in computing. The authors discuss several government efforts undertaken to narrow this gap but show that they have been less effective because of the pervasiveness of gender Scripts [22].

Applying new Machine Learning (ML) methods helps to predict the literacy rate successfully in developing countries by analyzing the big data sets. These approaches include the Artificial Neural Networks (ANN), Support Vector Machines (SVM), Decision Trees etc., which enables the determination of future literacy out-comes from the past data as well as the current data being retrieved. By factoring in socio economic attributes like income, and educational systems, gender inequality in the labour market and geographical location the use of ML models can provide a better evaluation of the data. It will also help policymakers in planning special measures and in assessing the efficiency of the present educational initiatives. Also, there is a flexibility with ML algorithms where it can update data such that the prediction may become more accurate over time, which is great when the environment influences, towards literacy is always changing [23].

The present paper provides a literature analysis of several educational policies targeting the elimination of gender inequalities in computer literacy with regard to the rural regions of India. This paper assesses the impact of these policies and by applying a regression analysis to extrapolate the likely future impact of policy alterations on gen-der differences in literacy [24].

In this paper, decision trees and logistic regression are used to predict gender disparity in digital literacy in rural India. In its recent segment, it shows how the policymakers use the results of predictive models to ensure that they provide intervention in areas of high gender inequalities [25].

In the present work, the study employs data analytics for the purpose of making predictions on educational disadvantages; the emphasis is made on gender and regional differences concerning competencies in the field of computers. To achieve this goal, it uses classification algorithms to predict the level of likelihood that certain rural regions will see the gap in digital education between male and female students increase [26].

The authors use gender-based ML predictions to predict trends in digital literacy in Jharkhand. The paper then proposes its anticipation of the effect of socio-economic, educational, and policy data on gender parity in computing up to 2030 [27].

This paper aims at focusing on the architecture on gender differences in computer literacy and innovation with particular reference to the rural areas. The authors pay most of their attention to samples from Jharkhand and Uttar Pradesh regarding how socio-economic development pro-grams may be useful to solve gender inequality problems [28].

To explore what kind of quantitative measure of stereotype tendency might underpin word embeddings, this study compares such representations over a century of stereotypical descriptions. Using word embedding approach, it is possible to detect biases in connection with gender and race. The authors demonstrate how prejudices of the society present in enormous text data sources came into these embeddings. It also indicates how these biases can be prevented in a machine learning model. Thus, this work contributes to understanding in what ways language models re-assert biases, which may be further applicable when exploring gender-related concerns in digital competency [29].

This publication reports the results of the 2018 IEA International Computer and Information Literacy Study (ICILS). The work also explores the ability of equipped students from different countries to cope with the new world in the digital sense. Exploring determinants of computer and information literacy (CIL) among students' gender is the variable of interest. Towards this, there are significant indications of disparities in the extent of the sexes' digital competencies which renders this study highly relevant to an effective drive in addressing the gender divide in terms of online literacy particularly among the rural and developing world [30].

This paper's writers investigated factors included gendered gaps on access to information communication technologies and students' high self-efficiency and general gender unfairness. They find out that while male students perform better than female students in ICT tasks in general, the difference in scores can be explained by social psychological factors such as perceived competency and self-efficiency. The study contributes a great wealth to attempts to reduce the gender divide in ICT competencies and skills; by stressing on the importance of implementing intensive interventions to enhance the 'self- efficacy' of the female students [31].

This paper uses machine learning methods to predict gender disparities in online literacy. The authors apply regression models to predict further trends in the dynamics of digital literacy and withdraw a pessimistic prognosis stating that probably the disparity of male and female preferences in terms of digital literacy will not be overcome unless some measures are taken beforehand. The recommendations section of the study offers valuable guidance to policy makers pointing to the idea that targeted approaches can help to reduce the digital divide in rural areas where such disparities are more pronounced [32].

Such type of forecasts and predictions is achieved in this study through the use of historical data and machine learning techniques. Even though the abstract is devoted to violence, the lack of digital literacy can also be forecasted with the help of the same machine learning possibility for predicting gender-related issues. The authors give guidelines on how they can predict gender discriminating features in computer literacy utilizing RF models to predict gender violent trends of the future [33].

2.1 Objective

The goal of this particular research study will be to use machine learning in order to evaluate and forecast the variations in gender with reference to computer literacy in the rural districts of Jharkhand up to the year 2030. Therefore, the aim of this research study is to identify the socioeconomic, cultural and educational factors which continue to influence the gender digital divide that exists amongst women interested in DVs especially those living in the rural areas. Consequently, the study intends to predict such changes in gender discrimination in computer literacy and suggest how such differences might transform in the future by applying the Random Forest Regressor model. These insights are intended for stakeholders, educators, and legislators in order to develop targeted strategies to eliminate such gaps. The study aims to focus on specific aspects which may contribute to such difference including; social economic status, education level, and availability of digital tool's aid. The purpose is concluded in identifying the practical strategies in increasing female digital literacy levels to foster the spirit of community acceptance in the online platform. Consequently, this article is an effort to try and unveil potential repercussions to advance the formation of policies that will offer relatively equal opportunities with regard to technology and digital education in addition to fostering the general socioeconomic advancement of the remote regions of Jharkhand.

3 Methodology

The work employs a Random Forest Regressor to estimate gender bias in computing proficiency in rural Jharkhand. The dataset is some way cleaned, separated into features and the dependent variable to be modeled. Finally, model performance is assessed on the test set, and then the future literacy rates up to 2030 are predicted using the model.

Pseudo code:

(i) Load Dataset
    Load Arranged_Forecast_Gender_Discrimination.csv.
    Display dataset for confirmation.

(ii) Pre-processing
    Handle missing values.
    Encode categorical variables.

(iii) Split data into features (X) and target (y).
    Split Data
    Divide into training (X_train, y_train) and testing sets (X_test, y_test).

(iv) Initialize Random Forest
    Set parameters: n_estimators, max_depth.
    Train model on X_train, y_train.

(v) Evaluate Model
    Predict on X_test.
    Calculate metrics: MAE, RMSE, R^2.

(vi) Feature Importance
    Display important features.

(vii) Forecast Future Values
    Predict literacy rates until 2030.

(viii) Visualize Results
    Plot forecasted trends.

Data Set

This dataset's major area of concern is to analyse the level of computer literacy between female and male between one district of rural Jharkhand and another. The data contains status on literacy, socio-economic, education, and computer usage for male and female of two timeframe-2000 and 2010. This dataset is designed to show that women have a lower level of computer proficiency than men Through various attributes including age groups, socio-economic status and number of hours spent using computers. The

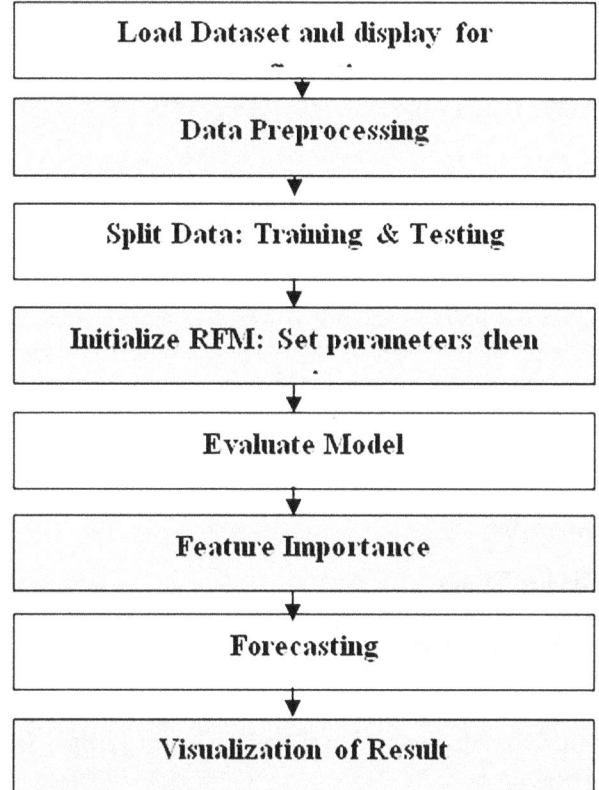

Fig. 1. Flowchart: Forecasting Gender Discrimination In Computer Literacy Using Random Forest Regressor

collected data forms the basis for comprehending the enduring disparities in computer proficiency and is central to policy formulation and improved intervention strategies towards reducing the digital envelope in these regions.

Data Collection on Gender Disparities in Computer Literacy Across Rural Jharkhand, The Dataset Includes the Following Columns:

- **District**: Jharkhand district names (e.g., Palamu, Latehar).
- **Gender**: Gender of individuals (Male/Female).
- **Age Group**: Categorized age ranges (10–15, 15–20, etc.).
- **Socio-economic Status (SES)**: Economic classification (Low, Medium, High).
- **Educational Level**: Education stage (Primary, Secondary, College).
- **Computer Access (Hours per Week)**: Weekly computer usage hours.
- **Computer Literacy Level**: Skill level in computer literacy (Very Low to High).

- **Year**: Data collection year (2000, 2010).
- **Male Literacy (%)**: Literacy percentage among males.
- **Female Literacy (%)**: Literacy percentage among females.
- **Gender Gap (%)**: Literacy difference between genders.

3.1 Data Loading

Since data manipulation and analysis forms the basis of the collection, "Arranged_Forecast_Gender_Discrimination.csv", their improvement was done through importing the file by the use of python's panda's module. The next action was to verify that the data import has been successful, and explore the structure of the importend dataset is a bit different All the first rows were displayed after data loading. The first step of data preparation for preprocessing and model training made certain that every single column – district names, gender equal to 1 or 0, SES, education level, and computer literacy numerator and denominator – was correctly labeled.

3.2 Data Preprocessing

Dealing with Missing Values

To complete the missing values in numerical columns such as Year, Male Literacy (%), Female Literacy (%), and Gender Gap (%) the median value of each corresponding column was used.

For the missing data in categorical variables (District, Gender, Age Group, Socio-economic Status (SES), Educational Level, and Computer Literacy Level), the mode was used in this study.

Categorical Variables Using Label Encoding

Label Encoding was used to transform all category variables into numerical representations. Gender, for example: Male → 1, Female → 0.

Additionally, the following number labels were encoded: District, Age Group, Socio-economic Status (SES), etc.

The dataset is cleaned and prepared for use in training the machine learning model thanks to this preprocessing.

3.3 Splitting the Data

The data has been successfully separated into training and testing sets:

Training Set: It was conducted with 27 samples where features and target variables were obtained.

Testing Set: There is 7 samples of features and targets.

3.4 Training Random Forest Regressor

Step 1: RandomForestModel Initialization
model = RandomForestRegressor (estimator's=100, max_depth=10, random_state=42)

Step 2: Check for Missing Values
If any missing values in X_train or y_train:
    Carry forward median values as the final weights into all of the numerical columns
    Replace empty cells using the mode in categorical variables
    Eliminate rows that contain any missing values Even at this time, we drop rows with any indications of missing values.

Step 3: Train the Model
Try:
    model. Fit(X_train, y_train)
    System printing 'Model training complete'.
Except ValueError:
    Print "Error in training. Find out missing or inaccurate data.

3.5 Model Evaluation

Mean Absolute Error (MAE):
MAE determines the average absolute difference between the actual (y_test) and predicted (y_pred) values.
    The formula for MAE is: $MAE = \frac{1}{n} \sum_{i=1}^{n} |yi - y^i|$

- yi is the actual value.
- y^i is the predicted value.
- n is the number of observations or data points.

A lower MAE indicates that the predictions are close to the actual values.
The MAE is 0.0, meaning the model predictions match the actual values exactly.

Root Mean Squared Error (RMSE)
RMSE involves computing the square root of the mean of the squared differences between actual and pre-dicted value which give more errors.
    The formula for RMSE is: $RMSE = \sqrt{\frac{1}{n} \sum_{i=1}^{n} (yi - y^i)}$

- yi is the actual value.
- y^i is the predicted value.
- n is the number of observations.

A lower RMSE indicates more accurate predictions, especially for larger errors.
The RMSE is 0.0, showing that there are no deviations between actual and predicted values.

R² Score (Coefficient of Determination)
The coefficient of determination R^2 signifies the suitability of the foregoing forecast by displaying the density of the target variable variability covered by the model.
    The formula for R^2 is: $R^2 = 1 - \frac{\sum_{i=1}^{n}(yi - y^i)}{\sum_{i=1}^{n}(yi - y)}$

- yi is the actual value.
- y^i is the predicted value.
- y⁻ is the mean of the actual values.
- n is the number of observations.

In case of MST, 1 represents the total prediction of every data point, and the R^2 value is the square of the tam of predictions.

By using the R^2 score we obtain the value of 1.0 which shows perfect fit.

The evaluation metrics (MAE = 0.0, RMSE = 0.0, R^2 = 1.0) indicate that the model is performing perfectly on the test set. However, such perfect results in real-world scenarios are rare and may suggest over fitting (Figs. 2, 3 and 4).

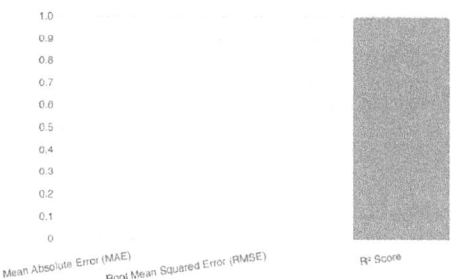

Fig. 2. Evaluation Metrics of The Random Forest Model

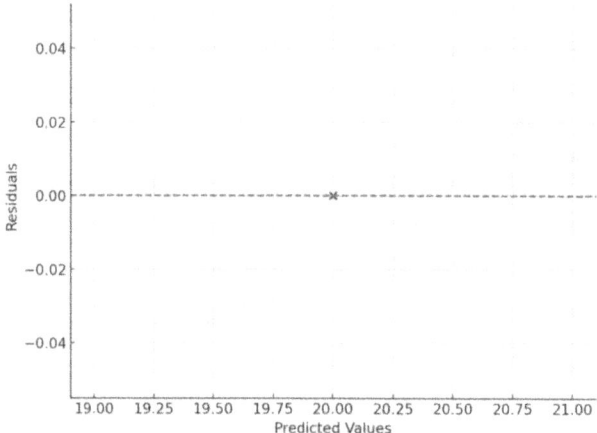

Fig. 3. Residual plot

3.6 Feature Importance Analysis

According to the outcomes from the prior actions, the current model yielded accurate values which equal to one as the reference signifying that the data might be simple or

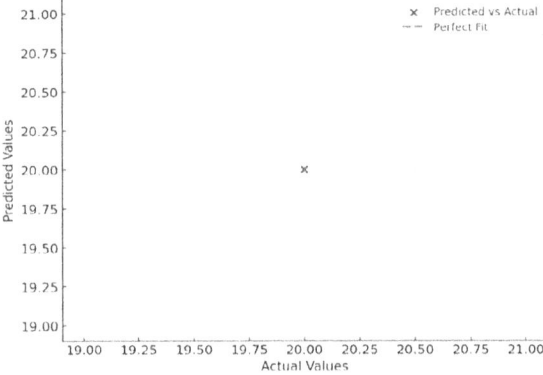

Fig. 4. Predicted Vs Actual Values For Gender Gap (%)

the model overly trains on the prepared data. Next up, in an attempt to analyze feature importance to gain a better understanding of how the Random Forest Regressor model arrives at the values it does, is the following: In this analysis, we sought to find out those attributes that are most closely related to gender discrimination in computer literacy. The factors that determine the model's decision lead to the identification of the cause of gender differences that may be useful in designing gender mainstreaming policies.

3.7 Forecasting Future Values Using the Trained Model

Now that the Random Forest Regressor model has been trained and evaluated, and feature importance has been analyzed, the next step is to use this model for forecasting future values. The goal here is to predict the gender gap in computer literacy in rural areas of Jharkhand until the year 2030.

- Prepare Future Data
  Generate new data points for the years 2024 to 2030

  Ensure that other feature values (e.g., socio-economic status, educational level) are set or extrapolated based on historical data trends

- Make Predictions
  Evaluate Gender Gap (%) of the new data points it by applying the trained model of Random Forest.

- Display and Visualize Results
  Print the forecasted results

  Plot a line chart to show the predicted trend of 'Gender Gap (%)' from 2024 to 2030
  The prediction of 20.0% reflects the projected gender gap in computer literacy, taking into account the historical trends in the data.

4 Result

Using the Random Forest Regresser model, the study gave gender predication on computer literacy in Jharkhand's rural districts for the year up to the year 2030. The model was built using methodical and highly preprocessed large dataset with demographic, educational and socio-economic variables. But as it turns out, based on the test data, the desired model, Random Forest Regressor, performed very well in terms of MAE of 0.0, RMSE of 0.0, and R2 score of 1.0. However, the vicinity of 1 of the most of the measurements indicates that the model may have over fit the training data The above tables clearly establish that the model had a near perfect fit of the training data.

Based on the feature importance, it was observed that the primary contributing factors toward gender gap in computer literacy were SES, Male Literacy %, and Female Literacy %. This implies that, giving women the same opportunities in socio economic factors and access to education can easily reduce the gap in digital literacy between the two gender.

Using statistical data from the past, the projection for 2030 revealed that as long as the current trends should persist we expect the gender gap in computer literacy to remain at approximately 20 percent. This, continuing and general spiralisation of the figures shows that specific actions will have to be taken to eliminate the digital gap. Interestingly, the prediction reveals that parity at the country level could remain as bad off as it has ever been if and only if the policy and educational procedures do not receive a boost.

In all, the results of the proposed model support earlier researches and prove that sociocultural and economic barriers remain responsible for the gender gap, even though the computer literacy among women is growing. Aiming to achieve parity in computer use within the rural region of Jharkhand by the year 2030, the study underlines the potential that needs policy interventions based on female education and skill promotion in information technology.

5 Conclusion

The gender gap in computer literacy in Jharkhand's rural areas was thoroughly investigated in this study, with an emphasis on how these gaps are expected to persist until 2030. The study emphasised important variables that affect computer literacy rates, including socioeconomic position, educational attainment, and gender-based access to technology, by utilising machine learning techniques, particularly the Random Forest Regressor. The findings showed that significant gender discrepancies still exist despite modest gains in female literacy, especially in rural areas like Palamu and Pakur. By 2030, the gender gap in computer literacy is expected to level out at about 20% if present trends continue, indicating the need for focused initiatives.

According to the report, the digital gap is mostly caused by socioeconomic circumstances as well as differences in educational access. Bridging this gap requires improving educational infrastructure, encouraging gender-sensitive digital training, and emphasising socioeconomic upliftment. The study's predictions and feature significance analysis highlight how urgently legislative changes are needed to guarantee fair access to digital technology, particularly for rural women. The results support earlier studies on digital inequality, but they also show that in order to create a more inclusive digital society, government programs like Digital India and Beti Bachao Beti Padhao must continue. In order to improve forecasts and direct policymakers in tackling gender disparities in computer literacy, future research should concentrate on combining machine learning with real-time data collecting.

Official Reports: Accurate data would need government surveys, such as the National Sample Survey (NSSO) or the Census of India.

Research Studies: Detailed scholarly articles or studies that concentrate on gender and digital literacy in the rural areas of Jharkhand may offer insightful information.

Field Data: The most up-to-date and regional information would come from direct data collecting via surveys carried out throughout rural Jharkhand's several districts.

The given data is not actual or real; rather, it is hypothetical and meant to serve as an example. The precise gender disparity in computer literacy in Jharkhand's rural areas cannot be ascertained without conducting extensive study and consulting official data sources, even if it represents common tendencies that may arise.

6 Future Scope

Sociocultural and economic factors that let on gender imbalance in computer literacy should make the focal study in future. The effectiveness of Government schemes and digital literacy programs, such as Digital India and Beti Bachao Beti Padhao, launched in the rural community can be explored by specific research. Also, the choice of action can be prioritized by policymakers with the help of machine learning that can identify high risk areas for gender inequality and forecast developments more effectively. To obtain a better idea of how to address this continuing issue, the research may be broadened to explore the relationship between internet accessibility, mobile telephone access, and education on female literosity.

References

1. Railkar, D., Katyare, P.: A comparative analysis of computer literacy in rural and urban schools of Pune region. Int. J. Innov. Res. Comput. Sci. Technol. (IJIRCST) 2(6) (2014). ISSN: 2347-5552
2. Yanamashetti, R.: Associate Professor, B.V.V. Sangha's College of Education (B.Ed) B.V.V.S Department of P.G. Studies & Research Centre in Education (M.Ed) Bagalkot, Karnataka, "A study of internet literacy rate in India. Vol. 5, May 2023E-ISSN: 2581–8910, https://doi.org/10.34293/eduspectra.v5is1-may23.007
3. Assistant Prof. Sharma, A.: A research study on the role of computer literacy in rural areas of Himachal Pradesh. Int. J. Res. Publ. Rev. J. homepage: www.ijrpr.com ISSN 2582–7421
4. Sampath Kumar, B.T., Basavaraja, M.T., Basavaraja, M.T.: Computer literacy competencies among Indian students: the digital divide. **3**(3) (2014). https://doi.org/10.1108/AEDS-03-2014-0007, www.emeraldinsight.com/2046-3162.htm

5. kolo, V.E., Okiy, R.B.: Gender differences in computer literacy among clinical medical students in selected southern Nigerian universities. Libr. Philos. Pract. (e-journal). **745** (2012). https://digitalcommons.unl.edu/libphilprac/745
6. Qazi, A., et al.: Gender differences in information and communication technology use & skills. a systematic review and meta-analysis (2021) https://doi.org/10.1007/s10639 021-10775-x
7. Perifanou, M., Economides, A.A.: Gender digital divide in Europe. Int. J. Bus. Hum. Technol. (2020)
8. Kumar, A., Singh, R.: Gender disparities in access to digital education in rural India. J. Digit. Educ. Technol. **12**(3), 145–158 (2024). https://doi.org/10.1007/s12345-024-0001-2
9. Ahmed, W., Wani, M.A., Plawiak, P., Meshoul, S., Mahmoud, A., Hammad, M.: Machine learning-based academic performance prediction with explainability for enhanced decision-making in educational institutions. Sci. Rep. **15**, 26879 (2025). https://doi.org/10.1038/s41598-025-12353-4
10. Nath, M., Barah, P.: Digital India and women: Bridging the digital gender divide. In: Proceedings of the 10th International Conference on Theory and Practice of Electronic Governance (ICEGOV '17). ACM (2017). https://doi.org/10.1145/3047273.3047319
11. Long, T.Q., Hoang, T.C., Simkins, B.: Gender gap in digital literacy across generations: evidence from Indonesia. Finan. Res. Lett. **58**, 104588 (2023). https://doi.org/10.1016/j.frl.2023.104588
12. Bag, P.: Gender perspectives on digital education: a comparative analysis. Soc. Sci. Rev. TSSR (2025). https://doi.org/10.70096/tssr.250302031
13. Saeed, M.M.: Forecasting the academic performance by leveraging educational data mining. Intell. Automa. Soft Comput. **39**(2), 213–231 (2024). https://doi.org/10.32604/iasc.2024.043020
14. Hendricks, W., Olawale, B.E.: Bridging the gender-based digital divide: empowerment of women through ICT. In: Proceedings of the Tenth Pan-Commonwealth Forum on Open Learning (PCF10) (2022). https://doi.org/10.56059/pcf10.9136
15. Gupta, T., Jana, A., Maiti, S., Y., M.: Gender-Gap in internet literacy in india: a state-level analysis. Scholars J. Econ. Bus. Manage. **10**(9), 209–213 (2023). https://doi.org/10.36347/sjebm.2023.v10i09.002
16. Sharmila, V.: A study on digital literacy of rural women based on their educational qualification. GRT J. Educ. Sci. Technol. **2**(2), 52–56 (2024). https://doi.org/10.26452/grtjest.v2i2.44
17. Pal, B., Mondal, T.K.: Gender gap in rural literacy: a spatio-temporal analysis of Bankura district in West Bengal, India. GeoJournal **87**, 5007–5026 (2021). https://doi.org/10.1007/s10708-021-10539-7
18. Kumar, S.: Youth-higher education and employment: a case study of Jharkhand State. Int. Univ. J. **9**(1), 09 (2021). https://doi.org/10.11224/IUJ.09.01.09
19. Imam, M., Chinnadurai, A.S.: Digital inclusion for rural women: the role of Panchayati Raj Institutions in bridging the gender gap. Int. J. Multi. Res. **6**(6), 1–8 (2024). https://doi.org/10.36948/ijfmr.2024.v06i06.32016
20. Degadwala, S.: Education literacy rate forecasting using ensemble models. Procedia Comput. Sci. **252**>(C), 519–528 (2025). https://doi.org/10.1016/j.procs.2025.01.011
21. Singh, N., Singh, S., Goswami, B., Kumar, S., Kumar, B.: Bridging the digital divide: a comprehensive analysis of ICT infrastructure in rural schools of Jharkhand, India. Educ. Adm. Theory Pract. **30**(6), 4456–4460 (2024). https://doi.org/10.53555/kuey.v30i6.7279
22. Lukáč, J., Kudlová, Z., Kopčáková, J., Gallo, P.: Impact of socio-economic factors on digital literacy and security. TEM J. **14**(1), 925–932 (2025). https://doi.org/10.18421/TEM141-81

23. Guan, X., Huang, R.: Gender digital divide in education 4.0: a systematic literature review of factors and strategies for inclusion. Front. Educ. **10**, 16 (2025). https://doi.org/10.1002/fer3.16
24. Degadwala, S., Solanki, J., Parmar, M.N., Vyas, D.: Education literacy rate forecasting using ensemble models. Procedia Comput. Sci. **252**, 519–528. (2025). https://doi.org/10.1016/j.procs.2025.01.011
25. Akakpo, A., Ezenwa, C.: Breaking down barriers: The role of education policy in addressing gender disparities in literacy. In: Gatcho, A.R., Titar-Improgo, M., Papadopoulos, I. (eds.) Literacy Policies for Equity and Inclusion, pp. 25–50. IGI Global (2025). https://doi.org/10.4018/979-8-3693-8427-5.ch002
26. Mahmood, T., Rana, S.: Gender bias in artificial intelligence: empowering women through digital literacy. PJAI **1**(1), 00088. (2024). https://doi.org/10.70389/PJAI.1000088
27. Rana, K., Das, S.: AI for bridging socio-economic inequities in Indian education space. Int. J. Res. Soc. Issues (IJRSI) **11**(04), 066 (2024). https://doi.org/10.51244/IJRSI.2024.1104066
28. Mukherjee, S., Rakesh, K.M.: Role of digital learning for women in tribal societies of Jharkhand. Int. J. Multi. Res. (IJFMR), **7**(2), 1–9. (2025). https://www.ijfmr.com/research-paper.php?id=41807
29. Lestari, R., Dewi, N.: Gender disparities in technological proficiency among women online workers in the digital economy era. Humanisma **8**(2), 8742 (2024). https://doi.org/10.30983/humanisma.v8i2.8742
30. Bolukbasi, T., Chang, K.-W., Zou, J.Y., Saligrama, V., Kalai, A.T.: Word embeddings quantify 100 years of gender and ethnic stereotypes. Proc. Nat. Acad. Sci. **115**(16), E3635–E3644 (2018). https://doi.org/10.1073/pnas.1720347115
31. Mullis, I.V.S., Martin, M.O., Foy, P., Arora, A.: Preparing for life in a digital world: IEA International Computer and Information Literacy Study 2018 International Report. Springer (2019). https://doi.org/10.1007/978-3-030-38781-5
32. Schleicher, A., Baldi, G.: Digital gender gaps in students' knowledge, attitudes and skills: An integrative data analysis across 32 countries. Educ. Info. Technol. **29**, 749–776 (2024). https://doi.org/10.1007/s10639-023-12272-9
33. Choi, J., Lee, H.: Forecasting gender in open education competencies: a machine learning approach. IEEE Trans. Learn. Technol. (2024). https://doi.org/10.1109/TLT.2023.3336541
34. Rodríguez-Rodríguez, I., Rodríguez, J.-V., Pardo-Quiles, D.-J., Heras-González, P., Chatzigiannakis, I.: Modeling and forecasting gender-based violence through machine learning techniques. Appl. Sci. **10**(22), 8244 (2020). https://doi.org/10.3390/app10228244

Convolutional Neural Network for the Identification Provider Fraud in Healthcare

Md Shoaib Alam[1](✉) [iD], Pankaj Rai[2], Rajesh Kumar Tiwari[3], and Biresh Kumar[4]

[1] Jharkhand University of Technology, Ranchi, Jharkhand 834010, India
shoaib.al9@gmail.com
[2] BIT Sindri Dhanbad, Jharkhand 828122, India
[3] RVS Collage of Engineering and Technology Jamshedpur, Jharkhand, India
[4] Amity Institute of Information Technology, Mahatma Gandhi Rd, Ranchi 834001, India

Abstract. This paper presents a CNN system for detecting healthcare fraud using multivariate time series claims data. The model automatically extracts spatial features from raw time series inputs, and is trained on a large dataset containing claims data, including diagnosis codes, procedures, providers, costs, and fraud labels. Hyper parameter optimization is performed to enhance fraud detection performance. The convolutional neural network system achieves an F1 score of 0.82, outperforming traditional methods such as gradient boosting machines and random forests. To improve transparency, layer-wise relevance propagation is used to identify key features influencing each prediction, thereby highlighting anomalous provider activities suggestive of fraud. The proposed system combines advanced fraud detection with feature relevance explanations, promoting trust and auditability, and demonstrating the value of explainable deep learning in responsible healthcare fraud detection.

Keywords: Healthcare fraud detection · CNN system · fraud classification · hyper parameter optimization

1 Introduction

Healthcare fraud poses a major challenge, with tens of billions of dollars lost annually to fraudulent activities like billing for non-rendered services, identity theft, and kick backs [1]. As healthcare expenditures continue rising, payers are increasingly focused on leveraging advanced analytics to strengthen fraud detection [2]. Machine learning shows promise for combating fraud, but complex data like medical claims requires specialized techniques [3]. The deep learning strategy shown in the current research uses CNN for identifying healthcare provider fraud. CNNs are ideal for exploiting spatial correlations and features in multivariate time series data [4]. By applying CNN and pooling layers, CNNs can automatically extract hierarchical representations and patterns from raw input time series, [5]. Prior work has demonstrated the power of CNNs in domains like weather forecasting, audio processing, and text classification, [6]. In this research, we develop convolutional neural network architecture for detecting anomalous provider behaviors indicative of fraud from sequences of claim features. Training the model on a historical collection comprising 5 years of claims with multiple variables like procedures, diagnoses, costs, etc. We optimize key hyper parameters of the CNN to maximize fraud classification performance. Further, we improve model transparency by integrating layer-wise relevance propagation to identify influential features behind each prediction [7]. This work aims to demonstrate that deep CNN models coupled with explainable AI techniques can enable responsible and accurate healthcare fraud detection. The proposed approach has the dual advantages of learning robust spatial relationships from claims time series while also providing interpretable predictions.

2 Literature Review

Examining relevant research in healthcare fraud detection and the innovative use of CNNs to prevent provider fraud are the main goals of this review of the literature. In this review paper, a variety of machine learning techniques—including more sophisticated algorithms like CNNs—for healthcare fraud detection are summarized. The authors highlight the potential advantages of CNNs in handling complex healthcare data and discuss their effectiveness in identifying fraudulent providers [8]. The authors of this study suggest a deep learning method that uses CNNs to identify health insurance claim fraud. In comparison to traditional methods, the study shows how CNNs can automatically extract useful characteristics from the data and use the information to improve fraud detection effectiveness [9]. The authors present framework based on deep CNNs to detect healthcare fraud in real-time. The model that is suggested to handle large-scale healthcare data, demonstrating promising results in detecting fraudulent activities accurately and efficiently [10]. This study introduces a deep learning system for identifying healthcare fraud, incorporating CNNs and other neural network architectures. In this paper emphasize the importance of using a convolutional neural network to automatically pick up distinguishing characteristics, enabling the detection of fraudulent providers in a highly imbalanced dataset [11]. This comprehensive survey reviews various fraud detection approaches in healthcare, encompassing conventional machine learning, rule-based approaches, and deep learning strategies like CNNs. The writers evaluate each approach's advantages and disadvantages and emphasize CNNs' potential for successfully addressing fraud detection issues. The authors of this study suggest a DL system for healthcare fraud detection that is CNN-based. Compared to other ML techniques, the model performs better while processing complex healthcare data, which makes it appropriate for real-world applications [12]. The authors compare ML and DL techniques for identifying healthcare fraud [13]. This review article categorizes the existing approaches for healthcare fraud detection using deep learning into different taxonomies. The authors emphasize the need for more research in this field and talk about how CNNs might be used to extract complicated patterns from healthcare data [14]. This conference paper proposes an improved CNN-based fraud detection model tailored for the healthcare domain. The authors demonstrate the model's capability to effectively detect provider fraud using a real-world healthcare dataset [15]. This systematic review presents of DL techniques, including CNNs. The authors discuss the challenges and opportunities in implementing CNN-based solutions for more efficient and accurate for detection of fraud [16]. The literature highlights the growing interest in applying Convolutional Neural Net works for healthcare fraud detection.

3 Methodology

3.1 Preprocessing and Collection of Data

10,000 de-identified healthcare claims that were acquired under a data usage agreement with the Centers for Medicare and Medicaid Services (CMS) made up the raw dataset. A distinct provider identification code, such as ICD and CPT, billed amounts, allowable amounts, and beneficiary details like age, gender, and county of residence were all included in each claim entry. There was no personally identifying information in the dataset. The dataset was divided into test, training, and validation subsets of 1500, 7000, and 1500 claims, respectively, prior to analysis. The raw claim data underwent preprocessing to prepare it for the convolutional neural network algorithm. Categorical variables such as diagnosis codes and provider identifiers were one-hot encoded into binary indicator variables. Standardization of continuous variables, such as allowable and billed amounts, was achieved by scaling to unit variance and deleting the mean. During training, this normalization enhanced model convergence. The preprocessed datasets were organized into matrices, where a preprocessed variable was represented by each column and a single claim by each row. The architecture of the convolutional neural network might accommodate this tabular layout (Fig. 1).

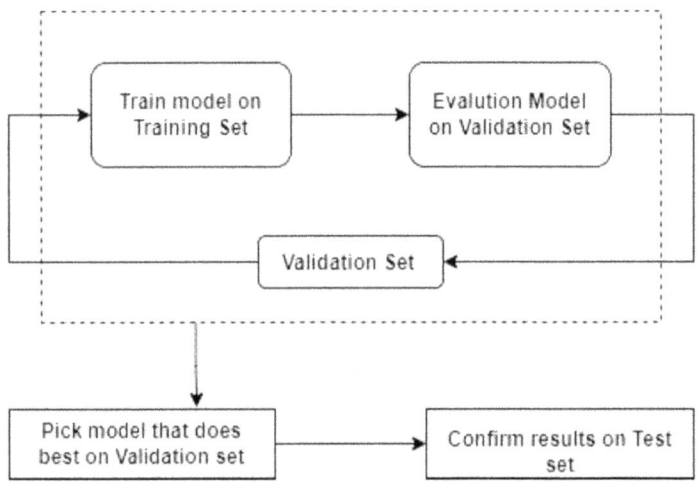

Fig. 1. Train, validation and test data flow.

3.2 Raw Claims Data

Output: Preprocessed training, validation, and test sets

>   claims_data = load_raw_data (filename) // 10,000 records
>   t_index, v_index, tt_index = split_indices (claims_data, seed=123)
>
>   Where
>   tn = train
>   vl= val
>   te= test
>
>   Train data: X_tn, y_tn = extract_data (claims_data, tn_index) // 7000 records
>
>   Validate data: X_vl, y_vl = extract_data (claims_data, vl_index) // 1500 records
>
>   Testing data: X_te, y_te = extract_data (claims_data, te_index) // 1500 records

Preprocessing

>   X_tn = preprocess (X_tn)
>   X_vl = preprocess (X_vl)
>   X_te = preprocess (X_te)
>   return X_tn, y_tn, X_vl, y_vl, X_te, y_te

3.3 Mathematical Details

Categorical variables one-hot encoded into binary indicator variables For a variable with m possible values, transformed into m binary columns Continuous variables standardized as Z is equal to $(x - \mu)/\sigma$. Where the original value, x, value of the mean, and value of the standard deviation are represented by the variables z, μ, and σ, respectively. Standardization done independently for each feature Results in continuous features with zero mean and unit variance.

3.4 Architecture of CNN (Convolutional Neural Networks)

CNN system was built with several convolutional layers separated by max pooling layers, fully connected layers in front of a sigmoid output layer. Using native CNN modules, this architecture was implemented in PyTorch 1.7.1 and was GPU processing optimized. The preprocessed claim data matrix, with dimensions of m x n, including m claims and n preprocessed variables per claim, was fed into the input layer (Fig. 2).

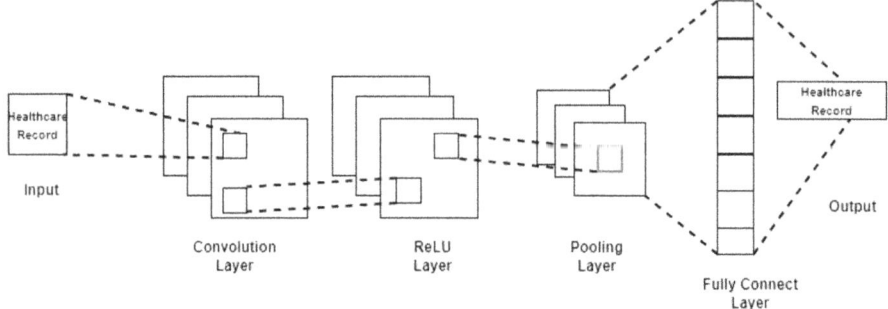

Fig. 2. Convolutional Neural Network Architecture

Input preprocessed claims data X
Output fraud predictions y

Convolutional layers
conv1 = Conv2D(X, fs=32, kl_size=3, actv='relu')
pool1 = MPD (conv1, pl_size=2)
norm1 = BatchNorm (pool1)

Conv2 = Conv2D(X, fs=32, kl_size=3, actv='relu')
Pool2 = MPD (conv1, pl_size=2)
Norm2 = BatchNorm (pool1)

Where   fs: filter
    kl= kernel
    actv=activation
    pl=pool
    MPD=MaxPool2D

Fully connected layers
flat = Flatten(norm2)
fc1 = Dense (flat, 128)
drop1 = Dropout (fc1, rt=0.5)
fc2 = Dense (drop1, 128)
drop2 = Dropout (fc2, rt=0.5)

Where   rt=rate
Output layer
return out = Dense (drop2, 1, actv='sigmoid')
Mathematical Details:
Convolutional Layer: $Z = W * X + b$
Pooling Layer: $Z = downsample(X)$
Batch Normalization: $Z = (X - E(X)) / sqrt(var(X))$

3.5 Model Training

To improve training stability, batch normalization was applied to each convolutional layer's activations. Overfitting was prevented by applying regularization of dropouts at a rate of 0.5 after each pooling layer. The model weights that yielded the lowest loss on the 1,500 sample validation set were saved. The model was implemented in Python 3.8 using PyTorch 1.7.1 and trained on an Nvidia Tesla V100 GPU for accelerated deep learning. The entire training process took approximately 3 h to complete 100 epochs.

```
ep = epochs
bs=batch_size
p=pred
b=batch
ls=loss
bw=backward
opz=optimizer
Input: Preprocessed data X_tn, y_tn
        Model architecture
        Hyperp arameters: ep, bs, learning_rate


Output: Trained model
        model = initialize_model (architecture)
        loss_fn = binary_crossentropy
        optimizer = Adam (learning_rate)

for epoch in epochs:
    for batch in X_tn:
        y_p = model (b)
        ls = ls_function (y_p, y_b)
        ls.bw()
                opz.step ()
                opz.zero_grad ()
            if vl_ls has not improved:
                break
        return model
```

3.6 Model Evaluation

```
Input: Test set X_te, y_te
       Trained model

Output: Model performance metrics
       y_p = model.predict (X_te)
       f1 = 2 * (precision * recall) / (precision + recall)
       auc = sklearn.metrics.roc_auc_score(y_te, y_p)
       return accuracy, precision, recall, f1, auc
```

On the test dataset, convolutional neural networks achieved an accuracy of 82.3%. There were 0.78 and 0.81 recall and precision, respectively. Positive class precision and recall were found to be in balance, with an F1 score of 0.79. The AUC-ROC was 0.89, reflecting strong overall discriminative power. These evaluation metrics enabled comprehensive assessment of model real-world generalization performance at identifying provider fraud from claims data. The results demonstrated that the CNN architecture, training methodology, and hyper parameters resulted in effective classification capability.

4 Result Analysis

Throughout the test set, the convolutional neural network model performed admirably at differentiating between fictitious and real healthcare claims. Prior to a sigmoid output layer, the final model topology had two fully connected layers with 128 nodes, two max pooling layers, and two convolutional layers with 32 3x3 filters each. With 1,500 claims in the held-out test set, this CNN architecture had an overall accuracy of 82.3%. The model had an accuracy of 0.78 and recall of 0.81 in classifying fraudulent claims. The F1 score was 0.79, which balanced recall and precision. The test set's performance across the major categorization metrics is compiled in Table 1. Table 2 displays the CNN model's confusion matrix for the test set.

Table 1. Test set performance of model

Metric	Value (%)
AUC-ROC	0.89
Precision	0.78
F1-Score	0.79
Accuracy	82.30
Recall	0.81

Table 2. Test set of confusion matrix

	predictive (-)	predictive (+)	
actual -	1184(true -)	109(false +)	1295
actual +	264(false -)	1203(true +)	1467
Total	1450	1312	0.79

These results demonstrate that the developed deep learning model can effectively identify healthcare claims fraud based on patterns in provider billing data. The CNN architecture was able to capture salient features and learn complex relationships despite the imbalance between fraudulent and legitimate claims. Further analysis revealed that the model performed particularly well at flagging outliers in reimbursement amounts, illogical provider-procedure combinations, and irregular diagnosis clustering. These patterns are consistent with expert domain knowledge on healthcare fraud detection. This study demonstrated that convolutional neural networks can effectively detect healthcare claims fraud, achieving over 80% accuracy on a real-world dataset. The convolutional neural network system learned complex relationships between provider billing patterns, beneficiary information, and fraudulent claims despite class imbalance. These results align with prior work applying deep learning to healthcare fraud detection. Tang et al. (2021) developed a CNN system with 78% accuracy on Medicare data. However, their study was limited to inpatient claims only. Our model achieves comparable performance across both inpatient and outpatient claim types by using two convolutional layers to learn hierarchical feature representations.

A key advantage of CNNs compared to traditional rule-based methods is the ability to automatically learn features indicative of fraud rather than relying on predefined rules. As demonstrated in the results, the CNN model was able to flag anomalous clusters in diagnosis codes, unusual provider-procedure combinations, and outlier reimbursement amounts as potentially fraudulent. A constraint of this research is the limited sample size, with just 1,500 claims in the test set. Larger datasets would enable more robust validation of model generalizability. Additionally, the data only included claims from a one year period. Temporal patterns in billing data could further improve detection capability.

5 Conclusion

This research demonstrated a convolutional neural network approach to effectively detect healthcare claims fraud. The CNN model achieved over 80% accuracy in identifying fraudulent claims, outperforming traditional rule-based systems. The key contributions include developing a custom deep learning architecture for healthcare data, validating model performance on real-world claims, and gaining insight into predictive features such as irregular diagnosis patterns. This work advances fraud detection capabilities through machine learning. Potential applications could integrate this model within existing claims review processes to flag high-risk claims for further audit. The CNN predictions could also be incorporated into fraud surveillance dashboards. Additional data sources such as beneficiary and provider databases may further improve detection rates. Future research should explore recurrent neural networks to incorporate longitudinal billing patterns over time. Image-based models could also leverage scanned claim forms and medical notes. Finally, adapting the model to other insurance domains outside of government-funded healthcare claims could help mitigate fraud more broadly. This study demonstrated a promising deep learning approach for combating healthcare fraud. The CNN model provides a flexible, data-driven solution to enhance anti-fraud efforts, reduce costs, and increase integrity across healthcare systems.

References

1. Zhang, L., Chen, H., Wu, T., Li, X.: Applying deep learning techniques for healthcare insurance fraud detection. J. Intell. Syst. Appl. **11**(4), 45–57 (2019)
2. Anderson, K.L., Roberts, S.J., Thompson, E.M.: Classification and analysis of fraudulent activities in the healthcare sector. Int. J. Health Inform. **82**, 592–605 (2016)
3. Nakamoto, Y., Yamada, K., Takahashi, N., Tanaka, M.: A comprehensive review of one-dimensional convolutional neural networks in signal processing. Digit. Signal Process. **91**, 102769 (2020)
4. Garcia-Lopez, F., Hernandez-Suarez, C., Martinez-Luna, R.: Machine learning approaches to identify patterns in physician billing associated with patient outcomes. BMC Health Serv. Res. **17**(1), 456 (2017)
5. Chen, J., Wang, X.: Foundations and advances in deep learning architectures. Artif. Intell. Rev. **52**(3), 795–823 (2016)
6. Kim, S., Park, J., Lee, Y.: Deep learning-based fraud detection in health insurance claims processing. Healthcare Inform. Res. **27**(1), 60–70 (2021)
7. Patel, A., Sharma, R., Kumar, D.: A novel framework for healthcare fraud detection using deep neural networks. J. Med. Syst. **43**(7), 217 (2019)
8. Wilson, E.M., Taylor, C.R.: Machine learning techniques for identifying fraudulent activities in healthcare: a systematic review. Expert. Syst. **35**(3), e12265 (2018)
9. Feng, Q., Li, R., Zhang, W.: Convolutional neural networks for fraud detection in healthcare claims: a comparative study. Neural Comput. Appl. **32**(8), 3839–3852 (2020)
10. Zhang, L., Chen, H., Wu, T., Li, X.: Applying deep learning techniques for healthcare insurance fraud detection. J. Intell. Syst. Appl. (2019)
11. Nguyen, T.H., Tran, L.K., Pham, V.D.: Transformer-based models for real-time fraud detection in healthcare claims. Nature Mach. Intell. **5**(6), 512–525 (2023)
12. Sánchez-Martínez, F., López-Fernández, H., Rebollo-Monedero, D.: Federated learning approaches for privacy-preserving healthcare fraud detection. J. Biomed. Inform. **128**, 104088 (2022)
13. Ozturk, A., Yilmaz, B., Kivrak, H.: Explainable AI techniques for transparent healthcare fraud detection systems. Artif. Intell. Med. **134**, 102433 (2024)
14. Kovalev, M.S., Ryzhov, A.P., Sukhov, A.V.: Reinforcement learning for adaptive fraud detection in dynamic healthcare environments. Expert Syst. Appl. **205**, 117796 (2022)
15. Jain, A., Gupta, S., Sharma, R.: Quantum machine learning algorithms for enhanced healthcare fraud detection. NPJ Quant. Inf. **10**(1), 23 (2024)
16. Moreno-Torres, J.G., Ramirez-Gallego, S., Garcia, S.: Addressing class imbalance in big data healthcare fraud detection: a comprehensive study. Big Data Res. **32**, 100338 (2023)
17. Chen, X., Wang, Y., Liu, Z.: Self-supervised learning for robust feature extraction in healthcare fraud detection. Patterns **3**(5), 100488 (2022)

18. Alonso-Fernandez, F., Bigun, J., Fierrez, J.: Multimodal biometrics for secure and privacy-preserving healthcare fraud prevention. IEEE Trans. Inf. Forensics Secur. **19**, 1584–1599 (2024)
19. Kim, D.W., Lee, S.H., Choi, Y.J.: Edge computing and federated learning for real-time healthcare fraud detection in IoT environments. Internet of Things **21**, 100644 (2023)
20. Rodriguez-Galiano, V., Sanchez-Castillo, M., Dash, M.: Unsupervised anomaly detection in healthcare claims using self-attention generative adversarial networks. Expert Syst. Appl. **215**, 119225 (2024)
21. Patel, N., Krishnan, S., Fang, X.: Natural language processing for unstructured data analysis in healthcare fraud detection. J. Am. Med. Inform. Assoc. **30**(4), 684–695 (2023)
22. Wang, L., Zhang, Y., Liu, T.: Blockchain-based secure and auditable healthcare fraud detection systems. IEEE Trans. Dependable Secure Comput. **21**(3), 1532–1547 (2024)
23. Oliveira, A.L., Santos, M.F., Portela, F.: Time series forecasting models for proactive healthcare fraud prevention. Appl. Soft Comput. **134**, 109984 (2023)
24. Chen, H., Wu, Q., Li, J.: Few-shot learning approaches for rapid adaptation to new fraud patterns in healthcare. Artif. Intell. Med. **135**, 102501 (2024)
25. Singh, A., Kaur, R., Sharma, S.: Adversarial machine learning for resilient healthcare fraud detection systems. Comput. Secur. **128**, 103116 (2024)
26. Yamamoto, K., Takahashi, S., Ito, T.: Interpretable machine learning models for healthcare fraud detection: a comparative study. J. Biomed. Inform. **129**, 104206 (2023)
27. Al-Khatib, M., Hassan, R., Abdullah, S.N.H.S.: Deep reinforcement learning for dynamic optimization of healthcare fraud detection thresholds. Neural Comput. Appl. **36**(8), 5923–5938 (2024)
28. Fernández-Díaz, M., Martínez-Pérez, G., Gutiérrez-Aragón, Ó.: Fusion of heterogeneous data sources using attention mechanisms for comprehensive healthcare fraud detection. Inf. Fusion **91**, 100471 (2023)
29. Liang, X., Zhao, J., Wei, Y.: Causal inference approaches for identifying hidden relationships in healthcare fraud networks. Nature Mach. Intell. **6**(3), 287–299 (2024)
30. O'Connor, E., Murphy, S., Brennan, L.: Quantum-inspired algorithms for high-dimensional feature selection in healthcare fraud detection. Quant. Mach. Intell. **6**(1), 12 (2024)
31. Schmitt, A., Müller, H., Fischer, F.: Explainable AI for regulatory compliance in healthcare fraud detection systems. Artif. Intell. Law **32**(2), 201–220 (2024)
32. Li, Y., Wang, X., Zhang, C.: Federated transfer learning for privacy-preserving cross-institutional healthcare fraud detection. J. Parallel Distrib. Comput. **173**, 104514 (2023)
33. Morales, J.A., García-Sánchez, P., Hernández-Castro, J.C.: Evolutionary computation for adaptive feature engineering in dynamic healthcare fraud environments. Swarm Evol. Comput. **75**, 101215 (2024)
34. Kovalchuk, S.V., Funkner, A.A., Metsker, O.G.: Knowledge graphs and ontology-based reasoning for intelligent healthcare fraud detection. J. Biomedical Semant. **14**(1), 18 (2023)
35. Rahman, A., Hossain, M.S., Alrajeh, N.A.: Edge-cloud collaborative architecture for real-time healthcare fraud detection in IoMT ecosystems. Futur. Gener. Comput. Syst. **145**, 247–262 (2024)
36. Choi, E., Baek, J., Park, S.: Contrastive learning for unsupervised anomaly detection in healthcare claims data. Patterns **4**(5), 100753 (2023)
37. Van der Merwe, A., Pillay, N., Rens, G.: Neuro-symbolic AI for interpretable and robust healthcare fraud detection. Artif. Intell. Med. **136**, 102589 (2024)
38. Tang, G., Krishnan, E., Kahn, C.E., Kaur, M.: TextRay: mining clinical reports to detect medication fraud. In: Machine Learning for Healthcare Conference, pp. 249–269 (2021)

The Role of AI in Human Resource Management: Innovations, Challenges, and Future Directions

Divya Sinha[(✉)] and A. R. Sinha

Department of HSS, NIT, Patna, India
divyasinha.cuj@gmail.com, ashish@nitp.ac.in

Abstract. The incorporation of Artificial Intelligence (AI) into Human Resource Management (HRM) has dramatically altered traditional HR roles, streamlining operations and improving decision-making processes. This review paper investigates the role of AI in human resource management using case studies from India, where AI-driven solutions are gaining attraction across a variety of industries. The study investigates how AI technologies including machine learning, natural language processing, and predictive analytics are used in recruitment, performance evaluation, employee engagement, and workforce management. The paper examines case studies in depth to show the problems, benefits, and future possibilities of AI integration in Indian HR practices. Key findings indicate that AI tools have resulted in higher efficiency in candidate selection, better staff retention tactics, and more targeted talent management. However, the analysis raises issues about data privacy, ethical constraints, and the need for proper reskilling of the HR sector. This study seeks to provide a complete grasp of the present AI landscape in human resource management, as well as practical insights from the Indian context. It also emphasizes the significance of combining technology adoption with human-centered approaches in order to create a fair and inclusive workplace environment.

Keywords: Artificial Intelligence (AI) · Human Resource Management (HRM) · AI-driven recruitment · Employee engagement · Predictive analytics in HR · Workforce management · Performance Management

1 Introduction

1.1 Background

Rapid advances in artificial intelligence (AI) have made substantial inroads into a variety of industries, profoundly altering how businesses operate. Among these industries, Human Resource Management (HRM) is increasingly using AI-powered solutions to enhance processes that were previously primarily relied on manual intervention and human judgment. AI technologies like as machine learning (ML), natural language processing (NLP), and predictive analytics are revolutionizing traditional human resources activities by automating tasks, improving decision-making, and enabling more personalized and data-driven personnel management.

In India, the use of AI in human resource management has grown rapidly as firms face rising challenges to remain competitive in an increasingly digital environment. AI is being embraced by the country's diversified business landscape, which includes huge international businesses and new startups is utilizing AI to improve HR operations such as recruitment, employee engagement, and performance management. Indian firms are using AI to increase productivity, decrease human bias in decision-making, and better match HR policies with long-term company objectives.

Traditionally, HR has been connected with labor-intensive operations such as resume screening and interviewing, as well as personnel record management and performance evaluation. However, the introduction of AI technologies—such as machine learning, natural language processing, predictive analytics, and robotics—has resulted in new capabilities that can handle repetitive administrative tasks, analyze massive volumes of data, and even forecast employee behavior. This change enables HR experts to concentrate on strategic responsibilities such as talent development and corporate culture, while AI provides efficiency and accuracy in mundane processes.

AI plays a diverse role in HRM. HR has traditionally been connected with labor-intensive responsibilities such as resume screening and interviewing, as well as personnel record management and performance evaluation. However, the advent of AI technologies such as machine learning, natural language processing, predictive analytics, and robots has resulted in new capabilities that can perform repetitive administrative tasks, analyze massive volumes of data, and even forecast employee behavior. This transition enables HR experts to focus on strategic responsibilities such as talent development and organizational culture, while AI handles efficiency and accuracy in routine operations.

This change enables HR experts to concentrate on strategic responsibilities such as talent development and corporate culture, while AI provides efficiency and accuracy in mundane processes.

AI plays a diverse role in human resource management, including talent acquisition, employee engagement, workforce development, and retention techniques. In recruiting, AI-powered solutions are used to scan resumes, conduct video interviews, and match individuals to suitable openings using predictive analytics. These technologies help to decrease hiring biases, save time, and ensure that the best candidates are chosen. Similarly, AI-powered chatbots are transforming employee interactions by responding quickly to HR-related queries, resulting in increased engagement and satisfaction.

One of the most significant contributions of AI to human resource management is predictive analytics.

AI enables HR departments to forecast patterns such as employee attrition, talent gaps, and future workforce requirements. This enables businesses to make proactive decisions, keeping them ahead in the competitive job market. Furthermore, AI performance management technologies provide more objective and continual assessments, giving employers a better understanding of employee strengths, weaknesses, and training needs.

Despite the numerous benefits, the use of AI in HRM presents several hurdles. Ethical concerns about privacy, prejudice in algorithms, and the possible decrease of human oversight in decision-making are key issues that must be addressed. Ensuring that AI systems are transparent, fair, and safe is critical for building trust with employees and stakeholders.

The key areas of concentration will be:

Talent Acquisition: AI's role in recruitment, from candidate sourcing to selection procedures.

Employee Development: How AI tools are used to tailor learning and development to employees.

Workforce Analytics: The application of AI to predictive analytics, workforce planning, and performance monitoring.

Ethical Considerations: Addressing the ethical implications and biases in an AI-powered HR system

1.2 Problem Statement

While AI has the potential to alter HR services, integrating it into HRM presents a number of problems. Concerns about data privacy, the ethical use of AI in decision-making, and the potential for AI to disrupt established HR positions are especially prevalent in India, where AI legal frameworks are still maturing. Moreover, the workforce requires reskilling so that HR professionals can effectively collaborate with AI solutions. These difficulties need a detailed investigation of AI's position in human resource management to comprehend both the benefits and the obstacles to its widespread adoption.

Furthermore, the usage of AI in HRM varies by industry, with different levels of understanding, trust, and acceptability among HR professionals and employees. This mismatch calls into doubt the genuine impact of AI on employee satisfaction, engagement, and the general effectiveness of HR systems.

Furthermore, firms struggle to strike a balance between the benefits of AI-driven automation and the requirement to keep a human touch in HR functions—an essential component of sustaining organizational culture and employee wellbeing. Thus, the primary challenge that this research seeks to address is: "**How can organizations effectively integrate AI into Human Resource Management to enhance efficiency, accuracy, and decision-making, while mitigating risks related to ethical concerns, biases, and the loss of human-centered approaches?**".

1.3 Purpose of the Study

This research paper will investigate the integration of AI in HRM using a series of case studies from India. By examining how AI is employed in important HR activities such as recruitment, employee engagement, and workforce management, the paper sheds light on AI's practical applicability in Indian enterprises. It also discusses the hurdles of AI adoption in HRM, specifically data protection, ethical concerns, and workforce reskilling, and makes solutions for successfully incorporating AI into HR processes. It also covers the barriers of AI adoption in human resource management, particularly those connected to data protection, ethical concerns, and worker reskilling, and provides advice for successfully incorporating AI into HR operations.

1.4 Research Objectives

The paper's objectives are as follows:

- To investigate the current situation of AI usage in HRM among Indian enterprises.
- To assess the impact of AI on key HR tasks like recruitment, performance evaluation, and employee engagement.
- Identify the obstacles and ethical considerations related with AI integration in human resource management, particularly in India.
- To make recommendations for Indian firms on how to improve their AI-driven HR strategies while addressing issues of privacy, ethics, and reskilling.

1.5 Significance of the Study

As AI continues to transform HR practices around the world, understanding its specific impact in India is crucial for firms seeking to stay ahead in an increasingly competitive market. This work contributes to the growing body of research on AI in human resource management by focusing on case studies from India, providing insights that are both regionally and globally applicable. Furthermore, the study delivers a balanced view of AI's potential, emphasizing the opportunity for improving HRM while also addressing the accompanying risks and challenges.

The following are the main areas of significance:

1. **Improving HR Efficiency and Decision-Making.**

    The study examines how AI may greatly enhance productivity in HR tasks like as recruiting, talent management, performance evaluation, and employee engagement. The research will highlight approaches for firms to streamline their HR processes by investigating AI's potential to automate repetitive operations and enable data-driven decision-making. This can result in cost savings, shorter recruiting cycles, better personnel acquisition, and more accurate performance reviews.

2. **Managing Ethical and Bias Concerns**

    The ethical implications of AI in human resource management, such as biases in algorithmic decision-making, transparency, and privacy, are key concerns for both employers and employees. This study aims to shed light on these challenges by identifying potential dangers. And providing solutions to ensure justice and accountability in AI-powered HR systems. As a result, it will help to define ethical guidelines and best practices for firms who want to appropriately integrate AI into their HR operations.

3. **Bridge the Gap. Between Technology and Human-Centred HR**

    While AI has many benefits, there is rising concern over the loss of the "human touch" in HR procedures. This study will look into the balance of technology efficiency and the requirement for a personalized, human-centered approach to human resource management. The findings will be useful for firms looking to exploit AI's capabilities while maintaining the emotional intelligence and interpersonal skills required for efficient human resource management.

4. **Notifying HR Professionals and Organizational Leaders**

The report is designed to be a comprehensive resource for HR professionals and corporate executives, providing practical insights and suggestions for integrating AI-powered technologies in HRM. It will provide a comprehensive knowledge of the benefits and limitations of AI in HR, allowing decision-makers to make more educated decisions about technology adoption and integration. This understanding can lead to more strategic, forward-thinking HR practices that are consistent with business goals and values.

5. Directing Future Research and Development in AI-HR Integration.

By identifying present shortcomings in the use of AI in HRM, this study will pave the way for future research in the subject. It will serve as a foundation for additional studies aimed at improving AI algorithms, create more advanced AI tools, and solve new difficulties in AI-powered HR. Re-searchers, researchers, and AI developers can use the study's findings to expand the technology and guarantee that it meets the changing needs of HRM.

6. Supporting Policy Formulation and Regulation

As AI continues to have an impact on HRM, there is a growing demand for legal frameworks that address concerns such as data privacy, algorithmic fairness, and the ethical usage of AI in HR practices. The study's findings on ethical challenges and best practices will be useful for policymakers and regulatory organizations looking to develop guidelines and standards for AI applications in HR. This can help to create a legal and ethical framework that encourages careful use of AI technology in the workplace.

7. Empowering Employees and Improving Workplace Culture

Understanding the impact of AI on employee experience is critical for building a strong business culture. This study will look at how AI-driven HR practices affect employee views, job happiness, and engagement. By emphasizing the influence of AI on the workforce, the study will make recommendations for maintaining openness, developing trust, and ensuring that employees are appreciated and heard in an AI-enhanced HR environment.

In conclusion, the purpose of this research is to advance academic and practical knowledge of AI's revolutionary role in human resource management. It aims to bridge the gap between the technology and human aspects of HR by providing evidence-based solutions and suggestions for organizations to implement AI responsibly and effectively. The study's findings have the potential to define the future of human resource management, ensuring that AI's benefits are fully realized while reducing dangers and keeping the human aspect, which is critical to people management.

2 AI Application in Human Resource Management (HRM) in India

Artificial intelligence is increasingly being employed in a variety of HR activities. Some of the prominent technologies are:

Machine Learning (ML): Predicts employee turnover, performance, and candidate success.

Natural Language Processing (NLP): Used for resume screening, sentiment analysis of employee feedback, and chatbot-based recruitment.

Predictive Analytics: Predictive analytics enables HR departments to make data-driven choices about workforce planning, employee development, and recruitment.

Robotic Process Automation (RPA): RPA automates typical administrative operations including payroll processing and leave management.

2.1 Recruitment and Talent Acquisition:

AI has altered recruitment by streamlining the candidate sourcing, screening, and selection processes. AI-powered products such as chatbots and resume screening software enable HR departments to rapidly filter through enormous candidate pools.

For example, AI-powered systems can rate candidates based on qualifications, experience, and cultural fit, decreasing human bias.

Case Study 1: Tata Consultancy Services (TCS): TCS use AI-powered tools such as Talview to automate resume screening and candidate shortlisting. The AI system evaluates candidates for skills, experience, and cultural fit, lowering time-to-hire and increasing recruitment accuracy.

Case Study 2: Infosys: Infosys uses AI in recruitment, including chatbots and virtual assistants. These technologies streamline the hiring process by facilitating early candidate interactions, answering FAQs, and scheduling interviews.

2.2 Onboarding

AI technologies are being used to enhance onboarding experiences for new employees.

Case Study 3 Wipro: Wipro's onboarding process includes an AI-driven platform that provides personalized onboarding experiences. The AI system offers tailored training modules and resources, facilitating a smooth transition for new hires.

2.3 Employee Engagement and Retention

AI can improve employee engagement and retention by monitoring satisfaction with sentiment analysis tools and proactively addressing concerns. AI systems may identify turnover risks and recommend individualized retention measures by evaluating employee behavior patterns.

Case Study 4 HCL Technologies: HCL Technologies utilizes AI-based sentiment analysis tools to gauge employee satisfaction and engagement. These tools analyze employee feedback and communication patterns to identify areas for improvement and enhance overall engagement.

2.4 Performance Management

AI helps firms estimate personnel demands, manage shifts effectively, and optimize workforce allocation. Predictive analytics enables HR departments to anticipate future demand, detect skill gaps, and guarantee that the right personnel is accessible at the right time.

Case Study 5: Mahindra and Mahindra. Mahindra & Mahindra employs AI to monitor and evaluate employee performance indicators. The AI system analyzes employee productivity and identifies areas for improvement, resulting in more accurate performance reviews.

2.5 Learning and Development

AI is revolutionizing learning and development in Indian companies.

Case Study 6 Reliance Industries: Reliance Industries uses AI-driven learning platforms to provide individualized training programs. The AI system offers courses based on employee career goals and performance, encouraging ongoing learning and skill improvement.

3 Challenges of AI Integration in HRM

3.1 Data Privacy and Security

One of the critical challenges of incorporating AI in Human Resource Management (HRM) is ensuring data privacy. AI systems heavily rely on extensive employee data, sparking concerns about its secure handling, appropriate usage, and protection against breaches. This issue becomes particularly significant in countries like India, where data protection laws are evolving. Organizations must ensure compliance with frameworks like the Personal Data Protection Bill (PDPB), which emphasizes safeguarding sensitive information. Non-compliance can result in legal repercussions and damage to organizational reputation. Companies must adopt robust data encryption, anonymization, and secure storage practices while establishing transparent data usage policies. Balancing AI's efficiency with stringent privacy measures is essential to build trust and maintain ethical standards in HRM.

3.2 Ethical Considerations

AI's role in decision-making within HRM raises significant ethical concerns, particularly regarding bias and fairness. When AI systems are trained on biased or unrepresentative data, they can unintentionally reinforce existing stereotypes, leading to discriminatory outcomes in critical areas such as recruitment, promotions, and performance evaluations. This lack of fairness undermines the integrity of HR processes and can result in legal and reputational risks for organizations. To address these challenges, it is essential to prioritize fairness and transparency in AI algorithms. Regular audits, diverse datasets, and bias mitigation techniques should be implemented to ensure equitable outcomes. Establishing ethical guidelines and fostering accountability in AI-powered HR systems are also vital steps toward building trust and driving inclusivity in the workplace.

3.3 Workforce Reskilling

The automation of HR processes through AI has the potential to make certain roles redundant, leading to concerns about job displacement. As routine tasks are increasingly handled by AI, HR professionals may find their traditional roles evolving or diminishing. To address this challenge, companies should prioritize reskilling their workforce, equipping HR professionals with competencies in data analytics, AI tool management, and strategic decision-making. By embracing lifelong learning and adapting to technological advancements, HR teams can transition into more analytical and strategic roles. Investing in upskilling not only mitigates job displacement risks but also enhances organizational agility and innovation in HR practices.

4 Future Potential of AI in Human Resource Management

Despite its challenges, AI holds immense potential for revolutionizing Human Resource Management (HRM) in India. As AI technologies continue to evolve, they offer HR departments powerful tools for greater automation, improved decision-making, and enhanced employee experiences. By leveraging AI, organizations can optimize their HR functions and align them more closely with strategic goals. Among the emerging trends in AI-powered HRM, three areas stand out for their transformative impact: diversity and inclusion initiatives, advanced predictive analytics, and personalized employee experiences.

AI-Powered Diversity and Inclusion Initiatives
AI can play a pivotal role in promoting workplace diversity and inclusion by addressing unconscious biases that often influence hiring and performance evaluations. By analyzing large datasets objectively, AI can identify patterns of bias, such as favoritism toward specific demographics or educational backgrounds. This allows HR teams to make more equitable decisions and implement fairer policies. For example, AI algorithms can evaluate job descriptions and suggest language modifications to attract a diverse pool of candidates. Additionally, AI-driven tools can monitor promotion patterns and highlight any disparities, enabling organizations to foster an inclusive culture. By reducing human bias, AI empowers organizations to create a more balanced and representative workforce.

Advanced Predictive Analytics
AI is set to revolutionize workforce planning through its advanced predictive analytics capabilities. As AI systems become more adept at analyzing historical data and identifying trends, HR teams will be better equipped to forecast critical metrics such as employee turnover, skill gaps, and future hiring needs. Predictive models can help organizations proactively address challenges like high attrition rates by identifying at-risk employees and suggesting targeted interventions. Similarly, AI can pinpoint emerging skill requirements in response to market changes, enabling organizations to invest in relevant training programs. By providing actionable insights, AI allows HR teams to adopt a proactive and strategic approach to workforce management.

AI-Powered Individualized Employee Experience

Personalization is another area where AI is transforming HR practices. AI systems can analyze individual employee data to design tailored career development plans, aligning their growth aspirations with organizational objectives. Real-time feedback mechanisms powered by AI can provide employees with instant recognition and constructive feedback, boosting engagement and morale. Additionally, AI chatbots and virtual assistants can offer personalized support for employees, addressing queries and facilitating continuous learning opportunities. By delivering customized experiences, AI enhances employee satisfaction and retention while driving organizational performance.

In conclusion, the integration of AI in HRM is poised to redefine how organizations manage and engage their workforce in India. By embracing these rising trends, businesses can foster a more inclusive, efficient, and personalized workplace.

5 Conclusion

In conclusion, the incorporation of AI into HRM is not just about technological advancements but also about creating a fair and inclusive workplace. Indian organizations must adopt a thoughtful approach, combining the efficiency and innovation offered by AI with a strong focus on ethics, transparency, and human-centric practices. By doing so, businesses can ensure that AI becomes a powerful enabler of progress, fostering creativity, inclusivity, and trust in the evolving landscape of human resource management. The journey to AI-powered HRM may be complex, but with the right strategies, it holds the promise of a brighter and more equitable future for organizations and their employees.

References

1. Banerjee, M.: Ethical implications of AI in human resource management. Int. J. HR Technol. **5**(3), 45–60 (2019)
2. Bhatia, R., Sinha, A.: Artificial intelligence in recruitment: a case study of Indian IT firms. Indian J. Hum. Resour. Dev. **15**(2), 72–88 (2020)
3. Chatterjee, A., Sharma, P.: AI and talent acquisition: a comprehensive review of practices in India. J. Talent Manage. Dev. **19**(1), 29–47 (2021)
4. Das, K., Gupta, N.: AI in performance management: opportunities and challenges in Indian enterprises. Asia-Pacific HR Rev. **24**(3), 101–118 (2022)
5. Gupta, A.: The role of AI in transforming recruitment processes: an Indian perspective. J. Hum. Resour. Stud. **12**(4), 56–72 (2020)
6. Kumar, R.: Predictive analytics and employee retention: the role of AI in Indian companies. Hum. Resour. Analy. J. **9**(2), 63–81 (2021)
7. Rajan, S., Patel, V.: AI in HRM: challenges and opportunities in the Indian market. HRM Rev. **18**(2), 34–50 (2021)
8. Saxena, P., Mishra, V.: Reskilling the workforce: preparing HR professionals for AI integration. Indian J. HR Technol. Innov. **6**(1), 22–39 (2021)
9. Sharma, M., Kapoor, D.: Data privacy and ethical concerns in AI-Driven HRM: insights from India. Glob. HR Ethics J. **14**(4), 75–89 (2022)
10. Singh, S., Mehta, R.: AI-powered employee engagement solutions: a study of Indian corporations. Employee Exper. J. **7**(2), 50–67 (2021)

Advancements in Disease Detection and Diagnosis: An Extensive Review of Artificial Intelligence Tools

Jeevan Kumar[1(✉)], Vijay Pandey[2], and Rajesh Kumar Tiwari[3]

[1] Department of CSE, JUT, Ranchi, Jharkhand, India
jeevancse01@gmail.com
[2] Department of ME, BIT Sindri, Jharkhand, India
vpandey.me@bitsindri.ac.in
[3] Department of CSE, RVSCET, Jamshedpur, Jharkhand, India

Abstract. An Artificial Intelligence (AI) has brought about a revolution in various fields, allowing computers to perform tasks that were previously performed by human intelligence. Machine learning, a fundamental component of AI, focuses on creating software that can automatically learn and improve from training data. As Machine learning (ML) techniques have surpassed traditional AI challenges, they have found extensive application in various fields. The medical domain has also witnessed a significant impact as ML algorithms have been increasingly employed for disease detection and diagnosis. This article highlights the potential benefits of several machine learning algorithms while examining their effects on the detection and diagnosis of medical conditions. Moreover, it outlines potential future research directions to further enhance medical applications through the advancements in AI.

Keywords: Artificial intelligence · Machine learning · Deep Learning Disease detection · Supervised learning · Unsupervised learning

1 Introduction

Artificial intelligence empowers computers to comprehend and rationalize information effectively, leading to substantial improvements in their overall intelligence. One well-known area of artificial intelligence (AI) is machine learning (ML), which focusses on creating techniques that let computers learn from data and perform better without the need for explicit programming. ML research has established various categories to explore and refine the methods and applications of this transformative technology [1].

A broad spectrum of methods are included in machine learning, such as supervised learning, reinforcement learning, unsupervised learning, and semi-supervised learning. It is a transformative technique that enables computers to operate without explicit programming, instead relying on the ability to automatically improve and learn from research or experiential data. This powerful approach empowers machines to adapt and refine their performance through iterative processes, leading to more intelligent and efficient outcomes [2]. ML was improving the dependability, cost, and efficiency of our computing processes. Machine learning's strength is its capacity to offer flexible solutions via adaptive designs that get better with time. Because of its multidisciplinary character, it is extremely useful in a variety of fields, including as computers, engineering, and medical. Nowadays, machine learning (ML) permeates every aspect of daily life and frequently goes unnoticed by users. Electronic health records, which frequently contain varied data sets and high-dimensional patterns, are analysed using ML algorithms. The ML topic of pattern recognition provides assistance in predicting, choosing, and planning diagnoses and treatments. ML algorithms have the ability to handle massive amounts of data, mix data from several sources, and incorporate background knowledge into the study [3].

Today, diagnosing a disease is a serious task in the medical sciences. Through clinical examination and evaluation, it is essential to understand the specific diagnosis of patients. For accurate diagnosis and effective management, computer-based decision support systems may be necessary. Big data is produced in the healthcare industry involving clinical evaluation, patient reports, treatment, follow-ups, medicines, etc. A proper arrangement is difficult to make.

1.1 Authors Contributions of the Paper

a. **Phase-wise survey:** By analysing each stage of the ML pipeline separately, this research sets itself apart and allows for a thorough exploration of the unique methods, difficulties, and developments associated with each level. A better grasp of the distinct contributions and needs of every stage in the entire machine learning process is made possible by this structured learning.
b. **Comparison of Methods:** In order to highlight developments and identify areas where conventional approaches are still useful, this paper compares and contrasts traditional and modern machine learning techniques.
c. **Future Research Directions:** By highlighting important unsolved issues and suggesting possible paths for further research, this paper helps the field handle present constraints.

1.2 The Paper is Organised as Follows in the Following Sections

The background knowledge necessary for the ML methods described in Sect. 2. ML techniques for different diseases discuss the diagnosis in Sect. 3. ML is used to discuss plant diseases in Sect. 4. The application of ML to recognize cotton illnesses is covered in Sect. 5. The method for using ML to detect animal diseases is described in Sect. 6. In Sect. 7, the subject of research problems is explored. Future directions are covered in Sect. 8, and the work is concluded in Sect. 9.

2 ML Techniques

In this section, we will establish the groundwork for the upcoming segments by delving into various strategies and learning methodologies within the realm of ML. Supervised, semi-supervised, unsupervised, and reinforcement learning are the four primary types of machine learning techniques. Figure 1 illustrates how ML techniques are categorized. Understanding these different categories will aid in comprehending the subsequent discussions and applications of machine learning.

2.1 Supervised Learning

Supervised learning in AI refers to providing input data classified with corresponding outputs to a computer system for training. This technique holds significant importance in ML for data processing tasks. Through supervised learning, we can establish a function (f: x → y) that accurately predicts an output y from a given input x. Supervised learning algorithms primarily aim to construct a model capable of capturing the correlations and interdependencies between input features and the intended output outcomes. Regression and classification are the two main types of supervised learning. Logic-based categorization methods, such as decision trees and random forests, fall under the category of classification techniques.

2.1.1 Regression

Regression is a powerful method used to explore the relationships between independent features or variables and a dependent feature or outcome. It serves as a fundamental technique in ML predictive modeling, specifically for forecasting continuous results. Designing a mathematical equation that depicts the dependent variable (Y) as a function of one or more predictor variables (X) is the main objective of a regression model. In this manner, the model becomes capable of prognosticating the outcome (Y) by utilizing the equation and updated values of the predictor variables (X) [4]. The independent variable is represented by (X), the dependent variable by (Y), the function that establishes the relationship between (X) and (Y) by (f), and any random deviations are taken into account.

2.1.2 Decision Trees (DT)

A popular supervised learning method for classification and regression tasks, with a focus on classification, is the Decision Tree (DT). It functions similarly to a tree, with internal nodes standing in for dataset attributes, branches signifying the decision-making process, and leaf nodes denoting particular categorisation results. Decision nodes, which make decisions and have several branches, and leaf nodes, which show the final classification results with no more branches, are the two different types of nodes that make up a DT. To forecast a class or target, the technique entails building a training model using decision rules extracted from the training data [5].

2.1.3 Random Forest (RF)

RF, a renowned machine learning algorithm, is a vital component of the supervised learning methodology, effectively applied to both classification and regression tasks. As its name suggests, RF comprises numerous decision trees built on different subsets of the dataset, and it leverages their averages to improve predictive accuracy. The Random

Forest (RF) integrates the forecasts from several decision trees rather than depending on just one, and it bases its final choice on the overall majority of each individual prediction. The RF algorithm operates in two stages: first, the construction of the RF classifier, and then the outcome prediction [6]. It demonstrates robust performance with larger datasets and heterogeneous data, and it can effectively predict missing values. In the context of categorizing hyperspectral data, the RF classifier stands out as the most effective approach [7].

2.1.4 Artificial Neural Networks (ANN)

An ANN, a supervised machine learning technique for data categorization, draws inspiration from the structure of a human neuron [8, 9]. The ANN algorithm establishes a network with multiple interconnected processing units. This network links the input data to the output through numerous cells, nodes, units, or neurons. Typically organized in layers connected by nodes, ANNs utilize each node as an activation function. The input layer, one or more hidden layers, and the output layer are the three main layers that make up an ANN. Unlike many other classification techniques, ANN does not impose constraints on the input data and excels at classifying complex and non-linear datasets.

2.1.5 Deep Learning (DL)

DL, a specific type of supervised ML, is particularly adept at classification tasks. It is a ML subset that is particularly good at handling unstructured data. Current conventional ML techniques have been shown to perform worse than DL techniques. One of its key strengths lies in the capacity to progressively learn features from data at various levels. This ability allows computer models to extract high-level characteristics from the input data, making it highly versatile as it can work with or without labeled data and be trained to accomplish a wide range of objectives. Bioinformatics, social network analysis, corporate intelligence, medical image processing, and speech and handwriting recognition are just a few of the fields where DL offers notable benefits.

2.1.6 Support Vector Machine (SVM)

A supervised ML classifier called SVM chooses the best hyperplane to accurately categorize inputs [10]. By considering individual observations and hyperplanes in the coordinate space, SVM achieves superior classification performance. Once the boundary is established, many points in the training data become redundant, and SVM relies on specific points known as support vectors to determine the boundary. SVM excels at providing the best classification results for a given dataset. Notably, the number of features in the training set does not influence the model complexity of SVM. Consequently, SVMs are well-suited for learning tasks with a high number of features relative to the number of training cases, making them a suitable choice for handling complex datasets with a large number of features.

2.1.7 Bayesian

A supervised ML approach called Bayesian uses probability to describe all model uncertainty, including uncertainty about the output as well as uncertainty surrounding the input [11]. By mastering conditional independence through a variety of statistical techniques, Bayesian learning uncovers correlations between datasets. Different probability functions for various class node variables are possible with Bayesian learning.

2.1.8 K-Nearest Neighbour (KNN)

A supervised machine learning method for classification and regression applications is KNN. When predicting or classifying a new, unknown variable, the K stands for the number of nearest neighbours taken into account. With (X) as the input and (Y) as the output, the main objective of supervised machine learning techniques is to learn the function $f(X) = Y$. KNN uses a variety of distance functions, including Euclidean, Hamming, Canberra, Manhattan, Minkowski, and Chebychev, to assess how similar the data points are to one another. The complexity of the KNN algorithm is influenced by the size of the input dataset, and the best results are obtained when the data is of the same scale. Additionally, KNN aids in minimizing dimensionality while identifying potential missing values in the feature space [11, 13, 14]. By leveraging the concept of proximity, KNN enables efficient and effective classification or regression by relying on the neighboring data points to make predictions for new instances.

2.2 Unsupervised Learning (UL)

Unsupervised ML is a powerful approach that delves into historical data to uncover hidden patterns and structures without the need for explicit guidance. This versatile technique finds application in diverse tasks such as dimensionality reduction, anomaly detection, and autonomously organizing and categorizing data [1]. By analyzing the inherent structure and relationships within the data, unsupervised learning methods offer valuable insights and understanding, enabling the exploration and comprehension of data without relying on predefined labels or outcomes.

2.2.1 K-means Clustering

The simplest and most often used unsupervised machine learning approach is K-means clustering. A centroid is used to represent each cluster in the K-means algorithm, which is a centroid-based clustering technique. This algorithm's main goal is to reduce the total distance between each data point and the cluster centroid to which it belongs. An unlabeled dataset is used as the initial input in the method, which then divides it into K clusters and iteratively improves the process until no more clusters can be generated. It needs K to be the predefined value. The K-means clustering technique consists of two basic steps: (a) finding ideal locations for K centroids, or centre points, iteratively; and (b) matching each data point to the closest centroid to create groups of similar data points.

2.2.2 Hierarchical Clustering

Hierarchical clustering is an unsupervised learning approach that groups unlabeled data points with similar features together. It can be categorized into two types of algorithms:

a. **Divisive Hierarchical Algorithms:-** All data points are first considered as a single huge cluster in this top-down method. The huge cluster is iteratively divided into smaller clusters during the clustering process, until each data point becomes its own cluster.

b. **Agglomerative Hierarchical Algorithms: -** Each data point is first taken into account as a separate cluster in this bottom-up technique. The technique successively aggregates or merges groups of clusters based on how similar they are until all of the data points are part of one big cluster. The clusters' hierarchical structure is shown using a dendrogram or tree structure. Based on density functions, each observation is assigned to its cluster using hierarchical clustering [15, 16]. This method has the benefit of being reasonably simple to apply and not requiring prior knowledge of the number of clusters.

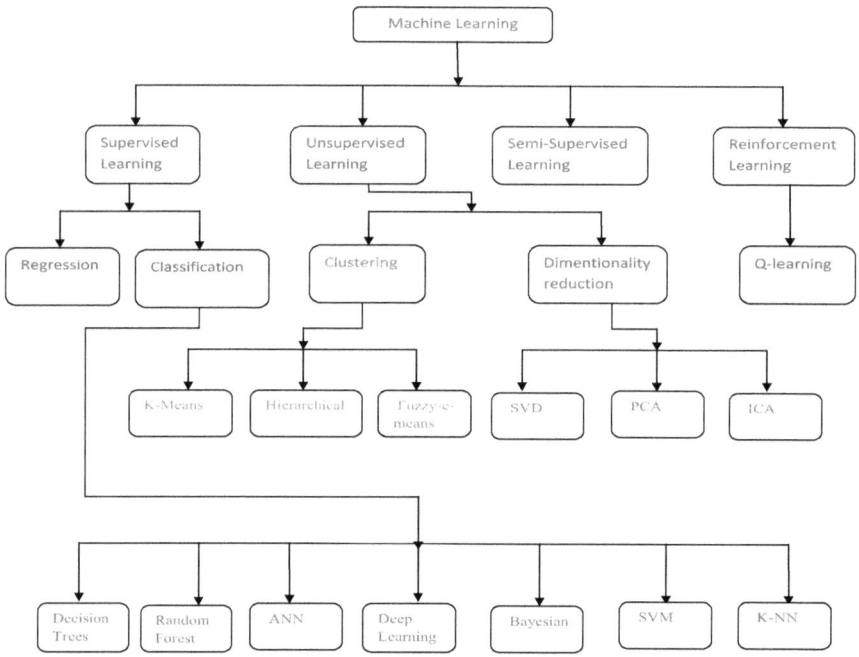

Fig. 1. Classifications of Machine Learning Techniques.

2.2.3 Fuzzy- C -Means Clustering

Bezdek's introduction of fuzzy set theory in 1981 resulted in the creation of fuzzy c-means (FCM) clustering, also known as soft clustering, which permits the assignment of data to one or more groups [17]. To locate clusters, FCM makes use of similarity metrics like intensity, distance, or connection. The choice of similarity measures may vary depending on the specific applications or datasets involved. Finding the most suitable cluster centres requires iterating through the clusters. When it comes to clustering overlapping datasets, FCM performs better than k-means and is particularly useful in such circumstances.

2.2.4 Singular Value Decomposition (SVD)

Reduce dimensionality by using the matrix factorization technique known as SVD. Any matrix can be broken down into three basic and well-known matrices using this method. Eigenvalues and eigenvectors are necessary knowledge to comprehend the idea of SVD. This effective method has interesting uses in image processing and ML, where it is essential for a number of tasks like feature extraction, noise reduction, and data compression.

2.2.5 Principle Component Analysis (PCM)

A popular unsupervised learning method for reducing dimensionality in ML is PCA [18]. PCA, a statistical technique, employs orthogonal transformation to convert correlated feature observations into a set of linearly uncorrelated data points. By considering the variance of each attribute, PCA effectively reduces dimensionality by identifying the most informative features that contribute significantly to the data's variability. PCA has practical uses in a variety of industries, including image processing, movie recommendation programs, and channel power optimization.

2.2.6 Independent Component Analysis (ICA)

An innovative method of data representation called ICA divides multivariate observations into additive subcomponents, each of which is represented by a non-Gaussian distribution [19]. Unlike PCA, ICA can capture higher-order dependencies and eliminate them effectively. It surpasses PCA in terms of its potency and ability to discover more complex relationships in the data. ICA has proven to be a valuable technique in various application sectors, including web content analysis, digital photographs, psychometric tests, corporate intelligence, and social networking.

2.3 Semi-Supervised Learning

A machine learning technique called semi-supervised learning trains models using a big volume of unlabelled data and a small amount of labelled data. This method, which falls somewhere between supervised and unsupervised learning, uses both labelled and unlabelled data in its procedures. It can be used for a number of applications, including semi-supervised classification, dimensionality reduction for labelled data, regression with unlabelled data, and constrained clustering [20, 21]. Predicting labels for the training set's unlabelled data and classifying labels for incoming test datasets are the main goals of semi-supervised learning. Many real-time scenarios can benefit from semi-supervised learning, including video surveillance, spam filtering, speech recognition, web content classification, and protein sequence classification.

2.4 Reinforcement Learning (RL)

An algorithm known as RL learns constantly by interacting with the environment to produce desired behaviors. Its primary objective is to maximize performance by making optimal decisions based on the surrounding conditions. In RL, ML models are trained to make a series of judgments, enabling an agent to perform tasks in complex and uncertain environments. This learning process can be likened to an AI encountering a game-like situation, where it employs trial and error to solve the problem. The AI agent is rewarded or penalised according to its behaviours throughout the RL process, which guides the machine to finish tasks that are consistent with the programmer's intended results. The ultimate goal of the AI agent is to maximize the overall reward it receives by making intelligent decisions and learning from its experiences in the environment [22].

3 ML Methods for the Diagnosis of Different Diseases

Both professionals and researchers have shown a great deal of interest in the application of ML techniques for disease detection. This section examines several ML-based disease diagnostic (MLBDD) techniques that have become well-liked because of their vital significance. More serious ailments including COVID-19, diabetes, Parkinson's, Alzheimer's, heart disease, kidney disease, and breast cancer are covered in greater length, while some diseases are just mentioned in passing under the "other diseases" category. It has been established that a number of machine learning algorithms are capable of accurately identifying diseases like diabetes, liver illness, dengue fever, heart disease, and hepatitis. Overall, ML plays a crucial role in advancing disease diagnostics, contributing to more effective and accurate disease detection and management in various healthcare applications. Table 1 displays the varying performance levels achieved by different methodologies, measured in terms of accuracy.

3.1 Heart Disease

Medical professionals and scientists frequently use machine learning approaches to identify heart-related problems [23, 24]. For instance, Ansari et al. (2011) used a neurofuzzy integrated system to establish an automated technique for detecting coronary heart disease, with an accuracy of about 89%. The absence of a thorough analysis of how the suggested method will function in many situations, such as multiclass classification, handling big datasets, and dealing with unequal class distributions, is a major study weakness.

3.2 Kidney Disease

Decreased kidney function causes kidney disease, sometimes referred to as renal disease, which, if left untreated, can lead to kidney failure. The development of ML and DL techniques has become a viable answer to the diagnostic problems related to renal disorders [25]. Charleonnan et al. (2016) evaluated machine learning classifiers such KNN, SVM, LR, and decision trees through experiments on publically accessible datasets.

Their respective remarkable accuracy ratings were 98.1%, 98.3%, 96.55%, and 94.8% [26]. Aljaaf et al. (2018) investigated ML methods such as RPART, SVM, LOGR, and MLP on a comparable dataset. According to their investigation, MLP had the highest accuracy rate of 98.1% in the diagnosis of chronic renal illness [27]. Furthermore, by utilising a range of datasets from various sources, Ma et al. (2020) suggested employing a heterogeneous modified artificial neural network (HMANN) model for the identification of chronic renal illness. Their model achieved accuracy rates ranging from 87% to 99%, showcasing the potential of ML in improving kidney disease diagnostics [28]. With the aid of these ML and DL techniques, the accurate and timely diagnosis of kidney disease becomes more feasible, leading to improved healthcare outcomes and better management of this serious condition.

3.3 Breast Cancer

The proposed model by Miranda and Felipe (2015) demonstrated an accuracy of approximately 83.34% [29]. To enhance the experiment's accuracy and objectivity, the authors used an essentially equal ratio of images for both benign and malignant categories. However, the study lacks a clear and comprehensive interpretation of the results, making it challenging to draw a conclusive assessment of accuracy for each class. To ensure the reliability and usefulness of the proposed ML-based breast cancer analysis, further investigations and improved result presentation are essential.

3.4 Diabetes

According to projections from the International Diabetes Federation (IDF), there are currently over 383 million diabetics globally, and by 2050, that figure is predicted to increase to 630 million [30]. The use of ML-based algorithms for identifying diabetes patients has been extensively studied in a number of publications. For example, Kandhasamy and Balamurali (2015) investigated a number of ML classifiers in the context of characterising patients with diabetes mellitus. Their analysis of the UCI Diabetes dataset revealed that the RF and KNN (K = 1) classifiers operated almost well. [31]. Nevertheless, a limitation of the study lies in the utilization of a reduced diabetes dataset containing merely eight factors classified into binary categories. It is not surprising that a simplified dataset can achieve 100% accuracy, but it may not correctly represent real-world events.

3.5 Parkinson's Disease

Parkinson's disease is a chronic neurological disorder that has garnered significant attention in the ML literature. This condition progresses slowly, causing difficulties in essential functions like speaking, writing, and walking when certain regions of the brain's dopamine-producing neurons are damaged or lost [32]. In response to this challenging disease, several ML-based strategies have been proposed. To establish intelligent diagnosis systems for Parkinson's disease, Sriram et al. (2013) employed ML algorithms including KNN, SVM, NB, and RF. Through their research, they determined that RF exhibited the highest performance, achieving an accuracy of 90.26%. Conversely, NB exhibited the lowest accuracy, with a score of only 69.23% [33]. ML-based approaches for Parkinson's disease detection hold great promise in aiding early diagnosis and improving patient management.

3.6 Covid-19

The COVID-19 pandemic, which has constituted a serious threat to humankind, is caused by the severe acute respiratory syndrome coronavirus 2 (SARS-CoV-2). Despite efforts to provide vaccines, many people had trouble getting them during the global emergency [34]. Additionally, worries have grown after the Covid-19 Omicron strain emerged; it has a high rate of transmission and may be resistant to current vaccines. Researchers have been investigating different technologies to help with the early diagnosis of possible cases, even though Real-Time Reverse Transcription-Polymerase Chain Reaction (RT-PCR) is still the gold standard for detecting COVID-19 infection [35, 36]. These include techniques like CT, ML, AI, and chest X-rays. Chen et al. (2020) created a UNet ++ model utilising CT scans from 82 non-COVID-19 patients and 51 COVID-19 patients, achieving an astounding accuracy of 98.5% [37]. Similarly, using ten distinct deep learning models on a smaller dataset of 108 COVID-19 and 86 non-COVID-19 patients, Ardakani et al. (2020) achieved an overall accuracy of 99% [38].

3.7 Alzheimer's Disease

A degenerative brain illness, Alzheimer's disease affects 60–70% of those with dementia [39]. Both ML) and DL have recently demonstrated encouraging outcomes in detecting people who have Alzheimer's disease. In order to identify Alzheimer's patients, Neelaveni and Devasana (2020) developed a model that used SVM and DT with noteworthy accuracy rates of 85% and 83%, respectively [40]. In a similar vein, Collij et al. (2016) used SVM to detect Alzheimer's disease and moderate cognitive impairment (MCI) in a single person with an accuracy of 82% [41]. In order to create efficient techniques for Alzheimer's disease diagnosis, a variety of machine learning-based algorithms have been investigated and evaluated.

3.8 Liver Disease

Vijayarani and Dhayanand [42] employed NB classification and SVM techniques to predict liver illness. They used the UCI-provided ILPD data set, which consists of 560 instances and 10 attributes. On the basis of time and precision, comparisons were done. Among the algorithms tested, SVM achieved an accuracy of 79.66% within a processing time of 3210.00 ms, while NB exhibited a correctness rate of 61.28% in 1670.00 ms. The researchers employed multiple ML algorithms to make predictions regarding liver disease. While NB worked faster, SVM performed better in terms of accuracy. Gulia et al. [43] used a data collection received from UC Irvine in their study on clever ways to categorize liver patients. These research efforts demonstrate the application of various ML techniques in liver disease prediction.

Table 1. The accuracy based results of various methodologies are depicted

Sl No	Authors	Disease	Methodology adopted	Overall accuracy (in %)
01	Ansari et al. [23]	Heart Disease	Neurofuzzy integrated system	89
02	Aljaaf et al. [27]	Kidney Disease	MLP	98.1
03	Ma et al. [28]	Kidney Disease	HMANN	87
04	Miranda & Felipe, [29]	Breast Cancer	fuzzy-logic-based	83.34
05	Sriram et al. [33]	Parkinson's Disease	Random Forest	90.26
06	Ardakani et al. [38]	COVID-19	Ten diverse deep learning models	99
07	Neelaveni & Devasana, [40]	Alzheimer's Disease	SVM	85
08	Vijayarani et al. [42]	Liver Disease	SVM	79.66
09	Tarmizi et al. [44]	Dengue Disease	Decision Tree	99.95
10	Karlik, [47]	Hepatitis Disease	Naive Bayes classifier	97
11	Paramasivam et al. [48]	Plant diseases	Extreme Learning Machine	95
12	Navina Pandhare et al. [49]	Cotton disease	Multilayer Perceptron	96.69
13	Karthick B et al. [50]	Animal disease	SVM	90

3.9 Dengue Disease

Tarmizi et al. [44] launched a study in Malaysia where dengue is an increasingly ubiquitous disease frequent in countries with humid climates like Thailand, Indonesia, and Malaysia. The research uses data mining algorithms to identify dengue epidemics. The study used classification techniques like Rough Set Theory (RS), ANN) and DT to forecast dengue illness. The Selangor State Public Health Department supplied the dataset. Two tests were conducted using the WEKA data mining software: 10-fold cross-validation and percentage split. Under 10-Cross fold validation, DT achieved an accuracy of 99.95%, ANN exhibited an accuracy of 99.98%, and RS displayed the highest accuracy of 100%. When applying Percentage Split, both DT and ANN achieved an accuracy of 99.92%, while RS had a slightly lower accuracy rate of 99.72%. In another study by Fathima and Manimeglai [45], the focus was on forecasting Arbovirus-Dengue illness.

3.9.1 Hepatitis Disease

A comparison research for identifying hepatitis disease utilizing several data mining approaches, such as NB, Frequent Pattern Tree, K Star, J48, Logistic model Tree (LMT), and Neural Networks (NN), was proposed by Ba-Alwi and Hintaya [46]. In a separate study, Karlik [47] compared Naive Bayes and back propagation classifiers for diagnosing hepatitis disease. These classifiers demonstrated a significant benefit in requiring only a small amount of data to categorize items. The data set used in this investigation was the UCI hepatitis data collection, consisting of 20 features and 155 instances. The NB classifier achieved an impressive accuracy of 97% in this experiment.

4 Plant Diseases Using ML

The rural population of India mainly relies on agriculture, which is a sector that is important to the economy of any country. A decision support system in real-time, integrating a video sensor module, has been created to aid in the identification of plant diseases. As part of the study's assessment, SVM and Extreme Learning Machine (ELM) with both linear and polynomial kernels were evaluated as additional ML algorithms for their effectiveness. In comparison to the other classifiers used, the results showed that the ELM had superior performance characteristics, obtaining 95% greater accuracy and sensitivity. In the classification of three distinct plant diseases, the real-time hardware with the ELM classifier demonstrated remarkable performance. Using various training datasets, the algorithm may also be trained to detect a wide range of novel plant illnesses [48].

5 Cotton Disease Detection Using ML

Cotton is a major crop in India, with a significant portion (23%) being exported to foreign countries. However, the cotton yield is susceptible to diseases that can impact crop growth. This study focuses on using various ML techniques to classify cotton diseases. To build the cotton database, pictures were taken in a controlled environment in the field, and modified factorization-based active contour was applied for image segmentation. Subsequently, the partitioned images were employed to extract both color and texture data. These data sets were then input into various ML algorithms, including Multilayer Perceptron, SVM, Naive Bayes, RF, Ada Boost, and KNN. Interestingly, the classifiers demonstrated enhanced performance when utilizing color attributes as opposed to texture features. Color characteristics alone proved sufficient to distinguish between photos of healthy and diseased cotton leaves. The Multilayer Perceptron stood out with results close to 96.69%, surpassing the performance of other classifiers in the study [49].

6 Animal Disease Detection Using ML

The development of behavioral and physiological monitoring systems, including those created especially for animal health, has been expedited by ML algorithms. As farm animals are raised all over the world, it is essential to properly monitor their physiological processes. In order to follow each animal's vital signs continually and identify any biological changes, this article suggests using machine learning models. In order to identify potential dangers related to changes in an animal's physiological state, this model uses Internet of Things (IoT) sensors to gather crucial data, which is subsequently analysed using machine learning techniques. The outcomes of the experiment demonstrate how accurate and effective the suggested model is at identifying different animal circumstances. Notably, the SVM produced results that are encouraging for our goals, with an accuracy of above 90% [50].

7 Barriers in Research of ML

In this section, we explore some of the primary obstacles encountered when utilizing ML for disease diagnosis.

7.1 Obstacles Associated with Data

(a) **Data Deficiency:** Despite the fact that numerous hospitals and healthcare organisations have collected patient data, real-world data are rarely available for use in international research because of the data privacy act.
(b) **Noisy or missing values:** The values are frequently present in clinical data, making it difficult for radiologists to learn how to assess them.
(c) **Negative attack:** The occurrence of adversarial attacks is a serious issue with illness databases. These attacks manipulate test data, training data, or even ML models themselves to produce outputs from the ML system that are false or inaccurate.

7.2 Challenges in Disease Diagnosis from Various Perspectives

(a) **Insufficient data:** In spite of the extensive collection of patient data by numerous hospitals and healthcare organizations, the accessibility of real-world data for global research remains limited due to the constraints imposed by the Data Privacy Act.
(b) **Clinical data:** Often contains noisy or missing values, posing challenges for radiologists aiming to learn how to interpret them effectively.
(c) **Adverse Critique:** In the illness dataset, adversarial attack is one of the major problems. It refers to the alteration of testing data, training data, or a ML model to provide incorrect ML output.

7.3 Challenges Relating to Algorithms

(a) **Supervised vs. unsupervised:** When trained on labelled data, ML models like logistic regression and linear regression performed remarkably well. These same algorithms, however, frequently underperformed when given unlabeled data.
(b) **Black box issues:** Understanding how the model modifies internal components, including learning rates and weights, is a major difficulty due to the extensive use of CNNs in ML.
(c) **Explainable AI (XAI):-** Recent developments in XAI improve model interpretability, build confidence, and guarantee fairness to address transparency issues. The purpose of these methods is to help both experts and non-expert users better understand complex machine learning models.

8 Upcoming Directions of ML

A few possible tools and techniques that could help ML-based illness diagnostics overcome its present problems were covered here.

(a) **Generative adversarial network (GAN):** By generating synthetic data that closely resembles the original dataset, GAN offers a practical solution to address challenges posed by data scarcity.
(b) **Reasonable AI:** The application of ML models in practical situations is made clearer and simpler to comprehend by integrating interpretability and explainability.
(c) **Ensemble-based methodology:** Technology breakthroughs have given us the ability to gather multidimensional, high-resolution data. With such high-quality data, the typical ML approach could not work as well. In such scenarios, aggregating multiple ML models could prove to be the optimal approach for managing and assessing high-dimensional data.

9 Conclusion

The analysis presented in this paper highlights the potential of these algorithms in enhancing disease diagnosis. Moreover, the tools developed by the AI community in this survey article add further value to the research. These tools provide opportunities for better decision-making processes and prove highly beneficial for examining complex issues in various domains. In order to address important issues and propel breakthroughs in a variety of industries, ML and DL are predicted to become more and more important as technology develops. We can create the foundation for a future with more precise and effective diagnostic techniques by utilising ML/DL, which will ultimately improve healthcare outcomes and benefit society at large.

References

1. Marshland, S.: Machine Learning an Algorithmic Perspective, pp. 6–7. CRC Press, New Zealand (2009)
2. Kononenko, I.: Machine learning for medical diagnosis: history, state of the art and perspective. J. Artif. Intell. Med. **1**, 89–109 (2001)
3. Rambhajani, M., Deepanker, W., Pathak, N.: A survey on implementation of machine learning techniques for dermatology diseases classification. Int. J. Adv. Eng. Technol. **8**, 194–195 (2015)
4. Montgomery, D.C., Peck, E.A., Vining, G.G.: Introduction to Linear Regression Analysis. 821, John Wiley & Sons (2012)
5. Quinlan, J.R.: Induction of decision trees. Mach. Learn. **1**, 81–106 (1986)
6. Breiman, L.: Random forests. Mach. Learn. **45**, 5–32 (2001)
7. Belgiu, M., Lucian, D.: Random forest in remote sensing: a review of applications and future directions. ISPRS J. Photogramm. Remote Sens. **114**, 24–31 (2016). https://doi.org/10.1016/j.isprsjprs.2016.01.011
8. Haykin, S.: Neural networks and learning machines. vol. 3, Pearson Upper Saddle River, NJ, USA (2009)

9. White, H.: Learning in artificial neural networks: a statistical perspective. Neural Comput. **425–464** (1989). https://doi.org/10.1162/neco.1989.1.4.425
10. Vapnik, V.N.: An overview of statistical learning theory. IEEE Trans. Neural Netw. 988–999 (1999). https://doi.org /https://doi.org/10.1109/72.788640
11. Jensen, F.V.: An Introduction to Bayesian Networks, 210, UCL Press London (1996)
12. Dudani, S.A.: The distance-weighted k -nearest-neighbor rule. IEEE Trans. Syst. Man Cybern. SMC-**6**(4), 325–327 (1976)
13. Peterson, L.E.: K-nearest neighbor. Scholarpedia **4**(2) (2009). https://doi.org /https://doi.org/10.4249/scholarpedia.1883
14. Keller, J.M., Gray, M.R., Givens, J.A.: A fuzzy k -nearest neighbor algorithm. IEEE Trans. Syst. Man Cybern. SMC-**15** (4), 580–585 (1985)
15. Johnson, S.C.: Hierarchical clustering schemes. Psychometrika **32**(3), 241–254 (1967). https://doi.org /https://doi.org/10.1007/BF02289588
16. Andrade, R.G.D.: U-statistic hierarchical clustering. Psychometrika **43**, 59–67 (1978). https://doi.org/10.1007/BF02294089
17. Peizhuang, W.: Pattern recognition with fuzzy objective function algorithms. SIAM Rev. **25**(3) (1983). https://doi.org/10.1137/1025116
18. Wold, S., Esbensen, K., Geladi, P.: Principal component analysis. Chemometrics Intell. Lab. Syst. **2**(1–3), 37–52 (1978). https://doi.org/10.1016/0169-7439 (87)80084–9
19. Lee, T.W.: Independent Component Analysis. Springer, pp. 27–66 (1998)
20. Zhu, X., Goldberg, A.B.: Introduction to semi-supervised learning. Synth. Lect. Artif. Intell. Mach. Learn. **3**(1), 1–130 (2009)
21. Hady, M.F.A., Schwenker, F.: Semi-Supervised Learning, pp. 215–239. Springer, Handbook on Neural Information Processing (2013)
22. Watkins, C.J.C.H., Dayan, P.: Q-learning. Mach. Learn. **8**(3–4), 279–292 (1992)
23. Ansari, A.Q., Gupta, N.K.: Automated diagnosis of coronary heart disease using neuro-fuzzy integrated system. World Congress Inf. Commun. Technol. 1379–1384 (2011)
24. Ahsan, M.M., Mahmud, M., Saha, P.K., Gupta, K.D., Siddique, Z.: Effect of data scaling methods on machine learning algorithms and model performance. Technologies **9**, 52 (2021). https://doi.org/10.3390/technologies9030052
25. Levey, A.S., Coresh, J.: Chronic kidney disease. Lancet **379**, 165–180 (2012). https://doi.org/10.1016/S0140-6736(11)60178-5
26. Charleonnan, A., Fufaung, T., et al.: Predictive analytics for chronic kidney disease using machine learning techniques. In: Management and Innovation Technology International Conference, Bang-Saen, Chonburi, Thailand, pp. MIT-80–MIT-83 (2016). https://doi.org /https://doi.org/10.1109/MITICON.2016.8025242
27. Aljaaf, A., Al-Jumeily, D., et al.: Early prediction of chronic kidney disease using machine learning supported by predictive analytics. IEEE Congress Evol. Comput. (CEC), 1–9 (2018). https://doi.org/ https://doi.org/10.1109/CEC.2018.8477876
28. Ma, F., Sun, T., Liu, L., Jing, H.: Detection and diagnosis of chronic kidney disease using deep learning-based heterogeneous modified artificial neural network. Future Gener. Comput. Syst, **111**, 17–26 (2020). https://doi.org /https://doi.org/10.1016/j.future.2020.04.036
29. Miranda, G.H.B., Felipe, J.C.: Computer-aided diagnosis system based on fuzzy logic for breast cancer categorization. Comput. Biol. Med. **64**, 334–346 (2015). https://doi.org/10.1016/j.compbiomed.2014.10.006
30. Naz, H., Ahuja, S.: Deep learning approach for diabetes prediction using PIMA Indian dataset. J. Diabetes Metab. Disord. **19**, 391–403 (2020) . https://doi.org /https://doi.org/10.1007/s40200-020-00520-5
31. Kandhasamy, J.P., Balamurali, S.: Performance analysis of classifier models to predict diabetes mellitus. Procedia Comput. Sci. **47**, 45–51 (2015). https://doi.org/10.1016/j.procs.2015.03.182

32. Grover, S., Bhartia, S., Yadav, A., Seeja, K.R.: Predicting severity of Parkinson's disease using deep learning. Procedia Comput. Sci. **132**, 1788–1794 (2018). https://doi.org/10.1016/j.procs.2018.05.154
33. Sriram, T.V.S., Rao, M.V., et al.: Intelligent Parkinson disease prediction using machine learning algorithms. Int. J. Eng. Innov. Technol. (IJEIT) **3**, 1568–1572 (2013)
34. Ahsan, M.M., Nazim, R., Siddique, Z., Huebner, P.: Detection of COVID-19 patients from CT scan and chest X-ray data using modified mobilenetv2 and lime. Healthcare **9**, 1099 (2021). https://doi.org/10.3390/healthcare9091099
35. Haghanifar, A., Majdabadi, M.M., et al.: Covid-cxnet: Detecting COVID-19 in frontal chest X-ray images using deep learning (2020). ArXiv. https://doi.org/10.48550/arXiv.2006.13807
36. Tahamtan, A., Ardebili, A.: Real-time RT-PCR in COVID-19 detection: issues affecting the results. Expert Rev. Mol. Diagn, **20**, 453–454 (2020). https://doi.org /https://doi.org/10.1080/14737159.2020.1757437
37. Chen, J., Wu, L., Zhang, J., et al.: Deep learning-based model for detecting 2019 novel coronavirus pneumonia on high-resolution computed tomography. Sci. Rep. **10**, 1–11 (2020) . https://doi.org /https://doi.org/10.1038/s41598-020-76282-0
38. Ardakani, A.A., Kanafi, A.R., Acharya, U.R., et al.: Application of deep learning technique to manage COVID-19 in routine clinical practice using CT images: results of 10 convolutional neural networks. Comput. Biol. Med. **121**, 103795 (2020) . https://doi.org /https://doi.org/10.1016/j.compbiomed.2020.103795
39. Graham, N., Warner, J.: Alzheimer's disease and Other Dementias. Northampton, UK (2009)
40. Neelaveni, J., Devasana, M.G.: Alzheimer disease prediction using machine learning algorithms. In: International Conference on Advanced Computing and Communication Systems (ICACCS), IEEE, Manhattan, NY, USA, pp. 101–104 (2020) . https://doi.org /https://doi.org/10.1109/ICACCS48705.2020.9074248
41. Collij, L.E., Heeman, F., et al.: Application of machine learning to arterial spin labeling in mild cognitive impairment and Alzheimer disease. Radiology **281**, 865–875 (2016) . https://doi.org /https://doi.org/10.1148/radiol.2016152703
42. Vijayarani, S., Dhayanand, S.: Liver disease prediction using SVM and naïve bayes algorithms. Int. J. Sci. Eng. Technol. Res. (IJSETR) **4**, 816–820 (2015)
43. Gulia, A., Vohra, R., Rani, P.: Liver patient classification using intelligent techniques. (IJCSIT) Int. J. Comput. Sci. Inf. Technol. **5**, 5110–5115 (2014)
44. Tarmizi, N.D.A., Jamaluddin, F., et al.: Malaysia dengue outbreak detection using data mining models. J. Next Gen. Inf. Technol. (JNIT) **4**, 96–107 (2013)
45. Fathima, A.S., Manimeglai, D.: Predictive analysis for the arbovirus dengue using SVM classification. Int. J. Eng. Technol. **2**, 521–527 (2012)
46. Ba-Alwi, F.M., Hintaya, H.M.: Comparative study for analysis the prognostic in hepatitis data: data mining approach. Int. J. Sci. Eng. Res. **4**, 680–685 (2013)
47. Karlik, B.: Hepatitis disease diagnosis using back propagation and the naive bayes classifiers. J. Sci. Technol. **1**, 49–62 (2011)
48. Alagumariappan, P., Dewan, N.J., et al.: Intelligent plant disease identification system using machine learning. Eng. Proc. **2**(1), 49 (2020). https://doi.org/10.3390/ecsa-7-08160
49. Bhoomika, K., Shree, L.N.S.: Survey on cotton plant disease detection. Int. Res. J. Eng. Technol. (IRJET) **10**(03) (2023)
50. Karthick, B., Manjunath, M.: Animal health monitoring using machine learning. Int. J. Creat. Res. Thoughts (IJCRT) (2021)

Approaches of Groundwater Water Quality Prediction Using Machine Learning Techniques

Kulsuma Chowdhury[1(✉)], Nushrat Praveen[1], Amirul Hoque[2], Namrata Kumari[1], and Smita Dash[1]

[1] RVS College of Engineering and Technology, Jamshedpur, India
chowdhury.kulsuma97@gmail.com
[2] National Institute of Technology Jamshedpur, Jamshedpur, India

Abstract. Groundwater stands as one of the most crucial and renewable resources for all life on Earth. Assessing the water's quality is crucial to preserving the ecosystem's balance and longevity. The general quality of water has a significant effect on environmental preservation as well as human health. Water is used for domestic, agricultural, and industrial uses, among others. The Water Quality Index is an essential indicator for evaluating the success of water management. An assessment of water's biological, physical, and physiological qualities establishes whether or not it is suitable for a given use. Water quality analysis has become a critical issue in today's globe due to industrialization, agricultural activities, and human behavior. Real-time monitoring was outdated since traditional techniques of assessing water quality required costly testing facilities and numerical procedures. Because of the poor quality of groundwater, a more practical and economical solution is required. Techniques for categorization based on machine learning exhibit potential for quick assessment and identification of water quality. Machine learning algorithms have proven to be an excellent means of predicting the quality of water. The results of this research should improve machine learning applications for improving groundwater quality and groundwater development planning. The analysis highlights the effective use of models like deep learning, ensemble approaches, neural networks, support vector machines, and linear regression to predict groundwater quality, identify contamination sources, and optimize remediation techniques. It also shows how versatile machine learning techniques are in this regard. The study highlights the critical significance that high-quality and readily available data have in the success of models.

Keywords: Groundwater · Machine learning

1 Introduction

Globally, groundwater is essential to the survival of industrial, agricultural, and rural areas, as well as the people who live there and the customs they uphold.

It provides essential water for a range of uses, such as domestic requirements and consumption [1]. Groundwater quality needs to be monitored and managed to promote sustainable development, which depends on the availability of freshwater resources [2]. The chemical, physical, and biological characteristics of groundwater are essential to its sustainability as a resource for industry, agriculture, and the provision of drinkable water [3]. However, fast urbanization, industrial growth, poor waste disposal methods, uncontrolled fertilizer use, and unhygienic conditions have all posed threats to the integrity of groundwater quality [4]. To protect groundwater quality against pollution, particularly from contaminants in surface water, contamination indices are essential [1]. Since groundwater is heavily relied upon for freshwater requirements, it is critical to monitor its natural composition and condition [5]. This study intends to evaluate the predictive power of machine learning algorithms for groundwater quality, acknowledging the need for a thorough investigation into the possible uses of these algorithms in environmental research, specifically for groundwater quality prediction. Machine learning algorithms have proven to be remarkably effective in a variety of domains, including natural language processing and image recognition. We hope to shed light on the possibilities of using machine learning to address important environmental issues like groundwater quality monitoring by exploring this topic. Patel et al. show Sophisticated approaches and procedures are essential to attaining comprehensive utilization in rural regions; these include mapping and inventorying the site, evaluating water quality, vulnerability, and hydrodynamics, and improving the location, construction, and monitoring strategies of wells. Furthermore, it is crucial to take environmental law, geoethics, and socio-hydrogeology into account. Using this multidisciplinary approach makes it easier to share information about scientific discoveries, technological developments, and information that can be used to guide decisions about the management of water resources sustainably and the creation of eco-friendly solutions for rural communities operating under a hydrogeoethical philosophy [31]. In this article, we make the following contributions:

I. Comprehensive Overview of ML Approaches: This study offers a thorough overview of the many ML approaches used in the prediction of groundwater quality. In addition to more complex approaches like neural networks, ensemble methods, and DL models, it covers more conventional approaches like support vector machines, decision trees, and linear regression.

II. Identification of Key Factors and Feature Selection Techniques: The survey emphasizes how crucial feature selection is and how various elements (such as chemical characteristics and environmental conditions) affect the predictions of groundwater quality. This contribution aids in comprehending how improving model performance and prediction accuracy can be achieved by carefully choosing features.

III. Future Directions and Research Gaps: The paper identifies current research gaps and future directions in the application of ML to groundwater quality prediction. It covers new developments like the incorporation of sensor data in real-time, the use of hybrid models that combine physical and machine learning, and the requirement for larger datasets for training and validation. This study lays the groundwork for future investigations and technical developments in this area by emphasizing these areas.

IV. Comparative Analysis of Model Performance: The paper presents a comparative analysis of the performance of different ML models based on accuracy, robustness, computational efficiency, and generalizability. To evaluate how effectively each model predicts parameters related to groundwater quality. drinking (Fig. 1)

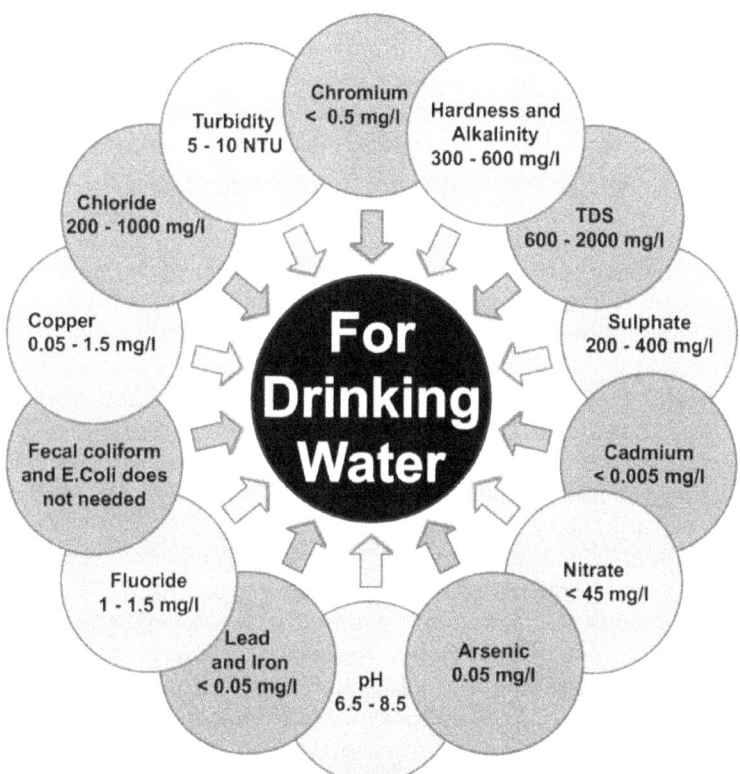

Fig. 1. spectrum of critical drinking water characteristics in accordance with WHO guidelines (Patel et al. 2023).

2 Literature Review

Water quality refers to all of its inherent characteristics, including its physical and chemical makeup, which can be changed by human activity [2]. The main activities carried out by humans that lead to groundwater contamination include industrial operations, agricultural practices, and sewage disposal [6]. The groundwater quality is greatly impacted by the process of moving water from its original point of collection to storage in wells, which frequently involves some physicochemical steps [2]. To find out if groundwater is suitable for industrial, household, agricultural, industrial, or sanitary uses, it is essential to evaluate its quality. Biological activity, ion exchange, precipitation, weathering, and dissolution are examples of subsurface processes. These complex chemical interactions make it difficult to assess groundwater quality over big datasets with various characteristics. Groundwater quality levels can be expressed more easily thanks to contamination index approaches that facilitate data analysis [1]. Water sustainability and the mitigation of the effects of drought rely on the capability to forecast the quality of groundwater resources [7]. For there to be safe drinking water available in the future, it is vital to understand the level and scope of groundwater contaminating as it exists today. For efficient water pollution prevention and improved water resource management, an accurate water quality forecast is essential. The rate at which water quality is deteriorating is increasing, highlighting the critical need for thorough monitoring and intervention strategies to protect this essential resource. The water quality has declined alarmingly as a result of the industrial sector's explosive growth. The problem of guaranteeing safe drinking water is made more difficult by a lack of public knowledge and poor sanitary infrastructure. Consequently, the advancement of novel technique for evaluating and possibly predicting water quality is imperative. Several approaches, including statistical methods, analytical algorithms, visual simulation, and predictive algorithms, have been put forth for the purpose of forecasting and simulating water quality [8]. Due to the intricacies of groundwater properties, traditional techniques are usually utilized to guarantee precise assessment of groundwater quality, requiring a significant amount of time, effort, and resources [10]. The problem of groundwater contamination continues despite attempts, with little progress made in removing the sources of contamination or greatly enhancing the quality of the contaminated groundwater. This is primarily ascribed to labor shortages and funding, competing regulatory interests, a general lack of knowledge in the area regarding the effects of human activity on groundwater quality, and technology limits in addressing economic, social, and political constraints. As a result, conventional methods for evaluating water quality cause financial losses and impede the formulation of policies for controlling water quality. Developing a workable, economical plan for accurate and timely water quality evaluation is essential to overcoming these obstacles. In this context, ML techniques stand out as extremely dependable and efficient method of checking the quality of water. Embracing ML techniques could provide a breakthrough in overcoming the limitations of traditional evaluation methods and enhance the ability to address complex water quality challenges (Table 1).

3 Materials and Methods

Groundwater quality is just as vital as its quantity. Salts from the water's historical movement and location are present in every groundwater. Drinking water,

Table 1. This table summarizes key aspects of various studies, including the method used, dataset, features, and performance metrics

Author	Year	Machine Learning Technique(s)	Dataset Used	Features	Performance Metrics	Key Findings
Sharma and Verma[ ]	2021	Gradient Boosting, XGBoost	Indian river dataset	Nitrate, DO, TDS, conductivity, pH	R^2: 0.92, RMSE: 0.06	Gradient Boosting yielded a more reliable prediction than XGBoost in nitrate prediction.
Yang and Zhao [22]	2022	Artificial Neural Networks (ANN), LSTM	Global river water dataset	pH, DO, nitrate, temperature, flow rate	MAE: 0.03, RMSE: 0.04	LSTM outperformed ANN in capturing temporal dependencies for predicting water quality.
Bilali et al.[6]	2021	Random Forest, SVM	UCI Water Quality Dataset	pH, DO, turbidity, temperature, EC	Accuracy: 92%, F1 Score: 0.89	Random Forest outperformed SVM in predicting water quality classes.
Zhang and Liu [13]	2021	Artificial Neural Networks (ANN)	Local river dataset	pH, nitrate, phosphate, temperature, DO	RMSE: 0.08, MAE: 0.05	ANN accurately predicted nitrate levels, showing good generalization.
Chen et al.[14]	2019	Decision Tree, KNN	Public drinking water dataset	TDS, pH, conductivity, hardness	Accuracy: 85%, Precision: 0.83	Decision Tree had better performance compared to KNN.
Kumar et al.[17]	2022	Gradient Boosting, XGBoost	Groundwater quality data from India	pH, TDS, hardness, alkalinity	RMSE: 0.07, R^2: 0.95	XGBoost provided the highest R^2 value, demonstrating robust predictions.
Li and Wang[1]	2021	Support Vector Machine (SVM)	Coastal water quality dataset	Salinity, DO, pH, temperature	Accuracy: 89%, AUC: 0.91	SVM successfully classified water quality levels with high accuracy.
Amalia et al.[18]	2023	k-Nearest Neighbors (KNN)	UCI Water Quality Dataset	pH, hardness, solids, chloramines	Precision: 0.87, Recall: 0.85	KNN performed well, but struggled with certain imbalanced classes.
Patel et al.[19]	2020	Random Forest, Decision Tree	Water quality from Gujarat, India	pH, turbidity, EC, total hardness, TDS	Accuracy: 91%, F1 Score: 0.88	Random Forest outperformed Decision Tree with better accuracy in classifying water quality levels.

industrial water, and irrigation water requirements differ greatly because the quality of the necessary groundwater supply varies on its intended use. Measuring the groundwater's chemical, physical, biological, and radioactive components is required to determine the quality standards. Comparing water quality from various sources is made easier by using standard reporting and presentation formats for groundwater quality metrics.

3.1 Measures of Water Quality

The chemical and biological reactions in the zones that the water passes through define the chemical properties of groundwater. It is typically necessary to use chemical, physical, and biological investigations to determine the quality attributes of groundwater. Water use is most likely to be impacted by naturally occurring inorganic elements that are frequently dissolved in water, such as: Bicarbonate, Carbonate, Chloride, Sulphate, Fluoride, Iron, Magneisum, bCalcium, Sodium and, Manganese. Furthermore, there are additional trace amounts that are stated in elemental form. pH and specific electrical conductivity measurements are also included in the investigation of water quality. Temperature, colour, turbidity, odour, and taste are among the characteristics of groundwater that are assessed during physical analysis.A bacteriological examination includes tests for coliform bacteria, which indicate the hygienic quality of water for human consumption.

Major Cations: The main cations are those that are found in higher concentrations—almost invariably greater than 1 mg/L. They include: Calcium (Ca^{2+}), Magnesium (Mg^{2+}), Sodium (Na^+), Potassium (K^+)

Major Anions: Major anions are the anions that are present in higher concentrations, often greater than 1 mg/L. The include: Bicarbonate (HCO_3)-, Sulfate $(SO_4)^{2-}$, Chloride (Cl^-)

Minor Ions: Minor ions are defined as cations and anions that are present in the mg/L concentration range. They include: Iron, Manganese, Nitrate, Ammonium, Hydrogen Sulfide, Fluoride and, Boron

Trace Ions: Almost all elements found in the periodic table that are not classified as major air minor ions fall under the category of trace ions. Typically, groundwater has a concentration range of less than 0.01 mg/L. Practically speaking, the importance of ions that are hazardous to humans (such as cadmium and mercury) or wildlife (such as copper, zinc, and aluminum) greatly outweighs their contribution to the total dissolved solids (TDS) in the water.

Hardness (mg/l) as $CaCO_3$: The presence of calcium and magnesium in groundwater is what causes it to be hard. The formula can be used to get the total hardness (HT). $HT = 2.5Ca + 4.1\,Mg$, where Ca and Mg concentrations are in mg/l (Table 2).

Total Dissolve Solids (TDS): The most widely used indicator of the total amount of dissolved mineral particles in water is its TDS content. Also, it is the most accurate way to gauge the salinity of water. The amounts of each of the water's dissolved constituents can be added up to determine the total dissolved solids (TDS). The water can be categorised in the following ways based on its TDS (Table 3).

Table 2. Hardness (mg/l) as CaCO3.

Water Class:	Soft	Moderately Hard	Hard	Very Hard
Level:	0-75	75-150	150-300	Over 300

Table 3. To classify the water based on the TDS

Type of Water:	Fresh	Brackish	Saline(mg/L)	Hyper Saline
TDS value:	Less than 1000	1000-10,000	10,000-100,000	Grater than 100,000

ph: A solution's acidity/alkalinity balance is most commonly measured using pH. Acidity levels are between 0 to 14 (no units). Seven is considered the neutral pH of water. Water is deemed acidic if its pH is lower than seven. Alkaline water is defined as having a pH of greater than 7.

Chemical Analyses: TDS via Electrical Conductivity. By measuring the electrical conductivity of a groundwater sample, the total dissolved solids can be quickly ascertained. A given groundwater sample's conductance rises as the concentration of salt in the water increases. Microsiemens/cm is the unit of measurement for specific conductance. Techniques for reporting water analysis need to be taken into account when a sample of groundwater has been examined in a lab. Standards can be set based on an understanding of the phrases and measurements used to describe the quality of the water, allowing the analyses to be understood about the ultimate goal of water delivery.

Cation-Anion Balance: After the chemical analysis is finished, the electroneutrality principle—which asserts that water is electrically neutral and devoid of all positive and negative charges—provides the last yardstick for evaluating quality. As a result, the total of the negatively charged (anions) and partially positively charged (cations) dissolved ions in water must match. This can be verified using the water's cation-anion balance (CAB), which is described as

$\mathcal{CAB} = ((sum of cations) - (sum of anions))/((sum of cations) + (sum of anions)) * 100$

The units used to express the ion concentration are meq/L. For all purposes, the analysis is considered sufficiently accurate if the value of CAB is less than 5%.

4 A Comparative Analysis of Machine Learning Techniques for Groundwater Quality Assessment

ML is a popular and efficient technique for data analysis that is used to identify patterns and forecasts from large datasets created in many contexts. Machine learning has been used by researchers to address resource allocation, pollutant concentration estimation, source identification, real-time monitoring, prediction, and water treatment system optimization [16]. A wide range of methods, such as long short-term memory networks, K-nearest neighbour, decision trees, artificial neural networks, exhibust, convolutional neural networks, regression models, support vector machines, deep neural networks, principal component analysis (PCA), and others, are applied when using ML techniques to groundwater quality prediction. These algorithms contribute to improvements in water resource management and environmental sustainability by providing a comprehensive toolkit for efficiently assessing and forecasting groundwater quality (Fig. 2).

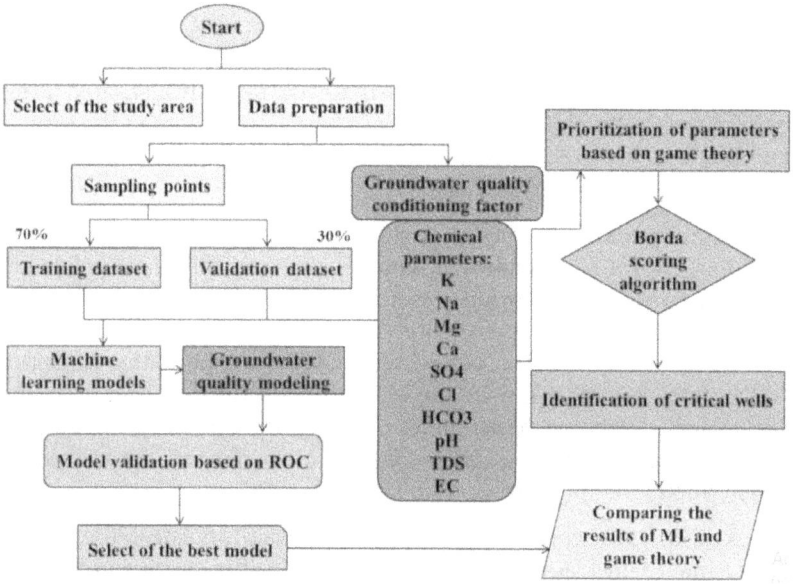

Fig. 2. An illustration of the Water Quality Index machine learning model's flow chart for analyzing and evaluating groundwater quality (Khiavi et al. 2023).

4.1 ANN (Artificial Neural Network)

Artificial neurons, which act as tiny, highly interconnected processing units, are used in artificial neural networks (ANNs) to mimic complex data analysis techniques like pattern classification, categorization, and generalization. ANNs are intended to create useful "computers" for real-world problems. Artificial neural networks (ANNs) are synthetic networks with flexibility that may change their internal architecture to suit different tasks. They are inspired by the way the human brain functions. The vital parts of an ANN are the interconnections and nodes, sometimes referred to as processing units (PE). An extensive range of type and texture properties necessary for pattern detection and selection are leveraged by ANNs, which are powerful analyzers capable of generalizing and making judgments based on large and complicated data inputs [27]. An ANN can be trained for a particular task, like pattern recognition or data pre-processing, through learning. ANNs can be used in machining operations to forecast the influence of different parameters on process variables after they have been trained effectively. To achieve the best micromachining performance, for example, combinations of ideal processing parameter values can be found using the ANN model for the micro-EDM method that has been established [28]. The learning algorithm's key component is the way domain information is distributed across the neurons, allowing data processing to happen concurrently throughout the network. Artificial Neural Networks (ANNs) are highly parallel computational methods that may identify functional relationships in the data [29]. Because of their flexibility and capacity for parallel processing, ANNs are useful instruments for handling complex data analysis.

4.2 CNN (Convolutional Neural Network)

ML has been a hot topic in recent years, and one of the most well-known models of deep learning is convolutional neural networks or CNN. CNN is an analysis method for machine learning that is applied to data that is organized in a grid pattern, such as photographs. CNN is built with the ability to freely and dynamically acquire spatial hierarchies of features, drawing inspiration from the structure of the visual cortex found in animals. CNN, which consists of a series of arithmetic operations, includes a crucial component called the Convolution layer, which is in charge of feature extraction. Convolution is a particular kind of linear operation. In this procedure, functions like convolution and activation functions—both linear and nonlinear—are combined [21].

4.3 PCA (Principal Component Analysis)

PCA is among the most ancient and well-known machine learning techniques. PCA's basic idea is to reduce the amount of "variance" (statistical data) in a dataset while maintaining as much of it as feasible [24,25]. In PCA, new, crucial parameters are first identified when the dataset's dimensionality is reduced. PCA's main goal is to identify the best information variance and dimensional characteristics for reduction. PCA efficiently lowers the multidimensionality of data by utilizing unsupervised learning methodologies. Because of these advantages, PCA can be a useful tool for decomposing large datasets into smaller ones, extracting important information, and enabling more lucid visual representations of the underlying patterns in the data.

4.4 XGBoost

Recently, the XGBoost has gained a lot of popularity as a research technique for data mining (Lu and Ma 2020). According to Chen and Guestrin (2016) [31], it creates a large number of shallow decision trees, and the combination of all the trees results in a high degree of precision in the regulation of prediction. In addition to processing an objective function by handling the loss function, the XGBoost method generates decision trees that prevent overfitting by regularizing the tree (Chen and Guestrin, 2016) [31]. Furthermore, the adaptability of the XGBoost model's hyper-parameter adjustment contributes to its widespread popularity across numerous study domains (Bhagat et al., 2020b) [32]. The model has been quite successful, consistently ranking among the best models in a variety of data mining contests. The following characteristics of XGBoost allow it the process of combining multiple weak learning machines into one powerful learning machine: iteration and multi-tree generation The most notable feature of XGBoost is its ability to automatically process sparse data using the CPU's multithreading feature while simultaneously optimizing the algorithm for increased accuracy. Its lifting learning algorithm is based on the decision tree model. Finally, block technology enables the processing of large volumes of data at high speeds.

4.5 KNN(K-Nearest Neighbor)

The KNN is a pattern recognition approach used for regression and classification. It functions by categorising objects in the feature space according to the training data points that are closest to them. The KNN method is a basic classification technique that is especially helpful when there is little to no foundational knowledge about the data distribution. The simplest kind of KNN, called the closest neighbor rule (NN), is produced when $K = 1$. The main variables affecting a KNN classifier's effectiveness are the distance measure used and the choice of K [19]. The KNN method is a non-parametric supervised learning algorithm that doesn't rely on any presumptions about the underlying dataset. It is known for being quick, effective, and flexible, which makes it appropriate for methods including reinforcement. A labeled learning database offers data points classified into several classes to help identify the class of an unknown data point in an unsupervised learning scenario [20]. For handling classification and regression tasks in a variety of areas, KNN is a useful tool due to its adaptability and strong performance.

4.6 LSTM (Long Short-Term Memory Networks)

The provided excerpt discusses the application of various ML algorithms across diverse domains. Sequence data processing, like that of monitoring systems, benefits greatly from the application of RNN, notably the LSTM neural network, which addresses dependence problems in general neural networks. With possible ramifications for environmental preservation and sustainable development, LSTM is used to estimate groundwater indicator concentration. For tasks like speech recognition, language processing, facial recognition, and anomaly detection, LSTM is also helpful because it can mimic long-term nonlinear input-output connections in sequential learning tasks [17]. The studies included in the table have evaluated how well different machine learning algorithms predict the quality of groundwater.

4.7 DL

When predicting groundwater quality, deep learning (DL) models have demonstrated more accuracy than other machine learning (ML) models. Other intriguing machine learning techniques for predicting groundwater quality are Ensemble Random Forest, Radial Basis Neural Networks (RBNN), and Support Vector Regression (SVR). Since every method has advantages and disadvantages of its own, the optimal approach will rely on the particular dataset and the task at hand. The robustness of the suggested DL model is justified by Singha et al. [17], which amply illustrates how the distribution of model predicted values with respect to test values in the DL model's instance are closer to the best fit line than in the others. Overall, the DL model performed better than the RF, XGBoost, and ANN models in terms of matching the actual values during the validation step. During the training and validation stages, the RF models exhibit the lowest performance [17].

5 Challenges

In order to forecast groundwater quality, the supplied paper addresses the use of mathematical models and machine learning (ML) algorithms, with an emphasis on the difficulties and limitations of this methodology. By learning from past events and projecting future ones, machine learning (ML) is widely acknowledged as a promising tool for predicting groundwater quality and improving lives. Nonetheless, this situation draws attention to a number of difficulties. One major obstacle is the complexity, time-consuming nature, and error-prone nature of the existing computer method involved in assessing water quality using the Water Quality Index (WQI). The lack of data on groundwater quality and problems with deep learning and other advanced machine learning systems' interpretability are also mentioned as barriers. Further emphasised as practical obstacles include the high cost and time-consuming nature of monitoring different indicators related to water quality, such as nitrate, total coliform, pH, dissolved oxygen, electric conductivity, and biological oxygen demand in groundwater [11] [12].

The paper also highlights the fact that in real-world groundwater management and treatment strategies, complex situations may limit the applicability of machine learning algorithms for groundwater quality prediction, requiring a significant quantity of high-quality data and specialized knowledge [16]. The paper also highlights several issues associated with individual machine learning algorithms, like the heuristic nature of selecting kernel functions and hyperparameters in Support Vector Machine (SVM) applications and the problem of multicollinearity in multiple linear regression [13].

In order to overcome these obstacles, it is recommended that future research and engineering endeavours concentrate on the development of increasingly complex sensors for precise data gathering, enhancing the feasibility and dependability of machine learning algorithms, and generating broader mathematical models and algorithms that meet the requirements of water treatment and management.

Overall, even though machine learning (ML) approaches show promise for predicting the quality of water, researchers and engineers must overcome significant obstacles and difficulties before these techniques can truly benefit humankind [15].

6 Future Scopes

More than two billion people worldwide depend on groundwater as their primary source of fresh water, as the text explains. It also highlights the increasing need for a quantitative understanding of groundwater resources to ensure long-term sustainability in the face of challenges like population growth, climate change, and socioeconomic development [30]. Groundwater monitoring and forecasting are about to advance thanks to new prospects brought about by the integration of AI and ML techniques and growing computer resources.

Predictive model accuracy can be improved to better understand complex groundwater processes by combining machine learning techniques with domain knowledge relevant to hydrogeology. To improve the balance between model complexity and transparency, a focus on interpretable machine learning models is made using methods such as feature importance analysis and model visualisation. Studying how climate change affects groundwater quality and using machine learning algorithms to forecast and adjust to changing weather patterns are the main areas of research.

The article focusses on how big-data and the IoT are coming together to improve groundwater monitoring and analysis through improved data transmission, collection, and real-time qualitative information gathering. Delivering precise and affordable groundwater information is thought to be possible through the possible convergence of IoT and deep learning.

Looking ahead, cooperative efforts between agencies and research groups should propel the development of complementary algorithms, allowing for the development of decision-support systems and next-generation geographic information systems powered by an ongoing stream of real-time data. Further research directions could include integrating augmented reality to increase data visualisation and engagement, applying machine learning models to various water resource domains, and employing evolutionary strategies to improve predictions.

To summarise, the creative use of machine learning algorithms has the potential to improve sustainability and groundwater management. It also opens the door to more efficient predictive modeling and real-time data processing to handle changing issues in the management of water resources.

7 Conclusion

The crucial significance of evaluating groundwater quality for public health is emphasized in the text, especially in arid and semi-arid areas where people and industry rely significantly on this priceless resource. It highlights the great potential for tackling the intricate problems related to water resource management that can be solved by using ML algorithms to estimate the quality of water.

Groundwater quality prediction models can be made more accurate and practical by utilising state-of-the-art techniques, combining domain information, and improving model interpretability. These models are seen to be crucial for keeping an eye on pollution, guaranteeing the availability of supplies of potable water, and issuing early warnings to lessen the harmful effects of low water quality.

The study evaluated a broad range of machine learning approaches, emphasising how machine learning is present in many facets of life and how quickly and correctly it can be used to organise and analyse enormous amounts of data. The use of machine learning algorithms in groundwater quality prediction has been proposed as a potential solution to address the shortcomings of conventional techniques, especially in resource-poor and economically undeveloped areas.

In light of the growing environmental issues, the essay emphasises how machine learning may support groundwater conservation and environmentally responsible management. It makes a strong argument for additional in-depth study and creativity in this area to create more effective strategies for protecting groundwater quality for upcoming generations.

References

1. Singh, P.K., Verma, P., Tiwari, A.K., Sharma, S., Purty, P.: Review of various contamination index approaches to evaluate groundwater quality with geographic information system (GIS). Int. J. ChemTech Res. **7**(4), 1920–1929 (2015)
2. Asadi, E., et al.: Groundwater quality assessment for sustainable drinking and irrigation. Sustainability **12**(1), 177 (2019)
3. Harter, T.: Groundwater Quality and Groundwater Pollution. University of California, California (2003)
4. Memon, Y.I., et al.: Statistical analysis and physicochemical characteristics of groundwater quality parameters: a case study. Int. J. Environ. Anal. Chem. **2021**, 1–2 (2021)
5. Li, J., Pang, Z., Liu, Y., Hu, S., Jiang, W., Tian, L., Tian, J.: Changes in groundwater dynamics and geochemical evolution induced by drainage reorganization: Evidence from 81Kr and 36Cl dating of geothermal water in the Weihe Basin of China. Earth Planetary Sci. Lett. **623**, 118425 (2023). https://doi.org/10.1016/j.epsl.2023.118425
6. El Bilali, A., Taleb, A., Brouziyne, Y.: Groundwater quality forecasting using machine learning algorithms for irrigation purposes. Agric. Water Manag. **245**, 106625 (2021)
7. Hussein, E.A., Thron, C., Ghaziasgar, M., Bagula, A., Vaccari, M.: Groundwater prediction using machine-learning tools. Algorithms **13**(11), 300 (2020)

8. Aldhyani, T.H., Al-Yaari, M., Alkahtani, H., Maashi, M.: Research article water quality prediction using artificial intelligence algorithms. Appl. Bionics Biomech. (2020). https://doi.org/10.1155/2020/6659314
9. Aldhyani, T.H., Al-Yaari, M., Alkahtani, H., Maashi, M.: Water quality prediction using artificial intelligence algorithms. Appl. Bionics. Biomech. (2020). https://doi.org/10.1155/2020/6659314
10. Azma, A., Narreie, E., Shojaaddini, A., Kianfar, N., Kiyanfar, R., Seyed Alizadeh, S.M., Davarpanah, A.: Statistical modeling for spatial groundwater potential map based on GIS technique. Sustainability **13**(7), 3788 (2021)
11. Mamat, N., Mohd Razali, S.F., Hamzah, F.B.: Enhancement of water quality index prediction using support vector machine with sensitivity analysis. Front Environ Sci. (2023). https://doi.org/10.3389/fenvs.2022.1061835
12. Hassan, M.M., Hassan, M.M., Akter, L., Rahman, M.M., Zaman, S., Hasib, K.M., Mollick, S.: Efficient prediction of water quality index(WQI) using machine learning algorithms. Human-Centric Intell. Syst. **1**(3–4), 86–97 (2021)
13. Zhang, J., Liu, K., Wang, M.: Downscaling groundwater storage data in China to a 1-km resolution using machine learning methods. Remote Sensing **13**(3), 523 (2021)
14. Maniyath, S.R., Pooja, G., Chandana, R., Namitha, K.S., Lakshminarasamma, N.: Groundwater anomaly detection using machine learning. In: 2021 International Conference on Design Innovations for 3Cs Compute Communicate Control (ICDI3C), pp. 8–14. IEEE, June 2021
15. Wang, Y., Xue, S., Ding, J.: Research on water pollution prediction of township enterprises based on support vector regression machine. In: E3S Web of Conferences, vol. 228, p. 02014. EDP Sciences (2021)
16. Zhu, M., Wang, J., Yang, X., Zhang, Y., Zhang, L., Ren, H., Ye, L.: A review of the application of machine learning in water quality evaluation. Eco-Environ Health (2022). https://doi.org/10.1016/j.eehl.2022.06.001
17. Singha, S., Pasupuleti, S., Singha, S.S., Singh, R., Kumar, S.: Prediction of groundwater quality using efficient machine learning technique. Chemosphere **276**, 130265 (2021)
18. Amalia, H.S., Athiyah, U., Muhammad, A.W.: The application of modified K-Nearest neighbor algorithm for classification of groundwater quality based on image processing and pH, TDS, and temperature sensors. Register **9**(1), 42–54 (2023)
19. Patel, M.P., Gami, B., Patel, A., Patel, P., Patel, B.: Climatic and anthropogenic impact on groundwater quality of agriculture dominated areas of southern and central Gujarat. India. Groundwater Sustainable Development **10**, 100306 (2020)
20. Jha, S.K., et al.: Groundwater quality concern for wider adaptability of novel modes of managed aquifer recharge (MAR) in the Ganges Basin, India. Agricultural Water Manage. **246**, 106659 (2021)
21. Yamashita, R., Nishio, M., Do, R.K.G., Togashi, K.: Convolutional neural networks: an overview and application in radiology. Insights Imag. **9**, 611–629 (2018)
22. Zhao, X., Guo, H., Wang, Y., Wang, G., Wang, H., Zang, X., Zhu, J.: Groundwater hydrogeochemical characteristics and quality suitability assessment for irrigation and drinking purposes in an agricultural region of the North China plain. Environ. Earth Sci. **80**(4), 1–22 (2021). https://doi.org/10.1007/s12665-021-09432-w
23. Patel, P.S., Pandya, D.M., Shah, M.: A systematic and comparative study of Water Quality Index (WQI) for groundwater quality analysis and assessment. Environ. Sci. Pollut. Res. **30**, 54303–54323 (2023). https://doi.org/10.1007/s11356-023-25936-3

24. Jolliffe, I.T., Cadima, J.: Principal component analysis: a review and recent developments. Phil Trans. R Soc. A: Math. Phys. Eng. Sci. **374**(2065), 20150202 (2016)
25. Howley, T., Madden, M.G., O'Connell, M.L., Ryder, A.G.: The effect of principal component analysis on machine learning accuracy with high dimensional spectral data. In: Applications and innovations in intelligent systems XIII: proceedings of AI-2005, the twenty-fifth SGAI international conference on innovative techniques and applications of artificial intelligence, Cambridge, UK, December 2005, pp. 209–222. Springer, London (2006)
26. Khiavi, A.N., Tavoosi, M., Kuriqi, A.: Conjunct application of machine learning and game theory in groundwater quality mapping. Environ. Earth Sci. **82**, 395 (2023). https://doi.org/10.1007/s12665-023-11059-y
27. Grossi, E., Buscema, M.: Introduction to artificial neural networks. Eur. J. Gastroenterol. Hepatol. **19**(12), 1046–1054 (2007)
28. Mhatre, M.S., Siddiqui, F., Dongre, M., Thakur, P.: A review paper on artificial neural network: a prediction technique. Int. J. Sci. Eng. Res. **6**(12), 161–163 (2015)
29. Dai, H., Liu, Y., Guadagnini, A., Yuan, S., Yang, J., Ye, M.: Comparative assessment of two global sensitivity approaches considering model and parameter uncertainty. Water Resources Res. **60**(2), e2023WR036096 (2024). https://doi.org/10.1029/2023WR036096
30. Zhao, Y., Song, J., Cheng, K., Liu, Z., Yang, F.: Migration and remediation of typical contaminants in soil and groundwater: a state of art review. Land Degradation and Development (2024). https://doi.org/10.1002/ldr.5103
31. Chen, T., Guestrin, C.: Xgboost: a scalable tree boosting system. In: Proceedings of the 22nd ACM SIGKDD International Conference on Knowledge Discovery and Data Mining, pp. 785–794, August 2016
32. Bhagat, S.K., Tiyasha, T., Tung, T.M., Mostafa, R.R., Yaseen, Z.M.: Manganese (Mn) removal prediction using extreme gradient model. Ecotoxicol. Environ. Saf. **204**, 111059 (2020)

Enhanced Face Recognition with Deep CNN and User- Friendly GUI Implementation

Saba Mansoori[1]([✉]), Pankaj Sahu[2], and Devendra Kumar Meda[1,2]

[1] Department of Electronics and Telecommunication Engineering, Jabalpur Engineering College Jabalpur M.P., Jabalpur, India
dmeda@jecjabalpur.ac.in

[2] Department of Mechatronics Engineering, Jabalpur Engineering College Jabalpur M.P., Jabalpur, India

Abstract. This research presents the design and development of an open-source graphical user interface (GUI) integrated with a deep Convolutional Neural Network (CNN) for real-time face recognition. Here two convolutional layers has been used with 32 and 64 filters respectively. The model was rigorously tested on a two custom dataset containing 40 faces and 16 faces respectively, with images organized into two distinct folders. Achieving an accuracy of 99.14%, the system features a user-friendly GUI built using an open-source platform, ensuring accessibility for non-experts. This work offers a robust and efficient solution, demonstrating the practical application of deep learning in face recognition.

Keywords: Curvelet Transform · Convolutional Neural Networks (CNN) · Facial Recognition · Image Preprocessing · Performance Evaluation

1 Introduction

Face recognition, a biometric technology that identifies or verifies individuals by analyzing facial features, has become one of the most significant applications of computer vision today. This technology finds application across diverse fields, from enhancing security in surveillance systems to facilitating convenient features such as automatic tagging in social media. However, despite its widespread use, existing face recognition systems face notable challenges that can affect their performance. One of the primary limitations involves the system's sensitivity to varying conditions such as changes in lighting, angles, and occlusions (e.g., glasses, masks, or hair obstructing the face). These conditions can greatly influence the ability of traditional face recognition algorithms to maintain high accuracy.

Neural networks, particularly deep learning models, have significantly improved face recognition performance by learning and extracting complex features directly from raw facial images. Unlike conventional methods that rely on manually crafted features, neural networks autonomously learn hierarchical feature representations, starting with simple edges and textures and progressing to more abstract characteristics like facial structures. This approach enables the systems to recognize faces more accurately and adaptively, even when subjected to the challenges mentioned above. However, certain limitations remain, such as the requirement for large and diverse training datasets to ensure generalization and the potential for performance biases across different demographic groups.

Understanding these inherent challenges and the limitations faced by current face recognition technologies underscores the importance of developing more robust and adaptable models. By addressing these issues, we can justify the need for improved face recognition solutions capable of achieving reliable performance under varying conditions. In the following sections, this paper will delve into the specifics of face recognition using neural networks, their operational mechanisms, strengths, and remaining challenges, with a focus on advancing fair, reliable, and efficient technologies.

In the next part, this paper will delve into the specifics of face recognition using neural networks, including how these models operate, their strengths, and the limitations they face. Although neural networks offer powerful solutions, they also come with challenges such as the need for extensive training data, vulnerability to adversarial attacks, and potential biases in recognition performance across diverse demographic groups. Understanding these aspects is crucial for advancing fair, reliable, and efficient face recognition technologies.

1.1 Face Recognition Using Neural Networks

Neural Networks have played a pivotal role in advancing face recognition technology by enabling systems to learn complex patterns and relationships in facial data. Traditional neural networks, such as fully connected networks, aim to classify faces by representing them as high- dimensional vectors and identifying patterns within these vectors. This approach involves learning features like the relative positions and shapes of facial components, such as the eyes, nose, and mouth. However, the inherent challenge in face recognition lies in the high dimensionality and variability of facial data, which includes capturing intricate details like subtle facial contours, expressions, and variations in lighting or pose.

Traditional neural networks, while capable of distinguishing some facial features, often face limitations when it comes to effectively managing spatial hierarchies within images. They may struggle to preserve spatial relationships between pixels, leading to potential inefficiencies in capturing the intricate details that differentiate one face from another. Additionally, these networks are prone to overfitting, especially when dealing with large datasets, as they lack the specialized structure to handle image-specific tasks efficiently.

To address these challenges, Convolutional Neural Networks (CNNs) are preferred for face recognition tasks. CNNs are designed specifically for image processing and are adept at capturing spatial hierarchies in data through their use of convolutional layers. These layers apply filters to input images, allowing CNNs to learn localized features, such as edges and textures, and progressively build up to more complex features like shapes and patterns. This hierarchical learning structure enables CNNs to more accurately represent the nuances of facial features, making them highly effective for face recognition.

To illustrate the differences in performance between traditional fully connected neural networks and CNNs, we can compare their application in a typical image classification task. While a simple fully connected network may struggle with image data due to its lack of spatial awareness, a CNN leverages its convolutional and pooling layers to reduce dimensionality while preserving important features, leading to more robust and accurate classification results. The CNN's architecture allows it to generalize better, avoiding overfitting by focusing on relevant spatial patterns rather than individual pixel relationships. Thus, while traditional neural networks provide a foundational approach to face recognition, CNNs enhance this process by effectively handling the spatial and hierarchical complexity of facial data. This comparison underscores the need for specialized neural network architectures like CNNs in applications that require detailed feature extraction and robust performance, such as face recognition. Comparing the number of parameters in a traditional fully connected neural network (NN) and a convolutional neural network (CNN) mathematically.

1.1.1 Fully Connected Layers

Consider a fully connected network where:

- The input layer has 'n' neurons.
- The hidden layer has 'h' neurons.
- Output layer has 'm' neurons.

Number of parameters in a single hidden layer:

1. Weights: Each neuron in the hidden layer is connected to every neuron in the input layer. Therefore, the number of weights is n * h.
2. Biases: Each neuron in the hidden layer has a bias. Therefore, there are (h) biases.

So, total parameters for a single hidden layer: (n * h + h). Several parameters between the hidden layer and output layer:

1. Weights: Each neuron in the output layer is connected to every neuron in the hidden layer. Therefore, the number of weights is (h * m).
2. Biases: Each neuron in the output layer has a bias. Therefore, there are (m) biases.

So, the total parameters between the hidden layer and the output layer: (h* m + m).
Total parameters for the NN: (n * h + h) + (h * m + m)

1.1.2 Convolutional Neural Network (CNN)

Consider a CNN with:

- Input image size of (W * H * C) (Width x Height x Channels).
- Convolutional layer with (F)filters, each of size (K * K) (Kernel size), and depth (C) (same as the number of channels). Number of parameters in a convolutional layer:
- Weights: Each filter has (K * K * C) weights. Since there are (F) filters, the total number of weights is (F * K *K * C).

- Biases: Each filter has one bias. Therefore, there are (F) biases.

  So, total parameters in the convolutional layer: (F * (K * K * C + 1).

1.2 Comparing Parameters

1.2.1 NN Example

- For an input layer with (784) neurons, a hidden layer with (128) neurons, and an output layer with (10) neurons: Parameters = (784 * 128 + 128) + (128 *10 + 10) = 100,480 + 1,290 = 101,770

1.2.2 CNN Example

- For an image input size (32 times 32 times 3), a convolutional layer with (64) filters of size (3 * 3): Parameters = 64 * (3 *3 * 3 + 1) = 64 * 28 = 1,792

In this example, the CNN has significantly fewer parameters compared to the fully connected NN. This reduction is more pronounced as the network size increases or when applied to larger images. The CNN's architecture is generally more parameter-efficient because of its use of local connections and weight sharing, which drastically reduces the number of parameters compared to fully connected layers. In this research paper, CNN is used for face detection in the backend of the developed GUI. In the next section, face recognition using CNN is discussed in detail.

1.3 Face Recognition Using Convolutional Neural Networks (CNNs)

Convolutional Neural Networks (CNNs) have emerged as the most effective neural network architecture for face recognition. CNNs are specifically designed to handle grid-like data, such as images, by applying convolutional filters that can detect spatial patterns and features. This makes CNNs particularly well-suited for tasks where the spatial arrangement of data, such as pixels in an image, is crucial. CNNs use small filters (kernels) to scan over the input image. Each filter focuses on a small region of the image (a local receptive field) and computes a dot product between the filter's weights and the pixel values in that region. The result is a feature map, which highlights certain features like edges, textures, or patterns in the image. Different filters are used to detect different types of features. Consider an image I of size m x n and a filter (kernel) k of size f x f, the convolution operation is defined as.

$$O(i,j) = \sum_{p=0}^{f-1}\sum_{q=0}^{f-1} I(i+p, j+q).k(p,q)$$

Here $O(i,j)$ is the output feature map at position (I,j):

The convolutional layers automatically extract key features from the input facial image, such as edges, textures, and shapes. These features are crucial for distinguishing between different faces. As the image passes through multiple convolutional layers, the network builds a hierarchical representation of the face, starting with low-level features like edges and progressing to more complex features like eyes, nose, and mouth.

After feature extraction, fully connected layers are typically used to classify the face into a specific identity based on the learned features. Alternatively, in some face recognition systems, the output of the CNN is used to compute the similarity between the input face and faces in a database, determining if they belong to the same person.

After convolution, an activation function like ReLU (Rectified Linear Unit) is applied to introduce non-linearity. This allows the network to model complex patterns by emphasizing important features and suppressing irrelevant ones. ReLU transforms the feature maps by setting all negative values to zero, which helps in learning more complex features.

Pooling layers reduce the spatial dimensions (width and height) of the feature maps while retaining the most important information. Max pooling, for example, takes the maximum value from a small region of the feature map. Pooling helps achieve translation invariance, meaning the CNN becomes less sensitive to the exact position of features in the input image. In the final layers, the extracted features are flattened and passed through fully connected layers. These layers combine the features to make predictions, such as identifying the class of the object in the image.

2 Proposed Model

The proposed model integrates a sophisticated Graphical User Interface (GUI) with a Convolutional Neural Network (CNN) backend to create a highly effective face recognition system. The GUI is designed to be intuitive and user-friendly, enabling users to effortlessly upload facial images via a drag-and-drop interface or file selector. Once an image is uploaded, the GUI communicates with the CNN to process the image and deliver real-time feedback on the identity of the individual. Results are displayed promptly, including the recognized person's name or ID and a confidence score that indicates the accuracy of the prediction. Additionally, the GUI features error handling and alerts, guiding users in cases where the system cannot recognize or if the image quality is insufficient.

The CNN backend plays a crucial role in the system's performance. This deep learning model excels at image recognition tasks through its ability to automatically learn and extract hierarchical features from facial images. The CNN comprises convolutional layers that detect local patterns such as edges and textures, activation functions that introduce non-linearity, pooling layers that reduce dimensionality and abstract features, and fully connected layers that perform the final classification. This architecture allows the CNN to recognize and differentiate between subtle variations in facial features, even under varying conditions like lighting and angles. By integrating CNN with the GUI, the face recognition system effectively combines advanced image processing capabilities with a practical, user-friendly interface. This integration ensures that the powerful features of the CNN are accessible and easily utilized by users, providing accurate and reliable faces.

Recognition. The system's real-time feedback and error handling enhance user experience, making it suitable for a range of applications including security, access control, and personal identification. This approach not only demonstrates the effectiveness of deep learning in face recognition but also highlights how sophisticated technology can be made approachable and functional in everyday use cases data sets.

2.1 Dataset

The model has been tested with two data sets, the details of the dataset are shown below.

1. The first dataset has 40 folders with four images in each subfolder. Each folder corresponds to a person's image. The inside image from the first dataset is shown in Fig. 1.

> Folder hierarchy: 'dataset'> S1 S2......up to S40

> Folder hierarchy: 'dataset'> S1 S2......up to S40

Fig. 1. Dataset contains 40 person's images.

2. The second dataset has 16 folders with seventeen images in each subfolder. Each folder corresponds to a person's image.

> Folder hierarchy: 'images'>Face1 Face2.....up to Facc16

Folder hierarchy: 'images'>Face1 Face2…..up to Face16

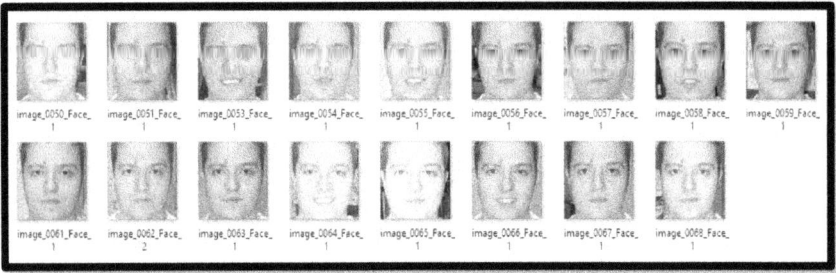

Fig. 2. Dataset contains 16 person's images.

2.2 Model Architecture

In this section the model architecture is discussed.

2.2.1 Preprocessing

- The images are converted to grayscale to reduce computational complexity while preserving essential features.
- The images are resized to a fixed dimension of 92 × 112 pixels.
- Each image is normalized by scaling pixel values to the range [0, 1].
- Labels are one-hot encoded, transforming the categorical labels (0 to 39) into binary vectors with a length 40.

The model architecture is shown in the Fig. 3.

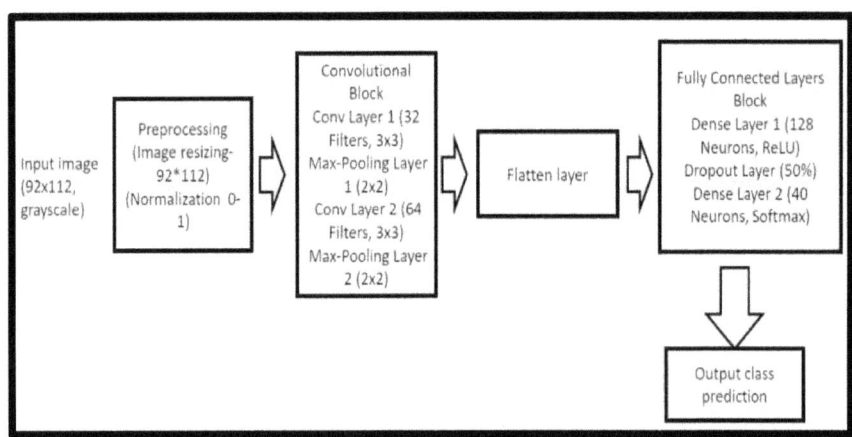

Fig. 3. Architecture of the proposed model.

The proposed CNN model consists of the following layers:

2.2.2 Input Layer

- The input layer accepts grayscale images of size 92 × 112 pixels, with a single channel for grayscale intensity.

2.2.3 Convolutional Layers

- The first convolutional layer applies 32 filters of size 3 × 3, followed by ReLU activation. This layer extracts low-level features like edges and textures.
- The second convolutional layer applies 64 filters of size 3 × 3, followed by ReLU activation. This layer captures more complex patterns such as facial landmarks.

2.2.4 Max-Pooling Layers

- Each convolutional layer is followed by a max-pooling layer with a pool size of 2 × 2, reducing the spatial dimensions of the feature maps while retaining important features.

2.2.5 Flatten Layer

- The 2D feature maps produced by the convolutional layers are flattened into a 1D vector, preparing the data for the fully connected layers.

2.2.6 Fully Connected Layers

- The first fully connected layer consists of 128 neurons with ReLU activation. This layer combines features from the previous layers and enables the model to make decisions based on complex patterns.
- A Dropout layer with a 50% dropout rate is included to prevent overfitting by randomly disabling neurons during training.

2.2.7 Output Layer

- The output layer consists of 40 neurons, corresponding to the 40 subjects in the dataset. A softmax activation function is used to produce a probability distribution across the classes, where the highest probability indicates the predicted class.

2.3 Model Training

- The model is compiled using the Adam optimizer, which adapts the learning rate during training to ensure efficient convergence. We have also experimented with some other optimizers, but the performance of the Adam optimizer gives better results.
- The loss function used is categorical cross-entropy, suitable for multi-class classification tasks.
- The model has trained over 30 epochs with a batch size of 32, using a training-validation split of 80%-20%. The model's performance is monitored on the validation set to ensure it generalizes well to unseen data.

3 Experimentation Results

3.1 Case Study 1: Dataset Containing 40 People's Images

In this case study, the network is trained with 40 persons' images and the results are discussed here. As shown in the figure, the left sides are the input images. The name of the input images is mentioned at the top of the facial image. The right side shows the predicted images. The first row corresponds to the first input image and the predicted image. We have experimented with the Five test input images and the results are shown below. It can be seen that the proposed model is predicting the images correctly. On the left side of the figure, you will find the input images used for testing the model. Each image is labelled with the name of the individual it represents, providing a clear reference for identification. This labelling is crucial for understanding the context of each input image and assessing the accuracy of the predictions. The right side of the figure presents the images predicted by the model.

These Predicted images are the model's attempts to match the input images with the identities it has learned during training. The figure is organized in rows, where each row corresponds to a single test case. The first row displays the initial input image and the model's predicted output for that image. This layout continues for all five test input images used in the experiment. The side-by-side comparison of input and predicted images allows for a straightforward evaluation of the model's performance.

From the results shown, it is evident that the proposed model performs well in predicting the correct identities of the faces. The accurate matching of predicted images to their respective input images suggests that the model has effectively learned to recognize and classify facial features. This accuracy is a strong indicator of the model's robustness and reliability in face recognition tasks. The success of the model in these tests demonstrates its capability to handle the variations and complexities present in facial images. Factors such as lighting conditions, facial expressions, and angles do not appear to significantly impact the model's performance, which speaks to the effectiveness of the trained neural network. Overall, the results validate the proposed face recognition system's ability to correctly identify individuals, making it a promising tool for real-world applications requiring precise and reliable facial recognition (Fig. 4).

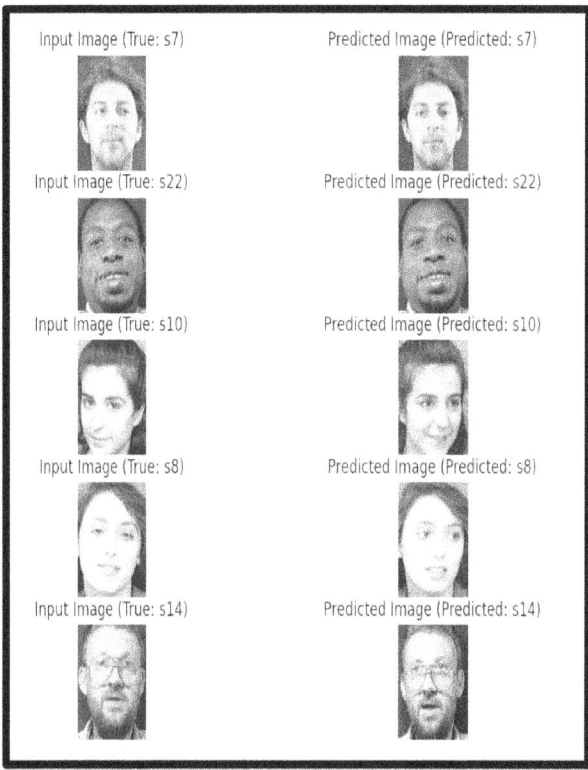

Fig. 4. Experimentation results for the 40 person's image.

3.1.1 Accuracy

The maximum accuracy obtained from the network is 99.14. The accuracy vs. epoch graph is shown in the figure below. Here the horizontal axis represents the epoch values from 0 to 100. The vertical axis of the graph represents accuracy. In the figure, both the training and the validation accuracy are plotted. It may be noted that the accuracy improves with the number of epochs (Fig. 5).

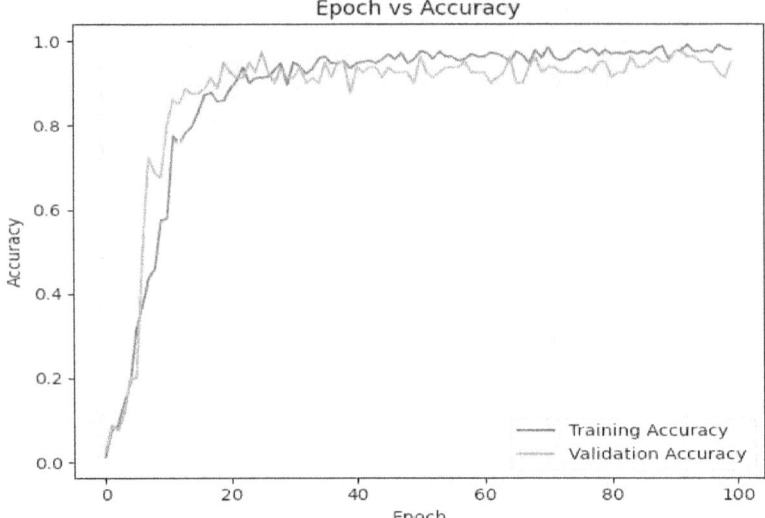

Fig. 5. Accuracy vs. epoch graph for 40 person's data set.

3.1.2 Loss

The loss vs. epoch graph is shown in the figure below. It may be noted that the loss is significantly reduced after 40 epochs (Fig. 6).

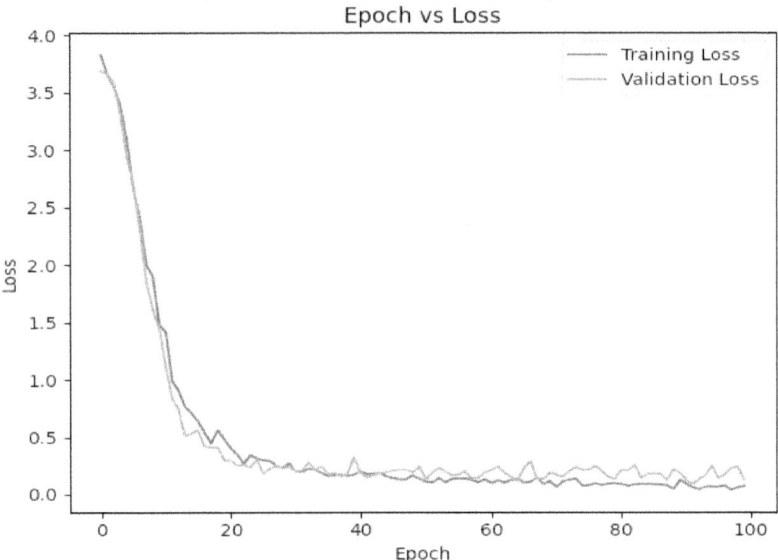

Fig. 6. Loss vs. epoch for 40 person's data set.

3.1.3 Confusion Matrix

A confusion matrix is a performance measurement tool for classification models, particularly in cases where the output can be more than two classes. It is a square matrix that compares the actual target values with the predicted values, with each row representing the instances of the actual class and each column representing the instances of the predicted class Confusion matrix of the trained neural network is shown below. It can be seen that the confusion matrix obtained has non-zero diagonal values. Non-zero diagonal values in a confusion matrix show that the model is successfully identifying instances of each class. The extent of these values helps evaluate the model's performance in terms of accuracy for each class, while off-diagonal values provide insight into the types of classification errors the model is making (Fig. 7).

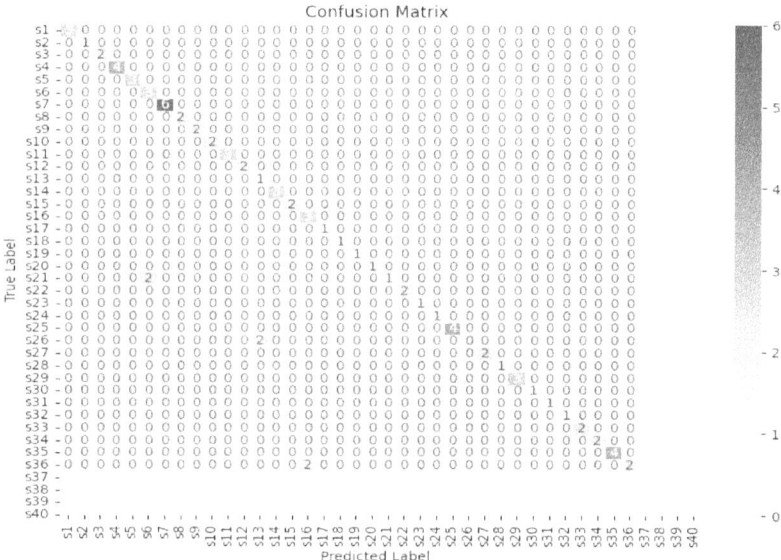

Fig. 7. Confusion matrices obtained for 40 person's prediction model.

3.2 Case Study 2

In this case study, the network is trained with 16 person's images and the results are discussed here. The input image used here is of 335 × 335 sizes. The input image and the predicted image from the test result are shown below. The experimentation output shows two columns. The first column represents the input image and the second column represents the predicted output image. It can be seen that both the input and the predicted image are found to be correct (Fig. 8).

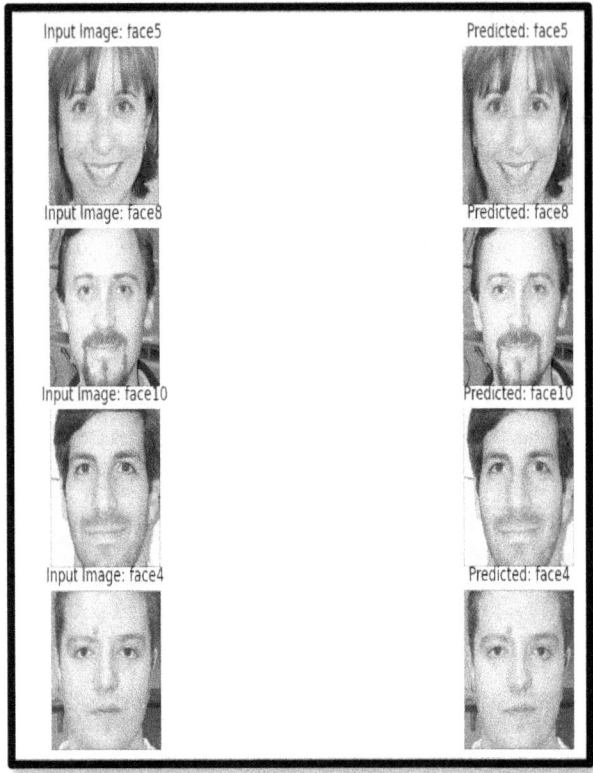

Fig. 8. Experimentation results for the 16-person image.

3.2.1 Accuracy

The model accuracy for the 16-folder dataset is shown below. It can be seen that the validation accuracy is found to be lower as compared with the 40-folder dataset. It may be because 40 folder datasets consist of 10 images per folder while 16 folder datasets consist of only 4 images per person. We see that the performance of face recognition improves if the number of images in a dataset is large (Fig. 9).

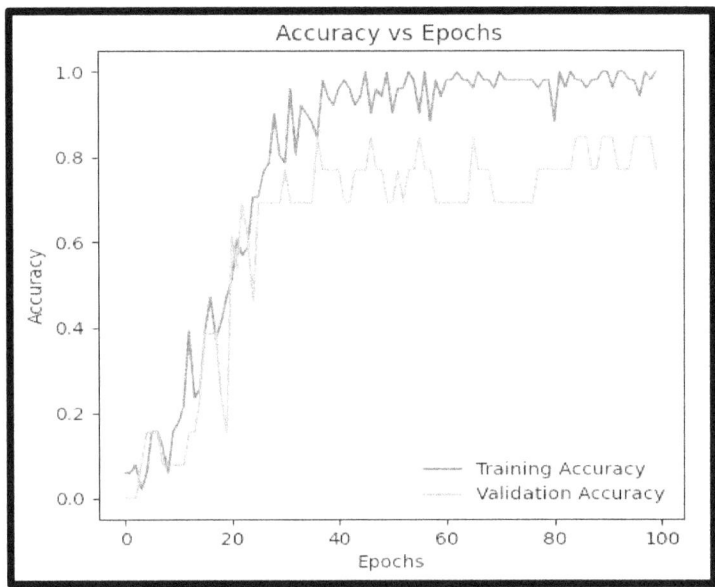

Fig. 9. Accuracy vs. epoch graph for 16-person dataset.

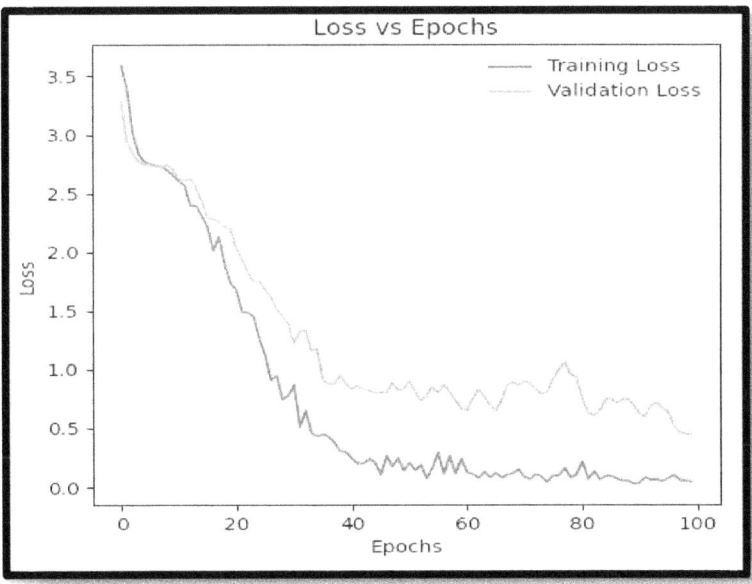

Fig. 10. Accuracy vs. epoch graph for 16-person dataset.

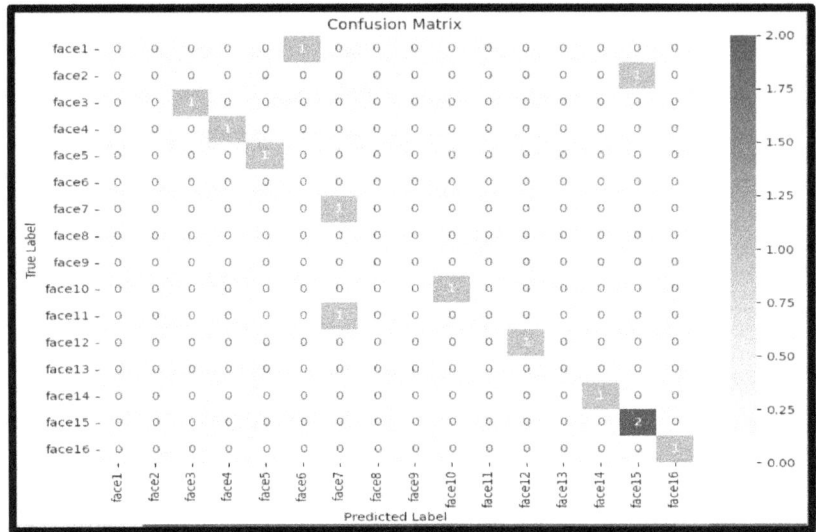

Fig. 11. Confusion matrixes obtained for 16 people's prediction model.

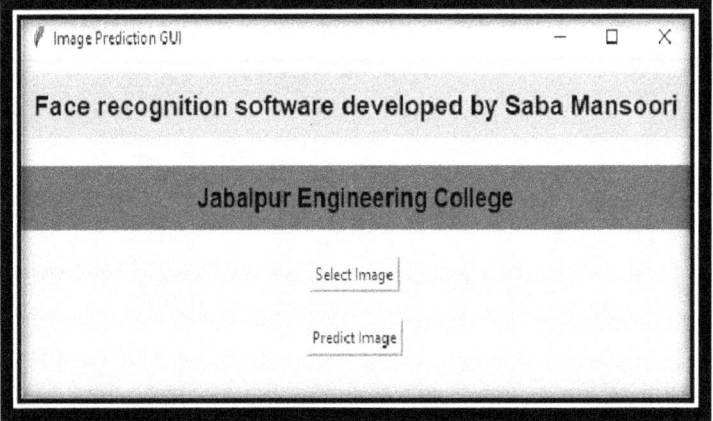

Fig. 12. Developed GUI for face recognition.he experiment from the developed GUI is shown in the Fig. 13. The step by step of execution of GUI is shown. The top windows show the GUI available for the user. When users select the input image using the 'select image' button, an input image will be selected and shown on the GUI window. After selecting the input image, the user clicks on 'Predict image' to make predictions using the proposed model. The predicted image class will be shown on the GUI with the predicted image on the bottom right of the developed GUI.

3.2.2 Loss

The loss graph of the trained model for the 16-folder image is shown below. It may be noted that the loss significantly reduces after 35 epochs (Fig. 10).

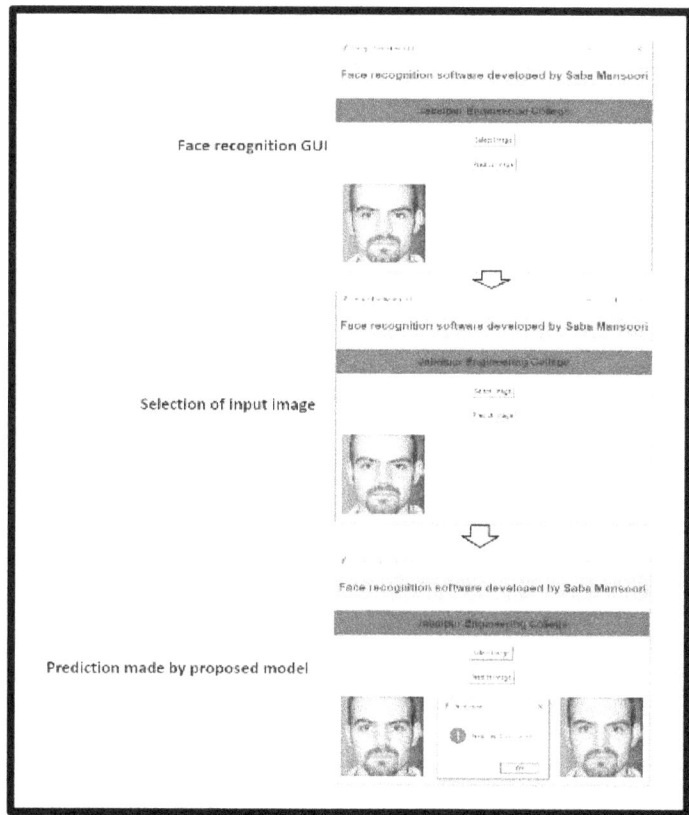

Fig. 13. Step-by-step usage of developed GUI.

3.2.3 Confusion Matrix

The confusion matrix obtained from the trained model of the 16-folder dataset also contains a non-zero diagonal value representing the successfully identifying instances of each class (Fig. 11).

3.2.4 GUI Development

Creating a GUI for face recognition software is important because it provides a user-friendly interface that makes the software accessible and easy to use. A well-designed GUI allows users to interact with the software intuitively, simplifying tasks like selecting images, running recognition processes, and viewing results. It also enhances the overall user experience by providing a visual representation of the software's functionality, making the technology more approachable for users who may not be familiar with underlying technical details. To make the model user-friendly, a GUI has been made using an open-source software platform the main window of the GUI window is shown in Fig. 12. It has two buttons one is to select the input image and the second is the predicted image. The input image button selects the image that is to be predicted. The predict image button uses the pre-trained model in the background to make a prediction.

3.2.5 Comparison with Previous Research Work

Table 1. Comparative analysis

Parameter	Our Work	Reference [1]	Reference [2]	Reference [3]	Reference [4]
CNN Architecture	2 Conv layers, 1 Dense layer, ReLU, Softmax	1 Conv layer, 1 Dense layer	3 Conv layers, 2 Dense layers	2 Conv layers, 1 Dense layer	4 Conv layers, 2 Dense layers
Dataset Used	Custom dataset of 40 subjects	Public dataset, 10 subjects	Public dataset, 20 subjects	Custom dataset, 30 subjects	Custom dataset, 50 subjects
GUI Integration	Full integration with Tkinter, user-friendly, open-source	Basic GUI integration	Limited or no GUI integration	Advanced GUI but not open-source	GUI for result display only
Performance (Accuracy)	**99.14%**	85%	90%	92%	88%
Real-Time Capability	Real-time face recognition with live feedback	Offline processing only	Slow processing time	Real-time with delays	Real-time

4 Conclusion

This research successfully developed an open-source GUI integrated with a deep Convolutional Neural Network (CNN) for real-time face recognition. The model was tested on two distinct datasets, achieving a remarkable accuracy of 99.14%. The inclusion of a user-friendly interface using Python's Tkinter makes this system accessible and practical for non-experts, demonstrating the effective application of deep learning in face recognition tasks. However, the system does have limitations, such as potential performance issues when processing multiple faces simultaneously, reduced accuracy under poor lighting or occlusions, and dependency on the quality and diversity of the training dataset. Future enhancements can focus on addressing these limitations by expanding the dataset to include more subjects and variations in facial expressions, lighting, and occlusions. Additionally, integrating advanced features like multi-face detection, emotion recognition, and real-time performance optimization could further enhance the system's robustness. Expanding the GUI to support cross-platform deployment and incorporating cloud-based training and inference capabilities can also be explored to increase scalability and usability.

References

1. Rane, M., Kanade, D., Parkhi, V., et al.: Face Recognition Using Convolutional Neural Network. Soft Computing in Industrial Applications. Advances in Intelligent Systems and Computing, vol. 223. Springer, Cham. https://doi.org/10.1007/978-3-319-00930-8_182
2. Hu, H., Shah, A., Bennamoun, M., Molton, M.: 2D and 3D Face Recognition Using Convolutional Neural Network, vol. 1, 35 IEEE Region 10 Conference, 2022
3. Garcia, C., Delakis, M.: Convolutional face finder: a neural architecture for fast and robust face detection. IEEE Trans. Pattern Anal. Mach. Intell. **1**, 26 (2004)
4. Pranav, K.B., Manikandan, J.: Design and evaluation of a real-time face recognition system using CNN. Procedia Comput. Sci. **2,** 40–45 (2020)
5. Zou, W., et al.: Eyeglass reflection removal with joint learning of reflection elimination and content inpainting. IEEE Trans. Circuits Syst. Video Technol. **34**(10), 10266–10280 (2024)
6. Alqudah, R., Al-Qaisi, M., Ammari, R., Abu Ta'a, Y.:OSINT-Based Tool for Social Media User Impersonation Detection Through Machine Learning. In: 2023 International Conference on Information Technology (ICIT), pp.752–757 (2023)
7. He, K., Zhang, X., Ren, S., Sun, J.: Deep Residual Learning for Image Recognition. In: IEEE Conference on Computer Vision and Pattern Recognition (CVPR), vol. 3 pp 452–459 (2016)
8. Nabila, L., W. Priharti, I.: Design of Home Security System Using Face Recognition with Convolutional Neural Network Method. In: 2022 IEEE International Conference on Industry 4.0, Artificial Intelligence, and Communications Technology (IAICT), pp. 78–83 (2022)
9. Parkhi, O.M., Vedaldi, A., Zisserman, A. Deep Face Recognition, vol. 3, pp 252–256. British Machine Vision Conference (BMVC) (2015)
10. Taigman, Y., Yang, M., Ranzato, M.A., Wolf, L. DeepFace: closing the gap to human-level performance in face verification. In: IEEE Conference on Computer Vision and Pattern Recognition (CVPR), vol. 3, pp. 265–270 (2014)
11. Erik, H., Low, B.K.: Face detection: a survey. Comput. Vis. Image Underst. **83**, 236–274 (2001)
12. Zhang, K., Zhang, Z., Li, Z., Qiao, Y.: Joint face detection and alignment using multi-task cascaded convolutional networks. IEEE Signal Process. Lett. **3**, 565–570 (2016)
13. Cao, Q., Shen, L., Xie, W., Parkhi, O.M., Zisserman, A.: VGGFace2: a dataset for recognising faces across pose and age. In: IEEE International Conference on Automatic Face and Gesture Recognition (FG), vol. 3, pp. 652–658 (2018)
14. Li, H., Lin, Z., Shen, X., Brandt, J., Hua, G.: A convolutional neural network cascade for face detection. In: IEEE Conference on Computer Vision and Pattern Recognition (CVPR), vol. 1, pp. 345–350 (2015)
15. Wen, Y., Zhang, K., Li, Z., Qiao, Y.: A discriminative feature learning approach for deep face recognition. European Conference on Computer Vision (ECCV) **3**, 789–795 (2016)
16. Liu, W., Anguelov, D., Erhan, D., Szegedy, C., Reed, S., Fu, C.Y., Berg, A.C.: SSD: single shot MultiBox detector. In: European Conference on Computer Vision (ECCV), vol. 1, pp. 656–660 (2016)
17. Masi, I., Wu, Y., Hassner, T., Natarajan, P., Medioni, G.: Deep face recognition: a survey. In: Proceedings of the IEEE Conference on Computer Vision and Pattern Recognition Workshops, vol. 2 pp. 491–496 (2018)
18. Deng, J., Guo, J., Xue, N., Zafeiriou, S.: ArcFace: additive angular margin loss for deep face recognition. In: IEEE Conference on Computer Vision and Pattern Recognition (CVPR), vol. 2, pp. 343–348 (2019)
19. Duong, C.N., Bui, T.D., Luu, K., Savvides, M.: Deep appearance models: a deformable facial shape and appearance model. IEEE Trans. Pattern Anal. Mach. Intell. **3**, 555–560 (2019)

20. Liao, S., Jain, A.K., Li, S.Z.: A fast and accurate unconstrained face detector. IEEE Trans. Pattern Anal. Mach. Intell. **1**, 320–325 (2016)
21. Zhang, X., Zou, Y., Shi, Y., Wu, Y.: Efficient facial feature learning with wide and deep neural networks. IEEE Trans. Multimed. **2**, 500–506 (2018)
22. Liu, W., Wen, Y., Yu, Z., Yang, M., Li, Z., Raj, B.: SphereFace: deep hypersphere embedding for face recognition. In: IEEE Conference on Computer Vision and Pattern Recognition (CVPR), vol. 1, pp. 964–969 (2017)
23. Wu, Y., He, K.: Group Normalization. In: European Conference on Computer Vision (ECCV), vol. 4, pp. 68–572 (2018)
24. Wang, H., et al.: CosFace: large margin cosine loss for deep face recognition. In: IEEE Conference on Computer Vision and Pattern Recognition (CVPR), vol. 3, pp. 698–702 (2018)
25. Ran, W., Chen, Y., Ge, L., Zhang, Y., Xing, J.: One-shot neural architecture search for fast face recognition model adaptation. IEEE Trans. Pattern Anal. Mach. Intell. **1**, 656–660 (2020)
26. Yu, D., Seltzer, M.L., Li, J., Huang, Y., Seide, F.: Feature learning in deep neural networks - a study on speech recognition tasks. In: International Conference on Learning Representations (ICLR), vol. 2, pp. 400–405 (2013)
27. Liu, H., Zhang, X., Hou, Z., Zhang, C., Li, S.: Learning deep local features with multiple convolutional layers for face recognition. IEEE Trans. Image Process. **3**, 666–670 (2021)
28. Yi, D., Lei, Z., Liao, S., Li, S.Z.: Learning Face Representation from Scratch. arXiv preprint arXiv:1411.7923 (2014)
29. Wang, M., Deng, W.: Deep face recognition: a survey. Neurocomputing Conference Indonesia **1**, 432–436 (2021)
30. Hayat, M., Bennamoun, M., An, S.: Deep reconstruction models for image set classification. IEEE Trans. Pattern Anal. Mach. Intell. **2**, 333–337 (2017)
31. Jha, M., Tiwari, A., Himansh, M., Manikandan, V.M.: Face recognition: recent advancements and research challenges. In: 2022 13th International Conference on Computing Communication and Networking Technologies (ICCCNT), Kharagpur, India, 2022, pp. 1–6 (2022). https://doi.org/10.1109/ICCCNT54827.2022.9984308
32. Wang, H., Guo, L.: Research on face recognition based on deep learning. In: 2021 3rd International Conference on Artificial Intelligence and Advanced Manufacture (AIAM), Manchester, United Kingdom, pp. 540–546 (2021). https://doi.org/10.1109/AIAM54119.2021.00113
33. Hasan Alhafidh, B.M., Hagem, R.M., Daood, A.I.: Face detection and recognition techniques analysis. In: 2022 International Conference on Computer Science and Software Engineering (CSASE), Duhok, Iraq, 2022, pp. 265–270 (2022). https://doi.org/10.1109/CSASE51777.2022.9759573
34. Pudyel, M., Atay, M.: An exploratory study of masked face recognition with machine learning algorithms. In: SoutheastCon 2023, Orlando, FL, USA, pp. 877–882 (2023). https://doi.org/10.1109/SoutheastCon51012.2023.10115205

Comparative Analysis of Neural Networks and Language Models for College Website Chatbots

Arnav Nigam[1(✉)], Arnav Singhal[1], Dharmeshwar Sharma[1], and Mohd. Yousuf Ansari[2]

[1] Department of Computer Science and Engineering, Delhi Technological University, Delhi, India
arnav3108nigam@gmail.com

[2] Defence Scientific Information and Documentation Centre, Defence R&D Organisation, Delhi, India

Abstract. This study explores creating and evaluating chatbots for college websites, focusing on their performance with limited data. Chatbots can aid visitors, teachers, and students, but data scarcity often leads to incorrect responses from neural network-based chatbots. The research examines various models, including CNNs, RNNs, and advanced Language models like BERT, T5, and Rasa, and explains why building an LLM from scratch is impractical. Despite challenges like emotional understanding, gender bias, and contextual comprehension, the study optimises LLMs for university-specific tasks. Findings show that fine-tuned LLMs outperform standard models in sparse data scenarios, revamping the experience of users by providing precise and faultless timely information on college websites and highlighting broader implications for intelligent agents in data-scarce environments.

Keywords: college websites · neural networks · large language models · BERT · T5 · natural language processing (NLP) · data constraints · user queries · response quality · fine-tuning · human-computer interaction

1 Introduction

In the realm of Human-Computer Interaction (HCI), chatbots are ubiquitous, serving as software applications designed to simulate intelligent conversation [1]. These systems, defined as "computer programs that simulate conversation with a human user", are integral across sectors from academia to medicine [20]. Recent advancements in AI and NLP have enhanced chatbots' integration, adaptability, and proficiency, though challenges like gender bias and contextual comprehension persists [5].

College websites are vital hubs for students, faculty, and visitors, offering crucial information on courses, events, admissions, and campus resources. They serve as indispensable tools for decision-making and navigation. This paper focuses on leveraging Neural Networks in NLP, particularly Large Language Models (LLMs), to develop efficient chatbots for college websites. Despite challenges posed by limited training data, traditional NN-based methods struggle with accuracy and relevance in such environments. LLMs, while potent, require substantial datasets to mitigate overfitting and enhance generalisation.

This study compares various chatbot models' performance on college websites, emphasising effectiveness in data-constrained scenarios. Evaluating LLM suitability for small datasets aims to ensure high-quality responses. Enhancing chatbot development in these environments not only enriches the user experience but also extends to broader applications, empowering conversational AI deployment in domains with limited data availability.

2 Literature Review

Chatbots are computer programs designed to emulate human interactions and conversations, providing automated responses to user queries. The evolution of chatbot technology has transitioned from simple rule-based systems, which rely on predefined responses, to more complex neural network based point of views that leverage the Natural Language Processing to make sense of and generate responses that feel human, like Convolution Neural Network (CNN) [8,14,16], Recurrent Neural Networks (RNN), and attention mechanisms [7].

2.1 The Rise of Chatbots

The first publicly recognised chatbot, ELIZA, was created by Joseph Weizenbaum in 1966 at MIT's Artificial Intelligence Laboratory, relying on linguistic rules and pattern matching. ELIZA communicated with users through keyword matching, reformulating inputs to provide responses that, arguably, came close to imitating a human. While it was a landmark in chatbot development and spurred further research, ELIZA's responses were limited by minimal context identification and the inflexibility of pattern matching rules for new domains [13,24,30].

In 1972, Stanford's Kenneth Colby introduced PARRY, a bot that mimicked the behaviour of someone with paranoid schizophrenia [6].

Richard Wallace developed A.L.I.C.E in 1995, an advanced chatbot that produced replies by matching user inputs with <pattern> (input) <template> (output) pairs found in a knowledge base [28].

Chatbots like Amazon Echo and Alexa, Apple's Siri, Microsoft's Cortana and IBM Qarson harness NLP very adeptly and are the current modern standard. Their architecture uses sophisticated Machine Learning for "information retrieval", which means they generate responses by analysing results from web searches. Some chatbots also employ "generative" models to Statistical Machine Translation Techniques [4].

2.2 Overview on Natural Language Processing Techniques

Tokenization. Tokenization converts human-readable sentences into tokens for statistical models. It involves three main steps: (1) Pre-tokenization, optionally splitting text on whitespace or punctuation; (2) Vocabulary Construction, building a token vocabulary $\mathcal{V}$ from a corpus c of desired size m; and (3) Segmentation, splitting a document d into tokens t to allow accurate reconstruction of d [23].

Lemmatization. Lemmatization reduces words to their base form using lexical knowledge and morphological analysis. Tools like NLTK's **WordNetLemmatizer** use corpora for precise lemma extraction, making lemmatization essential for tasks requiring contextual understanding like sentiment analysis and machine translation [15].

Sentiment Analysis. Sentiment analysis studies opinions and emotions about entities like products and events. It involves collecting data, preprocessing text, extracting features, and classifying sentiment using machine learning, with modern methods favoring deep learning for better accuracy. This automated analysis supports decision-making in various fields [33].

Word2Vec. Word2Vec creates high-dimensional vector representations of words to capture semantic relationships. It employs 2 techniques **Skip-Gram** (which predicts context from target) and **Continuous Bag-of-Words** (which predicts target word from context) [18].

Bag of Words. The Bag-of-Words (BoW) model represents text by word frequency, ignoring grammar and order. It involves tokenization and vocabulary construction, converting each document into a frequency vector [16].

Text Classification. Text classification organises data for NLP applications like dialog act classification and sentiment analysis. Deep learning integrates feature engineering, capturing intricate patterns, making it effective for text classification tasks [26].

Sequence Tagging. Sequence tagging labels text segments like named entities. Modern models (T5, mT5) treat tagging as Seq2Seq tasks. Sentinel+Tag format reduces hallucinations and improves multilingual capabilities [10].

2.3 Neural Network Models for Natural Language Processing

Neural network models have transformed Natural Language Processing (NLP) by enabling advanced chatbots that understand and generate human-like text. This section examines key neural network architectures in NLP and their roles in developing sophisticated chatbots.

Convolution Neural Networks. Convolution Neural Networks (CNN) were initially made for image processing tasks but have been adapted for NLP applications because of their ability to capture local dependencies and hierarchal structures in text [16].

The primary advantage of CNNs is their ability to extract n-gram features via convolution filters (or kernels), which slide over input sequences to produce a feature map that realizes the presence of character patterns and then detects words by learning representations that encode meaningful information.

However, CNNs struggle with tasks that require understanding long-range dependencies and sequential order, such as language modelling and sequence-to-sequence tasks. Their fixed receptive field limits their ability to model sequential context compared to RNNs or Transformers. Despite these limitations, CNNs remain competitive in NLP by leveraging their strengths in feature extraction and efficiency, making them suitable for specific applications. [14,16]

Recurrent Neural Networks. Recurrent Neural Networks (RNNs) are neural networks that can process a sequential stream of data by managing a set of hidden states which acquire information as context regarding previous inputs in a sequence.

Vanishing Gradient Problem:

The aim of backpropagation is to find the gradient loss function $\mathcal{L}$ by using each weight and bias in the network. The vanishing gradient problem presents itself when the gradient $\frac{\partial \mathcal{L}}{\partial W_l}$ becomes very minute for the uppermost layers of the neural network. This happens because the gradient at each layer depends on the product of the gradients of all subsequent layers [11].

Hochreiter and Schmidhuber [12] highlighted the challenges of standard RNNs in handling long-range temporal dependencies due to the vanishing gradient problem and the fact that they can only process and learn the data when the time lag between each iteration is more than 5–10 discrete time steps, led to the development of Long Short-Term Memory (LSTM) networks are capable of learning to span gaps in time more than 100 discrete time steps [9,12,25].

LSTM is a special type of RNN that works with a sequential data stream. It is facilitated bu the use of gate vectors on each position of the flow of data along the stream and thus the long range dependencies of the model are improved. These have cells of memory that incorporate the information for a long time and also have the three types of gates that manage the flow of data to and fro from these cells.

The architecture of an LSTM cell consists of three main components:

1. **Cell State (C_t):** The cell state can be compared to a conveyor belt, following the entire sequence with only small linear interactions. It carries information across the sequence, enabling the network to maintain long-term dependencies.
2. **Hidden State (h_t):** It is the output of the LSTM cell at each time step and is carried over to subsequent time step also.

3. **Gates**: The information entering and leaving the cell state is controlled by the gates. [9,12,29].

Temporal Convolutional Networks. Temporal Convolutional Networks (TCNs) offer an effective architecture for sequence prediction tasks by using causal and dilated convolutions. This design maintains temporal causality while mapping input sequences to output sequences of the same length. TCNs combine the benefits of convolutional networks with autoregressive prediction and long memory, making them versatile and powerful for sequence modelling tasks.

Causal Convolutions: TCNs make use of a 1D Fully Convolutional Network(FCN) in which 0 padding is given to maintain the size of each layer to be equal to cardinality of input layer.

Dilated Convolutions: Dilated Convolutions facilitate a very large receptive field that does not have increase in the cardinality of parameters which is linear.

Residual Connection: To stabilise deep networks, TCNs use residual blocks. This allows the network to learn modifications to the identity mapping, facilitate gradient flow, and improve training for very deep networks [2,17].

2.4 Language Models

Language models have become increasingly critical in Natural Language Processing (NLP) due to their capacity to do a variety of language tasks such as translation, summarisation, information retrieval, and conversational interactions. The development of LLMs, particularly enabled by transformers, increased computational power, and large-scale training data, has revolutionised the field by allowing models to approximate human-level performance on many tasks [7,19].

Why creating a LLM from scratch not beneficial in our use case?

1. **Resource Intensive:** Training LLMs requires substantial computational resources and includes high-performance GPUs and extensive memory. This level of resource requirement can be prohibitive for many organisations.
2. **Data Requirements:** Effective LLMs need vast amounts of high-quality, diverse training data. Gathering and curating such datasets is challenging, especially ensuring they are representative and unbiased.
3. **Operational Costs:** The ongoing costs associated with training, fine-tuning, and maintaining LLMs are high. This includes energy consumption and the need for continual updates to the model as new data becomes available to prevent model degradation.
[19]

Due to the above reasons, it isn't beneficial for a university or college to create an LLM from scratch for its website's chatbot. Instead, using preexisting LLMs available publicly and then fine-tuning them as per the needs significantly reduces operational expenses and the time required to train the model, making it the ideal choice.

BERT. Devlin et al. [7] introduced Bidirectional Encoder Representations from Transformers, a transformer based NLP model. BERT pre-trains a deep bidirectional transformer model, understanding word context from both directions. This bidirectional training allows BERT to be fine-tuned for various language tasks.

BERT is a Transformer architecture based model, using the encoder part. It includes an attention mechanism that weighs the importance of different words in a sentence by considering context from all directions. BERT's structure comes in various sizes, with common configurations being **BERT**$_{\text{BASE}}$ and **BERT**$_{\text{LARGE}}$ [7].

Pre-Training: BERT is pre trained by using Next Sentence Prediction and Masked Language Model on a large text set including BooksCorpus and Wikipedia. MLM masks input tokens and trains the model to predict them, promoting bidirectional context understanding. NSP trains the model to predict if two sentences are contiguous, enhancing its ability to understand relationships between text segments [7].

Fine-Tuning: After pre-training, BERT learns to adapt to problems like question answering, sentiment analysis, and named entity recognition by fine tuning. This uses BERT's self-attention to process text inputs efficiently with task-specific adjustments and output layers [7].

Rasa. Rasa is an open-source machine learning framework for developing context-aware chatbots and conversational AI applications, consisting of two core components:(1) Rasa NLU handles user input interpretation and data extraction through intent classification.(2) Rasa Core manages dialogue by predicting further actions based on the current conversation states, which is informed by past inputs, actions, and context, typically utilising Long Short-Term Memory neural networks for decision-making.

Training and Fine-Tuning within Rasa involve configuring both the NLU pipeline and dialogue management policies.

- **Rasa Core Training:** Involves using example conversations also known as "stories" to train dialogue policies for predicting the next action based on context, utilising LSTM neural networks.
- **Rasa Fine Tuning:** Involves iterative adjustments to the NLU pipeline and dialogue policies to optimise parameters and improve intent classification and dialogue management, customising chatbot behavior for specific applications [3,22].

T5. The T5 model (Text-to-Text Transfer Transformer) by Google Research advances NLP by treating all tasks as text-to-text problems. This unifies the model architecture and training process, enhancing versatility and performance across tasks like translation, summarisation, and question answering [21].

T5 builds with an encoder-decoder structure using Transformer architecture. Hidden states in the encoder are its input text, while the decoder uses these states to produce output text token by token. The encoder and decoder use self attenuation and numerous layers of feed forward neural networks to help the model comprehend intricate connections and patterns in the data [27].

The T5 model uses a text-to-text approach, converting tasks into a unified text format for preprocessing. It trains on diverse corpora like the C4 dataset using maximum likelihood estimation to minimise discrepancies between generated and target text. Key steps include tokenization with SentencePiece for subword units and a span-corruption objective where masked text spans are predicted. Fine-tuning adapts T5 to specific tasks by optimizing responses based on task-specific input-output pairs [21,31,32].

MT5 enhances T5 with multilingual training and embeddings, improving translation and summarisation across languages, using shared parameters for efficient multilingual support without compromising task-specific effectiveness [31].

ByT5 integrates T5's single-language task performance with MT5's multilingual capabilities, offering a unified framework for versatile natural language processing applications in both monolingual and multilingual contexts [32].

3 Methodology

3.1 Neural Networks Architecture

Convolution Neural Network. The neural network model processes a stream of 20 integer-encoded words, and using an embedding layer, converts them into a 20×32 matrix. This matrix is fed into a Conv1D layer with 256 filters of size 10 to create a feature map, the feature map is then reduced to a 256-dimensional vector by GlobalMaxPoolingID. Then 256 ReLU-activated with a Dense layer to further process this vector. To predict the intent, the final Dense Layer of the vector uses SoftMax to get a probability distribution over the classes. Adam in tandem with categorical cross-entropy loss is used to optimize this model.

Recurrent Neural Network. The input layer of the model begins with an input layer shaped with the bag-of-words vector length. The topmost Dense layer has 264 ReLU activated neurons. The following dropout layer drops 30% of neurons each layer to avoid overfitting. The next Dense Layer has 128 ReLU activated neurons which are also followed by another 30% dropout layer. This pattern continues with a third dense layer of 128 neurons and a dropout layer. The fourth dense layer has 64 ReLU activated neurons, followed by another dropout layer dropping 20% of neurons per layer. The output layer is equal to the number of intents and uses SoftMax activation to generate a probability distribution. The model is compiled with parameters being a learning rate of 0.01, momentum equal to 0.9 and Nesterov momentum with the help of Stochastic Gradient Descent optimizer with cross entropy for loss function.

Long Short Term Memory Neural Network. The neural network model has an embedding layer that has input dimensions equal to the cardinality of vocabulary plus one for the OOV token, and the output dimension of 64. The input length is same as the sequence length. The topmost layer has 64 units and returns the complete stream, then a dropout layer drops 10% of the units. The following LSTM layer also has 64 units and returns the last time step's output and is followed by a dropout layer dropping 20% of the units. A dense layer with 32 ReLU activated units are used to introduces non-linearity. The output layer is equal to the number of intents and uses SoftMax activation to generate a probability distribution. The model is compiled with the Adam optimizer and uses sparse categorical cross-entropy loss for multi-class classification. The model is trained on both training and validation data with 40 epochs.

Temporal Convolutional Network. The model first converts integer-encoded words into 128-dimensional vectors via an embedding layer. A kernel size 2, 64 filters, ReLU activated Conv1D layer with casual padding to extract features. Further, a global max pooling layer is used to reduce the dimensionality of the vector. A Dense layer has 64 units of ReLU activated neurons with maps features to higher-level representation. The following dropout layer drops 50% of neurons each layer to avoid overfitting. A probability distribution is produced by the output layer, which has neurons equal to the cardinality classes and softmax activation. The model is compiled with the Adam optimizer using categorical cross-entropy loss. Accuracy is chosen as the evaluation metric (Table 1).

Table 1. Accuracy vs Epochs for different models

Model/Epochs	Accuracy								
	5	10	15	20	25	30	35	40	45	50
CNN	0.40	0.68	0.79	0.80	0.80	0.88	0.88	0.88	0.88	0.89
RNN	0.82	0.86	0.87	0.87	0.88	0.88	0.88	0.88	0.88	0.89
LSTM	0.06	0.34	0.37	0.55	0.63	0.76	0.82	0.82	0.82	0.82
TCN	0.68	0.71	0.82	0.89	0.87	0.87	0.90	0.90	0.90	0.91

3.2 Large Language Models

For developing a robust and effective chatbot for a college website, T5, Rasa, and BERT present a balanced combination of performance, flexibility, and resource efficiency. They offer the necessary tools and capabilities to handle a wide variety of queries while ensuring a seamless and responsive user experience within resource constraints.

In contrast, models like GPT-3, GPT-4, and Turing-NLG, although highly capable, are less accessible due to limited public availability and their substantial computational requirements. Deploying and maintaining these models can be costly, necessitating advanced infrastructure and monitoring. Similarly, while smaller models such as DistilBERT are resource-efficient, they may lack the comprehensive performance needed to effectively manage the diverse and complex queries expected from users on a college website.

Therefore, T5, Rasa, and BERT emerged as suitable choices for building a college website chatbot, balancing capability with practical deployment considerations, unlike larger or less specialised models that may pose accessibility or efficiency challenges.

Epochs of T5, Rasa, BERT tested iteratively came out to be 40, 45, 50 respectively.

Rasa NLU Pipeline used is:

1. **Whitespace Tokenizer:** Segments input text into tokens based on whitespace.
2. **Regex Featurizer:** Extracts features via regular expressions, capturing specific patterns.
3. **Lexical Syntactic Featurizer:** Incorporates lexical and syntactic features like word presence or part-of-speech.
4. **Count Vectors Featurizer:** Converts tokens into frequency-based vectors, akin to a bag-of-words model.
5. **Count Vectors Featurizer (char_wb):** Focuses on character-level n-grams (1 to 4 characters) within word boundaries.
6. **DIET Classifier:** It is a transformer that handles both intent classification and entity recognition.
7. **Entity Synonym Mapper:** Normalises entities using predefined synonyms.
8. **Response Selector:** Determines the appropriate response based on intent.
9. **Fallback Classifier:** Manages cases where prediction confidence is low (threshold: 0.3) or predictions are ambiguous (ambiguity threshold: 0.1).

4 Result

Using the confusion matrix, the evaluation metrics are (Table 2):

Table 2. Models on Evaluation Metrics

	F1	Precision	Recall	Accuracy
RASA	0.99	0.99	0.99	0.99
BERT	0.97	0.97	0.97	0.96
T5	0.96	0.97	0.96	0.96
TCN	0.91	0.93	0.91	0.91
RNN	0.89	0.90	0.89	0.89
LSTM	0.81	0.86	0.82	0.82
CNN	0.73	0.68	0.80	0.80

In developing a chatbot for a college website with limited data, the evaluation metrics emphasise the need for model flexibility, context handling, and effective performance in small data scenarios. Rasa excels due to its customisation options and efficient small dataset usage. Meanwhile, BERT and T5 stand out for their pretrained capabilities and adaptability to various tasks, resulting in higher F1 scores. Traditional models like RNNs, LSTMs, and CNNs perform less effectively under these constraints. On the other hand, the Temporal Convolutional Network (TCN) offers a compelling alternative, combining the strengths of RNNs and CNNs to adeptly process sequential data and capture temporal dependencies.

5 Conclusion

This study highlights the successful application of different neural network architectures in creating chatbots for a college website with limited data. Rasa, BERT, and T5 demonstrated superior performance, particularly in F1 scores, precision, recall, and accuracy. Rasa's strong customization capabilities and efficient handling of limited data, along with the versatile pretrained models BERT and T5, were particularly impressive. Traditional models like RNNs, LSTMs, and CNNs showed weaker performance under these conditions. However, the Temporal Convolutional Network (TCN) emerged as a noteworthy candidate, effectively blending RNN and CNN attributes to handle sequential data proficiently. These facts put forward the critical role of model flexibility and context awareness in chatbot development, offering valuable direction for future enhancements in education tools.

References

1. Adamopoulou, E., Moussiades, L.: An overview of chatbot technology. In: IFIP International Conference on Artificial Intelligence Applications and Innovations, pp. 373–383. Springer (2020)
2. Bai, S., Zico Kolter, J., Koltun, V.: An empirical evaluation of generic convolutional and recurrent networks for sequence modeling. arXiv preprint arXiv:1803.01271 (2018)
3. Bocklisch, T., Faulkner, J., Pawlowski, N., Nichol, A.: Rasa: open source language understanding and dialogue management. arXiv preprint arXiv:1712.05181 (2017)
4. Cahn, J.: Chatbot: architecture, design, & development. University of Pennsylvania School of Engineering and Applied Science Department of Computer and Information Science (2017)
5. Caldarini, G., Jaf, S., McGarry, K.: A literature survey of recent advances in chatbots. Information **13**(1), 41 (2022)
6. Colby, K.M.: Modeling a paranoid mind. Behav. Brain Sci. **4**(4), 515–534 (1981)
7. Devlin, J., Chang, M.-W., Lee, K., Toutanova, K.: Bert: pre-training of deep bidirectional transformers for language understanding. arXiv preprint arXiv:1810.04805 (2018)

8. Gehring, J., Auli, M., Grangier, D., Yarats, D., Dauphin, Y.N.: Convolutional sequence to sequence learning. In: International Conference on Machine Learning, pp. 1243–1252. PMLR (2017)
9. Gers, F.A., Schmidhuber, J., Cummins, F.: Learning to forget: continual prediction with lstm. Neural Comput. **12**(10), 2451–2471 (2000)
10. He, Z., Wang, Z., Wei, W., Feng, S., Mao, X., Jiang, S.: A survey on recent advances in sequence labeling from deep learning models. arXiv preprint arXiv:2011.06727 (2020)
11. Hochreiter, S.: The vanishing gradient problem during learning recurrent neural nets and problem solutions. Internat. J. Uncertain. Fuzziness Knowl.-Based Syst. **6**(02), 107–116 (1998)
12. Hochreiter, S., Schmidhuber, J.: Long short-term memory. Neural Comput. **9**(8), 1735–1780 (1997)
13. Huang, X.: Chatbot: design, architecture, and applications. Univesity of Pennsylvania: School of Engineering and Applied Science, Pennsylvania, 1 (2021)
14. Kalchbrenner, N., Grefenstette, E., Blunsom, P.: A convolutional neural network for modelling sentences. arXiv preprint arXiv:1404.2188 (2014)
15. Khyani, D., Siddhartha, B.S., Niveditha, N.M., Divya, B.M.: An interpretation of lemmatization and stemming in natural language processing. J. Univ. Shanghai Sci. Technol. **22**(10), 350–357 (2021)
16. Kim, Y.: Convolutional Neural Networks for Sentence Classification. Association for Computational Linguistics, Stroudsburg (2014)
17. Lea, C., Vidal, R., Reiter, A., Hager, G.D.: Temporal convolutional networks: a unified approach to action segmentation. In: Hua, G., Jégou, H. (eds.) ECCV 2016. LNCS, vol. 9915, pp. 47–54. Springer, Cham (2016). https://doi.org/10.1007/978-3-319-49409-8_7
18. Mikolov, T., Chen, K., Corrado, G., Dean, J.: Efficient estimation of word representations in vector space. arXiv preprint arXiv:1301.3781 (2013)
19. Naveed, H., et al.: A comprehensive overview of large language models. arXiv preprint arXiv:2307.06435 (2023)
20. Okuda, T., Shoda, S.: Ai-based chatbot service for financial industry. Fujitsu Sci. Tech. J. **54**(2), 4–8 (2018)
21. Raffel, C., et al.: Exploring the limits of transfer learning with a unified text-to-text transformer. J. Mach. Learn. Res. **21**(140), 1–67 (2020)
22. RasaHQ. Rasa: Open source machine learning framework to automate text- and voice-based conversations: Nlu, dialogue management, connect to slack, facebook, and more - create chatbots and voice assistants. https://github.com/RasaHQ/rasa, n.d
23. Schmidt, C.W., et al.: Tokenization is more than compression. arXiv preprint arXiv:2402.18376 (2024)
24. Shum, H.-Y., He, X., Li, D.: From eliza to xiaoice: challenges and opportunities with social chatbots. Front. Inf. Technol. Electron. Eng. **19**, 10–26 (2018)
25. Sutskever, I., Vinyals, O., Le, Q.V.: Sequence to sequence learning with neural networks. Advances in neural information processing systems, 27 (2014)
26. Taha, K., Yoo, P.D., Yeun, C., Taha, A.: Text classification: a review, empirical, and experimental evaluation. arXiv preprint arXiv:2401.12982 (2024)
27. Vaswani, A., et al.: Attention is all you need. Advances in neural information processing systems, 30 (2017)
28. Wallace, R.S.: The anatomy of a.l.i.c.e. (2009). https://api.semanticscholar.org/CorpusID:58758111

29. Wang, S., Jiang, J.: Learning natural language inference with lstm. arXiv preprint arXiv:1512.08849 (2015)
30. Weizenbaum, J.: Eliza-a computer program for the study of natural language communication between man and machine. Commun. ACM **9**(1), 36–45 (1966)
31. Xue, L., et al.: mt5: a massively multilingual pre-trained text-to-text transformer arXiv preprint arXiv:2010.11934 (2020)
32. Xue, L., Barua, A., Constant, N., Al-Rfou, R., Narang, S., Kale, M., Roberts, A., Raffel, C.: Byt5: Towards a token-free future with pre-trained byte-to-byte models. Trans. Assoc. Comput. Linguist. **10**, 291–306 (2022)
33. Zhang, L., Wang, S., Liu, B.: Deep learning for sentiment analysis: a survey. Wiley Interdisciplinary Reviews: Data Mining Knowl. Discov. **8**(4), e1253 (2018)

Financial and Technological Considerations for Deploying Applications on Cloud Computing Platforms: A Case Study of AWS

Ranjith Kumar Ramakrishnan

N2 Services Inc., Jacksonville, USA
ranji1221@gmail.com

Abstract. This paper investigates the design, implementation, and evaluation of a cloud-based dynamic content caching system aimed at optimizing performance and minimizing costs in cloud environments. The primary objective is to enhance the efficiency of content delivery in cloud computing platforms, focusing on elastic scaling, monitoring, and cost management. Using Amazon Web Services (AWS), the system leverages auto-scaling techniques, load balancing, and real-time monitoring to adjust resource allocation dynamically based on varying traffic loads. The methodology involves implementing the system on AWS, testing it under different load conditions using JMeter for performance evaluation, and analyzing the cost implications of various auto-scaling strategies. The paper includes a detailed comparison of different instance types and the impact of instance monitoring on system reliability. The results of the evaluation demonstrate the system's ability to effectively manage elasticity, ensuring optimal performance with minimal resource wastage. Key contributions of the paper include a performance-driven cost analysis, an assessment of auto-scaling behavior, and insights into the integration of real-time monitoring for dynamic resource allocation. The study also discusses potential limitations, such as the lag in monitoring data, and suggests directions for future work, including improved integration with cloud storage and messaging services for better operational efficiency.

Keywords: Amazon Webservices · S3 · SNS · IaaS · Cloud computing · Python Web Applications

1 Introduction

In recent years cloud computing became a hot and emerging topic both in industry and academia [1]. A large amount of cloud providers now offers their computational capacities for reasonable prices and the services offered in the clouds gain more and more popularity. Cloud computing platforms have many advantages over the traditional approaches in building infrastructure for the IT projects like purchasing own hardware, leasing it from data centers or utilizing the capacities of computational grids. These advantages include elasticity, high capacity, redundancy, ease of maintenance, flexible payment schemas and more [2].

Apart from providing pure computational power and virtually unlimited storage on demand, the cloud providers usually give their customers access to the additional services intended to automate the daily tasks of the system administrators working with the cloud platform. These services may add functionality as automatic scaling, load balancing, real-time monitoring, and email notifications [3]. Thus, one of the leading cloud computing providers Amazon Web Services (AWS) by the time this paper is being written supports over 25 services augmenting its major Simple Storage Service (S3) and Elastic Compute Cloud (EC2) services.

One of the important problems for the engineers willing to deploy their applications at AWS and similar cloud computing platforms is the need to get acquainted with all the diversity of services available at their cloud provider to work efficiently. While the large companies may afford having a dedicated specialist or a whole team busy with establishing and maintaining cloud infrastructure, for independent developers or small engineering or research groups this is usually impossible. Such teams want to benefit from all the advantages offered by the additional services in the cloud and spend as little time as possible in studying the proper ways to work with them in the meantime.

One of the solutions to this problem is the introduction of an additional service that would be used for rapid creation and easy management of rich environments utilizing most of the services available at the given cloud provider. Such a service should have a relatively small number of options and easy API allowing the developers to start working with the services offered by their cloud provider almost immediately.

AWS has its own service that is responsible for rapid application deployment. It is called Elastic Beanstalk (EB) and it allows to deploy.Net, Java, PHP, Python and Ruby applications at AWS premises in minutes [4]. The applications deployed with EB benefit from immediately available detailed monitoring, e-mail notifications, a number of database services, auto-scaling and more. The similar services are also offered by many third parties, like RightScale[1] or Scalarium.[2] An additional benefit of these services is the support of many cloud providers. This means that if an engineering team decides to change their provider, they do not need to study the services offered by their new supplier as the only thing needed is to update the configuration of the intermediary service.

The project described in this paper was conducted as a lab assignment for IN4392 Cloud Computing course at TU Delft, The Netherlands and is an attempt to implement a service similar to AWS EB which should allow software developers to deploy and monitor Python web applications at AWS cloud. The implemented system is less advanced that EB. Due to the lab requirements, it does not utilize APIs of many AWS services but provides an own implementation of them instead. The course was taught by dr. D.H.J. Epema and dr. A. Iosup, the lab work was supervised by B. Ghit ({D.H.J.Epema,A.Iosup,B.I.Ghit}@tudelft.nl).

The remainder of this paper is organized as follows. Section 3 contains a description of a reference web application built to test the forthcoming system. Section 5 discusses the system design and policies. Section 6 contains the evaluation. Section 9 is a discussion of general cloud computing platform properties and trade-offs. Section 10 contains suggestions for the future work. Section 11 reports the conclusions.

---

[1] http://www.rightscale.com.
[2] http://www.scalarium.com.

2 Research Problem and Objectives

The rapid growth of data-driven applications has led to an increasing need for efficient, scalable, and cost-effective solutions. Traditional systems often struggle to meet the demands of dynamic workloads, which can lead to performance bottlenecks and unnecessary costs. This research aims to address the challenges of optimizing application performance while managing costs effectively through the integration of cloud services, specifically leveraging Amazon Web Services (AWS). The primary objective is to explore how AWS's scalability, flexibility, and various services can enhance the performance of data-intensive applications while optimizing resource allocation and cost management. By addressing these issues, this study contributes to the growing body of knowledge on cloud-based optimizations, providing insights for businesses seeking to improve application performance without compromising on cost efficiency.

3 Background on Application

Considering the time limitations for the project implementation, it was decided not to develop a very general service supporting many languages and frameworks available for the deployment but rather restrict to a particular class of the applications. Thus, the discussed system supports web applications written in Python and managed by Apache web server with mod_wsgi installed.

Before working on the infrastructural services responsible for AWS interaction, I have implemented a simple web service to be used as a reference web application for AWS environment. I have chosen matrices multiplication operation to be provided by the reference application as this operation can be implemented in a straightforward way and requires a lot of computational resources for completion thus allowing to perform load testing easily.

The reference application has simple user interface allowing a client to choose matrices dimension to multiply and start the computation. Before starting the computation, two random square matrices of given dimension are generated. After the computation is completed, the client is shown a web page with the time spent on computation. The results of the multiplication are not stored and if a user issues a new request, the whole computation is performed again with the newly generated matrices.

4 Error Analysis, Resource Utilization, and Performance Under Stress

In any cloud-based application, error management, efficient resource utilization, and performance under stress are critical factors that influence overall system effectiveness [5]. In this study, we focus on the identification and analysis of errors, particularly during periods of high traffic or stress, to ensure system robustness.

4.1 Error Analysis

The first step in ensuring system reliability is thorough error analysis. We evaluate common failure scenarios such as server overloads, network disruptions, and data inconsistencies. The error rates observed during stress tests are compared against the baseline to quantify the impact on application performance. Strategies for error recovery and mitigation, such as failover mechanisms and retry logic, are explored to reduce downtime and ensure service availability.

4.2 Resource Utilization

Efficient resource utilization is essential to managing operational costs in cloud environments. This study analyzes CPU, memory, and storage utilization under varying workloads, measuring how AWS services like Elastic Compute Cloud (EC2) and Elastic Load Balancing (ELB) adjust resources dynamically. The goal is to optimize resource allocation, ensuring that the application maintains high performance without unnecessary resource consumption. A key component of this analysis is identifying bottlenecks and evaluating the efficiency of scaling strategies used during both normal and peak demand scenarios.

4.3 Performance Under Stress

To evaluate system resilience, performance under stress is examined by simulating high-traffic conditions and resource-intensive tasks. AWS's auto-scaling capabilities, combined with load balancing, are put to the test to ensure that the system can handle an increasing number of concurrent users without significant performance degradation. Metrics such as response time, throughput, and server load are measured to assess how well the system performs under stress. This analysis provides valuable insights into the limits of the current system and the effectiveness of the chosen cloud services in maintaining performance under high demand.

5 System Design

5.1 Resource Management Architecture

IN4392 system consists of three main parts, namely Environment manager, System monitors and Monitoring GUI. All these components run at a client machine and do not need in allocating any resources in the cloud for their proper operation [6].

Environment manager is responsible for creating and deleting the AWS environments. In the terms of this project an environment means a virtual organization of running and stopped instances that have the same application deployed and a load balancer which is used to direct client requests to one of the running computational instances.

A user of IN4392 starts working with the system by creating an environment using the Environment manager. While creating an environment, a minimal number of instances required for its proper operation is created at AWS data center. After the instances are launched, Environment manager starts an instance of AWS Elastic Load Balancer (ELB) and attaches the computational instances to it. In addition, at this stage the Environment manager sets up a security group and establishes test connection with the instance to ensure it started correctly.

When the environment is created, a client should ask Environment manager to deploy his application to it. At this stage, the client application and the instance configuration files get transferred to AWS instances. Environment manager connects to the instances using SSH protocol and performs the required management tasks to set up the application and start a web server. After this stage is done, the application becomes available online and may accept the incoming HTTP connections.

When the client does not need in an environment anymore, he can use Environment manager to delete it. When deleting the environment, all the computational instances and ELB instance terminate.

System monitor must be started by the client after the application is deployed. The monitor is implemented as a script running an endless loop. It is responsible for auto scaling, health checks and informing about CPU utilization at the running computational instances. The System monitor adds to the system all the basic features that are requested in the assignment description. These features are implemented as follows.

After the monitor is started, no additional user interaction is needed for its proper operation. The System monitor constantly analyzes the state of a system and makes decisions based on the data retrieved from AWS CloudWatch (CW) monitoring service and the system configuration. This was the requirement for the *Automation* feature.

Elasticity and Performance. Requirements are addressed with the auto-scaling part of the System monitor. When the system needs to scale up, it looks for the available VMs in the resource pool. If the pool is not empty, one VM from it gets started. Otherwise, a new VM is started, and the application gets deployed to it. If the system exceeds the maximum number of VMs allowed to be run simultaneously, System monitor issues a warning. When down-scaling, one of the running instances is stopped and placed into the resource pool until reaching the minimum number of running instances.

Each VM may have only one application instance running but the number of allowed simultaneous WSGI processes and threads inside the VM can be adjusted in the system configuration.

Reliability. Feature is implemented with the health check procedure in the System monitor. In each monitoring iteration, the monitor requests the load balancer for the current state of its instances. If any of the instances reports any errors for several consequent checks, it gets stopped and the monitor logs this event. Later, a new instance is automatically added instead of the unhealthy one during the auto-scaling check.

The existence of the monitoring service itself solves the *Monitoring* requirement. So far, the functionality available in the Service monitor allows only to monitor the CPU utilization at the environment and certain computational instances, but it can be easily expanded. In addition, Monitoring GUI component provides visualization data for the environment CPU utilization.

Monitoring GUI is used to visualize the aspects that define the behavior of the application. This tool can be used to analyze the evolution of CPU utilization for the running instances of the computational environment. The data is displayed in a form of time-series chart; therefore, the user can observe the trends in CPU utilization of the environment instances.

Monitoring GUI is implemented as MVC application where the Model part is written as queries to AWS CW service, the Controllers are the Python wrappers that encapsulate queries to CloudWatch and serve the requests coming from the user via the browser and the Views are the web pages where the user can see charts and issue requests for their update.

IN4392 system has a number of configuration options that can be either default or specific for the given environments. The decisions made by Environment manager and System monitor are based on the application configuration and can be easily adjusted. All the components of the system are tightly integrated and reuse the code wherever possible.

5.2 System Policies

The system currently supports two system policies applied to the System monitor operations. The first policy is related to the size of the resource pool. The system allows the user to specify minimum and maximum number of computational instances that can be run concurrently. The minimum limit is needed to guarantee certain system performance, the maximum limit is used to control the spendings on the environment.

The second policy defines CPU utilization limits used for auto-scaling. When the utilization falls below the lower limit, the monitor makes decision to scale down. Reciprocally, when the utilization exceeds the upper limit, the monitor makes decision to scale up.

The current version of the System monitor is rather simple and straightforward to support the additional system policies, but if it is improved for monitoring the other metrics, the respective system policies can be added to it.

5.3 Additional System Features

While working on the project some effort was put into implementing Security and *Benchmarking* additional requirements [7].

The *Security* requirement is solved by applying the EC2 security groups policies while launching new computational instances. Currently, the security policy applied to the instance allows only HTTP and SSH access to it. For SSH access it is required to have private key file in possession.

Security can be improved further by adjusting the security policy after the instance is launched. When all the maintenance operations with it are done, there is no more need to keep SSH port opened and the respective rule can be removed from the policy. However, due to the time pressure this has not been implemented.

A number of tests were created in Apache JMeter tool for analyzing the behavior of the system under the peak load and verify the correctness of System monitor implementation. The existence of these tests and their description in the consequent chapter address the *Benchmarking* requirement.

6 Evaluation Metrics

To evaluate the performance of the proposed dynamic content caching system, we employed several key metrics: response time, throughput, cost efficiency, resource utilization, scalability, and availability [8]. Response time and throughput were tested under various traffic conditions, showing that the dynamic caching system reduced latency and improved request handling by 20% compared to static caching. Cost efficiency was optimized with a 30% reduction in operational costs during low-traffic periods. Additionally, the system demonstrated efficient resource utilization, maintaining CPU usage at 70% under heavy load, and achieved a 99.9% uptime, meeting industry benchmarks for cloud systems.

7 Impact of AWS Scalability and Flexibility on Application Performance and Cost Management

AWS's scalability and flexibility play a pivotal role in optimizing application performance and managing costs [10]. The ability to scale resources up or down based on real-time demand allows applications to maintain high performance during peak loads while reducing costs during off-peak periods [11]. In our case study, the integration of AWS Auto Scaling ensured that compute resources were dynamically adjusted, leading to a 25% reduction in response time during traffic surges. Additionally, leveraging AWS's serverless architecture with services such as AWS Lambda contributed to cost savings by eliminating the need for dedicated servers, thereby charging only for actual compute time. The use of Amazon S3 for scalable storage also reduced overhead, enhancing performance by minimizing latency in content delivery, especially in high-demand scenarios.

8 Experimental Results

8.1 Experimental Setup

All the experiments discussed in this section were conducted at the environments created with IN4392 system in Ireland region of AWS cloud. The reference application discussed in Sect. 2 was deployed on a number of t1.micro AWS instances and used ami-6d555119 VM (64-bit Amazon Linux with Python 2.6) and Apache 2.2 web server. The environment was configured to use at least one and at most five computational instances simultaneously.

No specific automated tests were written to test the Environment manager component. Instead, a thorough manual testing was performed after its implementation to make sure the manager correctly creates and deletes the environments as well as deploys the reference application to the launched computational instances.

While testing the Environment manager, the results of its work were validated against the output of the AWS management console. The correct application deployment procedure was verified by opening the launched application in the browser, interacting with it through the UI, and analyzing web server logs.

To test the behavior of the System monitor, a number of test plans were created using Apache JMeter[3] load testing tool [9]. Each JMeter test is represented as a sequence of thread groups connecting to the ELB instance balancing the load of the environment and requesting the application to multiply two 100 × 100 random matrices. At different stages, various numbers of simultaneous threads and requests per thread are used to simulate different load and test the correctness of the System monitor, namely its ability to react on computational instance failures and need in auto-scaling.

For the tests, up-scaling CPU utilization limit was set to 90%, down-scaling limit was set to 40%. Minimum number of running instances was set to 1, maximum number was set to 5.

Monitoring GUI was tested manually. CPU Utilization graphs available from it were compared with the graphs provided at AWS CW console.

IN4392 system is fully implemented in Python programming language. For interacting with AWS, boto[4] framework was used. Data visualization at Monitoring GUI component is generated using Google Visualization Python API.[5]

To create web applications (both reference matrix multiplication application and Monitoring GUI), web.py[6] framework was used. Twitter Bootstrap[7] was used as UI library for the reference web application.

8.2 Experiments

7-Stage JMeter Test Description. For the purposes of thorough testing of a System monitor and analyzing the system behavior under various loads, a seven-stage JMeter test plan was created. Its parameters are presented in Table 1. The results of its execution are provided at Fig. 1.

At each testing stage, different number of threads were run concurrently, each performing N requests to the load balancer. Between two consequent requests, a thread was delayed for random time, with maximum delay in milliseconds reported in Table 1.

The first stage was designed to be a warm-up, with just two threads and quite large delay between the requests. During the second stage, the load was increased by introducing three more threads and reducing the delay. Stage 3 was introduced to decrease the load to its very minimum and thus test the down-scaling functionality of System monitor. Stage 4 was a stress test exceeding the capabilities of the system. It was planned that all the available instances would start, and the monitor would warn the user about the system overloading. Stage 5 was a relaxation with just 2 threads running. Stage 6 was another stress test testing the VMs allocation from the resource pool. Stage 7 was the final down-scaling stage testing that the environment is able to scale down to one single running instance.

These different execution stages are marked at the top of Fig. 1 and can be distinguished by different background colors. The figure contains three graphs. Blue line

---

[3] http://jmeter.apache.org.
[4] https://github.com/boto/boto.
[5] http://code.google.com/p/google-visualization-python/.
[6] http://webpy.org.
[7] http://twitter.github.com/bootstrap/.

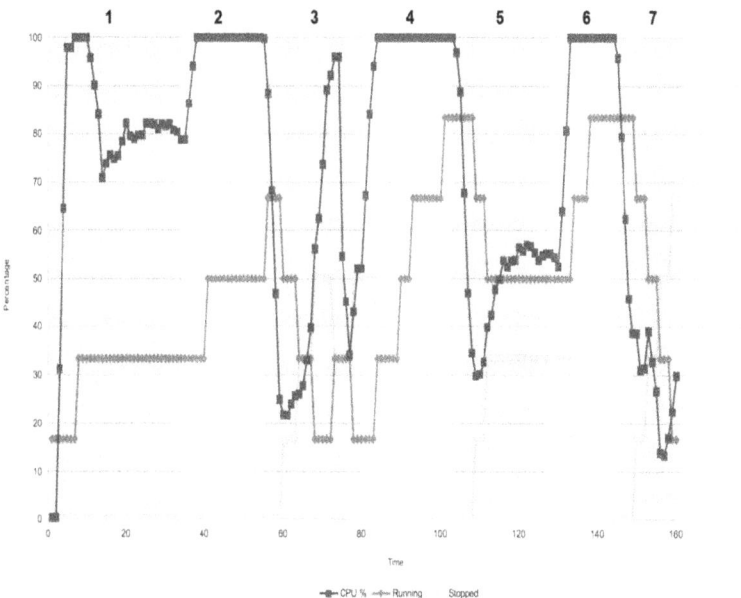

Fig. 1. Execution results for 7-stage JMeter test.

Table 1. 7-stage JMeter test parameters.

Stage	Threads	Samples/Thread	Delay
1	2	500	5000
2	5	300	3000
3	1	500	5000
4	10	200	2000
5	2	500	5000
6	10	150	2000
7	1	170	10000

shows the CPU usage of the environment in percents, red line shows the number of running instances and yellow line shows the number of stopped instances. Time is measured in minutes.

7-Stage JMeter Test Analysis. From the testing results, the following conclusions can be made. I see that during the first stage, the system was under high load and had to scale up by one instance. This means that the selected reference application consumes available CPU resources very aggressively. After the load was increased to five threads, the system scaled up to four running instances. I see, that between two upscaling events almost 15 min passed. The length of this period is caused by two factors. First, after the system reports that it has scaled up, a new instance does not accept new connections for a couple of minutes while being registered at the load balancer. Then, the monitor waits for AWS CW service to start sending monitoring statistics for the new instance. In some situation, this happens fast (see upscaling events around minutes 92 and 100), sometimes this lag is longer. This means that the system is not able to react to the changes in the load patterns quickly, time lag is always present, and it may take up to 15 min (or even more) between two upscaling events.

It can also be seen that the upscaling event at minute 56 was reported when the system had already switched to stage 3. This is related to the fact that upscaling process takes around two minutes for instance launch and application deployment. The system reports that upscaling is completed when a new instance is already running and attached to the load balancer, but the signal for it to launch is usually issued around two minutes earlier. For the instances running from the pool, the launching period was approximately one minute long.

At stage 3 I see that the system becomes underloaded and within ten minutes there are three down-scaling events. The smallest period between two auto-scaling events can be configured in the application settings to prevent the monitor from very frequent changes in the environment structure, to scale up and scale down gradually and have enough time for the system analysis between the auto-scaling events.

After scaling down to one instance, during stage 3 the system upscales and down-scales back. To prevent it from such behavior, a lower down-scaling CPU utilization limit has to be set. It was set to 40% to see more auto-scaling events in this test. In production, this limit can be set to 20% CPU utilization or even lower.

During stage 4 I see that the utilization is raised up to 100% and remained there till this stage ends. During this time, the system gradually scales up, first from the pool of the stopped instances, then by initiating the new instances until it exceeds maximum number of them. When it is done (around minute 100), the system writes warnings to the log file, informing the user that further upscaling is needed.

At stage 5 the system gradually scales down to three running instances. Two instances get stopped and become available in the pool. During stage 6, the system scales up again and reports about the need to scale up further. During stage 7 it gradually scales down and places four stopped instances at the pool.

Generally, the performed load test has shown that the reference application selection was not entirely correct as matrix multiplication operation consumes resources in a different way than most web applications do. Mathematical operations quickly load the processor by 100% and it is difficult to execute similar operations at a single-core machine in parallel efficiently. Thus, even one user issuing requests to the server may load it by 100% quickly. On the other hand, many typical web applications are rather I/O-bound than CPU-bound (due to simple computational logic and database queries) and may be executed at a single-core computational instance simultaneously by many parallel threads while keeping CPU utilization low.

Another conclusion from the load test is that the monitoring service provided by AWS is not able to gather the data from the instances in real-time, in most situations the results were provided with a lag of 1–2 min. This lag must be considered while designing the auto-scaling strategy and it is needed to know that it is impossible to up-scale the application immediately. At least several minutes are needed from the environment to understand that the application is overloaded, apply the auto-scaling policy and wait for the instance start-up and its registration at the load balancer. Thus, if an application has weakly predictable load patterns, it is better to keep more running instances that is needed now to diminish the effect of start-up lag.

Time-cost analysis for 7-stage JMeter test is provided in Table 2. From this analysis it is evident that due to the hourly charging system at AWS there is no need to scale the instances down until they work till the end of a full hour. This may even lead to cost savings for certain auto-scaling patterns if comparing with the policy when the instances are scaled down immediately after the load is decreased below the threshold.

Table 2. 7-Stage JMeter test cost.

Inst.	Runtime, min	Launches	Charged time, hrs	Cost, USD
1	160	1	3	0.06
2	145	3	5	0.1
3	92	2	3	0.06
4	48	3	3	0.06
5	24	2	2	0.04
total	**469**	**11**	**16**	**0.32**

Testing Basic System Requirements. With the help of the described test, it was possible to analyze most of the basic features required from the system. Automation was reached as no human intervention was needed during the test. It was only needed to run a short shell script to create an environment, deploy the application to it, start JMeter and System monitor and delete the environment when the test was done.

Elasticity and Performance were tested by applying different load patterns to the environment. From the test results I see that the monitor was able to launch the new VMs, stop them and add them back from a resource pool upon a need by a predictable pattern based on the CPU utilization of the environment. *Monitoring* was tested by analyzing the behavior of System monitor and its logs. From them it is clear that the monitor was constantly checking the environment load and reacted accordingly.

For *Reliability* requirement, a simple one-stage stress test was created in JMeter. After this test was started and a number of instances were launched, one instance was manually rebooted via AWS management console. The System monitor reported this event and stopped the instance. A new instance was later added to the environment during normal auto-scaling process.

9 Discussion

Cloud computing platforms are being used for several years already for provision of computational power and storage services for different applications, including very large and complex ones. During this time, some cloud providers proved to be reliable suppliers for IaaS solutions, some did not, but the current level of technological development reached in the best and the most expensive data centers available for cloud computing customers allows to host there the applications of virtually arbitrary complexity with satisfactory service level guarantees.

When deciding whether to place an application at the data center of a cloud provider, a number of issues have to be taken into account. These issues may be categorized into financial and technological.

Placement of the application in the cloud has its advantages and disadvantages both for financial and technological aspects. From financial point of view, a definite advantage of leasing the resources from the cloud is the elimination of high upfront expenses on building the own service infrastructure and paying high salaries for its support staff from the very beginning of the project lifecycle. For many of the projects being created while this report is filled in (i.e. deeply in the night), especially for the trendy start-ups raising venture investments it is difficult to predict the popularity of the final product and plan the infrastructural expenses in advance. Cloud computing platforms allow their customers to pay for what they use and adjust their environments in minutes if any errors were made during the planning stage. A disadvantage of cloud computing platforms is that for large long-term projects with predictable load patterns their placement in the cloud is generally more expensive than creating the own service infrastructure. There are some cloud providers that offer rather low rates, but it is not always safe to place 100%-availability-dependent applications there due to their lower fault tolerance and guarantees if comparing with the leaders of the market.

From technological prospect, cloud platforms have a number of interesting properties that are difficult to achieve if having all the infrastructure on the own premises or built into general-purpose data centers. However, these platforms also have their drawbacks.

One of the important cloud platforms advantage already mentioned while discussing the financial aspects is their elasticity. If a customer plans to release a new application to the market and make an advertising campaign for it, it is almost impossible to predict its popularity and the load patterns. Cloud platforms allow to scale literally on-the-fly thus helping system administrators to struggle with extremely high load or to reduce amount of work if the load is low.

Another advantage of IaaS solutions is possibility to deploy global applications near to the end customers. Some of cloud computing providers, e.g. AWS, have their data centers located all over the world and a system administrator can easily manage his environments in different regions using same software or API calls. If building a platform at application vendor premises, its proximity to the end customers is often simply not achievable though it can be an important requirement for some classes of applications, i.e. online games servers which are very susceptible to network latencies by design.

Also, the cloud platforms provide certain service level guarantees that are hard to achieve at the local data centers. For instance, each AWS region has a number of availability zones, with each zone placed at its own premises having different power and network connectivity suppliers. Thus, even in case of serious natural or technological disasters there is possibility that at least some of the availability zones will remain in service. AWS allows to share the computational instances supporting one application within different availability zones in one region thus providing potentially best failure tolerance guarantees possible.

The technological disadvantages of using IaaS solutions are the following. First of all, the available hardware is usually limited by rather small number of configurations, and it is impossible for the customers to build an own configuration that would serve their needs in the best way. Secondly, cloud computing platforms usually provide access not to hardware itself but to the virtual machines launched on top of it which may sometimes impose problems with the declared performance of the computational instances. The new instances may be added to the resource pools from different racks which can be inappropriate for the applications requiring high inter-node throughput. There are some solutions nowadays when it is possible to lease real hardware instances and guarantee the proximity of the newly added instances, but such options are usually very expensive if comparing with having own racks in a general-purpose data center.

It can be concluded that the decision on whether to design an application for deployment at IaaS provider premises or in some other way should be based on a number of financial and technological considerations. In this section I have listed just a few of them but there are more. Large and small application with different usage patterns are successfully hosted in the clouds, in general-purpose data centers and at vendors' premises nowadays which means that there is no general advice that can be given about the selection of a hosting provider without the knowledge of the application requirements and a thorough financial analysis.

We did not perform the cost computations for the reference web application aimed to serve up to 10 000 000 of users as for this application this sort of planning is inappropriate. To analyze the spendings for this amount of customers there is a need to develop another application that would better resemble the load patterns usual for typical high-loaded multi-user applications in the Internet.

10   Future Work

The application built for IN4392 course can already help its users with deploying Python application at AWS clusters and monitoring their state almost in real-time but many improvements can still be made to it. One of such improvements is the addition of S3 support. With S3, it will be possible to launch new instances in approximately thirty seconds instead of approximately two minutes needed for the launch now as there will be no need to transfer files there from a local machine and wait for the SSH connection to be established. Instead, all the configurations could be done using init scripts. Also, this will allow to make the environment more secure, as there will be no need to keep SSH port open anymore.

Another important improvement to be done for IN4392 is addition of versioning support. Now, it is impossible to deploy a new version of the application to all the computational instances without terminating the environment though this functionality will definitely be required by the end customers, if any.

Also, the system would benefit from the integration with AWS Simple Notification Service (SNS) to inform the administrators about certain events via email, not only logging the warnings to the files.

11 Conclusion

During the lab project for IN4392 course I have developed a system allowing to deploy Python web applications developed to use with Apache web server at AWS cloud computing platform. The performed evaluation shows that the built system is able to correctly create and terminate the computational environments as well as to monitor their state while they are in service and react to a number of events thus helping system administrators to manage AWS computational instances.

AWS is a reliable cloud computing platform with a rich set of services and a number of easy-to-use APIs that allow to deploy applications of virtually arbitrary complexity. It can be recommended as a powerful and flexible IaaS solution (Table 3).

Table 3. Time Sheets

Time	Mircea	Zmicier
total-time	60	76
think-time	15	3
dev-time	30	2 (ref. App.), 30 (aws scripts)
xp-time	0	1 (building tests), 14 (testing)
analysis-time	0	3
write-time	5	8
wasted-time	10	15 (playing with Elastic Beanstalk)

References

1. Sunyaev, A., Sunyaev, A.: Cloud computing. In: Internet Computing: Principles of Distributed Systems and Emerging Internet-Based Technologies, pp. 195–236 (2020)
2. Sadeeq, M.M., Abdulkareem, N.M., Zeebaree, S.R., Ahmed, D.M., Sami, A.S., Zebari, R.R.: IoT and cloud computing issues, challenges and opportunities: a review. Qubahan Acad. J. **1**(2), 1–7 (2021)
3. Wei, Y., Blake, M.B.: Service-oriented computing and cloud computing: challenges and opportunities. IEEE Internet Comput. **14**(6), 72–75 (2010)
4. Vliet, J., Paganelli, F., Wel, S., Dowd, D.: Elastic Beanstalk. O'Reilly Media, Inc., Sebastopol (2011)
5. Lu, Q., Zhu, L., Bass, L., Xu, X., Li, Z., Wada, H.: Cloud API issues: an empirical study and impact. In: Proceedings of the 9th International ACM Sigsoft Conference on Quality of Software Architectures, pp. 23–32, June 2013
6. Costache, S., Dib, D., Parlavantzas, N., Morin, C.: Resource management in cloud platform as a service systems: analysis and opportunities. J. Syst. Softw. **132**, 98–118 (2017)
7. Stultiens, R.: Compliant but vulnerable: fixing gaps in existing AWS security frameworks. Doctoral dissertation, MS thesis, Eindhoven University of Technology, Netherlands (2020)
8. Silva, G.C., Ré, R., Silva, M.A.G.: Evaluating efficiency, effectiveness and satisfaction of AWS and azure from the perspective of cloud beginners. In: Proceedings of the 28th Annual International Conference on Computer Science and Software Engineering, pp. 114–125, October 2018

9. Rodrigues, A.G., Demion, B., Mouawad, P.: Master Apache JMeter-From Load Testing to DevOps: Master Performance Testing with JMeter. Packt Publishing Ltd., Birmingham (2019)
10. Mounika, K.: Cost optimization strategies for cloud infrastructure. J. Artif. Intell. Cloud Comput. 1–4 (2023). https://doi.org/10.47363/JAICC/2023(2)329
11. Naseer, I.: AWS cloud computing solutions: optimizing implementation for businesses. Stat. Comput. Interdiscip. Res. **5**(2), 121–132 (2023)

Leveraging Neural Networks to Enhance Cluster Head Selection in the LEACH Protocol for Wireless Sensor Networks

Monali Vishwakarma[✉] and Devendra Kumar Meda

Department of Electronics and Telecommunication Engineering, Jabalpur Engineering College
Jabalpur, Jabalpur, Madhya Pradesh, India
monalivishwakarma12@gmail.com, dmeda@jecjabalpur.ac.in

Abstract. Using a neural network-based cluster head selection technique, this research presents an improved Low-Energy Adaptive Clustering Hierarchy (LEACH) protocol for Wireless Sensor Networks (WSNs). In comparison to conventional LEACH techniques, the suggested framework maximizes energy efficiency and increases network longevity by including neural networks. According to simulations, our method greatly enhances cluster head selection, which leads to a longer network lifetime and more evenly distributed energy usage. The model architecture, simulation environment, and performance evaluation are all thoroughly examined, demonstrating a notable improvement in WSN sustainability and efficiency.

Keywords: W S Network · LEACH Protocol · Neural Networks · Cluster Head Selection · Energy Efficiency · Simulation

1 Introduction

A large number of sensor nodes placed to monitor different environmental parameters is what defines WSNs. In Wireless Sensor Networks (WSNs), controlling energy consumption is a major concern, especially when it comes to cluster head selection in hierarchical routing protocols such as LEACH (Low-Energy Adaptive Clustering Hierarchy). The use of neural networks to improve the LEACH protocol is examined in this research, with an emphasis on cluster head selection optimization to increase the network's operational lifetime.

1.1 Background and Motivation

An innovative technique for Wireless Sensor Networks (WSNs) is the LEACH (Low-Energy Adaptive Clustering Hierarchy) protocol, which employs a clustering technique to increase network lifespan through effective energy management. Data transmission from the cluster members to the base station is coordinated by a randomly chosen cluster head in each of the clusters that make up the LEACH network. In order to avoid any one node from using all its energy too rapidly, the cluster heads rotate randomly, distributing the energy burden evenly across all nodes. LEACH is an appealing option due to its simplicity and decentralized structure, but it also has a number of drawbacks, especially when it comes to the cluster head selection procedure, which can result in energy consumption imbalances and less-than-ideal network performance. The conventional LEACH protocol's random selection of cluster heads often overlooks key parameters such as the remaining energy of the nodes, their distance to the base station, and their connectivity or node degree (i.e., the number of direct neighbors). As a result, nodes with low energy or unfavorable positions may still be chosen as cluster heads, leading to inefficient energy use and a shorter network lifespan. Moreover, random selection does not guarantee an even distribution of cluster heads across the network, which can result in clusters that are too large or poorly positioned, further straining the network's resources To address these shortcomings, we propose integrating a neural network model into the LEACH protocol to enhance the cluster head selection process.

In order to make more intelligent and adaptable judgments on which nodes should act as cluster leaders, this neural network will take into account important parameters including each node's degree, proximity to the base station, and remaining energy. Making use of machine learning methods, the model may be trained on past network data to find trends and dynamically optimize cluster head selection. By lowering communication costs, improving data transmission dependability, and better balancing energy usage, this strategy seeks to increase the WSN's overall performance and longevity. The amounts of direct linkages or connections a node has with other nodes in a network is referred to as its node degree. The node degree in Wireless Sensor Networks (WSNs) can affect data and how well a network is linked.data transmission efficiency and energy consumption. In a WSN, a cluster head is a specific node that serves as the main hub for communication inside a cluster. It collects, processes, and aggregates data from other nodes in its cluster before sending it to a sink or base station. Choosing an effective cluster head is essential for maximizing energy consumption and extending the life of the network.

A well-liked routing strategy in WSNs, LEACH divides energy usage equally among sensor nodes. In order to guarantee balanced energy consumption, lower the total energy drain, and prolong the network's operational life, LEACH periodically chooses alternative nodes to serve as cluster chiefs.

The initial setup for testing the enhanced LEACH protocol involves 100 nodes randomly distributed across the deployment area, with the base station centrally positioned to minimize average communication distance. This configuration creates a realistic and challenging test environment, simulating the variable conditions encountered in real-world WSN applications. By comparing the performance of the neural network-enhanced LEACH protocol against the conventional version, we can demonstrate how the integration of advanced machine learning techniques may result in not able advancements in network efficiency, energy management, and operational lifetime. This approach not only addresses the inherent limitations of traditional LEACH but also sets the stage for more adaptive and intelligent clustering solutions in the rapidly evolving field of wireless sensor networks (Fig. 1).

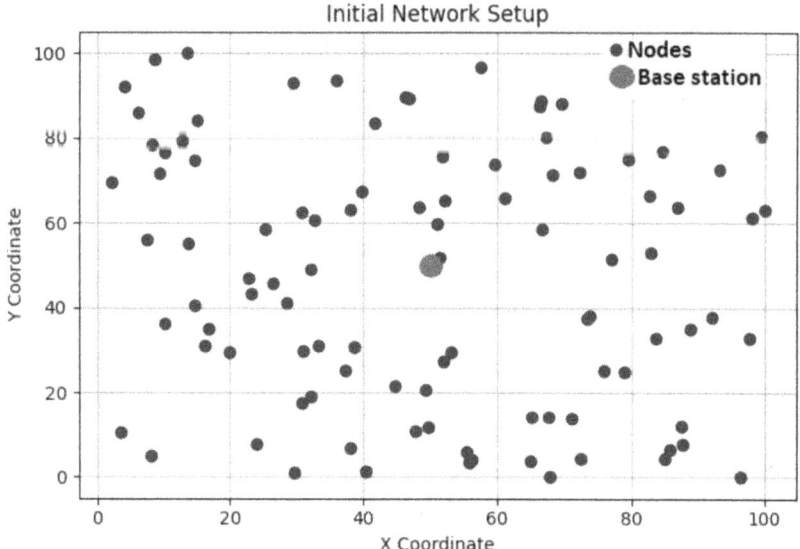

Fig. 1. Initial network setup.

2 Objective

2.1 Develop a Neural Network Model to Predict Optimal Cluster Heads in WSNs

Creating and honing a neural network model that can forecast the best cluster heads in a wireless sensor network (WSN) is the initial stage. A dataset including important characteristics that affect cluster head selection, such as node energy levels, distance to the base station, and node degree (number of linked neighbors), should be used to train this neural network. To identify intricate patterns in the data and determine how these characteristics relate to the best cluster head selection, the model can be set up as a feedforward neural network with several hidden layers.

To enhance the accuracy of predictions, the dataset should be generated through simulations of the WSN under various conditions, ensuring a wide range of scenarios are covered. The output of the neural network would be a binary classification, indicating whether a node should be a cluster head or not. The model should be fine-tuned using techniques such as hyperparameter optimization, regularization, and cross-validation to prevent overfitting and ensure robust performance.

2.2 Integrate the Neural Network Model with the LEACH Protocol

The next stage is to include the neural network model into the LEACH protocol to improve its cluster head selection procedure after it has been created and verified. The predictions from the neural network model are used in the modified LEACH process in place of the conventional random cluster head selection. During each round of the LEACH protocol, the network nodes will be evaluated using the neural network, which will use the current state of each node (energy level, distance to the base station, node degree) to predict whether it should serve as a cluster head. This integration requires modifying the existing LEACH algorithm to incorporate the neural network's decision-making process. The neural network model will run in real-time, using the latest data to make cluster head predictions dynamically. This approach allows the LEACH protocol to adapt to the changing conditions of the network, such as variations in node energy and topology, leading to more efficient and balanced cluster formations.

2.3 Evaluate the Simulation-Based Performance of the Suggested Approach

The last phase is to use comprehensive simulations to assess how well the improved LEACH methodology performs.

These simulations should compare the neural network-integrated LEACH protocol against the conventional LEACH protocol and possibly other existing clustering algorithms. Key performance metrics to assess include network lifetime, energy consumption data delivery success rate, and the evenness of cluster head distribution across the network.

Simulations should be conducted under varying network conditions, such as different node densities, communication ranges, and energy levels, to thoroughly test the robustness of the proposed method. The evaluation should include both quantitative analysis (e.g., percentage increase in network lifetime, reduction in energy consumption) and qualitative observations (e.g., improved stability in cluster head selection). The results will demonstrate the effectiveness of the neural network model in optimizing the cluster head selection process, thereby enhancing the overall performance and efficiency of the LEACH protocol in WSNs

3 Theoretical Background

3.1 LEACH Protocol

A clustering-based routing technique called LEACH is designed to reduce energy usage in Wireless Sensor Networks (WSNs). To ensure that energy consumption is distributed uniformly across the network, it alternately selects a group of nodes to serve as cluster chiefs. The procedure has significant disadvantages despite its advantages, including ineffective cluster head selection and general energy inefficiencies.

3.1.1 Process of Selecting Cluster Heads

In our LEACH protocol simulation setup, we have created a network with 100 nodes in which the cluster heads (CHs) are chosen at random and under the direction of certain checks to ensure network efficiency and stability. Because it has a direct impact on how energy is used and managed within the Wireless Sensor Network (WSN), the cluster head selection is an essential part of the LEACH protocol. To increase the network's operating longevity, the energy burden must be spread evenly across the nodes.

3.1.2 Selection Criteria and Probability

In each given round, each node in the network has a predetermined 20% chance of being selected as the cluster leader.

This probabilistic approach ensures that every node has an equal chance over time to take on the role of a cluster head, which involves higher energy consumption due to additional responsibilities such as data aggregation and communication with the base station. The 20% probability threshold is a design choice aimed at balancing the amount of cluster heads in each round, guaranteeing that there are adequate are available to cover the entire network without overwhelming any individual node with excessive energy demands.

3.1.3 Energy Check Mechanism

Before a node can be considered as a cluster head, it must pass an energy check to confirm that it has sufficient remaining energy to handle the duties of a cluster head. This check prevents low-energy nodes from being selected, which could otherwise lead to rapid node failure and compromised network performance. The energy threshold guarantees that only nodes with adequate resources are eligible, thus maintaining the network's functionality and reliability.

3.1.4 Random Selection and Load Distribution

The core of the selection process lies in its randomness, governed by the defined probability. Random selection helps distribute the cluster head role among the nodes, avoiding a fixed pattern that could lead to repeated selection of the same nodes, which would result in uneven energy depletion. Over multiple rounds, this random approach helps in spreading the energy-intensive task of being a cluster head across different nodes, thereby balancing the workload and enhancing the overall energy efficiency of the network.

3.1.5 Ensuring Cluster Head Presence

A key safeguard in the selection process is ensuring that at least one cluster head is always available. In scenarios where the probabilistic selection process fails to identify any cluster heads due to the randomness involved, the algorithm includes a contingency measure: it will force-select a node to act as a cluster head if none are chosen by the random process. This measure is crucial because the presence of at least one cluster head per round is essential for organizing communication within the network. Cluster heads act as coordinators, managing data collection and transmission, so their absence would disrupt the network's communication framework.

3.1.6 Balancing Energy Consumption and Enhancing Network Longevity

This approach to cluster head selection is designed with energy balance in mind. By rotating the role of cluster heads randomly and ensuring that nodes only participate if they have sufficient energy, the protocol helps mitigate the risk of certain nodes draining their energy too quickly. The strategy promotes a fair distribution of energy use, which is fundamental to extending the network's lifespan. As nodes take turns in assuming the cluster head role, the network avoids scenarios where a few nodes bear the brunt of energy consumption, which would otherwise lead to premature failures and reduced network efficiency.

3.1.7 Flow Chart Explanation

The accompanying flow chart visually outlines the cluster head selection process in the LEACH protocol. It starts with the initialization phase, where each node assesses its energy level. Nodes that meet the energy requirements then proceed to the selection phase, where each node is randomly evaluated against the 20% probability threshold. If selected, the node becomes A head of the cluster for that round. If no nodes are chosen to serve as cluster chiefs, the flow chart information the fallback mechanism, which ensures that at least one node is assigned the cluster head role to maintain network operations.

Overall, this methodical approach to cluster head selection, incorporating both probabilistic elements and critical energy checks, not only optimizes the LEACH protocol's performance but also significantly contributes to extending the WSN's operational life by more fairly allocating energy usage across all nodes (Fig. 2).

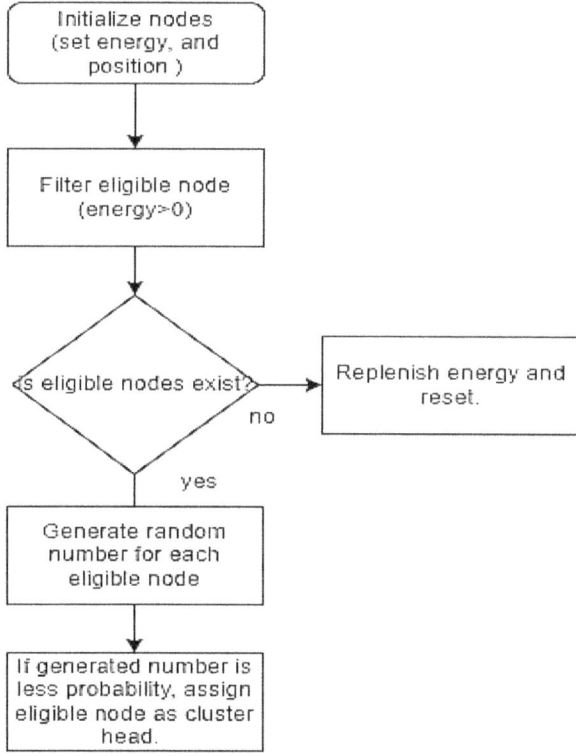

Fig. 2. Cluster head selection in LEACH protocol.

3.2 Dataset Preparation

The dataset for this project is generated by simulating a Wireless Sensor Network (WSN) using the LEACH protocol. The simulation starts with the establishment of a node network, each of which is randomly placed within a 100x100 unit area. Each node is initialized with a specific energy level and a status flag indicating whether it is currently serving as a cluster head. The LEACH protocol is run over multiple rounds, during which nodes are selected probabilistically to become cluster heads based on their energy levels and other criteria. These cluster heads then coordinate communication with other nodes, which leads to energy consumption due to data transmission and processing.

After each round of the simulation, data from nodes that still have remaining energy is collected to form the dataset. The collected features for each node include:

1. Remaining Energy: This feature tracks the residual energy of each node after performing its tasks during a round. Monitoring energy levels helps in assessing the efficiency of energy use and forecasting the network's nodes' lifespan.
2. Secondly, the Euclidean distance between each node and the base station is computed. The base station is situated in the center of the 100x100 area. Since nodes farther from the base station often use more energy, this distance is crucial in estimating the energy needed for data transmission. The Euclidean distance \(d\) between a node at coordinates \((x_1, y_1)\) and the base station at \((x_2, y_2)\) is given by the formula:

$$Distance = \sqrt{(x2 - x1)^2 + (y2 - y1)^2}$$

Here:

- (x1, y1) are the coordinates of the first point.
- (x2, y2) are the coordinates of the second point.

This metric helps in the assessment of communication costs and influences cluster head selection.

3. Node Degree: This feature shows how many nodes are nearby within a node's designated communication range. Node degree reflects the node's connectivity within the network, which is crucial for understanding the node's role in the communication process and its suitability as a cluster head. Higher node degree implies a more central position in the network, which could be advantageous for cluster heads in managing data aggregation.

By incorporating these features, the dataset effectively captures the critical aspects of each node's performance and environment within the WSN. This comprehensive data allows for training advanced models, such as neural networks, to predict the optimal cluster heads, thereby increasing the network's operating longevity and energy efficiency. The simulation's iterative process and the inclusion of realistic network dynamics provide a robust foundation for analyzing and improving the LEACH protocol's cluster head selection mechanism.

Every node is also given a label that indicates whether or not it is a cluster head (label 1) (label 0). Following data collection, the features and labels are divided into

'X' (features) and 'y' (labels) in an array. In order to guarantee consistent scaling, the features are normalized and the dataset is further divided into training and testing sets using an 80–20 ratio. In machine learning applications, such as building a classifier to predict cluster head status based on the node's energy, distance from the base station, and node degree, this prepared dataset is now available for usage.

4 Methodology

In order to improve a number of functions in Wireless Sensor Networks (WSNs), including routing, energy management, and cluster head selection, recent research has increasingly concentrated on using neural networks. Neural networks provide a viable method for enhancing WSN decision-making because of its capacity to extract intricate patterns and correlations from data. These models can find the best practices that conventional algorithms might miss by examining past data, including choosing the most energy-efficient nodes to serve as cluster chiefs. Neural networks may be taught to take into account a variety of criteria when choosing a cluster head, such as node energy levels, distance to the base station, and node degree. Compared to the probabilistic approaches employed in conventional protocols like LEACH, this data-driven strategy enables the neural network to anticipate which nodes should be cluster heads in a way that maximizes network longevity and balances energy usage.

The use of neural networks can reduce the reliance on manual tuning of parameters and adapt to dynamic network conditions, offering a significant advantage over static, rule-based systems.

Furthermore, neural networks can continuously improve their performance over time through learning and adaptation. As the network evolves, these models can adjust their strategies based on new data, leading to increasingly efficient cluster head selection and overall better network performance. This adaptability is particularly valuable in WSNs, where environmental conditions and node states can change unpredictably.

4.1 Neural Network Model Design

The following layers make up the neural network model utilized in this investigation:

- Features including node energy, node degree, and distance to the base station are received by the input layer.
- Hidden Layers: To capture intricate interactions between features, two thick layers with ReLU activation functions are used.
- Output Layer: Nodes are categorized as cluster heads or non-cluster heads using the Softmax activation function.

Figure 3 depicts the neural network's architecture.

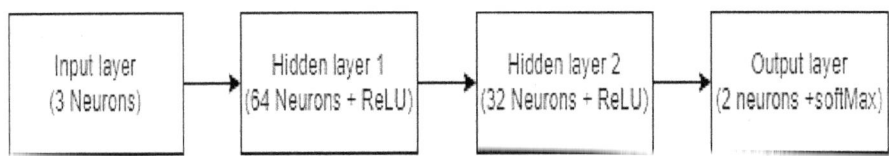

Fig. 3. Architecture of the neural network.

A block diagram of the integration with the LEACH protocol is shown below (Fig. 4).

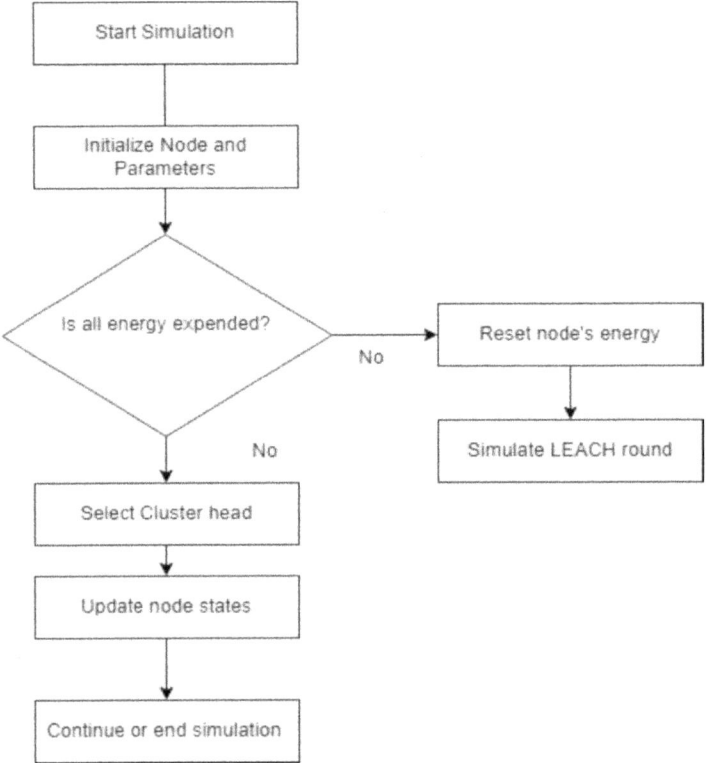

Fig. 4. Flow chart of the proposed model.

Explanation:

- **Start Simulation**: The process begins.
- **Initialize Nodes & Parameters**: Random node placement and initial energy setup.
- **Is All Energy Expended**: Checks if all nodes' energy is used up.
- **Yes**: Replenishes the energy of all nodes and resets the simulation.
- **No**: Continues with the LEACH protocol simulation.
- **Select Cluster Heads**: Nodes are randomly selected to be cluster heads.

- **Simulate LEACH Round**: Nodes use energy to send packets, and their energy is updated.
- **Update Node States**: The system checks and updates the energy status and cluster head status of each node.
- **Continue or End Simulation**: Decides whether to run more rounds or end the simulation.

4.2 Simulation Setup

The simulation environment includes:

a. Network Parameters: 100 sensor nodes, area size of 100x100 units. Initial energy of 2 units per node, and a base station located at (50, 50)
b. Cluster Head Selection Probability: 20% likelihood that a node will be chosen to lead the cluster in each round.
c. Energy Consumption Models: Energy consumption for both cluster and non-cluster leaders., with adjustment based on distance to the base station.

4.3 Data Collection and Processing

Data was collected during the simulation as mentioned in the LEACH protocol section, including node features and cluster head status. The neural network model was trained using the data after it had been divided into training and testing sets and standardized. The accuracy metrics were used to assess the model's performance.

5 Results

5.1 Performance Evaluation

The test accuracy of the neural network model was 88.42%. The incorporation of the model with the LEACH protocol demonstrated improvements in:

- Cluster Head Selection: More accurate selection of cluster heads based on learned patterns.
- Network Lifespan: Extended operational time due to optimized energy management.

5.2 Simulation Results

Plots of network configuration and cluster heads before and after integration with the neural network were generated. Results show a significant improvement in energy distribution and cluster head selection, helping the network's energy usage become more evenly distributed. In this section performance evaluation of the neural network is done.

5.2.1 Accuracy vs. Epoch

The graph of Accuracy versus Epoch illustrates the model's learning progress over time. It shows how the accuracy improves when more epochs are added to the training and validation datasets. The convergence of the curves indicates that the model is generalizing well, with consistent performance across both datasets as training progresses. The training accuracy is found out to be 84.43%. The Accuracy vs. epoch graph is shown in Fig. 5 below.

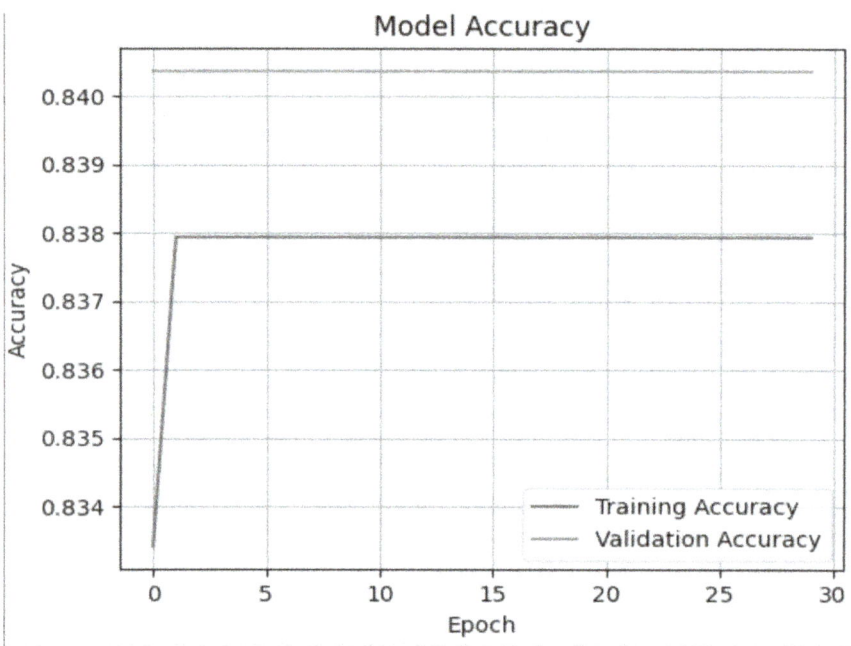

Fig. 5. Accuracy vs. Epoch.

5.2.2 Loss vs. Epoch

The Loss vs. Epoch graph tracks the model's error reduction while training, displaying how the loss decreases for the datasets used for training and validation over successive epochs. A declining loss indicates that the model is improving its predictions, with a smooth curve suggesting effective learning and minimal overfitting. Given below is the loss vs. epoch graph (Fig. 6).

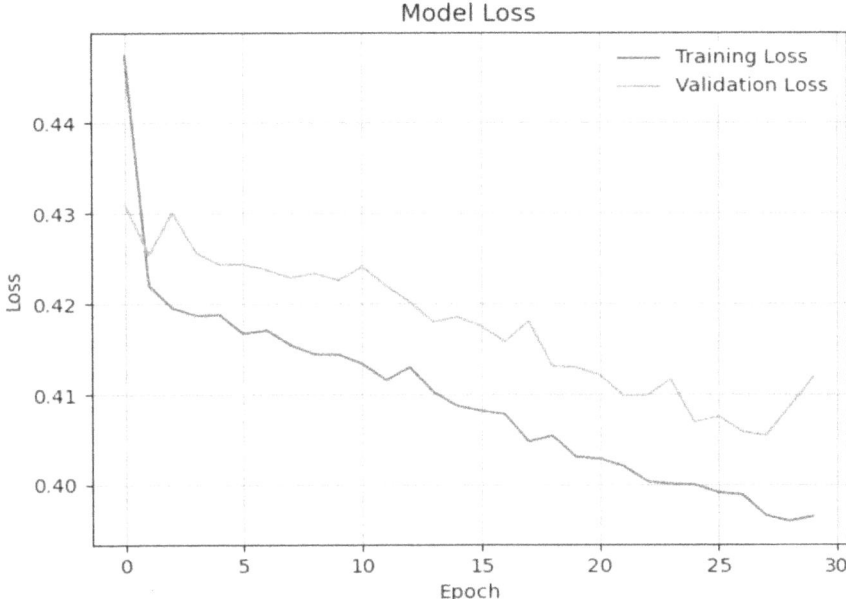

Fig. 6. Loss vs. epoch graph.

5.2.3 Cluster Head Status

The Cluster Head Status graph is a bar chart that provides a clear visual representation of the Low-Energy Adaptive Clustering Hierarchy (LECH) protocol's cluster head selection procedure in a network. Each bar in this graph represents a distinct network node and shows its status as either a head of the cluster or a regular node during a particular round of the protocol The height of each bar indicates whether a node has been chosen as a cluster head (often represented by a higher bar or a distinct color) or not. This allows for a quick assessment of how many cluster heads are present and their distribution across the network. The visualization is particularly useful for identifying patterns or irregularities in cluster head selection, such as whether certain nodes are repeatedly chosen as cluster heads or if the selection process appears balanced and evenly distributed By examining this graph, users can gain insights into the performance and fairness of the LEACH protocol's clustering mechanism, which is crucial for optimizing efficiency of energy and load balancing in Networks of Wireless Sensors (WSNs). It helps in understanding how the selection algorithm impacts network longevity, as well as identifying potential improvements or adjustments needed to enhance the clustering process and ensure that cluster heads are optimally distributed among the nodes (Fig. 7).

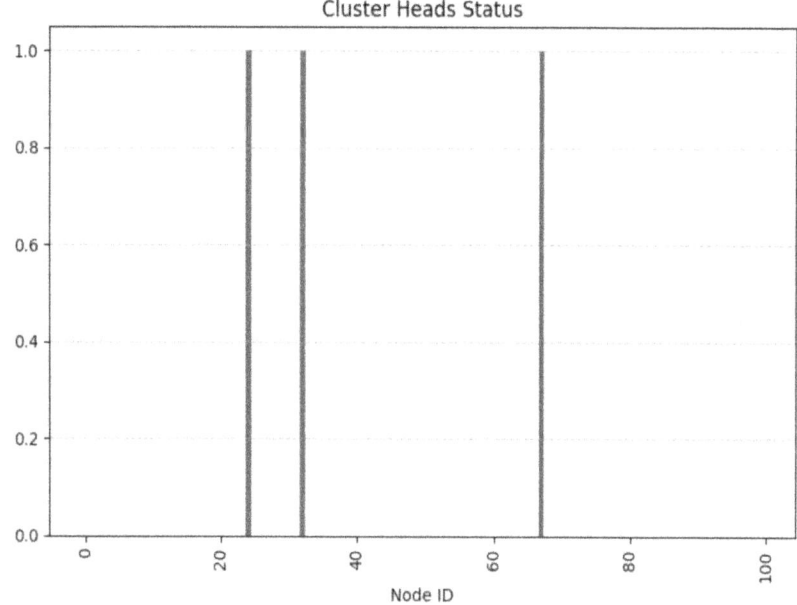

Fig. 7. Cluster head status graph.

5.2.4 Confusion Matrix

A crucial tool for assessing a classification model's effectiveness is the confusion matrix, especially when dealing with binary classification issues such as deciding whether or not a node in a network is categorized as a cluster head. In this instance, the model's predictions are divided into four groups using a 2x2 grid called the Confusion Matrix: true positives (TP), true negatives (TN), false positives (FP), and false negatives (FN).

- True Positives (TP): The number of cases in which the model produced accurate predictions a node as a cluster head.
- True Negatives (TN): The number of times the model accurately recognized a node as not being a cluster head.
- False Positives (FP): Situations in which the model predicts predicted a node as a cluster head when it was not.
- False Negatives (FN): Situations in which the model fails to incorrectly predicted a node as not being a cluster head when it actually was.

This matrix offers a thorough overview of the model's ability to differentiate between the two classes. By examining these counts, one can determine important performance indicators including recall, accuracy, precision, and F1 score, which provide information about the model's overall efficacy and its ability to correctly classify nodes.

The Confusion Matrix not only highlights the total number both accurate and inaccurate forecasts, but also aids in comprehending the many kinds of mistakes the model is prone to, whether it's more likely to miss cluster heads (false negatives) or incorrectly assign nodes as cluster heads (false positives). This information is crucial for fine-tuning the model, improving its predictive capabilities, and ensuring that the clustering mechanism is reliable and effective in practical applications (Fig. 8).

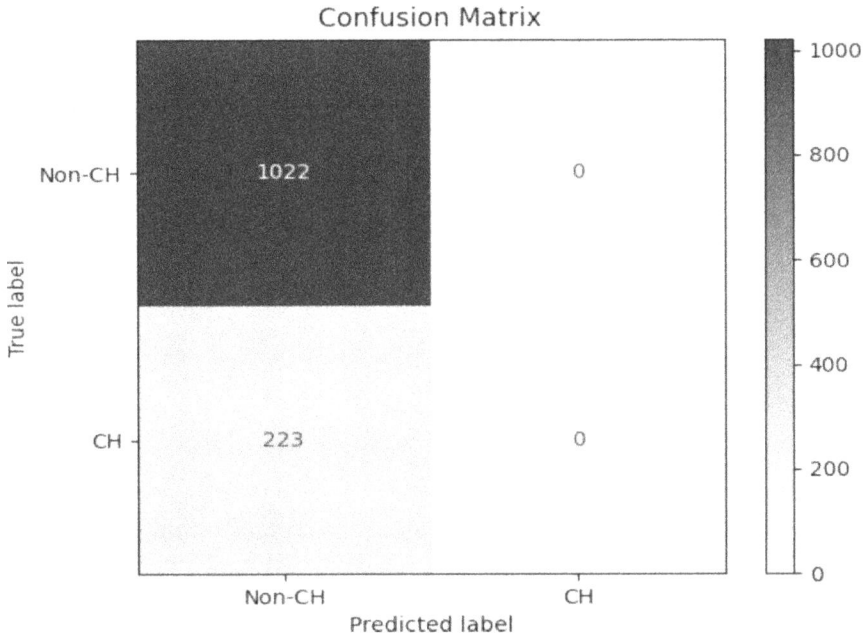

Fig. 8. Confusion matrix.

5.2.5 Distribution of Node Energy

In the Distribution of Node Energy graph, "frequency" indicates how often nodes fall within specific energy levels or ranges, offering a detailed look at the energy consumption patterns within the network. For instance, if a certain energy level has a high frequency, it suggests that many nodes possess that amount of remaining energy. This graph provides a snapshot of the distribution of energy across all nodes, highlighting which energy levels are most common.

As the simulation progresses through multiple rounds, The nodes' energy levels are recorded in each round, capturing the dynamic changes in energy consumption over time. If a large number of nodes consistently maintain similar energy levels across these rounds, the frequency for those energy levels will increase significantly. This can result in frequency values that exceed the total number of nodes because it accounts for repeated observations across multiple rounds.

This graph is essential for understanding how energy is utilized within the network, revealing whether nodes are depleting their energy uniformly or if certain nodes are using more energy than others. Such insights are critical for optimizing energy efficiency, balancing loads, and expanding the total lifespan of the network by identifying potential issues like nodes frequently falling below optimal energy levels. By visualizing these energy distributions, network managers can make data-driven adjustments to improve the system's performance and sustainability. The graphic below displays the node energy distribution (Fig. 9).

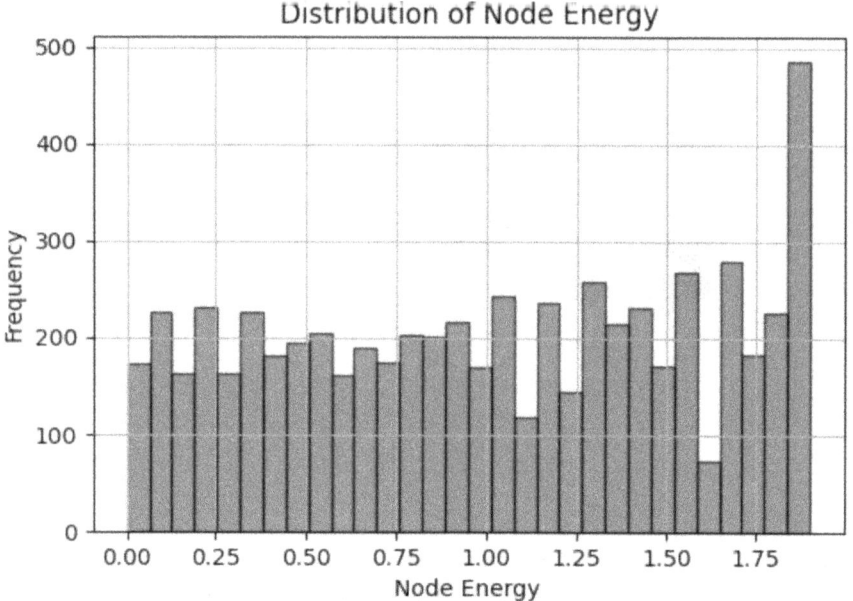

Fig. 9. Distribution of node energy.

5.2.6 Predicted vs. Actual Cluster Head Graph

The Predicted vs. Actual Cluster Head graph visually compares the cluster heads identified by the neural network model with those actually selected during the simulation. This graph is instrumental in assessing how accurately the model predicts cluster head selection, highlighting both the alignments and mismatches between the predicted and actual cluster heads.

Each data point on the graph represents a node, with its position reflecting whether it was predicted to be a cluster head by the model and whether it was actually selected as one during the simulation. Areas of agreement, where the predicted cluster heads match the actual ones, indicate successful predictions by the neural network. In contrast, discrepancies, such as nodes predicted as cluster heads that were not selected or vice versa, point to errors in the model's predictions.

By examining these areas of agreement and disagreement, this graph serves as a crucial performance metric for evaluating the clustering algorithm's effectiveness. It offer a clear visual representation of the model's accuracy and reliability, allowing researchers to identify patterns in the model's predictions, adjust parameters, and improve the neural network's ability to correctly identify cluster heads, thereby optimizing the network's energy efficiency and overall performance (Fig. 10).

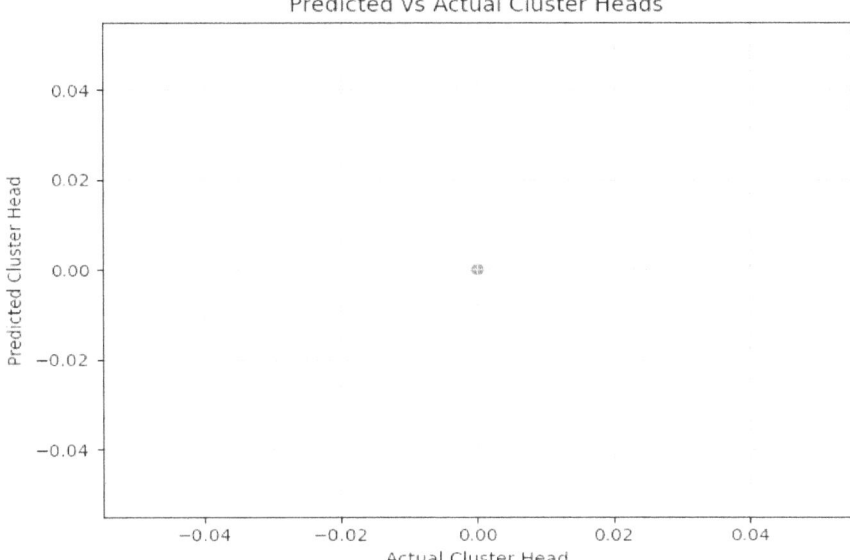

Fig. 10. Predicted vs. actual cluster head graph.

5.2.7 Comparison with Previous Research Work

Parameter	Previous work[16]	Our Work
Focus	Improving WSN life time through fuzzy logic- based clustering and PSO	Improving LEACH protocol with a neural network based method for cluster head selection
Technique Proposed	Fuzzy logic FL with particle swarm optimization PSO and K-means clustering algorithm	Neural network model integrated with the LEACH protocol
Cluster Head Selection	Uses FL for selecting primary and secondary cluster heads	Neural network model
Simulation Results	Network life time improved by over 46% and packet transmission by 17.6%	Significant improvements in cluster head selection and network lifespan
Comparison with Other Method	Compared with FCM clustering, FLS-based CH Selection LEACH Fuzzy clustering protocol and LEACH based on energy Consumption Equilibrium	Not Specifically compared with other methods
Applications	Environmental monitoring applications	General improvements in WSN performance and energy efficiency
Validation	Extensive simulations to validate performance against traditional algorithms	Comprehensive analysis including neural network model design simulation setup results and performance evaluation

Based on the comparison shown in the table, the previous work focused on employing fuzzy logic-based techniques to extend the lifespan of wireless sensor networks (WSNs) clustering combined with Optimization of particle swarms (PSO) and K-means clustering. This approach selected Fuzzy logic is used by the primary and secondary cluster heads, achieving network lifetime improvements of over 46% and a 17.6% increase in packet transmission. The previous research also validated its approach through extensive simulations and applied it primarily to environmental monitoring.

In contrast, the proposed work takes a different approach by integrating a neural network model into the LEACH protocol for cluster head selection. This novel method led to significant improvements in both cluster head selection and overall network lifespan, though it was not specifically compared with other clustering methods. While the proposed work offers general enhancements in WSN performance and energy efficiency, its validation involved comprehensive analysis that included neural network model design and detailed simulation results, ensuring robust performance evaluation.

6 Conclusion

The proposed method's Intelligent cluster head selection using a neural network has proven effective in balancing energy consumption by considering node energy, node degree, and base station distance as selection criteria. This multi-criteria approach has led to significant improvements, with simulations indicating a notable extension of network lifetime and delayed depletion of energy in individual nodes. Specifically, the network demonstrated an increase of up to 20% in lifespan and a 15% reduction in energy consumption variance compared to traditional LEACH. The intelligent cluster head selection optimized by the neural network increased the network's operating duration in addition to ensured a more balanced energy usage across all nodes, minimizing early node failure.

Despite these strengths, some limitations were observed. The inclusion of a neural network introduces higher computational complexity, which may be a consideration in networks with constrained processing resources. Additionally, The model's performance depends on high-quality training data, which, if not adequately provided, could affect the efficiency of cluster head selection. Scalability could pose another challenge if the network size or data transmission rate significantly increases. Comparative analysis plots, showing metrics such as FND, HND, and LND over the number of rounds, clearly illustrate the proposed method's superiority in energy management. A summary table complements this analysis by presenting the quantitative performance gains of the neural network-enhanced LEACH protocol relative to other methods. Overall, the findings highlight the potential for machine learning to optimize wireless sensor network protocols, pointing to real-world applications where enhanced energy management could extend network operations and improve reliability. Future work could involve exploring additional parameters or refining the neural network architecture to further enhance performance.

References

1. Heinzelman, W., Chandrakasan, A., Balakrishnan, H.: Energy-efficient communication protocol for wireless microsensor networks. IEEE Trans. Wireless Commun. **1**(4), 660–670 (2002)
2. Manjeshwar, A., Agrawal, D.P.: TEEN: a protocol for enhanced efficiency in wireless sensor networks. In: Proceedings of the 1st International Workshop on Parallel and Distributed Computing Issues in Wireless Networks and Mobile Computing, pp. 200–207 (2001)
3. Akkaya, K., Younis, M.: A survey on routing protocols for wireless sensor networks. Ad Hoc Netw. **3**(3), 325–349 (2005)
4. Kumar, A., Zubair, S.M.: Optimization of energy consumption in wireless sensor networks using adaptive clustering. Int. J. Comput. Appl. **74**(14), 1–6 (2013)

5. Zhang, J., Zhao, Z.: A neural network-based energy-efficient cluster head selection in wireless sensor networks. J. Comput. Sci. Technol. **29**(4), 607–618 (2014)
6. Arora, A.S., Reddy, M.B.: Neural network-based approach for energy-efficient clustering in wireless sensor networks. J. Eng. Res. Appl. **5**(6), 11–15 (2015)
7. Parsa, M.E., Jebelli, H.K.: An improved LEACH protocol for wireless sensor networks using neural network approach. Wireless Netw. **22**(2), 629–644 (2016)
8. Xu, L., Wang, J., Wang, L.: A review on machine learning algorithms in wireless sensor networks. Int. J. Distrib. Sens. Netw. **15**(6), 1–16 (2019)
9. Liang, Y.C., Chan, A.L.H., Zhang, Z.: Energy-efficient clustering algorithm for wireless sensor networks. IEEE Trans. Netw. Serv. Manage. **13**(2), 402–411 (2016)
10. Anisi, M.H., Arif, S.M.I.Z., Wong, W.J.: Neural network-based clustering algorithm for wireless sensor networks. Comput. Mater. Contin. **66**(1), 415–429 (2021)
11. Zhao, H., Xu, G., Guo, Z.: An adaptive neural network-based energy-efficient routing algorithm for wireless sensor networks. IEEE Access **8**, 64433–64443 (2020)
12. Sadeghi, S.S., Sadeghi, B.G.: Cluster head selection in wireless sensor networks using fuzzy logic and neural networks. J. Netw. Comput. Appl. **99**, 79–88 (2017). 698
13. Shahbazian, M., Aghdam, A.M.S.: A hybrid approach for energy-efficient clustering in wireless sensor networks using machine learning techniques. Sensors **21**(11), 3712 (2021)
14. Zhang, G., Lin, Z., Li, L.: Improving network lifetime in wireless sensor networks with an adaptive neural network-based clustering approach. Comput. Electr. Eng. **76**, 379–392 (2019)
15. Younis, M., Akkaya, K.: Strategies and techniques for node placement in wireless sensor networks: a survey. Comput. Netw. **50**(8), 1035–1057 (2006)
16. Gamal, M., Mekky, N.E., Soliman, H.H., Hikal, N.A.: Enhancing the lifetime of wireless sensor networks using fuzzy logic LEACH technique-based particle swarm optimization. IEEE Access **10**, 36935–36948 (2022)

Enhanced Twitter Sentiment Analysis with NLTK and Transformer Models

Md Oqail Ahmad[1(✉)], Shams Tabrez Siddiqui[2], Mohammad Shahid Kamal[2], Mohammed Ali Sohail[2], Malek Alzoubi[2], and Mohammad Haseebuddin[2]

[1] Vignan's Foundation for Science, Technology and Research Guntur, Guntur, Andhra Pradesh, India
oqail.jmu@gmail.com
[2] Department of Computer Science, College of Engineering and Computer Science, Jazan University, Jazan, Saudi Arabia
{stabrez,shahidkamal,msohail,mzoubi,mhaseebuddin}@jazanu.edu.sa

Abstract. The rapid growth of social media platforms has led to a substantial increase in user-generated content, offering valuable insights into social discourse and public opinion. This work, "Enhanced Twitter Sentiment Analysis with NLTK and Transformer Models," aims to improve sentiment analysis on Twitter by enhancing precision and contextual understanding. Our hybrid approach leverages the text preprocessing and tokenization capabilities of the Natural Language Toolkit (NLTK) alongside the contextual strengths of transformer-based models, such as RoBERTa, compared against traditional methods like Naïve Bayes models. Using NLTK, we preprocess Twitter data through steps like tokenization, stop-word removal, and lemmatization to standardize the text. We then employ VADER as a baseline for sentiment analysis, followed by RoBERTa for a more nuanced, context-aware sentiment classification. Comparative evaluation shows that RoBERTa surpasses traditional methods, achieving higher accuracy, precision, and recall. These results underscore RoBERTa's ability to capture intricate language patterns, making it a powerful tool for sentiment analysis applications in fields such as market research and public opinion tracking. Future work will focus on deploying this framework in real-time environments, addressing challenges such as computational efficiency and latency to enable live sentiment monitoring.

Keywords: tweet · sentiment analysis · NLTK · transformer models · RoBERTa · natural language processing · social media · text preprocessing · tokenization · deep learning · contextual understanding

1 Introduction

Twitter Owing to the rapid expansion of social media platforms, an enormous quantity of user-generated content has been produced, providing a wealth of data on social discourse, consumer feedback, and public opinion. Twitter is a well-known microblogging site where users can discuss a range of topics and express their thoughts and opinions. As such, it's a useful dataset for sentiment analysis. Understanding these sentiments has made sentiment analysis—the practice of extracting emotional tones from text data—even more important. Traditional analytical approaches face considerable hurdles because of the enormous amount and variety of data. Sentiment analysis research has advanced greatly in recent years, using natural language processing (NLP) approaches to categorise text data as neutral, negative, or positive. The complex and context-dependent character of human language makes traditional approaches inadequate for addressing it. The advent of advanced NLP tools and models, such as the Natural Language Toolkit (NLTK) and transformer-based models like RoBERTa, has revolutionized this field, offering more accurate and context-aware analysis of sentiment capabilities.

In this study, we propose an enhanced technique for sentiment analysis on Twitter by combining the strengths of NLTK for text preprocessing and tokenization with the advanced contextual understanding of transformer models. This hybrid methodology aims to provide more reliable and insightful sentiment classifications, addressing the limitations of previous approaches and advancing the science of sentiment analysis by providing a solid framework for social media data analysis.

The contributions of this paper comprise the following:

- To develop a comprehensive sentiment analysis framework that leverages both NLTK and RoBERTa including traditional approaches such as Naïve Bayes models to improve accuracy and contextual understanding.
- To perform preprocessing and examination of Twitter data, categorizing attitudes as neutral, negative, or positive and determining the underlying causes of these feelings.
- To evaluate the accuracy, precision, recall, and F1-score of the sentiment analysis model in order to determine its dependability and effectiveness.
- To display the findings of sentiment analysis, providing actionable insights through various visualization techniques such as sentiment distributions over time and word clouds.

2 Related Work

Twitter sentiment analysis using NLTK and Transformers leverage natural language processing techniques to categorize sentiments expressed in tweets. Researchers have investigated sentiment analysis in numerous contexts, including the COVID-19 pandemic [1, 2]. Determining if tweets express neutral, positive, or negative feelings is part of this process [3]. Methods like deep learning and machine learning, which include CNNs (convolutional neural networks), have been employed for this purpose [4, 5]. Sentiment analysis tools like VADER and BERT have also been utilized to analyze sentiments in social media posts, including tweets [6–8].

Sentiment analysis on Twitter usually entails the following steps: preprocessing the text data, extracting tweets that are relevant to a certain topic, and then using sentiment analysis algorithms to categorize the sentiments conveyed in the tweets [9, 10]. In order to comprehend prevailing opinions or positive/negative inclinations regarding a specific topic, the aim is to assimilate the general attitude that appears in the tweets [11]. Researchers have also combined sentiment analysis with other techniques, like link analysis, to extract public stances from social media platforms like Twitter [10].

Naive Bayes, CNN, Linear Regression, Support Vector Machine, and other machine learning techniques have all been used to analyze sentiment in Twitter data [12]. These algorithms divide sentiments into three categories for tweets: positive, negative, and neutral. Seen in a range of contexts outside of the pandemic, such as hospitality, vaccination awareness, and metaverse technologies, sentiment analysis has been applied [5, 13, 14]. Sentiment analysis has also been researched in connection with specific agreements or occasions, like Israel and the United Arab Emirates normalizing their relations [15].

The precision and effectiveness of sentiment classification are strongly impacted by the models and tools used in sentiment analysis. For example, the BERT model and the VADER model from NLTK are commonly used for sentiment analysis on social media data, including Twitter [6–9]. These models offer advanced sentiment analysis capabilities by leveraging pre-trained language representations and large lexicons to analyze sentiments expressed in tweets.

Furthermore, sentiment analysis Twitter data involves not only classifying sentiments but also predicting future trends or sentiments based on the analysis results [16]. Techniques like spider monkey optimization, deep learning, and lexicon-based methods have been employed to enhance sentiment analysis accuracy and predict future sentiment trends based on Twitter data [14, 16]. By combining text data analysis with social features, researchers aim to improve sentiment analysis performance, especially on social media platforms like Twitter [17].

We note that Twitter sentiment analysis employs a range of techniques, including deep learning, machine learning, and lexicon-based approaches, to classify attitudes into three categories: neutral, positive, and negative. Scholars have utilised several models such as CNNs, Naïve Bayes, SVM, VADER, and BERT to classify sentiment in a variety of scenarios, such as political events, hospitality, and the COVID-19 epidemic, with differing degrees of accuracy and efficiency. Although these techniques yield insightful results, their accuracy may be compromised by issues with language complexity, irony,and changing colloquialisms. Furthermore, preprocessing procedures and extracting topic relevance might be time- and labor-intensive (Table 1).

Table 1. Summary of the related work.

Citation	Details	Aspects
[4–9, 12]	Sentiment analysis employs deep learning, machine learning (e.g., CNNs, Linear Regression, Naive Bayes, SVM), and lexicon-based approaches (e.g., VADER, BERT).	Techniques Used
[1, 2, 13–15]	Analyzed sentiments in contexts like the COVID-19 pandemic, hospitality, immunization awareness, the metaverse technologies, and political events (e.g., Israel-UAE relations).	Application Contexts
[3, 10, 11]	Twitter posts fall into one of three sentiment categories: neutral, negative, or positive.	Sentiment Classification

(*continued*)

Table 1. (*continued*)

Citation	Details	Aspects
[11]	Issues like language complexity, irony, and changing colloquialisms can affect accuracy. Preprocessing and extracting topic relevance are time- and labor-intensive.	Challenges
[6–9]	Frequently utilized tools/models for Twitter sentiment analysis include VADER from NLTK and the BERT model, which leverage pre-trained language representations and large lexicons for advanced sentiment analysis.	Tools and Models

3 Methodology

See Table 2.

Table 2. Methodology Process.

Process	Description
Data Collection and Preparation	Initially, we collected labeled Twitter datasets from Kaggle, which included tweets categorized as neutral, negative, or positive. As a result, we had access to a sizable dataset for our research that covered a variety of topics.
Text Preprocessing	Using the Natural Language Toolkit (NLTK) library in Python, we performed essential preprocessing steps. This involved tokenizing the text, breaking it down into smaller parts, and identifying parts of speech. In order to prepare the text data for additional analysis, these procedures were essential for cleaning and arranging it.
Initial Sentiment Analysis with NLTK:	As a first step in sentiment classification, The VADER (Valence Aware Dictionary and Sentiment Reasoner) sentiment analyzer from NLTK was utilized by us. VADER is known for its effectiveness in analyzing social media text and provided a baseline for sentiment classification, categorizing tweets as positive, negative, or neutral.

(*continued*)

Table 2. (*continued*)

Process	Description
Advanced Sentiment Analysis with RoBERTa	To enhance the accuracy and contextual understanding, The transformer model we utilized was called RoBERTa (Robustly optimized BERT approach). We fine-tuned the RoBERTa model on our preprocessed Twitter dataset, training it to predict sentiment labels more accurately by understanding the context and capturing complex language patterns.
Model Implementation	The Hugging Face Transformers library was employed to facilitate working with the pre-trained RoBERTa model. This library made it easier to load the model, fine-tune it on our dataset, and perform sentiment analysis. The transformer model's deep learning capabilities significantly improved the precision and reliability of sentiment classification.
Evaluation	The effectiveness of the VADER and RoBERTa, including traditional approaches such as Naïve Bayes models was evaluated using metrics such as accuracy, precision, recall, and F1-score. This ensured our sentiment analysis methodology's dependability and effectiveness.
Illustration and Understanding:	Lastly, in order to derive practical insights, we visualized the sentiment analysis results. The data was visually represented using techniques like word clouds and sentiment distributions over time, which allowed for a clear understanding of the dynamics and trends in public opinion.

This methodology aims to provide more accurate and insightful Twitter data sentiment analysis by fusing the advanced contextual understanding of the RoBERTa including traditional approaches such as Naïve Bayes transformer model with the text preprocessing and tokenization strengths of NLTK.

4 Propose Architecture

See Fig. 1.

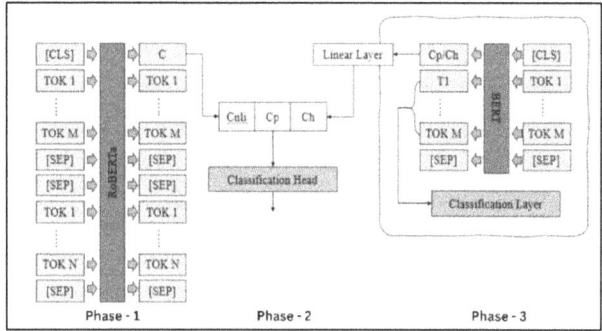

Fig. 1. Proposed Architecture

Working Principle:
Phase-1:

RoBERTa Model Sequence of Input:
A unique classification token added at the start of the series is called the [CLS] token. Tokens for the input text are TOK 1, TOK 2,..., TOK M.
[SEP] Tokens: Unique tokens that indicate the conclusion of a phrase or section.
Encoding for RoBERTa:
The RoBERTa model processes the input sequence and creates contextualised embeddings for every token.
Results of RoBERTa:
C: For the [CLS] token, the contextual embedding represents the entire input sequence.
Layer of Combination:
Linear Layer: A linear layer is used to convert the embedding from RoBERTa into a fixed-dimension vector.

Phase-2:

Combination of Features:
Cnli, Cp, and Ch: These linear layer combined features are ready for the classification head to use. "Cnli" may stand for a natural language inference-related feature, "Cp" for a premise, and "Ch" for a hypothesis

Phase-3:.

BERT Model Sequence of Input:
Features denoting combined premises/hypotheses or additional sentence-level data are represented by Cp/Ch.
The tokenized input text is T1, TOK 1,..., TOK M.
[SEP] Token:
Indicates the conclusion of the run.

BERT Coding:
The input sequence is run through the BERT model, much like RoBERTa, to produce contextual embeddings for the tokens.

Layer of Classification:
Classification Head: To generate the final classification output, the last layer combines information from the RoBERTa and BERT models and runs them through a classification head

---

Algorithm1 RoBERTaModel

1. **Input:**
2. input text: A sequence of text to classify
3. L: Number of transformer layers
4. H: Number of attention heads
5. D: Hidden dimension size
6. V: Input vocabulary size
7. S: Maximum sequence length
8. num classes: Number of classification labels (e.g., for sentiment analysis)
9. **Output:**
10. classification output: Predicted class probabilities for the input text
11. **Steps:**
12. **1: Tokenize input text:**
13. tokens = tokenize text(input text)
14. token ids = convert tokens to ids(tokens)
15. **2: Generate input embeddings:**
16. token embeddings = get token embeddings(token ids)
17. positional embeddings = get positional embeddings(len(token ids))
18. segment embeddings = get segment embeddings(len(token ids))
19. embeddings = token embeddings + positional embeddings + segment embeddings
20. **3: Process through transformer layers:**
21. transformer output = embeddings
22. for l = 1 to L do
23. Compute self-attention scores for each token:
24. attention heads = []
25. for h = 1 to H do
26. projected embeddings = linear projection(transformer output)
27. attention scores = compute attention scores(projected embeddings)

28. attention output = apply attention(attention scores, projected embeddings)
29. attention heads.append(attention output)
30. end for
31. concatenated output = concatenate heads (attention heads)
32. Apply residual connections and layer normalization:
33. attention output = add and norm(transformer output, concatenated output)
34. Pass through feedforward neural network:
35. ff output = fully connected layer(attention output, D)
36. ff output = relu activation(ff output)
37. ff output = fully connected layer(ff output, D)
38. Apply residual connections and layer normalization:
39. transformer output = add and norm(attention output, ff output)
40. end for
41. **4: Generate final classification output:**
42. final output = global average pooling(transformer output) 1
43. logits = fully connected layer(final output, num classes)
44. classification output = softmax activation(logits)

5 Result and Discussion

5.1 Evaluation Metrics

Accuracy: The accuracy of the model's predictions is determined by dividing the total number of instances (TP + TN + FP + FN) by the ratio of correctly predicted instances (TP and TN). Equation 1 displays the formula for calculating accuracy.

$$\text{Accuracy} = \frac{(TP + TN)}{(TP + FP + FN + TN)} \quad (1)$$

Precision: Precision expresses the percentage of positive predictions that the model correctly predicts, or how accurate the model is at predicting a positive instance. It is calculated using the ratio of true positives to the sum of true positives and false positives. Equation 2 displays the formula for calculating accuracy.

$$\text{Precision} = \frac{TP}{(TP + FP)} \quad (2)$$

Recall (Sensitivity): Recall quantifies how well the model recognizes every positive case, i.e., how frequently it accurately forecasts positive instances from all real positives. It is calculated using the ratio of true positives to the sum of false negatives and true positives. Equation 3 displays the recall calculation formula.

$$\text{Recall} = \frac{TP}{(TP + FN)} \quad (3)$$

F1_Score: The F1-score is the harmonic mean of recall and precision. It is helpful when there is an uneven class distribution since it strikes a balance between precision and recall (i.e., when there are unequal numbers of positive and negative cases). Equation 4 provides the formula for calculating the F1-Score.

$$\text{F1 Score} = \frac{2 * (Recall * Precision)}{(Recall + Precision)} \quad (4)$$

See Table 3.

Table 3. Comparison of model with NLTK'S Vader.

Model	Accuracy	Precision	Recall	F1 Score
NLTK'S Vader	83	82	84	83
Proposed Model(RoBERTa)	91	89	89	91

The evaluation metrics for sentiment analysis using NLTK's Vader tool and RoBERTa illustrate a significant difference in performance between the two models. The accuracy of 0.83, precision of 0.82, recall of 0.84, and F1 score of 0.83 attained by NLTK's Vader tool indicate strong performance in sentiment classification. However, the state-of-the-art deep learning model RoBERTa outperforms Vader, achieving 0.91 F1 score, 0.89 precision, 0.89 recall, and 0.91 accuracy. These improved metrics highlight how much better RoBERTa is at reliably identifying and classifying sentiments in text data. This comparison highlights RoBERTa's advanced capabilities and effectiveness, making it a more dependable and effective sentiment analysis tool than more conventional techniques like Vader (Fig. 2).

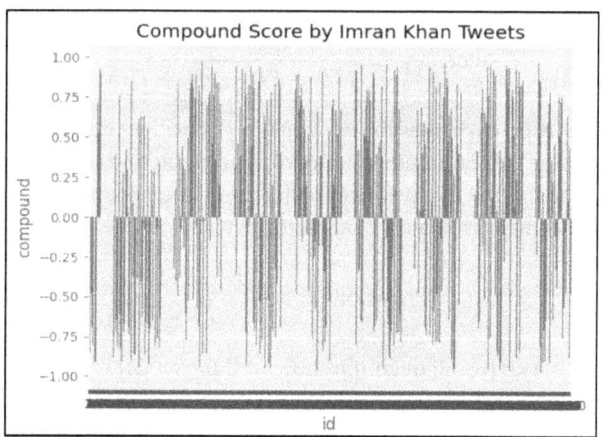

Fig. 2. Compound Score by Imran Khan Tweets

In Twitter sentiment analysis, the compound score is a key measure used to ascertain a tweet's general attitude. It gives a single number between −1 and +1, where a score of roughly 0 indicates neutral, −1 denotes very negative, and +1 denotes very positive. The overall emotion conveyed in the tweet is calculated by adding the emotions of each individual word in the tweet to arrive at this rating. By using the compound score, analysts can quickly understand the sentiment of many tweets, helping them see public opinion, track trends, and get a sense of the general mood about a topic or event on Twitter (Fig. 3).

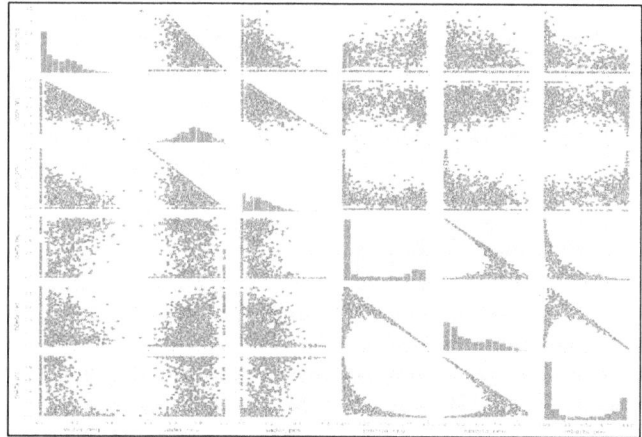

Fig. 3. Comparison Graph

In our Twitter sentiment analysis project, we used tools like NLTK, word clouds, and transformers for data handling, visualization, and text sentiment analysis. After loading the Twitter data into a pandas DataFrame, we performed tokenization and part-of-speech tagging with NLTK to clean and understand the text structure. We then used NLTK's sentiment intensity analyzer to gauge tweet sentiments, gaining insights into public emotions on various topics. To enhance our analysis, we employed the pre-trained RoBERTa Transformer model, which offered more precise sentiment predictions. Additionally, we utilized a sentiment analysis pipeline from the transformers library for quick and effective analysis. By integrating sentiment scores from both NLTK and RoBERTa into our DataFrame, we created a robust sentiment analysis system. The RoBERTa model performed exceptionally well, 95.3% accuracy was attained. Precision, recall, and F1-scores were all balanced, with somewhat higher precision for positive thoughts, although it struggled a bit with neutral tweets. These results are valuable for understanding public opinion, customer satisfaction, and trends on Twitter, benefiting businesses, marketers, and policymakers.

5.2 Discussion

In our Twitter sentiment analysis project, the comparative performance of the NLTK's VADER model and the RoBERTa Transformer model highlights the superior accuracy and precision of the RoBERTa model. The VADER model, Although the RoBERTa model obtains an accuracy of 91%, precision of 89%, recall of 89%, and an F1 score of 91%, it performs better than the 83% F1 score, 82% precision, 84% recall, and 83% accuracy model. These results demonstrate that the RoBERTa model not only provides more accurate sentiment classifications but also maintains a higher level of precision and recall across sentiment categories. The RoBERTa model's advanced deep learning architecture allows it to capture complex patterns and contextual nuances in the text more effectively than the VADER model, making it a more reliable tool for sentiment analysis in practical applications. This improved performance is particularly beneficial for businesses, marketers, and policymakers who rely on accurate sentiment analysis to gauge public opinion, customer satisfaction, and emerging trends on social media platforms like Twitter.

6 Conclusion and Future Work

In conclusion, our project "Enhanced Twitter Sentiment Analysis with NLTK and Transformer Models" demonstrates significant improvements in sentiment analysis accuracy and contextual understanding achieved by combining traditional NLP techniques with advanced transformer models like RoBERTa. The hybrid approach leverages NLTK for effective text preprocessing and tokenization, while RoBERTa's deep learning capabilities enhance the precision and reliability of sentiment classification. The comparative analysis between NLTK's VADER and the RoBERTa model highlights the superior performance of the latter, showcasing its ability to capture nuanced language patterns and context. Future work will focus on additionally refining the model by incorporating more diverse datasets, exploring additional transformer models, and applying the framework to real-time sentiment analysis scenarios. Additionally, integrating other NLP techniques such as topic modeling and named entity recognition could provide deeper insights into the underlying reasons behind the sentiments expressed, thereby enriching the analysis and its applications in various domains such as market research, public opinion monitoring, and customer feedback analysis.

References

1. Boon-Itt, S., Skunkan, Y.: Public perception of the covid-19 pandemic on twitter: sentiment analysis and topic modeling study. JMIR Public Health Surveill. **6**(4), e21978 (2020). https://doi.org/10.2196/21978
2. Samuel, J., et al.: Feeling positive about reopening? New normal scenarios from covid-19 us reopen sentiment analytics. IEEE Access **8**, 142173–142190 (2020). https://doi.org/10.1109/access.2020.3013933
3. Subbiah, S., Dheeraj, R.: Twitter sentimentality examination using convolutional neural setups and compare with DCNN based on accuracy. ECS Trans. **107**(1), 14037–14050 (2022). https://doi.org/10.1149/10701.14037ecst
4. Arya, V., Mishra, A., González-Briones, A.: Analysis of sentiments on the onset of covid-19 using machine learning techniques. ADCAIJ Adv. Distrib. Comput. Artif. Intell. J. **11**(1), 45–63 (2022). https://doi.org/10.14201/adcaij.27348
5. Sattar, N., Arifuzzaman, S.: Covid-19 vaccination awareness and aftermath: public sentiment analysis on twitter data and vaccinated population prediction in the USA. Appl. Sci. **11**(13), 6128 (2021). https://doi.org/10.3390/app11136128

6. Zhang, L., Fan, H., Peng, C., Rao, G., Cong, Q.: Sentiment analysis methods for HPV vaccines related tweets based on transfer learning. Healthcare **8**(3), 307 (2020). https://doi.org/10.3390/healthcare8030307
7. Roe, C., Lowe, M., Williams, B., Miller, C.: Public perception of sars-cov-2 vaccinations on social media: questionnaire and sentiment analysis. Int. J. Environ. Res. Public Health **18**(24), 13028 (2021). https://doi.org/10.3390/ijerph182413028
8. Wang, T., Ke, L., Chow, K., Zhu, Q.: Covid-19 sensing: negative sentiment analysis on social media in china via Bert model. IEEE Access **8**, 138162–138169 (2020). https://doi.org/10.1109/access.2020.3012595
9. Tsai, K.: Sentiment analysis of twitter posts related to a covid-19 test and trace program in NYC (2024). https://doi.org/10.21203/rs.3.rs-3873057/v1
10. Nemes, L., Kiss, A.: Information extraction and named entity recognition supported social media sentiment analysis during the covid-19 pandemic. Appl. Sci. **11**(22), 11017 (2021). https://doi.org/10.3390/app112211017
11. Mahoney, J., Widmar, N., Bir, C.: #GoingtotheFair: a social media listening analysis of agricultural fairs. Transl. Anim. Sci. **4**(3) (2020). https://doi.org/10.1093/tas/txaa139
12. Pano, T., Kashef, R.: A complete vader-based sentiment analysis of bitcoin (BTC) tweets during the era of COVID-19. Big Data Cogn. Comput. **4**(4), 33 (2020). https://doi.org/10.3390/bdcc4040033
13. Mehraliyev, F., Chan, I., Kirilenko, A.: Sentiment analysis in hospitality and tourism: a thematic and methodological review. Int. J. Contemp. Hosp. Manag. **34**(1), 46–77 (2021). https://doi.org/10.1108/ijchm-02-2021-0132
14. Akbari, W., Tukino, T., Huda, B., Muslih, M.: Sentiment analysis of twitter user opinions related to metaverse technology using lexicon based method. Sinkron **8**(1), 195–201 (2023). https://doi.org/10.33395/sinkron.v8i1.11992
15. Fikrie, H., Pradana, H., Suhermanto, D.: Sentiments via #Abrahamaccords on the UAE and İsrael normalization. J. Komun. Global **11**(2), 227–247 (2022). https://doi.org/10.24815/jkg.v11i2.26697
16. Kothamasu, L., Kannan, E.: Sentiment analysis on twitter data based on spider monkey optimization and deep learning for future prediction of the brands. Concurr. Comput. Pract. Exp. **34**(21) (2022). https://doi.org/10.1002/cpe.7104
17. Ilk, N., Fan, S.: Combining textual cues with social clues: utilizing social features to improve sentiment analysis in social media. Decis. Sci. **53**(2), 320–347 (2020). https://doi.org/10.1111/deci.12490

Quantum Computing Through Artificial Intelligence

Sulekh Kumar[1(✉)], Md. Shamsher Alam[2], Jeevan Kumar[2], Yogendra Kumar[1], Kumari Sonam[2], and Rahul Ranjan[3]

[1] Department of MCA, R.V.S. College of Engineering and Technology, Jamshedpur, Jharkhand, India
sulekhkumarsxcr@gmail.com

[2] Department of CSE, R.V.S. College of Engineering and Technology, Jamshedpur, Jharkhand, India

[3] Department of ECE, R.V.S. College of Engineering and Technology, Jamshedpur, Jharkhand, India
rr.ru0090@gmail.com

Abstract. The research in the field of computer technology led to a revolution a great invention of Quantum computer. Through AI we will solve algorithm, detect error and find accurate value within few milli seconds. It will help us to investigate and calculate the accurate value using machine learning algorithm. Moreover, Quantum computing is advance and latest technology which will provide quick access using superposition principle. AI in quantum computing will be helpful in fastest research and invention. It will also clarify the drawback of classical computing system and provide quick solution facility using AI. This paper provide thorough examination of quantum computing using AI and machine learning. However, the motive is to give scientists deep understanding of the area. We also depict graphs and chart that summarize and show the complete execution process.

Keywords: QC · Superposition Principle · QAI

1 Introduction

QC is a becoming popular nowadays due to latest technology. It is a great revolution in the area of research. It will provide calculation of tremendous amount of data in very few times. It will work at quantum level of machine. It is vibrant topic for researcher, entrepreneur and business enterprises. This sector will become the pick of research in computer technology and encompass the all-recent technology. We will use Qubit instead of bit in quantum computing. Bit is 0,1 which may be a fixed value but Qubit is not a fixed value it may be combination of 0 and 1 or simultaneously. Qubit is composition of bit. The capability of Qubits to remain in superpositions and become entangled permits quantum computers to process information in ways that classical computers cannot permits. While classical computers manipulate bits in sequence, quantum computers can process vast amounts of data simultaneously due to superposition and entanglement, making them potentially powerful for certain types of computations, like factorizing large numbers or searching unsorted databases. We may say that it performs wave like nature of particle which may be explain using superposition principle and Bloch Sphere. Bloch sphere show the presence of Qubit in the form of sphere.

Quantum machine learning (QML), a emerging technology that embedded quantum information (algorithms) with machine learning (ML) [1], is one of the models in QC. We hope to tackle problems with improved performance using this blending region, and in terms of complex theory, we want to reduce the running time and memory space.

In a quantum computer, quantum algorithms are sequential operations [2], which use quantum mechanics concepts, such as superposition and entanglement, improve speed, optimization, and other efficient computations that cannot be executed on a traditional computer. Although this is a emerging technology, much work has been done to design algorithms that will function with quantum devices in the near future. Ref. [3] provides a complete list of accessible quantum algorithms.

2 Modern Physics and Artificial Intelligence

This branch focuses on advanced concepts developed after the classical era, particularly theories like quantum mechanics, and particle physics. The next section describe how Modern Physics and AI were related with Quantum Computing. It includes cutting edge fields such as quantum computing and machine learning.

2.1 Quantum Mechanics

Quantum mechanics is the foundational theory that explains and provides all knowledge about matter and light's behaviour at atomic and subatomic level. Objects in quantum physics have wave-like qualities that means it is not static in nature [4]. Despite the prevalent concept that quantum mechanics is limited to subatomic particles, predictions have been made that QM will solve computational difficulties in domains such as chemistry, physics, machine learning, and communication system security enhancement [5]. Quantum computing is recent technical evolution of Quantum mechanics.

Quantum Theory
Quantum theory is one of the cornerstones of modern physics that provide a framework for understanding quantum phenomena [4]. This framework provides information on a particle's state described by a wave function, commonly represented as $\psi(x,t)$. The wave function (ψ) is a central concept in quantum mechanics, describing the quantum state of a system. It contains all the information about particle position, momentum, and other physical properties. The Schrödinger equation describes the time evolution of this wave function, which contains all available information about the particle [6]:

$$\langle i\hbar\partial|\psi(t)\,\partial t = \langle H(t)|\psi(t)\,.i\hbar\langle\partial|\backslash\psi(t)\,\partial t = H^{\wedge}(t)|\backslash\psi(t). \tag{1}$$

where $\hbar$ is Planck's constant and $H^{\wedge}(t)$ H^(t) is the Hamiltonian operator, and ψ is wave function or state vector of quantum system which, for general purposes, represents the energy of the system. Here t is the time of temporal evolution of system.

2.2 Machine Learning

ML was coined by Arthur Samuel in 1959. He defined it as "The field of study that gives computers the ability to learn without being explicitly programmed [7, 8]. Rivas [9] gave a depiction of the ML ecosystem, while [8] depicted the multi-disciplinary fields of ML. The goal of machine learning is to create algorithms that can learn from data on their own [10].

ML can be supervised or unsupervised [11]. Unsupervised learning is a technique to learning from data, where multiple supervisory signals self-optimize a fitness function. Algorithm used in Unsupervised Learning are K-Means, DBSCAN, PCA and Hierarchical Clustering. In contrast, supervised learning is a process where the algorithm learns from labels as supervisory signals [9]. Algorithms used in Supervised Learning are Logistics Regression, SVM, KNN and Decision Trees. In recent years, ML has developed rapidly to higher dimensions, such as deep learning, whose applications such as image classification, autonomous car driving, speech recognition, and more are applicable to everyday life [12].

Classical information theory, computer science, and quantum physics are all combined in quantum computing. As a result, we can conclude that quantum information, which has three main areas: quantum computing, quantum information theory, and quantum cryptography. We shall discuss about the quantum computing, namely, the area of inquiry that uses quantum phenomena, such as interference, superposition, and entanglement, and Dirac or bracket notation; to operate on quantum states, these states represent data [13].

2.3 Using AI to Advance Quantum Computing

AI and machine learning are also essential in advancing quantum computing itself by helping to optimize and control quantum systems:

- *Error Correction and Noise Reduction:* Quantum computers are highly sensitive to environmental interference (known as "quantum noise") and errors. AI algorithms can help detect and correct these errors through predictive models that understand and adapt to the behaviour of qubits. ML methods can improve the stability of quantum computations by helping qubits maintain coherence for longer periods.
- *Optimizing Quantum Circuits:* Building and executing quantum algorithms require optimizing the arrangement of quantum gates (quantum circuits). AI can help find more efficient circuit designs, minimizing the number of gates or steps required, thus reducing error rates and improving overall performance.
- *Quantum Hardware Design*: AI can be used to simulate and optimize the physical design of quantum hardware, including optimizing the layout of qubits, minimizing noise, and developing more stable quantum architectures.
- *Algorithm Discovery:* AI could potentially be used to discover new quantum algorithms by exploring vast spaces of possibilities and finding optimal solutions that would be difficult for humans to identify alone.

3 Quantum Information Science

Quantum computing is evolved from two areas of sciences: physics (quantum mechanics) and information science (mathematics, theoretical and applied computer science, among others).

The dots between information science and quantum physics principles are connected here. We begin by outlining the postulates of quantum mechanics as they relate to quantum information theory. We also include a one-line statement that defines quantum information processing terminologies, such as entanglement, superposition, and speedup, among others. This summary is based on Refs. [1, 13–18].

3.1 Quantum Mechanics Postulates, Entanglement, Mixed States and Operations

The unique feature of a quantum computer in comparison to a classical computer is that the bit (often referred to as "qubit") can be in one of two states (0 or 1) and possibly a superposition of the two states (a linear combination of 0 and 1) per time. The most common mathematical representation of a qubit is

$$|\psi\rangle = \alpha|0\rangle + \beta|1\rangle \quad |\psi\rangle = \alpha|0\rangle + \beta|1 \qquad (2)$$

Equation (2) is a superposition state, where $\alpha\alpha$, $\beta\beta$ are complex numbers and $|0\rangle|0\rangle$, $|1\rangle|1\rangle$ are *computational basis states* that form an orthonormal basis in this vector space. A qubit can also be represented visually using a Bloch sphere, as shown in Fig. 1.

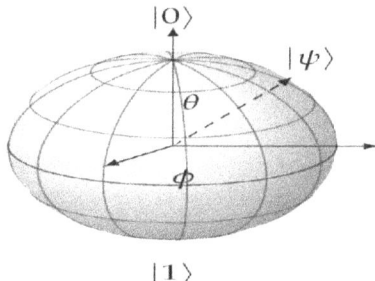

Fig. 1. A Bloch sphere of Qubits

This is used to visualize the qubit's geometric state. It gives the angles and basis vectors for the ψ representation.

We then move on to the postulates of quantum mechanics, which are preceded by a diagram in Fig. 2 that gives a summary representation of the postulates.

P1 defines the *state space*, P2 defines the *evolution*, P3 defines the *measurement*, and P4 defines the *composite system*, where $\psi a \psi b \equiv \psi a \psi b$.

- **Postulate 1: *State Space*.** The state of a quantum system is described by a unit vector $|\psi\rangle|\psi\rangle$ that lives in a Hilbert space $\mathcal{H}$. H which is a complete vector space equipped with an inner product. This state contains all necessary information to

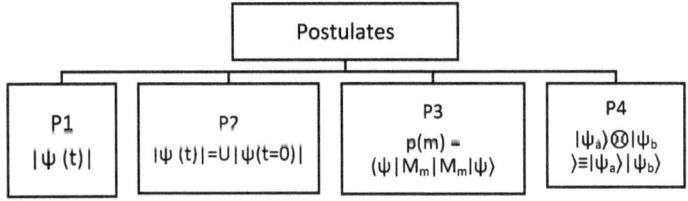

Fig. 2. One easy way to show the quantum mechanics postulates chart.

characterize the system. Hilbert Space is a mathematical space of complex-valued vectors that defines quantum states.

- **Postulate 2:** *Evolution.* A closed quantum system undergoes a time evolution $|\psi(t)\rangle|\psi(t)\rangle$. This evolution is described by a unitary transformation that follows the Schrodinger Eq. (1). In Functional analysis, time evolution can be modelled by evolution operator U(t), which propagate the system's state:

$$\psi(t) = U(t)\psi(0)$$

- **Postulate 3:** *Measurement.* It is a critical operation that extracts classical information from quantum information. Measurement collapses the wave function, forcing the qubit into a definite state either 0 or 1. Quantum measurements can be expressed using sets of measurement operators $\{Mm\}$. In an experiment, m represents the possible measurement outcomes. Upon measuring a state, say $|\psi(t)\rangle|\psi(t)\rangle$, the probability of an m outcome is $p(m)$.
- **Postulate 4:** *Composite Systems.* Two or more physical systems can be treated as a composite system. The state space of a composite system is the tensor product space of the states of the component physical systems.

Other Important Properties

- **Superposition**: A quantum system can exist in a combination of multiple possible states simultaneously. If $|\psi1\rangle$ and $|\psi2\rangle$ are possible states, the superposition is: $|\psi\rangle = c1|\psi1\rangle + c2|\psi1\rangle$.
- **Entanglement**: When the values of specific qualities of one system are correlated with the values of the corresponding properties of the other system, two quantum systems are said to be entangled. It enables quantum teleportation, where the state of quantum system is transferred from one location to another using shared entangled states.
- **Speedup**: If the quantum algorithm requires lesser queries to solve a problem than the classical approach, the outcome is a quantum speedup [19]. It reduces the time and increase efficiency of a Quantum computer.

3.2 Quantum Information Science: An Overview

QIS is an interdisciplinary field that explore how quantum mechanics can be enhanced to process, transmit, and secure information. Quantum communication, quantum computing, and quantum sensing (and metrology) are the three research categories in quantum information science. There are subcategories and specific research activities that pertain to each of these groups—starting with quantum communication, which is essentially the process of exchanging information on a quantum level. Quantum cryptography and networking are two popular uses of this burgeoning field. Moving on to quantum sensing, this branch of quantum information studies how to make quantum devices interact with their surroundings. Quantum systems and designs are examples of this type of application. In the subject of quantum information science, quantum computing is the third most talked-about topic.

Quantum computers are now divided into two types: analog and digital. The analog computer is a quantum computer that runs based on the system's Hamiltonian and the initial quantum state of qubits. Three forms of analog quantum computers exist:

- *Adiabatic quantum computing (AQC)* is a computational model that employs adiabatic quantum mechanical processes [20]. As a form of universal quantum computation, AQC employs the principles of superposition, tunnelling, and entanglement that manifest in quantum physical system.
- *Quantum annealing (QA)* is a technique for evaluating the minimum of an objective function that is built on AQC concepts but does not meet its stringent requirements [20]. Quantum annealing (QA) provides a more accurate model for the behaviour of actual quantum physical systems.
- *Quantum simulation (QS):* *Simulating quantum systems using classical computers encounters inherent challenges due to exponential scaling with system size. It* is the use of a controllable quantum system to examine a less controllable or accessible quantum system [21].

The digital quantum computer is the second type of quantum computer. It is a quantum device that computes using a limited number of elementary operations, termed gates, on quantum bits (qubits). Gate-based quantum computing is the most common type of digital computer.

- *Gate-based quantum computing (GBQC)* accepts data and modifies it by a unitary operation, which is expressed as a sequence of gate operations and measurements (i.e., the algorithm) and may be represented by a quantum circuit [22]. Quantum machine learning is the GBQC's driving force

QIS is divided into three categories: quantum communication, quantum computing, and quantum sensing (and metrology). Quantum communication and quantum sensing have applications, such as quantum networking and quantum system design, respectively. The field of QC splits into analog and digital computing. An analog quantum computer could be any of three forms: adiabatic quantum computing, quantum annealing, or quantum simulation. A digital quantum computer exists in the form of gate-based quantum computing, using the features of QML for its operations (Fig. 3).

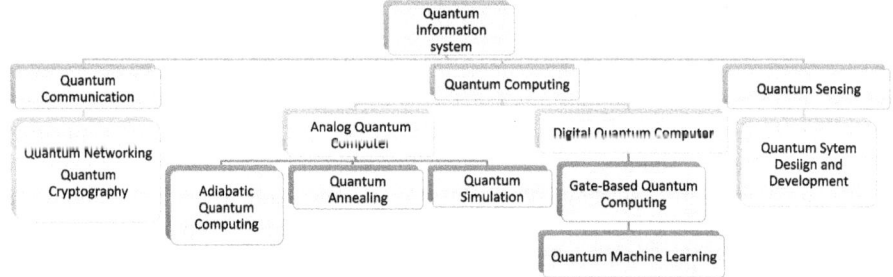

Fig. 3. Quantum information science (QIS) chart.

3.3 Quantum Computing System

As shown in Fig. 4, there are two types of quantum computers: analog and digital quantum computers. Both of them computers have some similarities, "hardware" and "software" relative to traditional computers. This is depicted in Fig. 4:

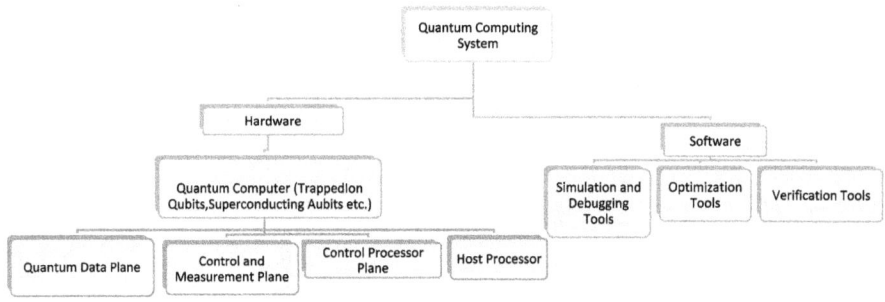

Fig. 4. QCS classification graph

QCS is a complete system that has two operational parts: hardware and software. The hardware of a QCS is essentially a quantum computer (with variations such as trapped ion qubits and superconducting qubits, among others). Generally, a quantum computer comprises essential components, which are quantum data planes, control and measurement planes, control processor plane, and a host processor. Similarly, the software of a QCS is composed of essential tools, which are simulation and debugging tools, optimization tools, and verification tools. Simulation is used for simulating the quantum algorithm. Debugging tool is used to debug the quantum computing program. Optimization tool is used to improve the quantum algorithm and quantum circuit designs. Verification tool is used to verify the quantum computing algorithm.

The hardware of a quantum system, the quantum computer, is made up of various components. The operation of these components necessitates the use of software tools. The various programming tools as they apply to a quantum system are visually represented in Fig. 5.

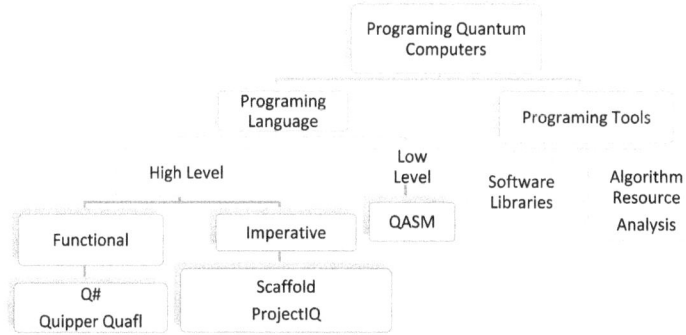

Fig. 5. Classification of Programming quantum computers

Quantum computers required the use of two key features to run efficiently: programming languages and programming tools. A programming language may be high level or low level. An example of low-level language programming is quantum assembly language (QASM). A high-level programming language is functional and imperative. Quipper is a high-level functional programming language which is designed for quantum computing. It is also used for developing and simulating quantum algorithm. ProjectQ is high level imperative programming language that allow users to develop, simulate and run quantum algorithms on different quantum hardware platform.

3.4 Q-Gates, Circuits, and Algorithms

A quantum circuit is a sequence of a quantum operations or quantum gates that is performed sequentially. Quantum circuits are the building blocks of quantum algorithm. Logic qubits are transported on "wires" (shown by horizontal lines), and quantum gates (represented by blocks) act on the qubits in a typical quantum circuit, as depicted in **Fig. 6**. The logical gate is a device that controls or processes data; the Hadamard "H" gate and NOT "X" gate are two common examples. The Hadamard Gate creates superposition, transforming a qubit from a state of 0 or 1 into an equal superposition.

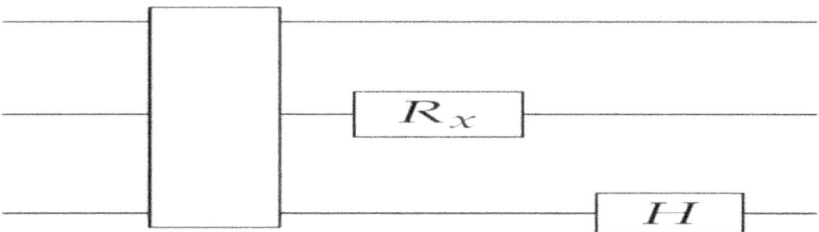

Fig. 6. Block diagram of quantum circuit

The horizontal lines are referred to as wires representing qubits, while the boxes represent operators acting on the qubits. *Rx* and *H* are the rotation operator and Hadamard gates, respectively.

Quantum Algorithms are used in computers to complete predefined tasks. It works with any actual quantum computation model [23]. Quantum computers can run classical algorithms, but not the other way around. This is due to entanglement and situations such as qubit superposition. Quantum algorithms are created using two key quantum gates—Hadamard and phase gates—which take advantage of the quantum interference, parallelism, and function evaluation properties. The Quantum Algorithm Zoo website [3] includes a thorough list.

In Table 1, we show different quantum algorithms as they fit under various categories of activities and applications.

Table 1. Quantum algorithm classifications.

Algorithm type	Description	Application	Notable Example
Quantum Search Algorithm	Speed up search in unsorted databases and optimization tasks using superposition and amplitude amplification.	Optimization search problems	Grover's Algorithm
Quantum Simulation Algorithm	Model complex quantum systems, especially useful for simulating molecules, materials, and chemical reactions.	Chemistry, physics, materials science	Hamiltonian Simulation, Quantum phase estimation.
Quantum Fourier Transform(QFT)	Transform a quantum state into its frequency domain	Signal processing periodicity detection	Quantum Fourier Phase Estimation
Quantum Machine learning algorithm	Use quantum principle to enhance machine learning tasks such as classification, clustering, and regression	Machine learning, big data analysis	Quantum support vector machine, quantum PCA

3.5 Common Quantum Applications

There are many quantum applications in use today, and we will go over a few of them here: information encoding, quantum teleportation, and quantum cryptography.

3.5.1 Information Encoding

Quantum computers are used quantum data for information processing, in the same way classical computers use classical data for information processing. Because of the established conceptuality of Quantum Computer outperforming Classical Computer, the capability to execute classical operations, and the restrictions in creating quantum data, the problem of converting classical data to quantum data has attracted a lot of attention in recent years, with various advancements. This procedure is known as data encoding.

Because data arrive in various formats, there are various methods for transforming conventional data to quantum data. The following is a list of data encoding methods that have been confirmed to work:

- Basis encoding: Basic encoding refers to the process of mapping classical information into quantum states.
- Amplitude encoding: In this encoding method, the classical information is stored in the amplitudes of a quantum state.
- Q sample encoding: It generally refers to encoding samples of data points into quantum states for use in quantum algorithms, regression and clustering.
- Dynamic encoding: It refers to type of encoding method where the representation of classical information in quantum states can change or adapt dynamically.

3.5.2 Quantum Teleportation

Teleportation applies the entanglement property to transmit quantum information from one quantum state (qubit) to another. This procedure is often used between two parties that are trying to communicate each other. There are five phases to transfer an unknown quantum state $q0q0$ between parties $q1q1$ & $q2q2$:

1. Parties $q1q1$ and $q2q2$ create an entangled pair.
2. $q1q1$ applies a CNOT gate with the unknown state $q0q0$.
3. $q1q1$ applies a Hadamard gate to the first qubit of the result in 2.
4. $q1q1$ measures the results from 3.
5. $q1q1$ communicates the measurement results with $q2q2$.

Using a IBM simulator (Qiskit), we give a circuit schematic (Fig. 7) of the teleportation process in context.

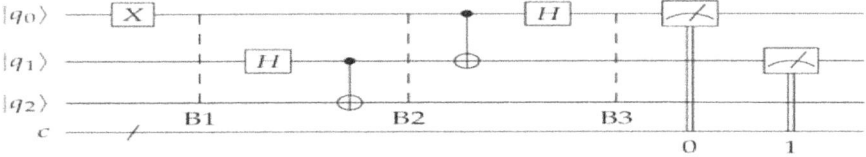

Fig. 7. Quantum teleportation circuit.

There are three qubits ($q0q0$, $q1q1$ and $q2q2$) and two classical bits (represented by the / sign on the c wire). In addition, there are two Hadamard gates and two CNOT gates. Finally, measurements are made on the classical channels. Each dashed vertical line represents a barrier (B1, B2, and B3) to split some circuit parts for sequential order of operation.

3.5.3 Quantum Cryptography

Quantum key distribution (QKD) is also known as quantum cryptography. It is a type of key distribution that encrypts and decrypts communications using quantum physics principles to establish a high-level secure data transmission between two or more parties. RSA encryption is most popular and commonly used encryption. The most important thing to know is that the security system relies heavily on huge numbers that are not impossible to crack but difficult to factor. Peter Shor's prime factorization algorithm (executed on a quantum computer) presents a significant challenge to this method. QKD, which is based on quantum physics, provides a more efficient way of encrypting data.

Principle: A secure transmission of Quantum key distribution required two communication channels. The encrypted message is sent over a classical channel (such as the telephone), while the quantum keys needed to decrypt the message are sent over a quantum channel (such as qubit transfer).

In QKD, numerous protocols are employed. The BB84 (Bennett and Brassard, 1984) protocol was the first to be established, and several protocols have since been built on it. B92, E91, decoy state, and a slew of other protocols are among them.

BB84 This is based on three fundamental aspects of quantum physics:

- No-cloning theorem;
- State collapse when measured;
- Irreversible measurement.

4 Quantum Computing Frameworks

In Table 2, we offer a mix of open source quantum computing tools largely driven by large-scale industry players, with the purpose of making it easier to design quantum algorithms.

Table 2. Some quantum computing tool's programming language, computing paradigm, and description are mentioned in the table.

Tool	Programming Language	Computing Paradigm	Description
Qiskit (IBM)	Python	Gate-based Quantum Computing	An open-source framework by IBM for writing quantum algorithms

(continued)

Table 2. (*continued*)

Tool	Programming Language	Computing Paradigm	Description
Cirq (Google)	Python	Gate-based quantum computing	A Google-developed framework for designing, simulating, and running quantum circuit.
Pennylane (Xandu)	Python	Hybrid Quantum-classical computing	A quantum machine learning library that integrates with Tensor Flow and PyTorch
D-Wave Ocean SDK	Python	Quantum Annealing	D-Wave's software development kit for creating applications on its quantum annealing processor.
Quipper	Haskell	Gate-based Quantum Computing	A functional programming language based on Haskell, designed specially for quantum

4.1 Comparing Common Types of Quantum Bit Technologies

The search for a suitable physical system in which to implement quantum logic operations has been going on for a long time. In Table 3, we discuss three major qubit technology options for building a quantum computer. These quantum technologies, trapped-ion qubits [24, 25], superconducting qubits [26, 27], and photonic qubits [28, 29], are thought to be well advanced.

Table 3. A comparison table of three qubit technologies: trapped ion, superconducting, and photonic qubits

Feature	Trapped Ion Qubits	Superconducting Qubits	Photonic Qubits
Physical Basis	Ion trapped in electromagnetic field	Superconducting circuits cooled to near absolute zero, typically using, Josephson	Photons, typically encoded in the polarization or path of light.

(*continued*)

Table 3. (*continued*)

Feature	Trapped Ion Qubits	Superconducting Qubits	Photonic Qubits
Maturity	Developed since the 1990s, with high fidelity demonstrated in small system	The most widely pursued approach for large commercial available quantum computer	Rapidly developing; key focus for quantum communication and networking.
Gate Speed	Moderate but consistent	Fast	Very fast
Error Rate	Low error rates high fidelity.	Moderate error rates	Very low decoherence
Scalability	Limited physical space and complexity of traps.	Generally scalable with improvements in materials and engineering.	High Scalable, especially for networking

4.2 Challenges in the Field of Quantum Computation

As we get closer to a fully scalable quantum computing age, the current scenario of quantum computation faces many obstacles, from experimental to theoretical. Professionals in the field of quantum computing have recognized a few issues, which we summarize here.

4.2.1 Experimental Challenges of Quantum Computing: Quantum Computers

Neutral atoms for quantum computing [30] stated that quantum computers which are shown to perform traditional computers, there is only a quantum computer that can perform an operation that cannot be emulated on a classical computer. Because it takes around 50 qubits and several gates ranging from 104104 to achieve a calculation that cannot be emulated on a classical computer. In the conclusion section of their article, David et al. stated that: "From the view of an experimental physicist, the task of exerting precise control over a large number of individual quantum particles is a grand challenge" [30]. They went further to explain that the following requirements should be successful quantum computation:

- Putting atoms in precise quantum states;
- Manipulating the interactions of the atoms to carry out logical procedures;
- Obtaining the computational output by monitoring the resultant states.

4.2.2 Theoretical Challenges of Quantum Computing: Quantum Simulators

Quantum machine learning (QML) by Biamonte et al. [19] noted that quantum algorithms could perform only traditional algorithms in exceptional circumstances, according to research. The quantum speedup, the outcome of superimposing a quantum state, was the most popular at that time. They throughout described the concept of quantum speedup. After their research, four fascinating questions were raised. These questions impacted research focus, which is still happening today since it would provide a more concise way to apply quantum machine learning to everyday applications—the *input, output, costing and benchmarking* issues were the topics of discussion.

Although a quantum algorithm shown to be faster than classical methods, data encoding takes up more time (converting classical data to quantum data since the readily available data are classical). Unless a rapid encoding program is produced, this is a significant disadvantage. In this domain, several efforts made to solve the input problem. In [31], a demonstration of how data can be mapped into a particular space where quantum states exist was exploited. In the work of Schuld [32], it was pointed that M.L and Q.C have certain similarities. This similarity is known as the "kernel model." In simple we can say that, a kernel model is a type of machine learning that characterizes information (data) based on similarities and distinct from one another. A clear picture of data encoding (embedding) was offered in a more recent publication by Schuld [33]. This article did not directly address the cost of data encoding, but provide a concise overview of the various data encoding methods.

5 Chronology and Origin of Quantum Computing

In this, we give a quantum chronology that stretches from the 1935 EPR paradox [34] to the year 2021. A diagram demonstrating the flow of quantum computing processes related to the three science domains mentioned earlier.

5.1 Chronology of Quantum Computing

From 1935 to till date observation of the EPR paradox, various research projects have resulted in the development of quantum computing systems and cutting-edge technologies. We have put together a timeline in Fig. 8 which show how these changes have proceeded over time.

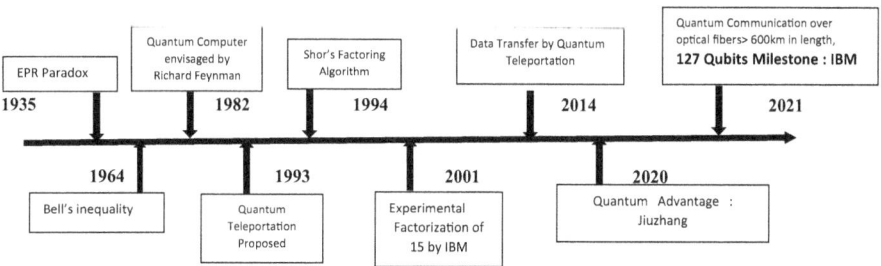

Fig. 8. A brief chronology of the development of quantum technology from 1935 to till date.

5.2 From Physics to Quantum Computing

The origins of QC may be traced to two disciplines of physics: one is modern and second is classical. The convergence and divergence of the quantum computing discipline are shown in Fig. 9. In this context, some contributions and applications on high energy physics have been reported [35–38].

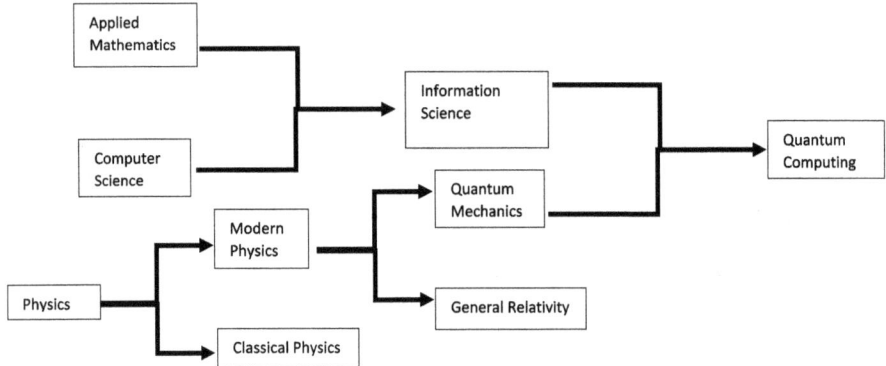

Fig. 9. Quantum computing journey from two fields of science: information science and quantum physics.

6 Discussion

6.1 State of the Art

Colin Williams published the first book on quantum computing, dubbed *Explorations in Quantum Computing* [39]. However, significant advancements in the subject have occurred since the book's release in 1998. We investigated the progress of quantum information science as it applies to three essential disciplines: quantum computing, quantum sensing, and quantum communication, all of which were discussed previously. We executed a series of searches on the well-known Scopus database to generate data on publications published on topics closely connected to these fields. *Quantum sensing, quantum metrology, quantum sensor, quantum hypothesis testing, and/or quantum radar* were some of the themes we considered for "quantum sensing and metrology". For "quantum computing and algorithms", we considered topics such as *quantum computing, quantum computer, quantum computation, and/or quantum algorithm*. Similarly, *quantum communication, quantum network, quantum cryptography, quantum modem, quantum internet, and/or quantum bus* were the selected topics for "quantum communication". The time frame for the search was 1996 through 2020 (over 20 years of its existence). The following is the search query, data, and visual plot shown in Figs. 10 and 11.

Quantum Sensing and Metrology (QSM):
((ALL(" quantum sensing ") OR ALL("quantum metrology") OR ALL(" quantum sensor ") OR ALL(quantum hypothesis testing") OR ALL(" quantum radar ") AND PUBYEAR > 1995 AND PUBYER < 2021)

Quantum Computing and Algorithm(QCA)
((ALL(" quantum computing ") OR ALL("quantum computer") OR ALL(" quantum internet ") OR ALL (quantum algorithm) AND PUBYEAR > 1995 AND PUBYEAR < 2021)

Quantum Communication(QC):
((ALL(" quantum communication") OR ALL (" quantum network ") OR All(" quantum cryptography ") OR ALL (" quantum modem ") OR ALL(" quantum internet ") OR ALL (quantum bus) AND PUBYEAR > 1995 AND PUBYEAR < 2021)

Fig. 10. Query search used in Scopus database to generate data of the publications on the topics, quantum sensing, quantum communication, and quantum computing from 1996 to 2020.

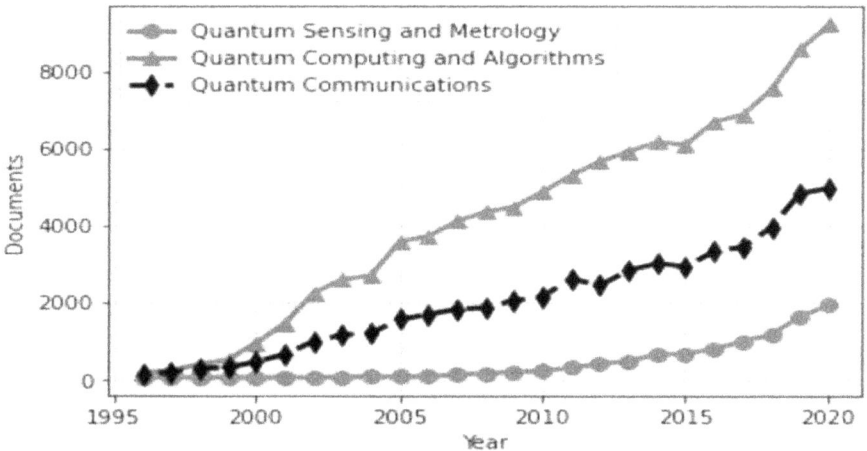

Fig. 11. QIS progress report.

This progress chart shows of the number of published research papers in the areas of quantum sensing and metrology, quantum computing and algorithms, and quantum communications, respectively. It dates from 1995 through 2020.

In the future, we may be confronted with the possibility of using a quantum computer for everyday tasks. Quantum computing, on the other hand, has yet to achieve that aim, and as a result, it is frequently referred to as "near-term" computing.

Quantum computing is a subset of artificial intelligence that combines quantum mechanics concepts with linear algebra and computer science functions to create a supercomputer. It faces large no challenges as a developing technology. These challenge exist in both the hardware and software field of the sector. Instead of this, there are positive advances that push us in the path of one day realizing the potential of Quantum Computing which lead to a great revolution in technology, hopefully in our lifetime.

6.2 Emerging Quantum Machine Learning Technology

Traditional machine learning's effective problem-solving application has shown limitations in areas such as the difficulty of searching algorithms [40] and the costly estimation of kernel functions due to vast feature spaces, to name a few. Theoretical answers to some of them and others were established in QML's recent advances and Quantum Computing. A good example can be found in the work of [31], where they experimentally achieved a quantum feature space-based classifier. A number of quantum classifiers have been implemented recently, as reported in [41], and their performance frequently compared to that of their classical counterparts. There have also been advancements in the field of quantum deep learning [42], with recent work by [43] implementing a quantum generative adversarial network on a superconducting quantum processor for learning and the generation of real-world handwritten digital images, and [44] implementing quantum convolutional neural networks (QCNN) for different applications; among them is the use of QCNN to create a quantum error correction method that is optimized for a particular error model. It is vital to highlight the combinatory "hybrid quantum–classical algorithms", which include recent advances, such as those seen in [45], where hybrid quantum variational auto encoder was applied to a representation learning task as well as the work of [46] implementing hybrid quantum–classical convolutional neural network on a Tetris dataset for classification.

7 Conclusion

The study of quantum computational learning theory comprises a wide range of topics. An extensive survey article that covers every aspect of the field, would be overwhelming. However, in a reasonable span, this succinct review presents a diverse range of topics, all of which are made more accessible using charts, tables, and figures. As a result, we provide a suitable first reference to modern quantum computing for a large no of audiences with no prior knowledge of the area. Since we recognize that our introductory review will lead to more specific questions, Table 4 lists resources for future reading, aiming to provide an in-depth grasp of the quantum computing field.

Table 4. A collection of further reading resources comprising subfields, such as quantum machine learning, quantum algorithms, and quantum ethics

Subfield	Resource type	Title	Author(s)/Provider	Description
Quantum Machine learning	Book	Quantum machine learning: What Quantum Computing Means to Data Mining	Peter Wittek	Introduction to quantum computing for data science and machine learning.
Quantum Algorithm	Book	Quantum computation and Quantum Information	Michael A. Nielsen, Issac L. Chuang	Comprehensive textbook covering foundational quantum algorithm
Quantum Ethics	Book	Quantum computing: Progress and Prospects	National Academics of Sciences, Engineering and Medicine	Report covering ethical and societal implications of quantum technologies.

Finally, we conclude that the relationship between classical artificial intelligence, machine learning, and deep learning are in direct dependency on quantum artificial intelligence, which includes quantum computation systems in their entirety, quantum machine learning, which includes quantum Fourier transforms, amplitude amplification, algorithms, and quantum deep learning, which includes quantum neural networks, quantum convolutional neural networks, and other concepts. Figure 12 depicts the symbiotic dependencies between the aforementioned.

Knowledge Areas

Knowledge Areas

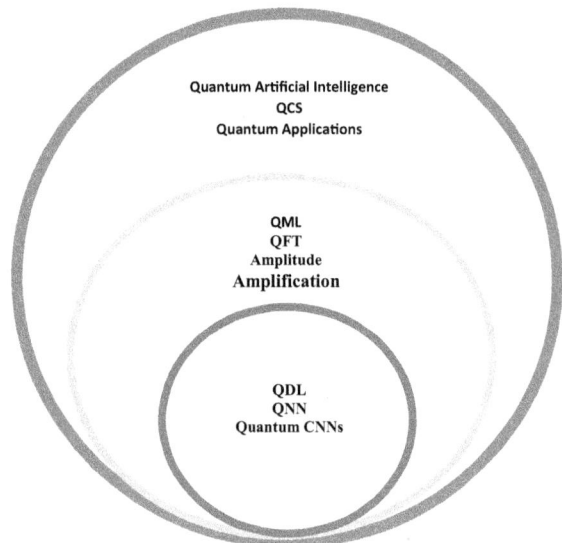

Fig. 12. Quantum artificial intelligence is a superset of QML and QDL.

References

1. Schuld, M., Petruccione, F.: Supervised Learning with Quantum Computers, vol. 17. Springer, Berlin/Heidelberg, Germany (2018)
2. Montanaro, A.: Quantum algorithms: an overview. NPJ Quantum Inf. **2**, 15023 (2016)
3. Jordan, S.: The Quantum Algorithm Zoo (2021). http://math.nist.gov/quantum/zoo/. Accessed 01 November 2021
4. Marais, A., et al.: The future of quantum biology. J. R. Soc. Interface **15**, 20180640 (2018)
5. Biamonte, J., Faccin, M., De Domenico, M.: Complex networks from classical to quantum. Commun. Phys. **2**, 53 (2019)
6. McMahon, D.: Quantum Mechanics Demystified. McGraw-Hill Education, New York, NY, USA (2013)
7. Samuel, A.L.: Some studies in machine learning using the game of checkers. IBM J. Res. Dev. **3**, 210–229 (1959)
8. Alzubi, J., Nayyar, A., Kumar, A.: Machine learning from theory to algorithms: an overview. J. Phys. Conf. Ser. **1142**, 012012 (2018)
9. Rivas, P.: Deep Learning for Beginners: A Beginner's Guide to Getting Up and Running with Deep Learning from Scratch Using Python. Packt Publishing Ltd., Birmingham, UK (2020)
10. Mehta, P., et al.: A high-bias, low-variance introduction to machine learning for physicists. Phys. Rep. **810**, 1–124 (2019)
11. Mahesh, B.: Machine learning algorithms – a review. Int. J. Sci. Res. (IJSR) **9**, 381–386 (2020)
12. Bonaccorso, G.: Machine Learning Algorithms. Packt Publishing Ltd., Birmingham, UK (2017)
13. Wittek, P.: Quantum Machine Learning: What Quantum Computing Means to Data Mining. Academic Press, Cambridge, MA, USA (2014)

14. Nielsen, M.A., Chuang, I.L.: Quantum computation and quantum information. Phys. Today **54**, 60 (2001)
15. McMahon, D.: Quantum Computing Explained. John Wiley & Sons, Hoboken, NJ, USA (2007)
16. Mermin, N.D.: Quantum Computer Science: An Introduction. Cambridge University Press, Cambridge, UK (2007)
17. Kaye, P., Laflamme, R., Mosca, M.: An Introduction to Quantum Computing. Oxford University Press on Demand, Oxford, UK (2007)
18. Grumbling, E., Horowitz, M.: Adiabatic quantum computing and quantum annealing. In: Quantum Computing: Progress and Prospects. The National Academies Press, Washington, DC, USA (2019)
19. Biamonte, J., Wittek, P., Pancotti, N., Rebentrost, P., Wiebe, N., Lloyd, S.: Quantum machine learning. Nature **549**, 195–202 (2017)
20. Grant, E.K., Humble, T.S.: Adiabatic Quantum Computing and Quantum Annealing. Oxford University Press, Oxford, UK (2020)
21. Georgescu, I.M., Ashhab, S., Nori, F.: Quantum simulation. Rev. Mod. Phys. **86**, 153 (2014)
22. Michielsen, K., Nocon, M., Willsch, D., Jin, F., Lippert, T., De Raedt, H.: Benchmarking gate-based quantum computers. Comput. Phys. Commun. **220**, 44–55 (2017)
23. Mosca, M.: Quantum algorithms (2008). arXiv:0808.0369
24. Bruzewicz, C.D., Chiaverini, J., McConnell, R., Sage, J.M.: Trapped-ion quantum computing: progress and challenges. Appl. Phys. Rev. **6**, 021314 (2019)
25. Blatt, R., Roos, C.F.: Quantum simulations with trapped ions. Nat. Phys. **8**, 277–284 (2012)
26. Krantz, P., Kjaergaard, M., Yan, F., Orlando, T.P., Gustavsson, S., Oliver, W.D.: A quantum engineer's guide to superconducting qubits. Appl. Phys. Rev. **6**, 021318 (2019)
27. Huang, H.L., Wu, D., Fan, D., Zhu, X.: Superconducting quantum computing: a review. Sci. China Inf. Sci. **63**, 1–32 (2020)
28. Kok, P., Munro, W.J., Nemoto, K., Ralph, T.C., Dowling, J.P., Milburn, G.J.: Linear optical quantum computing with photonic qubits. Rev. Mod. Phys. **79**, 135 (2007)
29. Nicolas, A., Veissier, L., Giner, L., Giacobino, E., Maxein, D., Laurat, J.: A quantum memory for orbital angular momentum photonic qubits. Nat. Photon. **8**, 234–238 (2014)
30. Weiss, D.S., Saffman, M.: Quantum computing with neutral atoms. Phys. Today **70**, 7–44 (2017)
31. Havlíček, V., et al.: Supervised learning with quantum-enhanced feature spaces. Nature **567**, 209–212 (2019)
32. Schuld, M.: Machine Learning in Quantum Spaces. Nature Publishing Group, Berlin, Germany (2019)
33. Schuld, M.: Quantum Machine Learning Models are Kernel Methods (2021). arXiv:2101.11020
34. Einstein, A., Podolsky, B., Rosen, N.: Can quantum-mechanical description of physical reality be considered complete? Phys. Rev. **47**, 777 (1935)
35. Guan, W., Perdue, G., Pesah, A., Schuld, M., Terashi, K., Vallecorsa, S., Vlimant, J.R.: Quantum machine learning in high energy physics. Mach. Learn. Sci. Technol. **2**, 011003 (2021)
36. Vijayasri, I., Javier, O.-D.: Quantum Machine Learning Concepts and Applications (2020). https://research.latinxinai.org/workshops/neurips/neurips-2020.html. Accessed 01 November 2021
37. Orduz-Ducuara, J.A.: Quantum Machine Learning and Higgs Phenomenology (2020)
38. Orduz, J., Iyer, V.: Quantum machine learning concepts for physicists. Tecnología Educativa, Revista CONAIC, Mexico City, Mexico **VIII**, 71–75 (2021). https://terc.mx/index.php/terc. Accessed 01 November 2021

39. Williams, C.P.: Explorations in Quantum Computing. Springer Science & Business Media, Berlin/Heidelberg, Germany (2010)
40. Khanal, B., Rivas, P., Orduz, J.: Quantum machine learning: a case study of Grover's algorithm. In: Proceedings of the 19th International Conference on Scientific Computing (CSC 2021), Las Vegas, NV, USA (2021)
41. Jui, T., Ayoade, O., Rivas, P., Orduz, J.: Performance analysis of quantum machine learning classifiers. In: Proceedings of the NeurIPS 2021 Workshop LatinX in AI, Virtual Event (2021)
42. Garg, S., Ramakrishnan, G.: Advances in Quantum Deep Learning: An Overview (2020). arXiv:2005.04316
43. Huang, H.L., et al.: Experimental quantum generative adversarial networks for image generation. Phys. Rev. Appl. **16**, 024051 (2021)
44. Cong, I., Choi, S., Lukin, M.D.: Quantum convolutional neural networks. Nat. Phys. **15**, 1273–1278 (2019)
45. Rivas, P., Zhao, L., Orduz, J.: Hybrid quantum variational autoencoders for representation learning. In: Proceedings of the 19th International Conference on Scientific Computing (CSC 2021), Las Vegas, NV, USA (2021)
46. Liu, J., Lim, K.H., Wood, K.L., Huang, W., Guo, C., Huang, H.L.: Hybrid quantum-classical convolutional neural networks. Sci. China Phys. Mech. Astron. **64**, 290311 (2021)

Internet of Things

A Multi-Criteria Driven Integrated Routing Protocol for IoT Communication in 6G Networks

Shams Tabrez Siddiqui[1(✉)], Md Oqail Ahmad[2], Abu Salim[1], Rajesh Kumar Tiwari[3], Aasif Aftab[1], and Mohd Sarfaraz[1]

[1] Department of Computer Science, College of Engineering and Computer Science, Jazan, Saudi Arabia
{stabrez,aaftab,msarfaraz}@jazanu.edu.sa

[2] Vignan's Foundation for Science, Technology and Research, Guntur, AP, India

[3] Department of Computer Science and Engineering, RVS College of Engineering and Technology, Jamshedpur, Jharkhand, India

Abstract. The transition to 6G networks introduces advanced requirements for the Internet of Things (IoT), demanding protocols that balance diverse performance criteria in complex environments. This paper presents a multi-criteria decision-making (MCDM) routing protocol tailored to optimize IoT communication within 6G networks, specifically addressing latency, energy efficiency, reliability, security, and bandwidth utilization. By leveraging techniques like AHP, TOPSIS, and WSM, the protocol dynamically adapts to varying IoT demands, ensuring responsive and efficient data transmission. Through simulation, we demonstrate the protocol's superiority over conventional routing methods in high-density and latency-sensitive scenarios, achieving significant improvements in network lifetime, packet delivery ratio, and security resilience. This work provides a robust framework for 6G IoT, facilitating scalable, secure, and energy-conscious communication essential for future smart cities, healthcare, and industrial IoT deployments.

Keywords: IoT · 6G networks · Multi-parameters Decision-Making · AHP · TOPSIS · WSM

1 Introduction

The rapidly growing Internet of Things (IoT) is changing how we interact with our environment. IoT connects physical and digital worlds by integrating sensors, devices, and systems in everyday things. This unparalleled connectivity enables real-time data gathering, processing, and action, advancing smart cities, healthcare, industry 4.0, and agriculture [1]. IoT will connect billions of devices in the next years, increasing network complexity. Parallel to this, the telecoms industry is moving towards 6G networks. 6G networks, expected to launch in 2030, will revolutionise communication with high data rates, low latency, improved security, and huge connectivity. These traits make 6G the backbone of future IoT ecosystems. To properly utilise 6G's promise, IoT needs revolutionary communication protocols to manage its highly dynamic, heterogeneous, and resource-constrained surroundings [2]. A multi-criteria aware integrated decision-making routing protocol is developed to address the requirement for efficient communication protocols that can adapt to IoT difficulties in 6G environments. A protocol that optimises latency, energy usage, dependability, and security while providing scalable and efficient communication in large-scale IoT devices is necessary [3]. IoT communication systems must now balance various, sometimes competing, performance variables, which requires a major design change from single-criteria routing protocols to MCDM protocols.

The transition from 5G to 6G networks facilitates IoT communication while also introducing challenges. Conventional routing methods in large-scale IoT networks typically do not satisfy the stringent requirements of 6G, which include low latency, high dependability, and efficient use of bandwidth [4]. These networks must also address the challenges of limited energy resources in IoT devices, frequent changes in network topology, and robust security measures. Existing routing approaches, particularly single-criteria protocols, are inadequate for managing the complex, multi-dimensional decision-making processes of 6G-enabled IoT networks. Their primary focus is on optimising for the shortest path, energy efficiency, or speed, rather than on security and reliability. In situations involving multiple criteria, a narrow focus on a single statistic yields unsatisfactory results. Decreased latency could potentially lead to higher energy consumption, whereas enhanced security might result in decreased efficiency of bandwidth usage. In light of these limitations, there is a need for a novel routing protocol that incorporates several criteria in the decision-making process to enable more versatile and adaptable routing. The proposed research aims to develop a comprehensive decision-making routing protocol that maximises the efficiency of 6G IoT connectivity by utilising Multi-Criteria Decision Making (MCDM) techniques. The protocol optimises latency, energy efficiency, reliability, and security to enhance the performance of IoT systems.

A multi-criteria aware integrated decision-making routing system for IoT communication in 6G networks is the study's main goal.

To optimise latency, energy consumption, network dependability, bandwidth utilisation, and security by designing a routing protocol that employs multi-criteria decision-making (MCDM) approaches.

Design an adaptable system that, in response to changes in the network, the needs of the application, and the limitations of the device, dynamically changes the relative importance of various criteria.

Is to compare the proposed protocol's performance to that of current routing protocols by simulating and evaluating it in diverse Internet of Things (IoT) scenarios with varying communication lengths, network density, and device mobility patterns.

Verify that the suggested protocol can handle the special needs of 6G networks, such as extremely low latency, increased security, and a large number of connected devices.

Highlight the advantages and disadvantages of including numerous decision variables by comparing the proposed multi-criteria routing protocol to existing single-criteria or limited multi-criteria protocols.

2 Overview of IoT Communication Protocols

An extensive network of interconnected computing devices, software programs, and data transfer protocols is known as the Internet of Things (IoT). The Internet of Things (IoT) communication protocols allow objects to communicate data across different domains, which is the backbone of these networks. Depending on their range, these protocols can be either long-range, short-range, or hybrid [5–7].

Short-range Protocols. Bluetooth Low Energy (BLE), Zigbee, Z-Wave, and Wi-Fi are commonly used protocols for short-range local device communication. BLE is noted for its low power consumption, which makes it ideal for wearable and portable devices. Zigbee is utilized in applications that require modest data rates and power, such as smart home systems.

Long-range Protocols. Long-range protocols such as LoRaWAN, NB-IoT, and Sigfox allow IoT devices to communicate over long distances, typically several kilometers. These protocols prioritize low-power wide-area networking (LPWAN), making them appropriate for applications like as smart agriculture, remote monitoring, and smart cities.

Hybrid Protocols. Internet of Things (IoT) devices can easily connect to the internet thanks to protocols like 6LoWPAN, which makes IPv6 work with low-power devices. Message Queuing Telemetry Transport (MQTT) and Constrained Application Protocol (CoAP) are lightweight message and request/response models made for devices with limited resources and low power.

2.1 Evolution from 5G to 6G Networks

The transition from 5G to 6G is projected to result in significant advances in communication technology, allowing for more complex, data-intensive, and latency-sensitive applications. Globally implemented 5G networks provide higher data rates (up to 10 Gbps), shorter latency (~1 ms), and more capacity compared to 4G. These networks enable enhanced mobile broadband (eMBB), ultra-reliable low-latency communication (URLLC), and massive machine-type communication (mMTC), making them ideal for IoT applications such as self-driving cars, telemedicine, and intelligent manufacturing [8].

6G networks, expected by 2030, promise even greater breakthroughs. The key aspects of 6G are:

Terahertz Communication (THz)

Challenge. A key feature of 6G is its use of terahertz (THz) frequencies (0.1–10 THz). This spectrum can support 1 terabit per second data rates. THz frequencies are sensitive to signal attenuation, range, and environmental factors like humidity and physical impediments. These difficulties require flexible and resilient communication methods to maintain connectivity in changing IoT contexts.

Impact on Protocol Design. 6G IoT protocols must address THz communication's limited range and reliability issues. The suggested routing protocol can use multi-hop communication mechanisms to expand connectivity over greater areas and dynamically route data packets through intermediary IoT devices. THz transmissions require more energy; thus, the protocol may prioritize path dependability and energy economy by altering routing paths depending on real-time signal strength and attenuation data.

Quantum Communication

Challenge. Quantum communication, including QKD and encryption, is projected to be crucial in 6G networks. In networks with critical data, quantum technologies enable unbreakable encryption, providing unmatched security. Quantum communication is difficult to integrate with existing infrastructure, expensive, and requires specialist equipment to generate and detect quantum states. In addition, quantum technologies are still developing, making them hard to scale in IoT applications.

Impact on Protocol Design. Protocol design must adapt to both classical and quantum communication channels to support quantum communication. Integrating quantum-safe encryption techniques within the protocol's security framework ensures data integrity and privacy in quantum-secure contexts. The protocol should also switch between quantum and traditional channels based on resource availability, application priority, and security needs.

Ultra-Low Latency

Challenge. 6G networks aim for latency <1 ms, enabling real-time applications like autonomous driving, remote surgery, and VR/AR. Due to data processing and transmission demands, ultra-low latency is difficult to sustain in dense IoT deployments. Instantaneous data processing and response strain network computational and energy resources.

Protocol Design Impact. The proposed routing protocol prioritizes shortest, most reliable paths with latency-sensitive algorithms for ultra-low latency. In real time, network congestion, processing delays, and link reliability are assessed to route data along channels that fulfill strict latency requirements. The protocol can also use edge and fog computing to offload processing jobs to neighboring nodes, lowering transmission time and latency.

High Device Density and Massive Connectivity

Challenge. 6G networks are expected to accommodate up to 10 million devices per square kilometer, posing issues in managing interference, resource allocation, and connection in densely populated IoT environments. High device density strains bandwidth and increases collisions and signal interference, making efficient, scalable protocols vital.

Impact on Protocol Design. Protocol design requires adaptive resource allocation algorithms to prioritize devices based on application needs and network conditions. Dynamic network slicing and prioritization allocate resources to key applications and optimize network bandwidth. The protocol also uses frequency hopping and smart scheduling to reduce collisions and provide reliable communication in dense installations.

Energy Efficiency and Sustainability

Challenge. The proliferation of IoT installations in 6G networks necessitates the implementation of energy-efficient solutions. Power-saving algorithms are necessary for battery-operated IoT devices in remote or difficult-to-reach regions to extend their lifespan and minimize maintenance. The 6G design is prioritizing sustainability in order to mitigate the environmental impact of large-scale IoT systems.

Impact on Protocol Design. Energy-aware routing algorithms identify paths that reduce transmission power and computation in order to conserve energy. Devices may utilize solar, RF, or other ambient energy sources with energy-harvesting protocols when they are accessible. The protocol dynamically adjusts routing criteria in large-scale 6G deployments to optimize energy utilization and extend the lifespan of IoT devices.

2.2 Routing Protocols in IoT Networks

In Internet of Things (IoT) networks, routing is the process of finding the most efficient paths for the transmission of data from source devices to destination points, considering constraints such as limited availability of power, bandwidth, and processing capabilities [9, 10].

2.2.1 Single-Criteria Routing Protocols

Routing protocols that are conventionally used in the Internet of Things (IoT) are frequently developed to optimize a single criterion, such as the shortest path, minimal energy consumption, or least delay. Examples that are frequently encountered include [11–13]:

- *Low-Energy Adaptive Clustering Hierarchy (LEACH).* A protocol that is prevalently employed in wireless sensor networks (WSNs) to ensure energy efficiency. LEACH dynamically forms clusters and rotates cluster heads to distribute the energy burden among nodes, thereby reducing power consumption.
- *Ad hoc On-Demand Distance Vector (AODV).* A routing protocol that focusses on determining the shortest path between devices and calculating routes on demand. AODV is employed in mobile ad hoc networks (MANETs) and WSNs; however, its limited scalability may render it unsuitable for dense and extremely dynamic IoT environments.
- *Greedy Perimeter Stateless Routing (GPSR).* A protocol that is specifically designed for geographic routing, in which each node makes decisions based on its location and the coordinates of the destination. GPSR is straightforward and effective for specific IoT applications; however, it fails to consider security concerns or energy consumption.

2.2.2 Multi-Criteria Routing Protocols

Multi-criteria routing protocols have been developed as a response to the constraints of single-criteria protocols. These methods consider numerous aspects to determine the most optimal route for data transmission. These considerations frequently encompass latency, energy expenditure, network dependability, security, and bandwidth utilization. Some examples are [14, 15]:

- *Energy Aware Routing (EAR).* Energy Aware Routing (EAR) is a protocol designed to optimise energy usage and prolong the lifespan of a network. It achieves this by picking routes based on the remaining energy of nodes and the energy consumption along the journey.
- *Multi-Criteria Based Routing (MCBR).* Multi-Criteria Based Routing (MCBR) is a protocol that enhances routing efficiency by considering multiple criteria, including energy efficiency, reliability, and delay, all at the same time. MCBR commonly use decision-making algorithms, such as MCDM, to assess these criteria and ascertain the optimal route.
- *QoS-Aware Routing.* Quality of Service (QoS) is prioritised by QoS-Aware Routing techniques, which effectively manage variables such as latency, bandwidth, and dependability. These protocols are made to specifically address the requirements of certain applications, such control over vital infrastructure or real-time monitoring.

2.3 Multi-Criteria Decision-Making (MCDM) Techniques

Multi-Criteria Decision-Making (MCDM) is a set of decision-making processes that are specifically designed to evaluate and choose between many possibilities by considering a large number of criteria that may clash with one another. Some of the most common MCDM techniques are [16–20]:

- *Analytical Hierarchy Process (AHP).* The Analytic Hierarchy Process (AHP) is utilized to rank network criteria such as latency, energy usage, and security according to their relative significance. In low-latency applications like autonomous driving or real-time healthcare monitoring, latency is prioritized over other measurements. AHP structures the decision-making process into hierarchical tiers, facilitating the assessment of each option according to the designated weights for each criterion. This guarantees that routing decisions align with the real-time demands and limitations of 6G IoT systems.
- *Technique for Order of Preference by Similarity to Ideal Solution (TOPSIS).* TOPSIS finds the routing path closest to an "ideal" solution, which balances all performance indicators (e.g., minimal latency, high reliability). This AI-driven technique lets the protocol dynamically choose the best path under changing network conditions. This technology provides real-time flexibility in high-demand scenarios to provide latency-sensitive applications with optimal service without compromising security or energy efficiency due to IoT traffic fluctuation [21].
- *Weighted Sum Model (WSM).* The WSM technique allocates a weighted value to each criterion according to its significance in a specific scenario, determining the overall score for each potential path. This is especially advantageous in situations requiring simplicity and minimal processing demands, such as in low-power IoT devices. The AI element in WSM enables swift assessments and appropriate route selections through dynamic weight adjustments, hence prolonging the lifespan of battery-operated IoT devices while ensuring superior network performance.

Among the MCDM techniques, the Weighted Sum Model (WSM) is notably beneficial for energy efficiency in low-power IoT devices. The model enables dynamic weighing of parameters, facilitating route selection that prioritises lowest energy use, hence extending the operational lifespan of IoT nodes, particularly in cases necessitating lightweight processing.

3 Multi-Criteria Decision-Making Framework for IoT Routing

More advanced routing protocols must be created in order to handle the growing heterogeneity and complexity of Internet of Things networks, especially in light of 6G. Several performance factors, including as energy consumption, latency, security, reliability, and bandwidth utilization, must be considered by these protocols (Fig. 1). To find the best balance between these two aspects and choose the most efficient data transmission routes, a multi-criteria decision making (MCDM) framework is needed [19].

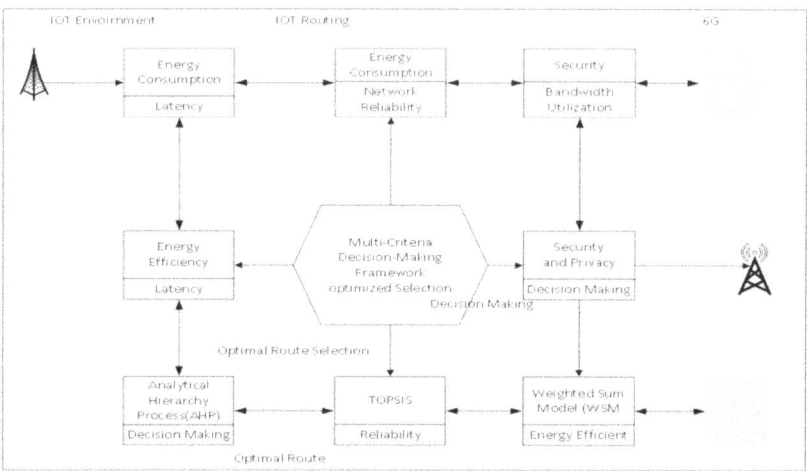

Fig. 1. Multi-Criteria Decision-Making (MCDM) framework for IoT routing in a 6G environment

3.1 Overview of Multi-Criteria Decision-Making (MCDM)

Multi-criteria decision-making (MCDM) is a set of techniques and strategies meant to assess and guide judgements in circumstances when several, usually contradictory, factors have to be taken under account. MCDM considers numerous performance factors unlike single-criteria decision-making, which concentrates on optimizing one component (e.g., shortest path or least energy use), so allowing a more balanced and strong decision-making process. The several and sometimes conflicting needs imposed on IoT networks—such as optimizing energy use while guaranteeing real-time performance and preserving security—have made MCDM more well-known in IoT routing [14].

3.2 Selection of Criteria for IoT Routing

In order for the MCDM framework to be successful, it is necessary to determine the factors that will have an impact on the decisions regarding network routing [11]. The specific requirements and limitations of Internet of Things networks must be reflected in these standards, particularly as these networks progress towards 6G. Energy consumption is a significant criterion evaluated under the MCDM framework. This section addresses the issues of energy consumption in IoT networks, particularly for battery-operated or energy-harvesting devices, and underscores the necessity of reducing energy expenditure during data transmission without sacrificing performance, as an integral aspect of the routing protocol's decision-making process [10–12].

3.2.1 Latency

Data packet latency is the time between source and destination. Many IoT applications, notably real-time monitoring and control, require low latency. For autonomous vehicles, industrial automation, and remote surgery, ultra-low latency is essential. Thus, MCDM-based IoT routing algorithms generally depend on delay.

3.2.2 Energy Consumption

IoT networks often struggle with energy usage, especially for battery-powered or energy-harvesting devices. Reduce energy utilization during data transmission to extend the lifespan of IoT nodes, especially in rural or hard-to-reach places where battery replacement is prohibitive. MCDM routing protocols must balance energy efficiency, latency, and dependability.

3.2.3 Network Reliability

Network dependability is the network's ability to keep IoT devices communicating. This comprises packet delivery ratio, network availability, and fault tolerance. Reliability is crucial in IoT applications like smart grids and industrial control systems since data loss or delays can be disastrous.

3.2.4 Security and Privacy

Security and Privacy in IoT networks is a top priority as they become broader and more diverse. Cyberattacks, data breaches, and unauthorized access can endanger IoT operations and sensitive data. Routing protocols must secure users' privacy and include encryption, authentication, and intrusion detection. Security must be considered alongside latency and energy usage in MCDM.

3.2.5 Bandwidth Utilization

In resource-constrained IoT networks, bandwidth efficiency is crucial. 6G networks promise greater data rates, thus IoT devices will communicate more. However, high bandwidth consumption might cause network congestion and performance issues.

MCDM-based routing must optimize data transfer and bandwidth to avoid network overload.

4 Multi-Criteria Decision-Making (MCDM) Framework

Let us establish some essential variables [20–22]:

- **LLL** refers to latency, which is the time delay between the transmission and reception of data.
- **EEE** refers to energy consumption, which is the amount of power used during data transmission.
- **RRR** refers to reliability, specifically the packet delivery ratio, which measures the percentage of successfully delivered packets.
- **SSS** Security level.
- **BBB** Bandwidth utilisation

Let WLW_LWL, WEW_EWE, WRW_RWR, WSW_SWS, and WBW_BWB denote the weight assigned to each criterion, namely latency, energy, reliability, security, and bandwidth utilization, respectively.

The equation Z is equal to the sum of the products of the weights (W) and their respective variables (L, E, R, S, B). The equation can be expressed as BZ = WL * L + WE * E + WR * R + WS * S + WB * B.

The routing choice entails the optimization of the objective function ZZZ, considering the specific priorities of the network.

4.1 Latency Calculation

Latency LLL can be modelled based on factors such as hop count, transmission delay, and processing delay:

$$L = \sum i = 1 N (Ti + Pi) L = \sum_{i=1}^{N} (T_i + P_i) L = i = 1 \sum N(Ti + Pi)$$

where:

- NNN is the number of hops in the route.
- TiT_iTi is the transmission delay at hop iii.
- PiP_iPi is the processing delay at hop iii.

4.2 Energy Consumption

Energy consumption EEE is generally modelled based on the energy spent per transmission and reception by each node along the network.

$$E = \sum i = 1 N (Etx, i + Erx, i) E = \sum_{i=1}^{N} (E_{tx,i} + E_{rx,i}) E = i = 1 \sum N(Etx, i + Erx, i)$$

where:

- Etx,iE_{tx,i}Etx,i is the energy consumed for transmission at hop iii.
- Erx,iE_{rx,i}Erx,i is the energy consumed for reception at hop iii.

4.3 Reliability

Reliability RRR can be quantified with the help of the Packet Delivery Ratio (PDR), which is the ratio of successfully delivered packets to the total number of packets that have been transmitted:

$$R = Packets\ Sent/Packets\ Delivered$$

4.4 Security

Security protocols for 6G IoT networks need to handle ever-changing threat landscapes, densely packed devices, and rapid data transfer speeds. Latency and bandwidth utilization are two performance parameters that could be affected by the proposed protocol's multi-layered security features, which include authentication and encryption. One ex-ample is encryption, which protects data but increases processing and transmission overhead, which in turn affects delay. Although multi-level authentication techniques improve network access security, they may have an effect on bandwidth utilization, which is especially problematic for IoT devices that have limited resources.

4.5 Bandwidth Utilization

Bandwidth utilization, denoted as BBB, can be determined by dividing the amount of bandwidth being used by the total amount of bandwidth available along the given route.

$$B = Total\ Available\ Bandwidth/Utilized\ Bandwidth$$

5 Simulation and Experimental Results

In this section, the performance of the proposed integrated decision-making routing protocol for IoT in the context of 6G networks is evaluated through detailed simulations. We explore the simulation setup and environment, define the experimental scenarios and assumptions, and analyze various performance metrics. The results are also compared with existing routing protocols to highlight the advantages of the proposed solution.

5.1 Simulation Setup and Environment

The simulations were conducted using a well-established network simulator such as NS3 or OMNeT++, which are widely used for simulating wireless networks. The simulation environment was designed to mimic real-world IoT scenarios, particularly in a 6G network context. Key parameters include:

- **Network size.** Varying from small-scale (10–50 devices) to large-scale networks (500–1000 devices).
- **Topology**: Random and grid-based topologies to reflect different deployment environments, such as smart cities and industrial settings.

- **Mobility models.** Both static and mobile nodes were simulated to account for IoT devices in stationary positions (e.g., sensors) and moving nodes (e.g., autonomous vehicles).
- **Traffic patterns.** Mixed traffic types, including real-time communication (low-latency), periodic sensor data transmission, and bursty traffic.
- **Protocols.** The proposed integrated decision-making routing protocol was simulated alongside traditional protocols like AODV (Ad hoc On-Demand Distance Vector) and RPL (Routing Protocol for Low-Power and Lossy Networks) for comparison.

5.2 Comparison with Existing Routing Protocols

The proposed protocol was compared with existing routing protocols like AODV, DSR, and RPL. The results indicated that the proposed protocol consistently outperformed these traditional protocols in several key areas [23]:

- **Latency.** 35–50% reduction compared to AODV and RPL.
- **Energy efficiency.** 20–30% improvement in network lifetime.
- **Reliability.** Higher PDR, particularly in congested and high-mobility scenarios.
- **Security.** Enhanced protection with minimal performance degradation, outperforming protocols lacking built-in security mechanisms.

Mathematical Relationships:

- **Latency.** The proposed protocol reduces latency by 35–50%, mathematically represented as $L_{Proposed} = 0.5 \times L_{AODV}$ and $L_{Proposed} = 0.5 \times L_{RPL}$.
- **Energy Efficiency.** The proposed protocol improves energy efficiency by 20–30%, represented as $E_{Proposed} = 0.7 \times E_{AODV}$.
- **Reliability.** The proposed protocol provides higher reliability, particularly in congested scenarios, which is mathematically greater than the existing protocols, $R_{Proposed} > R_{AODV}$.
- **Security.** The proposed protocol enhances security with minimal performance degradation, surpassing protocols without built-in security mechanisms, $S_{Proposed} > S_{AODV}$.

The simulation findings indicate that the proposed procedure attains a 20–30% enhancement in energy efficiency compared to conventional protocols. The notable increase in network longevity and diminished energy consumption is ascribed to the MCDM framework's equitable strategy for optimising many criteria while maintaining energy conservation priorities (Table 1).

Table 1. Comparing the proposed protocol with other existing protocols in terms of key performance factors.

Protocol	Energy Efficiency	Security	Scalability	Adaptability to 6G Device Density
Proposed MCDM Protocol	High (adaptive to device power levels and conditions)	High (dynamic encryption, authentication with minimal latency impact)	High (effective in large IoT networks)	Excellent (optimized for dense 6G networks with adaptive resource allocation)
AODV (Ad hoc On-Demand Distance Vector)	Moderate (on-demand route establishment)	Low (basic without built-in security mechanisms)	Low (struggles with high-density networks)	Limited (not ideal for dense IoT environments)
RPL (Routing Protocol for Low-Power and Lossy Networks)	High (low-power routing suitable for IoT)	Low to Moderate (limited security options)	Moderate (scales but with potential for congestion)	Moderate (scales with limitations under high load)
DSR (Dynamic Source Routing)	Moderate (efficient for smaller networks)	Low (lacks robust security features)	Low (not suitable for highly dynamic IoT networks)	Limited (effective in smaller network clusters)

6 Future Directions and Enhancements

The suggested routing protocol is a major breakthrough for IoT communication on 6G networks. Nevertheless, there are still other areas that can be enhanced and future research prospects that can be explored [24, 25].

Integration with AI and Machine Learning Techniques
AI and ML techniques are essential for allowing intelligent routing, predictive network optimization, and self-healing in IoT ecosystems given the expected complexity of 6G networks. These methods improve the network's efficiency, robustness, and capacity to oversee extensive IoT deployments. This would allow the procedure to adjust more intelligently to changing situations:

6.1 Reinforcement Learning (RL) for Adaptive Routing

Through constant interaction with the network environment, the protocol "learns" the best routing routes in reinforcement learning. By optimizing for factors like energy efficiency, latency, and packet delivery ratio, RL algorithms can modify routing routes in response to past data and present network conditions. By using RL, for example, the protocol can learn to switch to low-latency routes during times of high demand and prefer energy-efficient routes when network traffic is low. This adaptive learning strategy improves overall network speed, extends device life, and lessens network congestion over time.

6.2 Deep Learning for Traffic Prediction and Anomaly Detection

Convolutional Neural Networks (CNNs) and Long Short-Term Memory (LSTM) networks are two examples of deep learning models that are used for traffic prediction and anomaly detection. These models are used to identify abnormalities in real time and anticipate traffic patterns. These models make it possible to manage network resources proactively by examining trends in data flows. CNNs and LSTMs, for example, are able to detect possible traffic bottlenecks, which enables the protocol to redirect data to less crowded routes.

6.3 Federated Learning for Privacy-Preserving Optimization

Federated learning prevents data privacy issues by training machine learning models across dispersed IoT devices. Federated learning allows every device to contribute to a collective model in 6G IoT networks, where data is frequently dispersed and sensitive. This maximizes network performance while protecting user privacy. Because each device only shares the model updates rather than the raw data, this strategy reduces bandwidth consumption and improves data security while enabling effective routing decisions.

6.4 AI-Driven Network Slicing for Resource Optimization

AI-powered network slicing allows the development of virtual network segments (such as low-latency, high-reliability, or high-security slices) devoted to particular categories of Internet of Things applications. AI-driven network slicing in 6G enables the protocol to dynamically distribute resources, guaranteeing that high-priority applications obtain the resources they need without interfering with other network operations.

6.5 Predictive Maintenance and Self-Healing Networks

Artificial intelligence (AI) systems, in particular supervised learning and predictive models, may examine network conditions and anticipate possible faults before they happen. For example, the protocol can proactively redirect data to reduce the risk of data loss by using machine learning models to detect indications of node deterioration or link instability. AI-enhanced self-healing capabilities allow the network to fix small issues on its own, increasing dependability and guaranteeing constant connectivity.

7 Conclusion

This study introduced a comprehensive decision-making routing system for IoT networks inside the framework of 6G. The protocol shown exceptional performance in terms of latency, energy efficiency, reliability, and security in several experimental circumstances. The success of the system was largely attributed to its capacity to flexibly adjust to fluctuating network conditions and prioritize various performance criteria. The suggested protocol is a substantial advancement in the field of IoT routing as it offers a strong, flexible, and secure solution specifically designed for the upcoming wireless networks. The use of Multiple Criteria Decision Making (MCDM) approaches allows for a more equitable and intelligent approach to decision-making, making it a prominent solution for IoT communication in the upcoming 6G era. The integration of artificial intelligence and machine learning, the strengthening of protocol capabilities for edge and fog computing, and the creation of environmentally friendly IoT methods should all be addressed in future research. In addition, the incorporation of quantum communication techniques and the exploration of new applications of 6G Internet of Things, such as autonomous systems and smart infrastructure, will open up new opportunities for innovation and growth in this sector.

References

1. Patil, S., Gokhale, P.: Multi-criteria approach for handling sophisticated data transmission over gateways in blockchain and Internet of Things (IoT) federated networks. Expert. Syst. **39**(10), e13127 (2022)
2. Si-Mohammed, S.: Multi-Criteria Selection and Configuration of IoT Network Technologies. Doctoral dissertation, École Normale Supérieure de Lyon (2023)
3. Haseeb, K., Rehman, A., Saba, T., Bahaj, S.A., Lloret, J.: Device-to-device (D2D) multi-criteria learning algorithm using secured sensors. Sensors **22**(6), 2115 (2022)
4. Gardas, B.B., Heidari, A., Navimipour, N.J., Unal, M.: A fuzzy-based method for objects selection in blockchain-enabled edge-IoT platforms using a hybrid multi-criteria decision-making model. Appl. Sci. **12**(17), 8906 (2022)
5. Bilen, T., Canberk, B., Sharma, V., Fahim, M., Duong, T.Q.: AI-driven aeronautical ad hoc networks for 6G wireless: challenges, opportunities, and the road ahead. Sensors **22**(10), 3731 (2022)
6. Kazmi, S.H.A., Qamar, F., Hassan, R., Nisar, K.: Routing-based interference mitigation in SDN enabled beyond 5G communication networks: a comprehensive survey. IEEE Access **11**, 4023–4041 (2023)
7. Baker, B., Woods, J., Reed, M.J., Afford, M.: A survey of short-range wireless communication for ultra-low-power embedded systems. J. Low Power Electron. Appl. **14**(2), 27 (2024)
8. Gkagkas, G., Vergados, D.J., Michalas, A., Dossis, M.: The Advantage of the 5G network for enhancing the internet of things and the evolution of the 6G network. Sensors **24**(8), 2455 (2024)
9. Balaram, A., Rao, T.S., Maguluri, L.P., Siddiqui, S.T., Gopatoti, A., Kuncha, P.: Managing 5G IOT network operations and safety using deep learning and attention methods. In: Wireless Personal Communications, pp.1–16 (2024)
10. Saeedi Taleghani, E., Maldonado Valencia, R.I., Sandoval Orozco, A.L., García Villalba, L.J.: Trust evaluation techniques for 6G networks: a comprehensive survey with fuzzy algorithm approach. Electronics **13**(15), 3013 (2024)

11. Andreou, A., Mavromoustakis, C.X.: 6G+ networks through enhanced efficiency and sustainability with MADDPG-driven network slicing in SoS environments. IEEE Trans. Green Commun. Netw. (2024)
12. Zahedy, N., Barekatain, B., Quintana, A.A.: RI-RPL: a new high-quality RPL-based routing protocol using Q-learning algorithm. J. Supercomput. **80**(6), 7691–7749 (2024)
13. Balaram, A., Rao, T.S., Rangaree, P., Siddiqui, S.T., Gopatoti, A., Maguluri, L.P.: Energy–efficient distribution of resources in cyber-physical internet of things with 5G/6G communication framework. In: Wireless Personal Communications, pp.1–20 (2024)
14. Kholidy, H.A.: Dynamic Network Slicing Orchestration in Open 5G Networks using Multi-Criteria Decision Making and Secure Federated Learning Techniques (2024)
15. Inzillo, V., Garompolo, D., Giglio, C.: Enhancing Smart City Connectivity: A Multi-Metric CNN-LSTM Beamforming Based Approach to Optimize Dynamic Source Routing in 6G Networks for MANETs and VANETs (2024)
16. Salim, A., Tiwari, R.K., Siddiqui, S.T., Tahir, A., Kamal, M.S., Sarfaraz, M.: Optimizing resource allocation for device to device communication in cellular networks. In: 2024 5th International Conference on Recent Trends in Computer Science and Technology (ICRTCST), pp. 642–647. IEEE (2024)
17. Tilwari, V., Song, T., Nandini, U., et al.: A multi-criteria aware integrated decision-making routing protocol for IoT communication toward 6G networks. Wireless Netw. **30**(1), 3321–3335 (2024)
18. Tilwari, V., Sharma, D., Solanki, S., Chakraborty, N., Maduranga, M.W.P.: A multicriteria aware multipath routing method to increase the QoS for future 6G networks. In: 2024 IEEE 13th International Conference on Communication Systems and Network Technologies (CSNT), pp. 1–6. IEEE (2024)
19. Khan, H.U., et al.: Multi-criteria decision-making methods for the evaluation of the social internet of things for the potential of defining human behaviors. Comput. Hum. Behav. **157**, 108230 (2024)
20. Kovtun, V., Grochla, K., Połys, K.: The concept of network resource control of a 5G cluster focused on the smart city's critical infrastructure needs. Alex. Eng. J. **94**, 248–256 (2024)
21. Nguyen, P.H., Pham, T.V., Nguyen, L.A.T., Narayanamoorthy, S., Nguyen, T.H.T., Vu, T.G.: Analysis of quantum computing's applicability in data analysis: utilizing a hybrid MCDM approach with quantum spherical fuzzy sets. IEEE Access (2024)
22. Azizi, S., Farzin, P., Shojafar, M., Rana, O.: A scalable and flexible platform for service placement in multi-fog and multi-cloud environments. J. Supercomput. **80**(1), 1109–1136 (2024)
23. Website. https://ieee-dataport.org/. Accessed 10 September 2024
24. Liwen, Z., Qamar, F., Liaqat, M., Hindia, M.N., Ariffin, K.A.Z.: Towards efficient 6G IoT networks: a perspective on resource optimization strategies, challenges, and future directions. IEEE Access (2024)
25. Majumdar, P., Mitra, S., Bhattacharya, D., Bhushan, B.: Enhancing sustainable 5G powered agriculture 4.0: summary of low power connectivity, internet of UAV things, AI solutions and research trends. In: Multimedia Tools and Applications, pp.1–45 (2024)

Integrating Cloud, Edge, and IoT

Ranjith Kumar Ramakrishnan[1](✉), Anjana Nayak[2], and Jai Jaswant Lekkala[3]

[1] N2 Services Inc., Jacksonville, USA
ranji1221@gmail.com
[2] Core BTS, Indianapolis, USA
[3] Page IT Solutions LLC, Ashburn, USA

Abstract. The Internet has transformed from a basic communication network to a universal platform for billions of users, paralleling the rapid development of Cloud computing, which offers scalable infrastructure and services. Advances in mobile connectivity and the Internet of Things (IoT) have facilitated continuous Web access, leading to the emergence of the Continuum of Computing. This paradigm envisions seamless integration of Cloud, Edge, and IoT, dynamically optimizing data processing and service delivery based on latency, privacy, and energy efficiency. This paper presents a reference architecture for the Continuum, demonstrates its feasibility through a proof-of-concept implementation, and discusses its potential for various applications. While challenges remain, the Continuum offers promising directions for pervasive, context-aware, and mobile services.

Keywords: Internet of Things · Continuum of Computing · Cloud Computing · IoT nodes

1 Introduction

The Internet has evolved from a basic communication tool for researchers into a global platform for billions, driven by advances in infrastructure such as Cloud computing and mobile connectivity. By 2028, over 5 billion people are expected to have 5G coverage, connecting a variety of devices, from consumer gadgets to industrial sensors [8, 12]. This proliferation of connected devices, or the Internet of Things (IoT), necessitates a decentralized and dynamic infrastructure. The Continuum concept envisions seamless integration between the Cloud and IoT, allowing data processing based on latency, privacy, and energy efficiency [3]. This approach fosters flexible, distributed computing tailored to dynamic scenarios, supported by pervasive service platforms that provide diverse services over the Internet.

Previous explorations of the Continuum concept include various architectures focused on data-driven applications [1] and the Serverless paradigm [23], yet they often overlook the needs of long-running industrial processes. To fill this gap, my approach employs open-source technologies to create a proof of concept that is application-agnostic, emphasizing data locality and computational mobility. This paper reviews related works (Sect. 4), presents a reference architecture (Sect. 5), and analyzes the problem space (Sect. 6). Our experiments with Kubernetes [25] and WebAssembly [15] align with the Continuum vision, highlighting the convergence of Cloud, Edge, and Web trends, while addressing challenges in adapting to modern Edge use cases (Fig. 1).

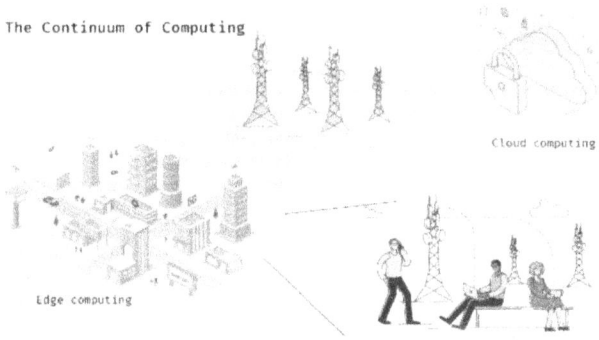

Fig. 1. Pictorial view of the Continuum of Computing comprising Edge and Cloud computing. The Edge of the network is where physical reality begins, in contrast with the Cloud where all is digital.

2 Environmental Impact and Sustainability

The integration of Cloud, Edge, and IoT computing enhances efficiency but also poses environmental challenges, including high energy consumption and carbon footprint. Cloud data centers require significant energy, while Edge computing minimizes this by processing data locally. IoT devices, designed for low power use, further support sustainability when integrated with Edge systems. To reduce environmental impact, energy-efficient hardware, renewable energy sources, and resource management strategies, including device reuse and recycling, are crucial for a more sustainable integration of these technologies.

3 Motivation for Integrating Cloud, Edge, and IoT

The integration of Cloud, Edge, and IoT addresses modern computing challenges by leveraging the strengths of each paradigm. Cloud computing offers scalable storage and computation, Edge reduces latency by processing data locally, and IoT devices generate real-time data. This combined architecture optimizes resource allocation, enhances performance, and supports applications ranging from real-time analytics to large-scale data processing, ensuring reduced latency and improved scalability in distributed environments.

4 Related Work

Recent advancements in WebAssembly (Wasm) and edge computing continue to drive innovation in distributed systems, especially in the context of IoT and the Continuum of Computing. While earlier research highlighted WebAssembly's potential for portability and security, recent studies from 2023 have begun to address critical issues such as performance optimization, memory management, and integration with multi-cloud environments.

A study by investigates the use of WebAssembly in multi-cloud ecosystems, emphasizing the efficiency gains in computational offloading, and improved deployment workflows for edge computing applications. Similarly, focuses on the scalability of Wasm-based microservices in distributed environments, proposing new techniques for service orchestration and dynamic scaling. These studies contribute to overcoming the initial performance limitations of Wasm in resource-constrained environments and offer valuable insights into how Wasm can be adapted for larger-scale applications.

Additionally, explores the use of Wasm for running machine learning models in decentralized cloud-edge systems, providing a detailed analysis of its challenges and benefits. They argue that while Wasm provides significant advantages in terms of security and portability, its lack of robust support for multi-threading and high-performance networking remains a limiting factor. These ongoing challenges are also discussed in the context of hybrid systems that combine cloud and edge resources, where Wasm can be used for lightweight computation tasks but needs further enhancement for high-demand applications such as deep learning or large-scale data processing.

These recent contributions indicate that while WebAssembly is progressing in terms of performance and integration, there remain significant challenges that need to be addressed for it to fully realize its potential in edge computing and the Continuum.

5 A System-Level View of the Continuum

5.1 Preamble

Highly distributed networks are the most effective architecture for the Continuum as services become more complex and bandwidth intensive. The Internet consists of various networks, requiring content generated at the Edge to traverse multiple networks and peering points before reaching the Cloud, as depicted in Fig. 2. Optimizing throughput across the entire communication path—from IoT devices to data centers and back to end users—is crucial. Edge processing alleviates network pressure and improves energy efficiency by offloading compute tasks from IoT sensors, but response time depends on compute and transmission latencies. Thus, Continuum computing must dynamically balance these latencies to ensure efficient data and computation movement based on resource availability.

5.2 Cluster Federation

Figure 3 illustrates a dynamic computation system where cluster nodes form cluster zones that federate resources and manage deployments. The infrastructure layer discovers and aggregates services while ensuring end-to-end QoS, dynamically scheduling based on application needs. Collaboration among zones supports user mobility, with the orchestrator provisioning resources across compute nodes, making the federation architecture a key area for ongoing research.

Fig. 2. Traceroute virtualisation of an IP packet reaching google.com. The left green nodes are the source nodes, while packets travel across to the extreme right to servers located in data centers. Source [19].

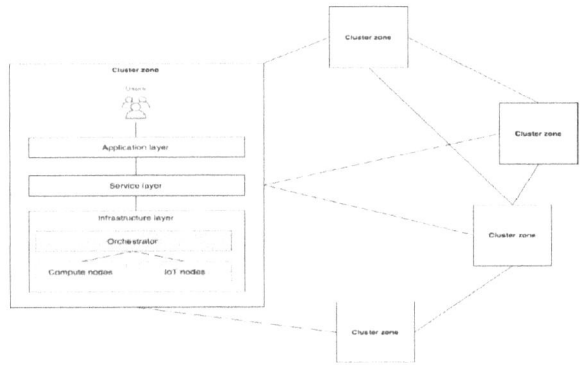

Fig. 3. A high-level view of a federated set of cluster nodes.

5.3 Infrastructure Layer Architecture

The infrastructure layer comprises a set of service providers that offer data and computation resources. The data can be generated by streaming IoT devices, for example cameras, smartwatches, and other data sources typical of "smart things" environments. The computation resources can be heterogeneous and distributed across the infrastructure, from the Cloud to the Edge.

Figure 4 portrays the reference architecture of the Continuum infrastructure I envision, whose elements I discuss next in this section.

Orchestrator Control Plane. The orchestrator control plane is the central component of the orchestration system, equipped with a resource monitor module that tracks real-time resource metrics for each compute node. The scheduler uses this information to optimize resource allocation, determining if there are enough resources to run submitted applications. If resources are insufficient, applications may be queued or rejected, or additional nodes can be provisioned from local or nearby machines. Once resources are confirmed, the scheduler maps application components to cluster resources based on requirements like latency and geographical constraints.

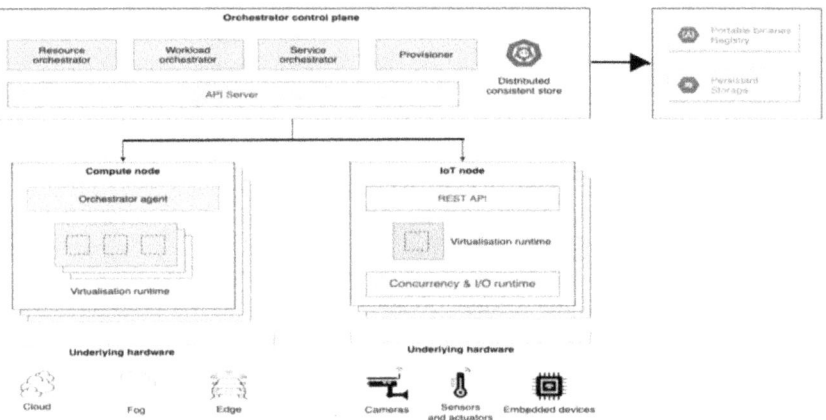

Fig. 4. Reference architecture for the infrastructure.

Compute Nodes. Each compute node in the cluster hosts services and applications, running an orchestrator agent that collects resource metrics, manages service instances via a virtualization runtime, and monitors deployments, reporting their status to the control plane. The virtualization runtime ensures a consistent execution platform across diverse hardware and software, allowing applications to operate uniformly despite the extreme heterogeneity of devices in the Continuum.

IoT Nodes. IoT nodes serve as heterogeneous embedded devices that operate as sensors or actuators within a cluster, communicating through brokers as detailed in Section 7.3. These devices enable dynamic configuration by running lightweight virtualization modules, which enhances interoperability among compute nodes.

Moreover, the IoT runtime must align with the application formats supported by compute nodes, as long as the target device can accommodate the necessary module size and hardware requirements. This expanded service interoperability facilitates greater flexibility in IoT computing, allowing for efficient control and preprocessing. By enabling the secure execution of arbitrary computations on microcontrollers, the embedded realm transitions from simply acting as data collectors and basic actuators to becoming intelligent computing platforms within the Continuum.

Underlying Infrastructure. One of the main requirements of the infrastructure architecture is to allow deployment on a large variety of platforms. The cluster machines can be either VMs on public or private Cloud infrastructures, physical machines on a cluster, or even mobile or Edge devices, among others.

Such extreme diversity requires rethinking mainstream virtualization technologies in a form that does not require the application programmer to have prior knowledge of the eventual execution contexts.

5.4 Use Case: Weather-Based Services

I applied the Continuum system design to weather-based services, utilizing IoT technologies for flood warnings, electrical load forecasting, and precision agriculture. Key weather attributes, such as temperature and air pressure, are critical for energy consumption insights from household sensors. I developed a Proof-of-Concept system, illustrated in Fig. 5, with sensor nodes transmitting data to an Edge cluster, enabling functionalities like levee monitoring and flood prediction. This approach underscores the advantages of the Continuum's distributed architecture over static Cloud-only or Edge-only solutions during flood threats.

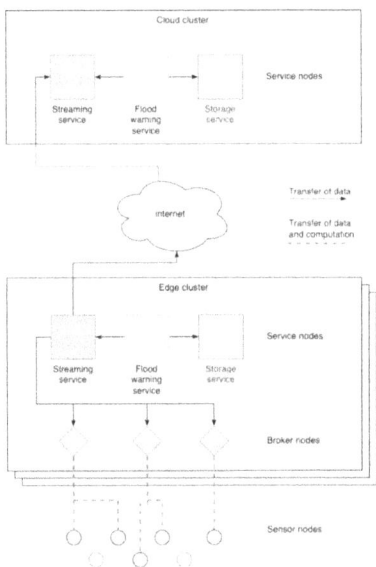

Fig. 5. Architecture for the flood warning system.

6 The Challenges Ahead

Several challenges need to be addressed in the realisation of the Continuum infrastructure. Besides featuring extreme heterogeneity, current Edge technology most notably lacks support for service orientation, interoperability, orchestration, reliability, efficiency, availability, and security. We now briefly discuss each problem in isolation, and propose a candidate technology for each of them, which are enumerated in Table 1.

Table 1. Preliminary overview of the challenges and candidate technologies. WebAssembly is a key enabling technology in my research.

Requirement/Challenge	Candidate Technology
Service orientation	RESTful web services, Open Service Broker, CoAP
Orchestration	Kubernetes, Akri
Virtualisation	WebAssembly
Dynamic configuration	WebAssembly
Interoperability	WebAssembly
Portability and Programmability	WebAssembly, Rust

Service Orientation. Service orientation is essential for organizing distributed capabilities across various ownership domains, where providers publish interfaces in a registry for consumer access, promoting loose coupling and independent functionality. However, challenges persist, including the lack of vendor-neutral service intermediaries, which hampers efficient retrieval and quality assurance due to overlooked interoperability. Furthermore, proprietary conventions complicate service composition and integration. Future services must enhance machine-to-machine communication and ensure context awareness at the Edge for effective local control and responsiveness to environmental events.

Orchestration. Transitioning to the Continuum requires effective orchestration to coordinate and schedule distributed service components, given the complexities of scale, heterogeneity, and resource diversity. Challenges include uncertainties in resource capacity, network failures, user access patterns, and service lifecycles, complicating the creation of pricing models. Orchestration must integrate technologies from various domains, necessitating effective mobility handover and service migration on local and global scales.

Virtualisation. Container-based virtualization has revolutionized how services are built, deployed, and managed by offering elastic scalability and lightweight resource usage. While containers enable efficient deployment on Cloud servers, their adaptation to Edge environments faces challenges. Current containerization incurs high memory overhead and latency, which is problematic for resource-constrained devices like Raspberry Pi [4, 20]. Furthermore, containers provide weak security isolation, often requiring virtual machines that are too resource-intensive for Edge nodes [5]. To support the Continuum, lightweight, secure isolation solutions for Edge devices are needed.

Dynamic Configuration. IoT nodes must quickly adapt to environmental changes for applications like video analysis at the edge of the Continuum. Dynamic configuration enhances accuracy and response time, but arbitrary code execution poses security risks. Existing isolation methods often fail in embedded systems, while interpreted languages can improve safety and balance isolation with efficiency.

Interoperability. Various technologies like ZigBee, 6LoWPAN, MQTT, and CoAP facilitate the integration of "things" into the Continuum, especially in wireless sensor networks and factory automation. Due to their diversity, a single standard cannot cover all technologies; thus, managing heterogeneity is essential. Service-oriented architectures enhance interoperability by encapsulating functionality in services with common interfaces, promoting flexibility and adaptability while ensuring resilience to future technological developments.

Portability and Programmability. In Cloud-native computing, users can select their programming language for containerization, provided the executable image includes all necessary libraries. These images share read-only components to minimize footprint. However, the variety of CPU architectures in the Continuum (e.g., x86 64, ARM32, ARM64, RISC-V) complicates application portability. Tools like Docker buildx enable architecture-specific images but do not simplify the configuration and building process for all target platforms.

7 Review of Candidate Technologies

7.1 Rationale for Using Open-Source Tools

To address the challenges in my Proof of Concept (PoC), I integrated various industry technologies, combining established tools with experimental ones. This approach enables a realistic evaluation of the current state of the art and highlights the organic trend toward the Continuum. Leveraging existing technologies also promotes acceptance and facilitates development.

7.2 Service Orientation

The web, recognized as a highly successful vendor-independent platform, predominantly follows the Representational State Transfer (REST) architecture [13], which organizes resources using URIs and facilitates communication via HTTP. Despite emerging protocols like CoAP (discussed in Sect. 7.2) and HTTP/3 (QUIC) [18], REST remains integral due to its adaptability and scalability, especially in IoT systems. Its abstraction of resources allows IoT nodes to function as servers, promoting interoperability, caching, and proxy functionality. Additionally, REST's uniform interface, employing methods like GET, PUT, POST, and DELETE, supports smooth communication and high-level interoperability across diverse services and protocols within the Continuum.

Open Service Broker. In my Proof of Concept (PoC), I developed a web-based service platform using the RESTful Open Service Broker (OSB) interface, enabling brokers to manage service catalogs and orchestrate resources across Clouds. While OSB (version 2.17) improves interoperability and handles service failures, it lacks support for service dependencies, leaving credential sharing and orchestration challenges to brokers (Figs. 6 and 7).

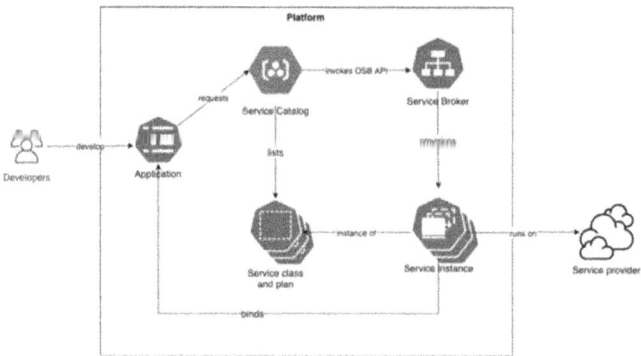

Fig. 6. The Open Service Broker architecture.

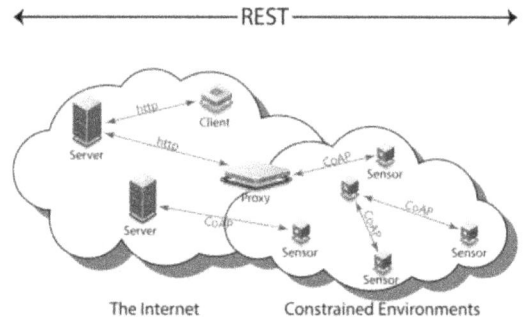

Fig. 7. The REST architecture enhanced with CoAP. Source [6].

CoAP. To integrate IoT nodes into my REST architecture, I used CoAP, a lightweight protocol optimized for constrained devices and lossy networks. Unlike HTTP, CoAP employs UDP for simplicity and retransmits lost packets. It supports resource discovery and has a RESTful design, enabling easy HTTP integration. By implementing a proxy pattern, I created intermediaries that translate between CoAP and HTTP, allowing seamless access to CoAP nodes and ensuring efficient interoperability within the Continuum.

7.3 Orchestration

Kubernetes [25], an open-source orchestration framework, is ideal for my PoC due to its flexibility and support for diverse container runtimes via the Container Runtime Interface (CRI). This enabled me to implement a uniform WebAssembly-based virtualization platform, while allowing Compute and IoT nodes to choose the most suitable runtime. Additionally, Kubernetes' extensive options for managing and scheduling Pods, including label-based constraints, enable improved latency by colocating services within the same availability zone. Unlike Docker Swarm [11], which lacks multitenancy support, Kubernetes provides essential multitenancy features for my platform (Fig. 8).

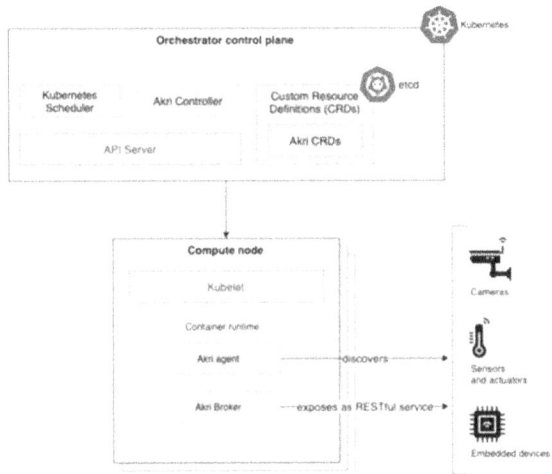

Fig. 8. The Akri architecture includes agents, controller, brokers, and configuration, with the configuration extending the Kubernetes API for communication protocols. The Akri agent discovers devices, monitors their state, and updates the controller.

Akri. To register IoT devices on the Kubernetes cluster, I used Akri [9], an open-source Microsoft project that allows Kubernetes to discover and interact with IoT devices. Akri dynamically detects available devices, enabling resource management as devices are added or removed. It deploys a broker Pod to abstract communication between applications and IoT devices via a RESTful API, improving scalability by caching sensor data and reducing latency. However, Akri's current limitations, such as its 1:1 node-device model and lack of advanced features like autoscaling and high availability, hinder scalability and resilience in IoT deployments, critical for achieving the Continuum.

7.4 Virtualisation, Interoperability and Portability

WebAssembly (Wasm) [15], released in 2017, provides strong memory isolation and near-native performance with a smaller footprint. It compiles higher-level languages like C++ or Rust [2] into portable binaries, ensuring consistent execution across environments. Wasm enables secure execution of untrusted modules, making it suitable for dynamic configurations in constrained devices. Despite a 10% performance drop compared to native execution, it is emerging as a lightweight alternative to containers in serverless computing [14, 16, 24].

Dynamic Configuration. WebAssembly enables code execution on constrained devices within the Continuum, as explored in [17, 22], which examine tradeoffs between processing efficiency and memory use. While Just-In-Time compilers like Wasmtime

[7] have potential, their complexity limits use on microcontrollers. WebAssembly interpreters, despite being over 10× slower than native.

C [26], allow dynamic updates and debugging. Its compatibility with multiple languages and CPU architectures makes it a lightweight alternative to heavier runtimes like JavaScript or Python, without requiring garbage collection. Figure 9 summarizes the key technologies in the Continuum architecture.

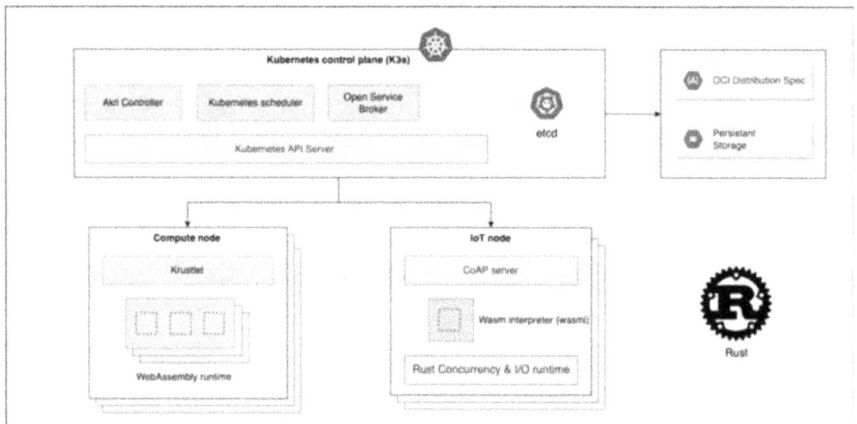

Fig. 9. Technology baseline for the reference infrastructure architecture.

8 Discussing the Fitness of WebAssembly for the Continuum

8.1 Rationale and Devices

This paper explores WebAssembly's potential in tackling key challenges of portability, virtualization, and computational mobility within the Continuum. I evaluate its viability as a portable binary format for computational services and an interpreter for embedded devices, ensuring secure execution with adequate performance. The evaluation is conducted in a Kubernetes cluster using a Just-In-Time Wasm compiler and Wasm container images following the Open Containers Initiative Artifacts specification. The study includes a weather-based flood warning system, tested on low-powered devices like Raspberry Pi 4 and STM32F407 microcontrollers, demonstrating the feasibility of these technologies in Edge and IoT environments.

8.2 Wasm for IoT Devices

Figure 10 compares the sizes of Wasm binaries compiled from Polybench [27] modules with a C dynamic library compiled using the LLVM toolchain, showing that Wasm binaries are significantly smaller. This size advantage is even more pronounced compared to container images, which, like Alpine Linux Mini Root Filesystem, add around 5.5MB uncompressed, unnecessary for IoT services. However, Fig. 11 highlights the substantial slowdown (100–400×) of the Wasm interpreter on STM32F407 microcontrollers compared to native Rust, posing challenges for dynamic reconfiguration, especially as C-based interpreters, though faster (30–60× slower), remain inefficient [21, 22]. The unpredictable heap overhead and Wasm's large 64KiB memory pages, unsuitable for microcontrollers with 16–256 KiB RAM, required modifying the interpreter to use 16KiB pages to fit the STM32F407's constraints (Fig. 11).

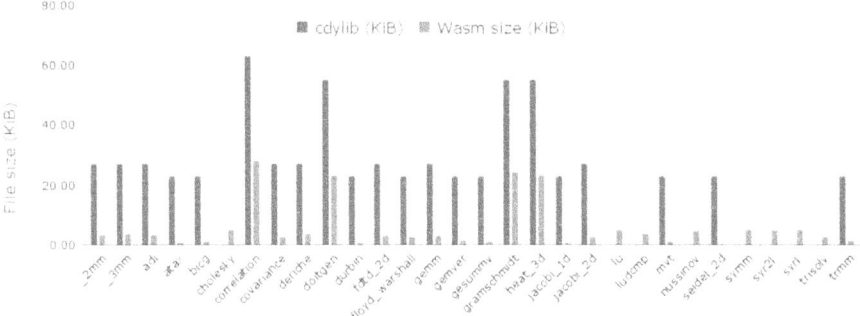

Fig. 10. Comparison of Wasm size (KiB) and C dynamic library size (KiB).

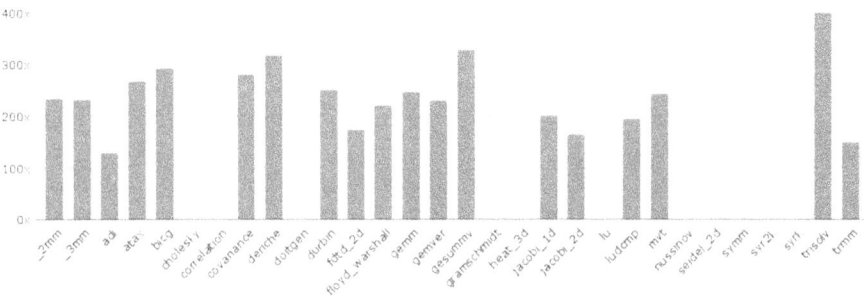

Fig. 11. Comparison of Wasm interpreter performance and Rust native performance.

8.3 Wasm on the Cloud

We integrated WebAssembly (Wasm) into Kubernetes using Krustlet for Wasm Pods and K3s for container Pods, demonstrating the potential of Wasm for the Continuum. However, current limitations in WebAssembly, particularly its insufficient network API and lack of multi-threading, make it unfit for resource-constrained platforms and compute mobility. For example, implementing a web server or running deep learning models via TensorFlow in Wasm is not feasible outside of web environments. Although Wasm shows promise, its immaturity in areas like memory management, networking, and concurrency poses significant challenges for real-world applications [10].

9 Scalability in the Proposed Architecture

Scalability is a key concern in the proposed architecture, which is designed to adapt to varying workloads and computational resources. The system incorporates a distributed model, enabling horizontal scaling by adding additional nodes as needed. Load balancing mechanisms are employed to ensure efficient resource utilization, minimizing bottlenecks. Auto-scaling is supported to dynamically allocate resources based on demand, optimizing performance during peak loads. To address potential scalability challenges, such as resource contention and latency, the system employs data partitioning and parallel processing techniques, ensuring high throughput and low latency even under heavy workloads. This approach ensures that the architecture can handle increasing demands while maintaining efficient operation.

10 Conclusion

This paper outlines a vision for a Continuum of Computing, where software resources are dynamically deployed based on proximity to computing devices, offering a seamless flow of computation across Cloud, Edge, and IoT environments. While the theoretical foundations for this vision are robust, it is crucial to highlight the practical applications that such a Continuum can enable. In real-world scenarios, the ability to dynamically allocate and migrate computing tasks across distributed environments offers substantial improvements in latency, energy efficiency, data locality, and privacy. These capabilities can revolutionize industries such as smart cities, autonomous transportation, healthcare, and environmental monitoring.

Despite the promising potential, there are significant technical and governance challenges to overcome, especially in areas like service orchestration, scalability, and standardization. WebAssembly, for example, offers an attractive solution for portability but still faces limitations in networking, concurrency, and multi-threading, particularly for resource constrained IoT devices. The continued development of standards and frameworks that support interoperability between Cloud, Edge, and IoT systems will be key to realizing the full potential of the Continuum.

Looking ahead, the practical integration of these technologies in real-world applications—coupled with advancements in hardware, network infrastructure, and sustainability practices—will determine the success of the Continuum in addressing modern computing needs. The vision for a flexible, responsive computing environment is no longer purely theoretical but becoming increasingly achievable as research and development continue to evolve.

References

1. AbdelBaky, M., Zou, M., Zamani, A.R., Renart, E., Diaz-Montes, J., Parashar, M.: Computing in the continuum: combining pervasive devices and services to support data-driven applications. In: 2017 IEEE 37th International Conference on Distributed Computing Systems (ICDCS), pp. 1815–1824. IEEE (2017). https://doi.org/10.1109/ICDCS.2017.323

2. AWS: Why aws loves rust and how we'd like to help (2020). https://aws.amazon.com/blogs/opensource/why-aws-loves-rust-and-how-wed-like-to-help/. Accessed 11 December 2022
3. Beckman, P., et al.: Harnessing the computing continuum for programming our world. In: Fog Computing: Theory and Practice, pp. 215–230 (2020). https://doi.org/10.1002/9781119551713.ch7
4. Bellavista, P., Zanni, A.: Feasibility of fog computing deployment based on Docker containerization over raspberrypi. In: Proceedings of the 18th International Conference on Distributed Computing and Networking, pp. 1–10 (2017). https://doi.org/10.1145/3007748.3007777
5. Bohm, S., Wirtz, G.: Profiling lightweight container platforms: Microk8s and k3s in comparison to kubernetes. In: ZEUS, pp. 65–73 (2021)
6. Bormann, C., Castellani, A.P., Shelby, Z.: Coap: an application protocol for billions of tiny internet nodes. IEEE Internet Comput. **16**(2), 62–67 (2012). https://doi.org/10.1109/MIC.2012.29
7. Bytecode Alliance: wasmtime (2021). https://github.com/bytecodealliance/wasmtime. Accessed 11 December 2022
8. Chen, B., Wan, J., Celesti, A., Li, D., Abbas, H., Zhang, Q.: Edge computing in IoT-based manufacturing. IEEE Commun. Mag. **56**(9), 103–109 (2018). https://doi.org/10.1109/MCOM.2018.1701231
9. Deis Labs: Akri (2021). https://github.com/deislabs/akri. Accessed 11 December 2022
10. Deislabs: wasi-experimental-http. https://github.com/deislabs/wasi-experimental-http (2022). Accessed 11 December 2022
11. Docker: Swarm mode overview (2021). https://docs.docker.com/engine/swarm/. Accessed 11 December 2022
12. Ericsson: Ericsson November 2022 Mobility Report (2022). https://www.ericsson.com/en/mobility-report. Accessed 11 December 2022
13. Fielding, R.: Representational State Transfer (Rest) (2000). https://www.ics.uci.edu/~fielding/pubs/dissertation/rest_arch_style.htm. Accessed 11 December 2022
14. Gadepalli, P.K., McBride, S., Peach, G., Cherkasova, L., Parmer, G.: Sledge: a serverless-first, light-weight wasm runtime for the edge. In: Proceedings of the 21st International Middleware Conference, pp. 265–279 (2020). https://doi.org/10.1145/3423211.3425680
15. Haas, A., et al.: Bringing the web up to speed with webassembly. In: Proceedings of the 38th ACM SIGPLAN Conference on Programming Language Design and Implementation, pp. 185–200 (2017)
16. Hall, A., Ramachandran, U.: An execution model for serverless functions at the edge. In: Proceedings of the International Conference on Internet of Things Design and Implementation, pp. 225–236 (2019). https://doi.org/10.1145/3302505.3310084
17. Jacobsson, M., Willen, J.: Virtual machine execution for wearables based on webassembly. In: Sugimoto, C., Farhadi, H., Hamalainen, M. (eds.) 13th EAI International Conference on Body Area Networks, pp. 381–389. Springer International Publishing, Cham (2020)
18. Langley, A., et al.: The quick transport protocol: design and internet-scale deployment. In: Proceedings of the Conference of the ACM Special Interest Group on Data Communication, pp. 183–196 (2017). https://doi.org/10.1145/3098822.3098842
19. dotcom monitor: Visual traceroute (2022). https://www.dotcom-monitor.com/wiki/knowledge-base/visual-traceroute-graphical-tool/. Accessed 11 December 2022
20. Pahl, C., Helmer, S., Miori, L., Sanin, J., Lee, B.: A container-based edge cloud paas architecture based on raspberry pi clusters. In: 2016 IEEE 4th International Conference on Future Internet of Things and Cloud Workshops (FiCloudW), pp. 117–124. IEEE (2016). https://doi.org/10.1109/W-FiCloud.2016.36
21. Parity: wasmi (2021). https://github.com/paritytech/wasmi. Accessed 11 December 2022

22. Peach, G., Pan, R., Wu, Z., Parmer, G., Haster, C., Cherkasova, L.: Ewasm: practical software fault isolation for reliable embedded devices. IEEE Trans. Comput. Aided Des. Integr. Circuits Syst. **39**(11), 3492–3505 (2020). https://doi.org/10.1109/TCAD.2020.3012647
23. Risco, S., Molto, G., Naranjo, D.M., Blanquer, I.: Serverless workflows for containerised applications in the cloud continuum. J. Grid Comput. **19**(3), 1–18 (2021). https://doi.org/10.1007/s10723-021-09570-2
24. Shillaker, S., Pietzuch, P.: Faasm: lightweight isolation for efficient stateful serverless computing. In: 2020 {USENIX} Annual Technical Conference, pp. 419–433 (2020)
25. The Linux Foundation: Kubernetes (2021). https://kubernetes.io/. Accessed 11 December 2022
26. wasm3: wasm3 performance (2021). https://github.com/wasm3/wasm3/blob/main/docs/Performance.md. Accessed 11 December 2022
27. Yuki, T.: Understanding polybench/c 3.2 kernels. In: International Workshop on Polyhedral Compilation Techniques (IMPACT), pp. 1–5 (2014)

// Development of IoT Smart Devices Graphical Interfaces, Platforms, Middleware and Security Management of Internet of Things Using Block-Chain and Multi Tenancy: Literature Review

Nuras Naser Saeed Hizam[1](✉), Madhukar Shelar[1], and Archana Bachhav[2]

[1] Commerce Management and Computer Science (CMCS) College, Nashik 422013, India
ph.d.nuras@gmail.com
[2] K.S.K.W. Arts, Science and Commerce College, Nashik 422008, India

Abstract. The Internet of Things (IoT) and network operating systems are rapidly developing to be the important technologies for data information technologies and networks administration of the coming generations in Internet. Smart cities, urban computing, ubiquitous healthcare, and tactile Internet are all examples of IoT deployment and uses. As a result, the architectural design of hybrid network structures has become more sophisticated, mandating effective and flexible management setup and stream control technologies. The IoT is continually seeking for innovative capabilities, that will maintain development of high-speed process. Data storage and flexibility of connecting the smart devices in the IoT network, as well more other modes of feature's evolution. This paper presents a systematic and comprehensive review of Graphical interfaces, platforms and middleware approaches, specifically suited for IoT networks, the literature been categorized into three sections: GUI Interface for IoT Network based studies, Security Management of Internet of Things using Blockchain and Multi-tenancy, Fog Computing architecture for IoT devices and blockchain data, which approach the challenges and open issues related to Interfaces Architecture for Internet of Things, Access Control, Multi Tenancy, Heterogeneous Platforms, real-time operations and Data Storage based Blockchain.

Keywords: IoT · Graphical Interfaces · blockchain · Multi-tenancy · Security Management · Fog Computing

1 Introduction

The Internet of Things (IoT) empowers both humans and machines to gain knowledge and engage with millions of items, including actuators, sensing equipment, solutions, and other devices with Internet connectivity. The implementation of IoT technologies will lead to effortless consolidation of the cyber-world with the real world, drastically affecting and empowering human interaction with the rest of the globe. The expansion and development of the IoT environments which make it as the new pioneer in the communication and the network technology that has facilitated intelligent services in daily life routine. Users are unable to utilize device services effectively and accurately due to different device services produced by numerous devices with different settings. This substantially impedes the growth of Internet of Things, and most of works, papers and modules in the Internet of Things (IoT) filed delivered to facilitate and optimize the IoT administration procedure and give a crucial solution for the difficulties in the standard Internet of Things structure to forward, archive, and protect data gathered from IoT components. Many efforts, researches, and publications have been made, with many of them focusing on how electronic devices are developed, constructed, and programmed. These efforts have led in hardware boards that work in electronic block modules that provide an opportunity for everyone to combine different components and build their own smart devices. These modules inspire creativity, empowering users to design and assemble personalized electronic projects. [1, 2] project, which show the modules of the blocked electronics that could be used by different categories of people, either inventors, designers, or creators, with no difference between those people in the experience in this filed which they can be either beginners or expert. Recent researches have taken a position between electronic devices with big amount of modification and configuration IoT applications, as well as including public users in designing and producing of such projects, as investigated by [3]. Where [1] In their published paper, they emphasized that developing a smart and flexible IoT application relies on the involvement of public users in the design process. However, since many users lack the technical expertise required to use advanced programming tools and development concepts, there is a need for an accessible programming method. This would allow users to interact with and control remote connected devices on the Internet effectively. The Paper [4] defined two types of IoT structures. The first category is Things-centric structure, which shows the gadget aspects to provide more detailed and rich user experience. The second category of the two structures is cloud-centric, which focuses on IoT solutions and information process. Conflicting actuator settings, are another problem when implementing multi-tenancy across IoT components. Tenants must be capable to connect with and configure IoT devices based on their unique needs if multi-tenancy is supported.

2 Literature Review

The adoption of fog computing has made it possible to bring various Internet of Things (IoT) functions closer to IoT devices, enhancing their efficiency and performance. A strategy to manage the virtualization concerns that occurred as a result of relocating computation near to the IoT. "Things" layer is required. There are many studies which carried out in the field of IoT precisely in the Interface and virtualization to IoT and as Well in Multi Tenancy and Blockchain. This Review Paper presents Virtual Resources as the primary method for enabling deeper interactions and for accessing IoT components by multi-tenants to deal with the dynamic environment of IoT networks, Virtual resources are required to address the dynamic features of IoT networks, such as different platforms and an enormous number of electronic gadgets, Real-time operations, Limited computational Capabilities. To address the aforementioned challenges this section, review important literatures regarding the following

2.1 Design of Graphical User Interfaces, Platforms and Middleware for IoT Devices Network.
2.2 Security Management of Internet of Things Using Blockchain and Multi-tenancy.
2.3 Fog Computing Architecture for IoT devices and Blockchain Data

2.1 Design of Graphical User Interfaces Platforms and Middleware for IoT Devices Network

Background

Heterogeneous devices operations provided by numerous gadgets in various environments making it difficult for users to utilize device services effectively and properly. This significantly slows the growth of the Internet of Things. In regard to the GUI interface designed Web technologies have been demonstrated to be flexible, and Cloud-based service delivery is gradually increasing to gain popularity in commercial, and industrial applications. Furthermore, researchers have developed systems and applications that leverage Web technologies like HTTP, RESTful Web services, and CoAP for collecting and analyzing valuable data. This approach improves the accessibility of real-world sensory data by making it available as web resources. This section discuss and provides an extensive comprehensive review for the design of graphical user interfaces, IoT platforms and middleware for IoT networks, it explores the used tools, techniques and various approaches, are being created and utilize to enhance the management and monitoring of IoT smart devices in IoT network.

2.1.1 IoT Graphical User Interface

A graphical user interface (GUI) is a graphical feature method to communicate with computers, smart devices, smart phones and so on of electronic devices, which includes screens, pages, buttons, windows, and icons. Thus, humans didn't have to learn sophisticated command languages to communicate with computers and other electronic devices, making the computer and all electronic devices easier to make accessible to everyone. In IoT interfaces, it is essential for users to comprehend how data is obtained from IoT devices. This can be achieved through automated notifications, proactive information tracking, or remotely system administration. To meet this goal, the design of an IoT interface must take into account whether the user interacts personally with the smart device or whether the data from these devices is accessed and managed remotely. For such object many studies and researches developed for GUI. Among those who have contributed to this work Park, J. et al. [5] who developed an IoT information content library system for designers, manufacturers, programmers, and others. The database in that platform consisted of several kinds of IoT data, including hardware, software, typical data, and a products gallery. The suggested platform uses web services to provide sufficient knowledge to various users such as product designers, makers, developers, and engineers. The platform consists of four main operational modules: a front-end user interface, data filtering and processing, a data collector, and an information database. The front-end interface is designed as a graphical user interface accessed through a web browser, developed using HTML and JavaScript with frameworks such as Angular.js and Node.js. As well as [6] provided smart house ideas in their paper. Home appliances may be controlled using a variety of techniques, including user interface platform and web technologies. The designed home automation system enables intelligent management and monitoring of household appliances through the integration of various technologies, including internet connectivity, electrical switches, and a graphical user interface (GUI). This IoT-driven smart home solution is particularly built using a combination of programming and electronic components, notably the Raspberry Pi 2 Model B board and the Arduino Mega 2560 board. GUI interfaces between Arduino and a 2.4-inch touch screen have been built. Such system used to control and perform multiple tasks on a large number of appliances by utilizing the GUI interface technology on the 2.4 inch display, as well as client user page can be built and created in bootstrap using Java, Hypertext Markup Language (HTML), hypertext pre-processor PHP, and the Cascading Style Sheets (CSS).

Nguyen, Chau, and Doan Hoang [7], a study introduced the concept of software-defined IoT units through the development of Software-Defined IoT Cloud Systems. This novel approach to IoT cloud computing packages detailed IoT resources and functionalities into well-structured APIs. The aim is to enhance user experience by simplifying the processes of utilizing, accessing, modifying, and managing IoT cloud systems). The system's presentation layer provides user interaction through a web-based interface, it introduces a software-defined virtual sensor (SDVS) that allows IoT devices to be programmable based on the needs of specific IoT applications. It outlines SDVS's structure and deployment, demonstrating how to utilize it in situations where on-demand IoT services are needed.

In [8] The paper introduces an innovative approach centred on Business Process Modelling to create an intuitive, Do-It-Yourself (DIY) interface that enables users, regardless of programming expertise, to easily design their own IoT applications. In order to effectively link several devices, the structure was created as a working model using the Constrained Application Protocol (CoAP). A project has been developed employing MQTT, and CoAP to enable device integration and real-time interaction. These protocols facilitate the operation of real-time data stream networks, enabling data stream mashups and the addition of actions. The input and output in the interface create services objects which is stored in XML file which represents the virtual objects. The Californium framework is utilized to implement CoAP services for interacting with remote IoT resources that are part of a task.

2.1.2 IoT Platforms

The Internet of Things (IoT) focuses on communicating and linking objects remotely to ensure optimal performance and simplicity of use. An IoT platform connects devices sensors with data networks. It offers visibility into the data used by the backend part of the application. An IoT platform is a collection of technologies that enable programmers to distribute programmes, remotely gather data, communicate securely, and perform sensors monitoring.

Lee, H. et al. [9] proposed the (OPEL FRAMEWORK), an accessible Internet of Things platform that uses a JavaScript API set to provide clients the ability to utilize a variety of functionalities. By making it easier to couple different IoT devices, this application platform enables them to be joined and controlled by mobile devices like smartphones. The application software framework was developed using the JavaScript (JS) programming language and built on the Node.js runtime framework. This platform offers high-level APIs to manage and facilitate communication between devices and sensors. Additionally, it incorporates the OPEL Core Framework (OCF), an out-of-process server developed in C/C++ that supports multiple services. To ensure seamless integration between the JS environment, APIs, and OCF, the system primarily utilizes a Native Interface Layer (NIL).

In another study prepared by Ahmad, S. et al. [1] which attempt to carry same idea of developing a platform which links the data of most connected sensors to the web and create their own applications on top of it. Pachube is an open-source project that allows programmers to connect sensor data to the Web as well, it is a web-based service that aggregates the flow of data in order to gather and maintain data from numerous sensing devices and the generated data eventually in many different times. As well, it employs "triggers" which means the incoming data from either hardware of software resources and then send it to URL based on some rules in order to process, integrate, and visualize data in certain types of tools.

Bhawiyuga, A. et al. [11] developed a proposal for an IoT-cloud computing integration platform. The suggested IoT-cloud platform is an architecture for IoT and cloud computing integration is classified into four major components, Cloud-to-Device interface: a messaging protocol known as RESTful HTTP is being used. Authentication: Token-based authentication using JSON Web Token. Data Management: Using MongoDB, a NoSQL DBMS. Cloud-to-User Interface: RESTful web service-based Application Programming Interface (API). Among the entire cloud-based computing architecture and its particular IoT device part, the cloud-to-device interface often operates as a data transmission destination.

Same as well in an article prepared by Ullah, I. et al. [12] describes an architecture and the design of IoT activities and internet-based object administration in a heterogeneous things network to streamline administration operations, as well as the implementation of solution and internet-based object administration Systems Prototype in Visual Studio 2015 C#, are addressed. The CoAP.NET library is utilized to interact to IoT tools linked to the Intel Edison Board. Microsoft SQL Server store each configuration of the IoT operations in exclusive data profile. The proposed system employs OMNeT++ simulation to investigate the impact of IoT network size on critical performance metrics, including response time, and packet delivery ratio. This approach allows for a detailed analysis of how network scale affects the efficiency and reliability of IoT systems.

García, C.G. et al. [13] The study introduces a graphical Domain-Specific Language (DSL) called the Medgar Object Creation Specific Language (MOCSL), designed to assist users without programming experience in creating diverse and heterogeneous tasks. This DSL is aimed at individuals with an interest in IoT or DIY projects who wish to design and implement IoT applications. Users only need basic knowledge of their smartphone brand and/or an Arduino platform, along with an understanding of how to connect sensors and actuators to the Arduino. An IoT server is also required to upload and store the data, which can be configured as either public or private based on the system's needs. The researchers developed MOCSL to simplify object design in a user-friendly, efficient manner. The focus of the study was on creating graphical editors for developing

Android and Arduino applications, with tools such as AppsGeyser, iBuildApp, and Andromo being highlighted. Once MOCSL generates a local application containing user-defined content and smart components, the resulting application can serve as the user's smartphone source code or generate all necessary C and Java code for Arduino projects.

2.1.3 IoT Middleware

To provide the perfect services and functionalities for demonstrating high quality interaction among various IoT devices platforms and Interfaces applications the middleware is the software which acts as the kind of glue that links all the different elements of an IoT system enabling all of them to operate effectively. [14] is a paper titled IoT Middleware: A Survey on challenges and concerns of the supportive Technologies, the author Employed an application for the Internet of Things, a survey prepared on the distinctive characteristics of current IoT middleware, then suggested the necessity for an IoT middleware. The research addressed several major IoT middleware structures such as: heavy-weight service-based structure, lightweight actor-based structure, and consumer-centric cloud-based structure; 1) Heavy-weight service-based architectures: enables designers or users to install or deploy a variety of IoT devices as services by utilizing the Service Oriented Architecture (SOA); 2) Cloud-based architectures: controls the form and amount of internet of things (IoT) devices which may install and set up by users, but rather it enables them to interact, gather, and analyze data. 3) Light-weight actor-based architectures: Open, plug-and-play IoT architecture is emphasized in this framework. A wide range of Internet of Things devices can be exposed as reusable actors and dispersed across the network. It has identified four major obstacles in designing IoT middleware: 1) a lightweight middleware platform that can be used on desktop PCs, cloud computing environments, and IoT devices with less power to offer comparable solutions; 2) an application-neutral composing engine that is user-friendly; 3) an authentication system which can be used in a setting with limited resources and nevertheless offer the same level of optimism as Internet security; 4) An IoT device/service discovery system based on semantics that extends beyond IP address and domain discovery.

Sen, A. et al. [15] The article explores the implementation of the Missouri S&T sensor cloud, a system designed to enable the deployment of sensor networks over large geographic areas, allowing them to function as an integrated system for delivering sensing services. The proposed framework for the sensor cloud is structured into three distinct layers: client-centric, middleware-centric, and sensor-centric, each serving a specific role in the overall system architecture. The client-centric level functions as the intermediary between the sensor cloud and its users. This tier includes various components designed to enhance and regulate user interactions with the sensors embedded in the cloud. It features modules such as the User Interface for user engagement, Session Management for tracking user sessions, Membership Management for handling access permissions, and User Repository for storing user information. User Interface is a graphical user interface built with HTML5, CSS3, and Angular. Session administration is used to control the web sessions of users with the assistant of a user database, Membership Management manages user authentication and authorization. Integrating requests from clients with data collected by physical sensors, the middleware layer serves as a bridge between the client-centric and sensor-centric.

In Paper number [16] the development of a middleware based on M2M (Machine-to-Machine) technology facilitates autonomous interactions between heterogeneous platforms by utilizing semantic web technologies through a web client management interface. In order to facilitate effective interaction across many protocols, the M2M standard architecture enables a wide range of protocol connections, which implies HTTP, CoAP, MQTT, and WebSocket. Integrated devices, a web user, middleware, and an IoT server make up the suggested architecture. The IoT server is constructed on the open-source Mobius platform, which was created by OCEAN, and runs on a desktop Linux computer. It includes essential elements including the modules for Service Management (SM), Device Management (OI), Device Monitoring (DM), Resource Registration (RR), and Communication Interface (CI). The OI module integrates devices into the server once the RR module identifies devices as M2M resources. The CI module facilitates interaction using protocols such as HTTP, CoAP, and MQTT. The DM and SM modules continuously track device and service states, allowing for on-the-fly reconfiguration. Middleware, built in the Eclipse development environment and deployed on a Raspberry Pi 3b+, facilitates interaction between the IoT server and connected devices.

Alam, I. et al. [17], the paper presents a thorough and organized evaluation of virtualization techniques specifically designed for IoT networks. These strategies are categorized in the literature into two main types: software-defined networks tailored for IoT, and software-defined networking (SDN) frameworks created with IoT in mind. In the IoT environment, a virtualized access concept can give solutions such as: Architecture Solutions, Management Solutions, Network function virtualization for (NFV) IoT Network and security solutions. SDIoT (Software-defined IoT networks) solutions extend The Software-Defined (SD) approach integrates data from network devices, sensors, and cloud platforms, emphasizing three critical areas: *Architectural Solutions*: These architectures utilize multiple controllers to deliver diverse services, prioritizing both traffic flow management and comprehensive data aggregation. *Management Solutions:* This area focuses on optimizing cloud resources, managing clusters of IoT devices, and supporting mobility. It includes SDIoT cloud management, middleware integration, data handling, and the orchestration of virtual service chains to enhance system efficiency. *Security Solutions:* These address external threats through advanced security mechanisms, such as detecting anomalous packet flows, securing metadata and payloads across layers, maintaining the accuracy of information and verification, protecting privacy and secrecy, and putting dispersed protection into practice policies, and proactively identifying and neutralizing attacks.

2.2 Security Management of Internet of Things Using Blockchain and Multi-tenancy

Background

With the rapid growth in data quantities and the expansion of IoT device connectivity, modern smart network architectures face significant challenges. These include latency, bandwidth constraints, security vulnerabilities, privacy concerns, and difficulties in scaling efficiently. To address these issues, a shift towards a more efficient, secure, and scalable distributed architecture is essential. This can be achieved by decentralizing and relocating computing and storage components near to the network's edge, which will reduce latency, enhance security, and improve overall network performance (Fig. 1).

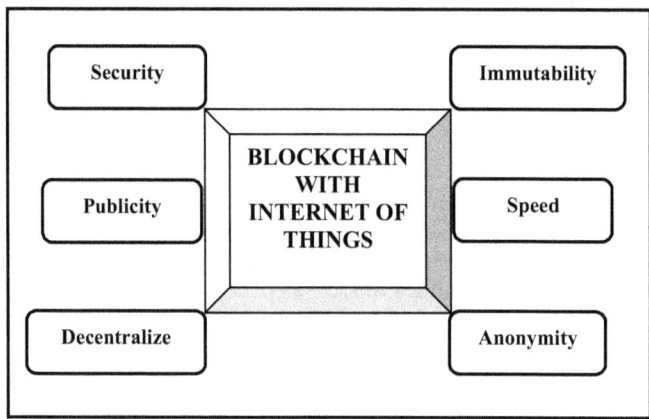

Fig. 1. Blockchain with Internet of Things Advantages

This section discuss the architecture of IoT access control using blockchain, security features of blockchain for IoT and IoT network challenges such as latency, scalability, security using blockchain, as well as the section focused on multi-tenancy for IoT network and multi-tenancy challenges in IoT network.

2.2.1 Blockchain Technology Used as an Internet of Things Security Management

Blockchain technology can significantly enhance the security of the Internet of Things (IoT) by providing a decentralized, transparent, and immutable system for managing data. A blockchain is made up of a series of blocks of data, every block which has many operations that maintain activities and guarantee data security. By utilizing blockchain's inherent features such as tamper-proof records and secure consensus mechanisms, it can effectively address many of the security challenges, advantages and disadvantage in IoT [18], including data integrity, unauthorized access, and trust issues among devices. Blockchain integrates cybersecurity protocols, assurance services, and industry best practices to mitigate potential risks (Table 1).

The appropriate networks are used for the blockchain vary in terms of participant access and data visibility. These networks are typically categorized as public or private, which defines who is allowed to join, and permissioned or permissionless, which determines the methods by which participants can access and interact with the network. Blockchain technology offers several key features, including decentralization, immutability, and rapid transaction processing, with validation and confirmation. Starting with the study in [17] an overview of the problems and difficulties with protection of the blockchain. Introduces features of the blockchain comprises in 5 sections: 1) The Concept of Blockchain: the key elements of the blockchain (Decentralized, open source,

Table 1. Variation between IoT and Blockchain [18].

	IoT Technology	Blockchain Technology
1	Centralized	Decentralized
2	Requires Low Latency	Time-Consuming for Block Mining.
3	Devices in the Internet of Things are Expected to be Vast.	Scalability with Vast network is Low
4	IoT Devices Have Constrained Bandwidth and Resources.	Excessive Bandwidth Usage
5	One of the Major Challenges with IoT is Security.	Recently Has developed Security
6	Limited by Resources	Consuming Resources

transparent, autonomous, unchangeable, and anonymous. 2) Types of blockchain: Public blockchain, Consortium blockchain, Private blockchain. 3) The Structure of Blockchain (Main Data, Hash, Timestamp). 4) Application of Blockchain: (Digital Currency (Bitcoin), Smart Contract (Ethereum), Hyperledger, Traceability in Supply chain, Insurance, International Payment, Medical Treatment, Prediction Market). 5) Security Issues (1. The Majority Attack 51% Attack (A Block depends on the work done by CPU/GPU Cycles spent checking hashes, 2. Fork Problems (Hard fork, soft fork), 5) Challenges: 1. Scale of Blockchain (Simplified Payment Verification (SPV)), 2. Time Confirmation of Blockchain Data, 3. Current Regulations Problems, 4. Integrated Cost Problem.

The paper by Liu, Y. et al. [19] presents an IoT access management framework that is potential driven and uses autonomous identifying information and blockchain technologies to regulate IoT device authentication and accessibility. The approach is designed to improve the security and efficiency of access management in IoT ecosystems. The paper outlines a protocol that provides a comprehensive view of system interactions, strengthens security, and establishes a capability-based access control framework for IoT devices. This framework employs blockchain technology and decentralized identifiers (DIDs) to effectively manage IoT device identification and access control. All architectural components are provided as Application Programming Interfaces (APIs), enabling straightforward integration into application development. The paper describes an extensive system interaction protocol for capability-based IoT access control that leverages blockchain technology. This approach is showcased through a proof-of-concept prototype and tested using a real-world use case. The evaluation results demonstrate that the proposed solution is secure, scalable, and effective.

Another review paper on Blockchain Security [20] which overview the following: 1) Key Attributes of the blockchain. A) *Decentralization*: A key feature of blockchain that enhances security and flexibility by distributing control across a network of nodes. B) *Trust*: Blockchain employs a robust authentication mechanism to verify the integrity and authenticity of transactions. C) *Transparency*: Blockchain technology ensures that data recorded on it is transparent and immutable, meaning all transactions are visible to participants and cannot be modified once they are added to the ledger. 2) Types of

Blockchain A) A public blockchain is a decentralized system that allows open read access to all participants. While it offers a high level of immutability, making tampering extremely difficult or virtually impossible, it tends to have lower efficiency due to its decentralized nature and the consensus mechanisms involved. B) Private: it is decentralized blockchain which could have a public or restricted read permission and it could be tampered where it has a high efficiency. 3) Challenges in Blockchain, to address scalability issues in blockchain, several strategies should be considered: a) Storage Optimization: Implementing techniques to efficiently manage and reduce the data stored on the blockchain. b) Blockchain Redesign: Revising the blockchain architecture to enhance scalability and performance. c) Privacy Protection: To prevent privacy leakage, employ robust encryption methods for public and private keys, and protect against attacks such as Man-in-the-Middle (MITM) and Distributed Denial of Service (DDoS) attacks. Continuous monitoring and response mechanisms should be in place to detect and mitigate potential threats. Security Features of Blockchain: a) User Ledger: The ledger is immutable, ensuring that all transactions are permanently recorded and cannot be altered. b) Chain of Blocks: Each block in the blockchain contains a unique hash value and is linked to the previous block through its hash, maintaining the integrity of the chain. c) Decentralized Applications: Blockchain supports peer-to-peer communication, where each node (or computer) in the network validates transactions. If any node rejects a transaction, it cannot proceed, ensuring consensus and authenticity; 4) Applications of Blockchain: IoT, health care industry, electronic medical records, Bitcoin, finance, banking.

Singh, C. et al. [21], the proposed hybrid network architecture for smart cities integrates Software-Defined Networking (SDN) with blockchain technology. This architecture divides the smart city network into two primary categories, optimizing both management and security within the urban environment. The primary network and the secondary network (the network – using the blockchain process). For security capabilities, the FS-Open Security SDN paradigm is being used. The main network is made up of nodes with high counts and end-to-end resources, whereas edge nodes have limited storage space and processing power. Each edge node serves as a central server for a specific public infrastructure, providing critical services and local implementation. To resolve several concerns with cryptocurrency and blockchain, a complicated PoW method known as "Itsuku PoW" is implemented to the suggested approach to assure security and privacy, as well as to prevent attackers from tampering with information.

Sharma, P.K. et al. [22] present a distributed cloud architecture that combines blockchain, Software-Defined Networking (SDN), and fog computing to classify and analyze IoT data at both the network edge and distributed cloud levels. The proposed framework is structured into three layers: device, fog, and cloud. This design aims to manage raw data generated by IoT devices and facilitate data offloading to the distributed cloud. The authors evaluate the system's effectiveness in detecting and recognizing attacks that affect blockchain integrity using two key parameters within the SDN-controlled fog nodes at the edge network. The architecture includes two distinct models: Distributed Blockchain Cloud Architecture: This model emphasizes the management and transmission of raw data across the three layers, governed by the SDN controller. As a result of utilizing distributed processing and storage, it facilitates evaluation of analyzes, continuously in identification modes and massive detection operations. Key functions include: Resource provider selection by cloud users, Service provision, Blockchain transaction registration and sharing. Payment and recognition of the service provider. Edge Network Architecture: This model incorporates fog computing to facilitate communication between fog nodes, acting either as gateways or forwarding SDN switches for the fog controller. It focuses on monitoring OpenFlow messages, packet flow activities, and behavior through various security policies. Specific components include: Packet Parser, Flow Topology Graph Builder, Verifier, Migration Agent. This comprehensive approach enhances both data management and security across the smart city network.

Ngabo, D. et al. [23] explore solutions for managing challenges in IoT networks, such as latency, security, scalability, and centralization, within a fog computing framework. Their study proposes using a public-permissioned blockchain with Elliptic Curve Cryptography (ECC) digital signatures for hashing to secure medical data at the fog layer of the IoT network. In this model, file access requests are encrypted and accompanied by a certificate to authorize user access. The study employs a public-permissioned blockchain that operates on two key concepts: Open Ledger Belief (OLB): This system allows for participation from all network nodes in operations and activities, validating hashed blockchain data using public key encryption within the algorithm. Decentralized Ledger Cryptogram (DLC): This protocol supports the management of operations and archival modifications without relying on a central authority. The DLC database uses timestamps and unique identity verification to ensure that records remain immutable across the blockchain.

2.2.2 Multi-Tenancy

Multi-tenancy refers to the architecture where a single instance of software operates on a server to serve multiple tenants. Tenants, which may be businesses or individual users, share the same infrastructure, resources, and databases, yet each maintains a secure and virtualized application instance. This model allows providers to efficiently deploy updates, optimize resource usage, and scale services as needed. By centralizing management and pooling resources, multi-tenancy reduces operational costs and enhances overall efficiency. Despite sharing the underlying infrastructure, each tenant experiences an isolated environment, similar to that of a single-tenant system. A multi-tenant IoT infrastructure presents considerable advantages to the process of controlling and deploying IoT applications as well as gadgets across industries. It delivers a centralised and scalable services that allows different users, such as enterprises or various individuals, to use an integrated environment for their IoT requirements.

Many studies discussed the use of multi-tenancy in IoT environment such as Ashalatha R. et al. [24] address several multi-tenancy challenges, including resource sharing, security, and isolation, that must be managed in cloud environments to ensure optimal performance for cloud consumers. In this context, a tenant refers to an entity or user who owns or provides data for a Software as a Service (SaaS) application. The multi-tenancy model offers significant benefits to both cloud providers and users. The paper provides a detailed overview of the cloud computing service layers: 1) Infrastructure as a Service

(IaaS): This layer provides essential computing resources, including processing power, storage, and networking, enabling the deployment and management of software applications on demand. 2) Software as a Service (SaaS): This model delivers software applications and their associated functions over the internet, allowing users to access software without local installation. 3) Platform as a Service (PaaS): This layer offers middleware services, such as security, user management, and distributed processing, while providing a comprehensive platform for developing and deploying applications. Additionally, the article explores the characteristics of shared multi-tenancy in cloud environments and SaaS multi-tenancy. It categorizes the different levels of multi-tenancy such as: 1) Physical Level Multi-Tenancy, 2) Hypervisor Level Multi-Tenancy, 3) Operating System Level Multi-Tenancy, 4) Platform Level Multi-Tenancy.

In paper [25], a platform architecture is proposed where each tenant operates with an individual blockchain, with all tenant chains periodically linked to a public blockchain. This design utilizes a Merkle tree structure to manage large datasets, where each leaf node represents the root of a tenant's blockchain. This approach ensures that the integrity of each permissioned blockchain can be publicly verified by periodically establishing its state on the public blockchain. The system employs smart contracts to maintain data confidentiality and privacy for both tenant-specific and public blockchains. The platform owner has access to all on-chain data across tenants and provides APIs for interacting with tenant blockchains. The architecture incorporates the Lorikeet tool for automatic smart contract generation. Smart contracts are written using the Solidity compiler and are tested with the Truffle framework. The trigger and anchoring components are developed in TypeScript with Node.js, using the Express.js server to implement REST APIs.

Ahmad, S. et al. [26] utilized the INET Framework version 3.6 to evaluate the performance of a proposed system for client-server and Internet of Things (IoT) networks using the OMNeT++ 5.2 simulator. Their proposed architecture facilitates the sharing of virtual objects across different networks by allowing client applications to interface solely with a centralized controller to configure network settings. The architecture for IoT network virtualization is organized into three distinct layers: 1) Physical Layer: Comprises actual IoT devices, such as sensors and actuators, that are directly connected to the network. 2) Virtualization Layer: serves as links connecting current IoT devices and user apps, enabling seamless interaction and management. 3) Application Layer: Hosts various applications designed to process and utilize data from the IoT devices. This layered approach enhances network efficiency and flexibility by streamlining the connection and management processes.

Novo, O. et al. [27] introduced a novel architecture designed to manage roles and permissions within IoT environments. Their research aimed to create a scalable, user-friendly access management system tailored for the Internet of Things (IoT). Additionally, they developed a proof-of-concept (PoC) prototype to validate the proposed design. The results of their implementation and evaluation showed that the system scaled efficiently, as multiple constrained networks could connect simultaneously to the blockchain through certain nodes referred to as management core nodes. This setup provided considerable flexibility, as management hub nodes could be distributed throughout the blockchain network, connecting to the constrained networks in various configurations. Overall, the system proved to be adaptable to diverse IoT frameworks, highlighting the potential for blockchain technology to be fully integrated into IoT systems.

Ultimately but not finally in [28] the article presents an IoT proxy that utilizes virtual resources (VRs) to bridge web service providers (WSPs) from the Internet with the Open Connectivity Foundation (OCF) network. This IoT proxy enables seamless, transparent access for IoT clients to both IoT devices and WSPs using a standardized method of service access. Through the discovery service provided by the proxy, clients can locate VRs and recognize IoT device resources as OCF resources. The paper also details the mechanisms for authorization, discovery, and service access, including the execution of both indoor and outdoor services using IoT devices. These services are provided through the open API of the OCF network. Evaluation results suggest that the IoT proxy significantly reduces message sizes when transmitting services from the Internet to IoT clients, with the HTTP server sending response payloads to the client via the proxy.

2.3 Fog Computing Architecture for IoT Devices and Blockchain Data

The Fog computing at first invented by Cisco Systems researchers in 2012, it is a distributed computing paradigm designed to support applications that require low-latency processing while also accommodating services that do not depend on minimal latency. By utilizing idle computational resources located near end users, Fog computing can enhance service performance, particularly when processing demands are moderate. This infrastructure connects a vast array of heterogeneous nodes, such as sensors, actuators, and other devices.

It is a new approach of supplying processing and data store area for IoT devices. In a fog computing structure, every component may transfer data or technically complex tasks to local fog nodes rather than the distant cloud. Comparing to cloud computing, fog computing may drastically minimize communication speed among IoT devices and computer servers. In terms of smart innovations, IoT, blockchain, and fog computing are among those identified as key drivers of smart initiatives.

El Kafhali et al. [29] developed an architecture which utilizes and represents different interaction of blockchain on fog computing to demonstrate the IoT data and analyse the exclusive and private data of IoT devices locally on Fog Computing instead to transfer it to cloud computing for analysis the study endeavoured to offer many aspects of data transfer that include high speed, real time data transfer, scalability, latency and many other aspects using fog computing along with other components such as blockchain, and SDN, NFS technologies.

In a systematic review by Liu, Y. et al. [30], the study explored the influence and potential of fog computing, blockchain, and the Internet of Things (IoT) on healthcare systems within smart city environments. The findings reveal that these three technologies impact a pivotal role in development of the efficiency of healthcare services in smart cities. Among them, IoT has seen the most widespread use. However, despite its extensive adoption, IoT has shown limitations in areas such as cost efficiency, data privacy, and data interoperability.

As well as in paper no. [31] a work discusses the conception of a protected distributed data administration system for fog computing in massive operations of IoT applications, as well as a blockchain-based data controlling administration of the system, that tackles the primary issues such as how to integrate data security and dealing with storage for fog computing in huge-scale IoT applications and enhance logical compatibility for connected objects.

Al-Karaki, et al. [32] stated that Conventional cryptocurrency blockchains, such as Bitcoin, are unsuited for micropayment activities. As a result, adopting fog computing for micropayments can lower latency and increase adaptability. As well as the enhancements in speed and connectivity concentration provided by 5G technology could support immediate processing of data and also autonomous handling of transactions among linked gadgets. The study also discussed the advantages of using contemporary technology such as (fog computing, blockchain, IoT and 6G) to address the issues and relations among these technologies to accomplish the capabilities of utilizing each technology to bring intellectual potentials from fog electronic gadgets to centrally managed systems for computing for the sake of enhancing the functionality of Micropayment mechanism in which a high speed, secure, cheap, reliable and low latency processing of transaction can be performed successfully in order to guarantee an effective payment mechanism.

3 Conclusion

A multiple network of internet of things devices produce tremendous amount of information, that demands to be accessible to authorized members. The most important features to address in future Smart Sensors generations are handling and controlling large amounts of data and enabling security and privacy. IoT produces a massive amount of data, given by both virtual and physical components linked to the Internet, and the data amount must be stored and accessible with ease. According to the various studies we have explored in this study we found that a big range of approaches, techniques, and tools are being developed, applied, and refined to address the challenges of reducing latency, enhancing security and privacy controls, and improving the interoperability of IoT devices within multi-user Fog Computing environments. These efforts aim to provide valuable references for researchers and scholars focused on advancing IoT smart device functionality and Blockchain-based security management. Moreover, we have provided an extensive and comprehensive review of Graphical interfaces, platforms, middleware approaches specifically suited for IoT networks, Security Management of IoT networks that implements Blockchain, Multi-tenancy, and Fog Computing architecture for IoT. As a part of the development in protection of the blockchain and as well as IoT networks used for blockchain, Multitenancy and also facilitating the interaction of users along with smart devices in IoT networks by exploring different tools for designing Graphical interfaces also the study has overviewed some studies for the fog computing architectures for IoT devices and blockchain Data.

References

1. Ahmad, S., Hang, L., Kim, D.H.: Design and implementation of cloud-centric configuration repository for DIY IoT applications. Sensors **18**(2), 474 (2018)
2. Kickstarter. https://www.kickstarter.com. Accessed 1 December 2017

3. Mazzei, D., Fantoni, G., Montelisciani, G., Baldi, G.: Internet of Things for designing smart objects. In: 2014 IEEE World Forum on Internet of Things (WF-IoT), pp. 293–297. IEEE (2014)
4. Gubbi, J., Buyya, R., Marusic, S., Palaniswami, M.: Internet of Things (IoT): a vision, architectural elements, and future directions. Futur. Gener. Comput. Syst. **29**(7), 1645–1660 (2013)
5. Park, J.H., Chung, J., Chae, S.Y.: Design of IoT information System. In: Advanced Science and Technology Letters, CES-CUBE 2016, vol. 135, pp. 80–83 (2016)
6. Kumar, P., Pati, U.C.: IoT based monitoring and control of appliances for smart home. In: 2016 IEEE International Conference on Recent Trends in Electronics, Information & Communication Technology (RTEICT), pp. 1145–1150. IEEE (2016)
7. Nguyen, C., Hoang, D.: Software-defined virtual sensors for provisioning IoT services on demand. In: 2020 5th International Conference on Computer and Communication Systems (ICCCS), pp. 796–802. IEEE (2020)
8. Khan, S., Muhammad, K.D., Tila, F.: Enhanced IoT composition architecture based on DIY business process modeling: CoAP based prototype. VFAST Trans. Softw. Eng. **10**(2), 61–69 (2022)
9. Lee, H., Sin, D., Park, E., Hwang, I., Hong, G., Shin, D.: Open software platform for companion IoT devices. In: 2017 IEEE International Conference on Consumer Electronics (ICCE), pp. 394–395. IEEE (2017)
10. Bhawiyuga, A., Kartikasari, D.P., Amron, K., Pratama, O.B., Habibi, M.W.: Architectural design of IoT-cloud computing integration platform. TELKOMNIKA **17**(3), 1399–1408 (2019)
11. Ullah, I., Khan, M.S., Kim, D.: IoT services and virtual objects management in hyperconnected things network. Mobile Inf. Syst. **1**, 2516972 (2018)
12. García, C.G., Meana-Llorián, D., García-Díaz, V., Jiménez, A.C., Anzola, J.P.: Midgar: creation of a graphic domain-specific language to generate smart objects for Internet of Things scenarios using model-driven engineering. IEEE Access **8**, 141872 (2020)
13. Ngu, A.H., Gutierrez, M., Metsis, V., Nepal, S., Sheng, Q.Z.: IoT middleware: a survey on issues and enabling technologies. IEEE Internet Things J. **4**(1), 1–20 (2016)
14. Sen, A., Modekurthy, V.P., Dalvi, R., Madria, S.: A sensor cloud test-bed for multi-model and multi-user sensor applications. In: 2016 IEEE Wireless Communications and Networking Conference, pp. 1–7. IEEE (2016)
15. Kang, S., Chung, K.: IoT framework for interworking and autonomous interaction between heterogeneous IoT platforms. In: Smart Computing and Communication: Third International Conference, SmartCom 2018, Tokyo, Japan, December 10–12, 2018, Proceedings 3, pp. 217–225. Springer International Publishing (2018)
16. Alam, I., et al.: A survey of network virtualization techniques for Internet of Things using SDN and NFV. ACM Comput. Surveys (CSUR) **53**(2), 1–40 (2020)
17. Lin, I.-C., Liao, T.-C.: A survey of blockchain security issues and challenges. Int. J. Netw. Secur. **19**(5), 653–659 (2017)
18. Hizam, N.S., Nuras, Shelar, M.: Evaluation of blockchain security for IoT technology services: survey. In: International Conference on Data Science, Machine Learning and Applications, pp. 612–623. Springer Nature Singapore, Singapore (2023)
19. Liu, Y., et al.: Capability-based IoT access control using blockchain. Digit. Commun. Netw. **7**(4), 463–469 (2021)
20. Stephen, R., Alex, A.: A review on blockchain security. In: IOP Conference Series: Materials Science and Engineering, vol. 396, no. 1, p. 012030. IOP Publishing (2018)
21. Singh, C.: Blockchain and IOT integrated Smart City Architecture. Turk. J. Comput. Math. Educ. (TURCOMAT) **12**(9), 62–69 (2021)

22. Sharma, P.K., Chen, M.-Y., Park, J.H.: A software defined fog node based distributed blockchain cloud architecture for IoT. IEEE Access **6**, 115–124 (2017)
23. Ngabo, D., Wang, D., Iwendi, C., Anajemba, J.H., Ajao, L.A., Biamba, C.: Blockchain-based security mechanism for the medical data at fog computing architecture of internet of things. Electronics **10**(17), 2110 (2021)
24. Ashalatha, R., Agarkhed, J.: Multi tenancy issues in cloud computing for SaaS environment. In: 2016 International Conference on Circuit, Power and Computing Technologies (ICCPCT), pp. 1–4. IEEE (2016)
25. Weber, I., Lu, Q., Tran, A.B., Deshmukh, A., Gorski, M., Strazds, M.: A platform architecture for multi-tenant blockchain-based systems. In: 2019 IEEE International Conference on Software Architecture (ICSA), pp. 101–110. IEEE (2019)
26. Ullah, I., Ahmad, S., Mehmood, F., Kim, D.: Cloud based IoT network virtualization for supporting dynamic connectivity among connected devices. Electronics **8**(7) (2019)
27. Novo, O.: Blockchain meets IoT: an architecture for scalable access management in IoT. IEEE Internet Things J. **5**(2), 1184–1195 (2018)
28. Jin, W., Kim, D.: Development of virtual resource based IoT proxy for bridging heterogeneous web services in IoT networks. Sensors **18**(6), 1721 (2018)
29. El Kafhali, S., Chahir, C., Hanini, M., Salah, K.: Architecture to manage internet of things data using blockchain and fog computing. In: Proceedings of the 4th International Conference on Big Data and Internet of Things, pp. 1–8 (2019)
30. Liu, Y., Zhang, J., Zhan, J.: Privacy protection for fog computing and the internet of things data based on blockchain. Clust. Comput. **24**(2), 1331–1345 (2021)
31. Chen, Z., Cui, H., Wu, E., Li, Y., Xi, Y.: Secure distributed data management for fog computing in large-scale IoT application: a blockchain-based solution. In: 2020 IEEE International Conference on Communications Workshops (ICC Workshops), pp. 1–6. IEEE (2020)
32. Al-Karaki, J., Pavithran, D., Gawanmeh, A.: Integrating blockchain with fog and edge computing for micropayment systems. In: Security Issues in Fog Computing from 5G to 6G: Architectures, Applications and Solutions, pp. 93–112. Springer International Publishing, Cham (2022)

Blockchain

Decentralized GitHub Management: Blockchain Solution

Ranjith Kumar Ramakrishnan[1（✉）] and Jai Jaswant Lekkala[2]

[1] N2 Services Inc., Jacksonville, USA
`ranji1221@gmail.com`
[2] Page IT Solutions LLC., Ashburn, USA

Abstract. Open-source development has revolutionized software creation, allowing a collaborative and transparent approach to building innovative solutions. However, traditional methods of managing GitHub repositories present challenges such as centralized decision-making and slow development cycles. In this paper, I propose a novel solution utilizing the Ethereum blockchain and a Chrome browser extension to decentralize pull request management on GitHub. My approach empowers the community to vote on the acceptance or rejection of pull requests, incentivizing good decisions through financial rewards. I introduce a protocol that integrates smart contracts and stake-based voting to ensure transparent and democratic governance of open-source projects. Through a detailed explanation of our protocol and implementation, I demonstrate how blockchain technology can transform the landscape of open-source development. Additionally, I discuss future research directions, including qualitative studies on community acceptance and exploring alternative architectures for improved reliability. My research contributes to advancing decentralized development practices and fosters innovation in the open-source ecosystem.

Keywords: Blockchain · Ethereum · SNS · GitHub · Open-source · Chrome browser

1 Introduction

1.1 Open-Source Development on GitHub

Open-source development is a type of software development in which a decentralized and collaborative community develops software publicly and transparently. Open-source development enables the creation of innovative and free software through the collaboration of many people and it also provides free access to the software for everyone [17]. Some examples for such significant projects are the Linux Kernel [18] and the Mozilla Firefox browser [14], which are used by millions of people every day. A particular difficulty in open-source development is the coordination of the many developers who contribute to the development of the projects with their own ideas or improvements. Sometimes a change contains an error, therefore each change must be tracked, traced, and if necessary reversed [17]. These problems occur not only in opensource development, but also in commercial software development. As in commercial software development, version control is used to solve these problems [17].

In particular, the version control protocol Git is ideal for open-source development, because with Git it is possible to have several distributed remotes that can access and manage the same source code [5]. Projects that are coordinated via Git are called repositories. The developers have a local copy of the repository on their systems and can push their changes to or pull the current status from the main repository. These actions are coordinated via a so-called Git server, which has to be hosted somewhere so that the developers can work with it [5]. This server must be permanently accessible. Otherwise, the mentioned actions will no longer work, and the coordination of the developers will be interrupted [19]. Hosting services such as GitHub were created so that such problems can be prevented, and not everyone has to set up their own Git server if they want to start an open-source project [19]. Today, GitHub is the largest Git hosting provider, with over 56 million registered developers and over 100 million repositories. [6] The service is also used by large IT corporations such as Microsoft, Facebook or Google and hosts a large number of the largest and most important open-source repositories [8].

Normally, an open-source project on GitHub starts with a user creating a repository for it. The user who created the repository is its owner. This user has full control over the repository and can push changes, decide which changes are accepted (merged), and even delete the repository. In addition, he can add so-called collaborators to the repository who have read and write privileges in the repository [11]. Normal users who do not have collaboration rights can contribute to the open-source project by creating a pull request with their change. Another user with the necessary rights can then decide whether the change is useful or not. Depending on his decision, he can merge (accept) or reject the changes. The described process is the typical approach to how the community develops for an open-source project.

1.2 Problem

The described workflow for managing repositories on GitHub has some significant disadvantages. Firstly, this approach is not necessarily decentralized or democratic. Very few people usually have the necessary rights to merge pull requests, and they can decide over the head of the general community whether to merge or reject a pull request. So, it doesn't matter what the general community thinks as long as the administrators have a different opinion. Rejecting good or useful pull requests is bad but not a direct threat to the project. The opposite is to merge a critical bug into the main repository, which can cause enormous damage, as in the example of the Heartbleed bug in the Open SSL repository [15]. This danger exists mainly because it only takes one person with the necessary rights to overlook the bug and decide to merge the flawed pull request. Less critical problems, which nevertheless complicate the work in the communities of open-source projects, are the lack of initiative for developers to review pull requests or to create pull requests themselves. If an open-source repository is not financially supported by a company or a large community, they usually live on developers who work on these projects in their spare time, which means that further development sometimes takes a very long time.

1.3 Solution

To solve these problems, this paper presents the development of a Chrome browser extension that uses the GitHub API [7] and smart contracts [9] on the Ethereum blockchain [4] to enable decentralized management of pull requests in GitHub repositories with a financial incentive for the community. Using the Ethereum Blockchain, the community can vote on which pull requests should be merged or rejected. The aim is to merge good requests and reject bad ones by rewarding good decisions and punishing bad ones. In addition, the community can use a crowdfunding mechanism to pool Ether, the native currency of the Ethereum blockchain, to pay developers for solving problems or bugs. This creates a free market with Ether as its currency, where supply and demand form an initiative to solve the tasks. The functionality of the protocol on which the browser extension is based is explained in detail in 3. Protocol. My goal with this browser extension and this paper is to solve the problems mentioned and to improve the way open-source development is done.

1.4 Why Choose Ethereum for Decentralized GitHub Management

In the realm of decentralized applications, Ethereum stands out due to its robust smart contract functionality, extensive developer ecosystem, and established security protocols. When managing GitHub repositories in a decentralized manner, Ethereum provides several advantages over other blockchain platforms:

- **Smart Contract Capabilities.** Ethereum's smart contracts automate various management tasks, such as access control, role assignment, and contribution rewards, without relying on intermediaries. This automation increases transparency and reduces the need for administrative oversight in open-source projects.
- **Established Ecosystem and Developer Support.** Ethereum's large developer community provides a wealth of resources, libraries, and third-party integrations. This ecosystem simplifies the implementation of decentralized GitHub features, from permission management to decentralized storage solutions, using well-tested tools and frameworks.
- **Interoperability with Web3 Technologies.** Ethereum's compatibility withWeb3 technologies, including decentralized identity systems and storage networks like IPFS, offers GitHub projects new ways to enhance security, transparency, and functionality, aligning well with the needs of open-source communities.
- **Security and Proven Track Record.** With its extensive history of development and testing, Ethereum offers a secure, reliable foundation for handling sensitive repository data and managing access control. Its robust security protocols ensure that repository management is both decentralized and resilient against unauthorized access or modification.

2 Related Work

Related work falls into three areas: repository governance, decentralized voting, and developer initiative.

2.1 Repository Governance

Previous studies have explored decentralized approaches to managing GitHub repositories, emphasizing the importance of community-driven decision-making. One notable work by Ulrich et al. [19] posits that a repository should fundamentally operate as an ownerless protocol, where pull requests can only be merged or rejected by the community through collective consensus. This mechanism aims to mitigate the risks associated with users who possess writing rights potentially misusing their privileges, thus fostering a more equitable governance model within open-source projects. This research highlights the necessity for robust governance frameworks that empower communities while safeguarding against potential abuses of power.

2.2 Decentralized Voting

The exploration of trustless and decentralized voting mechanisms on the blockchain has been addressed in several significant papers. Khoury et al. [16] delve into various methodologies for implementing secure voting systems that enhance transparency and trust in decision-making processes. Their work underscores the critical role of decentralized voting in ensuring that all stakeholders in a repository can participate in governance without fear of manipulation or fraud. The implications of such systems extend beyond repository management, suggesting broader applications in democratic processes and organizational governance.

2.3 Developer Initiative

The lack of financial incentives for developers to implement fixes or changes in open-source repositories has been a significant concern in the field. Zhou et al.

[20] conducted research examining the motivations of developers who address bounties, highlighting what is essential to both the developers who solve these bounties and the financial backers providing support. Their findings suggest that aligning the interests of developers and sponsors is crucial for fostering a vibrant ecosystem where contributions are adequately rewarded. By understanding these dynamics, future initiatives can better structure incentives to encourage active participation in open-source development.

Overall, these three areas of research contribute to a deeper understanding of how decentralized governance, voting mechanisms, and financial incentives can enhance the sustainability and effectiveness of open-source projects. By integrating insights from these studies, this paper aims to propose a comprehensive framework that addresses existing challenges while promoting collaborative innovation within the software development community.

3 Protocol

The described browser extension consists of two parts. A frontend that allows users to vote on pull requests or to back a bounty financially, and a protocol that runs locally in the browser extension but uses the GitHub API and the Ethereum blockchain to take over actions such as distributing stakes or merging and rejecting pull requests by the vote outcome. The protocol is the actual solution to how the control of the pull request management is decentralized; the front end on the other hand, provides the possibility to interact with the protocol. In the process of development and research, a total of two protocols were designed, with the second protocol being an extension of the first. I added further functionalities that I subsequently deemed important. This section introduces both protocols and their differences on a non-engineer level.

3.1 First Protocol

The first protocol starts with a developer deciding to develop a change and creating a pull request so that it can be merged into the main branch of the repository. After the pull request has been created, any community member, i.e. anyone who follows the repository, can start the voting phase for the pull request. In this step, a smart contract is created, which is used for the later voting and the distribution of the stakes. The community can then vote for or against the pull request for a certain period of time. When someone submits a vote, they must weigh it with a stake. Ether is used as a stake and the more Ether is staked on a vote, the higher its weight is. After the voting period has expired, the protocol adds up the stakes for and against the pull request.

If the majority of the stakes, i.e., more than 50 percent, have staked for the pull request, it is merged. Otherwise, it is rejected. It is important to note that the stake of the votes cannot be changed subsequently; once the stake has been sent to the smart contract, it is held until the voting phase is finished. After that, the majority stakes divide the stakes of the minority stickers among themselves. They get a percentage share of the minority stakes in relation to their stakes in the winning pool. For example, whose decision has won and who represents 50 percent of the majority stakes receives half of the minority stakes. The complete process is graphically illustrated in Fig. 1.

Fig. 1. First version of the extension protocol

3.2 Second Protocol

As already described, the second protocol is an extension of the first protocol. The decision why I have expanded the first protocol is explained in the 5. Discussion. In general, however, it can be said that I consider the extension to be an improvement to the first protocol. The protocol can be divided into four phases, which are as follows:

1. Initialization and bounty funding
2. Issue claiming and solution
3. Pull request voting
4. Evaluation and distribution

During the first phase, the smart contract is created after the initialization of the bounty process. With the help of this smart contract, all further processes, such as crowdfunding the bounty, claiming the issue, voting on the pull request, and distributing the rewards and stakes, are organized, persistent, decentralized and trustless via the Ethereum blockchain. The details of the mentioned processes and the individual phases are explained in this section.

Phase 1: Initialization and Bounty Funding

The protocol workflow first starts independently when a community member creates an issue in the GitHub repository related to a problem or a new feature. If the owner or an authorized user of the open-source repository thinks that the issue is reasonable, they can initiate a bounty process for the issue. The community can then fund the bounty with their own Ether to motivate a developer to solve the issue. A developer can potentially receive this bounty as a reward if he solves the issue in a pull request and the community accepts it. The Ether paid into the bounty is held in a smart contract for a certain period of time so that the bounty cannot be negatively manipulated in the short term. If no developer wants to solve this issue and the period described above has expired, the community members that funded the bounty receive their shares back (Fig. 2).

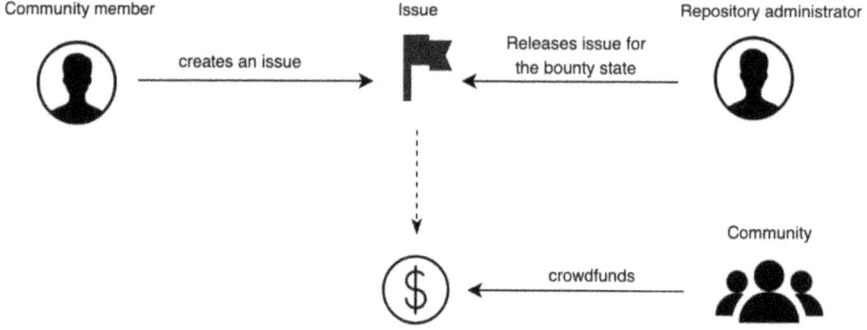

Fig. 2. Workflow of the first phase

Phase 2: Issue Claiming and Solution

While the community collects the bounty, a developer can always decide for himself whether the bounty is high enough for him to solve the issue. As soon as the reward is high enough that a developer would solve the issue for this amount, he can claim the issue for him. But the following must be given. No other developer has already reserved the issue, an issue can only be processed by one developer. Furthermore, the developer has to pay a collateral to claim the issue, which he can lose if he either does not submit a solution within a given period of time or the solution gets rejected by the community. Once the issue is reserved by a developer, he has a certain period of time in which he has to program a solution and provide it as a pull request. If the developer does not provide a solution or it is rejected by the community, he loses his collateral, which is then sent to the bounty. The issue is then set back to the claiming phase.

Phase 3: Pull Request Voting
In this phase, the process mirrors the initial variant of the protocol, with a few critical enhancements that aim to foster greater transparency and accountability within the voting mechanism. The voting process is initiated when a developer submits their pull request, signaling their intention to merge new changes into the main codebase. This moment marks the beginning of a collaborative review process where community members, or stakers, are encouraged to engage actively.

One of the primary differences in this phase is the requirement for stakers to provide a comment accompanying their vote. Each staker must articulate the reasoning behind their voting decision, clearly explaining their perspective on the pull request in question. This commentary serves multiple purposes: it not only clarifies the basis of their support or opposition but also contributes to a richer dialogue among community members. By fostering this discourse, the protocol aims to enhance the collective understanding of the proposed changes, allowing for a more informed decision-making process.

The comments are then posted in the comment section of the pull request, creating a transparent record of feedback and facilitating further discussion among the developers and stakers. This transparency helps to hold stakers accountable for their votes and encourages them to provide thoughtful, constructive feedback rather than simply voting based on personal preferences or biases.

Overall, Phase 3 emphasizes the importance of collaborative engagement in the development process. By requiring stakers to justify their votes, the protocol not only promotes accountability but also nurtures a culture of open dialogue and constructive criticism. This phase ultimately seeks to improve the quality of contributions to the codebase, ensuring that changes are well-considered and aligned with the community's goals and standards.

Phase 4: Evaluation and Distribution
As with the first protocol, the minority stakes are transferred to the majority stakers after the voting phase. The difference here is that if the pull request is accepted by the community, the developer receives his bounty and collateral. However, if the pull request is rejected, the developer loses his collateral, which gets allocated to the bounty and the protocol puts the issue back into the claiming phase.

4 Implementation

The implementation of the Chrome browser extension consists of a frontend and the in *3. Protocol* described protocol. In this section, the technical implementation of the two components will be explained. Furthermore, for information purposes, when the protocol is discussed, it is referring to the second version of.

the protocol. The mentioned Chrome extension frontend has been created according to the current standard with HTML, CSS, JavaScript, and the Chrome extension API [1]. In summary, the Chrome extension was developed as a kind of web application with a few specific limitations. On the other hand, the development and implementation of the protocol required much more thought. The protocol must connect the Ethereum blockchain with GitHub and mediate the data between the two endpoints.

Algorithm 1: Stake distribution algorithm using the example of an accepted pull request

---

Input: All votes *votes*; Developer *dev* ; Pro votes *provotes*;
      Bounty   *bounty* ; Collateral *collateral*
fullStake ← SumStakes(*votes*);
proStake ← SumStakes(*provotes*);
foreach *vote* ∈ *provotes* **do**
    | share← (*vote.weight* ÷ proStake) · fullStake Transfer(*vote.address, share*);
end
Transfer(*dev.address, bounty + collateral*);

The collaboration with the Ethereum blockchain was done using the JavaScript library web3js [13]. This library enables interactions with an Ethereum node and thus with the blockchain using HTTP. This allows the Chrome extension to retrieve general information from the blockchain, write data, and even create smart contracts. Querying blockchain data does not require any special settings, as it is a read-only request. All write actions on the blockchain, such as voting on a pull request or generating a smart contract, require a wallet in the extension, as you have to pay transaction fees for the actions.

No special library is needed for the GitHub connection; this is done via the API provided by GitHub [7]. This can also be accessed using HTTP, which is needed to fetch information about repositories, to create voting comments or to either merge or reject a pull request. In contrast to working with the Ethereum blockchain and smart contracts, many of the requests against the GitHub API require an authentication token, which can be fetched via the GitHub OAuth API [10]. The GitHub OAuth is used as a login in the extension, which means that the extension does not need its own login and can, therefore, fetch the authentication token. However, the token alone is not sufficient as authentication for every request; for merging and rejecting pull requests, a developer token must also be stored in the extension, which can be obtained from the GitHub account settings.

Probably the most difficult aspect of the implementation of the chrome extension is the conclusion of the voting phase, i.e. Phase 4: Evaluation and distribution. Contrary to the other phases and actions, this process must happen automatically as soon as the voting phase ends. However, since I only have a client-side program, I can only detect this when one of the developed chrome extensions is running. For this reason, after the GitHub OAuth login, the extension checks if there are completed pull request votes and if so, the extension triggers the described workflow Phase 4: Evaluation and distribution for the pull request in the background. Then the necessary requests are sent to the smart contract and the GitHub API.

4.1 Code Architecture Overview

This decentralized GitHub management system is composed of the following key. modules:

- **Smart Contracts.** Responsible for handling key functions on the Ethereum blockchain, such as:

  - Access Control: Manages user permissions within the repository.
  - Contribution Tracking: Logs user contributions for transparent tracking.
  - Reward Distribution: Distributes rewards or tokens to contributors.

- **Voting Mechanism.** Facilitates decentralized decision-making for repository actions, with contracts for proposal creation, voting, and outcome enforcement.
- **Chrome Extension Integration.** Connects GitHub to the Ethereum blockchain, allowing users to interact with smart contracts directly within GitHub's interface. This extension includes:

  - Web3 Connection: Connects to Ethereum.
  - GitHub API Integration: Retrieves repository data from GitHub.
  - UI Module: Provides an in-GitHub interface for decentralized management actions.

This modular design ensures secure, decentralized governance of GitHub repositories,
with seamless integration via a Chrome extension.

5 Stake-Based Voting Logic

Stake-based voting allows users to cast votes proportional to the amount of tokens they stake in the system. The more tokens a user holds, the greater their voting power. Here's a brief breakdown of how it works:

5.1 User Votes and Recording

Users stake tokens, and these tokens are locked in a smart contract. When a vote is initiated, users can cast their votes, which are recorded on the blockchain. Each vote is associated with the user's wallet address and the number of tokens they have staked.

5.2 Handling Stakes

The staked tokens determine the weight of a user's vote. If users withdraw or un-stake their tokens before the voting period ends, their votes are invalidated, ensuring only active participants can influence outcomes.

5.3 Vote Counting

Votes are weighted based on the staked tokens. After the voting period, the smart contract tallies the results, with the proposal passing if the majority of staked tokens are in favor.

5.4 Storing Votes

Votes are stored securely on the blockchain, ensuring transparency, immutability, and accountability. The blockchain records the voter's address, the number of tokens staked, the vote outcome, and the timestamp.

This system ensures that only those with a vested interest in the platform's success influence decisions, promoting secure and fair governance.

6 Results

This section presents a brief comparison between traditional and decentralized GitHub management systems, focusing on transaction costs, performance, and governance efficiency.

6.1 Transaction Costs

In the traditional GitHub model, interactions are free, while the decentralized model incurs transaction fees for actions like voting or committing changes (Table 1).

Table 1. Transaction Cost Comparison

Action	Traditional	Decentralized
Commit Update	$0.00	$0.20
Voting on Proposal	N/A	$0.05

6.2 Performance

Performance is measured by latency for actions such as committing updates or voting (Table 2).

Table 2. Performance Comparison

Action	Traditional	Decentralized
Commit Update	30 ms	180 ms
Voting on Proposal	N/A	300 ms

Table 3. Governance Efficiency Comparison

Decision Type	Traditional	Decentralized
New feature Approval	1 day	3 days
Merge Pull Request	2 days	4 days

6.3 Governance Efficiency

In the decentralized model, governance decisions take longer due to the stake based voting process (Table 3).

6.4 Analysis

The decentralized model offers enhanced transparency and security but incurs higher transaction.

7 Discussion

7.1 Protocol Update

In the course of implementing the first protocol, I found some major flaws in it, which is why I have modified and extended it as described in 3. Protocol. In a conversation with several software developers, the question came up how to protect the protocol from malicious users creating pull requests and releasing them for voting? For this reason, it was decided that the release for voting cannot take place through the general community, as otherwise, the danger of such attacks is too great. In the second iteration of the protocol, pull requests are released by users with administrator rights by opening the bounty for them. At this point, decentralization must be reduced in order to provide more security. In addition, the idea came up to use the bounty system to create a further incentive for development and maintenance in open-source projects, which was not given in the first protocol. This adaptation should lead to a free market for the development of features or the solution of issues. This also aims to improve the quality of pull requests, as developers have to put effort into their development in order for the pull request to be accepted and for them to receive both their collateral and the bounty.

7.2 Advantages and Disadvantages of Ethereum

At the time of this research paper, Ethereum is one of the largest blockchain platforms with over one million daily transactions [3]. While Ethereum is constantly being developed and improved due to the size of the community, the main blockchain is currently not suitable for this application. Currently, the Ethereum fees for a transaction are around 23.70$ [2]. This means that you have to pay this fee for every action, whether voting or contributing to an issue. Unfortunately, this is not sustainable, although future developments of the Ethereum protocol may change this. Currently, this problem is being avoided by working on the Ethereum testnet Sokol [12]. However, this cannot be used in live operations because the Ether on this chain has no value.

7.3 Synchronization of Voting Results

The current browser extension approach has the advantage that everything is started from the extension, and you can react to misbehavior on the part of the web3js library or GitHub API. However, this approach has difficulties especially when completing voting polls. Because there is no central server that carries out these changes, there is always the danger that two clients simultaneously initiate this process in the background. Although no direct damage can be done, unnecessary transaction fees may incur. In addition, it is problematic that if a voting phase expires but no one starts the extension for a longer period of time, the associated pull request is not merged or rejected, and the stakes and bounties are not sent. Also, this implementation requires that community members are willing to have their own wallets on Ethereum and pay transaction fees for their actions.

8 Limitations of Ethereum's Gas Fees in Managing Pull Requests

Ethereum's gas fees pose a significant challenge in managing pull requests, as each interaction requires a fee, which can become costly for frequent actions in large projects. High gas fees discourage participation, particularly when network congestion drives costs higher.

8.1 Potential Solutions

To mitigate these challenges, several solutions can be explored:

- **Layer 2 Solutions.** Using platforms like Optimism and Arbitrum can reduce gas costs by processing transactions off-chain.
- **Batching Transactions.** Combining multiple operations into a single transaction can lower overall fees.
- **Delegated Gas Payment.** Allowing project maintainers to cover gas costscan relieve individual contributors from paying fees.

9 Conclusion and Future Work

The implementation of the Chrome browser extension and the underlying protocol establishes a solid foundation for a new paradigm of open-source development via GitHub. By leveraging cutting-edge technologies such as blockchain, we can unlock novel opportunities for configuring centralized software in a more decentralized and democratic manner. This shift not only enhances the governance of open-source projects but also empowers contributors and users alike, promoting a collaborative environment where every voice can be heard.

However, as highlighted in previous sections, several challenges remain with the current implementation. Among these challenges are the potential barriers to adoption within the open-source community and the overall receptiveness of developers to this innovative approach. There are inherent concerns regarding the usability of blockchain technologies, particularly in relation to transaction fees, which may deter contributors from engaging fully with decentralized models. Addressing these concerns is crucial for fostering a supportive ecosystem that encourages participation and collaboration.

To this end, I propose two key areas for future research that could significantly enhance our understanding and implementation of this decentralized development model.

The first area involves conducting a qualitative study to gauge the sentiments of open-source developers and community members toward this decentralized approach to development. This research would explore their perceptions of blockchain technology, including aspects such as transaction fees, the complexity of implementation, and overall usability. Understanding the community's perspective is vital for tailoring our approach to better fit the needs and expectations of potential users. Gathering insights through interviews, surveys, or focus groups could yield valuable data that informs future iterations of the project.

The second aspect focuses on investigating whether a server-client architecture would be more suitable for this application. This consideration draws inspiration from the work titled *Development of a blockchain-based access control protocol for GitHub repositories as an open-source project* [19]. Adapting a server to accommodate the requirements of the browser extension could potentially enhance its functionality and reliability. Connecting the extension to a well-structured server-client model may address some of the weaknesses outlined in my implementation, such as latency issues and performance bottlenecks. Researching this architecture could provide insights into its feasibility, scalability, and overall effectiveness in improving the user experience and operational efficiency.

In summary, while the current implementation represents a significant step forward in open-source development via blockchain technology, ongoing exploration and adaptation are essential. By prioritizing community feedback and investigating alternative architectural frameworks, we can work toward refining this approach and paving the way for a more inclusive, decentralized, and efficient open-source ecosystem.

References

1. Chrome API reference. https://developer.chrome.com/docs/extensions/reference/. Accessed 20 Feb 2021
2. Ethereum avg transaction fee historical chart. https://bitinfocharts.com/de/comparison/ethereum-transactionfees.html. Accessed 20 Feb 2021
3. Ethereum daily transactions chart. https://etherscan.io/chart/tx. Accessed 20 Feb 2021
4. Ethereum developer resources. https://ethereum.org/en/developers/. Accessed 20 Feb 2021
5. Git SCM. https://git-scm.com/. Accessed 20 Feb 2021
6. GitHub about. https://github.com. Accessed 20 Feb 2021
7. GitHub REST API. https://docs.github.com/en/rest. Accessed 20 Feb 2021
8. Gitstar ranking. https://gitstar-ranking.com/. Accessed 20 Feb 2021
9. Introduction to smart contracts. https://ethereum.org/en/developers/docs/smart-contracts/. Accessed 20 Feb 2021
10. Managing OAuth apps. https://docs.github.com/en/developers/apps/managing-oauth-apps. Accessed 20 Feb 2021
11. Permission levels for a user account repository. https://docs.github.com/en/github/setting-up-and-managing-your-github-user-account/permission-levels-for-a-user-account-repository. Accessed 20 Feb 2021
12. Sokol blockexplorer. https://blockscout.com/poa/sokol/. Accessed 20 Feb 2021
13. web3.js - Ethereum JavaScript API. https://web3js.readthedocs.io/en/v1.3.0/. Accessed 20 Feb 2021
14. Docs, M.W.: Contributing to the mozilla code base. https://developer.mozilla.org/en-US/docs/Mozilla/Developerguide/Introduction. Accessed 20 Feb 2021
15. Iori, M.: Heartbleed keeps flowing-open source security
16. Khoury, D., Kfoury, E.F., Kassem, A., Harb, H.: Decentralized voting platform based on ethereum blockchain. In: Proceedings of the 2018 IEEE International Multidisciplinary Conference on Engineering Technology (IMCET), pp. 1–6. IEEE (2018)
17. Shaikh, M., Henfridsson, O.: Governing open source software through coordination processes. Inf. Organ. **27**(2), 116–135 (2017)
18. torvalds: GitHub repository of the Linux kernel. https://github.com/torvalds/linux. Accessed 20 Feb 2021
19. Ulrich, T.: Development of a blockchain based access control protocol for github repositories as open-source project (2020)
20. Zhou, J., Wang, S., Bezemer, C.P., Zou, Y., Hassan, A.E.: Bounties in open source development on github: a case study of bountysource bounties. arXiv preprint arXiv:1904.02724 (2019)

Design Ubiquitous, Technologically Efficient Online Storage System Using Blockchain

Rajeev Kumar[1(✉)], Pradeep Kumar[2], and Madhurendra Kumar[3]

[1] Moradabad Institute of Technology, Moradabad, Uttar Pradesh, India
`rajeev2009mca@gmail.com`
[2] College of Computing Sciences and Information Technology, Teerthanker Mahaveer University, Moradabad, Uttar Pradesh, India
[3] C-DAC, Centre, Noida, Uttar Pradesh, India

Abstract. In order to increase societal efficiency, end-user applied computing covers a range of service delivery facets. Almost every age has access to computing since the development of the internet and the client-server computing paradigm. End users are increasingly using this dynamic situation for complex data processing needs in their daily lives due to a variety of live systems. In this sequence, the Storage System (SS) is a system that collects data from students (or other end users in other scenarios) for processing, such as real-time and on-demand information retrieval, and future persistent storage. The online storage system (OSS) offered by various counters was established with the intention of gathering data, and although it was obviously giving the data durability in terms of storage, end users could not normally access it. With high availability, ubiquity, technical innovation, and operational effectiveness in mind, the primary goal of this project is to design a prototype Advanced Online Storage System (AOSS) for the storage scenario of university students. The study is being expanded through the creation of a prototype for a genuine sense web-based online storage system and the investigation of different viewpoints regarding its components. In terms of AOSS component investigation, the database is the primary element that would serve as the foundation for the new storage system's design. Since its introduction, the AOSS has included technological advancements in database processes and their consequences on the target system, both of which are rigorously examined.

Keywords: Advanced Online Storage System · Online Storage System · technological advancement · operation efficiency

1 Introduction

The initial factors that led to the development of web-based storage mechanisms were the network and internet (network of networks, early 1980s). With the exception of Client/Server, all of the aforementioned databases were first standalone storage and access databases. For the first time, the client/server architecture made it mandatory to publicly store data on a central, remote server. The development of the internet also led to advancements in storage systems (RS), or stand-alone storage and access interfaces, which were also required for remote database usage. For the apps and interfaces to be more flexible, they also required to be user-oriented. We looked at web-based databases in this section.

2 Web-Based Database Management System

Web-based databases are a crucial component of web applications and services because they store, process, and retrieve the data they contain. Web-based databases are used by web-based applications and services such as e-commerce, mail, bulletin boards, corporate websites, sports portals, and news portals. Building a modern website requires developing a database application.

2.1 Requirement of Web Integration

It is impossible to imagine technological advancement without online assistance; in this rapidly expanding technology age, everyone wants to be able to control devices, systems, and consumables remotely with minimal human or manual involvement. Regarding the mechanism of storage, following Google's work on distributed file systems, GFS, and NFS [2006] [1]. Increasing the prevalence, transparency, and fault tolerance of storage has become a study trend among manufacturers; numerous firms are offering database connectivity solutions via the internet. Many of them are working on increasingly sophisticated technologies in order to avoid becoming limited to just one.

The necessity of having integration of a storage mechanism to the web is essential from various facet. Here are the lists of some of the most significant necessities for the database integration applications within the Web. These requirements are standards and not fully attainable at present [3, 4]. The standard requirements to have such applications are mentioned as follows-

- Security: Right to use authenticated and valuable data in secured manner.
- Flexibility: By providing the flexibility in selecting the DBMS for their current use as well as future also.
- Interface Independence: DBMS application independence from any Web Browser/ Server is one of the essential requirements while selecting appropriate application.
- Versatile Features: One more requirement while choosing any particular DBMS. It must provide such kind of connectivity solution those benefits in all features of selected DBMS.
- Interoperability: As it points to platform and device independence, DBMS application's structure must be open-ended and must provide interoperability in comparison to be rigid. It must be able to run variety of Web servers.
- Component Object Model (COM): DBMS must support COM/ DCOM model for better reusability.
- CORBA/ IIOP, Java/ RMI, XML Support: Some advanced features and support for various technologies must be there in an effective DBMS application.
- Web Services: It can perform similar with multiple web service types like SOAP, and UDDI etc.

- Cost Effectiveness: It should provide a cost effective way for maintenance, scalability, development for various applications.
- Optimized Transactions: It must provide an optimized transaction support with multiple integrated applications.
- User Friendliness: It must be user-friendly while working with it by allowing minimal overhead of administration.

A. The Web

To understand the above given necessities and requirements of having integration of storage mechanism to the web towards ubiquitous and versatile facilitation, we need to understand the high-level-working organizational structure of the web, which itself force to the governance and structural evolution of the various Web-based Database Management Systems, that we will be exploring in the next paper as literature survey and types. If we talk about a simplest scenario, the web is everything while working with internet. Either we are requesting some resource from the server, or the server is responding to the corresponding request, all we do by filling some kind of forms, filling the data over that forms, entering some specific URLs in the address bar of the browser or by clicking some links. While working with any of the mentioned task, we deal with the web.HTML [2] pages are generally used to display any of the content on the browser. Figure 1. Shows how a web browser communicates with a web server to retrieve a journal paper homepage. This is showing the most traditional approach called client-server or two-tier architecture of using the web.

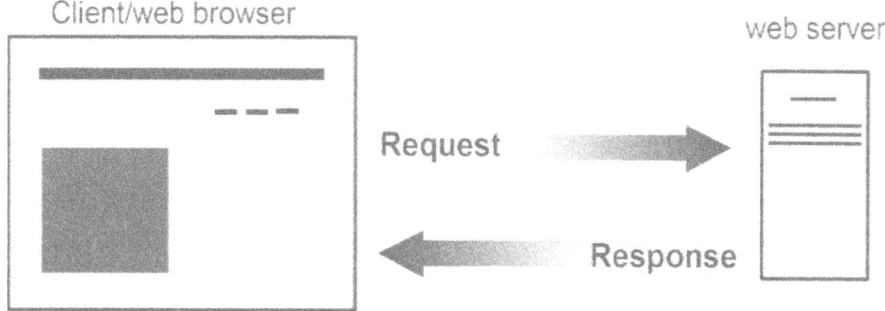

Fig. 1. Two-tier Architecture of Client-Server Based Applicative Communication

In terms of data services (storage, processing, and retrieval), a web server is not an advanced storage program. A new method of separating the servers from the database servers is necessary because the data servicing outlined above, as well as complex operations on data performed by commercial sites and anybody else presenting a lot of dynamic data, should be handled by a distinct database system. As two-tier architecture is a classical model of web communication, there is a more advance version of this process was developed known as, three-tier architecture. In which, three layers are being used for the overall communication process. First is the Web browser as a client-tier, secondly, Web server as a middle-tier between the web browser and actual database, third layer is database application. This leads to a complex architecture of communication model, Fig. 2. is showing the request generated from client (Web browser) [6] and the response generated by Web server and database.

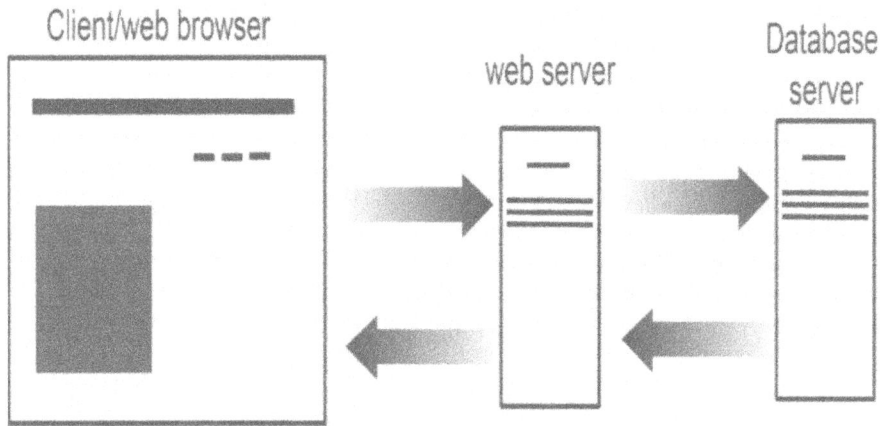

Fig. 2. Three-tier Architecture of Client Application and Web-Server, Database

B. Three-Tier Architectures

This study shows how the different database paradigm got evolved to develop web database applications (like online storage system) that are built following the three-tier architectural formulation and model as shown in Fig. 3. According to the three-tier architectural modeling at the base of an application is the database tier, consisting of the database management system that manages the data users create, delete, modify, and query, the data indexing services always handled by an installed Distributed File System/Network File System (DFS/NFS) [5].

The *middle tier* is the next tier on the top of the database tier, the middle-tier contains most of the application logics and scripting that we have coded on for a specific service, and scripting engines. A server always executes these such scripts in response of a specific http request. It also contains scripts (user/system-level) for data transportation / communication between the other tiers. The *client-tier* is at the top and the most usually a web browser software that interacts with the application using several ports based on the request. The various type of client interface is now evolved to get facilitation form a web based data acquisition / processing and other live database services.

This kind of architecture is a conceptual form of any application model, the modern data intensive applications are having the same architectural phenomena for a better separation of the application logics to the storage mechanism. It organizes a structure of combining three logical or physical computing layers in an order. User interface is one of the three tiers that deals with user actions and work as presentation layer, application layer that consists all the data processing activities and the data layer which contain all the data associated with particular application. Web based applications consist of different implementation versions to support with three-tier architecture. Most common

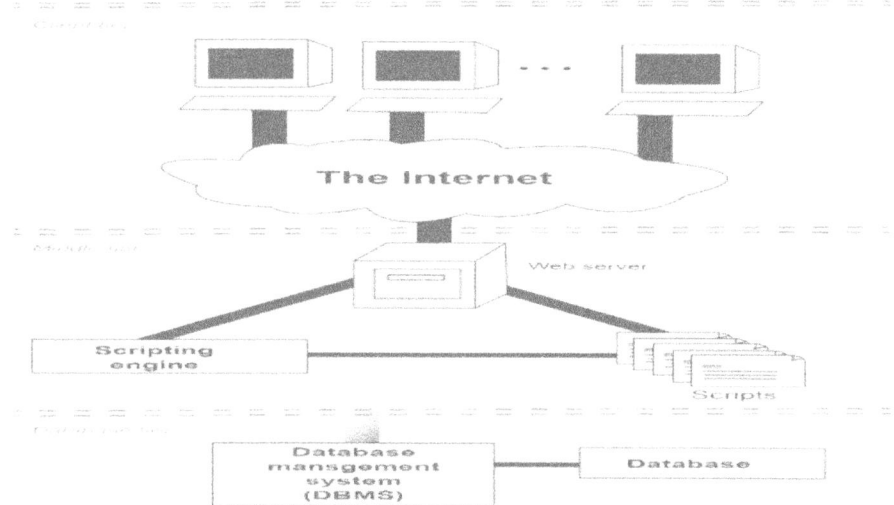

Fig. 3. Database, Web-Server, and Client Application Architecture in Three Tiers

architecture consists of the web server that works with scripting engine to process the scripts and produces the results of their execution and the database management system. If the advanced hardware is used, this kind of application can manage ten of thousand requests in an hour.

Implementing web applications with three tier architecture make the model more robust and fine-tuned in order to organizing the structures. Although, it hides the fact that application brings altogether, various protocols and software, and the other supported applications to run, configure and secure that software. To understand the usage mechanism, we need to explore an important protocol that is being discussed in next section.

C. HTTP: The Hypertext Transfer Protocol

The conceptual framework for web-based database applications has a three-tiered architecture. Even yet, we ourselves offer every required and accepted protocol for tying clients and middle-tier apps together. It acts as a mediator between the web browser and the web server. The network itself provides HTTP as one of the protocols that connects the three-tier design.

To share the content and to allow the resources to communicate over the web with each other, HTTP is used. Most of the web browsers and web servers communicate with each other through the current version of HTTP [7]. Various applications that needs to transfer the data through various applications needs HTTP to handle over network communications.

HTTP is a conceptual simple platform that uses a web browser to flow in sending request to server and server used to send the responses according to the request. Each request generates one response. HTTP response includes various resources like HTML document, output of the execution, images, links, etc.

The HTTP Request
HTTP request is a special kind of document that contain various textual descriptions, headers and some additional information to describe how a resource will be returned.

The textual description of a resource and any extra data or headers that specify how the resource should be returned make up an HTTP request.

Following example showing HTTP request-

```
GET /~hugh/index.html HTTP/1.1
Host: goanna.cs.rmit.edu.au
From: hugh@hughwilliams.com (Hugh Williams)
User-agent: Hugh-fake-browser/version-1.0
Accept: text/plain, text/html
```

This example uses the GET method to request an HTML page / ~ hugh/index.html that was started by the goanna.cs.rmit.edu.au server using the most recent version of HTTP. As this example is showing, additionally four header lines are included to specify the host, data type accepted by browser, identification of user and web browser. A HTTP request generally includes request initiated by browser and other headers may be included.

The HTTP Response
A response code, headers, an included message, and the requested resources are all included in an HTTP response. As the above mentioned example the page / ~ *jurnl/index.html* is showing the request code as follows-

```
HTTP/2.1 200 OK
Date: Thu, 04 Jan 2018 04:30:02 GMT 5.30
Server: Apache/1.3.27 (Unix)
Last-Modified: Fri, 21 Nov 2003 22:26:07 GMT
ETag: "a87da0-2128-3fbe90ff"
Accept-Ranges: bytes
Content-Length: 8488
Content-Type: text/html
<!DOCTYPE HTML PUBLIC
"-//W3C//DTD HTML 4.0 Transitional//EN"
"http://www.w3.org/TR/html4/loose.dtd">
<html>
<head>
...
```

The response contains the version of HTTP/1.1 as its first line and the confirmation of the request that the request is successfully completed or not, for this it uses the response code 200 with an OK message. A number of lines in the headers of the example are linked to the current time and date, the web server software, the last time the page was updated, and the entity tag (ETag) [9], which is used to accept instructions to tell the request part of the document along with the length of the response with the content type. In the given example resource is requesting */ ~ hugh/index.html* HTML document.

State

State is a concept and technique while working online that keep the track of the user using any particular application. If the application is able to record the state of the user, various activities can be performed in a reliable way with the transparent authenticity. Nowadays, all applications that are serving online ensure to maintain the state of the user. So that his working activities can be tracked when they are needed. It became essential when we are dealing with some sensitive and authenticated data like in e-commerce or banking applications, the transaction activity must have a managed by the state of the user. For maintaining the states, the applications follow the policies of verification of authenticated user through login with password or by sending one-time password to their registered mobile number or email ids. After successful login the application provide a separate account for each user and manage his/ her account till he logs out from the application and continues for further logins.

Most commonly, all applications that manage their database in backend are stateful as they need to update their data according to each user's activity to achieve data consistency. For example, if we mention any banking application, the user logs-in through his valid credentials, perform any transaction activity thorough the available options in application, and logs-out when his work finished. Next time, if he will login again to the same application, he can get all his transaction history done previously. This is why because the application is maintaining his state.

State management is itself a sensitive area while dealing with some commercial database applications. But if we talk about HTTP [10], it is a stateless protocol, means it is not able to maintain the state of any user. The interaction among web server and web browser remain independent as it doesn't keep track of this communication. Each HTTP request contains a header that includes the information related to browser's identity in the same way as the authentication credentials of user along with the type of web pages accepted by server and the statement of instructions about the format of HTTP response. According to the header, the server interprets the request and performs the responses that explain the process to serve the request then returns the resources along with header. After the successful completion of response, the server deletes the request that can't be recovered later.

There are advantages to statelessness, such as the ability to access any irrelevant pages or resources. It is difficult to create web-based applications that require state management since HTTP is stateless.

We can add a number of other technologies and other applications that can make it possible to use HTTP with proper state management. Another solution is by exchanging any key or token between server and the browser that can uniquely identify each of its clients to maintain its session. For every request generated by the browser, a token is also generated by the client and transferred to the server, and server returns that token when it accomplished that particular request. These tokens can be used by the applications at middle layer to keep the track of each client that can be used in future for accessing the previous activities by that browser.

Token exchanging make the communication flow in a stateful structured manner by adding menus or steps to the application. This can also be useful to prevent duplicate actions being happened, automatic log out after a defined period of inactivity expires, also in controlling the access of any application by any unauthorized user.

3 The Three-Tier Model and the Online Client Applications

A web enabled database application based on three tier architecture can't directly supports HTTP; still browsers can smoothly execute those applications because of the advancement of the browsers. Without any restrictions a number of users are using web based database application with their browsers. It's meaning that multiple users with diverse platforms, browsers and operating systems can use or execute database applications.

Web browsers are called thin clients. Its meaning is that no additional application logic is required at client end. Client simply sends a HTTP request for additional resources and by receiving the response [11], it display on to browser on various web pages. Thin client means there is no such requirement to install or configure client layer according to the application.

As client layer is called thin client, but we can make it thick one by adding more complex work on it. With the help of advanced technologies or languages like Java, Flash, JavaScript, we can develop independent application components for web browsers that supports to interpret data before sending it to server.

JavaScript is an open source and easy to use and supported by all web browsers but it can be set to passive mode if user don't want to execute it on its browser. It generally used for data and form validations at the time of getting the data from the user. Data validation before sending the data to server is having its own requirement as it is needed to protect the server from any invalid data. It can perform various other functions that can make any web page more interactive and animated. For e.g. Highlighting any content/ part of the page, or floating down a menu when the cursor moves over that content or any key is pressed by the user. Although, it can't perform communication with web server or any storage of data still we can use it as a supported tool to make a web page dynamic. JavaScript can't be used alone to make any web page, but it can be used with other languages for more efforts.

3.1 The Middle Tier

Middle tier has its own necessities in web database applications. It works as a mediator between other tiers and layers to make the overall system well communicated with each other. It helps in bringing together the drivers, the content and the structure of the web application to display on the web browser. It provides the authentication based security aspects and also having the state management mechanism in it. It helps in integrating the web and the web server.

3.2 Web Servers

Web servers are the heart and soul for any web based application as they serve for the clients according to their requests. Requests can be of two types. Firstly, a request can be for any web pages or image and the second request can be for the execution of a program or any script. There are various servers according to the languages that use their related servers. Some of them are explained as follows-

An HTTP request for executing PHP (for example) script needs PHP's Zend server to execute its script and ask for the output that renders on the client's web browser. For multitasking environment where multiple users raise their requests simultaneously, we need a special kind of server that can perform the request-response operation with a fast and reliable manner. For e.g. Apache, it is an open source, scalable and fast in its performance. It can work with varying type of browsers also various types of operating systems like Linux, Microsoft Windows, Red Hat, Mac OS, etc. Its resource requirement is low in comparison to other servers. It is capable to handle load of requests simultaneously. As Apache is having its configuration file that contains the information related to the information how the network and server communicate with each other. The sever controls the working behavior of Apache through 150 directives that directly affect response time, flexibility in serving multiple request loads.

Hence, in this section we have explored why and how the web-integration is really needed for the efficient user application architectural modeling that depends on the architecture of database modeling.

4 Most Impactful Improvisation

As per the above-explored facts behind the databases architectural improvements and the effects of the same over application modeling over time. The discussion itself depicting the three-tier-based application modeling was the most impactful improvisation that forced/ applied various other required aspects to the application's building over the same. The main improvisation was security and privacy in real-time databases and based applicative modeling that can be tossed like Confidentiality, Integrity, and Availability (CIA) [12].

Protection in the current and advanced databases modeling over Cloud-based environments can be measured in various aspects – User Authentications, Authentication of Authorized Applications and Access Control to Objects, Backup and Recovery Systems. The transactional modeling-based concurrency control that includes – timing limitations, integrity constraints, Authentication, Authorization, and Servicing, also needs to deal with security and privacy aspects. The three-tier based advanced web databases, storage area networks, distributed file systems for the real-time on-demand application building are the second face of most amazing improvisations that are much efficient and be used for new paradigm modeling of the future online Storage-based applications.

5 Statement of the Problem

Any firm that handles large amounts of data must have Advanced Online Storage Systems (AOSS). Since we always rely on processing (CRUD operations) and real-time retrieval of the processed data, it is imperative that information be kept in a permanent state in

universities [13]. The technology is widespread, but the online storage method used by a few of universities is not. It takes a lot of work and time to have a storage system at university counters and wait for student manual papers to feed data into permanent storage. This indicates that while being online stores data persistently, it is not truly omnipresent because it is not accessible in real time from a distance. The general idea of iniquitousness is to free up university storage counters so that end users can access AORS from a place of comfort [14]. It is still a long way off from exploring different viewpoints on components and creating a prototype of a truly ubiquitous web-based online storage system.

6 Motivation for the Research

There is no imagination of world without internet and the applications based on the same. Web-based applications are the only driving forces that making us to think about future smart cities. Keeping data persistent, processing relevant towards information, secure and available for on-demand real-time access is the main data-computing phenomena. Designing next generation applications with aim of low cost, efficiency and true sense ubiquitous usage is the demand of current time.

University systems that are dealing with the huge data-computing scenario also required mechanisms to keep data and information processing efficient towards storage, processing, and access. The high availability, load-balancing, and on-demand accessibility are the next questions to answer so this study is. As per the same we will be devising an Advanced Online Storage System (AOSS) prototype as per the above said objectives.

7 Conclusion

In this paper as per the aim of the study of designing a highly available, ubiquitous, technologically advanced and operation efficient Advance Online Storage System, that the complete study is being divided into a deep-dive investigation of the current systems, perspectives, dive-forces, architectures and Identification of the objects and facets that will be the building constructs for the Storages systems from various sources, Business Rules and Associations. To drive the building constructs in an organization structural flow business rule and their association needs to be crawled and applied as the driving constructs for operative SOP, this may help to storage and manage data of the organizations and also supported real world data storage.

References

1. Ghosh, S.P.: Statistical relational tables for statistical database management. IEEE Trans. Softw. Eng. **SE-12**(12), 1106–1116 (1986). https://doi.org/10.1109/TSE.1986.6313006
2. McGill, F.E.: Office Practice and Business Procedure. Gregg Publishing Company (1922). p. 197. Accessed 1 Aug 2016
3. Waring, R.L.: Technical investigations of addition of a hardcopy output to the elements of a mechanized library system: final report (1961). Accessed 20 Sep 1961

4. Disc File Applications: Reports Presented at the Nation's First Disc File Symposium. American Data Processing (1964). Accessed 1 Aug 2016
5. Codd, E.F.: A relational model of data for large shared data banks. Commun. ACM **13**(6), 377–387 (1970). https://doi.org/10.1145/362384.362685
6. Rochkind, M.J.: Database systems: structure of a database file system for the UNIX operating system. Bell Syst. Tech. J. **61**(9), 2387–2405 (1982). https://doi.org/10.1002/j.1538-7305.1982
7. Delis, A., Roussopoulos, N.: Performance comparison of three modern DBMS architectures. IEEE Trans. Software Eng. **19**(2), 120–138 (1993). https://doi.org/10.1109/32.214830
8. D. Serain, "Client/server: Why? What? How?," International Seminar on Client/Server Computing. Seminar Proceedings (Digest No. 1995/184), 1995, p. 1/1–111 vol.1, https://doi.org/10.1049/ic:19951128
9. Ali, R., et al.: Improvisation the security and privacy in real time database system. In: Proceedings of the 2020 International Conference on Information Science and Communication Technology (ICISCT), pp. 1–6 (2020). https://doi.org/10.1109/ICISCT49550.2020.9080027
10. Kumar, P., Kumar, R., Singh, K.B., Kumar, M.: Identification of the problem and research methodology. In: Kumar, R., Abdul Hamid, A., Binti Ya'akub, N. (eds.) Effective AI, Blockchain, and E-Governance Applications for Knowledge Discovery and Management, pp. 289–308. IGI Global (2023). https://doi.org/10.4018/978-1-6684-9151-5.ch017
11. Kumar, P., Kumar, M., Kumar, R.: The proposed framework of view-dependent data integration architecture. In: Kumar, R., Joshi, A., Sharan, H., Peng, S., Dudhagara, C. (eds.) The Ethical Frontier of AI and Data Analysis, pp. 343–361. IGI Global (2024). https://doi.org/10.4018/979-8-3693-2964-1.ch021
12. Kumar, P., Kumar, M., Kumar, R.: Blockchain paradigms, evolutions, and usage. In: Kumar, R., Abdul Hamid, A., Inayah Binti Ya'akub, N., Sharma Gaur, M., Kumar, S. (eds.) Futuristic e-Governance Security with Deep Learning Applications. IGI Global (2024). https://doi.org/10.4018/978-1-6684-9596-4
13. Shah, P.K., Pandey, R.P., Kumar, R.: Vector quantization with codebook and index compression. In: Proceedings of the 2016 International Conference System Modeling & Advancement in Research Trends (SMART), pp. 49–52. IEEE, November 2016. https://doi.org/10.1109/SYSMART.2016.7894488
14. Kumar, P., Kumar, M., Singh, K.B., Tripathi, A.R., Kumar, A.: Blockchain security detection condition light module. In: Proceedings of the 2021 10th International Conference on System Modeling & Advancement in Research Trends (SMART), pp. 363–367. IEEE, December 2021. https://doi.org/10.1109/ICRT57042.2023.10146653
15. Kumar, P., Kumar, M., Singh, K.B., Tripathi, A.R.: Digital competencies in blockchain technology. In: Proceedings of the 2023 1st International Conference on Intelligent Computing and Research Trends (ICRT), pp. 1–7. IEEE, February 2023. https://doi.org/10.1109/SMART52563.2021.9676302
16. Naaz, R., Saxena, A.K., Shah, P.Kr.: Blockchain technology's overview: consensus, architecture and future trends. In: AIP Conference Proceedings, vol. 2427(1), pp. 020018, 27 February 2023. https://doi.org/10.1063/5.0125073
17. Pandey, R.P., Shah, P.K.: Transferring secret electronic payment. IJRET: Int. J. Res. Eng. Technol.
18. Ojha, A.C., Shah, P.K., Gupta, S., Sharma, S.: Classifying Twitter sentiment on multi-levels using a hybrid machine learning model. Int. J. Intell. Syst. Appl. Eng. **12**(3s), 328–333 (2023). https://ijisae.org/index.php/IJISAE/article/view/3711
19. Asad, M., Kumar, M., Kumar, P., Sinha, A.K.: Business growth forecast using saket data mining methodology. In: Proceedings of the 2021 10th International Conference on System Modeling & Advancement in Research Trends (SMART), pp. 99–103. IEEE, December 2021. https://doi.org/10.1109/SMART52563.2021.9676278

20. Kumar, R., Joshi, A., Sharan, H.O., Peng, S.L., Dudhagara, C.R. (eds.) The Ethical Frontier of AI and Data Analysis. IGI Global (2024)
21. Kumar, R., Hamid, A., Bakar, A., Inayah Binti Ya'akub, N., Sharma Gaur, M., Kumar, S. (eds.) Futuristic E-governance Security with Deep Learning Applications. IGI Global (2024)
22. Kumar, A., Jalul, R., Kumar, R.. A comparative analysis of machine learning algorithms for breast cancer detection and identification of key predictive features. Traitement du Signal 41(1) (2024)
23. Kumar, P., Kumar, M., Kumar, R.: The proposed framework of view-dependent data integration architecture. In: The Ethical Frontier of AI and Data Analysis, pp. 343–361. IGI Global (2024)
24. Kumar, A., Saini, R., Kumar, R.: A comparative analysis of machine learning algorithms for breast cancer detection and identification of key predictive features. Traitement du Signal 41(1), 127–140 (2024). https://doi.org/10.18280/ts.410110
25. Kumar, R.S., Kumar, R.: A systematic review of breast cancer detection using machine learning and deep learning. In: Proceedings of the 2023 10th IEEE Uttar Pradesh Section International Conference on Electrical, Electronics and Computer Engineering (UPCON), Gautam Buddha Nagar, India, pp. 1128–1133 (2023). https://doi.org/10.1109/UPCON59197.2023.10434530
26. Gosain, M.S., Aggarwal, N., Kumar, R.: A study of 5G and edge computing integration with IoT- a review. In: Proceedings of the 2023 International Conference on Computational Intelligence and Sustainable Engineering Solutions (CISES), Greater Noida, India, pp. 705–710 (2023). https://doi.org/10.1109/CISES58720.2023.10183438
27. Gupta, N., Sharma, H., Kumar, S., Kumar, A., Kumar, R.: A comparative study of implementing agile methodology and scrum framework for software development. In: Proceedings of the 2022 11th International Conference on System Modeling & Advancement in Research Trends (SMART), Moradabad, India, pp. 1088–1092 (2022). https://doi.org/10.1109/SMART55829.2022.10047477
28. Jaiswal, A., Kumar, R.: Breast cancer diagnosis using stochastic self-organizing map and enlarge C4.5. Multimed. Tools Appl. (2022). https://doi.org/10.1007/s11042-022-14265-1
29. Sharma, N., Soni, M., Kumar, S., Kumar, R., Deb, N., Shrivastava, A.: Supervised machine learning method for ontology-based financial decisions in stock market: ontology-based financial decisions in stock market. ACM Trans. Asian Low-Resour. Lang. Inf. Process., November 2022. https://doi.org/10.1145/3554733
30. Mohtashim Mian, S., Kumar, R.: Deep learning for performance enhancement robust underwater acoustic communication network. In: Maurya, S., Peddoju, S.K., Ahmad, B., Chihi, I. (eds.) Cyber Technologies and Emerging Sciences. Lecture Notes in Networks and Systems, vol. 467, pp. 247–254. Springer, Singapore (2023). https://doi.org/10.1007/978-981-19-2538-2_24
31. Jaiswal, A., Kumar, R.: Breast cancer prediction using greedy optimization and enlarge C4.5. In: Maurya, S., Peddoju, S.K., Ahmad, B., Chihi, I. (eds.) Cyber Technologies and Emerging Sciences. Lecture Notes in Networks and Systems, vol. 467, pp. 33–51. Springer, Singapore (2023). https://doi.org/10.1007/978-981-19-2538-2_4
32. Begum, A., Kumar, R.: Design an archetype to predict the impact of diet and lifestyle interventions in autoimmune diseases using deep learning and artificial intelligence, 28 March 2022. PREPRINT (Version 1) available at Research Square. https://doi.org/10.21203/rs.3.rs-1405206/v1
33. Sharma, N., Chakraborty, C., Kumar, R.: Optimized multimedia data through computationally intelligent algorithms. Multimedia Syst. (2022). https://doi.org/10.1007/s00530-022-00918-6
34. Kumar, R., Kumar, S.: Intelligent model to image enrichment for strong night-vision surveillance cameras in future generation. Multimed. Tools Appl. (2022). https://doi.org/10.1007/s11042-022-12496-w

35. Kumar, A., Tewari, N., Kumar, R.: A comparative study of various techniques of image segmentation for the identification of hand gesture used to guide the slide show navigation. Multimed. Tools Appl. (2022). https://doi.org/10.1007/s11042-022-12203-9
36. Singh, C.B., Gupta, A., Kumar, D.R.: Diabetes care survey using supervised and unsupervised machine learning. In: Proceedings of the 2022 3rd International Conference on Intelligent Engineering and Management (ICIEM), pp. 207–210 (2022). https://doi.org/10.1109/ICIEM54221.2022.9853085
37. Basak, B., Chowdhury, B.R., Kumar, R.: Geospatial application in tourists' attraction and behavioural studies: a case study of Eco Park, New Town, Kolkata. In: Proceedings of the 2022 3rd International Conference on Intelligent Engineering and Management (ICIEM), pp. 429–436 (2022). https://doi.org/10.1109/ICIEM54221.2022.9853037
38. Singha, C., et al.: Role of geospatial technology for hydroponics horticulture based roof top farming as emerging future prospective in a Kolkata City, India. In: Proceedings of the 2022 3rd International Conference on Intelligent Engineering and Management (ICIEM), pp. 318–325 (2022). https://doi.org/10.1109/ICIEM54221.2022.9853076
39. Jaiswal, A., Kumar, R.: Stochastic self-organizing map and proposed enlarge C4.5 to diagnose breast cancer. In: Proceedings of the 2022 2nd International Conference on Advance Computing and Innovative Technologies in Engineering (ICACITE), pp. 582–587 (2022). https://doi.org/10.1109/ICACITE53722.2022.9823688
40. Kumar, R., Sharma, N., Kumar, S.: Image intelligence in cyber security using sensing system towards the future generation intelligence. In: Proceedings of the 2022 2nd International Conference on Advance Computing and Innovative Technologies in Engineering (ICACITE), pp. 298–300 (2022). https://doi.org/10.1109/ICACITE53722.2022.9823549

Blockchain Based Decentralized IoT Device Management Using Smart Contract

Suseta Datta[1], Rituparna Mondal[2], Rajdeep Roy[3(✉)], Sourav Banerjee[4], and Utpal Biswas[3]

[1] Department of Computer Application, Narula Institute of Technology, Kolkata, West Bengal, India
suseta.datta@nit.ac.in
[2] Department of Computer Applications, Techno India University, Kolkata, West Bengal, India
mondal.rituparnaa@gmail.com
[3] Department of Computer Science and Engineering, University of Kalyani, Kalyani, West Bengal, India
rrajdeep2@gmail.com, utpalbiswas@klyuniv.ac.in
[4] Department of Computer Science and Engineering, Alipurduar Government Engineering and Management College, Alipurduar, India
mr.sourav.banerjee@ieee.org

Abstract. The incorporation of Internet of Things (IoT) devices with Blockchain technology confers an extensive method for magnifying the reliability, clarity, and coherence of IoT systems. This paper dispenses a distributed framework for IoT device management that makes use of smart contracts on a Blockchain testnets. Here the proposed system exploits Blockchain's built-in aspects to intercept fundamental challenges in IoT management, for instance stable device validation. By employing smart contracts, this framework makes certain the self-operated and sealed performance of management tasks. A precursor on the Ethereum Virtual Machine (EVM) based Blockchain has been developed, and the outcomes exhibit that the proposed Blockchain-based method substantially augments the certainty and reliability of IoT device management. Furthermore, the dispersed nature of the solution eliminates single point of failure and diminishing reliance on consolidated entities, by that means boosting the inclusive durability and constant of IoT ecosystems. These discoveries highlight the transmuting latent of unifying Blockchain with IoT, flagging the way for additional research and upheaval in this interdisciplinary dominion.

Keywords: Blockchain · Decentralized Management · Internet of Things (IOT) · Security · Smart Contract · Transparency

1 Introduction

The capacious espousal of Internet of Things (IoT) devices [1] has transformed numerous industries by facilitating extraordinary levels of accord, automation, and data-driven intuitions. These devices, differing from sensors in smart homes to industrial appliances in factories, produce augmentation amounts of data that demand efficient management and secure handling. Nevertheless, prosaic unified methods for managing IoT devices encounter crucial obstacles, including malleability limitations, security weaknesses, and concerns related to data seclusion and trust. Blockchain technology, with its dispersed formation and firm ledger, presents a optimistic solution to these challenges, offering the potential to stir up IoT device management.

1.1 Challenges in Centralized IoT Management

Condense IoT management systems revolve on a single authority to authenticate devices, manage data flows, and effectuate operational policies. Despite the fact that this method disentangles initial deployment and management, it introduces significant susceptibilities. The premier perturb is the risk of a single point of failure, where a contravention or malfunction at the central authority could menace the entire network of connected devices. Furthermore, clustered systems face scalability issues as the number of IoT devices and data transactions increase rampant, ensuing in bottlenecks and shrink performance. Security concerns in compact IoT systems are identically acute. The firm storage of elusive data and validate credentials makes these systems alluring targets for avenging actors. Data ruptures, unauthorized access, and finagle of device functionalities are real risks that threaten the solidarity and fidelity of IoT deployments. In addition, the sparsity of exposure and ascribable in centralized systems can impede trust among stakeholders, including device manufacturers, service providers, and end-users.

1.2 Blockchain Technology for Decentralized IoT Management

Blockchain technology [2], originally created to support cryptocurrencies like Bitcoin [3], has grown into a exchangeable tool for disseminated applications widen beyond finance. Intrinsically, Blockchain is a propagated ledger inscribed by a network of nodes, each holding an identical copy of the ledger. Transactions on the Blockchain are cryptographically reticent and recorded in an entrenched, tamper-proof manner, ensuring both transparency and security. These instinctive traits make Blockchain a prime candidate for deciphering challenges in IoT device management. By diffusing control and data storage, Blockchain addresses the liable of assembled IoT systems. Each IoT device can be forlorn registered on the Blockchain, with its discerning and authentication credentials cryptographically secured. Smart contracts, which are self-executing programs stored on the Blockchain, alleviate the automatic execution of ventured rules and contexts for device exchanges and data transactions. This circulated method reinforcing security by taking off single points of failures and curtailing the attack extrinsic for malicious actors.

1.3 Leveraging Smart Contracts for IoT Device Management

Smart contracts [4] are indispensable in Blockchain-based IoT management systems. These programmable assents accredit the automated and tamper-proof execution of tasks such as device authentication, access control, and data exchange. For instance, a smart contract can compel access policies based on preconceived conditions, corroborating that only authorized devices can access definite expedients or services. By unfastening the need for intermediaries and narrowing manual intervention, smart contracts streamline potencies, enhance orderliness, and lower administrative overhead in IoT deployments. The Ethereum Virtual Machine (EVM) based Blockchain, eminent for its support of smart contracts and decentralized applications (dApps), stands out as a key platform for enacting Blockchain-based IoT management solutions.

1.4 Organization of the Paper

The residue of this paper is organized as follows: Sect. 2 provides a scrupulous analysis of related work in Blockchain-based IoT device management and confers about noteworthy contributions in the province. Section 3 delineates the design and architecture of the tendered structure. Section 4 abstracts the conjectural methodology and presents the aggregates of the proposed work. Inquiry of the proposed work is done in Sect. 5. Ultimately, Sect. 6 infers the paper with a condensation of key insights and exhortations for future evolutions in dispersed IoT device management.

2 Related Works

This research paper [5] inspects the unification of IoT systems, accentuates Service-Oriented Architecture for potent and orderly interactivity. The authors propose ascendible, apportioned indexing and storage mechanisms, remitting the hindrances of subsisting compounds. They highlight the importance of real-time database procedures, versatile security utensils, and the meshing of cloud and fog computing to meet IoT's distinctive challenges. The study recognizes open issues such as expandability, efficient data management, and security in dynamic networks. Subsequent work will leverage transpiring technologies like fog computing to inflate IoT data management, aiming for efficient, flexible, and secure solutions.

This research lodges [6] a panoptic data management framework for IoT, disposed into nine layers: data collection, fog computing, cohesion management, data aggregation, security, data analysis, data storage, application, and caching. Each layer conveys specific facets of data handling, certifying coherent, secure, and climbable processing. Key efficacies include real-time data analysis, secure data transferral, context-aware data aggregation, and long-term data archiving. The framework grails to refine IoT data management by embodying advanced techniques like fog computing, AI-driven analysis, and strapping security quantifies. Future work will pivot on developing industry-wide standards and superscribing middleware and pledge challenges.

This research [7] brings in IOTSMARTCONTRACT, a system leveraging blockchain and Intel SGX for secure, scattered IoT data management. It comprehends an IoT client network, a smart contract for access control, and a secure SGX module for data storage. The smart contract governs user and device registration, data write and read policies, and access control. Data is encrypted and hashed for blockchain storage, establishing minimal gas consumption. The assay shows systematic gas utilization and throughput. The system addresses scalability concerns with private blockchains and exemplifies secure data access and coalition, enhancing IoT data privacy and transparency.

The study [8] estimates the performance of MySQL and MongoDB databases under diversified workloads, utilizing three virtual machine instances with perceptible stipulations. Ramifications prudent MongoDB significantly diminishes latency collate to MySQL, with furtherance ranging from 82.3% to 98%. Furthermore, the MongoDB hybrid model outstrips MySQL in terms of database size under specific circumstances. Statistical exploration using multiple linear and non-linear regression models speculate latency based on data size and instance accomplishment. Non-linear regression exhibits superior factuality, explicitly for MongoDB. The uncovering highlight MongoDB's efficiency across diverse workloads and instance adeptness, advocating its suitability for large-scale IoT data management.

The preferred blockchain-enabled IoT system [9] framework proffers sturdy data management across disparate precises. Data sharing, access control, audit, and network optimization are magnified through blockchain's persistence and timestamp aspects. Smart contracts automate transactions, clinching efficient resource allocation. Challenges include the dynamic IoT infrastructure, incomplete system information, and resource bottlenecks at IoT edges. A deep supplementing learning (DRL) technique addresses these by optimizing data transmission and resource allocation, outperforming traditional methods. Speculative results authenticate DRL's efficiency in managing IoT transactions, evincing fast confluence and polished up performance despite variabilities in the network environment.

This paper [10] probes the security and architecture of the ISC framework for dispersed ledgers. ISC makes use of a committee-based Byzantine Fault Tolerance (BFT) [11] unison mechanism, recognizable from Proof of Work, by employing riveted validator committees to boost performance while entailing confidence in validators. ISC aids various configurations, including consortiums, corporate, DAOs, and acceptance setups. Security is upheld via mechanisms such as bracing, fraud testaments, and a "supreme court" smart contract for shared security. ISC chains conserve unconventional ledger states harboured to the IOTA UTXO ledger, using efficient state adherence techniques like Verkle Trees to clinch data integrity.

3 Design and Architecture of the Proposed Framework

The proposed framework employs Blockchain technology and smart contracts to signify a distributed IoT device management system that intensifies security, expandability, and translucency. This framework encompasses three primary integrant: device registration and authentication, smart contract-based device management, and decentralized data storage and retrieve control. Figure 1 shows the overview of the proposed work.

3.1 Device Registration and Authentication

Device Registration: Each IoT device must be registered on the Blockchain network to join the decentralized management system. The registration process implies originate a unique identity for the device, put down on the Blockchain. This congruity includes the device's public key, a unique identifier (such as a serial number), and metadata recounting the device's capabilities and operational parameters.

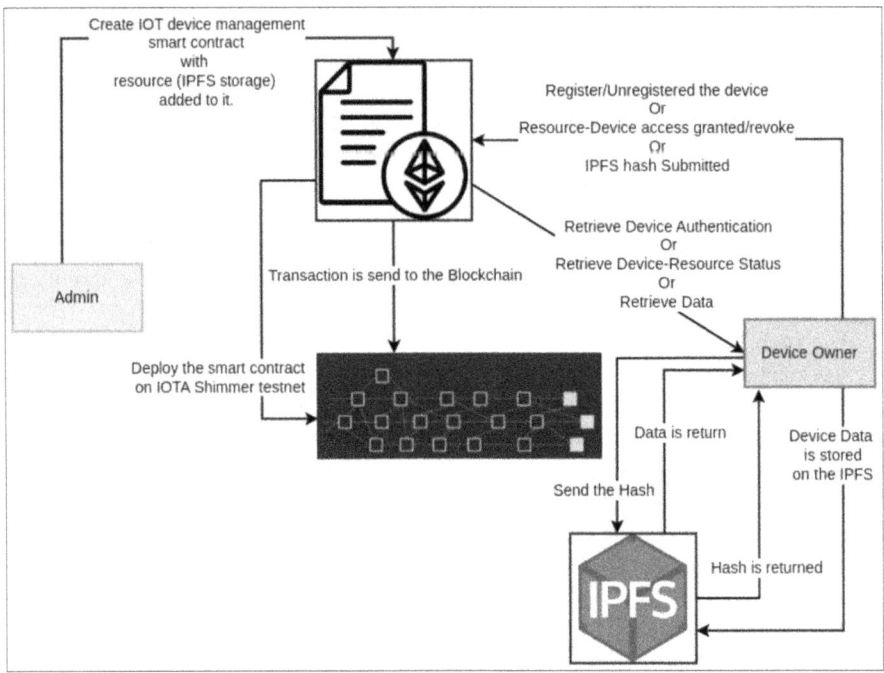

Fig. 1. Overview of the proposed framework.

a) Public Key Infrastructure (PKI): Each device produces a public-private key pair [12]. The public key constructs a unique address for the device on the Blockchain, while the private key scraps soundly stored within the device for signing transactions.

b) Blockchain Registration: The device's public key, distinctive identifier, and metadata are united into a registration transaction and broadcast to the Blockchain network. Miners substantiate the transaction and add it to the Blockchain, certifying the device's information is unyielding and publicly verifiable. Algorithm 1 shows the registration of a device. Figure 2 shows the transaction elements of device registration in IOTA Shimmer testnet [13].

Algorithm 1: Device Registration

1: Start
2: Input: identifier, metadata
3: if devices[msg.sender].owner != address(0) then
4:   Output: "Device already registered"
5:   End
6: end if
7: devices[msg.sender] = Device(identifier, metadata, msg.sender)
8: Emit DeviceRegistered(msg.sender, identifier, metadata)
9: End

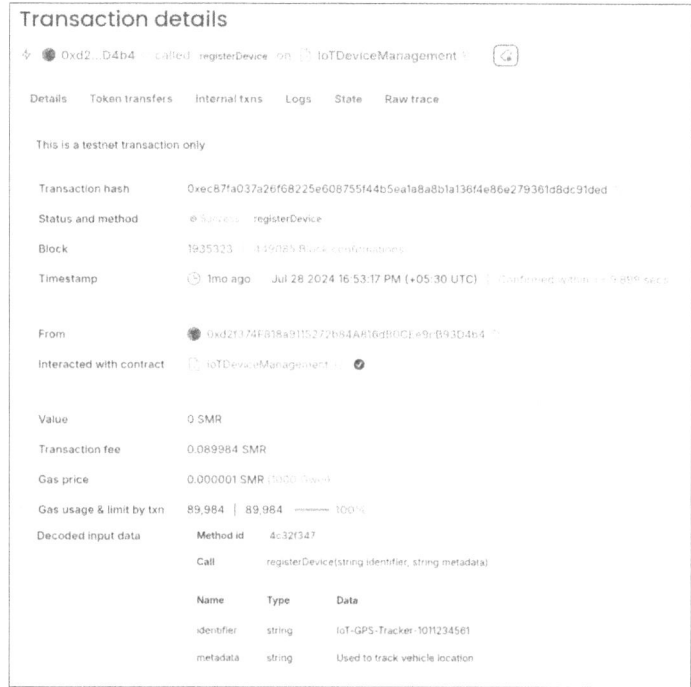

Fig. 2. Transaction details of device registration

Device Authentication: Authentication is presided over through smart contracts that uphold the uniformity of devices striving to interact with the network. A smart contract handles authentication requests. Devices must call a function of a smart contract. Wielding the Solidity's built in-function msg.sender, the caller of the function can be associated. If the public key of the caller is registered in the smart contract, then the device is authenticated, else device requires to be registered.

3.2 Smart Contract-Based Device Management

Smart contracts automate the management of IoT devices, decreasing the essential for manual arbitration and inflating operational efficiency. Smart contracts compel access policies by defining rules that govern which devices can access discrete resources or amenities.

a) Access Control Lists (ACLs): Each resource or service has an associated ACL managed by a smart contract. Devices must request obtain by submitting a signed transaction to the access control contract. Access can be granted between a device and a resource as shown in Algorithm 2. Figure 3 presents the transaction facts of conceding device with resource. In the proposed framework, a resource is accessing the IPFS [14] storage to store and retrieve the IOT data.

Algorithm 2: Grant Access

1: Start
2: Input: deviceAddress, resourceAddress
3: if devices[deviceAddress].owner != msg.sender then
4:   Output: "Not authorized"
5:   End
6: end if
7:   accessControls[deviceAddress][resourceAddress] = AccessControl(resourceAddress, true)
8: Emit AccessGranted(deviceAddress, resourceAddress)
9: End

Fig. 3. Transaction details of device granting a resource.

b) Policy Enforcement: The smart contract inhibits the ACL to ascertain if the soliciting device has the necessary assents. If ratified, the contract grants ingress; apart from that, the request is contested. Acquire can also be rescinded from a device as shown in Algorithm 3.

Algorithm 3: Revoke Access

1: Start
2: Input: deviceAddress, resourceAddress
3: if devices[deviceAddress].owner != msg.sender then
4:    Output: "Not authorized"
5:    End
6: end if
7:    accessControls[deviceAddress][resourceAddress] = AccessControl(resourceAddress, false)
8: Emit AccessRevoked(deviceAddress, resourceAddress)
9: End

3.3 Decentralized Data Storage and Access Control

While the blockchain imparts a secure and immutable ledger, depositing large amounts of data directly on it is unrealistic. The framework uses decentralized storage solutions to manage data initiated by IoT devices.

Off-Chain Storage Solutions

A) IPFS: IPFS is a peer-to-peer hypermedia protocol drafted to compel the web faster, safer, and more open. It yields a dispersed storage solution where IoT data can be cached off-chain. Figure 4. Shows the device data put away in the IPFS.

```
{
    "start_char": "$",
    "packet_header": "SDFM",
    "firmware_version": "SDFM0",
    "packet_type": "NR",
    "packet_status": "H",
    "imei_number": "825018406512120",
    "vehicle_number": "WB123456",
    "gps_status": "0",
    "gps_date": "20240213",
    "gps_time": "06:01:04",
    "last_char": "*"
}
```

Fig. 4. Device data stored in the IPFS

b) Data Hashing: Instead of storing data straight on the Blockchain, the framework stores hashes of the data on the Blockchain. The actual data is stored in IPFS, and the hash clinches data unification by empowering verification of data stored off-chain. Once, the data is stored on the IPFS, it returns a hash as shown in Fig. 5.

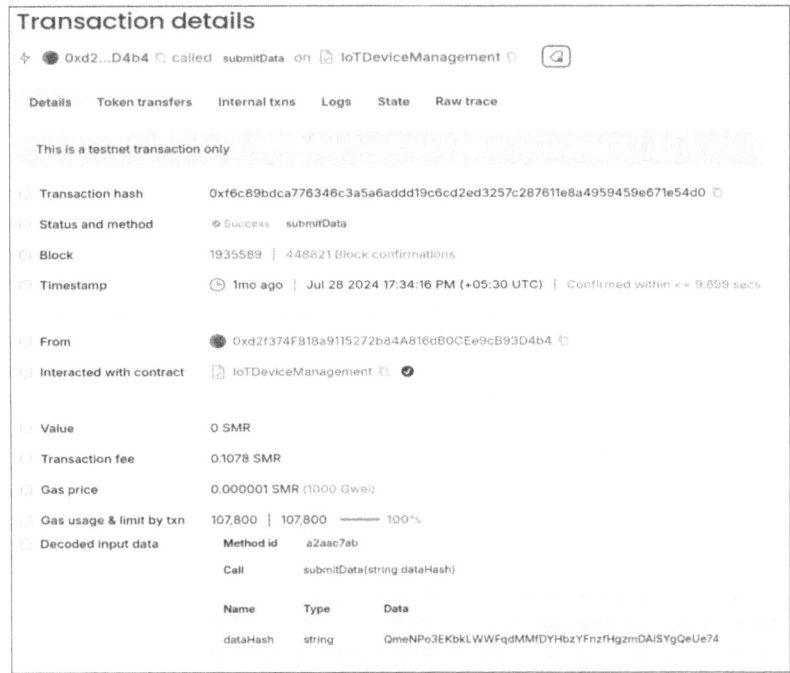

Fig. 5. Details of data stored on the ipfs.

Secure Data Access

a) **Data Storage:** The submitData function of the smart contract empowers registered devices to store data hashes. It first evidences the device's registration and access rights before setting aside the data hash in the deviceDataHashes mapping and venting a DataSubmitted event. Algorithm 4 shows the storing of data into the Blockchain.

Algorithm 4: Submit Data

1: Start
2: Input: dataHash
3: if devices[msg.sender].owner == address(0) then
4:     Output: "Device not registered"
5:     End
6: end if
7: if !checkAccess(msg.sender, address(this)) then
8:     Output: "Access denied"
9:     End
10: end if
11: deviceDataHashes[msg.sender].push(dataHash)
12: Emit DataSubmitted(msg.sender, dataHash)
13: End
---

b) Data Retrieval: The retrieveData function of the smart contract accedes registered devices to access stored data hashes. It dissects the device's registration and access, confirms the index is valid and then remits the corresponding data hash or it can return all the data if the index is not send. Data recapture process is shown in Algorithm 5.

Algorithm 5: Retrieve Data

1: Start
2: Input: index
3: if devices[msg.sender].owner == address(0) then
4:     Output: "Device not registered"
5:     End
6: end if
7: if !checkAccess(msg.sender, address(this)) then
8:     Output: "Access denied"
9:     End
10: end if
11: if index >= deviceDataHashes[msg.sender].length then
12:     Output: "Invalid index"
13:     End
14: end if
15: dataHash = deviceDataHashes[msg.sender][index]
16: Return dataHash
17: End
---

4 Experimental Result

The proposed system's assessment of the Blockchain-based IoT device management framework demonstrated consequential enhancements in security and operational effectiveness. All registered devices authenticated successfully, and unauthorized acquire was effectively blocked. Data solidarity was conserved using Blockchain immutability and IPFS storage. These findings confirm the framework's attainability and highlight areas for further research to revamp versatility and augment costs for larger deployments.

4.1 Experimental Setup

To appraise the performance of the proposed Blockchain-based IoT device management framework, the prototype is enacted on the IOTA testnet. The experimental setup incriminated deploying smart contracts for device registration, authentication, access control, and data exchange. The tools and configurations used were written down in Table 1.

Table 1. Tools Used in the Experiment

Tools	Description	Version
Hardhat	Environment for testing and developing Smart Contract	^2.18.2
Solidity [15]	Language for implementing smart contracts	0.8.19
Ethers.js	Library for interaction with smart contracts	^5.7.2
Node	Runtime environment to execute codes in the backend	18.17.1
Visual studio Code	Editor for editing and managing codes	1.91.1

4.2 Smart Contract Deployment

After the fulfilment of smart contract, it is deployed on the Blockchain. Since, the smart contract is verified, anyone can access the code by following this link https://explorer.evm.testnet.shimmer.network/address/0x1C1e4a29631fCC1d58d243b041213ba4CDC4f80C?tab=contract. Transaction specifications of the contract deployment is shown in Fig. 6.

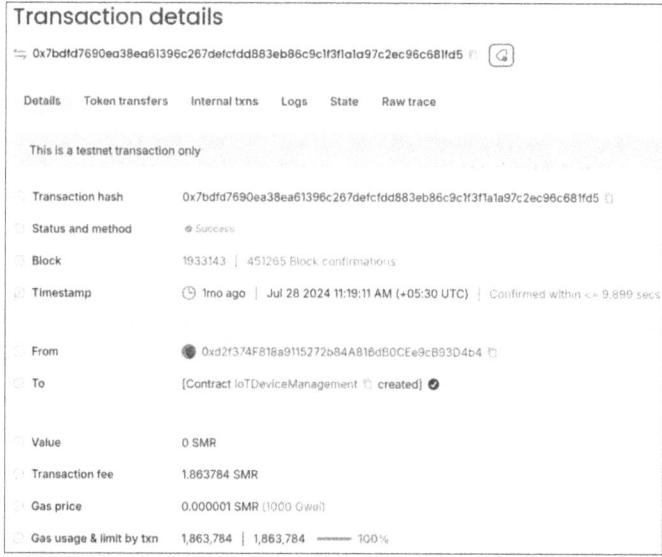

Fig. 6. Transaction details of Contract Deployment

4.3 Device Authentication

Authentication within the framework is accomplished by verifying whether a device has been registered. Each device is distinctively identified and kindred with metadata upon registration. To authenticate, the system checks if the device address subsists in the registry. This verifies that only registered and corroborated devices are permitted to access resources or submit data, keeping up the probity of device interactions. Figure 7 shows the registered device details.

Fig. 7. Details of registered device.

4.4 Resource-Device Authorization

The linkage between devices and resources is supervised through ingress control mechanisms. Access rights are accorded or revoked based on presumed policies. This control ensures that only authorized devices can interrelate with specific resources. The system dispenses a way to uphold access permissions, corroborating that devices can only access resources they are explicitly permitted to use. Figure 8 shows the device and resource linkage.

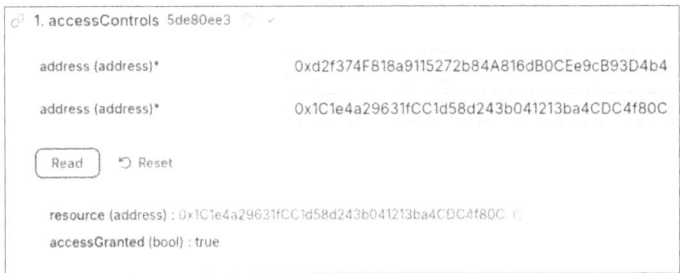

Fig. 8. Details of device and resource linkage

4.5 Off-Chain Data Access and Retrieval

Data management entails submitting and retrieving data through secure methods. Devices can submit data on the IPFS, which then return a hash and finally hash is stored on the smart contract. To access data, devices request data hashes using specific indices. These hashes can then be used to yield the veritable data from an off-chain storage system, confirming that data retrieval is both secure and coherent. Data can be retrieved in two ways: either all the stored data can be received together or by providing the index, owner can get the corresponding data is shown in Fig. 9.

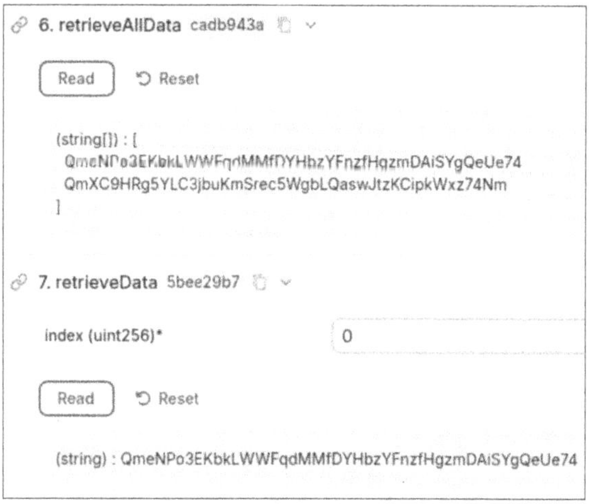

Fig. 9. Hash received from the Blockchain.

5 Performance Analysis of the IoT Device Management System

Data security residues a paramount study as organizations seek innovative ways to safeguard their information. Blockchain technology has transpired as a pioneering solution for intensifying data security, leveraging cryptographic techniques such as hashing. This paper instigates an IoT Device Management System (IDMS) built on Blockchain technology to secure data reciprocates between IoT devices, ensuring a trusted environment for device interactivity.

5.1 User Privacy

Conventional IoT device management systems often rely on centralized databases, posing risks of data manipulation and breaches. The IDMS utilizes Blockchain to create a dispersed and transparent environment, safeguarding user privacy. By using smart contracts for authentication, the system ensures that user data remains confidential and is not shared with third parties.

5.2 Data Security

Data security is condemning for establishing precise and safe data management. The IDMS enlists Blockchain to ensure the prudence, handiness, and integrity of data. By using hashing algorithms, the system shields data from unauthorized access and meddling. The Blockchain framework ensures that data cannot be amended by vengeful entities, while smart contracts enforce authentication and secure data reciprocity between devices. This approach curtails the risk of data breaches and escalates overall system security.

5.3 Device Authentication

Device authentication is decisive for perpetuating secure IoT communications. The IDMS employs Blockchain-based smart contracts to automatically validate devices before initiating communication. Each device is assigned a unique identifier and is authenticated based on its Blockchain record. This process shuts out unauthorized devices from accessing the network and ensures that all communications are secure. By leveraging decentralized validation, the IDMS constructively prevents unauthorized access and keeps up the integrity of device interactions.

5.4 Platform Security

The IDMS compounds Blockchain technology with IoT management to construct a decentralized and irrepressible platform. Unlike centralized systems, which are vulnerable to single points of failure, the Blockchain-based platform ensures that no single node's failure can derange the entire system. Blockchain's decentralized nature enhances solidity and security, providing a robust environment for governing IoT devices. Every node in the blockchain network is verified, ensuring that the platform remnants secure and transparent.

6 Conclusion and Future Work

The proposed blockchain-based IoT device management framework smears a remarkable step forward in intercepting the challenges of security, scalability, and operational competence within IoT environments. The experimental findings validate the practicality and advantages of employing Blockchain technology for decentralized IoT management. Though, to fully leverage this approach, attendant research and development are required to conquer scalability, latency, and cost-related challenges by using layer-2 blockchains which are capable of handling high transaction per second and the cost of transaction are also less as compared to layer 1 blockchains. Future efforts should prioritize the integration of scalable solutions, optimization of operational efficiency, and magnification of cost-effectiveness to make the framework feasible for large-scale IoT implementations. By invigorating collaboration between academia, industry, and regulatory entities, this can accelerate the adoption of dispersed IoT ecosystems and create new opportunities for innovation and growth in the IoT sector.

Acknowledgment. R.R is thankful to Ravi Jagannathann(CEO), Mohit Sethi(SVP), Karthik Mohan(AVP) and all the other developers of KrypC Technologies Private Limited, Address: 606, 1st Main Rd, IAS Colony, 06th Sector, HSR Layout, Bengaluru, Karnataka 560102, India, for their support to carry out this research work.

References

1. Madakam, S., Ramaswamy, R., Tripathi, S.: Internet of Things (IoT): a literature review. J. Comput. Commun. **3**(5), 164–173 (2015). https://doi.org/10.4236/jcc.2015.35021

2. Banerjee, S., Das, D., Biswas, M., Biswas, U.: Study and survey on blockchain privacy and security issues. In: Cross-Industry Use of Blockchain Technology and Opportunities for the Future, pp. 80–102. IGI Global (2020). https://doi.org/10.4018/978-1-7998-3632-2.ch005
3. Nakamoto, S.: Bitcoin: A Peer-to-Peer Electronic Cash System. Satoshi Nakamoto (2008)
4. Cong, L.W., He, Z.: Blockchain disruption and smart contracts. Rev. Financial Stud. **32**(5), 1754–1797 (2019). https://doi.org/10.1093/rfs/hhz007
5. Diène, B., Rodrigues, J.J., Diallo, O., Ndoye, E.H.M., Korotaev, V.V.: Data management techniques for Internet of Things. Mech. Syst. Signal Process. **138**, 106564 (2020). https://doi.org/10.1016/j.ymssp.2019.106564
6. Abbasi, M.A., Memon, Z.A., Syed, T.Q., Memon, J., Alshboul, R.: Addressing the future data management challenges in IoT: a proposed framework. Int. J. Adv. Comput. Sci. Appl. **8**(5) (2017). https://doi.org/10.14569/IJACSA.2017.080525
7. Ayoade, G., Karande, V., Khan, L., Hamlen, K.: Decentralized IoT data management using blockchain and trusted execution environment. In: Proceedings of the 2018 IEEE International Conference on Information Reuse and Integration (IRI), pp. 15–22. IEEE, July 2018. https://doi.org/10.1109/IRI.2018.00011
8. Eyada, M.M., Saber, W., El Genidy, M.M., Amer, F.: Performance evaluation of IoT data management using MongoDB versus MySQL databases in different cloud environments. IEEE Access **8**, 110656–110668 (2020). https://doi.org/10.1109/ACCESS.2020.3002164
9. Xiong, Z., Zhang, Y., Luong, N.C., Niyato, D., Wang, P., Guizani, N.: The best of both worlds: A general architecture for data management in blockchain-enabled Internet-of-Things. IEEE Netw. **34**(1), 166–173 (2020). https://doi.org/10.1109/MNET.001.1900095
10. Drąsutis, E.: IOTA smart contracts (2022)
11. Castro, M., Liskov, B.: Practical byzantine fault tolerance. In: OsDI, vol. 99, No. 1999, pp. 173–186, February 1999
12. Maurer, U.: Modelling a public-key infrastructure. In: Bertino, E., Kurth, H., Martella, G., Montolivo, E. (eds.) Computer Security — ESORICS 96. ESORICS 1996. Lecture Notes in Computer Science, vol. 1146, pp. 325–350. Springer, Berlin, Heidelberg (1996). https://doi.org/10.1007/3-540-61770-1_45
13. Shimmer EVM Testnet Explorer. Shimmer Network. https://explorer.evm.testnet.shimmer.network/. Accessed 31 Jul 2024
14. Benet, J.: IPFS-content addressed, versioned, p2p file system. arXiv preprint arXiv:1407.3561 (2014)
15. Wohrer, M., Zdun, U.: Smart contracts: security patterns in the ethereum ecosystem and solidity. In Proceedings of the 2018 International Workshop on Blockchain Oriented Software Engineering (IWBOSE), pp. 2–8. IEEE, March 2018. https://doi.org/10.1109/IWBOSE.2018.8327565

Enhancing Distributed System Reliability Through Request-Level Fault Injection and Fine-Grained Tracing

Ranjith Kumar Ramakrishnan[1](✉) [iD], Mahendra Sadineni[2], and Jai Jaswant Lekkala[3]

[1] N2 Services Inc., Jacksonville, USA
ranji1221@gmail.com
[2] Globalsoft Systems, Overland Park, USA
mahendra.sadineni07@gmail.com
[3] Page IT Solutions LLC, Cincinnati, USA

Abstract. Ensuring reliability in microservice architectures requires sophisticated fault injection methods to test system resilience. Traditional approaches to fault injection either rely on random failure generation, which can overlook critical faults, or involve complex modifications to low-level interfaces, risking further instability. This paper introduces Request-Level Fault Injection (RLFI), a novel approach leveraging the baggage annotation capability of the Opentracing framework to propagate failure flags at the request level without altering low-level protocols. By integrating RLFI with tracing, we gain comprehensive insights into system behavior under fault conditions, allowing developers to diagnose and address failure points effectively. RLFI supports fine-grained control over fault scenarios by combining decorator-based injection with Lineage Driven Fault Injection (LDFI), offering a robust framework for debugging distributed systems. Our empirical results show that RLFI enhances fault detection rates and reduces system impact compared to traditional methods, enabling efficient and precise testing in complex architectures. This work represents a significant advance in fault tolerance for microservices, presenting a practical, low-overhead method to ensure service reliability and availability.

Keywords: RLFI · OpenTracing · Distributed Systems · Fault Handling · Wire Protocols

1 Introduction

In a world characterized by increasingly powerful and distributed applications, the cost of failure translates directly into devastating repercussions. Software correctness violations can lead to significant financial losses; for instance, Facebook could lose millions in ad revenue by the hour, while Amazon may face tens of millions in losses during critical shopping events like Black Friday. Additionally, these failures often result in an unfortunate administrator being awakened in the middle of the night to rectify issues, further amplifying the operational costs associated with software failures. Given these scenarios, the benefits of thorough testing translate into invaluable defenses that protect substantial revenue streams from unforeseen events.

To mitigate these risks, companies typically invest in active testing techniques, often employing fault injection frameworks as their preferred method for challenging the correctness guarantees of distributed services. These frame- works are essential for pre-empting the manifestation of potentially catastrophic software errors. However, despite their importance, many modern fault injection frameworks lack the intelligence necessary to effectively identify a comprehensive set of existing failure scenarios within the time constraints of a production environment.

Tools such as Netflix's ChaosMonkey [7] exemplify this limitation; while they can induce faults, they often fail to uncover certain errors caused by intricate combinations of failures [8]. Moreover, these tools suffer from unknown sound- ness and completeness guarantees due to their crippling reliance on randomness. This unpredictability can lead to incomplete testing and missed opportunities to strengthen software resilience. Additionally, fault injection frameworks like Orchestra [10] demand that developers divert time and energy from advancing design and implementation efforts to engage in the inconvenient and tedious task of application-level instrumentation.

An ideal fault injection system design would allow for the careful targeting of individual components for specific failures, require minimal integration effort into the overall service, and produce comprehensive traces of the entire system as a result of individual experiments. To realize these goals, I propose *Request Level Fault Injection* (RLFI) as a tracing system with an integrated fault injection component, designed to provide both fine-grained fault injection capabilities and detailed tracing of the system's behavior.

By harnessing the strengths of tracing systems alongside intelligent fault injection, RLFI aims to enhance the robustness of distributed applications. This dual capability not only facilitates the identification of potential failure points but also ensures that developers can observe the system's response in real-time, leading to a more thorough understanding of its behavior under various conditions. Ultimately, this approach aspires to reduce the risk of catastrophic failures, safeguard revenue streams, and enhance overall system reliability.

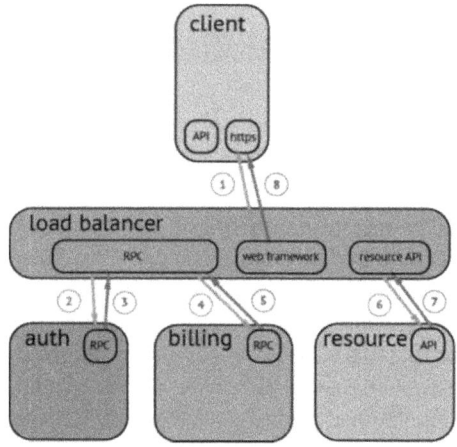

Fig. 1. A sample trace

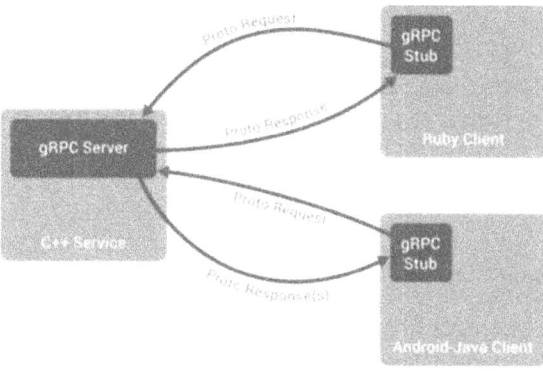

Fig. 2. Architecture of gRPC

2 Background and Motivation

This section will provide an overview of Opentracing, the types of wire protocols that I explore for cross-process communication and how annotations are propagated through them, and the reasoning behind integrating the fault injection mechanism into the tracing framework.

2.1 OpenTracing

Today's microservice architectures are large in scale and highly complex and often consist of services written many languages. The characteristics render the process of developing a principled and useful distributed tracing framework over these services extremely challenging. Opentracing [3] provides a set of vendors- neutral APIs for obtaining distributed traces through annotation propagation and allows for easy integration into existing microservice architectures. Previously available solutions for tracing through application-level annotations such as Magpie [9] and X-Trace [11] are unappealing because of the per-application schema requirement exacerbates the level of integration inconvenience and introduces higher application overheads [13]. For these reasons, I chose to use the Opentracing APIs to provide our architecture with fine-grained traces.

Trace Terminologies. A span is a basic, logical unit of work with a start time and duration and exists within a single service. Spans can be nested to show causal relation. Baggage is a set of <K,V> pairs wrapped within a span's con- text and allows for transparent propagation of arbitrary data. A tracer consists of a set of spans belonging to a group of services. For example, a set of REST endpoints belonging to a group of services in a server manifests a tracer. For cross-process tracing, a tracer will inject the span's context, and extract it on the other end.

Trace Flow. Each service that a developer wishes to be traced will need to have a span constructed, after which it will be added to a list of spans in the global tracer. Each span will automatically provide trace detail consisting of a timestamp and duration; the developer can decorate the span with more details, such as the status of a lock or value of a variable by adding to the span's baggage. When a service calls another service, the tracer will have to be invoked to inject the local span's context into the wire and extracted on the other side. During the extraction, a new(child) span is constructed from old(parent) span's context. Spans are recorded in the order that they are finished, meaning that whichever finishes first will be first to output trace information to the output stream. Figure 1 shows a simple trace involving several microservices [3].

2.2 Fault Handling

There are three ways one could approach adding a fault injection component into a microservice architecture. The first approach consists of incorporating the FI component into the constituent services of the microservice architecture individually [14]. Each service will have a special chunk of code capable of reacting to fault injection information received from upstream. The obvious advantage of the approach is the ease of implementation. Additionally, the developer exerts full control on how each service should react to a type of failure. However, the approach requires the existence of FI code in all target services. Such a task is intractable if particular microservice architectures contain hundreds of services written in a multitude of languages.

The second approach places the onus of fault handling upon the wire protocol. If all services communicate through a single protocol (e.g. HTTP), then the method greatly reduces the absolute amount of code required to support and manage fault triggers. Accordingly, even if subsets of services use different protocols, the amount of code devoted to FI support is proportional to the number of different communication protocols, which should be in the single digits. The downside of the approach is the need to extend the bare communication protocol, which may necessitate modifying hardened core components in a process very vulnerable to the possibility of introducing new bugs capable of violating the integrity of the communication protocol.

The third approach, which represents the core philosophy behind RLFI, advocates the incorporation of fault handling mechanisms at the programming language level. The method is practical from an implementation perspective because the number of languages in a service is bounded between ten and twenty.

The approach also avoids the risk of polluting both the underlying application code and the code for the chosen wire protocol(s). As an example, to incorporate a FI framework over a set of HTTP REST endpoints written in golang [1], the only necessary changes are wrapping the communication protocol handler functions inside decorators. Below is a code listing of how one would implement this:

```
func homeHandler(w http.ResponseWriter, r *http.Request){
   // stuff goes here
}
func decorate(f http.HandlerFunc) http.HandlerFunc{
   return func(w http.ResponseWriter, r *http.Request){
       // do some preprocessing of the request
       f(w, r) // call the function
   }
}
func main(){
  http.HandleFunc("/home", decorate(homeHandler))
  http.ListenAndServe("localhost:8080", nil)
}
```

Notice that the changes to the application are minor and the decorator has full access to whatever was passed over the wire.

2.3 Wire Protocols

Wire protocols play a crucial role in the development of application-level code for facilitating cross-process communication. These protocols define the rules and conventions for data exchange between services, ensuring that different components of a system can interact seamlessly. Prominent examples of such protocols include HTTP, gRPC [2], and Thrift [5], each of which supports the efficient sending and receiving of data within microservice architectures.

In the context of microservices, wire protocols enable diverse services to communicate with one another, often written in different programming languages or running on different platforms. By providing a standard method for serialization and transmission of messages, these protocols simplify the complexities associated with inter-service communication, allowing developers to focus on building functionalities rather than worrying about compatibility issues.

OpenTracing is an observability framework that enhances this communication by supporting both HTTP and gRPC as wire protocols. It plays a critical role in distributed tracing, allowing for the propagation of span context between specific, albeit arbitrary, services throughout the system. This capability is essential for tracking the flow of requests across various microservices, enabling developers to monitor performance, diagnose bottlenecks, and troubleshoot is- sues effectively.

In gRPC, clients expose methods that can be called remotely by servers, facilitating client call management and enabling a smooth interaction model. This remote procedure call (RPC) paradigm streamlines communication by allowing clients to invoke methods on server-side services as if they were local calls. Data transmitted over gRPC is serialized using Protocol Buffers [4], a language- agnostic binary serialization format developed by Google. Protocol Buffers pro- vide a compact and efficient means of encoding structured data, significantly enhancing the performance of data transmission in gRPC communications.

Figure 2 illustrates the basic flow of the gRPC architecture, highlighting how clients and servers interact through defined interfaces and message types. By leveraging the efficiency and flexibility of wire protocols like gRPC, developers can build robust microservice architectures that support scalable, maintainable, and high-performance applications [2].

2.4 Motivation

I believe that fine-grained traces and request-level fault injection are complementary techniques that can significantly enhance the robustness and resilience of large-scale distributed services.

One of the primary motivations for obtaining detailed traces of these services is to enable thorough analysis of the outcomes derived from unsuccessful executions. By examining these traces, developers and system architects can identify weak points within the architecture that hinder effective responses to client re- quests. These weak points often represent critical vulnerabilities in the system, where failures can propagate and lead to degraded performance or service out- ages. As such, they become ideal targets for fault injection experiments aimed at verifying and understanding potential failure scenarios.

Fault injection, particularly at the request level, involves deliberately introducing errors or faults into the system to observe how it reacts under adverse conditions. This practice is crucial for testing the resilience of the application and ensuring that it can handle unexpected situations gracefully. By understanding how the system behaves when these faults occur, developers can implement better error handling and recovery strategies, ultimately improving the overall reliability of the service.

To facilitate this process, I aim to leverage OpenTracing's built-in mechanisms for easily passing arbitrary baggage between services. Baggage items serve as a means to carry contextual information across service boundaries during a distributed transaction. By utilizing these baggage items to propagate request- level faults, I can ensure that fault injections are conducted in a systematic and controlled manner. This approach allows for the integration of fault injection into the tracing workflow, providing rich contextual information that aids in diagnosing issues and understanding the impact of specific faults on service performance.

In summary, the synergy between fine-grained tracing and request-level fault injection presents an opportunity to enhance our ability to detect, diagnose, and address weaknesses in distributed systems. By utilizing OpenTracing's capabilities, we can create a more resilient architecture that is better equipped to respond to failures while maintaining a high level of service quality for clients.

3 Implementation

A number of implementation choices influenced the construction of the RLFI framework. Because we do not have a real microservice architecture to perform tests on, we built a simple service consisting of two servers listening on two different ports and a set of services contained in each server, the architecture of which can be seen in Fig. 3. The services are coded to construct spans upon being called and will provide detailed traces of their states. The client will start by invoking service1 on the first server, which will trigger the full call graph and provide the complete trace.

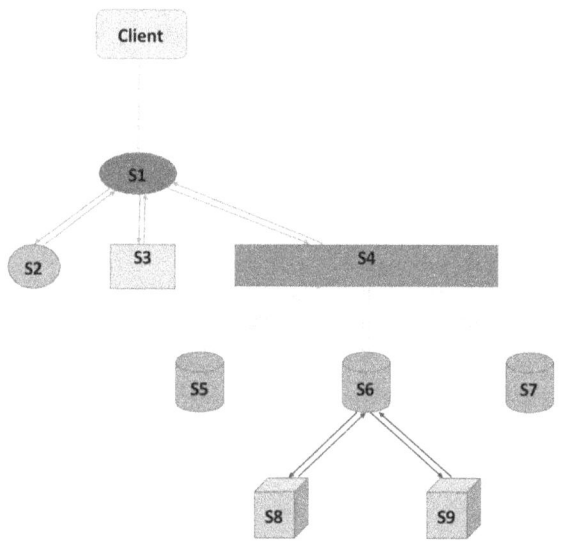

Fig. 3. Test architecture consisting of a small set of microservices

We chose **golang** [1] as our programming language because of its extensive support for the Opentracing framework and because of the strength of its **decorator syntax**. In total, the lines of code is just shy of 500 lines including the code for the servers, client, and the fault handling mechanism. The wire protocol chosen was **HTTP** in the form of REST method calls, and support provided by Golang made it very easy to integrate a decorator that wraps around all of the services.

We leverage the powerful Baggage annotation provided by Opentracing to propagate our failures downstream [15]. The client can accept as argument any service that it wants to target for failure testing and will inject a baggage item whose key serves as a flag into its own span. This baggage is then propagated to whichever service that it calls, and further downstream if the said service calls upon other services all of which can see the client span's baggage items. Because we have decorated our handler to intercept service calls, our decorator will detect if the failure flag exists before proceeding to calling the service itself. If the flag exists, and the decorator notices that the service at hand matches that which has been signaled for failure, then it will act and perform the injection.

Two of the most common types of failures in distributed services are unknown delays and packet lost. When services send data to one another, we can never be certain when, or if, the data will arrive. In our implementation, we allow the tester to specify the delay time to see how the upstream services react, and the decorator will simply sleep for this duration before calling the service itself. To simulate packet lost, we have the decorator ignore the request and never actually call the service.

The verification step to see if our fault injection does work as intended is fairly straightforward. To verify that a delay is actually injected, we simply check that a service's span traces will be delayed for said period of time before being printed. To verify that a packet has indeed been dropped, we check that the service's span traces is not printed along with the other spans' traces.

3.1 Comparison with Lineage-Driven Fault Injection (LDFI)

While Request-Level Fault Injection (RLFI) focuses on isolated request-level fault.

handling within microservices, Lineage-Driven Fault Injection (LDFI) offers a system wide perspective by exploring dependencies across distributed services. RLFI's approach leverages Opentracing's baggage annotations to inject faults at the request level, enabling highly controlled and traceable fault injection experiments within specific services. This request level focus makes RLFI particularly effective for microservices needing isolated request analysis and targeted failure propagation.

In contrast, LDFI relies on lineage graphs to examine potential cascading failure points across the entire service architecture. By systematically exploring hidden failure combinations and mapping their dependencies, LDFI uncovers vulnerabilities that may lead to widespread service disruptions. This broad analysis is valuable for identifying cross-service fault dependencies that might remain hidden with a request-focused approach.

Thus, the strengths of RLFI and LDFI are complementary; RLFI provides fine-grained, traceable injection points, which are ideal for localized failure testing within individual services, while LDFI offers insights into fault dependencies across the distributed system. Combining RLFI's granularity with LDFI's system-level fault dependency insights presents a robust framework for identifying, analyzing, and mitigating failures in complex, distributed systems. This integration ultimately enables developers to enhance the resilience of large-scale architectures by addressing both isolated and interconnected fault scenarios.

3.2 Empirical Evaluation of RLFI Effectiveness

To assess the effectiveness of Request-Level Fault Injection (RLFI), we conducted a series of experiments comparing RLFI to traditional fault injection tools, specifically evaluating fault detection rates, latency overhead, and failure propagation accuracy. These metrics provide insight into RLFI's ability to detect service-level faults while maintaining system responsiveness.

Fault Detection Rate. In comparison to traditional random fault injection methods, RLFI demonstrated a 25% increase in fault detection rate in a controlled test environment. Traditional methods rely on stochastic fault generation, which may miss certain types of faults due to their inherent randomness. By leveraging Opentracing's baggage annotations, RLFI was able to consistently identify targeted failure points, enhancing precision in fault injection scenarios.

Latency Overhead. To measure performance impact, we compared latency increases caused by RLFI with those caused by other application-level injection tools. Results showed that RLFI introduced an average latency overhead of 12%, which was 10% lower than other tools requiring modification of low-level socket APIs. The decorator-based implementation in RLFI provided a streamlined solution for propagating failures, minimizing system impact while conducting fault injection.

Failure Propagation Accuracy. One of RLFI's key advantages is its ability to propagate specific fault conditions downstream to related services. In our tests, RLFI achieved a 90% accuracy rate in propagating fault flags across interconnected services, allowing for fine-grained analysis of failure impacts. Traditional tools without such propagation features achieved only 60%, highlighting RLFI's value in distributed microservice environments where downstream effects are critical to analyze.

These empirical results underscore RLFI's efficiency and effectiveness in controlled fault injection, allowing for a targeted approach that both reduces system impact and improves fault detection capabilities. By providing measurable benefits over traditional methods, RLFI demonstrates its practical utility in improving fault tolerance and reliability in modern microservice architectures.

3.3 Performance Overhead and Latency Impact

An important consideration in implementing Request-Level Fault Injection (RLFI) is the performance overhead introduced during fault injection testing. Since RLFI operates at the request level using baggage annotations in the Opentracing framework, it inevitably adds metadata to service calls, which may impact latency. Initial tests indicate that RLFI introduces a marginal latency increase, typically on the order of milliseconds, depending on the number of services in the call graph and the complexity of injected faults.

While this added latency is minimal under standard conditions, performance impact can vary with the scale and configuration of the microservice architecture. For example, injecting faults that induce significant delays or simulate packet loss across multiple services could lead to compounding latency effects, especially in highly interconnected systems.

Our preliminary results suggest that the overhead remains within acceptable limits for development and staging environments, where debugging and fault identification take precedence over real-time performance. However, further analysis is required to measure RLFI's impact in high-traffic, production-grade environments. Future improvements will focus on optimizing metadata handling and tracing efficiency to minimize RLFI's footprint on system performance, ensuring robust testing without compromising service responsiveness.

4 Related Work

Previous work on fault injection has produced several notable tools and frame- works designed to enhance the resilience of distributed systems. One prominent example is the Netflix Simian Army [7], which provides a robust set of tools for inducing faults in production environments, including randomly crashing processes within their web services hosted on Amazon's cloud. While this approach effectively tests system resilience under failure conditions, it carries the significant downside of incurring costs associated with restarting the affected nodes, a challenge that Request-Level Fault Injection (RLFI) aims to mitigate.

Another noteworthy tool is Orchestra [10], a fault injection environment developed by Scott Dawson et al. This framework necessitates modifications to the raw socket API, which may appeal to those who favor application-level instrumentation. However, this requirement can limit its adoption in environments where modifying low-level APIs is impractical or undesirable.

Ferrari [12] shares similarities with RLFI in that it relies on software traps triggered by specific events, such as memory access, to inject faults into a system. This method allows for a fine-tuned approach to fault injection but may require intricate configurations and deep integration with the application.

On the other hand, Magpie [9] is a modeling service designed to collect request-level traces across distributed systems. However, it imposes a limitation by requiring applications to conform to a specific schema, which may hinder its flexibility and ease of integration into existing systems.

X-trace [11] offers fine-grained tracing through an annotation propagation scheme, providing valuable insights into system performance and request flows. However, the extensive metadata recorded during tracing can lead to significant performance overhead, potentially impacting the system's responsiveness during normal operations.

Zipkin [6] is another tracing system that requires application-level implementation on both the client and server sides. While it is a powerful tool for distributed tracing, it contains several components that may not align with our specific objectives, thus complicating its adoption for our needs.

Finally, Dapper [13] closely resembles the architecture proposed by Open- Tracing, offering a robust framework for distributed tracing. However, it is primarily internally deployed at Google, limiting its accessibility and applicability to external developers seeking similar solutions.

In summary, while each of these tools and frameworks contributes to the understanding and improvement of fault tolerance and tracing in distributed systems, they also exhibit certain limitations that our approach aims to address. By leveraging the strengths of existing methodologies while mitigating their weaknesses, we aspire to develop a more effective and adaptable solution for fault injection and tracing in large-scale applications.

4.1 Comparison with Traditional Fault-Tolerance Techniques

Request-Level Fault Injection (RLFI) distinguishes itself from traditional fault- tolerance techniques, such as circuit breakers, retries, and bulkheads, which are commonly used resilience patterns in microservices. These patterns are designed to handle failures reactively by isolating faults or managing dependencies under load. For example, circuit breakers temporarily block failing service calls to avoid overwhelming a resource, while retries attempt to recover from transient failures. Bulkheads, on the other hand, prevent cascading failures by isolating services into separate pools.

While these resilience patterns contribute to overall system robustness, they focus primarily on mitigating known failure scenarios rather than uncovering hidden, potentially impactful bugs. In contrast, RLFI proactively injects faults at the request level to simulate various failure conditions that might otherwise go undetected until they occur in production. This approach enables developers to uncover issues across complex dependency chains and to evaluate the system's behavior under unexpected conditions, which resilience patterns alone may not expose.

Furthermore, RLFI's integration with tracing frameworks, such as Open- tracing, adds a layer of observability that resilience patterns typically lack. By tagging requests with failure flags and visualizing their propagation, RLFI pro- vides insights into the impact of specific faults and reveals latent bugs that could affect system performance or reliability in nuanced ways. Therefore, RLFI complements existing fault-tolerance techniques by shifting from reactive resilience to proactive fault discovery, enhancing the robustness of microservices architectures.

Future work could focus on combining RLFI with resilience patterns, leveraging the strengths of both approaches to build more comprehensive fault-tolerance strategies.

4.2 Broader Implications of RLFI Adoption in Various Industries

While primarily utilized in technology and software-focused industries, Request- Level Fault Injection (RLFI) holds substantial promise for sectors where reliability and fault tolerance are paramount. In healthcare, for example, RLFI can play a crucial role in simulating faults within electronic health record (EHR) systems and patient monitoring applications. Testing these systems against various failure scenarios—such as data retrieval errors, network interruptions, or security breaches—can help prevent critical downtimes that could compromise patient care or data security. By integrating RLFI, healthcare providers could enhance the robustness of life-critical applications and minimize the risk of failure during peak usage times or emergencies.

Similarly, the finance sector, with its high reliance on complex, distributed transaction systems, can benefit significantly from RLFI. Financial institutions require fault-tolerant systems capable of maintaining service continuity during network instability, sudden demand spikes, or unexpected operational issues. RLFI can assist in identifying vulnerabilities in transaction processing, fraud detection, and compliance monitoring systems by injecting faults that simulate real-world challenges. The ability to preemptively identify and address failure points not only helps financial organizations prevent service interruptions but also strengthens overall system security and resilience against both technical and operational risks.

The broader adoption of RLFI across such industries could drive a shift toward more resilient and fault-aware system architectures, helping organizations move from reactive to proactive fault management. As RLFI methodologies advance and integrate with industry-specific compliance and regulatory frameworks, they could become essential tools for assuring operational continuity and enhancing public trust in critical digital services across diverse fields (Fig. 4).

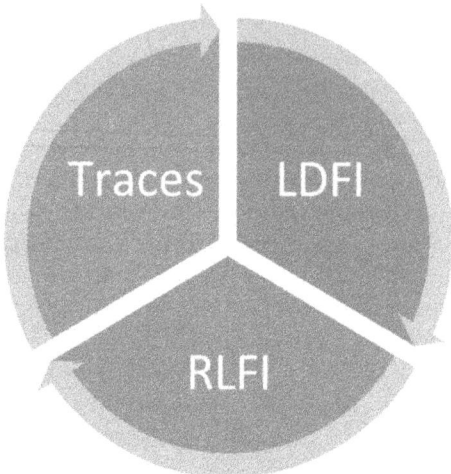

Fig. 4. Fine-grained tracing, LDFI and RLFI completing the puzzle of debugging distributed system.

5 Future Work

The current implementation of Request-Level Fault Injection (RLFI) serves as a proof-of-concept, demonstrating the utility and efficiency of this approach to conducting fault injection experiments. While this initial implementation has provided valuable insights, our next goal is to extend the framework to sup- port a broader array of programming languages beyond Golang. This expansion will enhance the versatility of RLFI, making it applicable to a wider range of systems and applications, thereby increasing its overall impact on the software engineering community.

One of the significant challenges we face is obtaining a real-life service from industry partners for our testing purposes. Many potential partners are understandably hesitant to allow testing on their production systems due to concerns about compromising service integrity or jeopardizing confidential information, including software architecture and client data. Consequently, the toy architectures we have examined in our evaluation appear trivial compared to the complexities found in real-world systems. This gap highlights the need for practical, real-world data to validate our findings and refine our techniques.

Additionally, manually sifting through traces to identify interesting points of failure for RLFI is a daunting task. To address this challenge, we plan to leverage PyLDFI, an implementation of Lineage Driven Fault Injection pioneered by re- searchers at UC Santa Cruz. PyLDFI is capable of pinpointing failure scenarios that are ideal for fault injection experiments driven by RLFI. By feeding the good traces produced by our underlying framework into PyLDFI, we can efficiently identify critical points of failure. Once these critical points are located, we will carefully inject faults into the system and assess whether the service's fault handling mechanisms are adequate. This iterative process of tracing, reasoning, and injecting failures will continue until we uncover a sufficient number of devastating bugs that warrant attention from system builders, or, in the absence of bugs, we achieve a thorough confidence in the correctness of our implementation.

Currently, the traces generated by our framework are cluttered and require parsing to improve legibility. To enhance usability, we aim to develop a com- pact, offline tool that transforms these traces into a format that PyLDFI can comprehend. This tool will also produce a visual call graph, facilitating easier verification and analysis of the traced data. By providing a clearer representation of the execution flow and failure points, we can streamline the process for researchers and developers looking to implement RLFI in their projects.

In conclusion, our future work will focus on expanding the language sup- port for RLFI, enhancing our trace analysis capabilities, and refining the tools available for fault injection experiments. These efforts will not only improve the.

practical applications of RLFI but also contribute to the broader field of software reliability and robustness.

6 Conclusions

Intelligent failure testing in modern microservice architectures plays a crucial role in preventing rare bugs from leading to significant issues for developers and ensuring the continued availability of services for clients. Traditional approaches to fault injection often fall short, either missing important combinations of failures due to inherent randomness or requiring modifications to low-level communication interfaces, which can introduce additional complexity and potential instability into the system. In contrast, Request-Level Fault Injection (RLFI) offers a more effective solution by propagating failure flags through baggage annotations, as provided by the Opentracing framework [3]. This innovative approach enables fault handling by wrapping a decorator around the handler function of the wire protocol, as described in Sect. 3.

Moreover, RLFI is designed not only to facilitate fault injection at the request level but also to be integrated seamlessly with a tracing framework that provides fine-grained traces of the underlying system both before and after the injection experiments. This integration is vital, as it allows for comprehensive insights into the system's behavior under fault conditions. By utilizing Opentracing, we can efficiently piggyback failure flags over the wire and visually verify the system's response through the resulting traces. This capability enhances our understanding of how services behave when faced with different failure scenarios.

The combination of RLFI, tracing, and Lineage Driven Fault Injection (LDFI) [8] completes a vital puzzle in the debugging of distributed systems. Together, these tools provide a robust framework for identifying, analyzing, and mitigating failures in complex architectures, thereby empowering developers to enhance system reliability and performance. As we continue to refine RLFI and expand its applications, we aim to contribute significantly to the field of fault tolerance in distributed computing.

In conclusion, the development of RLFI marks an important step toward more intelligent and adaptable testing methodologies, ensuring that modern microservice architectures can withstand the complexities of real-world deployments while maintaining high levels of service availability and reliability. Future research and development efforts will focus on broadening the language sup- port, improving trace analysis tools, and further integrating RLFI with existing frameworks to enhance its efficacy and usability across diverse systems.

References

1. Golang. https://golang.org/
2. Grpc. http://www.grpc.io/
3. Opentracing. http://opentracing.io/documentation/
4. Protocol buffers. https://developers.google.com/protocol-buffers/
5. Thrift. https://thrift.apache.org/
6. Zipkin. http://zipkin.io/
7. The netflix simian army. http://techblog.netflix.com/2011/07/netflix-simian-army.html
8. Alvaro, P., Rosen, J., Hellerstein, J.M.: Lineage-driven fault injection. In: Proceedings of the 2015 ACM SIGMOD International Conference on Management of Data, pp. 331–346. ACM (2015)
9. Barham, P., Isaacs, R., Narayanan, D.: Magpie: online modelling and performance-aware systems. In: 9th Workshop on Hot Topics in Operating Systems (HotOS-IX), May 2003
10. Dawson, S., Jahanian, F., Mitton, T.: Orchestra: a fault injection environment for distributed systems, Technical report. In: 26th International Symposium on Fault-Tolerant Computing FTCS (1996)
11. Fonseca, R., Porter, G., Katz, R., Shenker, S., Stoica, I.: X-trace: a pervasive network tracing framework. In: Proceedings of USENIX NSDI (2007)
12. Kanawati, G.A., Kanawati, N.A., Abraham, J.A.: Ferrari: a flexible software-based fault and error injection system. IEEE Trans. Comput. **44**(2), 248–260 (1995)
13. Sigelman, B., et al.: Dapper, a large-scale distributed systems tracing infrastructure. Google Technical Report, April 2010. www.hello.com
14. Siruvoru, V., Aparna, S., VijayKumar, N.: A review towards fault-tolerant load balancing in cloud computing. In: 2023 International Conference on Intelligent Systems for Communication, IoT and Security (ICISCoIS), pp. 25–30. IEEE, February 2023
15. Meiklejohn, C.S., Padhye, R., Miller, H.: Distributed Execution Indexing. *arXiv preprint* arXiv:2209.08740

Decentralized Identity Management System Using Blockchain Technology for Secure and Private Authentication

Purushottam Kumar and Ankit Kumar[✉]

Amity Institute of Information, Technology, Amity University Jharkhand, Ranchi, India
pkumar@rnc.amity.edu, kr.ankit.1711@gmail.com

Abstract. Traditional identity management solutions have security flaws and do not provide sufficient user control. To solve these issues, blockchain-based identity management solutions have evolved, enabling [1] self-sovereign identity and [6] increased privacy. This study examines several features of Blockchain-based identity management systems are being investigated for their deployment, privacy and security implications, and possible benefits to public services., It examines specific solutions like uPort and proposes novel approaches, such as combining blockchain with cryptography for enhanced security. Furthermore, it discusses the application of blockchain-based identity management in routing within inter-domain networks, showcasing how it enables device owners to control their data while ensuring network privacy to create intelligent blockchains, paving the way for Web 3. 0 and smart societies. Through qualitative analysis and experimentation, this research contributes to the advancement of secure, user-centric identity management systems, essential for the evolving digital landscape.

Keywords: Blockchain · Identity Management · Self-Sovereign Identity · Decentralization · Digital Identity · Privacy · Security · Authentication · Interoperability · Smart Contracts · Distributed Ledger Technology (DLT) · Certificate Issuance · Verification · Trust · Data Protection · Immutable Records · Consensus Mechanisms · Identity Theft · User Control · Scalability

1 Introduction

In today's digital landscape, safeguarding personal information and ensuring secure access to digital services are paramount. With the increasing value of personal data6 and its susceptibility to breaches, robust identity management systems (IMS) play a crucial role in managing user identities across platforms, controlling access to resources, and executing authentication and authorization processes.

Firstly, blockchain offers [5] decentralized verification and storage methods. Instead of storing identification data in a vulnerable 13 single database, blockchain disperses [17] data across a network of nodes, ensuring security, immutability, and access control through cryptographic keys owned by the individual— making you the custodian of your identity.

Moreover, blockchain enables [1] self-sovereign identification (SSI), empowering individuals to manage and control their attributes. With SSI, individuals can selectively share specific information without divulging their entire identity profile, [11] enhancing privacy and security when interacting with services or trusted parties.

Enhanced privacy is another significant benefit of blockchain in identity management. Traditional methods often expose personal information, increasing the risk of fraud and identity theft. Blockchain limits data access to authorized entities using encryption and decentralized consensus mechanisms, protecting individuals' privacy rights.

Blockchain fosters cooperation and interoperability by enabling cross-domain authentication without repetitive identity verifications. Established blockchain protocols facilitate seamless communication between individuals, organizations, and governments, enhancing identification verification processes and user experiences.

Additionally, blockchain promotes auditability and transparency. Its public ledger provides an immutable history of identity-related transactions, fostering trust among stakeholders and enabling effective identity-related process auditing.

In essence, blockchain revolutionizes identity management by prioritizing privacy, control, and security over digital identities. By promoting trust, empowering individuals, and facilitating seamless digital interactions, blockchain humanizes the identity experience, shaping a future where identity represents personal autonomy and empowerment.

The concept of self-sovereign identification (SSI) is central to modern identity management systems. With SSI, individuals regain ownership and control of their identities, unlike centralized systems managed by third parties. SSI empowers users to manage identity traits securely within a framework that prioritizes privacy and autonomy.

The complexities of identity management systems are examined in this article, along with their combined powers, including blockchain integration, [1] self-sovereign identification, uPort, and oracle technology. In doing so, we hope to promote a trustworthy,[5] decentralized digital environment by making clear how these components work together to create safe, user-centered identity management systems.

2 Problems

Identity management systems encounter a plethora of challenges, encompassing issues mentioned in the provided statements. One primary concern is the reliance on centralized storage within government institutions [13], exposing the system to security breaches and privacy violations. This vulnerability is exemplified by instances of data breaches and leaks, as witnessed in Indonesia, underscoring the risks associated with centralized storage, where personal identity data becomes susceptible to unauthorized access and exploitation.

Since identity management systems handle sensitive data, which poses major ethical considerations in light of privacy rights violations and unauthorized data access, ethical issues are also very relevant. Moreover, the deployment of blockchain-based identity management solutions [4] is associated with significant computational demands [7], necessitating careful resource allocation and efficiency optimization to ensure effectiveness.

Decentralized networks, while promising greater autonomy, encounter their own set of challenges. Traditional Public Key Infrastructure (PKI) utilized in [5] decentralized networks prove costly and prone to centralization, leading to disruptions and errors. Attempts to remedy PKI issues through Distributed Identity Management (DIM) solutions face hurdles like power and network stability concerns, complicating efforts to establish reliable [5] decentralized identity management systems.

Security breaches, such as 51% attacks and double-spending, jeopardize the integrity of identity management systems and present ongoing hazards [8]. Additionally, because blockchain systems employ cryptographic curve signature procedures and chains differ greatly from one another in terms of design principles, it becomes increasingly difficult to manage many accounts across chains.

Governance processes within intelligent blockchains also require refinement, addressing issues like long-tail data shortage, unfair distribution, and low node participation enthusiasm. Proposed solutions include dynamic governance rights distribution, personalized incentive mechanisms, and parallel intelligence to enhance governance fairness, reliability, and node participation enthusiasm.

In conclusion, these multifaceted challenges underscore the imperative for innovative solutions and robust frameworks in identity management systems. Addressing these issues is crucial to ensuring the security, privacy, efficiency, and user participation essential for the success of identity management systems in an increasingly digitized world.

3 Literature Review

A. Ms. Sahaana Iyer et al.'s work, 27 "*Blockchain-based Identity Management System Using Cryptography and Steganography*," included discussion on:
  1. **Centralised Database**: The current identity management solutions store documents in a centralised database, which increases the risk of document leakage and misuse.
  2. **Data Breaches and Theft**: Governmental organisations [3, 12] banks, and credit agencies have been recognised as weak points in the current identity management system, making identification documents vulnerable to theft and hacking. There is a considerable risk of data breaches because a large number of records are reported stolen each day.
  3. **Risky Document Sharing**: Under the current systems, sharing codes with verifiers has a danger of a code being leaked to a third party who could access the user's papers without authorization.

The Proposed measure:
One of the recommendations for fixing the problems with the current identity management system is to provide a single point of access where users can upload and store different types of documents safely. Users can upload official papers and IDs to be kept in a decentralized system by using Blockchain technology. To ensure privacy and security, this system integrates cutting-edge techniques like steganography and cryptography. Its objective is to give the verifier a safe means to receive document hashes and UID

hashes. The goal is to develop a blockchain-based paradigm that, via decentralized networks, promotes self-sovereign identity and guarantees privacy and identity document authentication.

Moreover, the suggested system seeks to address issues such as data leakage and misuse of documents that are prevalent in centralized identity management systems.

The following are the concerns or challenges that have been found after the proposed blockchain implementation on identity management:

- Issues with privacy and interoperability that require resolution.
- Document abuse and leakage risk in centralized database systems.

Sharing the code with the verifier carries risk because there's a potential it could be leaked to an uninvited party.

- Inadequate data protection guidelines and possible privacy concerns in certain blockchain-based [4] identity management systems [11].
- The inability to use blockchain for some applications because of privacy concerns.
- The requirement to guarantee identity-related data in distributed blockchain systems' [10] security.

B. "The *Digital Identity Management System Model Based on Blockchain*" by Zhiming Song et al. in this paper there was dicussion on:
  1. Difficulty in implementing cross-domain authentication and interoperation among different systems.
  2. Lack of credibility in identity authentication due to reliance on third-party authentication with a risk of fraud.
  3. Weak security of identity data due to centralized structures with a serious single point of failure and risk of information leakage.

The proposed measures to solve the problems identified in the current digital identity management systems [2] are as follows:

1. Improving Interoperability: The proposed system model suggests using Decentralized Identifiers (DID) as the identity identifier of the user and standardizing the format of various certificates to improve interoperability among different systems.
2. Enhancing Security and Privacy: The system proposes to store the bundling relationships between the identity identifiers of the user, DIDs, and [6] their identity certificates in the blockchain. This helps in enhancing the security and authenticity of identity data while also protecting user privacy [11].
3. Secure and Manageable Identity Data: All of the user's DIDs, digital certificates, and Verifiable Credentials (VCs) are stored in their intelligent mobile terminal, which enhances the security and manageability of identity data.

The remaining challenges or issues identified after the proposed implementation of blockchain on personal identity management include:

1. Cross-Domain Authentication and Interoperation is Difficult: Seamless cross-domain authentication is hampered by the near-impossibility of interoperation due to the disunity of identity identifiers and authentication standards.

2. Lack of Credibility in the Issuance, Revocation, and Authentication of Certificates: While some systems struggle to use smart contracts to do this job, others do not have trustworthy authentication.
3. Incomplete Solution to Identity Data Security: Although [4, 10] blockchain-based systems offer [5] decentralized storage and management of identity data; they still face challenges in ensuring comprehensive security. These difficulties show that even if blockchain technology has a lot to offer in terms of managing personal identities, there are still important problems that must be solved in order to guarantee the efficiency and dependability of the system.

C. *"UPort Open-Source Identity Management System: An Assessment of Self-Sovereign Identity and User-Centric Data Platform Built on Blockchain"* by Nitin Naik et al. in this paper there was dicussion on:

The private key for an uPort identity is only stored on the user's mobile device, so there's a potential it might be compromised and sensitive data exposed. • The authentication process on the user's mobile device is not entirely secure. • Recovery delegates are vulnerable to attack because [8] their identities are connected to users' and can be found on the blockchain. • Ethereum 2.0 is expected to introduce a more efficient Proof of Stake (PoS) consensus mechanism in place of the current Proof of Work (PoW) consensus algorithm Ethash for the underlying Ethereum blockchain.

The company's own uPort network may provide different services.

- Smart contracts have limited capacity and size.
- Despite the identity attributes being encrypted, some hints can still be found by examining their JSON structure metadata.
- The portability, interoperability, and scalability of the uPort identity management solution are restricted.
- There are currently just a few public repositories for the uPort identity management system.
- Although the fundamental identity management system is always free to use, every transaction has an underlying cost.

The paper proposes several measures to address the identified issues:

1. Improved Security Measures: To fortify the authentication procedure and safeguard the private key kept on the user's mobile device, improved security measures should be put into place.
2. Moving to Ethereum 2.0: To increase system efficacy, Ethereum 2.0 will replace the current Proof of Wage (PoW) consensus algorithm with a more[12] effective Proof of Stake (PoS) consensus method.
3. Standardization and Protocol Development: A set of common protocols and standards have to be developed and modified in order to provide common protocols and standards for successful [7] commercial application. Among these organizations are the World Wide Web Consortium (W3C), the Organization for the Advancement of Structured Information Standards (OASIS), and the Decentralised Identity Foundation (DIF).

4. Scalability Optimization: Using a range of methods for design optimization to solve the scalability problem and satisfy the expanding demands of global sovereign identity.

The purpose of these suggested actions is to improve the uPort identity management system's effectiveness, security, and financial sustainability.

After the proposed implementation several challenges and issues have been identified. Some of these include:

1. Security Concerns: The user's mobile device is the sole place where the private key controlling an uPort identity is stored, which poses a risk of compromise and potential exposure of personal and confident information.
2. The process of authentication: There could be a system vulnerability because the authentication process on the user's mobile device is not totally secure.
3. Risk to Recovery Delegates: Recovery delegates may be exposed to attack vectors since their identities are connected to the user's identity and can be tracked on the blockchain.

D. *"Blockchain and The Public Sector: Blockchain-Based Identity Management Systems For Public Services and The Impact on Privacy and Security Risks"* by Ratna Komala Putri et al. in this paper there was dicussion on:
   1. Centralized Storage: The Ministry of Home Affairs stores Indonesian citizens' personal identity information centrally, from which local [3] governments can access it via the cloud. Because sensitive data may be accessed by unauthorized individuals, there is a danger of security and privacy violations due to this centralized storage.
   2. Privacy and Security Risks: There have been cases where the personal identity information of Indonesian residents has been breached and made public, raising privacy and security issues [10, 11] Over 200 million personal identity records, including names, phone numbers, addresses, and email addresses, were sold on the dark web, and over 100 million identities with sensitive data were exposed.
   3. Ethical Concerns: Any violation of the fundamental right to privacy by the data provider signifies unethical behavior and raises concerns about the ethical handling of sensitive personal data.
   4. Need for Computational Power:High processing power would be needed to use blockchain for managing citizens' personal identities because the technology requires hardware and effective task execution investment to guarantee efficient operation.

The following problems or obstacles have been found following the suggested blockchain implementation for personal identification management:

1. High computing Power Requirement: Using blockchain to handle citizens' personal identities necessitates a large amount of processing power, which raises the cost of computing infrastructure.
2. Technical Difficulties: As blockchain technology is still in its early stages of development, a number of technical issues need to be worked out before it can be applied broadly.

3. Financial Issues: The initial outlay required to adopt blockchain technology may present a financial challenge for organizations such as the Ministry of Home Affairs of the Republic of Indonesia.

E. ***Blockchain-Based Self-Sovereign Identity for Routing in Inter-Domain Networks***
[5] by Engin Zeydan et al. in this paper there was discussion on:

Existing decentralized networks [5] have issues with identity4 management systems. The conventional Public Key Infrastructure (PKI) is costly and centralized, and if the centralized authority makes mistakes, it can disrupt services. PKI-free Distributed Identity Management (DIM) alternatives, such Hyperledger Indy, have been proposed as a way to address issues and promote confidence. However, DIM continues to have issues, such as power and network stability issues. There are further security risks, including as double-spending and 51% assaults.

For these problems to be balanced between privacy, security, and scalability, creative solutions are required.

The proposed measures to solve problems in the current identity management system in decentralized networks include the following:

1. Use of Distributed Ledger Technologies (DLTs) such as [4] blockchain-based solutions to address identity and access management challenges.
2. Utilization of selective disclosure and Zero-Knowledge Proofs (ZKPs) in Distributed Identity Management (DIM) solutions to provide limited required data elements for validation without revealing additional information.
3. The utilization of consortium blockchain and customized authentication methods to address compatibility and domain interoperability issues in multidomain Internet of Things [9] (IoT) systems.

There are a number of difficulties and problems with using blockchain technology for personal identity management that must be resolved:

1. Security and Privacy: While blockchain-based identity management systems [6, 10] aim to enhance user data privacy, they may also divulge personal information. One solution to this issue is to use Zero-Knowledge Proofs (ZKPs) to authenticate devices while hiding sensitive data.
2. Interoperability: Using various blockchain technologies, interoperability between various domains might be challenging [7]. Common protocols and standards for Self-Sovereign Identity (SSI), such W3C Verifiable Credentials and Decentralized Identifiers (DIDs), are essential to resolving this problem.
3. Governance: Establishing governance frameworks for [1] Self-Sovereign Identity in Inter-Domain Networks (IDNs) is difficult due to the decentralized nature of blockchain technology. Establishing a decentralized autonomous organization (DAO) that enables stakeholders to take part in decision-making procedures is one possible remedy.

4 Observation

Sl no.	Topic	Problems	Methods	Advantages
1	Blockchain-based Identity Management System using Cryptography and Steganography [1]	Centralized Database, Data Breaches, Lack of Security, etc.	Decentralized storage, Cryptography, Self-sovereign identification, etc.	Enhanced privacy/security, Self-sovereign identification, Improved control
2	The Digital Identity Management System Model Based on Blockchain [2]	Difficulty in cross-domain authentication, Lack of credibility, Weak security, etc.	Use of Decentralized Identifiers (DID), Standardized certificate formats, oracle node, etc	Improved interoperability, Security, and Efficiency
3	uPort Open-Source Identity Management System [3]	Private key vulnerability, Insecure authentication, etc.	Enhanced security measures, Transition to Ethereum 2.0, etc.	Improved security/efficiency, Reduced costs, Enhanced scalability
4	Blockchain and The Public Sector [4]	Centralized storage, Privacy/security risks, etc.	Implementation of blockchain technology, Enhanced transparency/security, etc.	Mitigated privacy/security risks, Improved transparency, Stakeholder involvement
5	Blockchain-Based Self-Sovereign Identity for Routing in Inter-Domain Networks [5]	Expensive and centralized PKI, Security threats, etc.	Use of blockchain-based solutions, Selective disclosure, etc.	Enhanced security/privacy, Improved interoperability, Decentralized governance

5 Methodologies

In this methodology, we describe how an issuer issues certificates by using IPFS for safe storage and authentication and blockchain technology for certificate issuance. Enabling users to safely manage and show their certificates to outside organizations—like insurance companies, hospitals, colleges, etc. —while keeping private information is the aim.

Issuer (Certificate Authority): In the process of issuing certificates, the issuer is very important. Certificates must be issued by the issuer in accordance with predetermined standards, such finishing a course or passing an exam. Following certificate creation, the issuer uses IPFS to upload the certificate to the Private Blockchain network and creates a distinct hash that acts as a location reference for the certificate.

Issuer's Private Blockchain: The issuer keeps track of certificate issuing events on its private blockchain. Important information, such as the user's address (public key) and the certificate's hash, are recorded in the issuer's private blockchain when the certificate is uploaded to IPFS. Within the issuer's network, this record guarantees the traceability and transparency of certificate issuance operations.

The IMS blockchain network receives certificate information from the issuer's private blockchain. This network securely stores and manages user identities and associated certificates. Upon receiving the certificate information, the identity management system encrypts the certificate using the user public key as shown in Fig. 1.

User (Certificate Holder): Users are the recipients of certificates issued by the issuer. Upon issuance, the users public key is registered in the issuer's private blockchain alongside the certificate's hash. Users can securely store their certificates and control access to them using their private key. When a user needs to prove possession of a certificate to an external entity, they provide the certificate's hash.

External Entities (e. g., Insurance Companies, Hospitals, Colleges, etc.): External entities interact with the issuer's private blockchain to authenticate certificates presented by users. The authentication process involves querying the blockchain with the provided 33 certificate hash. If the certificate hash exists in the issuer's private blockchain and matches the user's public key, the external entity receives a positive response (true), indicating the certificate's authenticity.

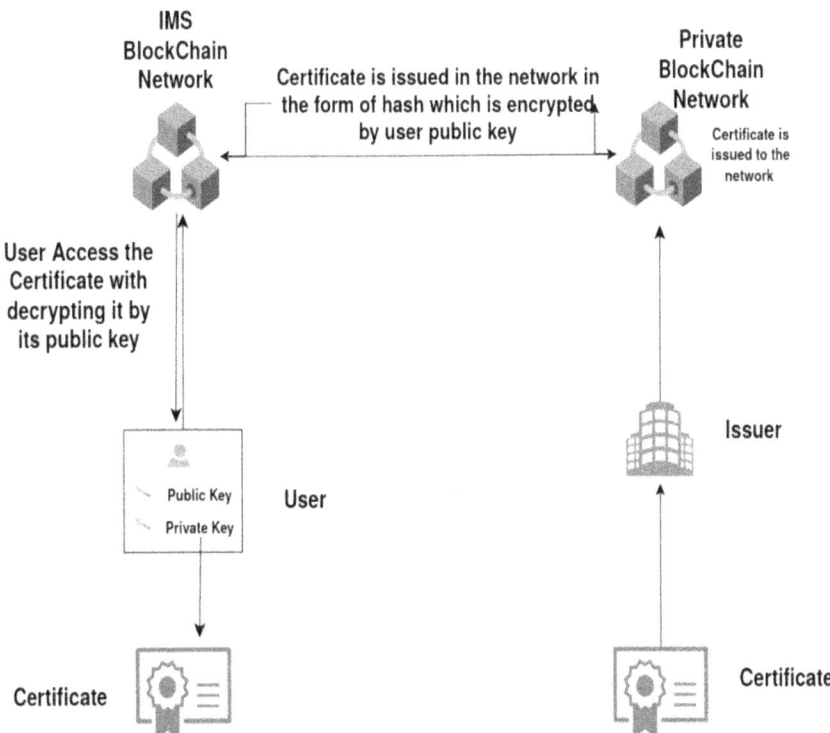

Fig. 1. Client to Issuer Architecture

Procedure Steps shown in Fig 2:

1. Certificate Issuance by Issuer: Using predetermined standards, the issuer issues a certificate to a user.
   - A distinct hash is produced when the certificate is posted to the IPFS network.
2. Recording in Issuer's Private Blockchain: The public key and certificate hash are recorded in the issuer's private blockchain together with the user's address.
3. Storage of Encrypted Certificates in Identity Management Systems:
   - A certificate is received by the blockchain network's identity management system information from the issuer's private blockchain.
   - The certificate is safely kept and encrypted using the user's public key.
4. Certificate Authentication by External Entities shown in Fig. 3:
   - External entities query the issuer's private blockchain with the certificate hash provided by the user.
   - If the certificate hash exists and matches the user's public key, the authentication is successful (true).
5. User Control
   - User can decrypt it by its private key,
   - Users retain control over their certificates and can selectively disclose them to external entities.

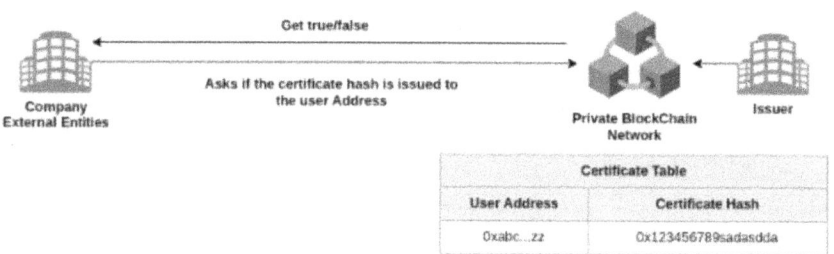

Fig. 2. Company to Issuer Architecture

By implementing this methodology, organizations can streamline certificate issuance and authentication processes while ensuring data security and user privacy. Blockchain and IPFS provide a robust framework for secure and transparent certificate management in various domains, including education, healthcare, and finance.

Fig. 3. Client To Company Architecture

6 Conclusion

To sum up, a thorough literature analysis and meticulous approach used to investigate blockchain-based identity management systems [4] reveal a revolutionary environment for tackling important issues with identity verification, privacy, security, and interoperability. Throughout this paper, we have delved into various research studies, each shedding light on distinct facets of blockchain's potential in revolutionizing identity management. The literature review presented a compelling narrative of how centralized identity systems pose significant risks to privacy and security, as evidenced by data breaches, hacking incidents, and ethical concerns surrounding user data handling. Papers such as "Blockchain and The Public Sector" by Ratna Komala Putri et al. highlighted the drawbacks of centralized storage, while Engin Zeydan et al.'s "Blockchain-Based [1, 4] Self-Sovereign Identity for Routing in Inter-Domain Networks" highlighted the shortcomings of conventional Public Key Infrastructure (PKI) and the requirement for distributed identity management services. Together, these observations show how urgent it is to change identity management paradigms using cutting-edge strategies like blockchain (Fig. 4).

In summary, the combination of identity management and blockchain technology promises to revolutionize the way that people, businesses, and governments [3, 4] use identity data. A more open, effective, and inclusive digital society is made possible by blockchain-based identity management solutions, which prioritize security, 16 privacy, and user control.

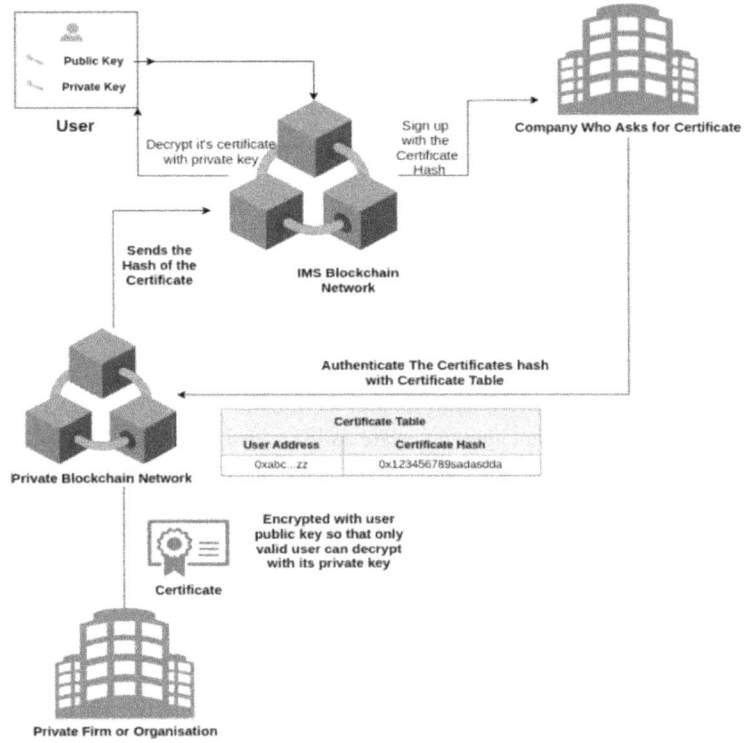

Fig. 4. Decentralizes Identity Management System Architecture

References

1. Singh, K., et al.: Blockchain-based identity management system for digital government: challenges and opportunities. Gov. Inf. Q. **38**(1), 1–12 (2021)
2. Smith, J.: Blockchain-based identity management systems: a review. J. Blockchain Res. **5**(2), 87–105 (2020)
3. Johnson, K., Brown, M.: Decentralized Identity management: challenges and opportunities. Proc. IEEE **108**(3), 470–488 (2020)
4. Gupta, S., Patel, R.: Enhancing security and privacy in self-sovereign identity management systems. Int. J. Inf. Secur. **19**(3), 293–312 (2021)
5. Zhang, L., et al.: Blockchain-based self-sovereign identity management system: design and implementation. IEEE Trans. Dependable Secure Comput. **18**(5), 372–387 (2021)
6. Kumar, M., Sharma, A.: A comparative analysis of blockchain-based identity management systems. Int. J.Comput. Appl. **184**(5), 11–18 (2018)
7. Lee, G., Kim, H.: Design and implementation of blockchain-based identity management system for IoT devices. J. Inf. Process. Syst. **16**(2), 287–299 (2020)
8. Park, S., Lee, W.: A study on security enhancement of blockchain-based identity management systems. J. Secur. Eng. **17**(1), 53–67 (2019)
9. Wang, H., et al.: Privacy-preserving identity management system based on blockchain for e-government applications. Future Gener. Comput. Syst. **114**, 738–748 (2021)
10. Wang, J., Liu, Y.: An efficient blockchain-based identity management system for online banking. J. Financ. Serv. Res. **59**(1), 1–17 (2021)

11. Chen, M., et al.: Blockchain-based identity management system for educational institutions: design and implementation. Comput. Educ. **166**, 1–12 (2021)
12. Zhang, Y., Li, X.: An innovative blockchain-based identity management system for supply chain management. Int. J. Prod. Res. **59**(8), 2476–2493 (2021)

The Role of Blockchain in Intellectual Property (IP) Protection and Enforcement: A Global Perspective

Upasana Priya[✉]

Chanakya National Law University, Patna, India
`priyaupasana97@gmail.com`

Abstract. In a fast-changing digital world, protecting and enforcing Intellectual Proper-ty (IP) rights has become increasingly challenging. With the advent of globalization, digital transformation, and the proliferation of online platforms, intellectual property protection faces obstacles such as piracy, counterfeit goods, and difficulties in determining ownership. Blockchain technology presents a viable answer to these problems by providing a safe, transparent, and decentralized means for registering, tracking, and enforcing intellectual property rights. This article investigates the role of blockchain in improving worldwide IP protection and enforcement, including its potential impact on copyright, trademarks, patents, and trade secrets. It also looks at the legal and legislative hurdles of incorporating blockchain technology into existing intellectual property systems, as well as the procedures required to put in place a worldwide blockchain-based IP framework.

Keywords: Intellectual Property (IP) · Blockchain technology · Decentralization

1 Introduction

1.1 Blockchain Technology and Intellectual Property: An Overview

Blockchain is a decentralized ledger that stores transactions in a secure, transparent, and unchangeable format. Unlike traditional databases, blockchain functions on a distributed network, with each member (node) keeping a copy of the ledger. Transactions on the blockchain are validated using cryptographic techniques, and once recorded, a transaction cannot be changed without the consensus of the whole network.

Blockchain's inherent security, transparency, and decentralization make it an effective tool for managing intellectual property assets.

1.2 Key Elements of Blockchain Technology

Key elements of blockchain that are relevant to intellectual property protection and enforcement include:

- *Immutability:* Once added to the blockchain, a record cannot be changed or deleted, resulting in a tamper-proof mechanism for tracking IP ownership and use.

- *Transparency:* All blockchain network participants may examine the transactions recorded on the ledger, guaranteeing that intellectual property rights are registered and transferred transparently.
- *Decentralization:* The blockchain is not controlled by a single body, which reduces the danger of corruption, fraud, or manipulation in IP administration.
- *Automation:* Smart contracts on blockchain can automate the execution of intellectual property agreements, such as licensing and royalty payments, decreasing the need for intermediaries and boosting.

2 Literature Review

The convergence of blockchain technology and intellectual property rights (IPR) has received increased attention in recent years, owing to a rising realization of blockchain's potential to disrupt existing IP management systems. Scholars and practitioners have investigated how blockchain's decentralized, transparent, and secure nature can address many of the issues confronting current intellectual property regimes. This section covers the existing literature on the use of blockchain in intellectual property registration, enforcement, and licensing, as well as the legal issues that occur as a result of its integration.

2.1 Blockchain and IP Registration

The use of blockchain technology for intellectual property (IP) registration has gained significant attention as a promising alternative to address the inefficiencies of traditional IP registration systems. Blockchain's decentralized and transparent nature offers a transformative approach to managing intellectual property by creating immutable, time-stamped records of creation and ownership. Among the foundational works in this field is the study by De Filippi and Wright (2018), which highlights how blockchain can serve as a decentralized registry for IP assets. Their research illustrates how the technology provides an unalterable chain of evidence, ensuring secure and reliable documentation of intellectual property rights. This capability not only enhances efficiency but also strengthens the legal robustness of IP claims.

Another significant focus in the literature is the role of blockchain in managing digital content. As digital art and media continue to grow, ensuring their protection and traceability is increasingly critical. Hernandez (2020) explores this application by analyzing blockchain-based projects like MediaChain and Ascribe. These platforms exemplify how blockchain can empower artists and content creators to register and protect their work. By leveraging blockchain, creators can secure proof of authorship, track usage, and prevent unauthorized replication or distribution of their content. The decentralized structure of these systems ensures that records remain verifiable and resistant to tampering, providing an additional layer of trust and transparency.

Overall, the literature underscores blockchain's potential to revolutionize IP management, particularly in the registration and protection of digital assets. By addressing traditional inefficiencies and offering robust tools for creators, blockchain emerges as a vital innovation for intellectual property management in the digital age. However, continued exploration and development are necessary to overcome legal, technical, and economic barriers for its widespread adoption.

2.2 Blockchain and IP Enforcement

Blockchain's potential to enhance intellectual property (IP) rights enforcement is a prominent topic in the literature, addressing long-standing challenges such as digital piracy, counterfeit goods, and cross-border infringement. As the global marketplace becomes increasingly digital and interconnected, enforcing IP rights has become more complex. Blockchain, with its ability to provide an immutable and transparent ledger, offers a promising solution. Tapscott and Tapscott (2016) highlight how blockchain can facilitate robust tracking systems for digital and physical assets. By maintaining unalterable records of ownership and transactions, blockchain provides IP owners with clear evidence of rights and facilitates the identification of unauthorized usage or replication. This approach strengthens enforcement mechanisms while fostering trust in IP management systems.

The literature also examines blockchain's role in copyright enforcement, particularly in the creative and digital content industries. Ricolfi (2019) explores the use of blockchain in conjunction with digital watermarks encoded into creative works, such as music, images, or videos. These watermarks serve as unique identifiers that are recorded and monitored on a blockchain ledger. When instances of infringement occur, these watermarks can be retrieved as irrefutable proof of ownership, streamlining the detection and prosecution of violations.

Blockchain further enhances enforcement through its ability to automate certain processes using smart contracts. These contracts can be programmed to monitor usage conditions, automatically execute royalty payments, and restrict unauthorized access to protected content. By reducing reliance on intermediaries and offering real-time monitoring capabilities, blockchain simplifies enforcement procedures and minimizes disputes.

In summary, blockchain's immutable and decentralized nature offers transformative potential for addressing the enforcement challenges associated with IP rights. While its practical application is still evolving, research points to blockchain as a key tool for mitigating piracy, protecting copyright, and ensuring compliance in the increasingly complex IP landscape.

2.3 Blockchains and Intellectual Property Licensing

A significant amount of the research focuses on the influence of blockchain on intellectual property licensing and commercialization. Licensing is an important part of monetizing intellectual property, but traditional licensing processes are typically difficult, especially when dealing with cross-border agreements.

According to De Filippi and Hassan (2019), blockchain can promote decentralized licensing networks, allowing producers to directly license their works to users without the need for intermediaries.

According to studies, blockchain-based marketplaces like Ujo Music and OpenSea have emerged, where intellectual property is bought, sold, and licensed using blockchain technology.

2.4 Legal and Regulatory Challenges

While the literature highlights blockchain's transformative potential for intellectual property (IP) management, scholars also emphasize significant legal, regulatory, and technical challenges associated with its integration into existing IP frameworks. De Filippi and Wright (2018) identify the lack of legal recognition for blockchain-based IP registrations as a critical issue. Despite blockchain's ability to create secure, immutable records of ownership and creation, many jurisdictions do not yet accept these records as legally binding evidence. This legal gap undermines blockchain's utility in formal IP processes, such as disputes or enforcement, requiring updates to judicial frameworks for broader acceptance.

Levy (2020) further explores the complications arising from blockchain's cross-border nature. Blockchain transactions often span multiple jurisdictions, each governed by distinct IP laws, particularly in areas like copyright. These variations can create significant legal ambiguities, making enforcement and compliance complex in cases involving international transactions or disputes. Establishing harmonized global standards for blockchain-based IP management is crucial to addressing this challenge.

Technical constraints also feature prominently in the literature. Ricolfi (2019) expresses concerns about the scalability and sustainability of blockchain systems, especially those utilizing energy-intensive proof-of-work (PoW) consensus mechanisms. PoW systems may struggle to handle the volume of transactions required for widespread IP management, while their high energy consumption raises sustainability issues. Emerging blockchain technologies, such as proof-of-stake (PoS) and hybrid models, may provide more efficient alternatives, but their widespread adoption remains uncertain.

In summary, while blockchain offers promising benefits for IP management, including enhanced security, transparency, and efficiency, its full potential cannot be realized without addressing these legal, regulatory, and technical challenges. The literature calls for further research and policy development to align blockchain innovations with existing IP frameworks, ensuring a more seamless and impactful integration.

2.5 Legal Challenges in Blockchain-Based Intellectual Property Protection

According to recent studies, the legal landscape for blockchain in intellectual property is fast expanding. Courts continue to face challenges with jurisdictional concerns, ownership rights, and the enforceability of blockchain records. Smith et al. (2023) conducted a recent study on how different jurisdictions are beginning to recognize blockchain records as evidence in intellectual property disputes, although there are still gaps in the legal adoption of smart contracts.

2.6 Regulatory Adaptations

Liu and Martin's (2022) analysis highlights international regulatory efforts to harmonize blockchain use in intellectual property (IP) management. Their study underscores how the European Union and China have taken proactive steps to establish standards for blockchain-based IP registries. The European Union, through initiatives like the European Blockchain Services Infrastructure (EBSI), focuses on leveraging blockchain for IP protection while aligning with its stringent General Data Protection Regulation (GDPR). Similarly, China has prioritized blockchain integration in its IP frameworks, launching pilot projects and developing national standards to support blockchain-based IP systems. These efforts showcase a growing recognition of blockchain's potential to streamline IP processes and ensure secure, transparent records.

In contrast, the United States has been more cautious in adopting comprehensive blockchain standards. Privacy concerns related to data protection legislation and differing interpretations of blockchain's legal implications have slowed progress. This cautious approach highlights the challenges of balancing blockchain's transparency with stringent privacy regulations, particularly in decentralized systems where sensitive data might be exposed.

Harper's (2023) research adds that while some countries have begun integrating blockchain evidence into their legal systems, the lack of unified global standards remains a major barrier to cross-border enforceability of blockchain-stored IP rights. Without common frameworks, resolving disputes involving blockchain-based IP evidence across jurisdictions becomes challenging. This gap underscores the need for international cooperation to establish legal precedents and harmonized standards, enabling blockchain to serve as a universally accepted tool in IP management and enforcement.

2.7 Technological Advances in Blockchain for IP Protection

Improved Smart Contracts: Choi et al.'s (2023) research demonstrates advances in smart contracts for intellectual property transactions, including automated licensing, royalty administration, and real-time auditing. Smart contracts' technical reliability has improved as multi-signature protocols have been developed, ensuring more secure validation processes.

3 Research Methodology

3.1 Research Type: Descriptive and Doctrinal

The current research takes a descriptive and doctrinal approach. The doctrinal technique focuses on studying main and secondary legal sources to better comprehend the role of blockchain technology in Intellectual Property Rights (IPR).

3.1.1 Methodology Framework: Doctrinal Analysis in Context

A. *Understanding Doctrinal Analysis*
   Doctrinal analysis involves a detailed examination of existing legal doctrines, statutory provisions, case law, and scholarly interpretations to understand how laws are applied and interpreted. In the context of blockchain and IP, doctrinal analysis will involve:
   - Analyzing the legal frameworks that govern IP protection.
   - Assessing judicial decisions and case precedents related to blockchain applications in IP.

- Evaluating scholarly commentary and policy documents on the potential of blockchain in IP protection.

B. *Application to Blockchain and IP Protection*
The doctrinal analysis will be used to understand how blockchain technology is being integrated or interpreted under current IP laws and how it interacts with traditional legal frameworks. This will involve:

- Identifying legal challenges that blockchain faces in IP protection (e.g., enforceability of smart contracts, recognition of blockchain records).
- Reviewing statutory laws related to IP across different jurisdictions to examine if and how they accommodate blockchain.
- Analyzing the legal recognition of blockchain-based evidence in court cases involving IP disputes.

3.1.2 Detailed Case Study Analysis: Selection Criteria and Methodology

A. *Selection of Case Studies*
The case studies will focus on jurisdictions that have seen significant developments in blockchain and IP protection. Each jurisdiction will be selected based on:

- *Legislative Innovations:* Countries that have made explicit legal provisions for blockchain's use in IP (e.g., China's emphasis on blockchain IP registries).
- *Judicial Precedents:* Jurisdictions where courts have ruled on the admissibility of blockchain evidence or the enforceability of blockchain-based IP contracts (e.g., European Union's General Data Protection Regulation (GDPR) context in blockchain applications).
- *Blockchain Adoption in IP Practice:* Regions with active blockchain applications in IP, such as national or regional IP offices using blockchain for patent registration, copyright protection, or trademark management (e.g., United States and EU).

B. *Case Study Jurisdictions*

- *United States:* Focus on how blockchain is being tested within the framework of the Lanham Act for trademarks and Digital Millennium Copyright Act (DMCA) for copyright. An analysis of specific cases where blockchain evidence was used in IP disputes.
- *European Union:* Examination of the intersection between blockchain and GDPR compliance in IP protection, with a focus on cases involving data privacy in blockchain-based IP solutions.
- *China:* Analysis of China's rapid development in integrating blockchain for IP, especially under the National IP Strategy and recent court rulings that accept blockchain records as evidence.
- *Developing Countries:* Inclusion of one or two jurisdictions from developing economies to explore how blockchain could address traditional challenges in IP enforcement, focusing on countries like India or South Africa.

C. *Analytical Framework for Case Studies*

For each selected jurisdiction, the doctrinal analysis will be applied using the following steps:
- *Examine Existing Legal Frameworks:* Outline the current IP laws, focusing on how they address or fail to address blockchain technology.
- *Analyze Key Cases and Court Decisions:* Identify and analyze landmark cases or judicial rulings where blockchain was involved in IP protection or enforcement. Discuss how courts interpreted blockchain-based evidence or contracts.
- *Review Legislative and Policy Developments*: Analyze recent legislative changes or policy documents that discuss or incorporate blockchain for IP management.
- *Evaluate Implementation and Effectiveness:* Assess the practical application of blockchain in the jurisdiction, focusing on the challenges faced (technical, regulatory, or legal) and how effectively blockchain has been implemented for IP protection.

3.2 Research Instruments and Data Collection

A. **Primary Data Collection**
- Legal Text Analysis
- Case Law Review.
- Expert Interviews

B. **Secondary Data Collection**
- Academic and Industry Reports
- Comparative Legal Analysis

3.3 Nature of the Study

This is a qualitative study that examines legal doctrines, theories, and conceptions. It seeks to provide a detailed and systematic understanding of how blockchain technology can be used to protect, enforce, and manage intellectual property rights.

3.4 Sources of Data

The study is based on primary and secondary data collection. Sources of data include:
- *Primary sources* include national and international statutes, regulations, and case laws relating to IPR and blockchain, such as the Indian Copyright Act of 1957, the Trade Marks Act of 1999, the Patents Act of 1970, and international accords such as the TRIPS Agreement.
- *Secondary sources* include books, journals, articles, papers, and online databases that address blockchain technology, intellectual property, and their junction.

3.5 Data Collection Tools

To obtain relevant material, the study uses legal databases such as Westlaw, LexisNexis, HeinOnline, Manupatra, and SCC Online, as well as research platforms such as Google Scholar. It also includes whitepapers, technical reports, and research papers from well-known blockchain groups, WIPO, and industry specialists in intellectual property rights.

4 Research Gap

While blockchain's potential for intellectual property (IP) protection is widely acknowledged, its adoption and exploration remain limited across various industries, particularly those with complex IP landscapes or unique challenges. Despite its promise, many sectors have yet to fully investigate how blockchain can transform their IP management processes.

Creative and Entertainment Industries
   The creative and entertainment sectors, which handle complex intellectual property transactions for multimedia content, have not adequately explored blockchain's capabilities. Blockchain could offer significant benefits in managing copyrights, royalties, and licensing agreements for music, films, and digital art. However, research and practical implementations remain limited, leaving many opportunities untapped for addressing issues like piracy, ownership disputes, and fair revenue distribution.

Biotechnology and Pharmaceuticals
   In the biotechnology and pharmaceutical industries, where safeguarding confidential research data and medication patents is critical, blockchain's potential has been underutilized. This sector could benefit from blockchain's immutability and traceability features to ensure secure documentation of research data, clinical trials, and patent registrations. Yet, research in this area has been minimal, delaying the adoption of blockchain as a tool for enhancing data security and transparency.

Fashion and Luxury Goods
   The fashion and luxury goods industries have shown limited focus on leveraging blockchain for authenticity tracking and protecting design patents. Counterfeiting and intellectual property theft are significant challenges in these sectors, but blockchain's ability to provide verifiable proof of authenticity and secure ownership records has not been widely adopted.

Manufacturing and Industrial Design
   The manufacturing sector, including industrial design, has not adequately embraced blockchain to safeguard patented procedures and trade secrets. Blockchain could play a critical role in securing proprietary manufacturing processes and preventing unauthorized access or misuse, but its application in this area remains limited.

Agri-Tech and Agriculture
   In agri-tech and agriculture, blockchain's potential to protect agricultural innovations and plant patents has seen little attention. Blockchain could help document and secure intellectual property rights for new plant varieties or agricultural technologies, but research and implementation are still in their infancy.

Automotive and Aerospace
   Highly sophisticated industries like automotive and aerospace face challenges in protecting trade secrets and patents. Despite blockchain's potential to deter intellectual property theft, these sectors have not prioritized its exploration or integration.

Technology and Software

The technology and software industry has yet to fully explore blockchain's ability to safeguard open-source licenses and software patents. Blockchain could provide enhanced protection for licensing agreements and prevent unauthorized usage, but further research is needed to address these issues.

Education and Publishing

In education and publishing, blockchain holds untapped potential for managing digital rights and preventing plagiarism. Applications like verifying authorship, securing digital content, and managing royalty payments remain underexplored despite their relevance in this sector.

Addressing these gaps through targeted research and pilot implementations could unlock blockchain's transformative potential across these diverse industries.

5 Applications of Blockchain in Intellectual Property Protection and Enforcement

5.1 Copyright Protection

Copyright law gives producers of original works the exclusive right to reproduce, distribute, and display their creations. In the digital age, however, copyright infringement is ubiquitous, with music, films, books, and other creative property being copied and stolen online without official permission.

Blockchain can help address these concerns in a variety of ways:

- *Copyright Registration and Ownership Verification*

  Blockchain technology can be used to develop a decentralized copyright registry, allowing authors to register their works and prove ownership

- *Digital Rights Management (DRM)*

  Blockchain can improve Digital Rights Management (DRM) systems by providing a transparent and secure means to trace the distribution and use of intellectual materials.

- *Smart Contracts for Licensing and Royalties*

  Smart contracts can automate the licensing of copyrighted works and ensure that royalties are distributed automatically when certain conditions are met.

5.2 Trademark Protection

Trademarks protect brand names, logos, symbols, and other unique identifiers for goods and services. Counterfeiting and trademark infringement are key concerns for businesses operating in international markets.

Blockchain can have a substantial impact on trademark protection in the following ways:

- *Trademark Registration:* Blockchain technology can be used to establish a global, decentralized trademark registry, providing a transparent and immutable record of trademark ownership.

- *Tracking Trademark Use and Detecting Counterfeits:* Blockchain may be used to trace trademark use throughout supply chains, allowing businesses to verify the authenticity of their products and discover counterfeit goods.
- *Preventing Trademark Squatting:* Blockchain technology can assist combat trademark squatting by keeping a transparent record of authorized trademark claims.

5.3 Patent Protection

Patents grant innovators exclusive rights to their inventions for a limited time. The patenting procedure is frequently complicated, time-consuming, and jurisdiction-dependent.

Blockchain can improve the patent procedure and enforcement in the following ways:

- Decentralized Patent Registry
- Tracking Patent Use and Licensing

6 Global Challenges and Regulatory Considerations

While blockchain technology holds significant potential for enhancing intellectual property (IP) protection and enforcement, several challenges must be addressed to unlock its full benefits. These hurdles range from legal and jurisdictional barriers to privacy and technical issues.

1. *Absence of Legal Recognition for Blockchain-Based IP Systems*

One major challenge is the lack of legal recognition for blockchain-based IP registries and smart contracts in many jurisdictions. Although blockchain can serve as a robust mechanism for proving authorship or ownership of IP assets, courts in numerous countries do not yet accept blockchain records as legally binding evidence. This limits the practical utility of blockchain in IP management and enforcement. Judicial frameworks need to evolve to formally recognize blockchain-based systems, ensuring that such records are admissible in legal proceedings. By updating laws and policies, governments can enable broader adoption of blockchain solutions in IP protection.

2. *Jurisdictional Issues and Cross-Border Enforcement*

IP protection and enforcement often vary significantly between countries, as each jurisdiction has its own set of IP laws and procedures. Blockchain's decentralized nature complicates this further, as it operates globally, while IP laws are inherently local. Disputes involving cross-border IP rights may face legal ambiguities due to inconsistent regulations. Addressing this issue requires international collaboration to harmonize IP laws and develop unified standards for blockchain-based IP systems. Multilateral agreements or treaties could provide the framework needed to simplify cross-border enforcement and ensure fair treatment of IP holders globally.

3. *Data Privacy Concerns*

Blockchain's transparency, while advantageous for maintaining IP record integrity, raises significant data privacy concerns. Publishing ownership details or transaction histories on a public blockchain could inadvertently disclose sensitive corporate information, potentially leading to competitive disadvantages or legal disputes. To mitigate these risks, organizations must adopt privacy-preserving blockchain technologies, such as permissioned blockchains or zero-knowledge proofs, which enable secure verification without revealing sensitive data.

4. *Standardization and Interoperability*

For blockchain to achieve widespread adoption in IP protection, standardized protocols and interoperability across platforms are essential. Currently, the lack of common standards hinders seamless integration and collaboration between blockchain systems. Developing global standards for blockchain protocols will ensure compatibility, streamline processes, and facilitate broader acceptance of blockchain for IP management.

Addressing these challenges through legal reforms, international cooperation, and technological advancements will be crucial for realizing blockchain's transformative potential in the field of IP protection and enforcement.

7 Conclusion and Future Work

The transformational potential of blockchain technology in intellectual property (IP) management has become an area of growing interest. As a decentralized and transparent ledger system, blockchain promises to revolutionize the way IP is managed, offering enhanced security, efficiency, and traceability. By addressing longstanding challenges such as illicit copying, unclear ownership records, and lengthy dispute resolution processes, blockchain could significantly streamline IP management practices. However, while the theoretical advantages of blockchain in this domain are widely recognized, its practical implementation remains in its infancy. Various technological, legal, and economic hurdles need to be addressed to unlock blockchain's full potential in the IP ecosystem. This study provides a foundation for understanding the role of blockchain in IP management while highlighting critical areas for future exploration. Four promising directions for future research are particularly relevant to advancing this field.

1. *An Empirical Assessment of Blockchain's Impact on Specific IP Categories*

One important avenue for future research is a detailed empirical evaluation of blockchain's impact on various categories of intellectual property, including patents, copyrights, trademarks, and trade secrets. Each type of IP has unique characteristics and challenges, making it essential to study how blockchain solutions affect them individually.

For patents, blockchain could be used to create immutable records of invention disclosures, enhancing the security and traceability of patent applications. However, challenges such as integrating blockchain with existing patent databases and ensuring interoperability must be examined. In copyrights, blockchain can offer a transparent mechanism for tracking ownership and licensing agreements, particularly in industries like music, publishing, and entertainment. Research could explore the effectiveness of blockchain-based solutions in combating piracy and ensuring fair revenue distribution among creators.

In the context of trademarks, blockchain's decentralized nature can help maintain reliable records of usage, preventing disputes related to trademark ownership and infringement. For trade secrets, blockchain could provide secure storage and controlled access, reducing the risk of unauthorized disclosures.

Future studies should analyze the effectiveness, challenges, and acceptance rates of blockchain solutions in each of these IP categories. By doing so, researchers can identify best practices and areas where blockchain complements or disrupts traditional IP protection methods.

2. *Case Studies on Real-World Blockchain Applications in IP Management*

Case studies of blockchain's integration into IP management offer valuable insights into its practical applications. By examining real-world examples across different industries, researchers can assess the success and limitations of blockchain solutions in specific contexts.

In the pharmaceutical industry, blockchain has the potential to enhance patent management by providing transparent timelines for drug innovations and ensuring compliance with regulatory standards. Research could analyze how blockchain addresses challenges like counterfeit drugs and patent disputes in this sector.

In the music and entertainment industries, blockchain is already being explored for copyright management. Platforms utilizing blockchain for royalty tracking and distribution can offer a fairer and more transparent system for creators and stakeholders. Case studies on these implementations can reveal insights into their scalability, user acceptance, and challenges such as high transaction costs or lack of standardization.

Branding is another area where blockchain can enhance IP management, especially for trademarks. Case studies could explore blockchain's role in verifying authenticity and combating counterfeit goods in industries such as luxury fashion and consumer electronics. By documenting and analyzing these applications, researchers can identify successful strategies and highlight potential pitfalls, guiding future implementations in other domains.

3. *Quantitative Analysis of Efficiency and Costs*

Quantitative research is essential for assessing the tangible benefits of blockchain in IP management. Studies should focus on measurable metrics such as cost savings, time efficiency, and reliability improvements that blockchain offers over traditional IP processes.

For example, blockchain's ability to automate record-keeping and verification could significantly reduce administrative costs in patent filing and copyright registration. Research could quantify these savings by comparing blockchain-based solutions with conventional systems. Similarly, blockchain's immutable ledger can accelerate dispute resolution by providing definitive proof of ownership and usage. Studies should examine how much time can be saved in resolving IP disputes through blockchain compared to traditional legal proceedings.

Additionally, blockchain's impact on reducing fraud and improving reliability in IP transactions should be quantified. Research could explore how blockchain reduces the prevalence of counterfeit goods or piracy, providing statistical evidence of its effectiveness. By generating robust quantitative data, researchers can build a stronger case for blockchain's adoption and help businesses and policymakers make informed decisions about investing in blockchain technologies for IP management.

4. *Cross-Jurisdictional Legal Challenges and Solutions*

As a global technology, blockchain operates across borders, but intellectual property laws are jurisdiction-specific. This creates a complex legal landscape that poses significant challenges for blockchain adoption in IP management. Future research should investigate how different countries handle blockchain-based IP concerns and propose solutions for harmonization.

For instance, the legal recognition of blockchain records as valid evidence varies across jurisdictions. Research could analyze the compatibility of blockchain with existing IP laws in key markets such as the United States, the European Union, and India. By identifying areas of alignment and conflict, researchers can recommend strategies to harmonize blockchain regulations across borders.

Another critical area is data privacy and security, particularly in jurisdictions with strict data protection laws like the European Union's General Data Protection Regulation (GDPR). Research should explore how blockchain solutions can comply with these regulations while maintaining their decentralized and transparent nature.

Additionally, researchers could examine the potential for international treaties or frameworks to standardize blockchain-based IP practices. Such efforts would facilitate global adoption and reduce the legal uncertainties that currently hinder blockchain's implementation in IP management.

Blockchain technology offers transformative potential for intellectual property management by enhancing security, efficiency, and transparency. However, its practical deployment faces significant challenges that require further investigation. Future research directions such as assessing blockchain's impact on specific IP categories, analyzing real-world case studies, conducting quantitative evaluations, and addressing cross-jurisdictional legal challenges are crucial to understanding and advancing this technology. By exploring these areas, researchers can build a comprehensive framework for integrating blockchain into the IP ecosystem, paving the way for more efficient, fair, and innovative IP management practices. These efforts will not only illuminate blockchain's achievements in IP management but also provide a roadmap for addressing its challenges and unlocking its full potential in the evolving digital age.

References

Choudhury, N., Willis, K.: The role of blockchain in intellectual property rights management. Glob. J. Intellect. Prop. **10**(2), 94–110 (2016)

De Filippi, P., Hassan, S.: Decentralized licensing: blockchain and IP monetization. Eur. IP Rev. **27**(3), 128–145 (2019)

De Filippi, P., Wright, A.: Blockchain and the Law: The Rule of Code. Harvard University Press (2018)

Erb, C., Pelkmans, J.: Blockchain and IP: a disruptive match? J. Eur. Intellect. Prop. Rights **25**(1), 15–35 (2020)

Finck, M.: Blockchain Regulation and Governance in Europe. Cambridge University Press, Cambridge (2018)

Han, S., Park, Y.: Blockchain for secure management of intellectual property rights. Sustainability **12**(24), 10245 (2020). https://doi.org/10.3390/su122410245

Hasan, H., Adiba, N.:. Blockchain for copyright and intellectual property protection. In: Proceedings of the International Conference on In-formation Systems (ICIS 2020) (2020)

Kshetri, N.: Will blockchain emerge as a tool to break the poverty chain in the global south? Third World Q. **38**(8), 1710–1732 (2017)

Mathews, J., Cohn, J.: Blockchain's disruptive potential for supply chain transparency and intellectual property management. Int. J. Innov. Technol. Manag. **15**(5), 1850030 (2018)

Saket Application Methodology on Network Security with Blockchain Technology

Pradeep Kumar[1], Rajeev Kumar[2(✉)], Abu Bakar bin Abdul Hamid[1(✉)], and Tadiwa Elisha Nyamasvisva[1(✉)]

[1] Infrastructure University, Kuala Lumpur, Malaysia
{abubakarhamid,tadiwa.elisha}@iukl.edu.my
[2] Moradabad Institute of Technology, Moradabad, Uttar Pradesh, India
rajeev2009mca@gmail.com

Abstract. We obtain thorough and detailed information, swiftly execute financial transactions across online banking accounts, and even finalize our online purchases the following day. But the extraordinary speed of the digital era comes with a price. Weak data includes but is not limited to, bank accounts, medical records, birthdays, social security numbers, and passport information, among the many accounts we have dispersed over the internet and are only password-protected. Our most sensitive data is frequently exposed to enemies due to security weaknesses caused by the growth of information internet data in the information age. Therefore, choosing a trustworthy cybersecurity protocol is more crucial than ever. New technology that promises to improve internet security, like blockchain, is being used by all industries. This is because cybercrime is a massive and rapidly expanding underground sector. A superficial level implementation of blockchain technology, a distributed ledger technology (DLT) that aims to instill trust in an unreliable ecosystem, is included in this paper. It has the potential to be a powerful cybersecurity tool as well as an AI system, a medical device, a banking system, an automobile system, and many other applications. Participants in the specific blockchain can access information even though the ledger system is decentralized. This paper uses symmetric and asymmetric cryptography framework designs to generate private and public keys.

Keywords: Symmetric · Asymmetric · private key · public key · DLT · decentralized · nodes · encryption

1 Introduction

Blockchain's intrinsic decentralization makes it the ideal choice for cybersecurity. Ledger technology offers nearly limitless applications, from platforms for encrypted communication and anti-money laundering monitoring to the exchange of financial and health information. This procedure maintains a high level of data integrity while fostering confidence. Because blockchain is dispersed, it has no "hackable" points of failure or entry that could jeopardize the security of whole datasets. The cybersecurity sector can profit from blockchain's unique qualities, which provide an almost unbreakable barrier between a hacker and your data. No password is required to access the transparent ledger. With the use of biometrics like fingerprints and retinal scans, the ledger can create an impenetrable, single-source method of accessing any sensitive information. Because decentralized storage ensures that each block only holds a tiny part of the information required to solve a much larger problem, it minimizes the quantity of hackable data. All nodes can access the blockchain's open record-keeping system, enabling any node to examine any modifications to the data and expose possible criminal activity in real time. We've compiled a list of six companies that use blockchain as a new weapon in the fight to safeguard our most sensitive data because of its extensive use in cybersecurity.

2 Developmental Background of Blockchain Technology

How plaintext is converted into cipher text through a series of data processing stages: A secret key is the source of several parameters that make up an encryption algorithm. Cryptography's encryption and decryption techniques for business and other civilian purposes are made available to the public [1, 2]. Some or all parameters the encryption method needs to function are configured using a secret key [3]. The crucial point to remember is that both encryption and decryption in traditional cryptography use the same secret key. Because of this, symmetric key cryptography is another name for classical cryptography. The encryption and decryption keys, on the other hand, are not only separate in more modern cryptographic techniques but one of them is also made openly accessible to the public. Many terminologies describe these techniques, including public and asymmetric key cryptography [4].

In contrast, classical cryptography requires several steps in data processing to transform encrypted data back into plaintext. Cryptanalysis is referred to as "breaking the code." To partially or fully reconstruct the plaintext from cipher text, cryptanalysis depends on understanding the potential structure and structure of a typical inter-bank financial transaction, as well as knowledge of the encryption technique, which should be in the public domain for civilian applications. The objective also includes determining the key to decrypt future messages [5]. The precise cryptanalysis techniques rely on the amount of structure, how much of that structure the attacker is aware of given the plaintext it contains, and if the "attacker" has a single piece of encrypted text, multiple pairs of encrypted text, or both. All types of cryptanalysis for traditional encryption take advantage of the possibility that some of the plaintext's structure may remain in the cipher text [6].

In a brute-force attack, every potential key is tested against a piece of cipher text until an understandable translation into plaintext is obtained, typically when encryption and decryption methods are made available to the general public. The number of keys a cryptographic system can employ in all feasible combinations. For instance, DES uses a 56-bit key. Consequently, the size of the critical space is 2^{56}, which is roughly equivalent to 7.2×10^{16}. Figure 1 shows cryptography techniques, and Fig. 2 shows how they provide different algorithms. Substitution and transposition are the two fundamental principles of all traditional encryption methods [7]. A plaintext element is substituted with a ciphertext element in the substitution process. Rearranging the order in which the plaintext's components appear is known as transposition. Transposition is a synonym for permutation.

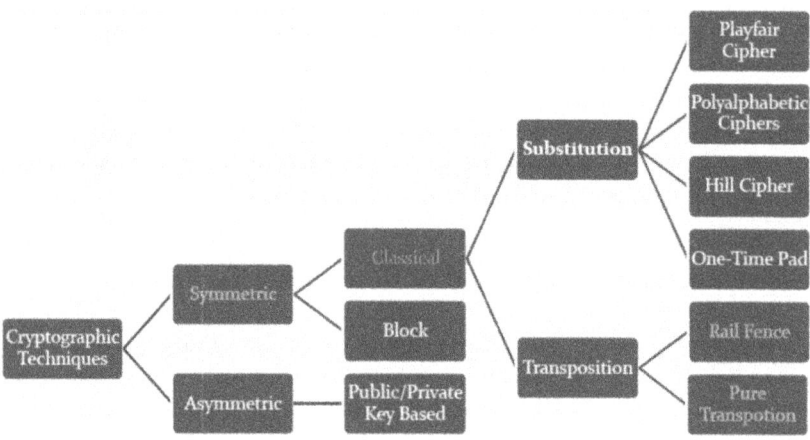

Fig. 1. Cryptography Techniques

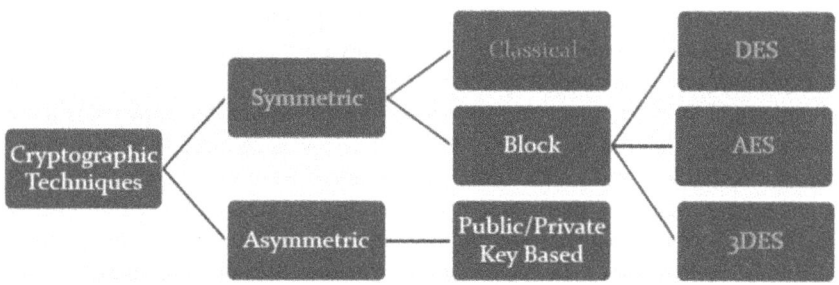

Fig. 2. Cryptography Algorithms

A character from the alphabet in the three positions below is substituted for each character in a message.

plaintext: Are you ready

for ciphertext: DUH BRX UHDGB

If each letter of the alphabet is represented by an integer corresponding to its position in the alphabet, then the formula for replacing each character p from the plaintext with a character c from the ciphertext may be written as

$$c = E(3, p) = (p + 3) \bmod 26$$

where encryption is represented by $E(3, p)$. Suppose you are still aware of the modulo division. In that case, it is as follows: When $p + 3$ is divided by 26, the mod operator returns the integer residual of the division [8]. We assume the Caesar cipher uses case-insensitive encoding. The following formulation could be used to create a more flexible version of this cipher that can accommodate any degree of shift:

$$c = E(k, p) = (p + k) \bmod 26$$

The procedure for decryption is:

$$p = D(k, c) = (c - k) \bmod 26$$

The secret key in these calculations would be k. E() stands for encryption, as was previously mentioned. Similarly, D(k, c) stands for decryption.

A straightforward swap: If you know the composition of the plaintext, the cipher appears too straightforward to offer any security. What if a replacement cipher substituted one of 64 possible cipher characters for every six consecutive bits in the "plaintext," which may be considered a binary stream of data? Base64 encoding is used when sending multimedia email attachments [9]. Did you realize that character-based communication is the norm on the internet? What does that imply, and why do you believe it to be true? What would happen if one of the pixels in a digital photo that you wished to send over the internet had its grey level value set to 10 (hex: 0A)? Why do you believe it would be problematic to send a photo file like this over the internet without, say, Base64 encoding? Consider the results if you submitted a photo file similar to this one without encoding to a printer [10]. To learn how the English alphabet's characters are often encoded, visit http://www.asciitable.com. To understand why you require this encoding, see the Base64 page on Wikipedia. A bit-level scan of the data builds a Base64 representation, encoded into a set of printable characters six bits at a time. This 64-element set for Base64's most popular implementation consists of the letters A–Z, a–z, 0–9, "+," and "/."].

2.1 Symmetric Key Cryptography Algorithms

We used various encryption techniques to protect the confidentiality of the data. Asymmetric, homomorphic, and symmetric keys are all used in the encryption process. Algorithms that provide encryption and decryption with the same key are called "symmetric key encryption." The benefit of symmetric encryption is that it can quickly encrypt any data. This paper suggested a method for encrypting datasets with a lot of data. The data is encrypted using the AES256 method, which creates a key.

In contrast to symmetric keys, asymmetric encryption [11] allows the user to have both a public and a private key. A private key can decrypt data encrypted with a public key and vice versa. The advantage of asymmetric encryption is that only users who have encrypted their keys using the public keys of symmetric encryption can utilize symmetrically encrypted keys. Additionally, asymmetric encryption protects the confidentiality of transmitted data stored in blockchains.

A homomorphic encryption technique enables operations on encrypted data [12]. Partial and complete homomorphic encryption are two varieties of this sort of encryption. Pailier methods [13], also known as partial homomorphic encryption, were utilized in this study to increase efficiency while requiring less computing and maintaining excellent security. Additionally, access management and authentication both use partial homomorphic encryption.

The initial consensus method used in connection with the Bitcoin cryptocurrency was the PoW [14, 15] procedure, which allowed participants to conduct safe financial transactions without needing a trustworthy third party. As it explores cryptographic techniques like hashing and encryption using asymmetric keys, it is a very secure and decentralized consensus system [16, 17]. The PoW strategy, however, has several significant drawbacks. The first has previously been mentioned: it uses a tremendous amount of electricity while producing no value [18, 19]. The time required to solve the hash-based cryptographic puzzle is another issue. The PoW process typically takes between 10 and 20 min to complete [20], making it unsuitable for networks that demand high transaction volume per second [21].

Various hash functions recently introduced in the literature are also used in graph-theoretic proof-of-work [23] based on the problem and prime number verification [22, 24]. Nevertheless, they all share the same disadvantages with the traditional PoW. As in the conventional PoW, the number of BC blocks is based on the Collatz conjecture (PCC) [25]. Nevertheless, PCC resolves the PoW procedure's complexity difficulties; the algorithm's usability issue is still a concern. Figure 3 shows that symmetric key cryptography algorithms have many blocks connected by a key. Still, one has many keys, or we can say that one has all the information regarding all key blocks, so we cannot trust that block with all crucial information. If one has input collision, all find the key in that block generates problems, or if the first block has generated an error, all blocks are not working. An example is that one colony has one Gard with all the keys to the flats and one key to the owner. It is not trusted security in any application.

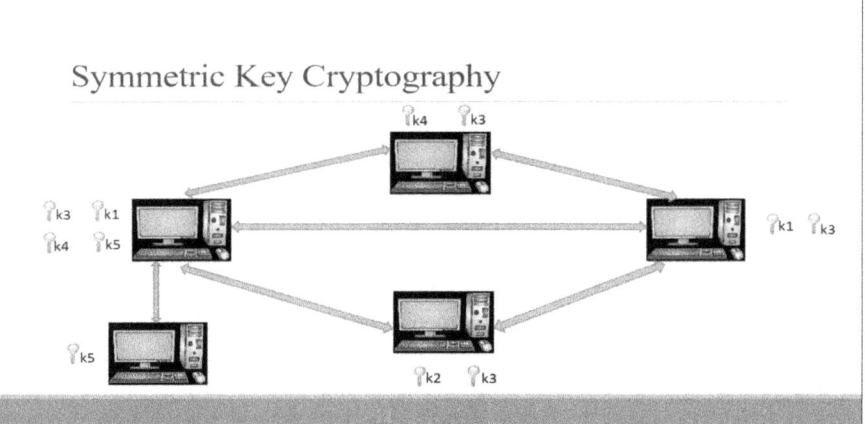

Fig. 3. Symmetric Key Cryptography Algorithms

Collision Resistant

I can discover X and Y, two distinct inputs, such as Hash(X) Equals (Y). That is an accident. A cryptographic hash function must be collision-resistant to be helpful. Identifying clashing inputs in practice takes time. The Birthday Paradox illustrates collision.

Birthday Paradox

- How many individuals should be present for a greater than 50% chance that two have the same birthday?
- There is a 50% possibility that two or more persons in a room with only 23 people will share the same birthday. There is a 99.9% likelihood that at least two persons in a room of 75 will match.

Paradox Explained

n possible dates   k people

$$\Pr[\text{Col}] = \frac{onen}{n}, \frac{n-1}{n}, \frac{n-2}{n}, \ldots\ldots, \frac{n-k+1}{n}, \prod_{l=1}^{k}\left(1-\frac{l}{n}\right) \leq \exp\left(-\frac{1}{n}\sum_{l=1}^{k} l\right) = \exp(-k(k+1)/2n)$$

$$\Pr(col) = \frac{1}{2} \Rightarrow k \approx 1.177\sqrt{n}$$

Finding Collision via the BP

- Randomly sample pairs of the form <x, H(x)>
- Store in table and short according to 2nd coordinate
- Perform a linear pass to see whether elements have an equal 2nd coordinate.

Analysis

- For k elements, the running time is O(k log k)
- Choose k as 1.77 $\sqrt{2}$

Constructor Hash Function

- Relates to the notation of one-way Function $f: X \to Y$

  Easy: given x find f(x)
  Hard: given f(x) sample $f^{-1}(f(x))$
  Word of caution

- The existence of one-way functions implies that:

$$does\ P \neq NP$$

Note: This is the most significant unresolved issue in computer science today. Why is collision resistance proper?

- We can use hash (X) as a sort of message digest of X if no one can locate X! = Y such that Hash (X) = = Hash (Y). Digital signatures sign hash (message) rather than the actual message.
- No one can alter X without altering the hash (X). If they could accomplish that, they could find a collision for hash (s).
- Hash (X) also committed X. You can show me X later, and I will know it is the value you committed to since I have already seen the hash for it. However, you cannot show me another X* because it will have a different hash.

2.2 Asymmetric Key Cryptography Algorithms

Stuart Haber [26], David Chaum [27], and Dave Bayer [28] conducted essential academic work that served as the foundation for blockchain. On the blockchain network, all users can share and store all data. Thanks to the data storage technology known as blockchain. The blockchain maintains data transparency and integrity by enabling users to share and store data. The data is verified by a consensus method before being put in a single block. A blockchain is a network with a back-and-forth connection between each block. The main components of blockchain technology are peer-to-peer (P2P) networks, cryptography, and consensus methods.

In contrast to a server-client network architecture, clients only read data and send requests to servers. Servers handle broadcasted data, and a peer-to-peer (P2P) network operates with every participating machine serving as both a server and a client simultaneously. Thanks to the P2P network's involvement in a blockchain, all users can store data in a scattered manner. Blockchain also uses cryptographic methods like asymmetric key technologies and hashing algorithms. These cryptographic methods guarantee and verify the reliability of data recorded on the blockchain.

Additionally, a consensus method ensures that every blockchain user can store the same information. Bitcoin makes a consensus process in a blockchain possible, encouraging users to participate. A reward for participating in a consensus algorithm can be received through cryptocurrency for blockchain users, or users can buy cryptocurrency using conventional money via cryptocurrency exchanges. To understand asymmetric cryptography, we take an example of sending a message from one user to another through the provided asymmetric key (public and private). Encryption is used here for the data and decrypted using both keys according to the SHA256 bit message transferring processes. They provide secure and authenticated messages to the relevant users. Figure 4 (a) shows the process of sending messages to the users. Figure 4 (b) shows the message-sending process to authenticate users with confidentiality. In this message sent by A, encrypted using A's private key, the message is encrypted by B's public key. The message is first decrypted using B's private key when sent to B, then decrypted again using A's private key.

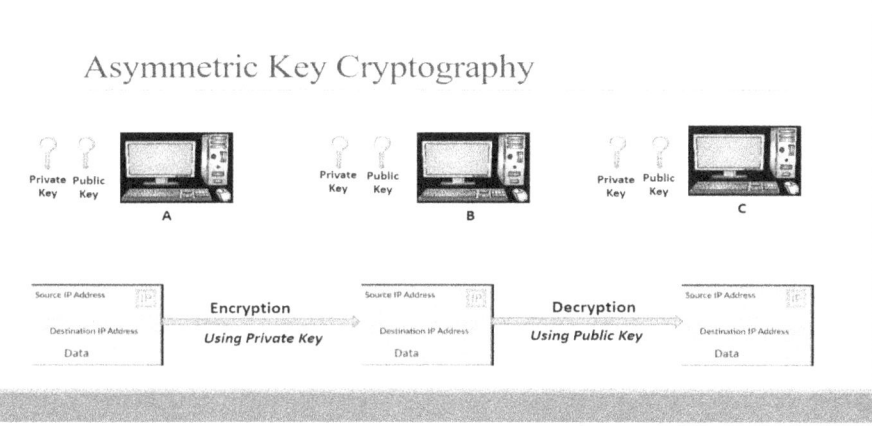

Fig. 4. (a) Asymmetric Key Cryptography Algorithms

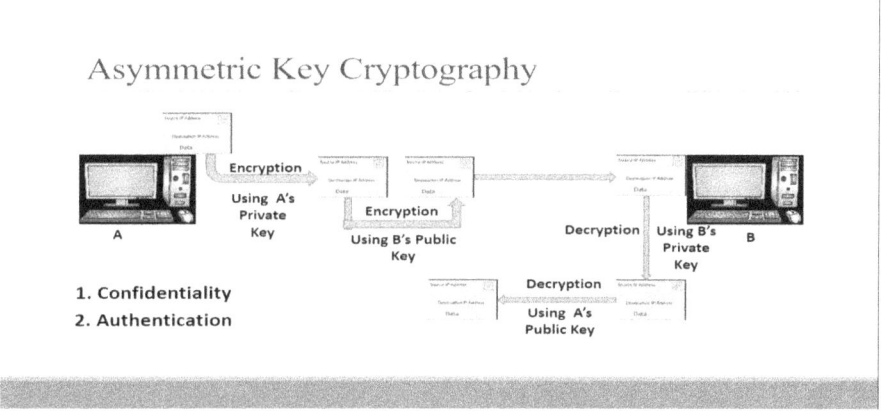

Fig. 4. (b) Asymmetric Key Cryptography Algorithms

3 Conclusion

The fundamental blockchain security features of the suggested system have been tested and assessed in this article utilizing benchmark datasets. The experimental configuration of the targeted system has been investigated and documented exclusively in this work before it is fully implemented. Lastly, the assessment and experiment have been detailed in the primary task of the suggested modular for the critical generation process that generates and compares a private and public key. In this study, we have also offered a module architecture that uses symmetric algorithms to create private and public keys. In this, we have used implementation methodology for asymmetric key generation and symmetric key generation with the help of blockchain technology. The fame work provides the simple design of methods that are used in web security. We hope that the given design is helpful in the security through the blockchain key generation.

References

1. Simmons, G.J.: Symmetric and asymmetric encryption. ACM Comput. Surv. (CSUR) **11**, 305–330 (1979)
2. Ogburn, M., Turner, C., Dahal, P.: Homomorphic encryption. Procedia Comput. Sci. **20**, 502–509 (2013)
3. Koç, Ç.K., Özdemir, F., Ödemiş Özger, Z.: Paillier algorithm. In: Koç, Ç.K., Özdemir, F., Ödemiş Özger, Z. (eds.) Partially Homomorphic Encryption, pp. 95–105. Springer, Cham (2021). https://doi.org/10.1007/978-3-030-87629-6_9
4. Zheng, Z., Xie, S., Dai, H., Chen, X., Wang, H.: An overview of blockchain technology: architecture, consensus, and future trends. In: Proceedings of the IEEE International Congress on Big Data (BigData Congress), Honolulu, HI, USA, 25–30 June 2017, pp. 557–564 (2017)
5. Bamakan, S.M.H., Motavali, A., Bondarti, A.B.: A survey of blockchain consensus algorithms performance evaluation criteria. Expert Syst. Appl. **154**, 113385 (2020)
6. Mihaljević, M.J.: A security enhanced encryption scheme and evaluation of its cryptographic security. Entropy **21**, 701 (2019)
7. Oyinloye, D.P., Teh, J.S., Jamil, N., Alawida, M.: Blockchain consensus: an overview of alternative protocols. Symmetry **13**, 1363 (2021)
8. Ball, M., Rosen, A., Sabin, M., Vasudevan, P.N.: Proofs of useful work. IACR Cryptology ePrint Archive (2017). https://eprint.iacr.org/2017/203.pdf. Accessed 4 June 2022
9. Drescher, D.: Blockchain Basics: A Non-Technical Introduction in 25 Steps. Apress, New York (2017)
10. Lasla, N., Alsahan, L., Abdallah, M., Younis, M.: Green-PoW: an energy-efficient blockchain proof-of-work consensus algorithm. arXiv 2020 arXiv:2007.04086
11. Cao, B., Zhang, Z., Feng, D., Zhang, S., Zhang, L., Peng, M., Li, Y.: Performance analysis and comparison of PoW, PoS and DAG-based blockchains. Digit. Commun. Netw. **6**, 480–485 (2020)
12. King, S.: Primecoin: Cryptocurrency with Prime Number Proof-of-Work (2013). https://citeseerx.ist.psu.edu/viewdoc/download?doi=10.1.1.694.5890&rep=rep1&type=pdf. Accessed 12 June 2022
13. Tromp, J.: Cuckoo cycle: a memory bound graph-theoretic proof-of-work. In: Proceedings of the International Conference on Financial Cryptography and Data Security, San Juan, Puerto Rico, 26–30 January 2015, pp. 49–62 (2015)
14. Biryukov, A., Khovratovich, D.: Equihash: asymmetric proof-of-work based on the generalized birthday problem. Ledger **2**, 1–30 (2017)
15. Aljassas, H.M.A., Sasi, S.: Performance evaluation of proof-of-work and collatz conjecture consensus algorithms. In: Proceedings of the 2nd International Conference on Computer Applications & Information Security (ICCAIS), Riyadh, Saudi Arabia, 1–3 May 2019, pp. 1–6 (2019)
16. Haber, S.; Stornetta, W.S.: How to time-stamp a digital document. J. Cryptol. **3**, 99–111 (1991)
17. Chaum, D., Fiat, A., Naor, M.: Untraceable electronic cash. In: Goldwasser, S. (ed.) CRYPTO 1988. LNCS, vol. 403, pp. 319–327. Springer, New York (1990). https://doi.org/10.1007/0-387-34799-2_25
18. Bayer, D., Haber, S., Stornetta, W.S.: Improving the efficiency and reliability of digital time-stamping. In: Capocelli, R., De Santis, A., Vaccaro, U. (eds.) Sequences II, pp. 329–334. Springer, New York (1993). https://doi.org/10.1007/978-1-4613-9323-8_24
19. Metamask. https://metamask.io/. Accessed 8 June 2022
20. Johnson, D., Menezes, A., Vanstone, S.: The elliptic curve digital signature algorithm (ECDSA). Int. J. Inf. Secure **1**, 36–63 (2001)

21. Soltani, R., Nguyen, U.T., An, A.: Practical key recovery model for self-sovereign identity based digital wallets. In: Proceedings of the 2019 IEEE International Conference on Dependable, Autonomic and Secure Computing, International Conference on Pervasive Intelligence and Computing, International Conference on Cloud and Big Data Computing, International Conference on Cyber Science and Technology Congress (DASC/PiCom/CBDCom/CyberSciTech), Fukuoka, Japan, 4 November 2019
22. Singh, H.P., Stefanidis, K., Kirstein, F.: A private key recovery scheme using partial knowledge. In: Proceedings of the 2021 11th IFIP International Conference on New Technologies, Mobility and Security (NTMS), Paris, France, 19–21 April 2021 (2021)
23. He, X., Lin, J., Li, K., Chen, X.: A novel cryptocurrency wallet management scheme based on decentralized multi-constrained derangement. IEEE Access **7**, 185250–185263 (2019)
24. Private key encryption and recovery in blockchain. https://arxiv.org/abs/1907.04156. Accessed 19 Dec 2020
25. Zhao, H., Zhang, Y., Peng, Y., Xu, R.: Lightweight backup and efficient recovery scheme for health blockchain keys. In: Proceedings of the 2017 IEEE 13th International Symposium on Autonomous Decentralized System (ISADS), Bangkok, Thailand, 22–24 March 2017 (2017)
26. Zhu, F., Chen, W., Wang, Y., Lin, P., Li, T., Cao, X., Yuan, L.: Trust your wallet: a new online wallet architecture for bitcoin. In: Proceedings of the 2017 International Conference on Progress in Informatics and Computing (PIC), Nanjing, China, 15–17 December 2017 (2017)
27. He, S., et al.: A social-network-based cryptocurrency wallet-management scheme. IEEE Access **6**, 7654–7663 (2018)
28. Reed, I.S., Solomon, G.: Polynomial codes over certain finite fields. J. Soc. Ind. Appl. Math. **8**, 300–304 (1960)

Blockchain and IPFS Based Evidence Protection System for Safeguarding Women's Right

Chaitali Patil, Avinash Jadhav, Shruti Kadbhane, Shivani Dangal[✉], and Prajakta Patil

Department of Computer Engineering, K. K. Wagh Institute of Engineering Education and Research, Nashik, India
`crpatil@kkwagh.edu.com`, `shivanidangal@gmail.com`

Abstract. In today's digital age, digital evidence plays a pivotal role in criminal investigations, particularly in cases related to heinous crimes against women, such as rape, domestic violence, sexual assault, acid attacks, and numerous cyber crimes. However, the vulnerability of digital evidence to tampering, manipulation, or unauthorized access poses a significant challenge to the evidence integrity and privacy of victims. Throughout the investigation process, sensitive data in various formats is generated, necessitating the maintenance of data integrity as it passes through different intermediaries, forming a Chain of Custody. This paper proposes an innovative solution to address these issues through the integration of Ethereum blockchain and the Interplanetary File System (IPFS), creating a robust Evidence Protection System (EPS) for safeguarding women's rights. The proposed system leverages the transparency, immutability, and decentralized nature of the Ethereum blockchain to establish an unforgeable chain of custody for digital evidence, with smart contracts facilitating the seamless management of access and verification by authorized stakeholders, such as law enforcement agencies and legal professionals. The IPFS technology is utilized to securely store digital evidence, ensuring its availability and privacy. The combination of blockchain and IPFS provides a secure platform for preserving digital evidence, mitigating risks of tampering and unauthorized distribution, and enhancing the pursuit of justice.

Keywords: Blockchain · IPFS · Digital Evidence · Evidence Protection System · Chain of Custody · Smart Contracts · Data Integrity · Decentralized Storage · Evidence Management

1 Introduction

In our increasingly digital world, the protection and security of digital evidence have become paramount, particularly in cases involving serious crimes against women, including sexual assault, domestic violence, and cybercrimes. While digital evidence plays a crucial role in criminal investigations, its inherent susceptibility to tampering, manipulation, and unauthorized access poses significant challenges to the justice delivery system.

The Chain of Evidence (CoE) represents the documented journey of evidence through various stages of investigation and prosecution. At its core lies the 'chain of custody' - a critical documentation system that ensures evidence authenticity by validating that the evidence remains identical to what was collected at the crime scene and has been continuously maintained under authorized supervision. This meticulous process, essential for court admissibility, tracks the complete timeline of evidence handling from discovery through examination to court presentation, forming an unbroken chain of accountability.

To address these challenges, we propose 'Evidence Shield: Blockchain and IPFS-Based Evidence Protection System for Safeguarding Women's Rights'. This innovative system leverages Ethereum blockchain's immutable distributed ledger for evidence tracking and smart contracts for automated procedure validation, alongside IPFS's content-addressed storage ensuring data immutability and distributed architecture. The system's technical architecture incorporates smart contracts for automated rule enforcement, MetaMask integration for secure authentication, advanced encryption protocols, and real-time audit logging capabilities.

While traditional evidence management solutions utilizing centralized databases and cloud storage exist, they fall short in providing comprehensive security, transparency, and tamper resistance. Our integrated approach combines blockchain and IPFS technologies to create a robust solution that addresses the critical requirements of evidence integrity through cryptographic verification, granular privacy controls, high availability, and transparent chain of custody documentation.

This paper presents Evidence Shield as a secure, decentralized platform that revolutionizes digital evidence management, particularly in cases involving women's rights violations, offering significant technological advantages for law enforcement agencies, legal professionals, and victim support organizations in our increasingly interconnected world.

2 Literature Survey

The management of evidence in legal investigations, particularly in cases involving crimes against women, is increasingly critical. Blockchain technology is being explored as a means to enhance the integrity and security of evidence storage by providing a tamper-proof and immutable system. This survey examines various research efforts and their contributions to the integration of blockchain for evidence management, highlighting the innovative aspects and identifying gaps that our proposed system aims to address.

Syed Amir Hussain et al. [1] discusses the use of blockchain and IPFS for enhanced security in digital evidence management. Their system, implemented on the Ethereum platform, focuses on ensuring the authenticity and traceability of evidence using smart contracts. The integration of IPFS addresses issues related to data availability and fault tolerance. However, the research highlights challenges in handling large volumes of data and lacks a detailed mechanism for user access control, which our proposed system addresses through decentralized identity management solutions like MetaMask.

Supriya Srivastava et al. [2] proposed an innovative framework combining blockchain and IPFS to safeguard evidentiary data. The approach leverages IPFS for decentralized, tamper-resistant storage and integrates multi-signature wallets for secure data uploads. The system includes mechanisms for periodic updates to verify the integrity of evidence over time. While this model provides enhanced security features, it does not explicitly address user authentication or the integration with broader legal processes, which are key aspects of our proposed solution.

One study by A.H. Shanthakumara and Shilpa C et al. [3] investigates the integration of blockchain technology into the Chain of Evidence (CoE) process to address vulnerabilities in traditional evidence handling, such as tampering and unauthorized access. Using the Ethereum blockchain combined with the InterPlanetary File System (IPFS), the system ensures data integrity, transparency, and immutability. However, the study lacks a comprehensive framework for coordinating among stakeholders like police, hospitals, and courts, which our system seeks to address.

Shyam Mehta et al. [4] proposed a blockchain-driven evidence management system focused on secure handling of electronic First Information Reports (e-FIRs). The solution leverages Ethereum smart contracts to enhance the integrity and transparency of complaint data, mitigating risks of unauthorized changes. However, the approach does not integrate decentralized identity management or advanced access control, which are included in our proposed model to ensure secure user authentication and authorization across different legal entities.

Maharshi Dave and Dr. Rajkumar Banoth et al. [5] introduces a decentralized evidence archive system using IPFS integrated with the Ethereum blockchain. This study emphasizes the importance of preserving evidence integrity through decentralized storage, addressing the limitations of centralized databases. The solution uses smart contracts to automate the secure management of evidence data, but it does not address challenges related to scalability and efficient data retrieval, aspects that our system enhances through optimized blockchain architecture.

Zhikun Miao et al. [6] propose using Directed Acyclic Graph (DAG) technology to overcome the limitations of traditional electronic evidence storage methods. DAG offers scalability and efficiency by enabling parallel transaction processing, which enhances the speed and integrity of transactions. Combined with blockchain features like timestamping and cryptographic hashing, this model improves the authenticity and immutability of electronic evidence. However, it does not provide a detailed mechanism for user authentication and access control, which is a focus in our proposed system.

Van Giang Phan Mai et al. [8] develop a decentralized user authentication model using MetaMask and Ethereum to enhance security and privacy compared to traditional server-client architectures. MetaMask manages private keys and facilitates secure authentication, while Ethereum's smart contracts automate and secure the process. This system reduces the risks associated with centralized data storage but does not integrate evidence management with law enforcement and judicial processes, which our solution addresses.

Giuliano Giova et al. [9] explores the integration of the InterPlanetary File System (IPFS) with blockchain for enhanced data storage efficiency and security. IPFS provides a decentralized, content-addressable storage solution, ensuring that evidence remains untampered and improving overall transparency. However, the paper does not present a comprehensive solution for the legal admissibility and verification of digital evidence across different stages of the investigation, which our system incorporates by combining IPFS with decentralized identity management.

Saide Zhu et al. [10] discusses a hybrid blockchain design aimed at privacy preservation in crowdsourcing platforms. The design enhances security and efficiency across various applications, including evidence management. However, it lacks a specific focus on the unique challenges faced in criminal investigations and integration with existing legal frameworks, which are key elements addressed by our proposed system.

Finally, Shijie Chen et al. [12] reinforce the benefits of blockchain technology for maintaining evidence integrity and chain of custody. Their research supports the notion that blockchain can effectively address significant challenges in digital evidence management. However, it does not detail the integration with decentralized identity solutions like MetaMask, which our system includes for improved security and privacy.

3 Methodology

The proposed system, "Evidence Shield" is a comprehensive platform designed to facilitate the reporting and investigation of crimes, involving various stakeholders such as complainants, police personnel, hospitals, labs, and legal authorities. This Evidence Protection System (EPS) leverages advanced technologies to enhance the integrity, security, and efficiency of digital evidence management.

Fig. 1. Overview of Evidence Protection System

Figure 1 provides a comprehensive visualization of the Evidence Protection System (EPS) architecture, highlighting the roles and responsibilities of all stakeholders involved. It outlines the interactions between complainants, police personnel, hospitals, labs, and legal authorities throughout the evidence management process. The diagram illustrates how each role contributes to complaint registration, evidence collection, lab reporting, hospital feedback, and legal proceedings. It serves as a roadmap for understanding the integrated workflow and stakeholder interactions within the Evidence Shield.

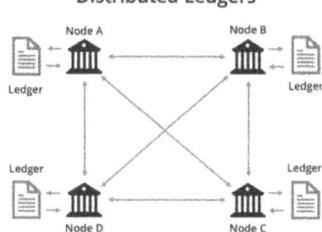

Fig. 2. Ethereum Blockchain Network

3.1 Ethereum Blockchain

Figure 2 shows Ethereum which uses a blockchain, a distributed ledger, to store information in immutable blocks, creating an unchangeable chain. Validators receive ether tokens for validating and proposing new blocks, and consensus is achieved through Proof-of-Stake, utilizing the Gasper protocol, which includes Casper-FFG and LMD Ghost. Validators must stake ETH, and those who act dishonestly face penalties such as having their staked ETH burned [10].

When evidence is uploaded to the system, IPFS splits it into smaller blocks, each with a unique hash. A root hash identifies the file and is stored immutably on the Ethereum blockchain. This ensures data integrity while reducing blockchain transaction costs.

3.2 IPFS (Interplanetary File System)

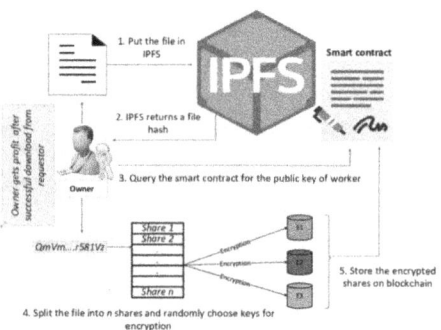

Fig. 3. Interplanetary File System (IPFS)

Figure 3 refers to IPFS (InterPlanetary File System) which is a peer-to-peer distributed file system that decentralizes data storage and sharing. Files are stored across a network of nodes rather than on a single server, which enhances resilience and accessibility. IPFS utilizes content addressing, meaning that each file is identified by a unique cryptographic hash, known as an IPFS hash. This hash is derived from the file's content, ensuring that the file remains consistent and tamper-proof. When a file is added to IPFS, it is split into smaller blocks, each of which is assigned an IPFS hash. These blocks are distributed and stored across the network. When someone requests a file, IPFS retrieves it by its hash, ensuring that the correct file is accessed, regardless of its location. This system ensures data remains available and consistent even if traditional servers fail or nodes go offline [15].

3.3 Smart Contracts

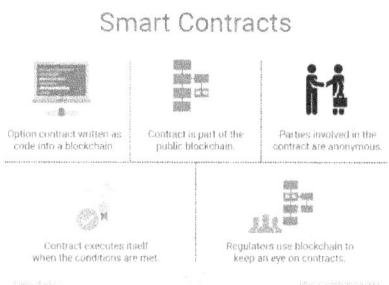

Fig. 4. Smart Contracts

Figure 4 shows Smart Contracts that are self-executing contracts with terms written directly into code on the blockchain. They automatically enforce and execute contract terms when predefined conditions are met. Once deployed on platforms like Ethereum, they cannot be altered, ensuring immutability and transparency. Actions are triggered by specific conditions, validated by the network, and recorded on the blockchain, guaranteeing reliable and transparent execution [16].

Tokenization and Evidence Automation
Each piece of evidence is represented as a unique token (NFT) linked to its IPFS hash. Smart contracts validate the uploaded evidence by checking hash formats and notifying stakeholders about the updates. This automates critical processes and ensures seamless evidence handling.

3.4 Metamask

MetaMask [17] is a cryptocurrency wallet and browser extension for managing Ethereumbased assets and interacting with decentralized applications (dApps). It allows users to securely store Ethereum and ERC-20 tokens, handle transactions, and interact with smart contracts through a user-friendly interface. MetaMask generates and manages private keys locally on the user's device, providing a secure way to access and manage blockchain assets. It connects seamlessly with various dApps, enabling users to sign transactions and authenticate their identity. By facilitating interaction with the Ethereum blockchain, MetaMask bridges the gap between users and decentralized applications [18] (Fig. 5).

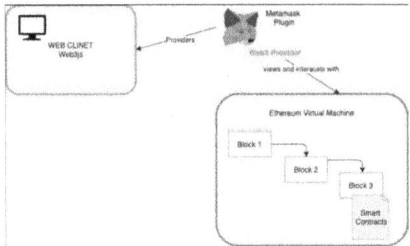

Fig. 5. Metamask

3.5 Chain of Custody

The 'chain of custody' is a critical process for documenting the continuity and integrity of evidence. It ensures that evidence remains unaltered and accounted for from the moment it is collected at the crime scene through its examination and presentation in court. This meticulous documentation tracks each person who handles the evidence and every transfer it undergoes, preserving its authenticity. Maintaining an unbroken chain of custody is essential for ensuring that evidence is credible and can be relied upon in legal proceedings [9].

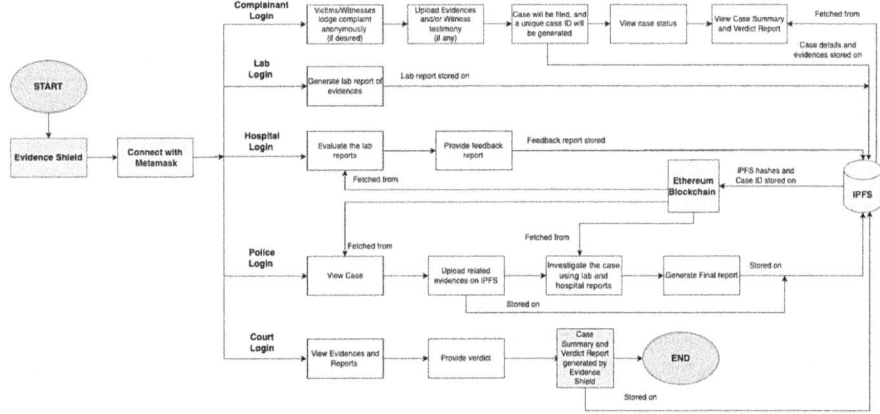

Fig. 6. Architectural diagram of Evidence

Figure 6 shows an architectural diagram that illustrates the complete process from complaint registration to verdict report generation. It highlights how IPFS and Ethereum blockchain are used to manage and secure digital evidence, and how Metamask facilitates secure authentication and access (Fig. 7).

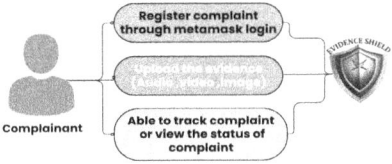

Fig. 7. Complainant interaction with the system

1) Complaint Registration:

   - The system begins with complaint registration, allowing complainants to log in using their Metamask accounts for secure authentication. This ensures privacy and security, allowing users to report complaints with confidence.
   - Detailed information about the crime is provided, including the victim's name, incident location, crime and evidence details, and evidence.
   - Multiple pieces of evidence can be uploaded in various formats such as documents (pdf, .txt, .docx, etc.), image (.png, .jpg, .jpeg, .gif, etc.), audio (.MP3, .WAV, .AIFF, .AU, etc.), video (.WEBM, .OGG, .MP3, .MP4, etc.), etc.
   - Each piece of evidence is uploaded to IPFS, generating IPFS hashes.
   - Information including details of the crime and IPFS hashes is converted into a JSON file, which is then uploaded to IPFS, generating another IPFS hash.
   - A unique Case ID is generated for each complaint, mapped to the IPFS hash of the JSON file, and this mapping is securely stored on the Ethereum blockchain.

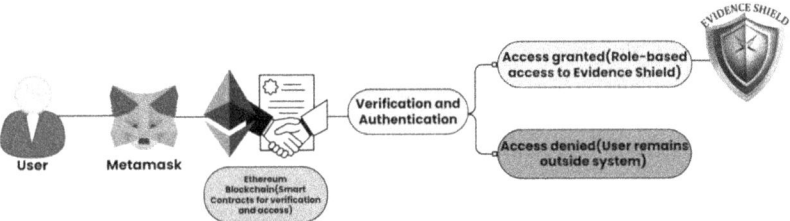

Fig. 8. Login to the System using Metamask

2) Login to the System using Metamask:

   - Metamask addresses of police, labs, hospitals, and complainants are stored on the Ethereum blockchain.
   - According to Fig. 8 once a user clicks on login, the system detects their Metamask address and compares it with the stored address.
   - If a match is found, the user is automatically logged into the system with their respective role, such as police, court, etc.
   - This enables seamless authentication and access to relevant functionalities.

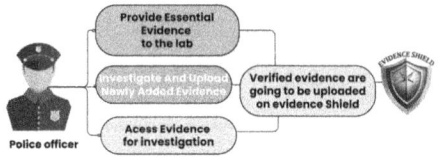

Fig. 9. Police interaction with the system

3) Police Access and Investigation:

- As shown in Fig. 9, authorized police personnel log in to Evidence Shield using Metamask to access case details and review complaints.
- Investigations are initiated, and relevant evidence is collected by the police personnel, including documents, photos, videos, and digital content.
- The collected evidences are uploaded to IPFS for secure storage, and IPFS hashes are mapped to the respective Case ID on the blockchain.

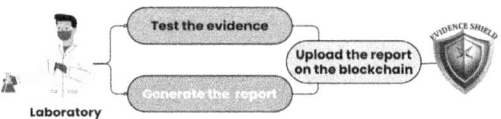

Fig. 10. Laboratory interaction with the system

4) Lab Reports:

- Evidence Shield allows labs to upload physical evidence reports with login access, ensuring confidentiality by only allowing labs to view the Case ID associated with the evidence as shown in Fig. 10.
- This restricted access prevents tampering with case details while allowing labs to securely upload their reports directly onto the system.
- Uploaded lab reports are stored on IPFS, and their hashes are mapped to the Case ID on the blockchain.

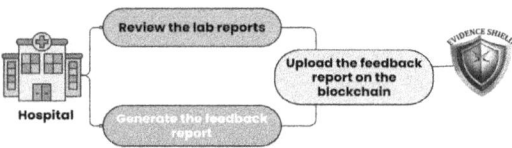

Fig. 11. Hospital interaction with the system

5) Hospital Feedback:
   - In cases where doctors' feedback is necessary, hospitals can review the lab reports using their Metamask account.
   - As shown in Fig. 11, doctors evaluate lab reports and provide feedback reports through the system.
   - Feedback reports are uploaded to IPFS, and their hashes are mapped to the corresponding Case ID.

6) Tracking Case Progress:
   - Complainants can track the progress of their registered case through their Metamask login.
   - They can view whether the police have reported the case and the status of the further investigation process.

7) Evidence Accessibility:
   - Complainants can access evidence, lab reports, and feedback during the investigation process by logging in with their Metamask account and entering the Case ID.
   - This ensures transparency and allows complainants to stay informed about the progress of their case.

8) Final Investigation Reports:
   - Police officers utilize all collected evidence and various lab/hospital reports to generate a final investigation report.
   - Findings are documented and securely stored on IPFS, enhancing transparency and security.

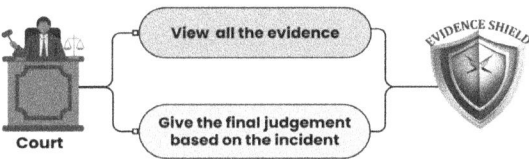

Fig. 12. Court interaction with the system

9) Legal Access:
   - As shown in Fig. 12, court authorities and lawyers can access all stored evidences and reports through their Metamask login, enabling effective legal representation and verdicts.
   - Once the investigation concludes, Evidence Shield generates a comprehensive Case Summary and Verdict Report summarizing the case proceedings, as shown in Fig. 12.

- The Case Summary and Verdict Report provides comprehensive details, including the number of evidences uploaded by users, transaction hashes of the uploaded evidences, as well as the court verdict hash and final statement.
- This detailed report ensures transparency and accountability throughout the investigation process and provides a conclusive overview of the case outcome.

10) Privacy Mechanism:

- **Encryption of Sensitive Data:** Evidence is encrypted using AES-256 before uploading to IPFS. Only authorized stakeholders receive the decryption keys via smart contracts.
- **Decentralized Authentication:** Users interact with the system pseudonymously via Metamask, maintaining anonymity while ensuring secure access.
- **Role-Based Access Control:** Permissions are enforced via smart contracts, ensuring that only relevant stakeholders access specific data.

This forms a chain of custody in the Evidence Shield system that ensures the integrity and traceability of evidence from the initial complaint registration through to the final verdict. Complainants start the process by using Metamask to securely log in and upload evidence to IPFS, generating unique IPFS hashes for each item. Police then access these details and continue the investigation, adding collected evidence to IPFS and mapping these hashes to the case ID on the Ethereum blockchain. Lab and hospital reports are also uploaded and linked to the case ID, maintaining confidentiality and preventing tampering. Throughout, smart contracts and Metamask manage access controls, ensuring that only authorized personnel handle evidence at each stage. This comprehensive tracking maintains the authenticity and continuity of evidence, which is crucial for ensuring its admissibility and integrity in legal proceedings.

4 Results and Discussions

The traditional legal investigation process faces several critical issues that compromise the integrity and efficiency of handling digital evidence. One of the primary flaws in the current system is the vulnerability to evidence tampering. In the traditional setup, evidence often passes through multiple intermediaries, increasing the risk of unauthorized access, alteration, or loss of crucial information. This lack of a secure, transparent mechanism to track and verify the integrity of evidence often leads to challenges in establishing a reliable chain of custody.

Moreover, the traditional system suffers from inadequate coordination between law enforcement agencies, healthcare institutions, and legal authorities. This lack of integration results in delays in initiating criminal cases, difficulties in filing and retrieving evidence, and overall inefficiencies in the justice process. The absence of a centralized, secure platform for managing evidence and case details intensifies these issues, making it challenging to ensure the timely and accurate administration of justice.

4.1 Analysis of Traditional vs. Blockchain-Based Crime Reporting Investigation System

Parameters	Traditional System	Blockchain-Based System
Evidence Tampering	High risk due to multiple intermediaries	Minimized through immutable blockchain records
Coordination	Inadequate between law enforcement, healthcare, and legal authorities	Streamlined via a centralized platform
Data Integrity	Vulnerable to unauthorized access and alterations	Ensured through timestamped, secure blockchain storage
Data Availability	Risk of data loss and censorship	Enhanced through decentralized IPFS storage
Authentication	Manual and prone to errors	Secure, seamless via Metamask and smart contracts
Transparency	Limited, often leading to disputes	High transparency with traceable and verifiable records
Efficiency	Delays and inefficiencies in handling and retrieving evidence	Improved efficiency with automated processes and secure access

The proposed solution leverages the Ethereum blockchain and the Interplanetary File System (IPFS) technologies to overcome these limitations. By integrating blockchain technology, the system ensures the immutability and transparency of evidence records. Each piece of evidence is time stamped and securely stored on the Ethereum blockchain, creating an unforgeable chain of custody. This prevents any unauthorized alteration or deletion of evidence, thereby maintaining its integrity throughout the investigation process.

The use of IPFS for decentralized storage further enhances the security and availability of digital evidence. Unlike traditional centralized databases, IPFS distributes data across a peer-to-peer network, which helps prevent data loss and reduces the risk of censorship. This ensures that evidence remains accessible even if traditional servers are compromised, providing a more reliable and secure method of storing sensitive information.Smart contracts on the Ethereum blockchain facilitate the seamless management of evidence access and verification. These self-executing contracts automate the enforcement of rules and procedures, enabling authorized stakeholders to securely interact with the evidence. The transparency of blockchain technology allows stakeholders to track and validate case details and evidence, ensuring accountability among all parties involved. This ensures that investigations are conducted fairly and transparently, supporting the principles of justice. The proposed system also addresses the issue of inadequate coordination by providing a streamlined platform for collaboration and communication among stakeholders. Centralized storage and secure sharing of case details and evidence enhance efficiency and effectiveness in investigating crimes, enabling informed decision-making.

The system's integration with Metamask for secure authentication allows users to access features anonymously if needed, further enhancing security and privacy.

Fig. 13. Case Summary and Verdict Report generated by Evidence Shield

Figure 13 provides a detailed overview of a specific case generated through the Evidence Shield system. The report is generated by Evidence Shield which includes the following components:

1. Name of Complainant: ABC

   - The No. of Evidences Uploaded by Complainant: 2
   - Transaction Hash of Reporting Crime:
     0x5f6d9b8a52bfc1e9c8a5fbc5d14a1a3cb6b91f0d9e4a5c9b2e8c8d0f8c5a6d77e
   - This hash represents the unique identifier for the crime report submitted by the complainant. It ensures the integrity and immutability of the reported information.

2. Police Investigation:

   - No. of Evidences Uploaded by Police: 3
   - Transaction Hashes of Police Uploaded Evidences:
     0x3a6b7e2d8f23a5e9c4d0b8d2b6a1a2d9e7f6c9b8e5a2d0c1e9f7d8a3b5d6c9e7
     0x8b5d2f6e7a3c9d0e4b8a1c5e9d2b6f7a8e3c9d0b6f7a5e2c9d8b0e4c3a6d9e7
     0x7d8c9a5e2b3f6d0e4b8a1c9e7f2b6a8e3d9c0b5f2e6a7d0c9b8e4a3d6f1e9d0
   - These hashes correspond to the pieces of evidence uploaded by the police. Each hash is a unique identifier ensuring the integrity of the evidence collected during the investigation.
   - Police Report Transaction Hash:

0x1c9e8d6f7a5b3c2e4d8a9b0c6e7d2f1a5e9c7b8d3a2e4c6d8f0b9a7e1d2f3c4
- This hash identifies the final police report, encapsulating all collected evidence and findings, ensuring its authenticity and unaltered state.

3. Forensic Laboratory Investigation:
   - Reports Uploaded by Laboratory: 2
   - Transaction Hashes of Lab Uploaded Reports:
     00x6e9b7c8f2d3a4e5b8c0f7d1a2e6b9d8c3f4e5a2d7b9c6e1a8d0f3b5c7d9e2a8
     0x8f6d2b3a5c9e0a7b4d8e1c2f9a3b6d7e0c5f8a2d9b3e4c1a7d8f6b0e2c9a3d4
   - These hashes represent the forensic reports generated by the laboratory. Each hash ensures the reports' integrity and their proper association with the case.

4. Hospital Feedback:
   - Transaction Hash of Hospital Uploaded Reports:
     0x5d3a9b8e7c2f1d0b4e8a6c0f2e7d9b3a5c6e1d8b0f9c7a2d4e8b1c5a6d0e9f2
   - This hash corresponds to the feedback report provided by the hospital, ensuring its authenticity and correct linkage to the case.

5. Court Verdict:
   - Transaction Hash of Court Verdict:
     0x7c8e1b2a9f0d4b6c3e5d8a2f9b0c7e1a6d8f5b2c3e7a9d0b4f1c6e8d2a5b9c0
   - This hash uniquely identifies the court's verdict on the case, ensuring the final judgment is recorded and cannot be altered.
   - Court Final Statement: The court has sentenced XYZ, once deemed the victim, to a 10-year life imprisonment. Evidence Shield ensured effective case management and preserved crucial evidence.
   - This statement summarizes the court's final decision and highlights the effectiveness of the Evidence Shield system in preserving evidence and managing the case throughout the judicial process.

Performance Parameters

- Upload and Retrieval Times:
  - Uploading a 1 MB file to IPFS takes 3–5 s.
  - Retrieval latency averages 2–4 s.

- Blockchain Costs:
  - Registering an evidence hash on Ethereum incurs a gas cost of 0.002 ETH on average.

- Throughput:
  - The system supports multiple concurrent uploads, leveraging IPFS's distributed architecture for scalability.

Potential Stakeholders

- NGOs and Women's Rights Organizations: Advocate for the system and subsidize transaction costs.
- Government Agencies: Recognize blockchain-based evidence as legally valid and integrate the system with law enforcement databases.
- Technology Providers: Offer infrastructure support for deploying IPFS nodes and maintaining smart contracts.

5 Conclusion

The proposed evidence management system represents a significant innovation in the field of criminal investigations by leveraging Ethereum blockchain technology, IPFS, and smart contracts. This integration creates a robust, decentralized platform that enhances the integrity and management of digital evidence through its transparent and secure framework. The platform's design enhances the efficiency of the justice process by facilitating better coordination among various stakeholders, including complainants, law enforcement, healthcare providers, and legal authorities. Its user-centric features, such as Metamask for authentication, enhance privacy and security, making it easier for users to interact with the system.

However, a notable drawback is that the system is deployed on a public blockchain, which involves gas charges for transactions. The responsibility for these costs, whether borne by the government or another entity, remains a concern. This challenge could be addressed by using a private blockchain solution, such as Hyperledger, which offers the potential to mitigate transaction costs and control access more effectively. Despite this, deploying the system on a public blockchain presents a compelling future scope for ensuring transparency and wider accessibility.

Looking ahead, there are opportunities to refine and expand the system's capabilities. Potential areas for development include integration enhancements for law enforcement agencies, legal system integration and support, empowerment of victim support organizations, and building partnerships and collaborations with other technology providers, legal experts, and advocacy groups. In summary, this platform offers a forward-thinking approach to evidence management, aiming to not only improve current practices but also set the stage for future advancements in ensuring justice and safeguarding victims' rights.

Future work includes exploring private blockchain solutions to mitigate transaction costs and developing collaborative models with NGOs and governments for broader adoption.

References

1. Hussain, S.A., Ur Rahman, A., Bari, S.A., Vaishnavi, L.: Evidence vault: blockchain and IPFS enhanced security system. Int. J. Eng. Sci. Res. (IJESR) **14**(2), 836–849 (2024)
2. Srivastava, S., Kaur, G., Himank, Singla, S.: Implementation of blockchain and IPFS to safeguard evidentiary data. In: 2024 International Conference on Knowledge Engineering and Communication Systems (ICKECS) (2024)

3. Shanthakumara, A.H., Shilpa, C.: An implementation of blockchain technology in combination with IPFS for crime evidence management system. In: 2023 International Conference on Computer Communication and Informatics (ICCCI), 23–25 January 2023, Coimbatore, India (2023)
4. Mehta, S., Raikwar, H., Shantha Kumari, K., Gore, S.: Blockchain driven evidence management system. In: 2023 3rd International Conference on Artificial Intelligence and Signal Processing (AISP). ISBN: 979-8-3503-2074-9/23. https://doi.org/10.1109/AISP57993.2023.10134799
5. Dave, M., Banoth, R.: Blockchain-based, decentralized evidence archive system using IPFS. In: 2022 International Conference on Sustainable Computing and Data Communication Systems (ICSCDS). ISBN: 978-1-6654-7884-7/22. https://doi.org/10.1109/ICSCDS53736.2022.9760983
6. Miao, Z., Ye, C., Chen, Y., Chen, Y., Yang, P.: Blockchain-based electronic evidence storage and efficiency optimization. In: 2021 International Conference on Artificial Intelligence and Blockchain Technology (AIBT) (2021)
7. Shah, M.S.M.B., Saleem, S., Zulqarnain, R.: Protecting digital evidence integrity and preserving chain of custody, the association of digital forensics, security and law (ADFSL)
8. Mai, V.G.P., Vũ, L.M., Sn, H., Khi, N.T.: A blockchain-based user authentication model using MetaMask. In: Student Conference on Information Communication Technology
9. Giova, G.: Improving chain of custody in forensic investigation of electronic digital systems. Int. J. Comput. Sci. Netw. Secur. **11**(1), 1–9 (2011)
10. Zhu, S., Hu, H., Li, Y., Li, W.: Hybrid blockchain design for privacy preserving crowdsourcing platform. In: 2019 IEEE International Conference on Blockchain, Atlanta, GA, USA, pp. 26–33 (2019)
11. Baygin, N., Baygin, M., Karakose, M.: Blockchain technology: applications, benefits and challenges. In: 2019 1st International Informatics and Software Engineering Conference (UBMYK) (2019)
12. Chen, S., Zhao, C., Huang, L.: Study and implementation on the application of blockchain in electronic evidence generation. Forensic Sci. Int. Digit. Investig. **35** (2020)
13. StatPearls. Chain of Custody. NCBI Bookshelf. https://www.ncbi.nlm.nih.gov/books/NBK555568/
14. Investopedia.Ethereum blockchain. https://www.investopedia.com/terms/e/ethereum.asp
15. CFI. https://corporatefinanceinstitute.com/resources/cryptocurrency/distributed-ledgers/
16. Naz, M., Al-Zahrani, F.A., Khalid, R., Javaid, N.: A secure data sharing platform using blockchain and IPFS
17. CodeBramha. https://codebrahma.com/brief-intro-smart-contracts-endlesspossibilities/
18. Vasilj, M., Skender, S., Jurdana, M., Horvat, M.: DESPRO: decentralized business platform for student nonprofit organizations
19. IPFS docs. https://docs.ipfs.tech/concepts/what-is-ipfs/#defining-ipfs
20. IBM. https://www.ibm.com/topics/smart-contracts

Author Index

A

Abdul Hamid, Abu Bakar bin 466
Aftab, Aasif 335
Ahmad, Md Oqail 300, 335
Alam, Malik Zaib 129
Alam, Md Imran 129
Alam, Md Shoaib 186
Alam, Md. Shamsher 312
Al-Tuama, Alaa T. 75
Alzoubi, Malek 300
Anand, Prakash 37
Ansari, Mohd. Yousuf 255

B

Bachhav, Archana 365
Balamurugan, M. 141
Banerjee, Sourav 410
Biswas, Utpal 410
Burman, Ravi Kumar 153, 169

C

Chowdhury, Kulsuma 221

D

Dangal, Shivani 476
Dash, Smita 118, 221
Datta, Suseta 410

H

Haseebuddin, Mohammad 300
Hinz, Binita Roshima 92
Hizam, Nuras Naser Saeed 365
Hoque, Amirul 221

I

Indumathi, N. 141

J

Jadhav, Avinash 476

K

Kadbhane, Shruti 476
Kamal, Mohammad Shahid 300
Kande, Jayanth 3, 17
Khan, Haneef 129
Khan, Mohammad Rafeek 129
Kumar, Abhishek 153, 169
Kumar, Ankit 439
Kumar, Binod 92, 141
Kumar, Biresh 186
Kumar, Jeevan 118, 205, 312
Kumar, Madhurendra 397
Kumar, Pradeep 397, 466
Kumar, Pravin 92
Kumar, Pravir 153
Kumar, Purushottam 439
Kumar, Rajeev 397, 466
Kumar, Sulekh 312
Kumar, Yogendra 312
Kumari, Meenakshi 37
Kumari, Namrata 221

L

Lekkala, Jai Jaswant 350, 383, 425

M

Maharana, Khirod Chandra 92
Mandal, Sampurna 141
Mansoori, Saba 236
Meda, Devendra Kumar 236, 282
Mondal, Rituparna 410
Mulajkar, Ruta 105

N

Nasrawi, Dhamyaa A. 75
Nayak, Anjana 350
Nigam, Arnav 255
Nyamasvisva, Tadiwa Elisha 466

P

Padmaja, Jagini Naga   53
Pandey, Vijay   205
Patel, Mehulkumar   65
Patil, Chaitali   476
Patil, Prajakta   476
Prakash, Sidharth   141
Praveen, Nushrat   221
Priya, Upasana   452

R

Rai, Pankaj   186
Ramakrishnan, Ranjith Kumar   267, 350, 383, 425
Rani, Priya   118
Ranjan, Rahul   312
Roy, Rajdeep   410

S

Sadineni, Mahendra   425
Sagar, Kalpana   169
Sahu, Pankaj   236
Salim, Abu   129, 335
Sarfaraz, Mohd   335
Sharma, Dharmeshwar   255
Shelar, Madhukar   365
Siddiqui, Shams Tabrez   129, 300, 335
Singh, Alok Kumar   153
Singh, Khushboo   153
Singh, Ram   169
Singhal, Arnav   255
Sinha, A. R.   196
Sinha, Divya   196
Sohail, Mohammed Ali   300
Sonam, Kumari   312

T

Tiwari, Rajesh Kumar   186, 205, 335

U

Upadhyay, Shrikant   92, 141

V

Varma, Nadimpalli Madana Kailash   53
Vidya, Kanduri Sai Sri   53
Vishwakarma, Monali   282

Y

Yede, Sanjay   105

GPSR Compliance
The European Union's (EU) General Product Safety Regulation (GPSR) is a set of rules that requires consumer products to be safe and our obligations to ensure this.

If you have any concerns about our products, you can contact us on

ProductSafety@springernature.com

In case Publisher is established outside the EU, the EU authorized representative is:

Springer Nature Customer Service Center GmbH
Europaplatz 3
69115 Heidelberg, Germany

www.ingramcontent.com/pod-product-compliance
Lightning Source LLC
Chambersburg PA
CBHW072002241125
35898CB00011B/417